DEFENDING NORMANDY
VOL. 1B
GERMAN INFANTRY DIVISIONS ON THE COTENTIN - PART II

Published in 2024 by Panzerwrecks Limited

Design by Toni Canfora
Maps by Niels Henkemans
Printed by Finidr. s.r.o.
Website www.panzerwrecks.com

Panzerwrecks Limited
Great Priors
Church Street
Old Heathfield
Sussex TN21 9AH
United Kingdom
lee@panzerwrecks.com

©2024 Henkemans. All rights reserved. No part of this publication may be reproduced or transmitted in any form or by any means, electronic or mechanical, including photocopy, recording or any information storage and retrieval system, without permission in writing from the publisher. Mention of company names or individual people are only included for historical documentation purposes. We recognise that some of the company names or designations mentioned in this publication may be registered trademarks or protected under copyright law. Their use in this publication is strictly for historical/technical documentation and does not constitute or imply endorsement of the holders of these titles. The purpose of this book is to document the history of World War 2. The author and publisher distance themselves from fascism, anti-Semitism or racism in any way.

Table of Contents

Part 2 (continued): Heer Infantry Divisions

243. Infanterie-Division — 4
- Organisation and Equipment — 7
- History — 24
- Combat — 29

265. Infanterie-Division — 48
- Organisation and Equipment — 48
- History — 60
- Combat — 66

353. Infanterie-Division — 82
- Organisation and Equipment — 82
- History — 94
- Combat — 99

709. Infanterie-Division — 120
- Organisation and Equipment — 122
- History — 143
- Combat — 156

Appendix — 192
- A Timeline of the occupation of Lower Normandy — 193
- B Coastal Defence Sectors — 200
- C Grundgliederungen — 204

Glossary
- German Military Symbols — 206
- Comparative Table of Ranks — 207
- Terminology and Abbreviations — 208

Bibliography — 213
Index — 217
Endnotes — 230
Acknowledgements — 264

Part 2 (continued):
HEER INFANTRY DIVISIONS

*Archives du Calvados, 10Fi/4, photo 361
(Agence Fama, France et Atlantic, Berlin)*

243. Infanterie-Division

The 243. Infanterie-Division was raised as a static (bodenständig) division outside of the "wave" system in June 1943.[1] Provisionally called "Division B" (as part of a group of five similar divisions named "A" to "E"), it was redesignated as the 243. I.D on 9 July.[2]

The division was formed in Döllersheim, Austria (*Wehrkreis XVII* / Vienna);[3] it moved to northern France in **August** and then to Bretagne, where it was assigned to the *XXV. A.K.* in early **October**.[4] Beginning in **November**, attempts were made to transform it into a mobile division and, in **January 1944**, it moved to Normandy, becoming part of the *LXXXIV. A.K.*[5] On **13 May**, *AOK 7* was able to remove its training status;[6] the division had an approximate strength of 11,500 men.[7]

The 243. I.D. was stationed on the west coast of the Cotentin on D-Day. It was not deployed as a single formation against the invasion, but in *Kampfgruppen* operating under different divisions. When US forces reached the west coast of the peninsula in mid-**June,** forces near the east coast were cut off and eventually destroyed in the fighting for Cherbourg and the Jobourg Peninsula. The bulk of the division, however, assembled south of the American breakthrough, where it held the left flank of the *Nordfront*. During **July**, the front was pushed back to Lessay. As a result of *Operation Cobra*, many forces on the *Nordfront* risked being cut off, with the result that the division attempted to breakout to the southeast, suffering heavy losses in the process. Surviving elements were regrouped as a battlegroup under the 353. I.D. and stayed with the division as it withdrew east in **August**. The division was formally disbanded in early **September**.

On **19 July 1943**, *Gen.Maj.* Hermann von Witzleben was appointed commander.[8] He would be succeeded by *Gen.Lt.* Heinz Hellmich, who led the division from **10 January 1944** until his death on **17 June**.[9] *Obst.* Bernhard Klosterkemper, the senior regimental commander, then took over and remained in charge of the remnants of the division until early **August**, when he was attached to *AOK 7*.[10]

The divisional insignia was a shield with three lions in repose (yellow on a red background), similar to the coat of arms of Normandy, albeit with

Left: Gen.Maj. Hermann von Witzleben was the division's first commander, having been appointed on 19 July 1943. In January 1944 he was transferred the OKH officers reserve of Wehrkreis VII and released from active duty on 31 December. (BArch, PERS 6/301383)

Centre: Gen.Lt. Heinz Hellmich was appointed as the division commander on 10 January 1944 and still was in charge on D-Day. On 8 June, being the senior commander on the Cotentin he was put in charge of all troops on the peninsula. He commanded Gruppe Hellmich until he was killed in action on 17 June. (BArch, PERS 6/299828)

Right: On 10 December 1943 Obst. Bernhard Klosterkemper became the commander of GR 920, a position he still held on D-Day. That day he was given temporary command of the 91.LL.I.D., after Gen.Lt. Falley had been killed. On the 10th the Oberst returned to his division, of which he became the commander after the death of Gen. Hellmich on 17 June. (BArch, MSG 2/7763)

an additional lion. The insignia was removed from all vehicles in **May 1944** and not replaced before the invasion.[11]

The division is reasonably well documented, with the records of *AOK 7* furnishing much useful information for the period leading up to the invasion. While records of the *XXV. A.K.* do the same for much of **1943**, those of the *LXXXIV. A.K.* for **1944** are mostly missing; as a result, many pre-invasion details and developments are not covered in depth. This also applies to its combat history; only some daily reports for the second half of June 1944 have survived. Moreover, the division is inadequately covered in the Foreign Military Studies programme; none of its senior officers contributed to the studies, with the exception of the combat school commander. The evaluation section of the *OKH* (*Abwicklungsstab*) did compile a preliminary combat report, but it was also short on details. That such lacunae exist is hardly

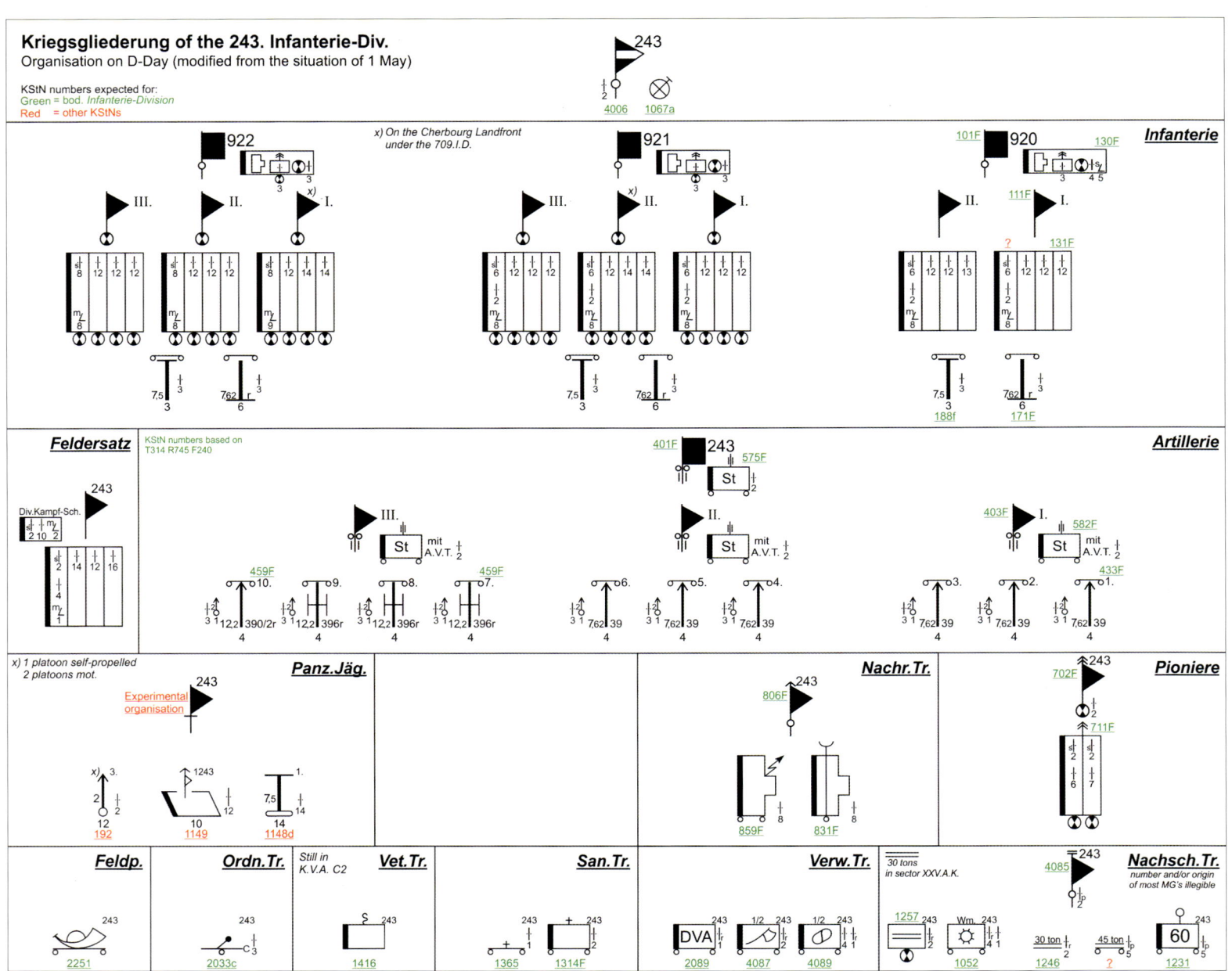

The 243.I.D. was an anomaly among the divisions which would fight in Normandy. Having started out as a static division, the mobility programme provided it with considerable means of transportation. With a motorised artillery regiment and two infantry regiments on bicycles it exceeded the mobility of regular infantry divisions.

surprising, since a detailed account is only available from one of the artillery battalions. However, since its elements frequently operated under other divisions, their records offer some information, although details on the fighting remain elusive.

Organisation and Equipment

The condition of the division on D-Day is fairly well recorded, at least as far as organisation and heavy weapons are concerned. Reports from the corps or division are not available, however, with the result that details on personnel, transportation, secondary weaponry and other topics are lacking.

The lack of surviving records is a problem, as the division was affected by the efforts to make divisions more mobile (*Beweglichmachung*) and, in **April 1944**, there were orders to transform it to an *Inf.Div.44*.[12] The lack of records can make it difficult to determine which *KStN's* were actually used, how units were made mobile or how they deviated from a standard organisation. To some extent, these questions can be answered by information from prisoners, whose accounts offer details not covered by official records.

The division's organisation was originally to match that of the static *266. I.D.*, raised in **May 1943**. This gave the division an organisation of a divisional headquarters with a motorcycle dispatch-rider platoon, three infantry regiments (each with three battalions and three heavy weapons companies), an artillery regiment (with two light and one heavy battalion), an engineer battalion and various support troops.[13]

On **9 July**, this organisational scheme was superseded by an intended organisational document (*Sollgliederung*) specific to the division. This was accompanied by all the *KStN* numbers which, as before, were specifically for static units and thus included little mobility. The changes were mostly minor; for example, changes were made to the headquarters companies of the infantry regiments by removing the fourth machine gun from the engineer platoon. A more significant change was made to the artillery battalions, in which the signals platoon was replaced by a headquarters battery (minus a surveying section), while the horse-drawn transport section (*Bespannungsstaffel*) was eliminated.[14]

To build the cadre, *Heeresgruppe Mitte* (Army Group Centre) was ordered to transfer 2,000 NCO's and 1,000 men: 55% infantry, 25% artillery, 5% anti-tank, 5% engineers, 5% signals troops and 5% supply troops. Meanwhile, the Replacement Army provided convalescents from the *387. I.D.*, a division destroyed on the Eastern Front and also raised at Döllersheim. The rest of the troops came from *Wehrkreis VII* (Munich) and *XVII* (Vienna) (contributing 30% each) and *Wehrkreis IV* (Dresden), which relied on the Military District of Poland and *Wehrkreis XVIII* (Salzburg), providing about 20% each.[15]

The orders illustrate some characteristics of the NCO's and men in a static division. Men with a protected status (last sons and fathers of large families) could be assigned to combat units, while men from the *Panzertruppen* could also be used if their age (born in 1910 or earlier) or status (garrison duty in the field / *garnisonsfähig Feld* / *g.v.F.*) no longer matched the requirements of that service branch. Members of *Volksliste III* could be used as well, but only as supply troops and to a maximum of 5%. Convalescents of the Army in the East (*Ostheer*) could only be used as an exception for critical positions; most significantly, this pertained to those who were no longer suitable for service on the Eastern Front (e.g., victims of third degree frostbite) and older men. Personnel from Alsace, Lorraine and Luxembourg were not to be used. The age of men and NCO's in the combat troops could not exceed an average age of 36 years. Most men were born in the period from 1901 to 1913, although those with a protected status could be born in 1914 or later.[16] Since no detailed personnel records are available for the situation on D-Day, the information above offers clues as to origin and characteristics of the men at that time, although admittedly much could have changed in a year.

A third authorisation document was issued in **September**. Compared to **July**, the organisation had changed little, although the infantry companies were now authorised to have an extra medium mortar (a total of three) and light MG's were added to several headquarters and units: Two to the headquarters of *Pi.Btl. 243*; four to the *1.* and three to the *2./Nachr.Abt. 243*; two to the field hospital (*Feldlazarett 243*); and one to the military police section (*Feldgendarmerie-Trupp 243*). This gave the division an extra 36 medium mortars and 12 light MG's.[17]

This organisational document is interesting as it shows the division's theoretical organisation just before it was selected for increased mobility. As such, it offers a useful comparison to the order of battle (*Kriegsgliederung*) of **1 May 1944**, which provides the latest information in the lead-up to the D-Day invasion. Many of the changes throughout this period pertained to the new mobile role given the division in late **1943**, which meant it could not maintain

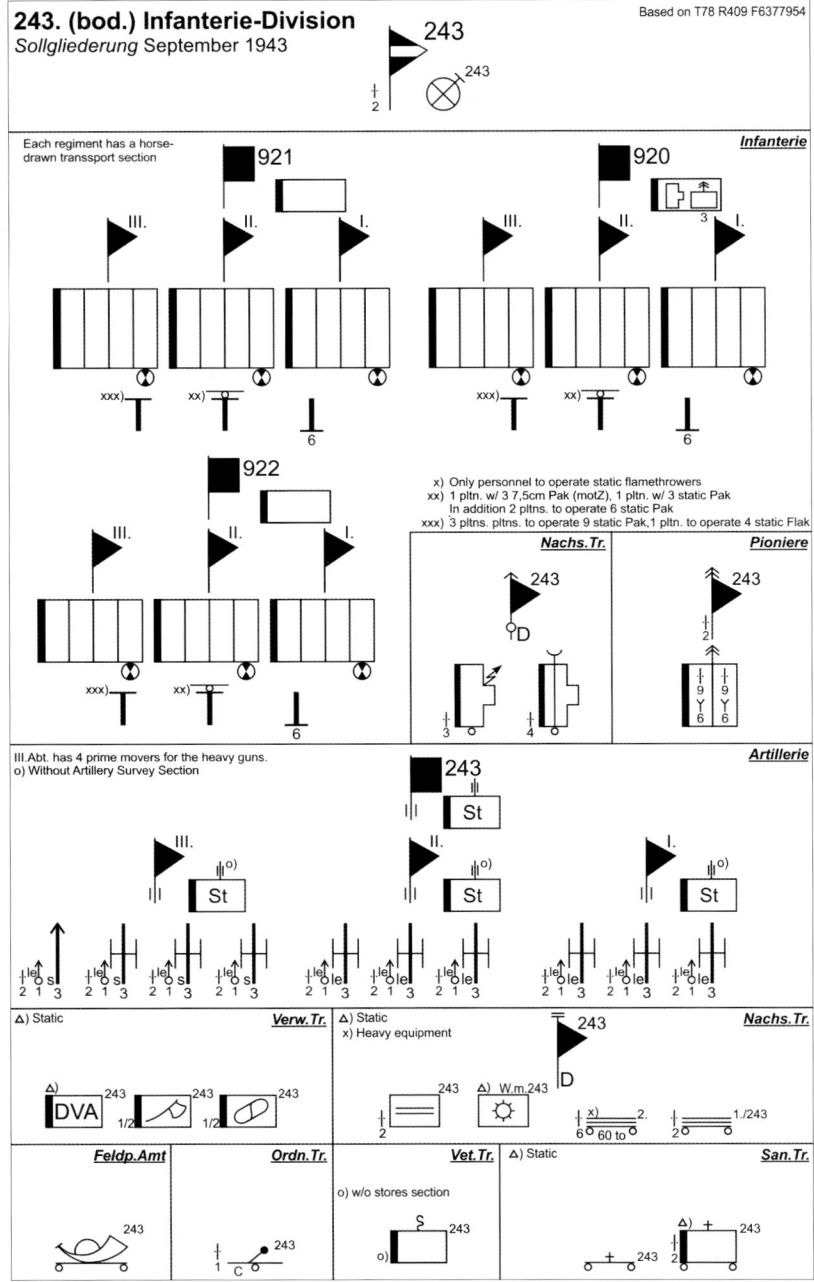

its organisation as a static division and instead received increased mobility and additional troops.

Without a status report from the time of the invasion, there are no authorised and on-hand numbers to show the division's condition or to pinpoint issues related to personnel, weaponry or mobility. Still, on **1 April**, the division was short 266 German personnel, while having a surplus of 442 *Hiwi's*.[18]

The last known organisational document (**1 May**) does show the division's organisation and on-hand numbers of personnel and small arms. On this date, it had a total strength of 11,529 men, although the exact composition is unknown. Accurate age group numbers are only available for 9 December 1943, when they were specified for both the combat (84.8%) and support troops (15.2%). At that time, the division had 11,226 men. Among the combat troops, just 0.1% was born in or before 1899, 2% in 1900-05, 63% in 1906-13, 20% in 1914-22, and 15% in 1923 or later. For the support personnel, these numbers were, respectively, 1%, 17%, 53%, 24% and 5%.[19] A week before, the average age of the combat troops had been given as 30.5 and as 34.6 for the support troops.[20]

	≤1899	1900-1905	1906-1913	1914-1922	≥1923
Dec. 1943	0.2%	3.9%	61.8%	20.9%	13.2%
KIA/MIA	0.4%	3.0%	51.9%	28.3%	16.5%
Difference	0.2%	-0.9%	-9.9%	7.4%	3.3%

Table 1: Comparison of age groups in the *243. I.D.* in December 1943 and 237 KIA*/MIA in the summer of 1944.

The situation at the time of the invasion is unknown, but the division was included in the MIRS paybook study, where 616 paybooks were examined.[21] They showed that 36% of the men were born in or before 1909, 52% in 1910-24, 11% in 1925, and 0.3% in 1926. These numbers are close to the results of a study of 237 KIA/MIA, which mainly differ in a lower percentage born 1909 or earlier and a higher percentage of those born 1910-24.[22] 64% of the KIA/MIA sample were members of the infantry regiments, which appears to be a fair representation considering the division's eight infantry battalions.

In September 1943 the division was still a fairly standard static division. It was not until later in the year that it was forced to give up one of its nine infantry battalions.

Even so, the complexity of the division makes the exact bias towards front-line troops difficult to determine.

Sample size		≤1909	1910-24	1925	1926
MIRS	616	36.4%	52.3%	11.0%	0.3%
KIA/MIA	237	31.6%	55.7%	11.4%	1.3%
Difference	379	-4.8%	3.4%	0.4%	1.0%

Table 2: Comparison of age groups in the *243. I.D.* between MIRS and KIA/MIA numbers.

By taking a closer look at the KIA/MIA it is possible to extract additional details. 54% of the men were 30-40 years old (born 1904-13). The number of 20-30 years old amounted to 31% and only 14% were aged 20 or younger (born 1924 at the earliest). Just over 1% were older than 40 (born in 1903 or before). The relative size of the three dominant age groups is very different to the 25th Wave divisions, and the high number of older troops betrays the division's origin as a static division. Yet, compared to the *265. I.D.* and the *709. I.D.*, the *243. I.D.* stands out in having few men born in 1924 or later. The samples of the two static divisions have about twice that amount. In fact, the *243. I.D.* reached only 13% born in 1925-26, well below the 20% target of *Ob.West* for static divisions. This is not a weakness, because the division scores much higher than the two static divisions in the more preferred age group of 20-25 (1919-23). There the division was pretty much on par with regular infantry divisions. This suggests that for its new mobile role, the division was allowed to keep better personnel, whereas static divisions had to exchange them for younger men. In addition, compared to the two static divisions, the 1909-13 age group was larger, while the number of older men was lower. The *243. I.D.* thus had fewer very young and very old troops. With some 60% aged 20-35, its age build-up was considerably more balanced than in the static divisions, which scored about 45%. Nonetheless, within this combined age group it was the older men (aged 30-35), who made up about half of the personnel.

	≤1903	1904-1908	1909-1913	1914-1918	1919-1923	1924	1925	1926
KIA/MIA	1.3%	22.8%	31.2%	14.3%	16.9%	0.8%	11.4%	1.3%

Table 3: Age distribution in the *243. I.D.* (Based on 237 KIA/MIA)

On **1 May 1944**, the division's small arms were mostly German and consisted of 6,878 *K98k's*, 179 self-loading rifles (*G41's*), 179 sniper rifles, 72 *G98* rifles, 499 rifle-grenade launchers, 729 machine pistols and 2,942 pistols. The number of captured small arms was lower, yet still considerable: 677 French, 58 Russian, 70 Polish, 51 Czech and 4 Yugoslavian rifles, as well as 5 Russian machine pistols. Among the heavier weapons were 17 Italian medium mortars and 16 Russian light MG's, with at least 15 of the latter assigned to the division's supply elements.[23] Detailed data on the types of German MG's assigned to the division on D-Day could not be found, but numbers reported on **1 January** provide the best available information. At that time, it had an authorised strength of 560 MG's, including 551 *MG 42's*; the actual strength, however, was 475, of which 416 were *MG 42's*.[24] In addition, there were five *MG 13's* and nine of an unidentified type.[25] In the months leading up to the invasion, the division reported receiving another 36 *MG 34's* and 86 *MG 42's*. By that time, however, the authorised number of MG's had changed.[26] Without a status report providing the authorised numbers at the time of the invasion, it is difficult to ascertain the precise figures for small arms. There were, however, some shortcomings. For example, a staff officer of *GR 922* reported a shortfall of 4 out of 12 grenade launchers in the rifle companies of his regiment.[27]

Although the organisational document of **1 May** only provides an overview of weapons and organisation, it is useful in understanding the changes in the months preceding the invasion. The **September 1943** authorisation document illustrates that the division had been a fairly regular static infantry division. It called for the division headquarters elements (*KStN* 4006) to be protected by two MG's and supported by a motorcycle dispatch-rider platoon (based on *KStN 1067a*). There was no mapping section.[28] By **1 May 1944**, the divisional headquarters was partially motorised and had three MG's instead of two. There were no changes to the messenger platoon.[29]

At the core of the division were *Grenadier-Regiment 920, 921* and *922*, with three infantry battalions each. The authorisation document for these regiments is not surprising. They had a headquarters (*KStN 101f*) and each headquarters company (*KStN 130f*) had a signals platoon and an engineer platoon, each with three MG's. The infantry battalions had the typical structure of a static formation: A headquarters (*KStN 111f*) and four rifle companies. There was no MG company. The companies had 2 heavy MG's, 12 light MG's and 3 medium mortars (*KStN 131f* and *KStN 170*). They also had personnel to man static flamethrowers. Some mobility was provided by bicycles in the first company of each battalion.[30] The regiments also had three heavy weapons companies. The 13th Company (*KStN 171f*) was outfitted with six light infantry guns. The 14th Company (*KStN 186f* and *KStN 188f*) was an AT company with one platoon of three motorised 7.5 cm AT guns, one platoon of three static 3.7 cm AT guns (presumably in a mobile role) and two platoons to operate three static AT guns each (presumably immobile). The company was thus only partially motorised. The 15th Company had three platoons to man a total of nine static AT guns and one platoon of four static 2 cm *Flak*.[31] To offer some mobility, each regiment had a horse-drawn transport section; these were able to transport eight heavy MG's and 12 medium mortars. When grouped together, this element was attached to the headquarters company.[32]

On D-Day, the regiments were commanded by *Obst.* Klosterkemper, *Obstlt.* Simon and *Obstlt.* Müller, respectively.[33] The order of battle of **1 May** shows an organisation that differed slightly from the earlier authorisation document. *GR 920* had only two battalions, as the *III./920* had been transferred to the East in **October 1943** and joined *GR 290 (98. I.D.)*.[34] The other two regiments still had three battalions.[35]

The headquarters of *GR 921* and *922* were partially motorised and their battalions equipped with bicycles, but this did not apply to *GR 920*. The battalions in all three regiments were reorganised to have three rifle companies and one MG company, as was standard in regular infantry divisions.[36] This change had been suggested by the division commander, *Gen.Maj.* von Witzleben, and was approved by *Gen.Obst.* Dollmann and *Gen.d.Art.* Fahrmbacher on **21 December 1943**;[37] it appears to have taken place between **1-13 January 1944**.[38]

By **1 May**, changes had also been made in the heavy weapons companies. A 15th Company was a typical feature of static divisions, but the reorganisation meant it was no longer required. In **December**, however, it was decided that those companies in each regiment were to remain intact as a cadre unit, in case they needed to be equipped as an extra AT company. The cadre for a field-replacement battalion was to be formed and two companies had been absorbed by this new battalion by D-Day.[39]

The personnel makeup suggests that, like the rest of the division, the infantry mainly consisted of Austrians and Germans; there were also Polish, Czech and Russian personnel. The infantry companies each appear to have

Obstlt. Franz Müller was given command of GR 922 on 12 February 1944. Previously he had been the commander of (replacement) battalions and Gren.Ers.Rgt. 78. After the beginning of the invasion he was in charge of KG Müller which operated under the 709. I.D. Together with his battlegroup, Müller continued to fighting after the liberation of Cherbourg, before being captured on the Jobourg Peninsula on 30 June. (NARA)

had about 20 Poles and four Russians (apparently *Hiwi's*), the latter usually taking care of the horses or performing work details.[40]

The regimental headquarters reportedly consisted of the commander, his adjutant, the first and second officer assistants (*Ordonnanzoffizier*) and 11 other ranks.[41] The adjutant of *GR 922* did not mention a second assistant officer in his regiment, but he did offer other details: A signals officer, a paymaster, a clerk, six bicycle dispatch riders and another three messengers on motorcycles.[42]

On **1 May 1944**, the organisation of the headquarters companies had changed from the earlier authorisations. All three embraced the usual signals and engineer platoons, but they had been expanded to include a bicycle platoon (*Infanterie-Radfahr-Zug*) that could be used for reconnaissance. This was a logical addition considering the division's intended more mobile role. The headquarters company of *GR 920* was not supposed to have a bicycle platoon, most likely because the increased mobility would be from horses. Regardless, the division had established such a unit on its own initiative, and it was formalised by *AOK 7* in early **February**.[43] This particular company was unusual in having a platoon of five heavy mortars; these 12 cm *Gr.W. 42's* had arrived in **April** and were not used elsewhere in the division.[44]

Detailed information on the headquarters company of *GR 921* and 922 is available.[45] The source of the latter is believed to be more reliable as it is from a regimental staff officer. His account forms the basis of the following information.[46] The command group comprised the company commander and eight men. The signals platoon had a strength of 1 officer and 28 men. The bicycle platoon had a *Feldwebel* in charge of 41 men; among its weaponry was one light MG. The engineer platoon had a *Feldwebel* and 59 men;[47] in *GR 921* and 922, this platoon was equipped with bicycles. The platoons consisted of the authorised six sections, which had a strength of one NCO and eight or nine men each. The number of MG's is difficult to read on the order of battle, but it appears to be five for each regiment.[48] However, the engineer platoon in *GR 922* reportedly only had two light *MG 42's* and possibly one heavy MG.[49]

Finally, the headquarters company had a tank destroyer section (*Panzerzerstörer-Trupp*) with three men; its equipment is not listed, but the company possessed 12 of an authorised 16 *Faustpatronen*.[50] A second source states that the company also carried *Ofenrohre*, *Hafthohlladungen*, mines, mine detectors and two self-loading rifles.[51] The *Ofenrohre* would be standard equipment for an AT section, although they may also have served as a reserve for the regiment. The additional equipment noted was commonly used by combat engineers and may therefore have belonged to the engineer platoon.

GR 921 also had a regimental aid station composed of a medical officer, two medical NCO's and three medics.[52] This is unusual, because it was not called for by any *KStN*. It was commonplace for the most senior battalion surgeon to assume the role of regimental surgeon. Even so, this was only advisory and did not include running a regimental aid station.

Quite a lot is known about the motorisation for the headquarters and headquarters company of *GR 922*. This information will be presented later in the text to illustrate the variety of vehicles in the division as a whole.

The organisation of all eight infantry battalions appears to have been similar on **1 May 1944**. Each had three rifle companies and a MG company, with differences in the number and type of MG's and, as stated, the level of mobility.[53]

According to the aforementioned staff officer of *GR 922*, each battalion staff had four officers: The commander, his adjutant, an officer assistant and a medical officer. It included three distinct sections: signals, administrative and transportation. The signals section consisted of a *Feldwebel* and 25 men, the administrative section had 14 troops and the transport section 50-60 men.[54] An examination of various battalion headquarters reveals a more diverse number of men. The signals section of the *II./922* reportedly had 17 men under a *Feldwebel*: 8 telephone operators, 3 wireless operators and 1 man as a reserve. In combat, two telephone men and two wireless operators would be attached to each company (most likely excluding the MG company). The wireless operators were outfitted with the usual infantry Caesar (*Torn.Fu.c*) or Dora (*Torn.Fu.d2*) backpack wireless.[55]

The headquarters of the *III./921* consisted of three officers: The commander, his adjutant and an assistant adjutant; they were assisted by a *Hauptfeldwebel* and an *Oberfeldwebel*. The signals section was considerably stronger than in the *II./922*, having a reported strength of 5 NCO's and about 40 men. The motorcycle dispatch-rider section had 2 senior NCO's, 1 junior NCO and 18 men. Transport was handled by a senior NCO, a junior NCO and 20 men. The armourers included a senior NCO, a junior NCO and six men. Administration comprised an officer, a senior NCO, a junior NCO and one man. The battalion aid station was run by a medical officer, assisted by two senior NCO's and four men. All told, the battalion headquarters had a strength of 5 officers, 10 senior NCO's, 8 junior NCO's and 89 men.[56]

The weapons enumerated on the **September 1943** authorisation document suggest that the rifle companies were following *KStN 131f*. This *KStN* was specifically designed for static rifle companies and called for 2 heavy MG's, 12 light MG's, 3 medium mortars and crews for a static flamethrower.[57]

By **1 May 1944**, the organisation of the rifle companies had changed, and this was reflected in the number of weapons. The first two companies of the *II./921* and the *I./922* had 14 MG's, while the *5./920* had 13; the other companies had 12. They no longer had mortars or heavy MG's, as these were now in the MG companies.[58] This suggests that the companies had become more comparable to the *Inf.Div. 44* organisational model.

243. Infanterie-Division

The companies consisted of the command group (including the company headquarters section), three platoons and trains.[59] In many of the companies, there was also an AT section, unusual for a rifle company but apparently common within the *243. I.D.*[60]

In the *9./921*, the command group consisted of the company commander and second-in-command, both officers. The company headquarters section was led by a senior NCO supported by a second one. There were four runners, one dispatch rider and two medics. The trains of this company was led by a *Hauptfeldwebel*, while two junior NCO's were responsible for pay and rations. The remaining men included a clerk, two cooks, an armourer, a bicycle mechanic and six drivers. The weapons in the company headquarters section and the trains were *K98k* rifles and a few pistols.[61]

Different figures were given for the rifle companies in *GR 922*. Evidently, the command group consisted of just one officer, a junior-grade NCO, three or four dispatch riders, a medical orderly and a clerk. No numbers were provided for the trains, except 30 men for transport.[62]

The primary combat power for the rifle companies was provided by their platoons. These consisted of a platoon leader, a few men in support and four infantry sections, although some platoons may have had only three.[63] In the *II./921*, each section consisted of an NCO and nine men. Weapons included a light *MG 42*, a rifle-grenade-launcher, a sniper rifle and a self-loading rifle.[64] The *6./921* is said to have matched this number of platoons and MG's, but it reportedly only had six to eight men per section.[65]

The situation in the *9./921* differed, as its first and third platoons had three sections instead of four and thus had fewer MG's. The rest of their weaponry was more or less the same as the *II./921*. The platoons also had four or five *Faustpatronen* and three or four *Hafthohlladungen*.[66] The most intriguing anomaly compared to other companies was in the 1st platoon. It reportedly had a 3.7 cm AT gun, with a crew of one NCO and four men; 600 rounds were available for this gun.[67] The presence of this gun has not been verified, although the earlier authorisation document for the 14th Company in the regiments had three motorised static 3.7 cm AT guns.[68] Perhaps these were assigned to the companies. A soldier from *GR 922* even stated that six tractor-drawn 3.7 cm AT guns were kept at regimental headquarters, although this is questionable.[69] Considering that the authorisation document linked the regiments to 3.7 cm AT guns, it is possible they were kept "off the books".

By **1944**, this gun was no longer effective as an AT weapon. Although units were allowed to keep them if they had them, reporting them may have been considered pointless.[70] In any case, no evidence has surfaced to prove that the division had 3.7 cm guns at the time of the invasion.

The possible presence of AT guns was not the only anomaly involving AT weapons in the companies. As already stated, it appears that a tank-destroyer section was in many of the division's rifle companies. The presence of these sections is unexpected, as they were not included in the *KStN's* used for rifle companies. It may have been a response to the introduction of the *Ofenrohr*, without having to create two such platoons for each 14th Company, as was standard in a *Inf.Div.44*. A section consisted of three men trained to operate an *Ofenrohr*.[71] A staff officer of *GR 922* stated that these sections were in all his regiment's rifle and MG companies, but that *Ofenrohre* were not issued.[72] This is refuted by men of the *3.* and the *9./922*, the latter company apparently receiving two of these weapons.[73] For most companies, no information is available, although an *Ofenrohr* was also reported in the *6./921*.[74] This may indicate that many, even all, of the rifle companies in the three regiments had *Ofenrohre* on D-Day.

Additional AT weapons in the *6./921* were to include two *Faustpatronen*, but none were delivered.[75] In contrast, the *9./921* reportedly had 10 *Hafthohlladungen* and 13 Faustpatronen. *Ofenrohre* were not mentioned.[76]

The actual strength of the rifle companies is difficult to determine. Prisoners provide various numbers. Although their reliability may be questionable, they give us an impression. The *5./921* reportedly had a strength of 193 men, while for the *6./921* and the *9./922* the number was allegedly 130 men.[77] The strength of the *9./921* was reported as 149 men, with a combat strength of 135.[78] The rifle companies in the *II./922* are said to have had a strength of 160-170 men.[79]

Most of the personnel were German or Austrian, although the *3./921* had three Poles and four Russians.[80] The companies in the *II./921* included 60 Austrians and 20 Poles each, with the rest of the personnel being German[81]. The men in the *9./921* were 42% German, 24% Pole, 16% Austrian, 10% Russian and 8% Czech. The Russians were *Hiwi's*, used only for work details. There were also six French drivers. Not surprisingly, they vanished after the invasion began.[82] The *9./922* reported only nine Poles, while the *10./922* was 30% ethnic German and 70% German.[83]

Data on the men's ages is difficult to confirm. The most detailed numbers are for the *9./921*: 25% 18-20; 20% 20-25; 20% 25-30; 25% 30-35; and 10% 35-40.[84] The average age in the *10./922* was given as 32.[85] Less specific numbers are available on the *3./921*, but its men were apparently 18-31.[86]

As noted, the battalions in *GR 921* and *922* were bicycle formations.[87] Detailed information on other means of transportation is also available. The rifle companies in the *II./921* each had two or three lorries, two horse-drawn wagons and a motorcycle.[88] The *10./922* had four light lorries, while the field kitchen was horse-drawn.[89] This contradicts a regimental staff officer, who claimed that only the *I./922* had horses (ca.15), yet did not specify how these were distributed.[90]

There is significant information available on the *9./921*. The command group had a motorcycle, a staff car and a cross-country lorry. Additional lorries were available for the paymaster, the armourer, the rations personnel, the field kitchen and the bicycle mechanic.[91]

On **1 May**, every MG company in the infantry regiments had eight medium mortars and eight MG's. In *GR 922* these were all heavy MG's, while the other regiments also had two light MG's.[92] When there were seven or eight heavy MG's, they were distributed between the first and second platoons.[93] If there were only six heavy MG's (as in the *4./920*), they were used in a single platoon.[94] The guns were organised in sections of two.[95] As a result, depending on the number of machine guns, some MG platoons had two sections, while others had three.

Since all companies had eight mortars, their organisation was identical. The mortars were divided between two mortar platoons with four mortars each; as such, they were either in the 2nd-3rd Platoons or the 3rd-4th Platoons.[96] A member of *Waffenmeister-Zug 243*, the division's armourer platoon, confirms that the division was equipped with German 8 cm and Italian 8.14 cm mortars. The Italian mortars were unpopular because they were highly inaccurate and had to be aimed by judgement and aiming sticks. The shortage of Italian ammunition also meant that German 8 cm rounds had to be used, further decreasing accuracy.[97]

The weaponry of the MG companies was not limited to the heavy and personal weapons. For example, the company weapons store of the *8./922* held eight *Faustpatronen* and a number of *Teller* mines and pole charges. On **7 June**, two *Faustpatronen* were issued to each platoon and an *Ofenrohr* was

Bicycles did not only allow troops to move more quickly, they could also be used to transport their weapons and equipment. The soldier in front has strapped the tube of a medium mortar to his bicycle, demonstrating his unit's mobility to Feldm. von Rundstedt. (Collectie CegeSoma – Rijksarchief (OD4))

assigned to an NCO from one of the MG platoons, who had been trained on the weapon.[98] This shows that *Ofenrohre* were not just present in the rifle companies, but in some MG companies as well. According to a staff officer, the three MG companies each had an AT section.[99] The example of the *8./922* could indicate that the activation of these sections may have depended on the availability of *Ofenrohre* or a combat situation.

Accounts of prisoners offer different estimates as to the strength of these companies. The *4./920* is said to have had a strength of 160 men. They were mostly Austrians, but there were also 20 Germans, 30 Poles, a few Czechs and 4 Russian stable hands (*Hiwi's*).[100] The *12./922* reportedly had a strength of 170 men, including 30 Poles and 15 Russians.[101] A similar figure was reported for the *8./922*, although another prisoner stated its strength was 220.[102]

Detailed data on the companies' transportation is lacking, with the *8./922* being an exception. This company had four staff vehicles: two Citroën's, a Morris and a Ford. An Opel *Blitz* lorry was used for troop transport, and there were a number of lorries used for weapons and supplies. Four lorries towed trailers, each of which carried two mortars and ammunition. There was also a mess lorry. A 3.5-tonne Renault lorry was used for rations and a 2.5-tonne Renault transported ammunition. There were also two *Kettenkräder*.[103]

Elements of the MG companies were used to support the rifle companies in combat, which was standard practice. In the case of the *5./921*, the *6./921* and the *9./921*, two mortars from their battalions' MG company were attached to each, suggesting this was standard practice within the regiment.[104] The *9./921* reportedly also had two heavy MG's from the 12th Company. The weapons from that company were assigned as a mortar- and machine-gun "platoon", with a total strength of 19 men each (1 senior NCO, 2 junior NCO's and 16 men).[105] It is plausible this was also the case in the other companies, but it is not mentioned in existing sources.

Information regarding the *8./922* indicates that when it was committed, it would still operate as a single formation with four mortars and four MG's (two light, two heavy). The remainder of the company's weapons and some of the men were distributed among the remaining companies in the battalion.[106] Unfortunately, reliable information from the rifle companies is not available to show how they were supported by the MG companies.

As usual, the heaviest weapons in the infantry regiments were in the heavy weapons companies. On **1 May**, the 13th Company of each regiment fielded six light infantry guns, matching the earlier authorisations and *KStN 171f*, which called for three platoons of two guns each.[107] Although the order of battle only shows them as Russian 7.62 cm infantry guns, they had earlier been identified as *7,62 cm I.K.H.290(r)'s*.[108] The description from one of the company commanders also matches this weapon.[109] In addition to these guns, the companies had three MG's and, except for the *13./920*, were motorised.[110] In action, each platoon supported an infantry battalion within its regiment.[111]

Reliable details on the organisation of these companies are not available. The *13./921* reportedly consisted of a headquarters and three platoons, each with two sections with a single gun. The platoons were led by an officer, aided by a *Feldwebel* and two signal men. The gun crews consisted of a junior NCO and nine men; four of the crew had pistols, the rest carried rifles. The platoon leaders were armed with machine pistols.[112]

The guns were towed by open-topped lorries and the basic load of ammunition was 170 rounds per gun, including 25 armour-piercing rounds; a demolition charge was also provided.[113] According to the commander of the *13./922*, his infantry guns were towed by *Chenillettes*, which points to Renault UE tractors. The guns had originally been horse-drawn, but they had proved too heavy.[114]

Personnel details are vague, but the headquarters of the *13./921* is said to have had an officer, a signals section, an administrative section, two dispatch riders, a messenger with a bicycle and three cooks.[115] According to a staff officer from *GR 922*, the 13th Company in that regiment had a total strength of 3 officers and 140 other ranks. The gun platoons had 25 men each, while the company transportation (presumably the trains) had 37 men. In addition, there was an AT section with three men.[116]

On **1 May 1944**, the organisation of the 14th Company in the three regiments varied from the authorisation document. As intended, each company had three motorised *7,5 cm Pak 40's* and three light MG's, but there were no static 3.7 cm AT guns or personnel listed for such weapons.[117]

The origin of these three companies is noteworthy. They had been listed on combat organisation documents in late **1943**, but they were not in the records of *AOK 7* on **13 January 1944**.[118] It appears they were finally formed later that month using *Panzerjäger-Kompanie 243*, which had nine heavy AT guns.[119] This company was no longer required, because the division had just been ordered to form an AT battalion, which would not be equipped with towed AT guns.[120]

The infantry AT companies appear on the **February** order of battle with three heavy AT guns each.[121] Although listed as companies, there is no evidence they were larger than a platoon, and it is doubtful they were expanded later. As late as **1 May**, the only other weapons listed were three light MG's, which also suggests there was just one platoon.[122] Prisoners indicated that some men in the infantry companies were trained to operate *Ofenrohre*. In other divisions (like those of the 21st to 25th Wave), such personnel and weapons were organic to the infantry AT companies as a tank-destroyer platoon. The fact that these weapons are linked to the infantry in the *243. I.D.* supports the supposition that each of its 14th Companies consisted of just a heavy AT platoon. This is confirmed for *GR 922* by a regimental staff officer and the officer who was in command of the combined 13th and 14th Companies. According to the latter officer, the situation was the same in the other regiments, an assertion that seems to be supported by at least one officer from *GR 920*, who stated there was no 14th Company in his regiment.[123] In a mixed company, the single platoon of the 14th Company would have been easy to overlook.

It is not entirely clear what the prime movers were for the AT guns in this combined company, but they were halftracks or *Chenillettes*. For example, Renault UE *Chenillettes* were being used by the combined heavy weapons company of *GR 922*.[124]

On D-Day, there was no longer a 15th Company in any of the regiments (these were last listed on the order of battle of **1 November 1943**).[125] Orders were given to retain them as personnel units (*Personal-Einheiten*) in case they could be equipped after all.[126] In addition, it was decided that a cadre for a field-replacement battalion should be formed, and the companies could be used for this, too.[127] Ultimately, this was the fate of two of these companies. The *15./921* and the *15./922* were used to form *Feldersatz-Bataillon 243* (*Hptm.* Zwanzig), with the *11./921* providing additional men.[128] It is not clear why the *11./921* was selected, but since the *9./920* had not moved east and the *8./921* had been re-established, the division had possessed an extra company since **October**. The formation of the battalion apparently commenced in **January 1944** and a *Feldpost* number was assigned on the **18th**.[129]

On **1 May**, the battalion consisted of three rifle companies and a MG company. The divisional combat school (*Major* Maurer) was also attached.[130] On paper, it was *Maj.* Maurer who commanded the battalion, and he was given the assignment in **April**.[131] Maurer had a long career in infantry training and, despite being 60 years old, was now given a field assignment. In view of his qualifications, it is not surprising he was also made head of the divisional combat school by *Gen.* Hellmich. The official head of the school, a captain, reportedly lacked teaching skills and suffered from health issues.[132] Instead of acting as both head of the combat school and battalion commander, it appears Maurer's role focused more on the former. This explains why prisoners said their battalion was commanded by *Hptm.* Zwanzig.[133] Although it was not possible to determine, it is assumed he was in charge of the battalion on D-Day. After the invasion, the activities of the combat school were halted, and *Maj. Maurer* appears to have taken on other assignments.[134]

In the battalion, the first three companies were armed with 16, 12 and 14 MG's respectively (on **1 May**). 4th Company was equipped with two heavy MG's, four light MG's, one medium mortar and an unknown type of equipment. The combat school also had significant armament with 2 heavy MG's and 10 light MG's; it also possessed two medium mortars.[135] Based on information from the men, it appears the rifle companies had three or four platoons, each with four sections and each section with a light *MG 42*.[136] This suggests the intended strength had been 16 MG's per company, which matches the number of machine guns in the 1st Company. The personnel strength of the companies is not clear. Members of the 3rd Company gave their strength as 100-150 men.[137] Although not mentioned on the last order of battle, the men all insisted that the rifle companies had bicycles.[138] This is confirmed for the 3rd Company and highly plausible for the 1st and 2nd Companies. According to one member, the battalion's transport was horse-drawn and, although this cannot be confirmed, it would match the organisational document.[139]

Little is known about the 4th Company. Based on information from a Polish soldier in it, it boasted a strength of about 150 men, including 25 Poles and 6 Russians. The organisation is said to have been three platoons of four sections, with each platoon having four Italian mortars. Since this does not match the order of battle, it is possible the number of mortars only applied to his platoon. If this assumption is correct, the platoon in question was probably the 1st Platoon, which had two French lorries. The company also had two "armoured troop carriers", although it is not clear how these were used or by whom.[140] It is possible that the remaining platoons were MG platoons, as the 4th Company was listed with several (heavy) machine guns. A soldier from the

3rd Company states the MG company did not have bicycles and was therefore immobile.[141] If correct, this probably applied to the MG platoons, with the 1st Platoon as the exception.

The authorisation document for *Pionier-Bataillon 243* of **September 1943** called for a headquarters (*KStN 702f*) with two MG's and two companies (*KStN 711f*) with nine MG's and six flamethrowers each.[142] This was the standard organisation of a static division. The battalion was also affected by the plan to mobilise the division. For some time, the intent was to have it fully motorised;[143] over time, these plans were altered, and it became a bicycle formation.[144]

On **1 May 1944**, the battalion was commanded by *Hptm.* Reicherzer.[145] It had two companies with bicycles, just like the headquarters. Otherwise, the battalion was close to the organisation of the authorisation document. No flamethrowers were listed. The headquarters had two light MG's and the two companies each had two heavy MG's and seven and six light MG's, respectively.[146]

The battalion staff consisted of a command section and a so-called "subordinate staff" (*Unterstab*). The command section included the commander, his adjutant, an assistant officer, a clerk and a messenger; the second staff had a medical officer, medic, paymaster, clerk, rations NCO and drivers.[147]

According to POW's, each company had three platoons with three sections. Each section had 10 men and a *MG 42*.[148] This would have put them at the authorised strength of nine MG's. However, an officer from the 2nd Company and several men stated that their company only had six or seven *MG 42's*.[149] This would match the order of battle. Additional weapons in the companies included six self-loading rifles, several machine pistols, and *K98k* rifles. As usual, the section leaders had machine pistols and the other men carried rifles.[150] Both companies had two flamethrowers of two different types (*Flammenwerfer 39* and *41*). In addition, there was a supply of *Tellermine 42's* and *S-Mine 35's*. The strength of the 2nd Company was given as 140 men, 20 of whom were Poles, with the remainder German.[151] Some motorisation was available, and each company had a motorcycle and one or two 3-tonne lorries. The rest of the companies had bicycles.[152]

Major Reicherzer was killed on **12 June**, and buried in Orglandes.[153] In **August**, *Hauptmann* Klein was reported as in command of the battalion, but it is not clear, when he had assumed command.[154]

In comparison to the authorisation document, the organisation of *Artillerie-Regiment 243* (*Oberst* Hellwig) changed little from **September 1943**. It called for a headquarters and headquarters battery, one heavy battalion and two light battalions. The light battalions were authorised a headquarters and headquarters battery, with the latter not having a surveying section. The batteries would each receive three light howitzers, a light *Flak* and two MG's. The heavy battalion was identical, but equipped with three batteries of heavy howitzers and a fourth battery with heavy cannon; it would also have four motor vehicles to tow the guns, most likely the *Sd.Kfz. 7* that were called for in earlier authorisation documents.[155]

The regiment used the following *KStN's*: Regimental headquarters (*KStN 401f*); regimental headquarters battery (*KStN 575f*); battalion headquarters (*KStN 403f*); battalion headquarters battery (*KStN 582f*); light battery (*KStN 433f*); heavy howitzer battery (*KStN 459f*); and heavy cannon battery (*KStN 454f*). Except for the latter, all of these were dated **1 December 1942**. Since *KStN 454f* (**20 May 1943**) had not actually been published, *KStN 459f* was used as a guideline.[156]

By **1 May 1944**, much of the authorised levels had been met. The transport situation was actually far better, as the regiment was now fully motorised. The regimental headquarters battery had a MG and the headquarters battery of all three battalions had two. The headquarters batteries in the battalions now also had surveying sections.[157]

All batteries had been formed with just three artillery pieces each and the authorisation document of **September 1943** still called for that number of guns.[158] In mid-**December**, it was decided to expand the batteries to four guns each, the guns arriving in the final weeks of the year.[159] There was a slight delay with the 10th Battery and, on **3 January 1944**, its final gun was still on its way, arriving on the **31st**.[160]

All artillery pieces in the regiment were of Russian origin. The first two battalions had three batteries of four *7,62 cm FK 39(r)'s* each. As was standard, the heavier guns were in the 3rd Battalion; its first three batteries were each equipped with four *12,2 cm sFH 396(r)'s*, while the 10th Battery had four *12,2 cm K 390/2(r)*.[161] Each battery had a German *2 cm Flak* and three MG's.[162] The antiaircraft artillery in the 3rd Battalion is said to have been *2 cm Flak 38's*, but the type used by the other two battalions is not clear.[163]

The use of 2 cm *Flak* is noteworthy, given it is unlikely they were used one per battery as prescribed by the authorisations. The orders of battle of the division through **1 January 1944** show that the 10 *Flak* had been consolidated in a dedicated "11th Battery".[164] *Gen.* Dollmann approved this battery for training purposes, yet insisted that the *Flak* be distributed among the battalions when moving and deployed.[165] It appears the battery was indeed split up, but with the guns divided among the battalions rather than their individual batteries. To that end, the *Flak* of each battalion were grouped together in platoons to protect the entire battalion. This method was reported for the 3rd Battalion.[166] In late **May**, ULTRA intercepted a message noting that a *Flak* platoon from *AR 243* was in position at Virandeville with five 2 cm *Flak*. This could indicate that the *Flak* was still partially organised as an independent element within the regiment.[167]

The regiment's mobility was excellent, because it was fully motorised. Most of the guns in the 3rd Battalion were towed by *RSO* prime movers.[168] This, however, did not apply to the 10th Battery, as its guns were much too heavy for them; instead, they probably used *Sd.Kfz. 7* or heavier halftracks. The lighter equipment of the other battalions was likely towed by *RSO's* or lorries. Much of the regiment's transport was reportedly French, but numbers and types are not known.[169] According to a soldier of the 7th Battery, his battery carried 600 rounds of ammunition. Of these, 50 rounds were carried in each of the prime movers and the rest carried in four ammunition vehicles. The vehicles in the battery were 10-12 lorries and five or six light cars.[170]

Personnel numbers are sketchy and accounts differ considerably. The 2nd Battery is said to have had a strength of 90 men, all Austrians with the exception of 20 Russians and five Poles.[171] The forward observer of the 5th Battery reported a strength of about 65 men, including 15 Georgians.[172] The 7th Battery reportedly had a strength of about 120 men. In the 8th Battery, all of the officers and most of the NCO's were Germans, with a total of 75 men.[173]

As a static formation, the division originally had limited AT capabilities, but this changed with the formation of *Panzerjäger-Abteilung 243* in early **1944**. To avoid confusion, the battalion's establishment will be examined first, followed by a closer look at the organisation and condition of one of its companies.

The **September 1943** authorisation document did not list any form of divisional AT elements — normal for a static division.[174] The first step in establishing divisional AT units was the formation of *Pz.Jg.Kp. 243* (with nine motorised 7,5 cm *Pak 40's*), most likely in early **November**.[175]

On **11 January 1944**, OKH ordered the establishment of *Pz.Jg.Abt. 243*. In addition to a headquarters, it was to have three companies. The 1st Company was to receive self-propelled AT guns, the 2nd Company would have assault guns and the 3rd Company would be outfitted with *Flak*. The battalion was to be ready for deployment on **1 February**.[176]

On **15 January**, *AOK 7* informed the *LXXXIV. A.K.* of the decision to form the battalion; information regarding the battalion headquarters would be provided later in a special order. The *Flak* company would be raised elsewhere and sent to the division in early **February**.[177] It was decided to use the headquarters of *Pz.Jg.Abt. 251* (which would be disbanded) to form the new battalion's headquarters. It used the *Feldpost* number of the former unit, suggesting it was simply redesignated.[178] While *Pz.Jg.Kp. 243* was not used in the formation of the new battalion, it probably supplied the AT companies of the three infantry regiments with AT guns. This was in contrast to the *352.* and the *353. I.D.*, which had both been ordered to form an AT battalion at the same time as the *243. I.D.* The two divisions were instructed to use their "AT companies" to form the 1st Company of their own AT battalions.

Orders for the battalion's formation, dated **11 January**, provide details about its organisation and the origin of the men. The *KStN's* employed were standard for the type of headquarters and companies involved. *KStN 1148d* was used for the self-propelled AT company (1st Company). This called for three platoons of four SP guns and two more with the command group.[179] Personnel were provided by *Wehrkreis XVII* (Vienna) from *Panzerjäger-Ersatz-und-Ausbildungs-Abteilung 17* (Antitank Replacement and Training Battalion 17), which became the battalion's official source of replacements. *KStN 446a* was initially used for the *Panzerjäger-Sturmgeschütz-Kompanie* (antitank assault gun company - the 2nd Company). This *KStN* was probably superseded by *KStN 1149*, introduced in **February**. A total of 10 assault guns were authorised, distributed among three platoons, each with three assault guns; the remaining vehicle was with the command group.[180] Personnel were provided by *Pz.Jg.Ers.u.Ausb.Abt. 18* (*Wehrkreis XVIII*). The assault gun companies of the infantry divisions were redesignated in **February 1944**, with the 2nd Company officially becoming *Sturmgeschütz-Abteilung 1243*.[181] As nothing changed other than its designation, this author will continue to refer to it as the *2./Pz.Jg.Abt. 243*. The *KStN* used by the *Flak* company (3rd Company) is not clear. The division later reported having the standard number of 12 2 cm *Flak*, but the guns were in two motorised platoons with a third SP

On D-Day Pz.Jg.Abt. 243 fielded the heaviest and most modern German armour of all the forces on the Cotentin. It was the only formation equipped with Sturmgeschütz III assault guns. It would loose several in the early fighting around Ste.Mère-Église, including this one. The number identifies it as the 2nd vehicle in the third platoon of 2nd Company. It was captured fairly intact, and here American mechanics are trying to replace the final drive by one taken from the vehicle in the background. As is evident from the pattern of their Zimmerit coating, the front vehicle was built by MIAG and the other one by Alkett. The camouflage pattern with its thin lines, typcial for the battalion, are clearly visible on the commander's cupola. (NARA)

platoon.[182] Two different *KStN's* for 2 cm *Flak* were authorised for this kind of company but neither match.[183] The history of the *Feldpost* number suggests it was originally formed as an unnumbered SP company. This means it probably followed *KStN* 192 and the towed guns were the exception.

Except for the 3rd Company, the battalion was reportedly formed at Freistadt, Austria in **January 1944**, and soon transferred to Tribehou. Equipment was received from Magdeburg (Germany) and Olmnitz (Czechoslovakia).[184] The division's order of battle (**1 February**) shows the battalion was in formation, but it had yet to receive its heavy weapons. While the AT company was no longer listed, all three infantry regiments now had a 14th Company, each with three motorised heavy AT guns.[185]

The battalion's heavy weapons arrived between **February** and **April**.[186] Eight *Sd.Kfz. 138 Marder III's (Ausführung M)* arrived on **19 February**, and another six on **16 April**.[187] The first five assault guns for the 2nd Company arrived on **7 March**.[188] On **23 March**, *AOK 7* recorded that the five remaining assault guns had been assigned by *OKH*, and these arrived on the **29th**.[189] On **1 March**, the division reportedly received 12 self-propelled 2 cm *Flak* 38's, but this must have been an error since only one platoon was ever reported with SP *Flak*, the remainder being towed.[190] An order of battle from this period confirms that 12 *Flak* were indeed assigned to the 3rd Company, but the type of vehicles is unclear.[191] The SP guns were most likely *Sd.Kfz. 10/5's*. Three assault guns were mechanically unserviceable in early **May** and still under repair when the invasion began.¹⁵² This may help explain how elements of the battalion were used after the start of the invasion (more on that later).

Motorised AT battalions required a large number of vehicles, as is made clear by *7. Armee* records. On **24 February**, the *OKH* assigned 1 medium motorcycle, 4 light cross-country cars (*Kfz. 1's*), 2 light lorries and 32 medium lorries to the battalion; this was followed by another 39 vehicles on the **28ᵗʰ**.¹⁹³ In **March**, the *OKH* assigned some special equipment to the battalion: A *Sd. Kfz. 8* (12-ton halftrack) (on the **6ᵗʰ**), followed by an entire maintenance section, 2 halftracks and 12 motor vehicles (on the **16ᵗʰ**).¹⁹⁴ On **5 April**, it was issued additional motor vehicles by the directorate responsible for for the formation of units in the west (*Aufstellungsstab West*): seven medium lorries and a *Kfz. 17* (light radio lorry). On **16 April**, the assault gun companies of the *243.* and *353. I.D.* were both assigned a 22-tonne flatbed trailer, capable of transporting an assault gun.¹⁹⁵ The 18-ton *Sd.Kfz. 9* prime movers, needed to tow the trailer, followed on **4 May**, as did one each for *Pz.Jg.Abt. 352* and *353*. Fuel, of course, was required for training and, in late **March**, the senior quartermaster for the western theatre allotted 30,000 litres to the new AT battalions.¹⁹⁶ Another special allowance of 15,000 litres was allocated on **5 May**.¹⁹⁷

Although reports show the battalion's evolution, they provide little information on its condition and organisation. The *KStN* numbers provide the theoretical strength, but this was often not met. Fortunately, a soldier from the 1ˢᵗ Company provided details on the organisation of his unit. Although his information is incomplete, it is reliable enough to provide a useful impression of the condition of the company at the time of the invasion. The company had a strength of about 140 men. Most were Germans, but there were some 60 Austrians, 3 Yugoslavs, and 8 Poles.¹⁹⁸

The command group had eight men to crew its two self-propelled guns (the aforementioned *Marder III's*). The company commander also commanded one of the vehicles. Additional personnel were two drivers, a paymaster and his assistant, a *Hauptfeldwebel* and an assistant clerk (junior NCO). Transport consisted of a motorcycle with sidecar and a *Volkswagen*.¹⁹⁹

The trains reportedly encompassed three kitchen personnel, two rations men, five men in the fuel section and a medic with driver. The unit was fully motorised and included a Renault lorry for the kitchen. Another Renault lorry was used for rations, and it carried supplies sufficient for two days. The fuel section had two lorries, carrying a total of 12 200-litre drums of fuel and 2 more drums of oil. A Tatra car was available to the medic.²⁰⁰

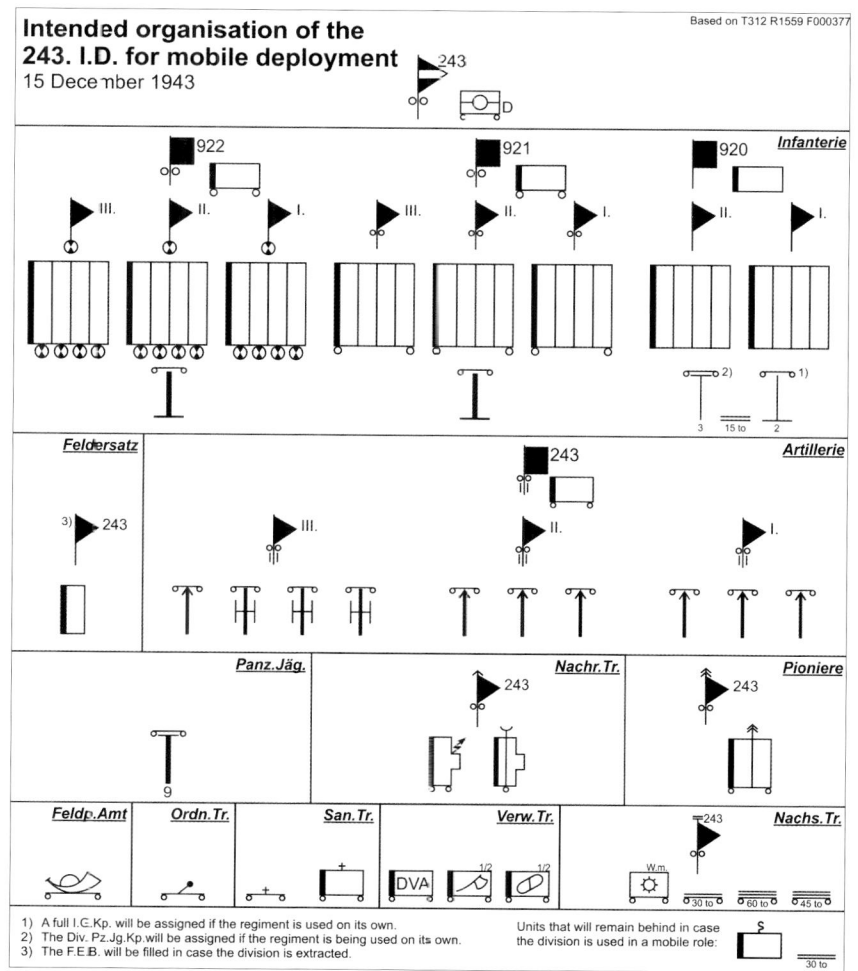

7ᵗʰ Army's mobility programme started out very ambitious, aiming to provide nearly the entire division with bicycles or motorisation. The infantry regiments would receive different forms of mobility, with GR 920 restricted to horses and foot marches, GR 921 would be motorised, and GR 922 would move mostly by bicycle.

The maintenance section had about 20 men. Of these, 12 were mechanics and one was a radio repairman. There were also a transport NCO, a carpenter, a cobbler, a tailor and around three *Hiwi's*. This section was equipped with three Renault lorries for transporting spare parts. Another Renault was available to the shoemaker, tailor and carpenter, and the transport NCO was provided with a Tatra car.[201]

The three combat platoons with their self-propelled guns had 23 men each. As expected from the *KStN*, the platoons each had four *Marder III's* crewed by four instead of five men. The vehicle crews consisted of a commander, gunner, loader/radio operator and driver. The platoon leader also commanded the first gun in his platoon.[202] The vehicles reportedly carried no less than 58 rounds for their *7,5 cm Pak 40's*, a number of rounds well above the standard basic load of 27. Yet this included only 3 armour-piercing rounds, as these were in short supply, 26 hollow-charge rounds and 29 high-explosive rounds.[203] Every vehicle also had a MG. In the platoons, these were three *MG 34's* and one *MG 42*; each MG had 2,000 rounds of armour-piercing ammunition, with every seventh round a tracer. There were 50-100 rounds for the machine pistols and 10 egg hand grenades. Each vehicle also carried a demolition charge to destroy the main gun on the vehicle to prevent capture. In addition to the weapons on their vehicles, the crews were armed with Belgian pistols.[204]

The personnel were not limited to the *Marder* crews. In line with the *KStN*, each platoon also had an observer in officer rank, who operated a range finder. He was allocated a Tatra car and driver. For ammunition transport, each platoon possessed one halftrack lorry (*Maultier*) instead of the two as prescribed by the *KStN*. The halftracks were loaded with 200-300 7.5 cm rounds, but they carried no armour-piercing rounds.[205]

On **1 March**, *Maj.d.R.* Bethge was put in command of the battalion. On **16 May**, Bethge and his adjutant were killed in a mine accident near Barneville.[206] *Hauptmann* Nesselhauf took command four days later, assigned from the *OKH* officer manpower pool in *Wehrkreis XVII*. He was formerly an assistant staff officer in *Pz.Jg.Abt.* 387 and had assumed acting command of the battalion for a month in the autumn of **1943**. Like his predecessor, he was only with the new battalion for a short period and died near Écausseville on **9 June**.[207] It was not until later in the month that he was formally succeeded by *Oblt.* Stratmann, who had commanded *Flak-Kompanie 243* under *FJR 6*.[208] His transfer was urgently requested by the division after the battalion's third commander was killed.[209] As he was the battalion's fourth commander, there must have been one more commander after *Hauptmann* Nesselhauf, whose identity is not known.[210]

The available information enables an examination of *Feldgendarmerie-Trupp 243*, the division's military police. The section was commanded by *Leutnant* Heimbach, and he had 32 NCO's and men armed with pistols or rifles. The section was supposed to have *Volkswagens*, but it used eight commandeered private vehicles instead. There also was a lorry that carried materials for putting up road signs.[211]

Mobility and Beweglichmachung

The military police section offers another example of the wide variety of motor vehicles in the division. Although the division had been raised as a static force, this started to change in late **1943**. In **November**, following *Führer* Directive 51, the *243. I.D.* was one of two divisions under *AOK 7* that was selected to be made "mobile"; the other being the *346. I.D.* The *243. I.D.* was considered suitable because of its position on the Atlantic coast — an area considered at limited risk of invasion — and the quality of its leadership, equipment and training.[212] The efforts to increase mobility meant that the division would ultimately surpass that of a standard infantry division in terms of its ability to move on its own and permit its employment as a mobile reserve.

In mid-**December**, most of the division was intended for mobile deployment and motorisation. Exceptions were *GR 920*, which would rely on horses and the battalions in *GR 922*, which would be bicycle formations. The field-replacement battalion would also be horse-drawn. Only two elements, the veterinary company and the logistics trains (*Veterinär-Kompanie 243* and *Große Fahrkolonne 243*, both horse-drawn) would remain behind in case of transfer.[213] Towards the end of the month, the mobility plans for *GR 921* and 922 were switched but little else changed.[214]

The situation remained the same in **January 1944**, when the mobility of the headquarters company of *GR 921* was reduced to bicycles.[215] Equipment numbers are thin on the ground for **1944**, but do exist for **1 January**. At that time there were 128 motorcycles (including 19 in short-term repair) with an authorisation of 167. The number of cross-country vehicles was 31 (2 in short-term repair) with an authorisation of 56 and the remaining vehicles were 32

(5 in short-term repair) with an authorisation of 33. The aggregate transport capacity of the lorries was authorised to be 283 tonnes. The division had 234 tonnes of lift available, although 23.5 tonnes were in repair. These numbers can be further broken down to an authorisation of 5 off-road lorries and 130 regular lorries. In the former category, the division had eight operational lorries and one in repair; the numbers for the regular lorries included 111 operational and 7 in repair. As authorised, the division also had three medium or heavy halftrack prime movers; these were probably the 8-ton *Sd.Kfz. 7* vehicles in the *III./AR 243*. The division's number of *RSO*'s also matched its authorisations, although 5 out of 30 were in repair. A final entry is for armoured ammunition transporters; the division had an authorisation of 22, of which 17 were operational and 1 was in repair. This vehicle has so far not been identified, but they may be Renault UE tractors. Although there were considerable shortages among some of the motor vehicles, this was not the case for horses. Against an authorisation of 1,216, the division had 1,168, a shortage of just 48.[216]

The numbers illustrate that there were already problems in providing the division with its organic mobility. The divisional commander reported that the intended motorisation was falling short due to the poor condition of the issued *Organization Todt* vehicles: 50% were not operational.[217]

In light of the above, it is hardly surprising that motorisation would not be achieved for all elements of the division as originally intended by the mobility programme. On **3 February**, the *2./Pi.Btl. 243* and most of *GR 922* were ordered to become bicycle formations, a decision that mostly affected the *I./922*, which had already been motorised in an ad hoc fashion in late **January**.[218] Those efforts were cancelled, and the battalion made a bicycle formation instead. The vehicles were returned to the motor vehicle company of the *XXV. A.K.*, which made sense, since the battalion was intended to rejoin its division under the *LXXXIV. A.K.*[219] The other battalions also became bicycle formations, but these had never been more than only partially motorised.[220] The engineer battalion was another example of downgraded mobility. On **1 February**, the entire battalion was still listed as partially motorised on the order of battle.[221] By mid-**March**, the 2nd Company was equipped with bicycles, while the battalion headquarters was still listed as partially motorised and the 1st Company as fully motorised.[222] The entire battalion had become a bicycle formation by **1 May**.[223]

Even though the division's mobility was not as ambitious as originally planned, its increased mobility still brought new challenges. Additional training was required to prepare the troops for mobile deployment, and exercises made clear the divisional command was also not ready for such deployment. On **16 February**, this was reported to *Ob.West*. Mobility itself

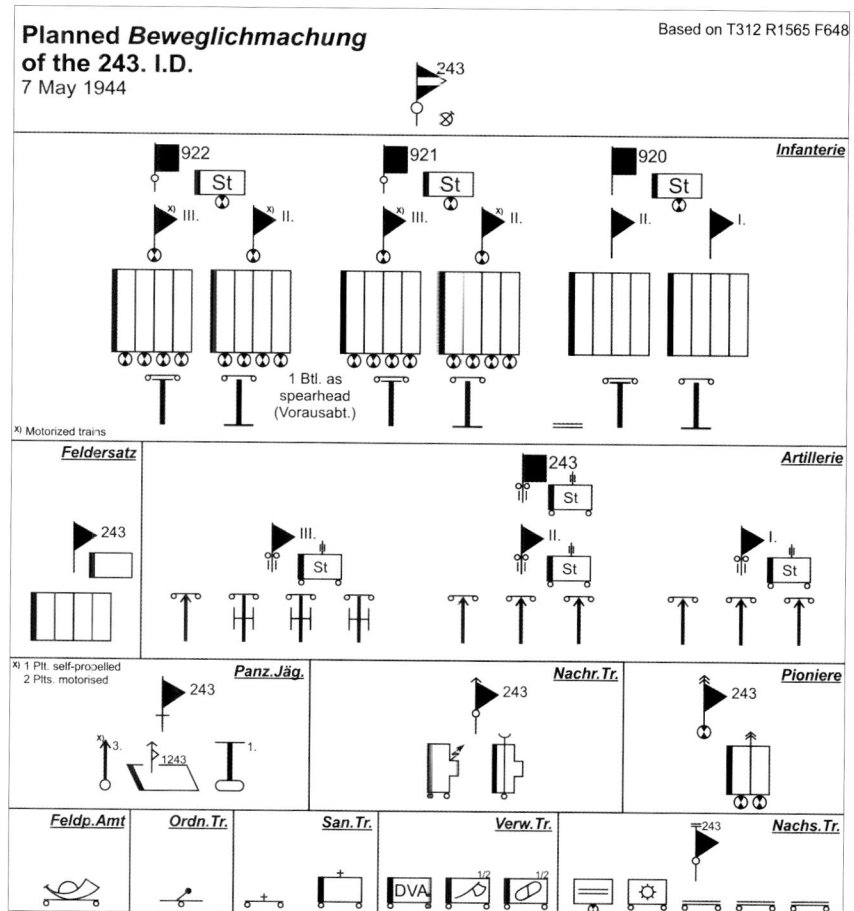

By 7 May 1944 the intended motorisation of the division had been considerably reduced compared to the plans of late 1943. GR 921 and 922 were now both bicycle mobile.

243. Infanterie-Division

was not the issue, but mobile deployment required additional equipment, such as radios. Permission was sought to change the *KStN* of the divisional headquarters and signals battalion from "static" to that of a regular infantry division. The personnel and standard vehicles for this change could be covered by the division, but special vehicles and equipment would have to come from outside the *7. Armee*.[224]

When, on **14 March**, further orders were issued regarding the enhanced mobility efforts (*Beweglichmachung*) of five infantry divisions, the special status of the *243. I.D.* was again confirmed. Whereas the other divisions were only to mobilise a limited number of units, all elements of the *243. I.D.* were to retain the mobility they already possessed.[225] This situation changed on **7 May**. Although the trains of the bicycle elements were to retain their motorisation, this did not apply to the *II./921* and the *I./922*, which were assigned the static duty of holding the Cherbourg *Landfront* (land defences).[226]

The special mobility of the division at this time is best illustrated by an order from **7 May** showing the mobility status of different divisions. For most of these divisions, their mobility amounted to a *Kampfgruppe* of two or three infantry battalions, a few engineer companies and, on occasion, an artillery detachment. For the *243. I.D.*, almost the entire division was listed with increased mobility, of which only the field-replacement battalion and *GR 920* had to fully rely on horses. All other formations were partially motorised or had bicycles.[227]

On **12 May**, the tonnage lift capacity of the division was an impressive 1,180 tonnes.[228] Compare this figure to **1 January 1944**, when the authorisation had been 283 tonnes.[229] By D-Day, the level of mobility of the infantry and the trains and the fully motorised artillery regiment, made the division unique among the infantry divisions in Normandy.

On **19 May**, *AOK 7* issued new orders from von Rundstedt's *Ob.West*. These affected the division in particular. *Ob.West* stated that motorised elements were not to consider their motorisation to be assigned assets; rather, it was deemed necessary to collect the vehicles in motor companies (*Kraftfahr-Kompanien*). Moreover, it might be necessary to strip the motorisation of the trains of the advance guard as well. These vehicles were to become part of the motor transport company, although they could remain with the troops for the time being. As an option, the troops were to keep horse-drawn trains available.

With a lack of motorisation, bicycles were some of the most important means of transportation in the German Army. This was especially true for infantry which otherwise mostly had to move on foot. Here we see an emergency drill to test a unit's readiness. (Archives du Calvados – 10Fi-2, photo 185, Agance Fama, France et Atlantic, Berlin)

The formation of motor transport companies was to be finished by **10 June** and their strength reported to *AOK 7*.[230] This suggests that the vehicles may not have been taken before D-Day.

The wide variety of motor vehicles was a complicating factor. This is characteristic of the *Wehrmacht* as a whole, for which the issue was quite serious. Since detailed information is available for the headquarters and headquarters company of *GR 922*, they will serve as an example. The headquarters was equipped with three medium motorcycles, one motorcycle combination, three light cars, three medium cars, one *Kfz. 12*, and a 1-ton Hotchkiss lorry. The regimental commander and adjutant had a light Renault car and, in action, the commander used the *Kfz. 12*. Two medium vehicles (including a Ford) were available for the dispatch riders, and the assistant staff officer had a medium Opel. The final light vehicle in the headquarters was another Ford. The headquarters company had considerably more motor transport: 1 motorcycle-combination, 3 light cars, 4 medium cars, 5 light lorries, 10

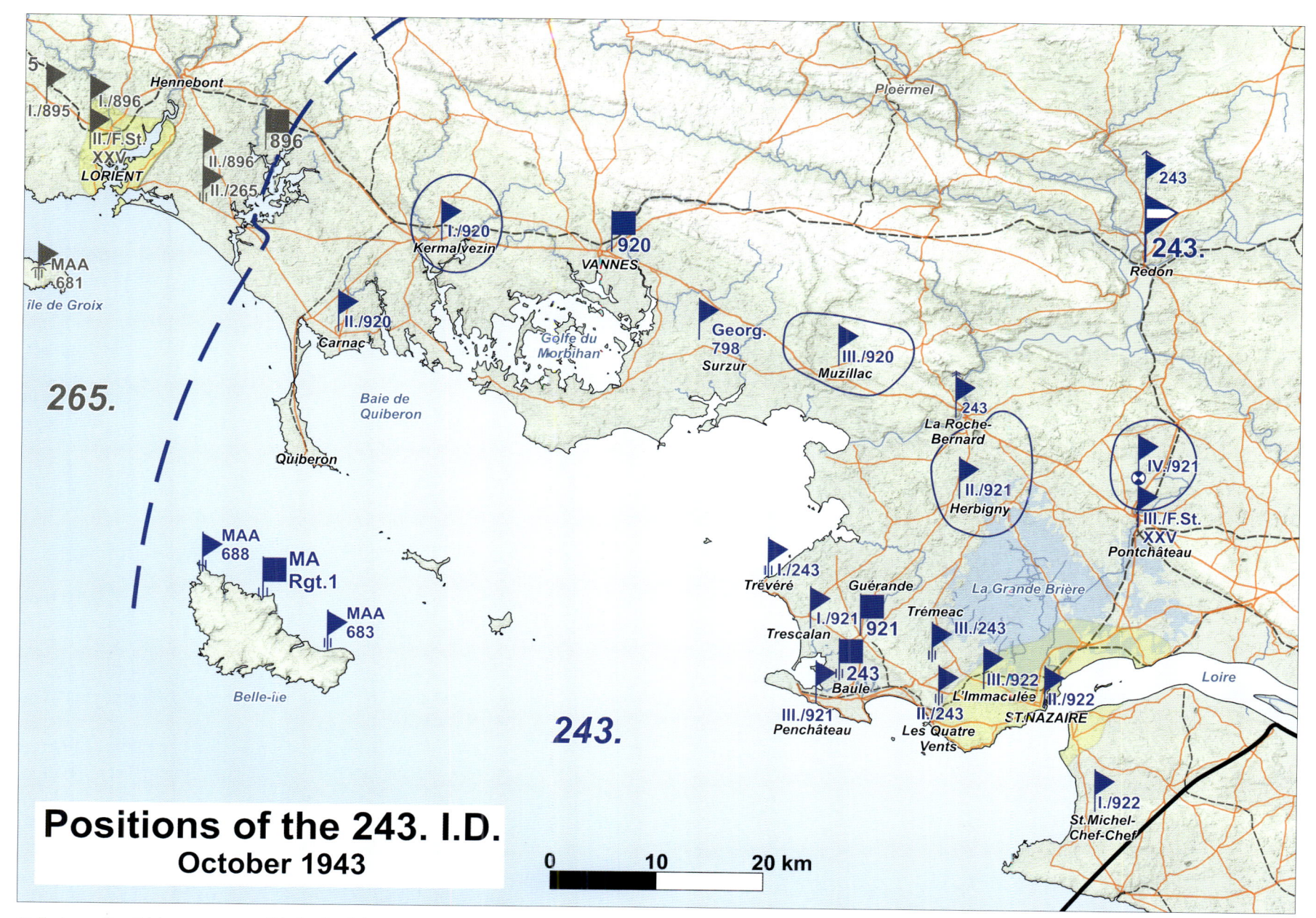

In Bretagne the division was responsible for the defence of KVA 'C2', the left most sector of 7th Army. The U-Boot base of St. Nazaire was the sector's most important installation and is where the main strength of the division was assembled.

medium lorries and 2 rented wood-gas generators. The light vehicles were an Opel, a Renault and a Ford. Of the medium vehicles, one was a Citroën, another a Ford and the remaining two were Renaults. Two of the light lorries were Renaults; the others were a Morris, a Ford and an Austin. The medium lorries were a Citroën, Reo, Unic, Delage, Studebaker and Panhard. Finally, there were two medium Renault and two Chevrolet lorries.[231] Not counting motorcycles, this constitutes more than 20 different makes and models within the battalion headquarters. There is no reason to assume the situation in the rest of the division was any better.

According to a member of *GR 921*, 70% of the vehicles were old and unreliable. After about 50 km, barely half of them would still be operational. On divisional manoeuvres in Bretagne, only one lorry in the regiment had not broken down by the second day! Poor tyres were responsible for 30-40% of the breakdowns. Mobility was further hampered by the ongoing lack of fuel. Manoeuvres could only be conducted sporadically, and even then the number of vehicles was restricted.[232]

History

As described earlier, the *243. I.D.* was formed as "*Division B*" on **22 June 1943**.[233] Orders to establish the division were issued by the *OKH* on **19 June**, and the division was to be ready for deployment by **15 August**, a fairly tight schedule. The working staffs were established between **1** and **10 July**, with convalescents from the *387. I.D.* beginning to arrive on the **8th**. Transfers from forces in the field started arriving on the **15th**. Weapons and equipment were brought up between **20 July-10 August**.[234]

As early as **4 August**, *Wehrkreis XVII* was ordered to transfer the division to *Ob.West* beginning on **11 August**, with the destination of Lisieux in the *15. Armee* sector. On **14 August**, the division was already listed as being in France and reporting directly to *Ob.West*, which was responsible for completion of its formation.[235]

The division would not remain with the *15. Armee* for long. On **8 August**, *AOK 7* was informed that elements would be transported to the area south of Carentan as soon as the *389. I.D.* had left the region.[236] In late **August**, *AOK 7* learned that the *243. I.D.* was to relieve the *384. I.D.* on the southern coast of Bretagne in late **September**. The *384. I.D.*, in turn, would take over the old positions of the *243. I.D.* A reinforced regiment from the *243. I.D.* would also relieve the reinforced regiment from the *384. I.D.* deployed in Normandy.[237]

On **13 September**, *AOK 7* provided more details to its corps regarding the new division. It would primarily be in *KVA "C2"* under the *XXV. A.K.*, but a regimental headquarters and two bicycle battalions would be moved to the *LXXXIV. A.K.* in the area of Caen - St. Lô as a field-army reserve.[238]

Later, the regiment's plans were clarified and three trains transferred it to Carentan, arriving on **1 October**.[239] This force, which consisted of the headquarters of *GR 922*, with one bicycle battalion each from *GR 920* and *922*, became a corps reserve.[240] The battalions were not standard, having been formed from the bicycle companies of the two regiments.[241] Essentially, the newly formed battalions were regarded as the 4th Battalion of the two regiments.[242] It also meant that the battalions in these regiments now had only three companies instead of four. It appears that the regiments reverted back to four companies per battalion in early **January 1944**.[243]

Transfer of the main body of the division to Bretagne began on **29 September**, with 29 trains shepherding it from Lisieux to Redon.[244] The move was completed on **2 October** and, at 18:00, the division assumed command of the entire sector, relieving the *384. I.D.*[245]

Apparently, it took time to relieve all of the *384. I.D.*, thus the locations of *243. I.D.* elements were not listed until **24 October** (down to battalion level). The divisional headquarters and *Nachr.Abt. 243* were located at Redon and *Pi.Btl. 243* at La Roche-Bernard. The right (northern) coast sector was held by *GR 920*, with its headquarters at Vannes. The 2nd and 3rd Battalions were on the coast, at Carnac and Muzillac respectively. The 1st Battalion was further inland at Auray, but it moved to Kermalvezin in early **November**. *Georg.Inf. Btl. 798* was also in this sector at Surzur.[246]

Most of the division's forces, including the artillery, were near and northwest of St. Nazaire. The headquarters of *GR 921* was at Guérande, with two of its battalions on the coast: The 1st Battalion in Trescalan and the 3rd Battalion in Penchâteau. Further inland were the 2nd Battalion and the ad hoc (bicycle) 4th Battalion at Herbignac and Pontchâteau, respectively. The *III./Festungs-Stamm-Regiment XXV* was also located in Pontchâteau.[247]

At this point, the headquarters of *GR 922* (with the *IV./920* and the *IV./922*) was still on the Cotentin, but three of its organic battalions were located in and around St. Nazaire. The 1st Battalion was south of the Loire,

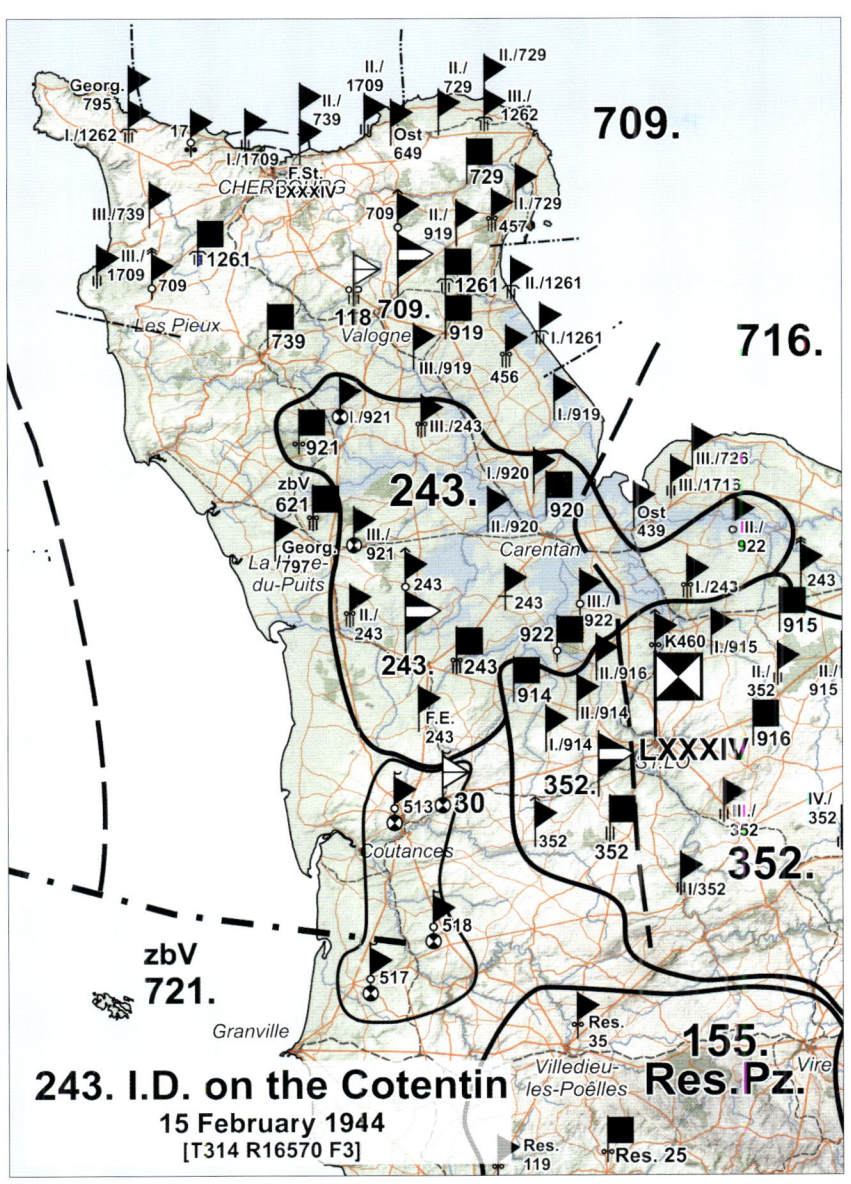

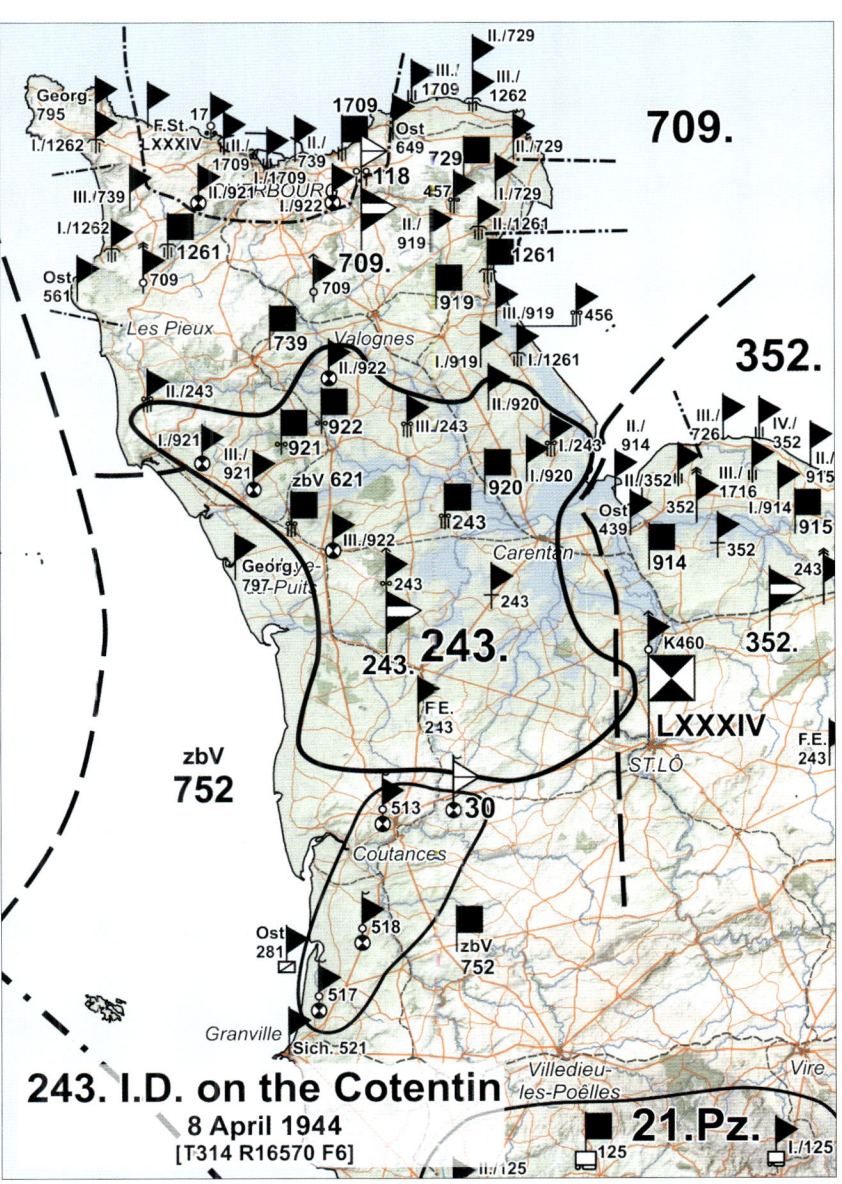

After moving to Normandy in early January, the division initially held a sector along the base of the Cotentin, with some elements stationed in the Calvados.

By 8 April the division had moved further north, up the Cotentin, holding positions from where it could support both the east and west coast.

at St. Michel-Chef-Chef, the 2nd Battalion was in St. Nazaire and the 3rd was at l'Immaculée.[248]

The headquarters of *AR 243* was in La Baule and the regiment's three battalions in Tréveré (1st), Les Quatre Vents (2nd) and Trémeac (3rd).[249] The battery positions were not reported except for the 10th Battery, which was north of La Trinité-sur-Mer covering the neck of the Quiberon Peninsula and the mouth of the Étel River.[250]

Although there were movements after the division's arrival, the most significant change concerned the transfer of the *III./920* to the east on **27-28 October**.[251] It only took its 10th to 12th Companies, since the 9th (Bicycle) Company was still in Normandy, but the battalion was brought up to strength by assigning it the *8./921*. This company was re-established through "command channels" on **8 November**.[252] As a replacement for the battalion, the division received *Ost-Btl. 636*, which arrived at Vannes on **19 November**.[253]

In the second half of **1943**, arrivals, departures and other activities in the *7. Armee* area of responsibility forced *AOK 7* to update its plans for redeploying forces as reinforcements for areas that might come under attack, the so-called Contingency Measures I - III (*Maßnahmen I - III*).[254] In early **November**, the *243. I.D.* was selected for Contingency Measure I, the transfer of entire divisions. To make this possible, motorisation and rail transportation were prepared.[255]

Shortly thereafter, *AOK 7* was informed of *Führer* Directive 51, which prioritised strengthening the defences in the west. *AOK 7* was ordered to select two divisions to be turned into mobile formations, and it picked the two divisions already selected for Contingency Measure I. **November 1943** thus marked the beginning of the efforts to increase mobility of the division.

Because transfer of the division would be complex, the *7. Armee* carried out an exercise in **December**. In this manner, the arrival and loading of the vehicles could be tested, as well as the division's relief on the coast; it would also be possible to train the division for mobile deployment. The exercise lasted several weeks, and the regiment from Normandy returned to the division to participate in it.[256] The relief forces began to arrive on **1 December** and most arrived within a few days.[257] The regiment in Normandy rejoined the division about the same time, starting with the *IV./922* on **1 December** followed by the *IV./920* two days later.[258] The headquarters of *GR 922* arrived on **6 December**.[259]

While the positions after its movement were not reported, they were shown down to battalion level on a situation map on **30 December**. The headquarters, signals battalion and the engineer battalion were not relocated. The headquarters of *GR 920* was still at Vannes, with its 1st Battalion at Theix, the 2nd Battalion at Arradon and the 4th Battalion at Elven. The headquarters of *GR 921* was in Kerflis (today Kerfélice), its 2nd Battalion in Herbignac and its 3rd Battalion in Kerdavy (all southwest of La Roche-Bernard). Its 1st Battalion was to the northwest, at Muzillac, and the 4th Battalion at Pontchâteau. The headquarters of *GR 922* was established in a radio station south of La Gravière, between St. Nazaire and Pontchâteau; the *II.* and *III./922* were in the same area, at Montoir-de-Bretagne and Besné, respectively. The 1st Battalion was at Savenay and the 4th Battalion at Guenrouet. *AR 243* had moved to Missillac on **9 December.** Its three battalions were at Péaule (1st), Campbon (2nd) and St. Dolay (3rd).[260]

Plans for the division continued to evolve and, on **10 December**, *AOK 7* ordered it to prepare for transfer to Normandy.[261] This was still only a plan, however, and on the **19th**, the *XXV. A.K.* ordered the division to return to the coast by the **30th**.[262] This was not carried out as the redeployment to Normandy became firm on **28 December**. The *OKW* expected enemy landings to begin as early as mid-February, and it realised that bringing up reinforcements once the invasion had started could be difficult. It was therefore decided to reinforce the most threatened sectors in advance, including the Cotentin. To this end, the transfer of the *243. I.D.* to Normandy was moved forward, with the division to be ready in its new sector by **1 February**. This change effectively ended plans for the division to return to its coastal sector in Bretagne. That sector would be taken over by the *275. I.D.*[263]

The *243. I.D.* would not move to Normandy all at once. On **23 December**, the decision was made for *Pi.Btl 243* to relieve *Pi.Btl. 346* in Normandy to allow the latter formation to return to its division.[264] *Pi.Btl. 243* was transferred to the *LXXXIV. A.K.* on **4 January**;[265] two days later, its headquarters and 1st Company were at Le Molay and the 2nd Company in a Château 1.5 km east of Balleroy.[266] The battalion, supported by a company from *Pi. Btl. 265*, was supposedly employed working on the second defensive position (a basic inland defence line) under *Festungs-Pionier-Abschnitts-Gruppe Beger* (aka *Sonderstab Beger*). Yet this appears to have been a cover for work it was doing on *V*-weapons sites in the Calvados. The battalion would be used for mine laying once it was relieved.[267] Over the next few months, the battalion mostly operated separately from its division. In late **April**, it was transferred to the west coast of Manche. On the **20th**, the headquarters moved to Montmartin-sur-Mer (9 km southwest of Coutances), the 1st Company to Agon (9 km west of Coutances) and the 2nd Company to St. Germain-sur-Ay (5 km northwest of Lessay).[268] Five days later (**25th**), the headquarters moved to Blainville-sur-Mer, while the 2nd Company moved to the Lessay airfield the next day.[269] In **May**, the battalion moved further south, with the headquarters in Donville-les-Bains (4 km northwest of Granville) and the 2nd Company in the area of Queron (today Kairon) – Jullouville (on the coast south of Granville).[270] The battalion rejoined the division later that month.

The main body of the division was transported from Redon to Périers by train between **7** and **9 January**;[271] its sector in Bretagne taken over at 18:00 on **7 January** by the *275. I.D.*[272] Some elements of the *243. I.D.* stayed in Bretagne, with the *II./921* and *I./922* temporarily in direct support of the new division.[273] *GR 922*'s motor transport was to remain as well.[274] Both infantry battalions were finally relieved by the *275. I.D.* on **20 March**.[275] Four days later, the *II./921* arrived west of Cherbourg and the *I./922* east of the city, becoming part of the *Cherbourg Landfront*. As such, they were attached to the *709. I.D.*, which was responsible for *Festung Cherbourg*. Because of their new mission, the two battalions became known as the *Landfront* Battalions.[276] Other elements that stayed in Bretagne were the division's veterinary company and its main horse-drawn transport column (minus 15 lift tonnes of vehicles). The latter returned to the division on **27 June**.[277]

When the bulk of the *243. I.D.* division arrived in Normandy in **January**, it was initially deployed along the base of the Cotentin. The division headquarters was at Périers and the headquarters of *AR 243* was at nearby Château le Perron. *GR 920* held the area behind what would become Utah Beach, which itself was defended by the *709. I.D.* The regimental headquarters was at Carentan; the headquarters of its two battalions at La Coquerie (just south of Ste. Mère-Église) and St. Côme-du-Mont, respectively.[278] *GR 921* first moved to the area around St. Sauveur-Lendelin (south of Périers) and later in **January** to the St. Sauveur-le-Vicomte area. The regimental headquarters moved accordingly from Château Rupalet to a Château 4 km west of St. Sauveur-le-Vicomte. As expected, its battalions also moved. The 1st Battalion headquarters moved from Gorges to a château 2 km north of St. Sauveur-le-Vicomte; this battalion defended the area along the Douve River north of the town. The 3rd Battalion was initially in Montsurvent, 7 km northwest of Coutances; it then moved to the La Haye-du-Puits area.[279] *GR 922* was furthest east, with its headquarters in Le Dézert and two available battalions at St. Jean-de-Daye (2nd) and Colombières (3rd).[280] The regiment moved onto the Cotentin in mid-**February**. The headquarters moved to St. Sauveur-le-Vicomte, the 2nd Battalion to Golleville and the 3rd Battalion to La Haye-du-Puits.[281] The artillery followed a similar pattern to the infantry regiments, since its battalions were essentially each supporting a specific infantry regiment. The 1st Battalion, initially around Les Oubeaux (southeast of Isigny-sur-Mer) moved to Ste. Marie-du-Mont in mid-**February**;[282] the 2nd Battalion, initially near St. Sauveur-Lendelin, moved to Lessay in **January** and to Hatainville in mid-**February**;[283] the 3rd Battalion was first quartered at Sainteny and a week later at Pont-l'Abbé.[284] In early **February**, the recently formed *Pz.Jg.Abt. 243* was deployed in the wider Sainteny area.[285]

The positions did not change significantly before **May**. The arrival of new formations, specifically the *91. LL.Div.*, affected deployment of the *243. I.D.*, which now moved to the west coast of the Cotentin with only a few elements remaining at their previous locations.[286] Until it could be relieved by *AR 191*, the *I./AR 243* was to stay in position around Ste. Marie-du-Mont.[287] The *Landfront* Battalions also remained in place.[288] *GR 920* was tasked with defending the Vauville Bight (on the west coast of the peninsula) and put under command of the *709. I.D.*[289] The divisional boundaries on the northwest of the peninsula soon changed, with the *243. I.D.* responsible for the coast west of the Cherbourg *Landfront*. The regiment thus returned to divisional control.[290]

Although deployed on the west coast, the division was ordered to retain mobile reserves. Should mobility become less important to certain elements, the bicycles and other means of mobility would be temporarily reissued to other units.[291] As the defence of Normandy increased in importance, the possible use of the division in other sectors of *Ob.West* was cancelled. By late **May**, it was only intended for deployment under *AOK 7*.[292]

Positions on D-Day

In its coastal sector, the divisional headquarters was established at Château Malassis (3 km southwest of Bricquebec).[293] *Nach.Abt. 243* was first at Le Haut du Neuf Clos, before moving further north to Le Cressonnière (1 km south of Quettetot).[294] The headquarters of *AR 243* was in Chambert, between

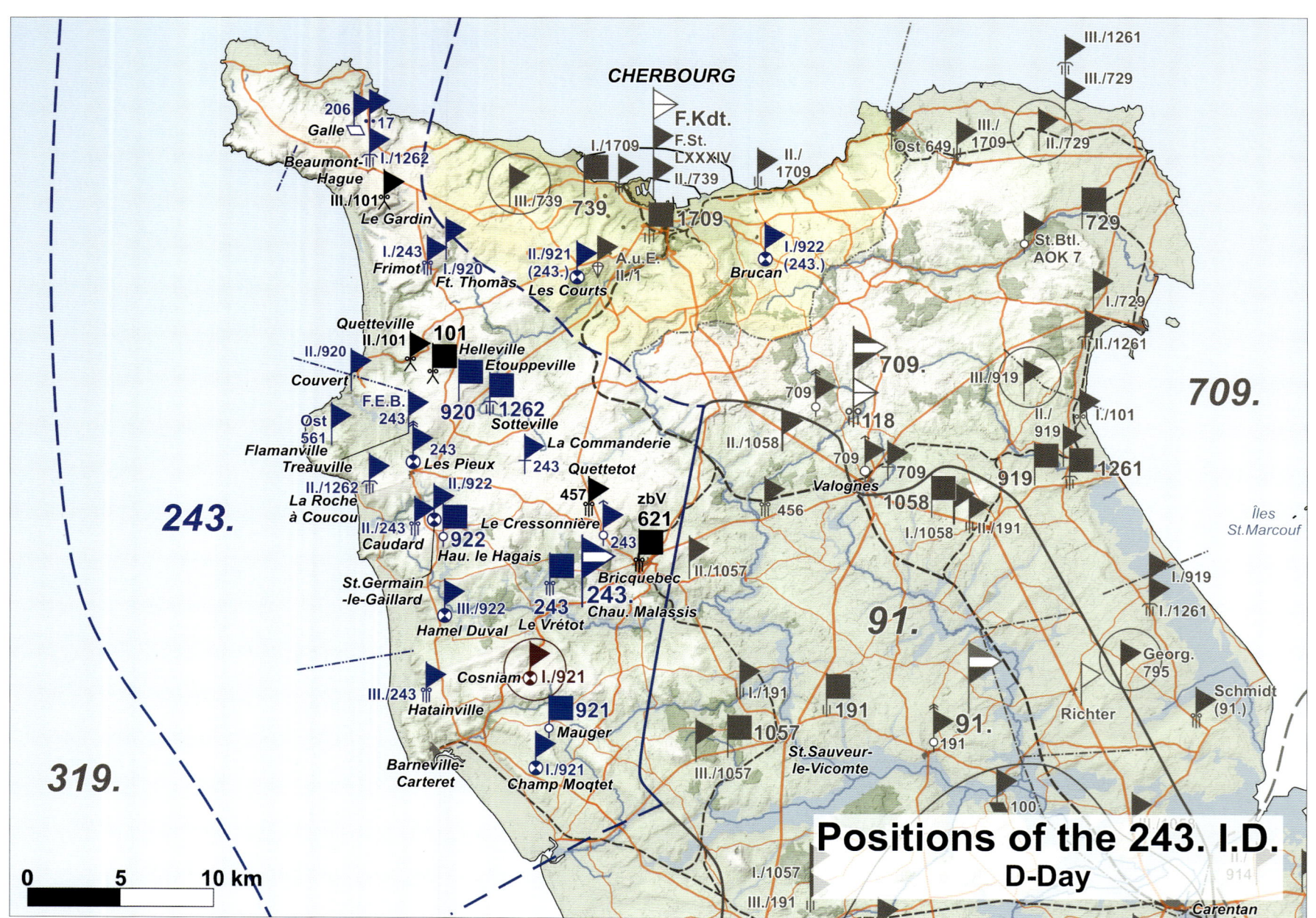

In May the defences of the Cotentin were reorganised. The 91.LL.I.D. assembled in the centre of the peninsula while the 243.I.D. assumed command of the west and north coast between Portbail and Festung Cherbourg. Two of its battalions defended the Cherbourg Landfront, under the 709.I.D.

Les Pieux and Grosville, and later moved to Le Vrétot, the same area as the divisional headquarters.²⁹⁵ *Pi.Btl. 243* had been in Les Pieux since the **22ⁿᵈ**, while *Feld-Ers.Btl. 243* was in position around Tréauville.²⁹⁶

The *GR 920* headquarters was in Étoupeville (1 km west of Virandeville), the 1ˢᵗ Battalion in Fontain du Bienheureux Thomas (1.5 km southeast of Vauville) and the 2ⁿᵈ Battalion in Hau. Couvert (southwest of Siouville-Hague). Artillery to support the coastal defences was provided by the 1ˢᵗ Battalion after its relief by *AR 191*. The battalion arrived on **19 May** and the headquarters was at Frimot.²⁹⁷

To the south of *GR 920* was *GR 922*, with two battalions. Its headquarters was at Hameau le Haguais (just northeast of Pierreville). The headquarters of the *II./922* and the *III./922* were in St. Germain-le-Gaillard and Hamel Duval (today Hameau Duval), respectively.²⁹⁸ The *III./AR 243* provided artillery support for the regiment and was located at Caudard.²⁹⁹

The southernmost divisional sector was held by *GR 921*. The regimental headquarters was at Mauger (today Hôtel Mauger, 3 km east of Barneville). The 3ʳᵈ Battalion was on the coast; its headquarters situated east of St. Jean-de-la-Rivière at Champ Moqtet (today La Charlerie). The 1ˢᵗ Battalion was in reserve further inland at Cosniam (today La Maison Quoniam).³⁰⁰ Artillery support was provided by the 2ⁿᵈ Battalion (headquarters at Hatainville).³⁰¹

Pz.Jäg.Abt. 243 was also moved. On **11 May**, the headquarters relocated to an area 2 km north of Besneville. Its 1ˢᵗ Company was about 2 km further north, around Hau. aux Petits; the 2ⁿᵈ Company still in the area of Le Pont aux Moines.³⁰² Two days (**13ᵗʰ**) later, the headquarters moved again, this time to La Commanderie.³⁰³ The 3ʳᵈ Company remained in the Sainteny area, where it supported *FJR 6* and the *17. SS-Pz.Gren.Div.* during the fighting in **June**.³⁰⁴

When the *243. I.D.* assumed responsibility for the west coast of the Cotentin, several non-organic formations were attached, including troops on the Jobourg Peninsula. This briefly included the headquarters of *GR 739* and its 3ʳᵈ Battalion. The intention was for them to relieve the *Landfront* Battalions, but this was never carried out.³⁰⁵ Instead, the battalion and regimental headquarters were transferred to the *709. I.D.*, and the battalion became a corps reserve.³⁰⁶ *Pz.Abt. 206* and *MG-Btl. 17* were still subordinated to the division on D-Day.³⁰⁷

Also attached to the *243. I.D.* was the bulk of *schwere Stellungs-Werfer-Rgt. 101*, including its headquarters and 2ⁿᵈ and 3ʳᵈ Battalions. The two battalions supported *GR 920*.³⁰⁸ *Ost-Btl. 561* defended the area around Flamanville, while the *2./Georg.Inf.Btl. 797* was on the division's southern boundary at St. Lô-d'Ourville, just east of Portbail.³⁰⁹ It is quite likely that this company was no longer in the divisional sector on D-Day, but that it had become its left neighbour.³¹⁰ Another small but intriguing attachment was the *1./Georg.Inf.Btl. 795*. This company had been assigned to *KVU Vauville* since early **February**;³¹¹ when *Georg.Inf.Btl. 795* moved to the southeast corner of the Cotentin in mid-**May**, its 1ˢᵗ Company stayed behind and came under command of the *243. I.D.*³¹² The division's defences were further augmented by *H.K.A.R. 1262*. The regimental headquarters was at Sotteville and those of its 1ˢᵗ and 2ⁿᵈ Battalions were at Beaumont-Hague and La Roche à Coucou, respectively.³¹³

Combat

The division saw little action on D-Day, as the nearest landings took place on the eastern part of the Cotentin. As early as that morning, the division was ordered to prepare for a move east to the beachhead. The west coast was to be held by covering forces.³¹⁴

Although the division did not have its own sector until **18 June**, it still influenced the initial fighting. On the evening of **8 June**, *Gen.Lt.* Hellmich took charge of all forces on the Cotentin for better coordination. This plan had been drafted before the invasion, with the combined forces known as *Gruppe Hellmich*.³¹⁵ On **10 June**, his headquarters was reported at Les Perques (4 km southwest of Bricquebec).³¹⁶ Some examples of his authority: On two occasions, Hellmich ordered the transfer of a heavy coastal artillery battery from the west coast to be used elsewhere. His overall control is also evident from requests for ammunition, weapons and equipment of types used by units other than his own division.³¹⁷

Despite not occupying a divisional front of their own, the division's assigned forces were heavily involved in the fighting.³¹⁸ East of the Merderet, elements supported the *709. I.D.* on the beachhead's *Nordfront*. West of the river, they reinforced the *91. LL.D.*, which covered an area south to Carentan, on the *Westfront*. When the *77. I.D.* was later deployed between these divisions, it too was supported by the *243. I.D.* Because the division was distributed over a wide area, it is easier to address the units by sector, rather than chronologically.

One of the earliest results of the invasion for the division was the transfer of *Obst.* Klosterkemper, the commander of *GR 920*. On D-Day, *Gen.Lt.* Falley,

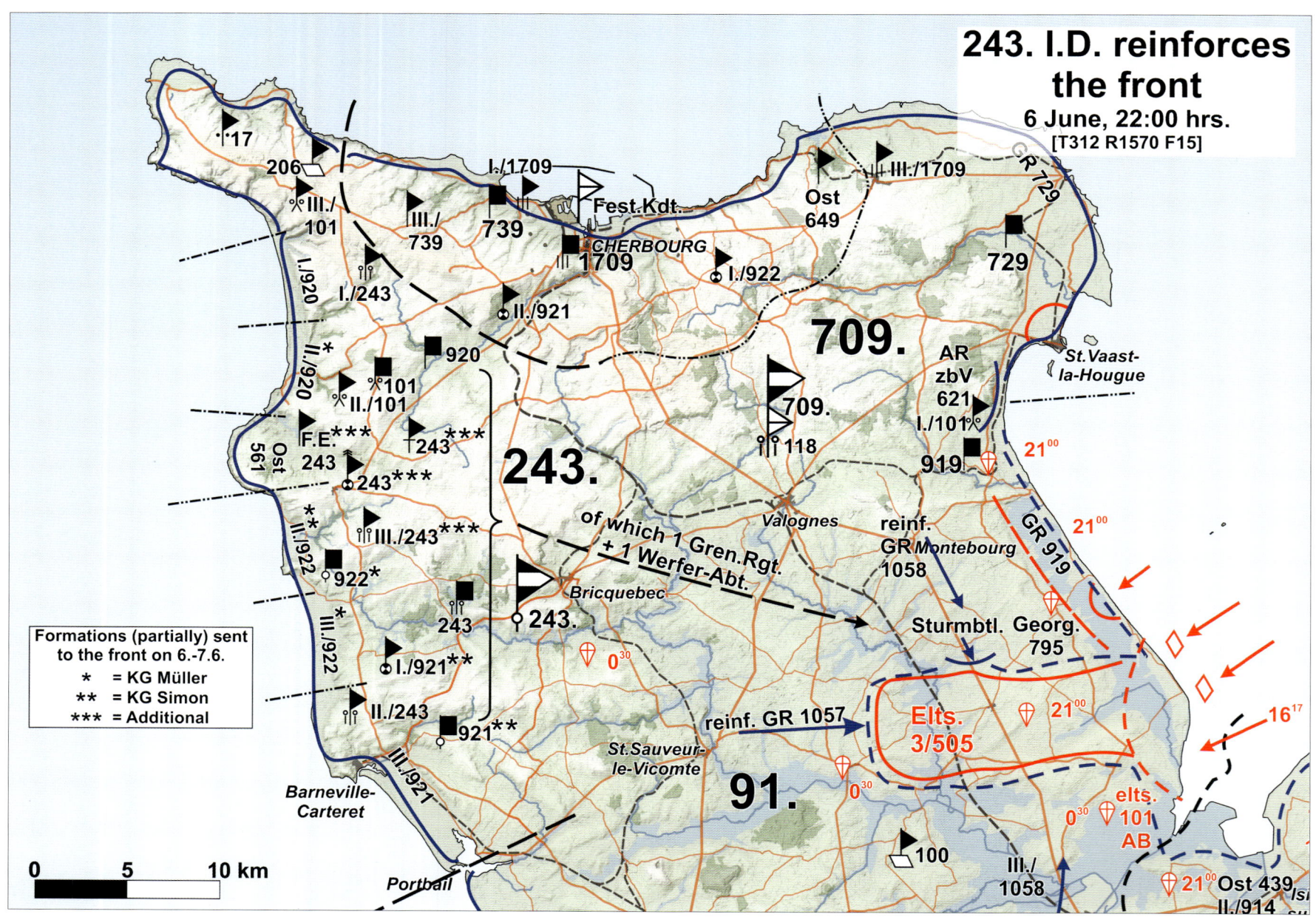

On D-Day the division was ordered to sent troops to the beachhead. Although the day's situation map shows only one regiment, the forces involved were considerably stronger and would support both the 91.LL.I.D. and 709.I.D.

the commander of the *91. LL.D.*, was killed and Klosterkemper temporarily took command.³¹⁹ The new division commander, *Obst.* König, arrived on **10 June**, allowing *Obst.* Klosterkemper to resume command of his regiment.³²⁰

Although many of the division's troops were dispatched to the front, it remained responsible for the coastal defences in its sector. The forces available were seriously reduced in strength by these transfers, which sometimes only left skeleton crews behind. In other cases, companies were overtaxed to relieve other units.³²¹ This probably applied to the *11./921*, which stayed on the coast, when the rest of the battalion was sent to the front or placed at disposal of the division. The latter is what happened to the 10th Company, which was used for security at divisional headquarters.³²² The *5./922* was also not deployed with the rest of its battalion.³²³

The impact of these troop transfers is best illustrated by looking at the situation maps for the initial days after the invasion. At 22:00 on **8 June**, the division's coastal defences were already severely weakened. *MG-Btl. 17* still held on to the Jobourg Peninsula, but the rest of the coast was defended by just two infantry and two artillery battalions (the *I.* and the *II./AR 243*). (The infantry units were probably the *I./920* (*Obstlt.* Bayer von Bayersburg) and *Ost-Btl. 561*.³²⁴) By **10 June**, the *I./920* had also been subordinated to the *91. LL.D.* and, two days later, the coast was only defended by covering forces; even *MG-Btl. 17* had relocated and was now in the fortress.³²⁵

Although they occurred in stages, the transfers robbed the division of virtually all of its combat troops. Throughout **June**, most of the transferred forces returned to the division, but some were cut off on the peninsula and eliminated as fighting forces.

The first major transfer of the division's combat units to the front took place on the evening of D-Day. An infantry regiment and a battalion of *schwere Stellungs-Werfer-Regiment 101*, were sent to the beachhead to join the German attack against Ste. Mère-Église (planned for the 7th) from the north.³²⁶ The *709. I.D.* was in charge of this sector and all reinforcements in the area were subordinated to it.

On the night of **6-7 June**, *Obstlt.* Müller (Commander of *GR 922*), leading an ad hoc regiment, advanced to the beachhead. His own regimental forces, among them elements of the heavy weapons companies, as well as infantry from the *II./920* (*Hptm.d.R.* Flockerzi) and the *III./922* (*Hptm.* Combosch), *Pi.Btl. 243*, and the *3./F.E.B. 243*, were part of the force.³²⁷ There are indications

Large parts of the Cotentin were a mixture of hedgerows, meadows and orchards. Taken shortly after D-Day, this photo is said to show a German patrol looking for stray American paratroopers. (Collectie CegeSoma - Rijksarchief (OD4))

that the *II./920* did not move to the front with all four of its companies, because men from this battalion, in particular from the 7th and 8th Companies, were captured west of the Merderet in mid-June. Yet east of the river, the US 4th Infantry Division (4ID) took no prisoners from these companies. However, men from the *I./920* were captured east of the Merderet, which could mean they were used to bolster the incomplete *II./920*. The company from the field replacement battalion may also have been attached to Müller's force to make up for missing companies.

Most of the *III./AR 243* was also transferred to the beachhead to provide artillery support, but not to support *KG Müller*. Its 10th Battery remained on the west coast, subordinated to the *II./H.K.A.R. 1262*. The battalion moved at daylight on D-Day, arriving in the Écausseville area that evening and taking up positions during the night.³²⁸

On **7 June**, the *LXXXIV. A.K.* launched its counterattack against the Utah Beachhead. This included *Obstlt.* Müller's troops, who had arrived during the night and moved into the area north of St. Marcouf - Azeville. In the morning, they attacked towards the south and captured the village of St. Marcouf before being forced to pull back.[329] Over the next few days, these elements from the *243. I.D.* helped the *709. I.D.* defend against the American advance to the high ground northeast of Montebourg.[330]

Further west (**7 June**), other elements of the division supported the attack on Ste. Mère-Église, the key objective of both American and German forces. The *III./AR 243* supported the attack along the N13 Highway, which was executed by the reinforced *GR 1058* (*91. LL.D.*, but under *709. I.D.* control). Direct support came from the assault guns of the *2./Pz.Jg.Abt. 243*, which lost two assault guns in the ensuing combat (including the company commander's) in front of the town. It is not known how many were committed, as several vehicles were not operational ready and four were reportedly attached to *Pz.Jg.Abt. 709*.[331] It is possible these four were those committed to the attack. The *1./Pz.Jg.Abt. 243* also participated in the fighting along the highway, and the number of vehicles it employed is clearer. Reportedly, its first platoon was attached to the 2nd Company.[332] This suggests that four *Marders* were involved, with one captured around Neuville-au-Plain that day and two more destroyed in the surrounding area.[333]

By dusk, the main German counterattack from the north had been decisively beaten back and was never resumed. Instead, the German troops on the *Nordfront* went onto the defensive. The entire front south of Montebourg (between the Merderet River and the east coast) was placed under the command of *Obst.* Rohrbach, the commander of *GR 729* (*709. I.D.*). *Obstlt.* Keil (Commander of *GR 919, 709. I.D.*) requested that the *III./922* and the *III./739* be placed under his command, since their communications already ran through his headquarters. His request was approved and *KG Müller* was subordinated to him, forming the left flank of the *Nordfront* (excluding the coast). That evening, *KG Müller* consisted of the *II./739* (*709. I.D.*) on the left (east) and the *III./922* on the right. The *II./920* was positioned to the right of the *III./922*, apparently subordinated to *Kampfgruppe Rohrbach*.[334] The *III./AR 243*, which had been joined by its missing 10th Battery on **8 June**, remained on the right wing of the *Nordfront*. It gradually pulled back northwest until the front stabilised around the Le Ham - Montebourg railway about **11 June**.[335]

On the morning of **9 June**, the organisation of the *709. I.D.* at the front was *KG Rohrbach* on the right (west) and *Kampfgruppe Keil* on the left. The boundary between the two battlegroups ran from Joganville to Ozeville church. From right (west) to left *KG Rohrbach* comprised the *II./729*, *Sturm-Bataillon AOK 7*, the *III./919* and the *II./920*. *KG Müller* was still under *KG Keil*, and from right (west) to left this group deployed the *III./922* and the *III./739*. *Pz.Jg.Abt. 243* was attached to *KG Rohrbach*, while *Pi.Btl. 243* was in Azeville, where the 4th ID captured 31 personnel on **8 June**, identifying the 1st and the 2nd Company. About 800 metres northwest of Émondeville, the 1/359 IR (90th ID) took 30 prisoners from *Feld-Ers.Btl. 243* on the **9th** and identified its 3rd Company[336]

That afternoon, *AOK 7* approved *Gen.* Marcks' petition to release the two *Landfront* Battalions (with subsequent approval of *Feldm.* Rommel).[337] The *I./922* (*Hptm.* Weindl) joined the line east of Montebourg.[338] On **11 June**, 35 men from the battalion were captured near the town and other prisoners taken by the Americans in the area St. Floxel – Ozeville.[339] The *II./921* (*Maj.d.R.* Rentsch) was reportedly attached to *FJR 6* on **13 June**, but this was a mix up with the *II./914*;[340] instead, it was committed southwest of Montebourg, near *Sturmbataillon AOK 7*, and identified by the 8th Infantry Regiment (4th ID) on **10 June**.[341] The troops in this area — between the Carentan - Cherbourg railway and Montebourg — were formed into *KG Hoffmann*, a sub-group of *KG Rohrbach*. The commander, *Obstlt.* Hoffmann, later confirmed that his troops included a battalion from the *243. I.D.*, although he misidentified it as the *III./922*, which was part of *KG Müller*.[342] Moreover, several men from the *II./921* were captured in the area of Montebourg - Éroudeville on **10-11 June**;[343] among them was the commander of the 5./921, who confirmed that his battalion had been in the Éroudeville area.[344] This implies that it had been inserted between *Sturmbataillon AOK 7* on the left (east) and the *II./739* on the right.[345]

Obstlt. Keil assumed command of the *Nordfront* about **12 June**. At his request, *KG Müller* became a separate element with responsibility for the left wing. Of the forces from the *243. I.D.* present on the *Nordfront*, Keil had control over the *I./922* and the *II./920*.[346] This left *Pi.Btl. 243* and the *III./922* to Müller. This was still the situation on **15 June**.[347] Although belonging to two groups, these four battalions from the *243. I.D.* held the centre of the *Nordfront* between Montebourg and the coast.

Although the fighting on the *Nordfront* embraced major elements of the division, the majority of its forces were not committed there. Instead, they were in action west of the Merderet under the *91. LL.D.* According to *Obstlt.*

On 7 June elements of Pz.Jg.Abt.243 supported the attacks of GR 1058 against Ste. Mère-Église. Two of its Sturmgeschütze were knocked out in front in the town and the attack was repulsed with heavy German casualties. This vehicle was numbered 201 and belonged to the company commander. To the right of the wreck is the airborne 6-pounder AT gun which had destroyed it. The gun was then manhandled forward to also engage the second StuG, which can be seen at the upper left of the gun shield. (NARA)

The lead assault-gun made it to the outskirts of Ste.Mère-Église before it could be destroyed by elements of the 82nd AB. In the background is a M32 tank recovery vehicle from the 746th Tank Battalion which supported the American counter attack later in the day. Despite the damage done to the assault gun, spare tracks are still wrapped around the reserve wheels; one of the identifying characteristics of 2./Pz.Jg.Abt. 243 vehicles. (NARA)

von Criegern (chief of staff of the *LXXXIV. A.K.*), a second regiment had already been rushed to the beachhead on the night of D-Day. He suggests it was built around *GR 921* and eventually attached to the *91. LL.D.*[348] Von Criegern's assertion is entirely credible, although the date it reached the front has not been found. On **8 June**, *KG Simon* (Commander of *GR 921*) was left (north) of *GR 1057*; this put it on the Merderet front north of the line Les Landes (west of Amfreville) - Château d'Amfreville (aka "The Grey Castle") - Les Noires Terres (2 km northwest of Ste. Mère-Église).[349] No records have been located detailing the organisation of the regiment at this time but, like *KG Müller*, it was likely an ad hoc regimental force. Based on later records and information from prisoners, it consisted of the *I./921* and *II./922* (minus the 5th Company).[350] Regimental troops from *GR 921* were probably included.

Although *KG Simon* was probably the first formation of *243. I.D.* to reinforce the *91. LL.D.*, it would not be the last. The *Luftlande* division held a large area, stretching roughly from Carentan, along the Merderet, to southwest of Montebourg.[351] The length of its front required more troops than the division possessed, thus it was assigned numerous reinforcements. An overview of the division on **10 June** shows a large number of these reinforcements, including troops of the *243. I.D.* The forces under its control included *GR 921* (*KG Simon*) with the *I./921* and the *II./922* (*Hptm.* Siepmann) and *GR 920* (*Obstlt.* Bayer von Bayersburg) with the *I./920* and the *II./1057* (*91. LL.D.*). The *III./921* (*Maj.d.R.* Hallmayer) was attached to the *91. LL.D.*, but it was not part of a regimental force, since it was not committed as a complete formation.[352] The headquarters, the 9th Company and the 12th Company fought together around Pont-l'Abbé, while the 10th Company was put at the disposal of the *243. I.D.*; the 11th Company remained on the coast.[353] The headquarters of *AR 243* was also attached to the *91. LL.D.* and directed the artillery west of the Merderet. Since its 3rd Battalion had gone to Montebourg, the regiment had its 1st and 2nd Battalions. In addition, *AR 191* was subordinated with its 1st and 3rd Battalions (two batteries each).[354]

It is difficult to determine when and where elements of the *243. I.D.* operating under the *91. LL.D.* were committed. By using statements of prisoners along with captured documents and other sources, it is possible to find some answers. Allied forces first identified the *II./922* east of the Merderet on **10 June**, where it was in the wider Le Ham area, between the river and the Cherbourg - Carentan railway;[355] this signifies that it held *KG Simon*'s left wing and, with it, the left of the reinforced *91. LL.D.* To the left (east) was the *709. I.D.* with *KG Hoffmann* (under *KG Rohrbach*). The *I./921* probably held *KG Simon*'s right wing, as the area east of the river (between the river and railway) was relatively small and did not require two battalions. This battalion was also not identified by American troops east of the Merderet; instead, it likely covered the west bank of the river to the southeast, making contact with units of *GR 1057* and/or *KG Bayer* on its right flank.[356] On **11 June**, the 2/325th GIR (82nd AB) captured Le Ham and the high ground west of the railway. The *II./922* pulled back across the Merderet to Urville, where the river became both the frontline and the boundary of the *91. LL.D.*[357]

Far less is known about the battlegroup formed around *GR 920*. Specific dates are lacking, but it may have been kept in reserve until US forces pushed *GR 1057* back and established a bridgehead west of the Merderet on **9 June**.[358] That morning, the *I./920* was a reserve force at a railway junction east of an unknown locality (based on the railway network, this may be the area around Sottevast).[359] The presence of the *II./1057* in *KG Bayer* on **10 June** may shed some light on where the battlegroup was committed. This battalion had previously been south of *KG Simon*, to the left of *GR 1057*.[360] This suggests that the new force was inserted in the centre of *91. LL.D.*'s sector west of the Merderet, placing it between *KG Simon* on the left (north) and the bulk of *GR 1057* (*KG Saldern*) on the right. Although *Obstlt.* Bayer von Bayersburg was listed as *Kampfgruppe* commander of "*GR 920*" on **10 June**, *Obst.* Klosterkemper soon returned to take over his own regiment (*Kampfgruppe*).[361] This would have allowed von Bayersburg to resume command of the *I./920* until killed in combat on **14 June**.

The arrival of the *77. I.D.* around **10-12 June** had a significant impact on those elements of the *243. I.D.* that were committed southwest of Montebourg. The new division took over the line on both sides of the Merderet;[362] this freed up forces of the *243. I.D.*, but also split them into two groups: Those subordinated to the *709. I.D.* on the *Nordfront* and those with the *91. LL.D.* on the *Westfront*.[363] Due to increasing pressure west of the Merderet, the 9. and the 10./*AR 243* had been moved to the southwest into the sector of the *91. LL.D.* The rest of the *III./AR 243* remained around St. Cyr and was in direct support of the *77. I.D.*, where it was attached to *AR 177*.[364]

Following the arrival of the *77. I.D.*, the *II./921* was relieved of its attachment to *KG Hoffmann*, which was disbanded. The battalion was transferred to

The 243. I.D. committed considerable elements of its anti-tank battalion in the battle for Ste.Mère-Église. Apart from assault guns, it lost three Marders in the fighting on D+1. This is one of the two destroyed in Neuville-au-Plain by Shermans of the 746th Tank Battalion. Behind the wreck are a number of If.8 infantry carts, a clear indication the town had been used as an assembly area before the attack. (NARA, via Steven J. Zaloga)

the southwest, as it was listed with the main body of the *243. I.D.* on **18 June**, indicating that it had been in a position to escape the Cotentin.[365] However, its precise location after arrival of the *77. I.D.* is not known. No encounters were reported by US forces, except for the 90th ID, which captured 20 men around Gourbesville on **15 June**.[366] The *77. I.D.* also relieved *KG Simon* (with the *I./921* and the *II./922*) and *KG Klosterkemper* (with the *I./920*). These actions probably took place after the relief of *KG Hoffmann*.[367] Just like the *II./921*, the two forces appear to have been reinserted in the southwest.

Some clues are available for some forces. The commander of the *I./921*, *Hptm.* Weindl, was killed near Reigneville-Bocage on **15 June**, giving an indication of the battalion's location.[368] For the period up to **17 June**, the 82nd AB captured 33 men of the battalion, suggesting there was contact — most likely on the right flank as the American airborne troops pushed towards St. Sauveur-le-Vicomte or, possibly, as the Germans attempted to escape through the town.[369] At some point, the *II./922* was subordinated to the *77. I.D.*, which suggests it was committed nearby and may have left *KG Simon* at some point.[370]

By **14 June**, the main American advance had shifted from the *Nordfront* to the *Westfront*.[371] For the Germans, the defence of Cherbourg remained a priority and plans were made accordingly. In case of an impending breakthrough around Valognes or the cutting of the Cotentin Peninsula, the troops in the north were to move to *Festung Cherbourg*, either on orders from the corps or — in an emergency — on *Gen.Lt.* Hellmich's authority.[372]

The situation on the *Westfront* continued to deteriorate and, on **15 June**, *Gruppe Hellmich* was divided into two groups. The boundary between them was the line Ste. Mère-Église - Orglandes - Ste. Colombe - St. Jacques-de-Néhou. *Gruppe von Schlieben* would defend the *Nordfront* with the reinforced *709. I.D.*, while the new *Gruppe Hellmich* would hold the *Westfront* with the *91. LL.D.* and the *243. I.D.*[373] In case of an enemy breakthrough to the coast, *Gruppe Hellmich* would pivot with its left flank to the line Beuzeville-la-Bastille - Portbail, building a new line across the base of the Cotentin — the new *Nordfront* of the *LXXXIV. A.K.*[374]

Although the situation west of the Merderet was growing ever more critical, a direct order from Hitler forbade a withdrawal to Cherbourg on the morning of the **16th**. At 13:00, the corps informed *AOK 7* that there was now a 5 km wide gap between Étienville and Orglandes.[375] At 16:11, *Gen.* Hellmich issued new orders in an effort to stabilise the front east of St. Sauveur-le-Vicomte. *KG Saldern* (*GR 1057*) was to establish physical contact with *KG Simon* (*GR 921*) at St. Clair.[376] *KG Simon*, in turn, would move its left flank to La Basseour. These orders indicate that *KG Simon* had moved southwest after the arrival of the *77. I.D.* The battlegroup remained under the *91. LL.D.* and was in the area north of the St. Sauveur - Pont-l'Abbé road, more or less in the centre of the Merderet bridgehead. St. Sauveur-le-Vicomte fell to the 82nd AB during the day, giving the Americans a bridgehead across the Douve. To the north, the 9th ID also built a bridgehead at Néhou. With the German defences shattered, the stage was set for the Americans to break through to the coast.[377]

Early on **17 June**, Hitler finally allowed *Gruppe von Schlieben* to withdraw to Cherbourg, a move that also made it possible for *Gruppe Hellmich* (including the *III./AR 243*) to withdraw to the south.[378] The withdrawal was successful, and it rejoined the *243. I.D.* at La Haye-du-Puits on the **18th**.[379] Of all the division's elements west of the Merderet, the situation for the *II./922* was the most difficult. The battalion had been subordinated to the *77. I.D.*, putting it north of the American breakthrough to the west coast. This division had problems escaping from the peninsula. Among the elements attempting to escape was *KG Bacherer*, to which the *II./922* had been attached and which only managed to break out after sustaining serious losses.[380]

On **17 June**, the *243. I.D.* headquarters was already at Le Tot (4 km southwest of La Haye-du-Puits), but *Gen.* Hellmich was no longer there to take command of the new *Nordfront*. That day, he was killed in a strafing attack.[381] Command of the division and the *Gruppe* temporarily passed to *Obst.* Klosterkemper, then to *Obst.* König (commander of the *91. LL.D.*) as *Gruppe König*. Although König was not the senior commander in the area, his division had already been responsible for the sector where the battlegroup had its new frontline.[382] *Obst.* Klosterkemper remained in command of the remnants of the division, now referred to as *KG 243. I.D.*[383] On **4 July**, *Obst.* Klosterkemper was decorated with the Knight's Cross (*Ritterkreuz*).[384]

On **21 June**, in recognition of their role in the fighting on the Cotentin, *AOK 7* requested that *Gen.* Hellmich and the *243. I.D.* be mentioned in the Armed Forces Daily Announcement (*Wehrmachtsbericht*).[385]

> *Gen.Lt. Hellmich, the commander of the 243. I.D. and leader of a Kampfgruppe has, together with his division, distinguished himself in the fighting on the Cotentin Peninsula. Again and again, he organised scattered troops and units from his division, which had become intermingled and for days he was able to prevent an enemy breakthrough to the west coast of the Cotentin Peninsula through aggressive personal action in critical situations. In this fighting, Gen.Lt. Hellmich died a hero's death on 17 June.*

On **2 September 1944**, Hellmich was posthumously awarded the Knight's Cross.[386]

The Cotentin was finally cut by the 9th ID on **17-18 June**, trapping elements of the *243. I.D.*[387] These were primarily those forces operating under the *709. I.D.* The bulk of *GR 922* (minus the 2nd Battalion), the *II./920* and *Pi. Btl. 243* were thus lost to the division.[388] On **19 June**, the *Nordfront* began to pull back to Cherbourg and, on **21 June**, 721 men from the division were reported in the *Festung*.[389] There, the *Landfront* was divided into four regimental sectors; three were held by the *709. I.D.* and the fourth by *GR 922*.[390] Nearly all the elements from the *243. I.D.* were assembled in this regiment under *Obstlt.* Müller; they held the right (west) flank defending the Jobourg Peninsula. Since the *Landfront* had not included this peninsula, the frontage of *KG Müller* actually was outside the fortifications. It ran along the high ground north of the Ruisseau de la Grande Vallée (a significant natural obstacle) roughly from the main road to Beaumont-Hague (D901), then southwest to Vauville where it reached the sea. At Resistance Nest 482 (*Widerstandsnest 482 / Wn. 482*) (on the D901), the front joined with *GR 919*, Müller's left neighbour.[391]

When the *II./920* arrived with *KG Müller*, it was down to 80 men.[392] The strength of the *III./922* was similar, a little more than 80 men. The *I./922* was the strongest, with a combat strength of 178 men.[393] Instead of joining Müller's forces, the remnants of *Pi.Btl. 243* (40 men under a *Leutnant*) were incorporated into *Pi.Btl. 709* on **22 June**. Combined with the latter battalion, they formed a reserve company of about 80 men.[394]

The weakened *III./922* was soon taken from Müller's command. American troops had penetrated German lines southeast of Cherbourg, with the result that the *709. I.D.* sent lorries to pick up the battalion to counter the threat. Two battlegroups were built from the *III./922*, one to be used in La Glacerie (with *GR 739*), the other at an unknown location. The former, however, never reached La Glacerie, since it was deployed on the railway between Tourlaville and Cherbourg under the command of an *Oberleutnant*.[395] The company of *Pi.Btl. 709* was dispatched to *GR 729* on **23 June**, and launched a successful counterattack in the evening. The next morning, it came under such heavy and unremitting attack that it disintegrated completely.[396]

The American drive on Cherbourg cut off the Jobourg Peninsula from the town and pushed elements of *GR 919* towards it. The regimental commander, *Obstlt.* Keil, assumed control of the peninsula and its forces on **24 June**. *U.KG Hadenfeldt* (*II./919*) was on the left (north) and *GR 922* (now called *U.KG Müller*) on the right.[397] One battalion of *GR 922*, apparently the *I./922*, was committed at the front, while a second was in reserve. This was the remnants of the *II./920*: 80 men under a *Feldwebel*, located in the woods east of Herqueville. Keil put this force under his direct command as his reserve and also sent what remained of *Pz.Abt. 206* to the woods as another reserve.[398] On **29 June**, the *I./922* and the *13./922* were still listed under *U.KG Müller*.[399] *Obstlt.* Müller was captured on **30 June**, and the forces on the Jobourg Peninsula surrendered on **1 July**.[400] This marked the end for the Germans trapped on the northern part of the Cotentin.

Those units of the *243. I.D.* that managed to retreat south held out longer. On **18 June**, the division was placed under *Gruppe König*, which was in control of the frontage stretching across the base of the Cotentin, the new *Nordfront* of the *LXXXIV. A.K.*[401] At 08:00 on **18 June**, the forces under Klosterkemper nominally held the line Neuville-en-Beaumont - the crossroads southeast of Besneville - St. Lô-d'Ourville.[402] Along this line, it formed a battlegroup on the left (west) wing of *Gruppe König*.[403] The division's frontage was difficult to consolidate, however, and it was pulled back to more favourable terrain. On the **19th**, the division closed the gap between the coast and the Praires Marécageuses along the shortest possible line. By securing two crossings over the Ollonde River, the division also allowed the cut-off forces under *Obst.* Bacherer (*77. I.D.*) to join the German forces south of the river.[404]

On **20 June**, the front of the battlegroup stretched from the southern edge of the Praires Marécageuses, via St. Sauveur-de-Pierrepont, Rue Bouillie and then La Groudière Château to the coast.[405] The 7 km frontline was held by the *I./1050* (*77. I.D.*), supported by assault guns. The lack of troops and difficult terrain did not allow for a continuous frontline. Instead, 12 strongpoints were established, some with 1 km gaps in between. Attacks to reduce these gaps were only partially successful, while elsewhere American attacks proved costly to the German defenders.[406] The *243. I.D.* headquarters was 1,200 metres southwest of Angoville-sur-Ay.[407] While *Gruppe König* held the front, the fresh *353. I.D.* was brought up to the rear to build and occupy a second defence line with the *77. I.D.*: The *Mahlmann-Linie*.

The records for *Gruppe König* on **18 June** list the forces in *KG Klosterkemper* but little beyond that. Especially for the infantry units, their

Gen.Lt. Hellmich was killed by Allied aircraft on 17 June. Today he rests at the German Military Cemetery at Orglandes, as do the two other generals killed on the Cotentin.

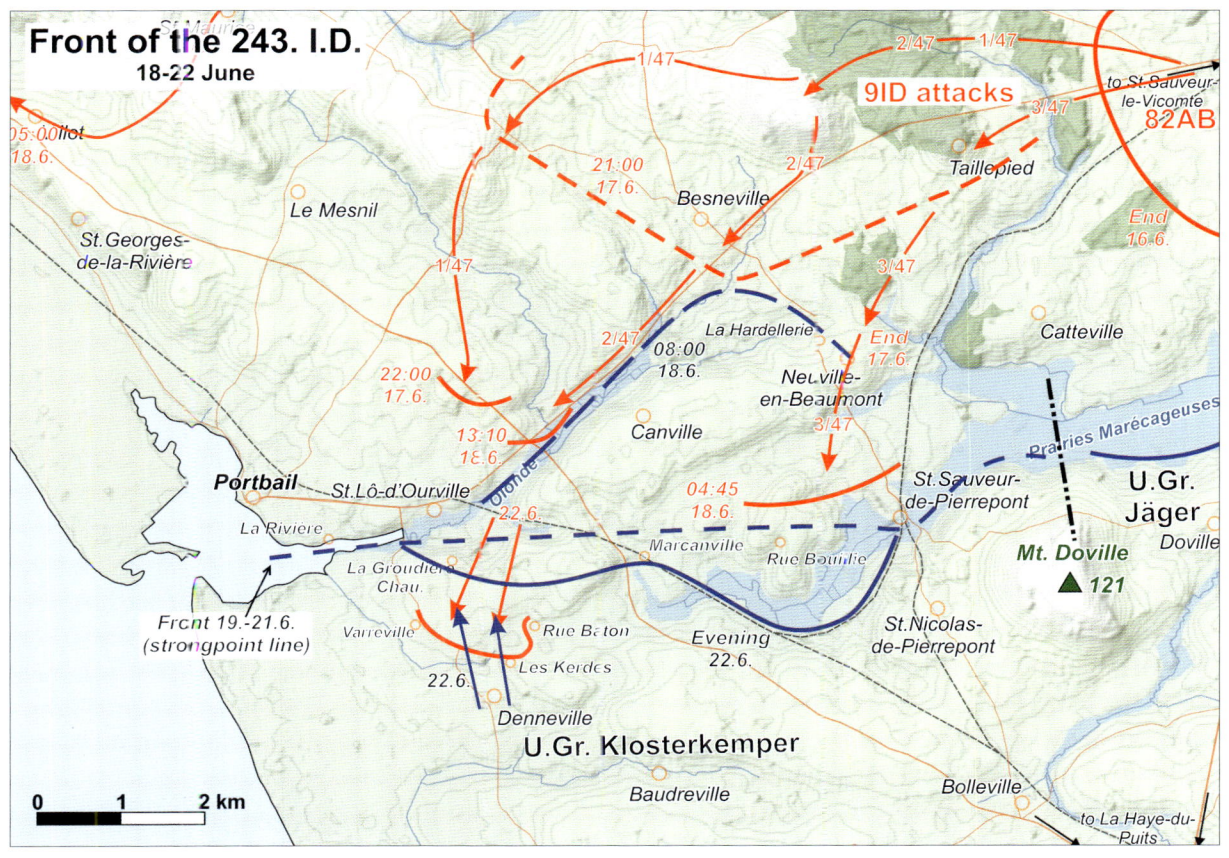

On 17-18 June the 243.I.D. was unable to prevent an American breakthrough to the west coast. Instead the division established a defence line to seal of the peninsula as part of Gruppe König. Against repeated attacks from the 90th ID, it was able to consolidate the front along the most favourable terrain.

presence says nothing about their actual strength. As expected, two regimental headquarters (including their headquarters companies) were available: *GR 920* and *921*. These were in command of six infantry battalions. It appears that the *II./1057*, the *I./920* and the *I./921* were subordinated to *GR 920* The two supporting heavy weapons companies probably belonged to *GR 920*.[408] This organisation indicates that *KG Bayer/Klosterkemper* had not changed much since **10 June**, except for taking over the *I./921* from *KG Simon*.

GR 921 consisted of the *II./921*, the *III./921* and the *II./922*; the two heavy weapons companies were the *13.* and the *14./921*. Although the *III./921* was present, it was not available as it was deployed with *GR 1057* (*91. LL.D.*).[409] This is not surprising, since it had already operated with this force, *KG von Saldern*, north of the Douve. Compared to **10 June**, *KG Simon* had given up the *I./921*, but it had received the *II./921*.

While *AR 243* was listed with the same four battalions as **10 June**, the headquarters of *AR 191* had left and the *5./AR 243* was not on hand. The remaining nine batteries had four guns each. The strength of *Pz.Jg.Abt. 243* was given as two assault guns and eight *Marders*.[410] The 3rd Company was not listed, as it was still attached to the *17. SS-Pz.Gr.Div.*[411] *Feld-Ers.Btl. 243* was also part of *Gruppe König*, and it seems to have had three companies plus the combat school of the *77. I.D.* (in company strength).[412] The 3rd Company may have been trapped on the Cotentin, as it had been on the *Nordfront* under the *709. I.D.*

If these situation reports provide information on the organisation of *Gruppe*

König, they say little about its strength, let alone that of the *243. I.D.* Fortunately, these details are found in other records. The losses of those elements that escaped to the south were significant. Personnel losses from **6-24 June** were: 55% of the infantry, 25% of the artillery, 90% of the engineers and 30-40% of the anti-tank units.[413] The losses of the division can be ascertained in more detail by looking at POW's. By the evening of **5 July**, 2,268 men from the division had been counted in POW cages in the UK, a figure that is unlikely to have included prisoners from the VIII Corps July offensive. After the *709. I.D.* (6,652) and the *716. I.D.* (3,359), this was the third highest among the divisions defending against the invasion. Most of the prisoners belonged to *GR 920* (519), *GR 921* (496) and *GR 922* (914); there were also 115 men from the division's engineer battalion, 150 from the field-replacement battalion and 58 from *AR 243*. The remaining prisoners were: A single man from the divisional staff, 5 men from *Pz.Jg.Abt. 243* and 10 from the support troops.[414]

The fighting in the division's sector continued on **22 June**. The lack of a continuous and observable frontline allowed American forces to infiltrate the German lines and attack the strongpoints from behind. In the afternoon, the division was forced to commit its reserve of one company and four assault guns;[415] an American attack between two strongpoints had reached the roads Rue Batôn - Les Kerdes and Les Kerdes - Varreville. *Hptm.* Riess (*I./1050*) organised an immediate counterattack, which managed to restore the main line of resistance. That evening, the front followed the line St. Sauveur-de-Pierrepont - the railroad to Marcanville - the crossroads north of Rue Batôn - Omonville - the bridge at La Groudiere - the crossing at La Rivière.[416]

23 June was quiet. A reconstituted battalion from the *243. I.D.* was used to take over the right wing of the *I./1050*, which had suffered considerable losses. The left wing of the latter battalion was strengthened by establishing three additional strongpoints.[417] That evening, the division's front was held by *GR 921*, which primarily consisted of the *I./1050* and the *III./921*; providing support were the *3./Stu.Gesch.Brig. 902*, the heavy AT platoon of the *14./920*, the heavy mortar platoon of the headquarters company of *GR 920* and an infantry-gun platoon from the *13./921* and the "*1./922*". The latter was probably a typographic error since this company was with *KG Müller*; instead "a single company" may have been meant. The commander of *GR 921*, *Obstlt.* Simon, had taken over command of the front from *Obst.* Klosterkemper. This is in line with other battlegroups on the *Nordfront*, which were also effectively under a regimental commander. *Obst.* Klosterkemper, it seems, had assumed the role of division commander further to the rear. His former headquarters, probably at Le Tot, was taken over by Simon. *AR 243* was reported with its regimental headquarters at Le Tot, and the positions of its 1st to 3rd Battalions at La Chapelle, 1.9 km southwest of Angoville-sur-Ay, and 3 km south of St. Rémy-des-Landes, respectively.[418]

The reorganisation of the front continued on the **24th**. Since *Wolga-Tat. Btl. 627* was due to relieve the *I./1050*, organic elements of the *243. I.D.* were deployed in the most important sector: St. Sauveur-de-Pierrepont - Marcanville. Attempts to establish additional strongpoints on the left wing of the division succeeded only after heavy fighting. By the end of the day, eight such positions controlled the frontline from Marcanville via the crossroads south of Château Duprey to La Groudiere. This was now considered to be a fairly strong defence line, and the eastern battalion was expected to be able to hold it successfully. On the right wing, a forward strongpoint protected the flank of the positions along the railroad. Yet, the division was concerned about its left and right flank. On the coast, men from *Georg.Inf.Btl. 797* had deserted and abandoned several resistance nests; on the right flank, the division could no longer could rely on *SS-Pz.Aufkl.Abt. 17* — which had been relieved by *Ost-Btl. Huber* in the sector Varenguebec - St. Sauveur-de-Pierrepont on the previous day.[419]

By the **25th**, the division's front stretched from La Cuiroterie (south of the Bois de Limors) to the coast, although this would have included *Ost-Btl. Huber*.[420] The fighting in the final week of **June** was of limited intensity, with only minor attacks and advances against the German lines. Reconnaissance patrols were frequent, however, and artillery and mortar fire continuously harassed German positions and supply routes.[421]

The order of battle for *Gruppe König* for **18-28 June** provides details on how this force, including *U.Gr. Klosterkemper*, was reorganised after the German escape from the peninsula. It would appear that all of the available units of the *243. I.D.* had returned.[422]

U.Gr. Klosterkemper (*KG 243. I.D.*) consisted of a headquarters, two divisional regiments and some additional infantry. The artillery regiment was also present, as were *Pz.Jg.Abt. 243*, *Nachr.Abt. 243* and *San.Kp. 243.*. *GR 920*, now commanded by *Hptm.* Siepmann, had been reorganised to include the *I./920* and the *II./922* (Siepmann's original battalion). It was supported by two AT guns, but there were no infantry guns. *GR 921* was still led by *Obstlt.* Simon, and it included two of the regiment's battalions: The 1st and 3rd. The regiment was supported by two infantry guns but no AT guns.[423]

Compared to **18 June**, *U.Gr. Klosterkemper* no longer commanded the *II./921* and the *II./1057*. The latter had returned to the *91. LL.D.*, while the *II./921* was no longer listed, having apparently been disbanded. The battlegroup did receive some additional infantry. The *I./1050*, was still listed under the division, as was a new company identified only as *Laumann* (possibly the *1./F.E.B. 177*).[424] The final infantry formation was *Wolga-Tat.Inf.Btl. 627*, commanded by *Rittmeister* Sörensen.[425]

AR 243 was still relatively strong — a fact that can largely be attributed to its motorisation, which allowed it to escape from the peninsula with its 1st and 2nd Battalions, losing few, if any, guns.[426] They were both listed as having three 2 cm *Flak* and three gun batteries. These batteries each had four Russian 7.62 cm guns, no different from D-Day.[427] The losses for the 3rd Battalion were more serious. Up to **18 June**, the 7th and 8th Batteries combined had lost four howitzers and six *RSO's*. The loss of three of these guns was directly caused by the loss of their motor transport. As a result, the 7th Battery was consolidated with the 8th Battery.[428] When the battalion assembled south of the breakthrough, its losses amounted to 4 artillery pieces, 6 *RSO's*, 25 lorries, 15 cars and 2 motorcycles.[429] The battalion still had its *Flak*.[430]

The order of battle shows that *Pz.Jg.Abt. 243* was now commanded by *Oblt.* Stratmann and still relatively strong. The 1st Company had nine *Marder's* and nine MG's, while the 2nd Company had five assault guns and eight MG's. This was an increase of one *Marder* and three assault guns compared to **18 June**. Replacements are unlikely, but vehicles may have been repaired or reappeared after the chaos chaos of the retreat. The 3rd Company was listed with 12 2 cm *Flak* and 6 MG's; 4 *Flak* were on tracked chassis, the rest were motorised.[431] This would mean that the company still possessed its original strength, but the numbers have not been confirmed by other records. As the 3rd Company had not been listed on **18 June** (it had only recently returned to the battalion), it is possible that accurate numbers were unavailable and that it was simply listed at its original strength.

The numbers of *Marder's* and assault guns from **18** and **28 June** can be compared to those reported by the *7. Armee* on **27 June**. At that time, 10 self-propelled 7.5 cm guns were listed under *Gruppe König*.[432] Since no other unit in *Gruppe König* had such vehicles (after *Pz.Jg.Abt. 353* returned to its division), they must have belonged to the *1./Pz.Jg.Abt. 243*. As no information on replacements has been found, this means the *Marder* losses amounted to just four vehicles, which was quite low given that three were lost around Neuville-au-Plain on **7 June**.

The **27 June** strength report offers little information about the number

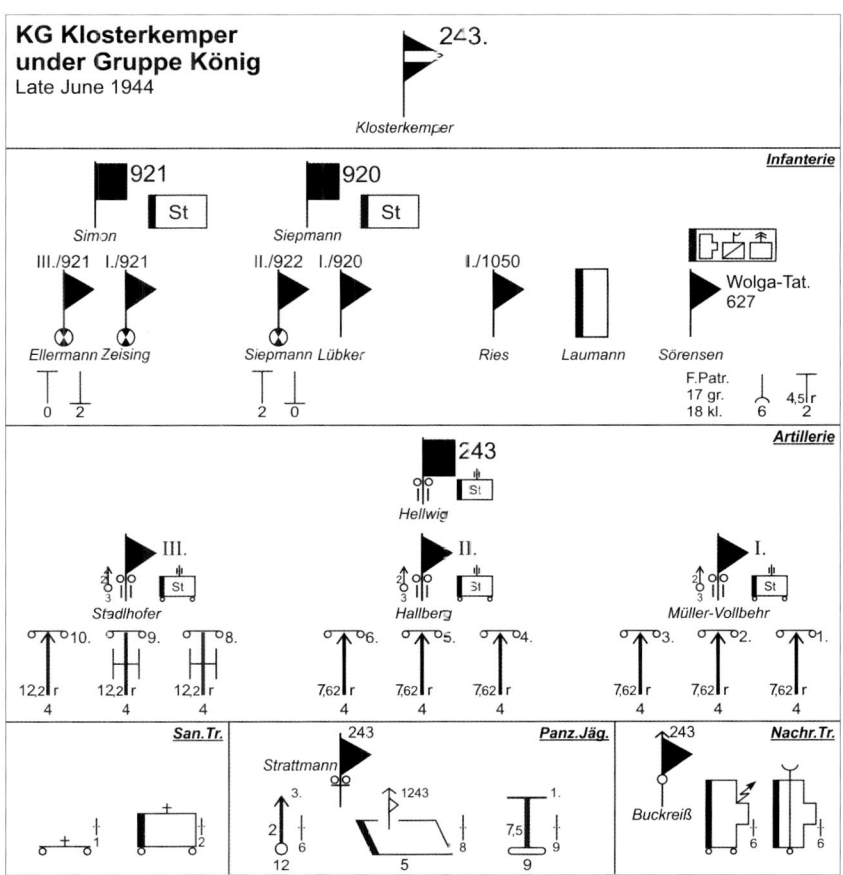

As Untergruppe Klosterkemper, the 243.I.D. provided a considerable percentage of Gruppe König's forces. Klosterkemper's forces were further augmented by I./1050 (77.I.D.) and Wolga-Tat.Inf.Btl.627, although both would soon leave the Untergruppe.

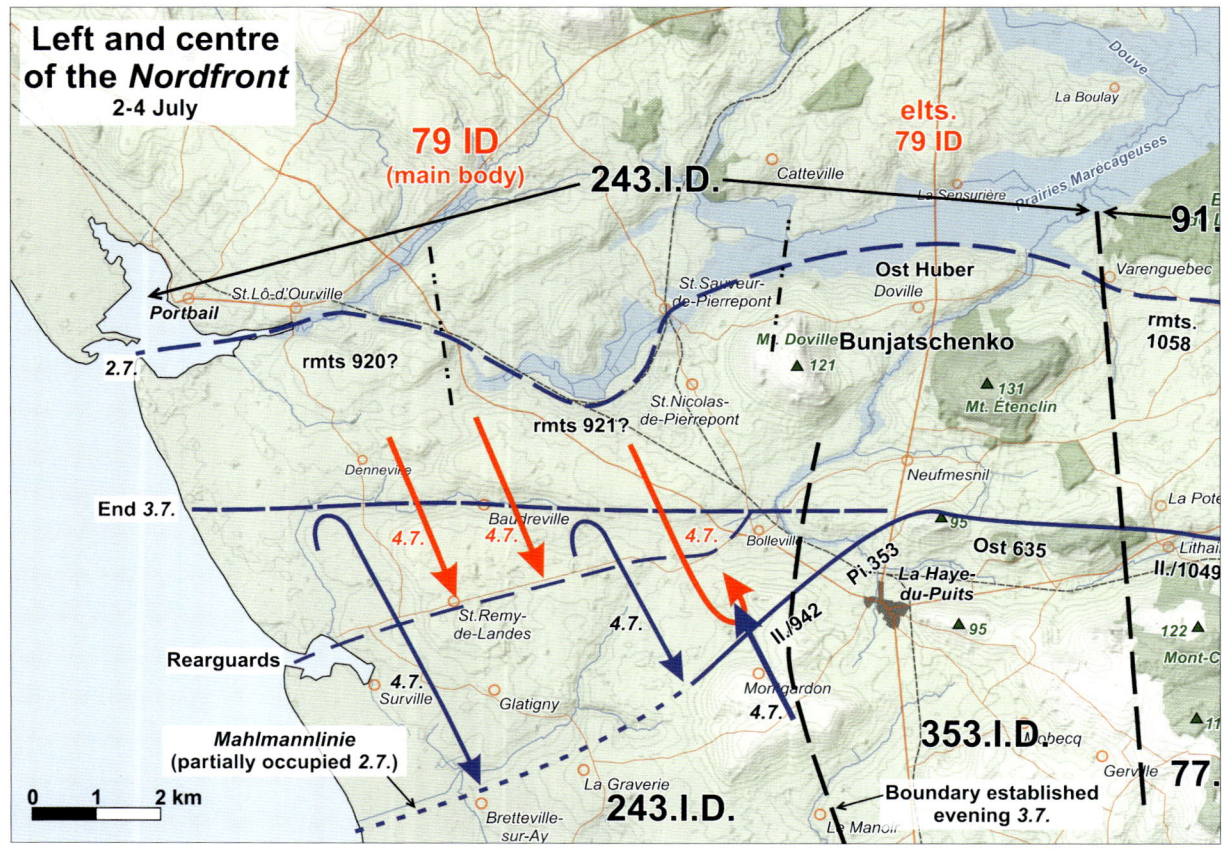

When the VIII Corps launched its offensive on 3 July, the 243.I.D. held both the centre and the left wing of the Nordfront. To its rear, the Mahlmannlinie was no longer as strongly held: the 353.I.D. had largely been extracted and the 77.I.D. had redeployed to the right wing of the line. On 4 July the 243.I.D. was forced to pull back to the Linie in order to stabilize the front.

of assault guns in the *2./Pz.Jg.Abt. 243*. A total of 21 were reported in *Gruppe König*, which raises more questions than answers.[433] The company only had 10 assault guns on D-Day, and reported 2 vehicles on **18 June** and five on **28 June**.[434] This illustrates that the vast majority of these 21 vehicles must have belonged to *Stu.Gesch.Brig. 902*, meaning the number of assault guns in *Gruppe König* must have been much higher as the brigade was at full strength with 31 vehicles on **1 July**.[435] The lower number is probably explained by vehicles that were not combat-ready, but it is not possible to determine how many vehicles in the *2./Pz.Jg.Abt. 243* needed repair. The five reported on **28 June** could have been all that was left in the company.

Between **18 June** and **3 July**, the division continued to hold the left wing of the *Nordfront* with a number of changes in its sector, its rear and its right flank. On **28 June**, *Wolga-Tat.Inf.Btl. 627*, freshly arrived from Bretagne, began to relieve the *I./1050*, which returned to the *77. I.D.*[436] The following day, the new battalion held the left wing of the divisional sector, while the remnants of *GR 921* held the right wing. *GR 920* was in reserve south of St. Rémy-des-Landes, while the remnants of *GR 922* were south of La Haye-du-Puits.[437] The commitment of the eastern battalion made sense, as it was both fresh and had an excellent reputation. It soon proved unreliable, however, and had to be replaced, likely by *GR 920*, which was nearby.[438]

Meanwhile, the *LXXXIV. A.K.* formed an ad hoc *Ost-Regiment*, named *Regimentsgruppe Bunjatschenko* after its commander; its mission was to hold the centre of the *Nordfront*, to the right of the division. It is not clear if *Wolga-Tat.Inf.Btl. 627* belonged to this force.[439]

On **29 June**, the *LXXXIV. A.K.* issued new orders for the organisation of its troops. *Gruppe König* was disbanded, and the *91. LL.D.* and the *243. I.D.* were to take command over the right and left wing of the *Nordfront*. This was to go into effect early on **1 July**. The *243. I.D.* would be reinforced by a battery of *Stu.Gesch.Brig. 902*, by *Wolga-Tat.Inf.Btl. 627* and by *Ost-Btl. Huber*. The boundary between the two divisions would run from La Ronde-Haye (*91.*), via Millières (*91.*) - Pissot (*243.*) - Varenguebec (*243.*) to the existing boundary between *U.Gr. Lewandowski* and *U.Gr. Jäger*; from there, it would continue to Rauville-la-Place (*243.*). As a result, *U.Gr. Jäger* would come under the *243. I.D.*; this sector, however, was to be taken over by *Rgts.Gr. Bunjatschenko*, allowing the headquarters of *U.Gr. Jäger* to be transferred to the *91. LL.D.*[440] These plans appear to have been carried out, for on **1 July** the right boundary of the *243. I.D.* was reported to run along the line Millières-Varenguebec - Rauville-la-Place.[441] The regimental group formed the division's right wing, covering the St. Sauveur-le-Vicomte - La Haye-du-Puits highway.[442]

To the rear of the division, the *Mahlmann-Linie* stretched west from La Haye-du-Puits and was held by the *77. I.D.* on the left and elements of the *353. I.D.* on the right. The latter committed the *II./942* on its left wing and *Pi.Btl. 353* at La Haye-du-Puits. Artillery support was from the *IV./AR 353*. In early **July**, the *353. I.D.* was largely withdrawn from the *Mahlmann-Linie*, and the *77. I.D.* shifted to the east to replace it in the most important sector, around Mont-Castre. For the time being, the formations of the *353. I.D.* behind the *243. I.D.* nonetheless remained where they were.[443]

On **2 July**, while the front remained quiet, the division headquarters moved to Angoville-sur-Ay. Indeed, it was noted that the frontline had not changed since its report on **20 June**, but this situation was about to change, and dramatically.[444]

The US VIII Corps launched its offensive on **3 July**. The division suffered serious losses on its left wing against the 79th ID and on its right (*Rgt. Gr. Bunjatschenko*) against the 82nd AB. That evening the boundary with the right-hand neighbour, the *353. I.D.*, which had been rushed back into the line, was changed to run east of Lessay - west of Angoville-sur-Ay and Montgardon - east of St. Sauveur-le-Vicomte.[445] Further east, elements of the *91. LL.D.* were absorbed by other formations or withdrawn. The *91. LL.D.* ceased to exist as a fighting force, while the *243. I.D.* remained in action as an separate battlegroup, continuing to fight on the *Nordfront* along with the *353.* and the *77. I.D.*, which were to the east.[446]

On the morning of **4 July**, the *243. I.D.* faced an enemy breakthrough with tank support in the direction of La Chapelle - Le Mouinerie. Its attenuated forces, however, were too weak to do much about it.[447] An immediate counterattack managed to temporarily push the US forces back and re-establish the main defence line running Bolleville – Baudreville; four US officers and 60 enlisted personnel were taken prisoner. Yet this defensive success along the *Nordfront* was only achieved at heavy cost and by committing the final reserves.[448] By evening, the division was left with just 500 men to hold the front and had to withdraw to the *Mahlmann-Linie* to avoid a total collapse.[449] After an evening counterattack south of La Mouinerie, the division could finally begin to pull back. It left rearguards along the line Bolleville - St. Remy-des-Landes - Surville (on the coast), with the new main line of resistance running from Bretteville-sur-Ay via Biémont to north of La Haye-du-Puits.[450] The move of the left wing also compelled a withdrawal of the rest of the *Nordfront*.[451] Having reached the *Mahlmann-Linie*, the *II./942* became available as a reinforcement, with fire support from the *IV./AR 353*.[452]

On **5 July**, replacements in the form of *Marschbtl. zbV 364* and a company of *Marschbtl. zbV 369* were on their way to the division. These included older men, some born as early as 1907.[453]

Meanwhile, the fighting continued. The rearguards conducted a fighting withdrawal and units that were briefly cut off around Montgardon were freed.[454] Along its entire front, the division was struck by American attacks with significant armoured support, the centre of gravity of the enemy assaults in the area southwest of Glatigny.[455] In the evening, the lines west of La Haye-du-Puits were reported to run from St. Symphorien, via Biémont and La Fairie, to Bretteville-sur-Ay.[456] The divisional headquarters was moved to 2.5 km southeast of Vesly.[457]

On the morning of **6 July**, it was reported that American forces had pushed back the front at Biémont and northeast of Bretteville-sur-Ay before being thrown back by immediate German counterattacks. Only Montgardon church was in enemy hands as the counterattack continued.[458] That afternoon, it was reported that the division, despite serious losses, had repulsed enemy attacks around Le Moulin.[459]

On **7 July**, the *243. I.D.* and the *353. I.D.* were chosen by the corps to receive march battalions. Both were suitable candidates since they were still fairly well organised.[460] The day itself witnessed intense combat around La Haye-du-Puits. The division's right neighbour, the *III./SS-Pz.Gr.Rgt. 4 "Der Führer"*, supporting the *353. I.D.*, was defending a gap southwest of the town. The Americans had already broken through the previous evening, but the penetration was sealed off on the line La Surellerie - Le Mont (today Carrefour de la Croix), more or less on the boundary with the *353. I.D.* The sector of the *243. I.D.* remained fairly quiet.[461] This finally changed in the evening, when the positions north of Biémont were attacked but successfully defended.[462]

8 July was a relatively calm day in the division's sector, although there was continuous bombing of the artillery positions, while heavy artillery fire raked the sector.[463] To the right of the division, the *III./DF* fought tenaciously to prevent La Haye-du-Puits from being outflanked.[464] On this day, the division was recognised in the Armed Forces Daily Announcement for its earlier successes:[465]

Under command of Obst. Klosterkemper, Kampfgruppe 243. Div. has prevented a breakthrough by superior enemy forces along the west coast of the Cotentin. After the enemy had succeeded in capturing the isthmus between the Praires Marécageuses and St. Lô-d'Ourville in front of the division, the division again threw the enemy from this key position in heavy fighting and inflicted heavy casualties.

9 July appears to have been fairly quiet, too. The division faced a company-sized attack near Biémont, but was able to seal off the penetration on the line Biémont - Carbonnet - Le Mont.[466] A successful counterattack brought in prisoners.[467]

On **10 July**, the division sought to defend a sector 7 km wide with just 700 men. Its right-hand boundary ran from Lessay along the railway to Beauvais, and from there northwest via the church at Angoville-sur-Ay to La Haye-du-Puits. During the day, US troops broke through west of Le Mont and were pushing forward with weak forces either side of the road from Le Mont - Les Coeuries (presumably the D528); the Germans, of course, immediately counterattacked.[468]

Although the division appears to have held its lines on **11 July**, US forces to the east advanced on both sides of the railway to Lessay. To close the gap and free up reserves, the decision was made to withdraw that afternoon to shorten the frontline. The retrograde movement commenced during the night and enabled the *II./942* to return to the *353. I.D.*[469] West of the highway, new lines were established from Angoville-sur-Ay to St. Germain-sur-Ay. The withdrawal was closely pursued by the Americans in the area around Angoville-sur-Ay; although their advance was brought to a halt, they managed to capture the town. To the east, Hierville (*353. I.D.* sector) was seized by the Americans on the **12**th. Although the Americans pushed into the western part of St. Germain-sur-Ay in the sector of the *243. I.D.*, an immediate withdrawal towards the *Wasserline* was not deemed necessary.[470]

The following afternoon, the Americans broke through south of Hierville and reached the area of La Motte, on the boundary with the *353. I.D.* This advance was soon contained by German reserves while, to the west, an attack on Le Bot was also repulsed.[471] The *Nordfront* was pulled back to the *Wasserlinie* on the night of **13-14 July**. In its new sector, the *243. I.D.* still continued to hold the extreme left wing of the *LXXXIV. A.K.*[472] During the withdrawal, the divisional headquarters moved to La Tringale (3 km southwest of Périers) on the **13**th.[473] On the **15**th, it was at La Laisnerie (2.5 km southeast of Geffosses).[474] On **17 July**, the division was reported to be holding the front with two battalions and the remnants of the *91. LL.D.*, with two battalions in reserve. One was south of Lessay, the other north of Créances. The divisional headquarters was still in La Laisnerie.[475]

Records show that on **19 July** the *243. I.D.* held a sector 7 km wide. *GR 920* was responsible for the left wing. On the left it deployed a battalion formed by the remnants of *GR 922* and a similar one formed by *GR 920* on the right. These battalions had a strength of 240 and 324, respectively. *The 3./Pi.Btl.343 (343. I.D.)* was in regimental reserve, as was an emergency company formed by the *GR 920*. The latter had a strength of 35 men. The division's right wing was held by *GR 1058 (91. LL.D.)* with a single battalion formed by *II./1057, III./1058* and *Füs.Kp. 91*. It had a combined strength of 461 men. The divisional reserve was formed by *I./921* and *III./921*, but their combined strength is illegible. As a whole, the division had a combined combat strength (*Kampfstärke*) of 1,643. Three days earlier it had been 1,060.[476]*

When the *353. I.D.* was pulled from the *Wasserlinie* on **22 July**, it left a gap between the *243. I.D.* and the *91. LL.D.* (which had now taken over the combat elements and sector of the *77. I.D*). The sectors of both formations - especially the 91st's - were simply widened to close the gap, while receiving

The withdrawal to the Wasserlinie had stabilised the Nordfront. Confronted by the crisis that had developed between the Taute and Vire rivers, LXXXIV. A.K. decided to transfer the 353.I.D. as a reserve to that sector. The 91.LL.I.D. and 243.I.D. were forced to widen their sectors, yet received no reinforcements.

Since the publication of Vol. 1A, new information has surfaced. This makes it possible to add additional details regarding various regiments and battalions on 19 and 25 July. The latter is assumed here to have been identical to the end of 23 July. Holding the 243. I.D.'s front were "battalions" of GR 922 (left) and GR 920 (centre). GR 921 held the right, likely with the reinforced III./921. Elements of I./921 were in reserve. On the 19th the 91. LL.D. held a 6.9 km front with GR 1050 on the left (west) and GR 1049 on the right. GR 1050 consisted of merely the combined remnants of both II./1049 and I./1050, with a strength of 161 men. It held the remnants of KG 265 (77 men) in reserve. GR1049 committed III./1049 on the left and I./1049 on the right. These were 249 and 151 men strong, respectively. In division reserve were the II./1050 and Pi.Btl. 177, combined 304 men strong. By the 25th, the division's front was still held by GR 1050 and GR1049. The former now deployed III./1058 on the left and II./1050 on the right. II./1057 was in division reserve, slightly to the rear. The GR 1049 held the 91. LL.D.'s right wing with III.Btl. on the left and I.Btl. on the right. Pi.Btl. 191 was in reserve west of Périers. (Captured document, 19 July, via Simon Trew; Captured map, 25 July, reproduced by the 665th Eng. Top. Co., Simon Trew Collection)

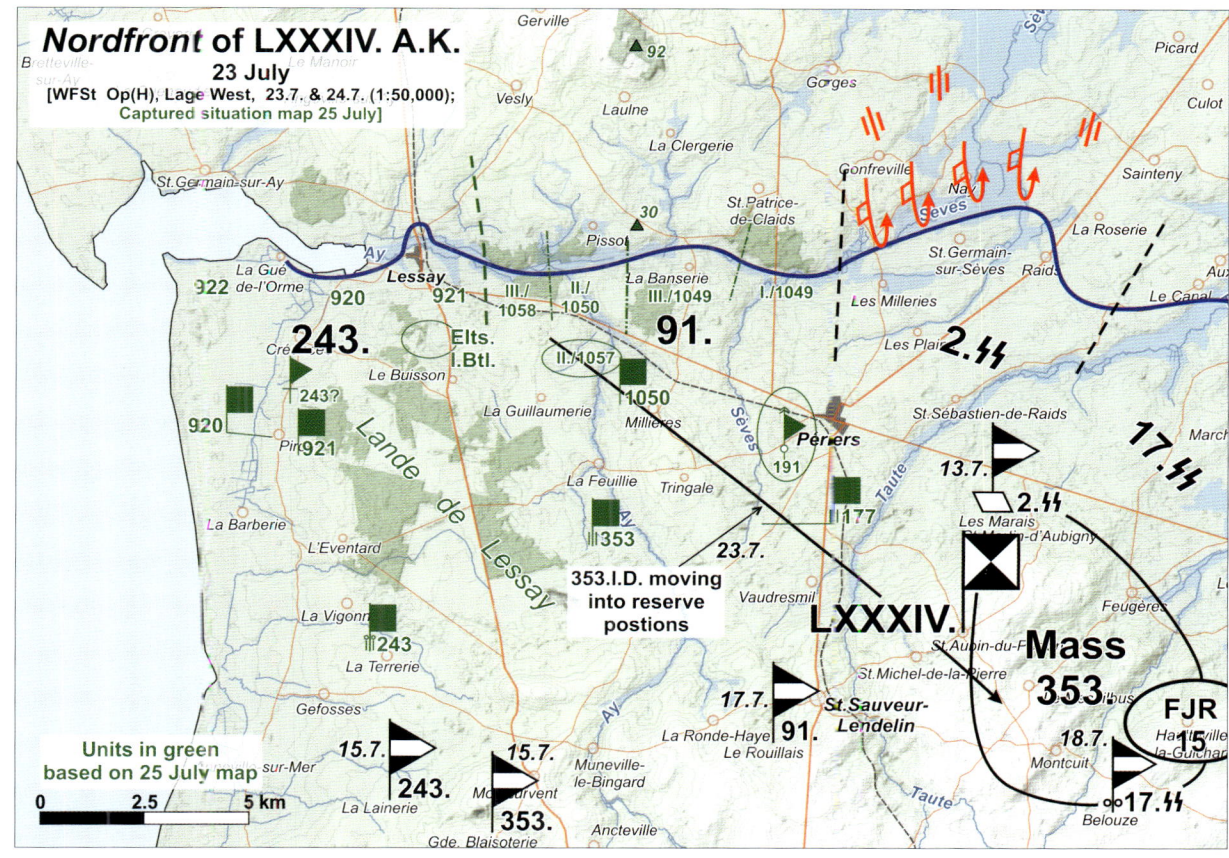

no additional forces.[477] The boundary between the two ran from Orval via Bactol to Village ès Noels.[478] The next day, GR 1058 was relieved by the I. and III./921, so it could take over part of the sector from the 353. I.D.[479] The 91. LL.D. elements were apparently used to hold the left wing of that division, which was covered by G.R. 1050. The HQ elements of G.R. 1058 appear to have been pulled back as an emergency reserve.

On **23 July**, the eve of *Operation Cobra*, the division was in a very poor condition and rated at *"Kampfwert V"*, the lowest possible combat rating. Mobility was 90% for horse-drawn and 50% for motorised units. The infantry consisted of two average and two weak battalions; these were the I./921 and the III./921, and most likely the I./920 and the II./922, but the condition of the individual battalions is not clear. One strong battalion from the 91. LL.D. was also attached. The heavy AT weapons consisted of eight heavy AT guns and three assault guns. The number of AT guns suggests some were self-propelled, but numbers cannot be confirmed. Attached to the division were eight assault guns from *Stu.Gesch.Brig. 902*, but this entry was crossed out on the document, suggesting these armoured vehicles were attached to another unit. The artillery consisted of six light and three heavy batteries, signifying the loss of just a single heavy battery since D-Day. In addition to its own artillery, the division was supported by three light batteries and three 8.8 cm batteries from the *91. LL.D.*[480] An overview from the **21st** gives the exact strength of the artillery. The six light batteries of AR 243 had at least three 7.62 cm cannon each, while the 1st, the 4th and the 5th Batteries still had four. The *3./Ost-Art. Abt. 752* was attached to the 2nd Battalion with two unidentified field pieces. The 8th Battery had three 12.2 cm howitzers and the 9th Battery four. The 10th Battery had four 12.2 cm cannon.[481] The eastern battery was also listed in the overview of **23 July**, but it was crossed out at some point.[482]

The division's precise losses (killed, wounded, captured and missing) are difficult to determine, but on **12 July** *Ob.West* recorded that it had lost 8,189 men since D-Day.[483] By **14 July**, POW camps in the UK had processed and identified 2,816 of the division's men. This compared with a figure of 2,268 on **5 July**, which may not have included those captured on the Jobourg Peninsula (*KG Müller*) in late **June**. This view is supported by the fact that 330 more soldiers of *GR 922* had been captured, while the numbers for *GR 920* and *921* were just 50 and 138. The number of new POW's from other units was small and consisted of 19 from *AR 243*, 3 from the field-replacement battalion and just 1 from the support troops.[484] Unfortunately, later overviews of the number of prisoners have not been found, rendering it impossible to ascertain how many were captured in **July** and **August**.

Documents with additional strength numbers were taken from a prisoner in late **July** or early **August**. These revealed that the division had received 5,200 replacements since **11 June**. On **28 July**, its strength was 5,868; losses amounted to 2,800 killed, 4,600 wounded and 4,000 missing (a total of 11,400), although the rounded numbers indicate that these were approximations.[485] The increase compared to the *Ob.West* loss figures on **12 July** suggests those numbers had been incomplete, since an increase of more than 3,000 men to **28 July** seems improbable considering the limited fighting during this period.

Due to *Operation Cobra*, the *Nordfront* had to be withdrawn further south to prevent the *LXXXIV. A.K.* from being cut off by the rapid American advance. Until late on **26 July**, the division's front was unchanged, but that night the *Nordfront* was pulled back to a new line that ran from St. Sebastian-de-Raids in the east via Millières to Pirou on the west coast.[486]

The withdrawals continued and, on the morning of **28 July**, the division was still crossing the Soulles River around Coutances, while establishing a new line from Roncey to Montpinchon. The division's new sector shows that it had moved away from the coast. To the right (south) of the division were elements of the *353. I.D.*, while a mixed force of *"Das Reich"*, *"Götz von Berlichingen"* and *FJR 6* was on the left (north).[487] All these elements were cut off by the American advance to their south, trapping them in a pocket.

The corps ordered the division to break out by heading southeast through Roncey – Hambye (D58 road). It was intended that the *243. I.D.* would hold the area Sourdeval-les-Bois - Gavray (west), with the *353. I.D.* on its left and elements of the aforementioned *SS* and airborne forces on its right. During the night, the division encountered strong enemy opposition in front of Hambye, and even an attack by three battalions, supported by the remaining assault and self-propelled guns, was unable to break through. In the rear, the artillery took up positions on both sides of the D58, but at dawn on the **29th**, the Americans counterattacked from the east, driving into those positions, separating the artillery from the division's forward elements. The *Kampfgruppe* moved southwest instead, making contact with the *91. LL.D.* Finally, *Obst.* Klosterkemper arrived on foot at *Obst.* König's command post south of St. Denis-le-Gast. He informed König that his division had been destroyed in its attempt to break through. In similar fashion, the corps informed *AOK 7* that the division had lost most of its artillery and vehicles, reaching the combat outpost line with about 200 infantry and a few guns. For the time being, the remnants of the division covered the area northeast of La Baleine.[488]

On **30 July**, what was left of the division retired to a blocking front on the line Briqueville-sur-Mer - Percy, along with elements of *Das Reich* and the *353. I.D.*[489] When they arrived, they occupied a sector along the Sienne River, east of La Baleine.[490] The following evening, the division and a regimental force from the *363. I.D.* held a line from south of La Faye, along the western edge of Villedieu-les-Poêles, to Hill 184.[491]

On **1 August**, the division's few surviving troops were operating under the *353. I.D.*[492] The thin German lines were once again breached by the American advance and the *Kampfgruppe* pulled back to directly east of Villedieu-les-Poêles, where it remained for several days.[493]

The division was now well east of the American breakthrough. This meant it would not be trapped in Manche or Bretagne, but it risked becoming trapped in the Falaise Pocket. After **1 August**, the division was no longer mentioned in the operational records, but on the situation maps it was still listed with the *353. I.D.*, until finally disappearing from the maps on **17 August**.[494]

With the division effectively destroyed, the role of the divisional headquarters would have been minimal, which may explain why *Obst.* Klosterkemper

The Roncey pocket was the end for much of LXXXIV. A.K.'s heavy equipment. These two guns ended up at the town's school, both apparently in good condition. On the left is an 8,8 cm Pak 43, mounted on its limbers for transport. Among the infantry divisions in the Cotentin, this type of gun is associated with the 77. I.D. and 91. LL.D.

The gun on the right is an ex-Soviet 76.2 mm USV field gun, towed by an ex-French Unic P107 halftrack. This type of weapon was used by the Germans as both an anti-tank gun and an artillery piece. Designated the 7,62 cm F.K.39, the 243. I.D. had 24 motorised pieces in its artillery regiment. This gun may well have been lost by the division as it tried to escape towards the southeast. (NARA)

was assigned other tasks under *AOK 7* during **August**.[495] It is unclear who was in charge of what was left of the *243. I.D.* following his departure.[496]

On **10 August**, the decision was made to reconstitute the division using elements of the *182. Res.Inf.Div.* This plan, however, was cancelled a few days later.[497] On **28 August**, *Heeresgruppe B* described the division as merely the remainder of the division headquarters with a few stragglers, some 200-300 men in total. It considered the division dissolved.[498] On **1 September**, the division's strength was still estimated by *Ob.West* at 3,000 men, although the accuracy of this number and composition of the force is far from clear.[499] Be that as it may, the division was informally disbanded on **8 September 1944**.[500]

Administratively, the formal end came on **20 November** with a report on the allocation of the remaining elements. Losses had been so enormous that combat units no longer existed. The same applied to the support units; some were reported as destroyed, while the locations of others was not known: A good indication that they had also been destroyed.[501]

Pz.Jg.Abt. 243 was a notable exception. The *1./Pz.Jg.Abt. 243* was sent back to Germany in **September** and eventually became *Pz.Jg.Kp. 1363b* of the *363. Volks-Grenadier-Division*.[502] The headquarters of *Pz.Jg.Abt. 243* and its 2nd Company were also in good enough shape to be reassigned, joining the *176. I.D.*, where they were used to form *Pz.Jg.Abt. 1176*.[503] Although not listed on the overview of reassignments, the *3./Pz.Jg.Abt. 243* also became part of this battalion.[504] The *176. I.D.* became trapped in the Ruhr Pocket in **April 1945**, surrendering to US forces.

265. Infanterie-Division

The *265. Infanterie-Division* was raised on **20 May 1943** outside of the "wave" system as a static division for France.[1] It did most of its service in and around Lorient (Bretagne) under the *XXV. A.K.* and was still there on D-Day.[2]

Initially, a battlegroup from the division took part in the Normandy fighting, later joined by an additional battalion. Almost all of these forces were eventually destroyed. In early **August,** other parts of the division were sent towards Dinan to oppose the American forces that had broken out into Bretagne. Pushed back towards Brest, these elements were also annihilated. The majority of the division, however, did not leave its sector on the coast. During **July-August**, this core withdrew to *Festung Lorient* and *St. Nazaire*, where they survived the rest of the war in relatively peaceful isolation.[3] The division itself was formally disbanded on **2 October**.[4]

The division had only two commanders during its existence. Its first was *Gen.Lt.* Walter Düvert, who was appointed on **1 June 1943**. Still in command on D-Day, he was succeeded by *Gen.Maj.* Hans Junck on **3 August 1944**.[5]

The division is well covered in the records of the *XXV. A.K.* and *AOK 7*, but corps records for **August 1944** are missing, making it difficult to follow its operations in Bretagne during those crucial days. Unlike other divisions, the *265. I.D.* is not directly represented in the Foreign Military Studies, but it is mentioned in a number of these studies, for example, that of the corps commanding general. Its battlegroup is also not specifically covered in any of these sources, but other records are available. Among the more interesting documents are after-action reports and other accounts in *OKH* records. Even so, coverage of the division in the summer of **1944** remains sketchy.

Organisation and Equipment

As a static division, the *265. I.D.* had the weak organisation one would expect, not having either an AT or fusilier battalion and with little mobility. This is illustrated by the authorisation document that was issued with the orders to raise the division.[6] Although it does provide the authorised strength and organisation, it lacks details on some of the heavy weapons. However, a later

Left: Gen.Maj. Walter Düvert commanded the 265.I.D. from 1 June 1943 to 28 July 1944, when he joined the OKW officer reserve. On 30 November he was released from active duty. (BArch, PERS 6/299580)

Right: Gen.Maj. Hans Junck was given command of the division on 3 August. On 26 September he was also appointed commander of Festung S.Nazaire to which his HQ had withdrawn. (BArch, PERS 6/299951)

authorisation document (**September 1943**) provides this detail on weapons and will be used here to present the division's theoretical and authorised organisation around the time of the invasion.[7]

The divisional headquarters had two machine guns and a motorcycle dispatch rider platoon. There was no divisional mapping detachment.[8]

The infantry was organised into three regiments: (*Festungs-*)*Grenadier-Regiment 894, 895,* and *896*. The first regiment had three battalions, while the others had two. The regiments included a headquarters and headquarters company. This company included signals and engineer platoons, the latter with four MG's. Each regiment had a horse-drawn section that offered at least a bit of mobility. The seven infantry battalions each had four rifle companies, all outfitted with 2 medium mortars, 2 heavy MG's and 12 light MG's. Each company also had men to man a static flamethrower. In each battalion, the first company was equipped with bicycles. As was typical for static divisions, the regiments had three heavy weapons companies: One was an infantry-gun company with six Russian guns, the other two were AT companies. One of the latter had a platoon with three motorised 7.5 cm AT guns, a platoon with

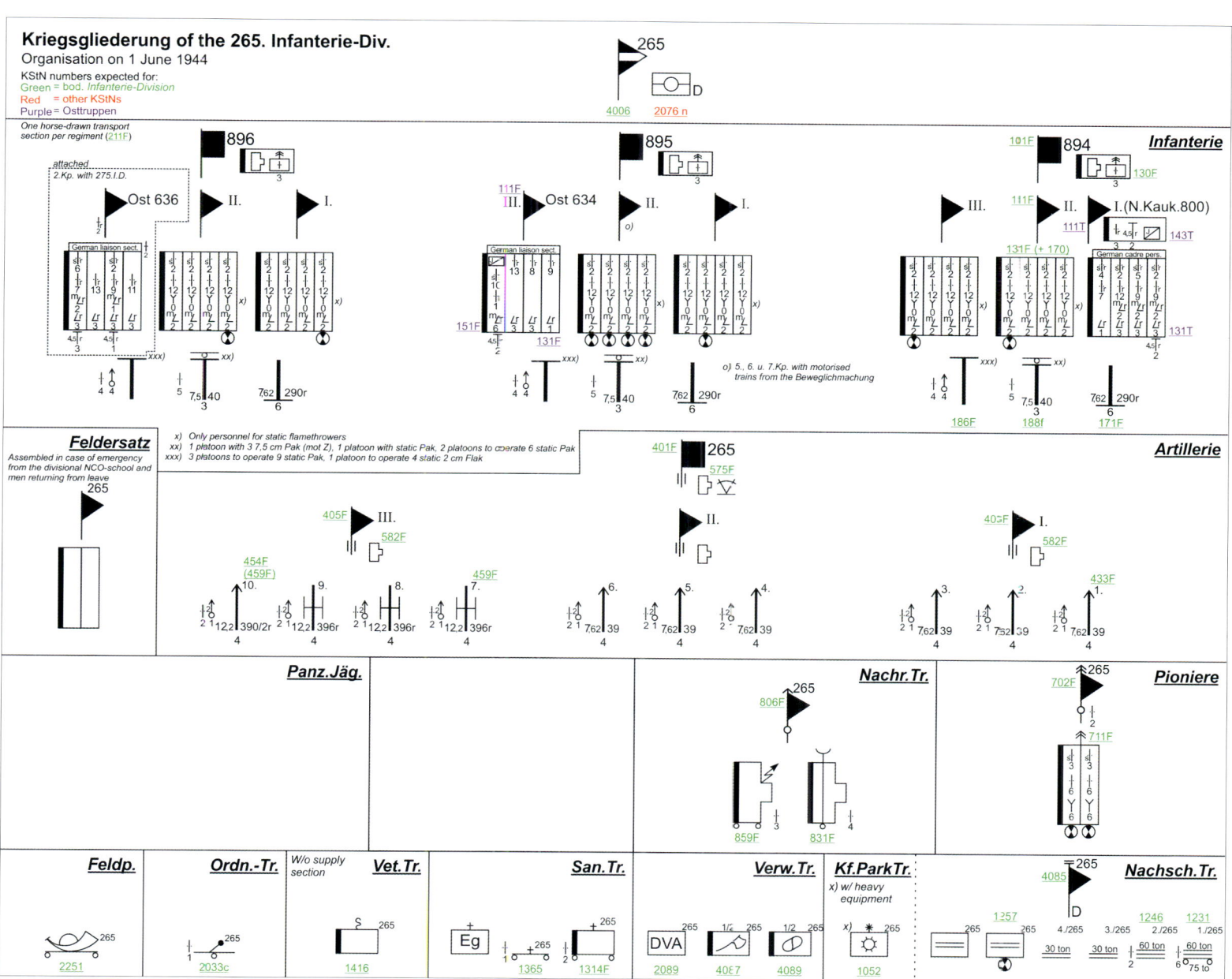

On D-Day the 265.I.D. included six German and two eastern battalions. The organisation of the division was unsurprising, except for the field-replacement battalion which was being prepared.

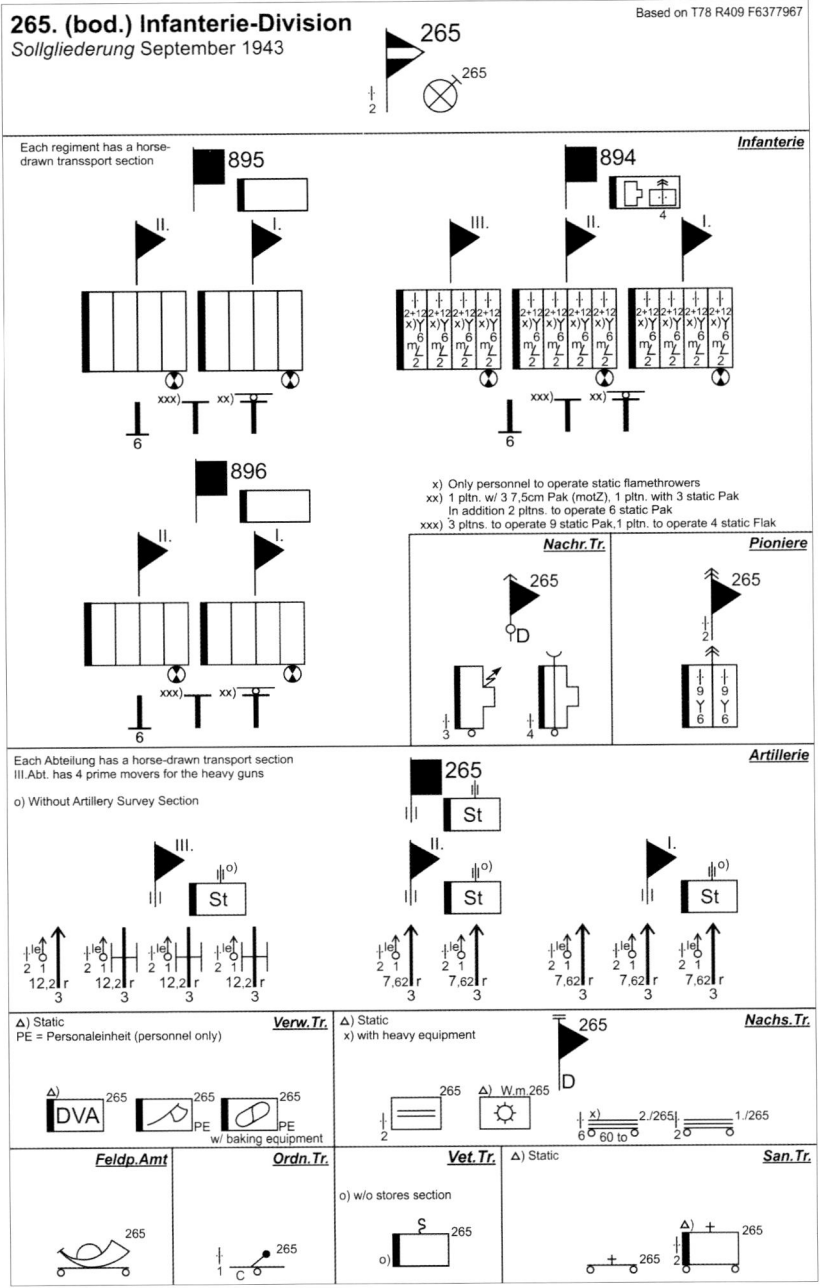

three static AT guns (presumably mobile) and two platoons to operate three more static AT guns each (presumably immobile). The other AT company had three platoons to operate three static AT guns each (presumably all immobile) and a fourth platoon with four static 2 cm *Flak*.[9] Oddly, these companies carried unusual numbers until they were renumbered in 1944. The infantry-gun company went from being the 15th Company to the standard 13th Company, the (static) 14th AT company became the 15th Company and the partially motorised 13th AT Company was redesignated as the 14th.[10]

Artillerie-Regiment 265 had a headquarters and headquarters battery. This was the same for the three battalions, none of which included a survey section.[11] The original order only called for a signals platoon instead of a headquarters battery.[12] The first two battalions in the regiment were light battalions; both had three batteries, each with three Russian 7.62 cm guns, one light *Flak*, and two MG's. The 3rd Battalion had four batteries: The first three each equipped with three Russian 12.2 cm howitzers and the fourth battery with three Russian 12.2 cm cannons. Each battery had a light *Flak* and two MG's. The battalions in the regiment also had a horse-drawn transportation section.[13] This was not part of a particular battery, but it belonged to the battalion as a whole. In addition, the 3rd Battalion had four 8-ton halftracks (*Sd.Kfz. 7's*) to transport its heavy guns.[14]

Pioneer-Bataillon 265 consisted of a headquarters and two companies. While the former was armed with two MG's, the companies each had nine MG's and six flamethrowers.[15] This differed from the original order, which had only called for six MG's per company and none with the headquarters.[16]

As a static division, its mobility was quite limited, and this is reflected in the relevant *KStN's*.[17] Except for the motorised AT gun platoons, the authorisation document only listed (partially) motorised units among the support elements and *Nachr.Abt. 265*.[18]

Of course, the division's theoretical and authorised strength in **1943** does not inform us about its condition on **6 June 1944**. Fortunately, a wealth of information is available. An additional source of data is prisoner interrogations,

---

The theoretical organisation of the division in September 1943 was rather typical for a static division. It still had seven German infantry battalions, but I./894 was transferred to the east in October. Instead the division received two eastern battalions.

but most of these relate to the battlegroup and are not necessarily relevant to the rest of the division.

On **1 June**, the division had 217 officers, 1,651 NCO's, 7,513 men and 341 *Hiwi's* assigned. With a combined strength of 9,722 personnel, it was close to full strength, having a shortage of just four officers.[19] According to the closing report about the division, 25% of the troops had combat experience (some of whom had suffered severe frostbite), 50% of the troops came from militia formations (*Landesschützen*) and were poorly trained and the remaining 25% were young soldiers, born in 1925.[20] Unfortunately, it is unclear to what extent these details were based on actual records, leaving some questions that require further investigation.

Official age numbers are available, but not after late **1943**. On **2 December**, the average age of the combat troops was 31.4 and 37.8 among the support troops. The latter was highest of all the *7. Armee* divisions.[21] A week later, more detailed numbers were reported. At that time, the division had 9,759 men, 89.8% of which were part of the combat elements. Of that group, 0.6% were born in or before 1899, 9% in 1900-05, 56% in 1906-13, 16% in 1914-22 and 19% in 1923 or later. For the support personnel, these numbers were, respectively, 3%, 62%, 26%, 8%, and 0.8%.[22]

In the summer of **1944**, an Allied study of 135 paybooks, captured up to mid-**July**, revealed that 79 of the documents (59%) belonged to recruits and 56 (41%) to experienced personnel; 48% of the men were drawn from training divisions; 54 (40%) were born in 1924-1925; and the remaining 81 (60%) were older soldiers.[23] The division was not included in the MIRS study, but additional information is available. Examining data of 130 KIA/MIA[24] (including rear area elements and troops remaining in Bretagne) paints a different picture than the paybook analysis. Above all, it shows only 25% born in or after 1924. Another 24% of the sample were 20-30 years old (born 1914-23) and 45% were 30-40 (born 1904-13). 6% were older than 40 (born 1903 at the latest). This means that a minority (43%) of the division was of the preferred 20-35 years old (born 1909-23), while the rest was either rather young (25%) or old (33%). This pattern is rather common for static divisions and differs considerably from regular divisions, but also from the *243. I.D.* which had a more favourable balance of its age groups. Within the 20-35 age group, the *265. I.D.* leaned quite heavily towards the older age groups, something that can also be observed in the *709. I.D.* where it was even stronger.

	≤1903	1904-1908	1909-1913	1914-1918	1919-1923	1924	1925	1926
KIA/MIA	6.2%	26.2%	19.2%	14.6%	9.2%	1.5%	22.3%	0.8%

Table 1: Age distribution in the *265. I.D.* (Based on 130 KIA/MIA)

While the data derived from the paybook and KIA/MIA studies are in-teresting, the samples are both small and biased towards (frontline troops of) the battlegroup, which cannot be expected to be representative of the entire division. Considering the *Ob.West* objective of 20% born in 1925, the paybook study — with 40% born in 1924 or later! — reveals an especially heavy bias. While not perfect, the KIA/MIA sample appears to be considerably better. It is also close to the results of a slightly larger sample for the static *709. I.D.* and the MIRS study of the *266. I.D.*[25] Not only was the latter static division raised as a sister unit of the *265. I.D.*, it also sent a similar reinforced regimental battlegroup to Normandy.[26] Moreover, in **December 1943**, the two divisions had also had a very similar age build-up.[27] Using that data as a reference point, it is clear that the sample of KIA/MIA for the summer of **1944** still varies a fair bit in certain age groups. Without further research it is, unfortunately, impossible to determine to what extent the differences can be explained by the bias of the sample, or by actual personnel changes before the invasion — such as 1925-26 increasing to the intended 20%.

	≤1899	1900-1905	1906-1913	1914-1922	≥1923
Dec. 1943	0.8%	14.1%	52.7%	15.4%	17.1%
KIA/MIA	0.0%	7.7%	43.8%	22.3%	26.2%
Difference	-0.8%	-6.4%	-9.9%	7.4%	9.1%

Table 2: Comparison of age groups in the *265. I.D.* in **December 1943** and 130 KIA/MIA in the summer of **1944**.

On **1 June 1944**, the division's weaponry was close to its authorisations, with all heavy AT guns and artillery pieces on hand; there were, however, some issues with the machine guns. Although the division had shortage of just three MG's (authorised 557), only 420 were *MG 42's*, 126 short of the authorised number of 546.[28] There is a discrepancy of four *MG 42's* between the figure in the division's status report and that of the accompanying order of battle

(542). The latter document indicates a shortfall of 98 light *MG 42's* (464 vs. 366) and 24 heavy *MG 42's* (78 vs. 54). The on-hand number of 54 heavy *MG 42's* was enough to equip all rifle and engineer companies. Other machine guns included 11 light *MG 13's* (authorised 12), 71 *leichte Maschinengewehre 120(r)'s* (the German designations for the Soviet DP-27) (authorised 0), and 22 Maxim *MG's* (authorised 0).[29] The latter two can only be linked to the two eastern battalions which had joined the division in **January** and caused the *MG 42* shortfall. On **1 December 1943**, the division's authorisation had been 431 MG's, including 420 *MG 42's*, and this had already been met.[30] This illustrates the fact that the division (especially the *Osttruppen*) had little priority in receiving *MG 42's* before the invasion.

The division did have the authorised number of 48 German medium mortars (*mittlerer Granat-Werfer 34*), while the *Osttruppen* battalions had a total of 16 5.2 cm and 13 8.2 cm mortars, all Soviet.[31] The German small arms included 6,974 rifles, 680 machine pistols, 3,079 pistols, 350 sniper rifles, 200 G41 self-loading rifles and 336 grenade launchers.[32]

Grenadier-Regiment 894, 895 and *896* were commanded by *Obst.* Reese, *Obst.* Habersang and *Obst.* Coep, respectively.[33] The organisation of two of the regiments was quite different from the **September 1943** authorisation document. In **November 1943**, the *I./894* was relinquished by the division to become the *III./854* of the *344. I.D.*[34] It was then decided to reinforce the division with two battalions of *Osttruppen*.[35] *Nordkaukakisches Infanterie-Bataillon 800* (North Caucasian Infantry Battalion 800 / *Nordkauk.Inf.Btl. 800*) had arrived in **October**, and *Ost-Btl. 634* arrived just as the *I./894* was leaving.[36] In **January 1944**, these battalions were formally consolidated into *GR 894* and *GR 895*, with *Nordkauk.Inf.Btl. 800* designated as *I.(Nordkauk.)/Fest.G.R. 894* and *Ost-Btl. 634* becoming the *III.(Ost)/Fest.G.R. 895*.[37]

Despite such changes, the organisation of the infantry regiments on D-Day was still close to the earlier authorisation document. As planned, each regiment had a headquarters company, several infantry battalions and three heavy weapons companies.[38]

Each headquarters company included a signals platoon and an engineer platoon with three light MG's.[39] Some additional information is available on the headquarters company of *GR* 896, which reportedly also had dispatch riders and horse-drawn transport. The dispatch riders were equipped with five motorcycles and one motorcycle-combination.[40] The signals platoon in this company had a strength of some 30 men — close to the authorised strength of 29 — and consisted of a telephone and a wireless section. The telephone section had three subsections, two for cable laying and one to operate six telephones. The wireless section had four subsections, each equipped with a *Torn.Fu.d2*.[41] The engineer platoon had three sections (each divided into two subsections); it had three light *MG 42's* and the rest of the men were armed with *K98k* rifles. Heavier weapons included one light and two heavy *Faustpatronen*, but there were no mines. The entrenching tools had been obtained from civilians. The platoon had a strength of 40 to 55 men, considerably lower than the authorised 71. Prisoners suggest that the company had about 100 to 120 men in total, which can be compared to the *KStN* number of 135 all ranks, not counting the horse-drawn transportation section. The men in the company were a motley crew. Most had been wounded, were unfit for field service, were more than 40 years of age or were the only sons of soldiers fallen in WWI. There were also 15 Poles or as much as 30% of the company.[42] The organic transport relied on horses, but numbers are not known. The transportation section reportedly had 20 men, 30 horses for four-wheel carts and three *Panjewagen*.[43] On paper, the latter had a strength of 34 men, 46 horses and 28 wagons and carts and a single bicycle.[44] When the headquarters company of *GR 896* was transferred to Normandy, it was provided two or three French buses and several vans or lorries, none of which belonged to the company. The busses were provided by *Organisation Todt* and driven by *Osttruppen*.[45]

Little has been found regarding the battalion headquarters but, in the *II./895*, it reportedly comprised 4 officers, 2 officials, 18 NCO's and 47 other ranks.[46] Information is also available for the headquarters of the *II./894*, which was sent to the battlegroup in **June**. It had a number of sections. No details are noted about the "administrative section", but the signals section consisted of just one NCO and one soldier; it was equipped with a *Torn.Fu.d2*. The dispatch rider section was composed of six dispatch riders equipped with two motorcycles and bicycles for the rest of the section.[47] The battalion headquarters of the *II./895* had 38 horses, 3 staff cars, 3 motorcycles and, possibly, 6 lorries. The battalion trains reportedly had 118 horses.[48] In contrast, the transport for the *II./894* reportedly consisted of just two lorries, with the remainder horse-drawn.[49]

As was typical for static divisions, the infantry battalions had no MG companies. Instead, there were just four rifle companies. This applied to all three regiments and matches the authorisation documents, as did the weaponry of 2 medium mortars, 2 heavy MG's and 12 light MG's per company. Some of the personnel manned static flamethrowers.[50]

The organisation of the individual companies was basically uniform. There was the company headquarters, three rifle platoons, one heavy platoon and some transport capability. The rifle platoons consisted of four sections each. These sections had a strength of 1 NCO and 9 or 10 men, although it reportedly could be as low as 7 or 8 in some companies. The rifle sections were armed with a single light *MG 42*, a sniper rifle, a grenade launcher, a machine pistol, a self-loading rifle and the ubiquitous *K98k* rifles.[51] It has been asserted that not every section in the *8./895* had a self-loading rifle or a grenade launcher.[52] This may have also applied to other companies, since the number of self-loading rifles in the division was below the number required to equip every rifle section. The heavy platoons (4th Platoon) had two sections: The MG section had two heavy MG's and the mortar section two medium mortars. The mortar sections had a strength of 15 men divided into two half-sections; each of these had one medium mortar and each man had a pistol. This also applied to the heavy MG crews, but one man per crew had a rifle.[53] In action, handheld AT weapons were available for the infantry, although numbers are vague. The *II./895* was reportedly equipped with *Faustpatronen*, *Hafthohlladungen* and two *Ofenrohre*.[54] This is supported to some extent by a soldier of the *8./895*, who stated there were about five *Faustpatronen* in his company.[55] An unknown number of *Faustpatronen* were available in the *8./894*, but there were reportedly no *Faustpatronen* in the *12./894*.[56]

Different strengths are reported for the various battalions and companies. The companies of the *II./895* each consisted of two officers, 25 NCO's and 148 men.[57] The number of officers is also confirmed for the *5./894*, but there reportedly were only 120 other ranks. Most of the men were from the year groups of 1908-1912. In addition to German soldiers, there were six Poles and two Italians.[58] Captured documents give the original strength (most likely before the invasion) of the *II./894* as 657 NCO's and men, 28 "foreigners" and 15 Italian *Hiwi's*.[59] The *12./894* is said to have had a strength of 180 men until **October 1943**, when 80 were sent to Russia. These men had not been replaced by D-Day.[60] Some soldiers of the *II./895* state that most men in the battalion were Czechs, Poles and Yugoslavs, with only a few Germans;[61] however, this is contradicted by an officer in the battalion headquarters, who stated it only contained about 6% Yugoslavs and Poles.[62] A soldier of the *8./895* supports this, stating there were only about 5% foreigners in the company.[63]

Thirty-three enlisted men of *GR 894* were captured in early July and interrogated. Their numbers on the strength and compositions of the battalions and companies illustrate the issues that arise when evaluating information provided by junior enlisted personnel. Claims were made as to 30% Poles in the 2nd Battalion and 10% in the 3rd Battalion. Yet, the numbers for the individual companies were rather different: 30% Poles in the 5th Company; just an unidentified number of Russians in the trains of the 6th; 12 to 15 Polish ethnic Germans in the 7th; five or six Poles and two Italians (in the mess) in the 8th; six Russians in the 9th; 25 Poles, 3 Czechs and 10 Russians (drivers) in the 10th; and about 40 Poles and 20 Russians in the 11th. Similar disparities exist for the over-all company strengths reported: 140 men in the 5th Company; 180 men in 6th; one officer and 117 men in the 7th; 180 men in the 8th; 140 to 150 men in the 9th; about 120 men in the 10th; and about 150 men in the 11th.[64]

The **September 1943** authorisation document listed the first company of each battalion as a bicycle company, similar to most static divisions.[65] Yet by **1 June 1944**, the entire *II./895* had become a bicycle battalion (the 8th Company had been its original bicycle company), while the other battalions still had just one bicycle company. These companies were the 7. and the *12./894*, the *3./895* and the *1.* and the *5./896*.[66] Even after the invasion, the division received additional motor vehicles and bicycles.[67] Some of these were apparently used to equip the *II./894*, which became a bicycle (mobile) battalion.[68]

There was limited motor transportation for some companies. According to the order of battle of **1 June**, the *5.-7./895* were provided with vehicles from the over-all efforts to increase mobility, which enabled these companies to have motorised trains.[69] The information for this battalion is conflicting. Some members of the battalion stated that all its transportation was motorised, but another member provided detailed numbers that still showed a large number of horses. According to him, the companies of the *II./895* each had 20 horses, 1 staff vehicle, 3 motorcycles and, possibly, 3 lorries. The battalion headquarters had 38 horses, 3 cars, 3 motorcycles and, possibly, 6 lorries, while the battalion trains had 118 horses.[70]

The *III./894* had less mobility. Originally, it had mostly relied on horse-drawn vehicles; the 9th through 11th Companies are said to have had two 8-10 horse-drawn wagons and 25 to 30 horses each. For the march to Normandy, the battalion was assigned some motorisation. The headquarters received one French bus, two 4-tonne lorries, four light lorries and two cars. Motor vehicles were also provided to the three rifle companies for the movement to Normandy; each company received three French busses. In addition, the 9th Company was provided three lorries and a car from a naval artillery formation. The 10th Company received three lorries from an unidentified source, while the 11th Company got two lorries from naval artillery, one requisitioned French lorry and a staff car.[71] Most men of the *12./894* moved by bicycle, but the company reportedly had one Ford lorry and two staff cars, while the rest of the transportation relied on horses to pull French carts. The company's guns and mortars were transported by bicycle. The machine guns were simply strapped to bicycle frames, while the mortars were split into three loads and attached to the rear of the bicycles.[72]

When the *II./894* left for the front in late June, each of its companies reportedly had about two or three lorries (one for supplies and one for the heavy platoon), one or two other cars and about two motorcycles. The company trains had four horse-drawn wagons. The 7th Company motorisation included a requisitioned taxicab and three motorcycles. Again, this motorisation was only made available when the battalion moved to Normandy. Upon arrival at the front, the battalion gave up its bicycles to be used elsewhere.[73]

The three regimental heavy weapons companies were organised similarly to many others in static divisions. By **1 June**, the company numbers differed from the authorisation document and were now aligned with more conventional numbering. The 13th Company was an infantry-gun company armed with six *7,62 cm I.K.H.290(r)'s*, but it had no MG's or motorisation.[74] A member of the *13./896* states that the company had a strength of 105 men, including some 30 Poles and 16 Rumanians. When the company moved to Normandy, lorries were borrowed from a naval unit.[75]

The 14th Company (AT) had one platoon with three motorised *7,5 cm Pak 40's* and three platoons with nine static AT guns. Two of the latter platoons "manned" static guns, while the third was "equipped" with static guns. This seems to suggest the some guns were in fixed positions and others were mobile. The company also had three MG's in its motorised platoon.[76] According to a soldier in the *14./895*, his company also had four platoons. One was armed with a number of 3.7 cm AT guns, a second had 5 cm and 7.5 cm guns and a third had one 7.5 cm and two 5 cm AT guns. His own platoon had three sections; these were each equipped with a 7.5 cm AT gun and a light *MG 42* and had a strength of one NCO and eight men. The platoon was motorised with three prime movers, five lorries and two light cars.[77] Another soldier offered slightly different information about the motorised platoon, claiming it went into action with three lorries to tow the guns and three more vehicles for the trains.[78] The platoons of the other regiments were probably similarly equipped, but exactly how is not clear.

The 15th Company was dedicated to manning static weapons: Three platoons for the AT guns (a total of nine) and a fourth to serve as crews for four 2 cm *Flak*. The company also had four MG's, but their distribution is unclear.[79]

Artillerie-Regiment 265 (*Obst.* Hett) had three battalions with a total of 10 batteries, all outfitted with Russian/Soviet artillery. In addition to headquarters, the authorisation document had called for a headquarters battery at both regimental and battalion levels. On **1 June 1944**, however, the regiment no longer had such batteries. They were last listed on the order of battle of **1 April**; thereafter, the regiment and battalions only had a signals platoon to support the headquarters. At regimental level, there was still a surveying section.[80]

The **September 1943** authorisation document had called for just three guns per battery.[81] In **November**, it was decided to add a fourth gun to each battery, and these arrived in **December**.[82] The 10th Battery was the last to receive its fourth gun, which arrived in **January**.[83] On **1 June 1944**, the three batteries of both the 1st and 2nd Battalions were each equipped with four *7,62 cm F.K. 39's*. The 3rd Battalion had three batteries with four *12,2 cm sFH 396(r)'s* and the 10th Battery with four *12,2 cm K 390/2(r)'s*.[84] Moreover, all 10 batteries had a *2 cm Flak 30 or 38* and two MG's. Mobility was poor, as none were motorised.[85] There were also differences within the regiment, as the mobility efforts had apparently provided for horse-drawn transportation for the *I./AR 265* as well as for the 2nd, 3rd and 9th Batteries.[86]

Pionier-Bataillon 265 (*Hptm.* Sabotha) was typical for a static division with only two companies. The headquarters was armed with two MG's and both companies had three heavy and six light MG's as well as six flamethrowers. Originally, the companies had no mobility, but on **1 June** they were shown with bicycles and the headquarters as partially motorised.[87] This was a fairly recent change, as the battalion had first been listed as such on **1 May**.[88]

Personnel from the 2nd Company, which was part of the battlegroup sent to Normandy, have provided some additional details. The company had a strength of some 120 men, including 20 to 24 Poles, a Czech, 12 Russians and 6 Italians. The nine machine guns were *MG 42's*, although only two were classified as heavy. The other weaponry included *K98k* rifles, 9 MP's, 3 pistols, 2 self-loading rifles, 16 flamethrowers and 2 *Faustpatronen*. The company was equipped with bicycles, 1 lorry, 1 staff vehicle, 1 motorcycle and 12 horse-drawn wagons. For the move to Normandy, it also received additional requisitioned lorries and one light car. Two lorries were used for the mess and rations, one for equipment, mines, etc. and a fourth as a bicycle repair shop.[89]

Although not listed on any authorisation document, *F.E.B. 265* had two companies on paper on **1 June 1944**.[90] The battalion was first listed on the order of battle of **1 February 1944** with a headquarters and two companies, but its organisation was far from standard.[91] On **14 February**, the *XXV. A.K.* informed *AOK 7* that the division had refrained from forming a field-replacement battalion, because to do so would seriously weaken the coastal defences. Instead, personnel reserves were collected in the NCO school, which consisted of 4 officers, 18 junior NCO's and 128 NCO candidates (*Unterführer*).[92] In case of combat (*"Fall A2"*), the academy would be increased to a proper battalion by taking in men returning from leave, from attachment to other units and convalescents.[93] Even on **1 July**, the battalion was still listed as "not yet formed".[94]

Information is plentiful concerning the division's signals battalion, *Nachrichten-Abteilung 265* (*Maj.* Mehner). On **1 June**, it consisted of a headquarters and two companies. The 1st Company was a telephone company, while the 2nd operated radios. The headquarters and 1st Company were partially motorised and the 2nd fully. The 2nd Company had three MG's, while the 1st Company had four.[95] The only difference with the authorisation document was the mobility of the 2nd Company; initial planning had only called for partial motorisation.[96]

The 1st Company reportedly consisted of four motorised and three horse-drawn cable laying sections. The other sections operated the telephones. More information is available for the 2nd Company, although the details are somewhat conflicting. It consisted of a headquarters, three platoons and an intercept section. The 1st Platoon was organised into four sections. Two of these (*mittlerer Fu.Tr. 100 Mw. (mot)*) each operated one 100 watt transmitter and one *Torn.E.b* receiver. The two remaining sections (*mittlerer Fu.Tr. 5 Mw (mot)*) each had a *Torn.E.b*, but a 5 Watt transmitter instead. This would differ from the *KStN* which called for two 80 watt transmitters in these sections.

The German forces in Normandy used a wide variety of artillery. Although photographed in the Canadian section, this photo shows several types of guns also used by the 265. I.D. On the front left is the ubiquitous 7,5 cm Pak40, which was used by the anti-tank companies of its infantry regiments. On the right is a 7,62cm le.F.K.39. 24 of these equipped the six batteries of the 1st and 2nd Battalion in A.R. 265. To the left and behind this gun are two 12,2 cm s.F.H.396 (r). Four of these were used in the 7th to 9th Batteries of the regiment's heavy 3rd Battalion. (LAC)

The four sections (*mittlerer Fu.Tr. 5 Mw (mot)*) of the 2nd Platoon are said to have each been equipped with a *Torn.E.b* and a 5 watt transmitter. This equipment would match the *KStN*, although there should have been six sections. The sections in both platoons consisted of one NCO and four men. Three of these were wireless operators, while the fourth was a driver who was trained in cipher. On paper there would have been a fifth man. Each section was transported by a *Kfz. 17* (signals wheeled vehicle) or similar vehicle. The organisation of the 3rd Platoon was different, but little is known about it, and its description is difficult to match to a *KStN*. It was putatively operated by NCO's and troops from the trains, such as drivers trained in cipher. One of its sections was a "C" section, equipped with a 15 watt transmitter and one ultra-short-wave receiver. It could communicate with reconnaissance aircraft. The other section had a 30 watt transmitter and a receiver; this is said to have been the only transmitter in the division that could transmit to *Ob.West*. The company's intercept section (*Empfängertrupp*) was equipped with four *Torn. Fu.b*. The first three were always on short wave, while the fourth monitored longer waves (*Mittelwelle*). The #1 receiver followed corps communications; #2 listened to the announcements of *Ob.West*, the standard channel for alarms, etc.; and #3 listened to Signals Command West (*Nachrichtenführer West*, commanded by *Gen.Lt.* Gimmler). The channel monitored by the #4 receiver is not known.[97]

As noted, two non-German battalions were incorporated into the division in **January 1944**. A third battalion, which arrived in **April**, was subordinated to it as well. Although none of the division's *Osttruppen* battalions took part in the Normandy fighting, there is enough information to discuss them briefly.

Osttruppen

On **1 January**, *Nordkauk.Inf.Btl. 800* consisted of a headquarters, headquarters company, three rifle companies and an MG company. The headquarters company included a mounted and an engineer platoon. According to the records of *AOK 7*, German personnel took the form of a liaison section. Yet corps records also note cadre, which makes more sense, since the number of German personnel was reasonably high, consisting of 7 officers, 1 official, 44 NCO's and 34 men.[98] *AOK 7* records on **1 May** indeed list cadre personnel instead of a liaison section, suggesting the earlier information was incorrect.[99] On **1 June**, the battalion's cadre personnel were still listed in the corps records. This also applied to the headquarters company, which included a mounted platoon and was armed with two Russian light MG's and two *4,5 cm Pak 184/1(r)*'s. Compared to **1 January**, it had lost its engineer platoon and some of its weaponry. For some reason, the 1st Company was listed as the MG company. Like the rest of the battalion, it was equipped with Russian weapons. It had one heavy MG, nine light MG's, two medium mortars (8.2 cm), three light mortars (5.2 cm), and one 4.5 cm AT gun. Both the 2nd and the 3rd Company had the same number of mortars, but the number of machine guns differed. The 2nd Company had 5 heavy MG's and 9 light MG's, while the 3rd Company had 2 and 12, respectively. The 4th Company was armed with four heavy MG's, seven light MG's and a single light mortar.[100]

When *Ost-Bataillon 634* arrived at Quimperlé on **10 November 1943**, its strength was 13 officers and 624 men; it also had 191 horses and 121 wagons.[101] Because it had been the second battalion in a regiment, its companies were still numbered from 5th through 8th.[102] By late **May 1944**, the companies had finally received standard numbers.[103] On **1 January 1944**, the battalion consisted of a headquarters, a headquarters company and three rifle companies.

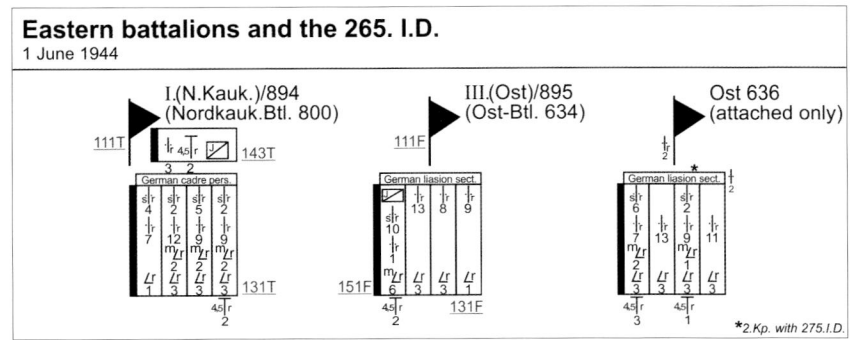

On D-Day the divisions controlled three eastern battalions. Ost-Btl. 636 was merely attached to the division, while the other two were incorporated in it. Despite their identical background, Ost-Btl. 634 and 636 differed somewhat in their organisation, but generally used the same KStN's. Being a turkic battalion, Nordk.Inf.Btl. 800 used a completely different set of TO/E's.

Its personnel were principally of eastern origin. To allow for communication with other units and headquarters, a German liaison section was attached to the battalion, consisting of 1 officer, 1 official, 1 NCO and 86 men.[104] By the time of the invasion, the battalion had been reorganised into three rifle companies and a heavy company, while retaining the liaison staff. The rifle companies were armed with Russian MG's and light mortars, although numbers varied.[105] It should be noted that some changes occurred after **1 May**. At that time, the 1st Company had been the strongest with 13 MG's and 3 mortars and the 3rd Company the weakest with 9 MG's and 1 mortar.[106] On **1 June**, however, the 1st Company was weakest with nine light MG's and one light mortar (5.2 cm); the 2nd Company had one less MG but three light mortars; and the 3rd Company had three light mortars along with 13 light MG's.[107] This suggests the 1st and 3rd Companies may have switched numbers or just transferred weapons for some unknown reason. The battalion's MG company was formed in **February** at the expense of its headquarters company. On **1 January**, the latter had included an engineer and a mounted-infantry platoon; its weaponry had been Russian, with four 4.5 cm and one 7.62 cm guns as well as two light MG's and two heavy MG's.[108] By **1 June**, the mounted platoon had become part of the MG company.[109] The daily logs of *ACK 7* listed the mounted platoon as an engineer platoon, but the records of the *XXV. A.K.* show it as an infantry platoon.[110] Until **1 April**, the 4th Company actually did have two platoons: a mounted infantry and an engineer platoon.[111] *AOK 7* appears to have listed these as a mixed platoon later, but the records merely list a mounted-infantry platoon after **1 May**. Since the corps was in closest contact, its records are probably more accurate. As in the rifle companies, the heavy weapons were Russian: 10 heavy MG's, 1 light MG, 6 medium mortars (8.2 cm), and 3 4.5 cm AT guns.[112]

Ost-Bataillon 636 was only attached to the division and never fully incorporated, while its 2nd Company remained in the area of the *275. I.D.*[113] The battalion originated from the same regiment as *Ost-Btl. 634*.[114] On **1 May**, it consisted of a headquarters, three rifle companies and a MG company. German personnel consisted of a liaison section with two German MG's. The rest of the heavy weapons were Russian. The headquarters had two MG's. The 1st Company had 12 MG's and 3 light mortars; the 2nd Company was listed with 1 heavy and 4 light MG's, 1 AT gun, 3 light mortars and 1 medium mortar; the 3rd Company had 13 MG's and 3 light mortars;[115] The 4th Company had six heavy and seven light machine guns, three Russian light mortars, two German medium mortars and three Russian 4.5 cm AT guns.[116]

Mobility and Beweglichmachung

Mobility of the division as a whole had improved since its arrival in Bretagne. In **February 1944**, it had about 600 horse-drawn wagons of all types; these included French wagons that had been purchased, although they were to be replaced by regular army horse-drawn wagons. Horses had also been purchased, but only in limited numbers. There was a shortage of 573 drivers, who had to be taken from the combat units. This shortage would be reduced to 400, when the promised 180 tonnes of lorry-lift capacity arrived. This reduced need for drivers would still weaken the combat strength of the troops, hence a request was made for more to be assigned to the division. The need for drivers could be further reduced, if fewer troops than intended were extracted; leaving the support troops and parts of the artillery behind. Even ignoring the lack of vehicles and personnel, transforming the division into a more mobile formation was further complicated by the deployment of its forces. Many were stationed on the coast and simply could not be moved inland for training.[117]

On **12 May**, the division's enhanced mobility lift capacity was only 33.3 tonnes. This put it above only the *77.*, the *275.* and the *343. I.D.*, each of which had none at all. All other divisions under *AOK 7* varied between 46 and 1,180 tonnes.[118] This extra tonnage in the division was mainly provided by horses. On **1 June**, the division had 2,380 horses, considerably more than the authorisation of 1,603. That noted, motorisation was only at 193 tonnes of lift capacity out of an authorised 301 tonnes, with another 49 tonnes in short-term repair.[119] All told, the mobility of the motorised units was rated at 50% and the horse-drawn troops at 85%.[120] The latter statistic illustrates that numbers alone do not tell the whole story: Horses cannot be used without the proper personnel, harnesses, wagons and carts.

After the invasion and the battlegroup's departure to the front, additional transport continued to arrive, yet it was insufficient to make the rest of the division mobile. Some formations, however, did benefit from this and the *II./894* was among them. On **18 June**, the battalion was reported to be bicycle mobile.[121] Its trains were mostly horse-drawn, although there was some motor transport.[122] Given that on **1 June** only its 7th Company was equipped with bicycles, it seems the battalion had taken advantage of a recent delivery of bicycles and motor vehicles. On **14 June**, the military administration at Quimper (*Feldkommandantur 752*) had supplied the division with a 1,000 confiscated bicycles, 60-tonnes of lift capacity and 18 vehicles.[123] The battalion would later join the battlegroup in Normandy.

The transfer of the battlegroup to Normandy significantly lowered the mobility of the rest of the division. On **1 July**, *Gen.Lt.* Düvert reported that the on-hand mobility capability of the motorised elements was just 22.6% and that of the horse-drawn troops was 93.4%.[124] This signifies that most of the motor vehicles had been taken to Normandy by the battlegroup. The division still had two mobile artillery batteries available, with the 5th Battery horse-drawn and 10th Battery partially motorised.[125]

Kampfgruppe

As a static division, the ability of the *265. I.D.* to provide support in other areas was limited. A partial solution was the formation of a mobile battlegroup, which naturally became the focus of mobility-enhancement efforts. Preparations for this force began in early **November 1943**, and it was related to "Contingency Measure II" — the plans of *AOK 7* to relocate a reinforced regiment to threatened sectors in the event of enemy landings.* [126] The *265. I.D.* was one of the divisions selected for possible implementation of those plans.[127]

At first, the battlegroup consisted of a reinforced infantry regiment with three battalions. The regiment would have a headquarters company, an infantry-gun company and sufficient signals equipment; support would be provided by a light artillery battalion with three batteries, an engineer company and three motorised AT platoons.[128] This force was to be motorised in an ad hoc fashion, using available vehicles. For elements not included in this motorisation process, six pre-configured trains (*I-Bereitstellungszüge***) would be available as rail transport. The force was to be ready to move within 33 hours of receiving orders.[129]

By late **November**, almost all of *GR 896* (with exception of its 1st Battalion) was selected for the battlegroup. To bring it up to the required three infantry battalions, the *II./894* and the *II./895* were attached. All three infantry regiments provided a (partially motorised) AT platoon, since there was no divisional AT company. The *II./AR 265* would provide fire support with three batteries. A single engineer company (*1./Pi.Btl. 265*) was also part of the battlegroup.[130] Most of elements were earmarked for rail transport. The exceptions were the *II./895*, the artillery battalion and the AT platoons, which would road march, although rail transport was considered for the AT platoons of *GR 894* and *GR 896*.[131]

While the corps was focused on the preparations for the battlegroup, *AOK 7* had already started to draw up other plans. In response to *Führer* Directive No. 51 (**3 November 1943**), which sought to improve defensive capabilities of the forces in the west, *AOK 7* intended to modify its force redeployment plans (Contingency Measures I - III). Contingency Measure I — the transfer of almost entire divisions — had hitherto only addressed the *243.* and the *346. I.D.*, but planning was now started for other divisions. One of these was the *265. I.D.*, and it would affect virtually the entire division.[132] After the aforementioned divisions, the *265. I.D.* was third in priority for possible redeployment.[133] Since an extraction for Contingency Measure I would mean mobile deployment, the division's mobility needed to be brought up to par with that of a regular infantry division. Initially, preparations were made to transform the division into a "new type" infantry division.[134] This plan was overly optimistic and subsequently amended in early **December** to the division merely receiving horse and motor transport, matching similar elements in the "new type" infantry divisions. A regimental headquarters and two reinforced infantry battalions were excluded from increased mobility, as they would remain static.[135] Later that month the plan was revised again to exclude one regimental headquarters, one and a half battalions and the division's *Osttruppen* battalions from increased mobility. The division was also ordered to form a bicycle battalion as an advance-guard battalion, without affecting the existing bicycle companies in the other battalions. Mobility would largely rely on horses; any missing horses were expected to arrive in mid-**January**. The drivers would be *Ostsoldaten*, but orders regarding their arrival would be issued at a later date.[136]

The plans for possible redeployment became more specific in **January 1944**. The forces pulled out would leave only the headquarters and headquarters company of *GR 895* in *KVA "C1"*, along with the *I./895* and the *I./896*.[137] The mobile parts of the division now included *GR 894* and *GR 896*

---

* Contingency Measure I (Maßnahme I): Extraction of complete divisions and the necessary relief forces from the same or other corps; Contingency Measure II (Maßnahme II): Extraction of reinforced regiments and battalions; Contingency Measure III (Maßnahme III): Relocation of division and corps reserves to neighbouring sectors. [T312 R1563 F000015]

** I-Zug: A standardised train configuration to transport mainly infantry formations. Bereitstellungszug: A train held in reserve to quickly provide mobility when required.

(minus formations but with the *II./895*); however, problems with enhancing the division's mobility soon undermined these plans. The shortage of horses and horse-drawn vehicles was expected to be resolved by mid-**February**, but difficulties were already foreseen in procuring sufficient drivers. Because of this, *AOK 7* suggested to hold only one *Kampfgruppe* fully mobile and ready (one grenadier regiment, one artillery battalion, one AT company and one engineer company). Preparations were to be made so that only when the division was to be extracted would other elements be made mobile. This approach would prevent the division's defences from being weakened by pulling out personnel required for the enhanced-mobility efforts.[138] As a result, the *Kampfgruppe* again became the focus of the mobile elements.[139]

By **10 February**, the enhanced mobility of the division's battlegroup had been completed, and the force was pulled out for training. At the end of this period (**21-29 February**), it carried out an exercise to become ready for operating as a single formation.[140] The *II./895*, the bicycle battalion, had been equipped with motor vehicles;[141] as such, it had a number of *Organization Todt* vehicles at its disposal: 15 light and 7 medium cars and 6 light, 6 medium and 9 heavy lorries. One of these lorries was a field-expedient ambulance.[142] The *2./Pi.Btl. 265* had bicycles, but it lacked the requisite motor vehicles to be fully mobile; instead, its mobility had been completed by assigning horses and horse-drawn vehicles. Other elements of the battlegroup were equipped with horses and vehicles and, thus, were fully mobile. The drivers, *Ostsoldaten*, had also been assigned.[143] The training period allowed *Gen.Lt.* Düvert to make some important observations. For example, the limited training would only enable the battlegroup to be deployed with limitations. Moreover, the battalion and company commanders lacked capabilities and experience. While a training programme was started to correct these deficiencies, the results would be limited, since the officers were suitable for static divisions and not for field deployment.[144]

The final composition of the *Kampfgruppe* before the invasion was reported in **April**, and it was still used in the *AOK 7* order of battle of **May**.[145] Another organisational document gives the status for **1 June** but it appears to have been modified to reflect the situation after D-Day.[146] Combined, they provide a good overview of the battlegroup about the time of the invasion. The headquarters of *GR 896* commanded the battlegroup. It was supported by its headquarters company, which included a signals and an engineer platoon; the company was armed with three MG's. The infantry consisted of the *III./894* and the *II./895*. Heavy weapons were provided by the *13./896* (six Russian 7.62 cm guns) and the AT platoons of the *14./895* and the *14./896* (each with three 7,5 cm Pak 40's and five MG's). The selection of just one platoon from these companies was an obvious choice, since only they were motorised, with the other platoons

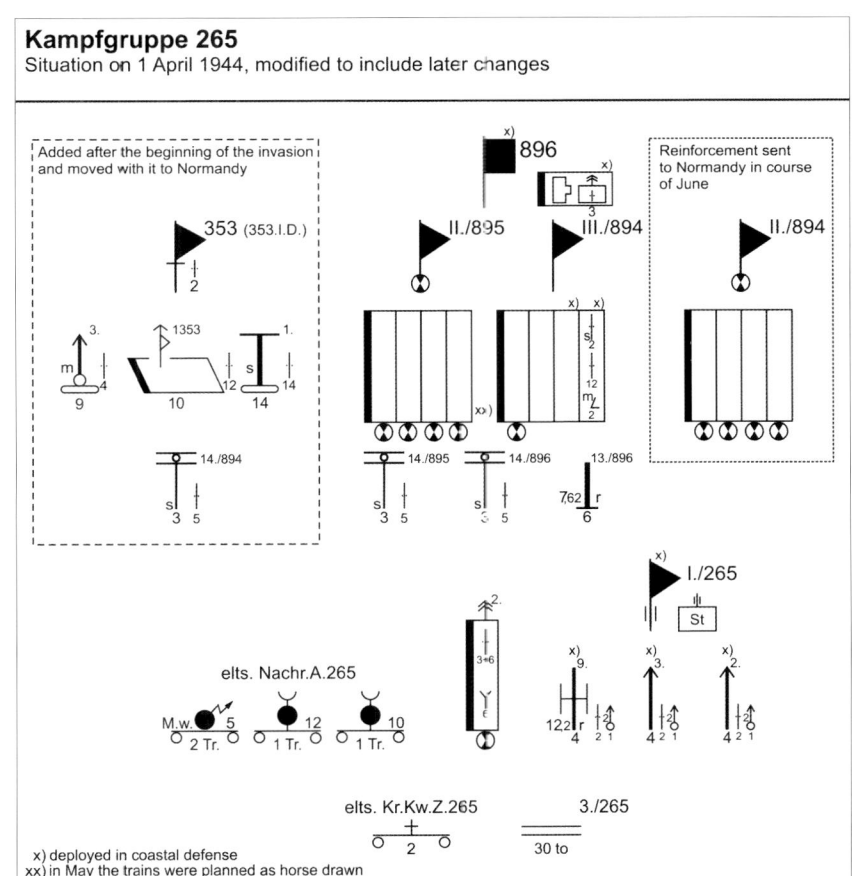

The division's ability to operate in other sectors depended almost entirely on its mobile battlegroup. After the invasions it was assigned Pz.Jg.Abt. 353 for additional support and a third infantry battalion (II./894) was sent to reinforce the Kampfgruppe it in late June.

265. Infanterie-Division

manning static guns. Artillery was also attached. The headquarters of the *I./AR 265* was in command of three batteries: The 2nd, 3rd and 9th. In addition to artillery pieces, each battery had a 2 cm *Flak* and two light MG's.[147] The final combat element was the *2./Pi.Btl. 265*, which was armed with three heavy MG's, six light MG's and six *Flammenwerfer 41*'s. Support was provided by a 30-tonne horse-drawn column, elements of the divisional field ambulance platoon, half of the medical company and parts of the signals battalion (two telephone and two wireless sections with a *mittlerer Feldkabeltrupp 12 (mot)*, a *mittlerer Feldkabeltrupp 10* and two *mittlerer Funktrupp 5 Mw (mot)*, respectively).[148]

Except for some clarifications, the **June** organisational document added the motorised heavy AT platoon from the *14./894* (three *7,5 cm Pak 40's* and five light MG's) to the battlegroup along with *Pz.Jg.Abt. 353*.[149] Both changes were apparently made after the invasion. On **2 June**, the battlegroup had 38 motorcycles, 28 light cars, 30 3-tonne lorries and 3 ambulances. To provide transport for the entire *Kampfgruppe*, another 59 motorcycles, 43 cars, 51 buses, 195 3-tonne lorries and 77 4.5-tonne lorries were required. If bicycles (722 of them) also were to be carried, another 25 lorries would be needed.[150]

History

On **20 May 1943**, orders were given to establish the *265. I.D.* along with the *266. I.D.* Both would be static divisions and were to be ready for deployment by **1 August**. The *265. I.D.* was formed at the Bergen Training Area (aka Fallingbostel) in *Wehrkreis XI*. The schedule called for establishment of the division headquarters by **10 June**, and the formation of the requisite cadres elements in various military districts by **15 June**, with the process of assembling and equipping the division beginning the next day. The divisional headquarters would be formed by the staff of the *403. Sicherungs-Division*, while most of the other elements were newly formed in *Wehrkreis I-III, VI* and *X-XI*.[151] *GR 895* was formed entirely in *Wehrkreis XI*, while both other regiments were drawn from elements in three different military districts.[152]

The division was first listed on the schematic order of battle of **21 June 1943** produced by the Commander-in-Chief of the Replacement Army.[153] It was transferred to France, relieving the *94. I.D.* in the *XXV. A.K.* sector and taking command on **1 August**.[154] Between **18** and **24 July**, 25 trains transported the division to Quimperlé, and it was listed under the corps the next day.[155] Potential plans to reassign *GR 894* and the *I./AR 265* to the *709. I.D.* after the *265. I.D.* left Germany were soon cancelled.[156]

In Bretagne, the division was assigned the defence of *KVA "J"*, a sector on the southern coast later renamed *KVA "C1"*. It assumed command at 12:00 on **1 August**. The *343. I.D.* was to the division's right and on the left (southeast) was the *384. I.D.*[157] The latter was relieved by the *243. I.D.* on **2 October**.[158] The right divisional boundary was approximately the line Crozon - Châteaulin – Carhaix, while the left boundary was the Étel River - Locminé - Josselin. The main city was Lorient, with its important U-Boot base.[159]

As was typical after the arrival of a new division, the locations of its units were not all reported. The first overview is a *7. Armee* situation map for **23 August**. The divisional headquarters was at Quimperlé, along with that of *Nachr.Abt. 265*. The headquarters of *AR 265* was in Château du Talhouët. The headquarters of *Pi.Btl. 265* was further west, at Rosporden. On the coast, *GR 894* held the right sector; its headquarters was initially located at Quimper, the main town in the area.[160] In **September**, it moved to Château Lanroz (6 km south of Quimper).[161] Its three battalions formed an arc between the town and the coast, with the 1st Battalion at Fouesnant, the 2nd at Plogastel, and the 3rd Battalion at Locronan. The divisional artillery in the area was the *I./AR 265*, with its headquarters at Plonéour-Lanvern. The area west of Lorient was in the sector of *GR 895*, with its headquarters at Guidel. Its two battalions were at Le Puil (I.) and Clohars-Carnoët (II.). The *III./AR 265* was also in the area, at Kervergant.[162] *GR 896* was in and east of Lorient; its regimental staff initially at a Château near Hennebont before moving to Merlevenez in **September**.[163] The regiment's 1st Battalion was at Lorient with the *II./Fest.St.Rgt. XXV*, while its 2nd Battalion and the *II./AR 265* were located in Plouhinec.[164]

In **October**, the division held a coastal sector of 270 km. *Ob.West* deemed its level of training insufficient, in part due to the division having to deploy immediately after its formation. The problem was exacerbated by exchanges of personnel (*Jahrgangaustausch*) and activities carried out by the division.[165] The level of training would prove difficult to improve. For one, the coastal defences in the division's sector were poor. As a result, the division was building defensive positions, leaving little time for training in the winter and spring of **1944**.[166]

In October, *Nordkauk.Inf.Btl. 800* (aka the *1. Nordkauk.Inf.Btl.*) was assigned to the division. The battalion arrived between **11** and **13 October**, and it was dispatched to the area southwest of Quimper.[167] On the **16**th, the

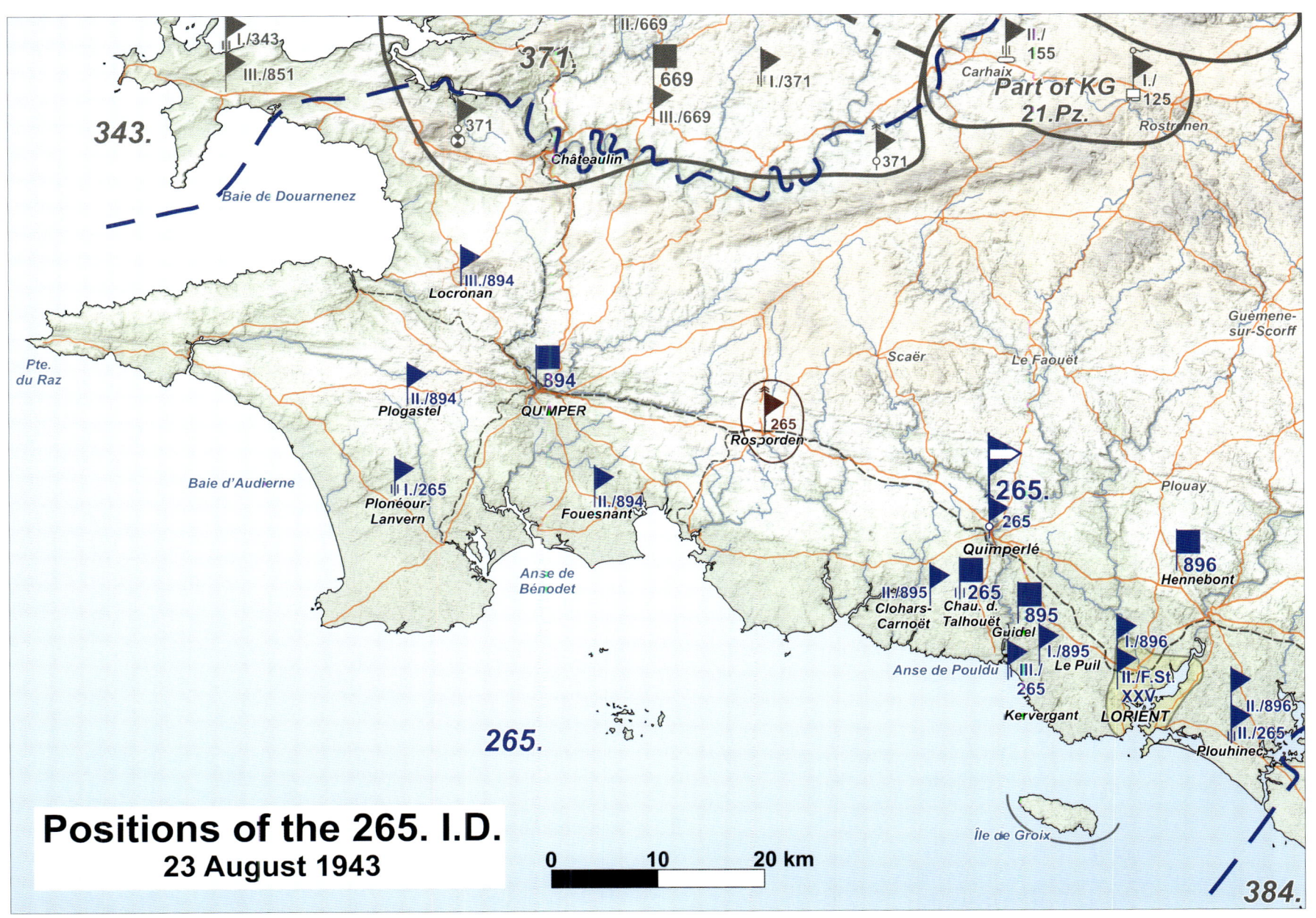

When the 265. I.D. arrived it took control of a large sector of the southern coast of Bretagne. In January 1944 its right (northern) boundary was moved south a bit but the left boundary remained pretty much unchanged up to D-Day.

corps was informed that the division was to hand over one battalion for service on the Eastern Front and the *I./894* was selected.[168] This battalion was largely relieved by elements of the *II./894* and the *II./895* on **18 October**, and moved to Quimper on the **21st**.[169] These developments may explain why the headquarters of the *II./894* moved to Fouesnant on **29 October**.[170] To replace the *I./894*, the division received *Ost-Btl. 634*, which arrived at Quimperlé on **10 November**, with the *I./894* leaving the next day.[171] The newly received battalion was deployed on the coast south and southwest of Quimperlé.[172]

In late **December**, the *1./Pi.Btl. 265* was ordered to the sector of the *LXXXIV. A.K.* in Normandy to work on the construction of the so-called "2nd Position".[173] The move was carried out in **January**, the company transferred by train from Rosporden to Caen.[174] The absence of this company affected the training of the battalion's 2nd Company, which would be completely occupied with the construction of coastal defences.[175] The 1st Company returned on **8 March** and moved to Rosporden.[176]

In **January 1944**, the division's sector was reduced by enlarging the area assigned to the *343. I.D.*, the right boundary moving south to include Douarnenez on the **16th**.[177] Another change involved the *II./895* (the division's bicycle battalion), which became a reserve battalion. On **13-15 January**, it moved to Gestel and Pont-Scorff, which would remain the battalion's home base, even while it conducted missions in other areas during the spring of **1944**.[178]

In mid-**March 1944**, the division received another reinforcement: *Ost-Btl. 636* minus its 2nd Company, which remained in the area of the *275. I.D.*[179] (The *275. I.D.* had relieved the *243. I.D.* in **January**) On **19 March**, the battalion took up positions on the eastern bank of the Blavet River, opposite Lorient. The battalion headquarters was at Carnac, with the 1st and the 3rd Companies at Resistance Nest Lorient 70 (*Wn.Lo. 70*); the 4th Company was at Port Louis.[180] The battalion was never truly incorporated into the division. Instead, it was subordinated to *Festungs-Kommandant Lorient*.[181]

In **April**, *Ost-Radfahr-Abteilung 285* (Eastern Bicycle Battalion 285 / *Ost-Radf.Abt. 285*) was transferred to *KVA "C1"*. On **4 April**, the battalion was relieved on the north coast of Bretagne by elements of the *353. I.D.*[182] On the **6th**, it was transported by rail from Landerneau, arriving in *Festung Lorient* two days later.[183] The battalion took up temporary positions in the resistance nests around Port Louis — on the south side of the Rade de Port Louis and the Rade de Pen Mané — opposite Lorient.[184] On **9 April**, it moved southwest of the city, to Ploemeur and on the coast.[185] Later that month and in **May** there were additional relocations, but most of the battalion remained in *Festung Lorient* throughout this period.[186]

Positions on D-Day

Around D-Day, the division held the same areas as when it arrived in the summer of **1943**. The divisional headquarters was at still at Quimperlé with *Nachr.Abt. 265*. KVA "C1" was divided into three sectors. On the right (northwest) was *GR 894* (*KVG Quimper*), the centre was held by *GR 895* (*KVG Anse de Pouldu*), and the left (southeast) by *GR 896* (*KVG Plouhinec*).[187]

The headquarters of *GR 894* was in Resistance Nest Quimper 504 (*Wn. Qu. 504*),* near Fluguffan, southwest of Quimper.[188] The headquarters company was at Lanroz and the 13th Company in reserve at Kéraval.[189] The *III./894* was on the far right, in the area between Douarnenez to Plouhinec; its headquarters was at Kerviny, the 9th Company at Ploaré, the 10th at Cléden-Cap Sizun, the 11th at Pont-Croix and the 12th (bicycle) at Pouldergat.[190] In the spring of **1944**, the 11th and 12th Companies were not committed on the coast.[191] On **31 May**, however, the 12th Company was sent to Plovan to take part in construction of beach obstacles.[192] *Nordkaukakisches Inf.Btl. 800* was in position west and southwest of Quimper and held the coast to Benodet, including the Baie d'Audierne; its headquarters was located at Lestréminou, the headquarters company at Kerfoular, and the horse-mounted platoon at Languivoa.[193] The 1st through 4th Companies were at Le Bren (today Brenn), Chau. Le Beuzec (today Beuzeg), Plobannalec and Plovan, respectively.[194] The headquarters of the *II./894* was at Fouesnant and responsible for the area to Trégunc;[195] the battalion's 5th Company was in reserve in the same village, except for one platoon, which was attached to the 8th Company and deployed on the coast. The 6th Company was in Trégunc, defending the coast around Concarneau. Much like the *12./894*, the 7th Company (bicycle) was kept in reserve at Pont-l'Abbé; on **2 June** it was sent to the Audierne Bight to support the building of beach obstacles. It was then located at Kerbascol.[196] The 8th Company was reportedly at Fouesnant and covered the coast from Trégounour to Cap Coz.[197]

---

* Wn.: Widerstandsnest, resistance nest. "Qu"was used for positions near Quimper. In similar fashion "Lo" referred to Lorient and "Va" to Vannes.

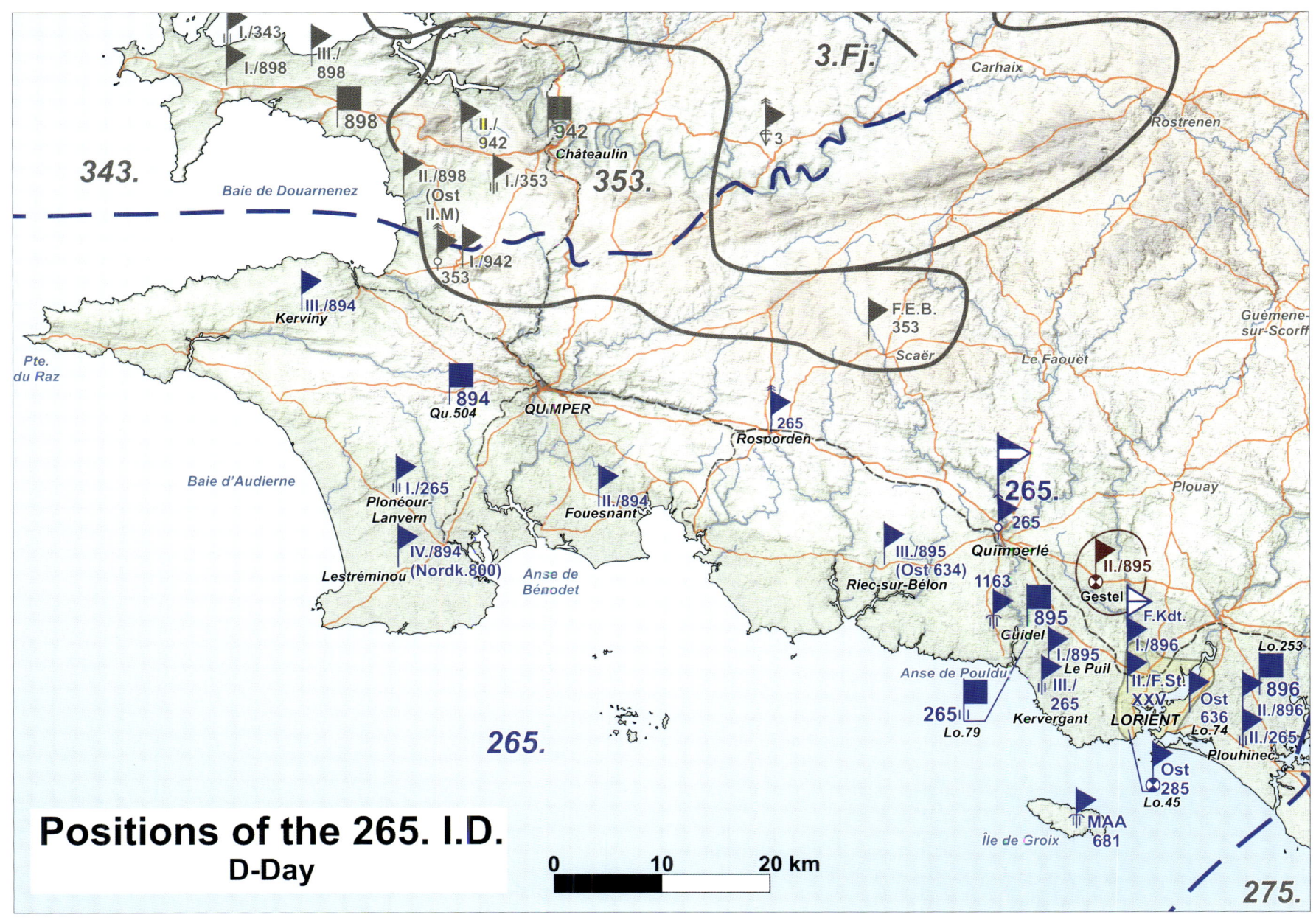

From its arrival, the 265.I.D. defended KVA 'C1' on the southwest coast of Bretagne. Its forces were strongest around the port of Lorient with its important U-Boot base.

The headquarters of *GR 895* was in Guidel.[198] The 13th Company was moved to Le Pouldu on **21 May**.[199] The motorised AT platoon of the *14./895* was at Guidel.[200] *GR 895*'s right flank was held by *Ost-Btl. 634 (III./895)* on the coast southwest of Quimperlé; the battalion commander had assumed control of *KVU Clohars* on **13 January**. This sector stretched to Clohars-Carnoët. The battalion headquarters was located at Riec-sur-Bélon.[201] The last report for the 1st Company was on **25 November 1943**, when the company was at Moëlan-sur-Mer.[202] On **11 January**, the 2nd Company assumed command of Resistance Nests Quimper 73-76 (*Wn.Qu. 73-76*).[203] On **24 May**, new positions were reported for two companies: The 3rd Company was at Resistance Nest Lorient 2 (*Wn.Lo. 2*) and the 4th Company on Hill 46 (1.7 km southwest of Clohars).[204] The *I./895* held the coast to Le Courégant. The battalion headquarters was at Le Puil, the 1st Company at Le Pouldu, the 2nd at Resistance Nest Lorient 29 (*Wn.Lo. 29*) and the 3rd at Ploemeur.[205] The location of 4th Company is not clear; it had been at Kerhouel in **July 1943**, but it had since moved from there.[206] As already noted, the *II./895* was a divisional reserve, positioned around Gestel and Pont-Scorff.[207] The 5th and 6th Companies were in a wooded area just east of Gestel. The 7th Company was just west of Pont-Scorff and the 8th Company was at the town itself.[208]

GR 896 held the area between Le Courégant and the Étel River, including Lorient.[209] The headquarters was at *Wn.Lo. 253* (2 km north-northwest of Merlevenez) and the headquarters company in Merlevenez.[210] The 13th Company was at Hennebont, and the 14th Company was reported in Pouldreuzic on **8 May**.[211] *Ost-Radf.Abt. 285* was southwest of the town; its headquarters at Resistance Nest Lorient 45 (*Wn.Lo. 45*) and its troops (companies) in the same area. The 1st Troop was at Point 64 (*Wn.Lo. 64*), the 2nd at 47 (*Wn.Lo. 47*), the 3rd at 46 (*Wn.Lo. 46*) and the 4th at 44 (*Wn.Lo. 44*).[212] The 1st Troop took part in *Operation Landgraf*, the *15./896* taking over its sector in Lorient.[213] It is not clear where the company was located after that. *Festung Lorient* was commanded by the *Festungs-Kommandant* and mostly defended by the *II./Fest.Stamm-Rgt. XXV* and the *I./896*. The *3./896* was deployed in the coastal defences, with the 14th and elements of the 15th Companies of *Fest.Stamm-Rgt. XXV*.[214] The *3./896* itself was at Resistance Nest Lorient 61 (*Wn.Lo 61*).[215] The *I./896*, with its 2nd and 4th Companies, was in the interior defences. Artillery support was from the 7th and 10th Batteries of the *III./AR 265*. There were also three companies from *Fest.Stamm-Rgt. XXV*: The 12th, 13th and elements of the 15th. If required, the *II./895* could be transferred to the north of the interior defences in a matter of hours. The *1./896* formed the fortress reserve, along with a naval *Flak* section from the *IV. Marine-Flak-Brigade*.[216] The majority of the artillery in the fortress was Navy. The aforementioned naval element provided *Flak* defence, while artillery of *Mar.Art.Abt. 264* and *681*, the latter stationed on the Île de Groix, provided conventional artillery support.[217] *Ost-Btl. 636* was on the eastern bank of the Blavet, opposite Lorient;[218] its headquarters was at Resistance Nest Lorient 74 (*Wn.Lo. 74*), while its 1st, 3rd and 4th Companies — all of which arrived on **8 April** — were at Resistance Nests 75, 70 and 73, respectively.[219] The 2nd Company was further south, in the sector of the *275. I.D.*, and it was placed under the *II./984 (275. I.D.)*, which took over *KVU Plouharnel* from the battalion.[220] Finally, the *II./896* held the coast up to the Étel River (*KVG Plouhinec*); its headquarters was at Kergatorne, with the 5th Company at the woods encampment (1.8 km northeast of Plouhinec) ever since **13 May**.[221] The rest of the battalion's locations were last reported on **17 February**. At that time, the 6th Company was in *Wn.Va.101*, the 7th in Resistance Nest Lorient 87 (*Wn.Lo. 87*) and the 8th at Resistance Nest Lorient 79 (*Wn.Lo.79*).[222] These resistance nests were south, 4 km southeast and 2 km southwest of Plouhinec, respectively.

The division's artillery was distributed throughout the sector. The headquarters of *AR 265* was in Resistance Nest Lorient 209 (*Wn.Lo. 209*), roughly mid-way between Quimperlé and Lorient. On the division's right, the regiment's 1st Battalion defended the Baie d'Audierne southwest of Quimper, with its headquarters in Plonéour-Lanvern; the *II./AR 265* was on the left with its headquarters in Plouhinec (Resistance Nest Lorient 79 / *Wn.Lo. 79*); the *III./AR 265* was near Lorient, with its headquarters in Kervergant.[223] This dovetailed with the plans made for the distribution of the artillery in **November 1943**.[224]

Pi.Btl. 265 was in Rosporden.[225] On **8 March**, its 1st Company returned from duties with the *LXXXIV. A.K.* and was also in Rosporden.[226] The 2nd Company is said to have been at Melgven.[227]

Fighting the Résistance

Compared to Normandy, Bretagne had an active armed resistance movement, referred to as *Terroristen* or *Banden* by the Germans. Officially, these terms were used for different groups. *Banden* (bandits) was used to replace the word *Partisan,* which had been glorified by Soviet propaganda.[228] To the Germans, *Banden* officially referred to well organised groups of armed bandits, whereas the term *Terroristen* was used for activists, mainly communists.[229] In France, the Germans used both terms rather indiscriminately to describe the *Résistance*. These resistance forces became a growing threat to the Germans. In a two week period between **1-15 April**, 12 men were killed and another 12 wounded in the *XXV. A.K.* sector.[230] On the afternoon of **13 April**, there were three attacks on German military vehicles on the road from Pontivy to Locminé. That evening, *Gen.* Fahrmbacher responded with an immediate deployment of the *I./984 (275. I.D.)* into the heart of the resistance area. The operation began with two reinforced companies and grew more substantial over the next few days.[231]

On **16 April**, the *XXV. A.K.* ordered an anti-resistance operation carried out in the area south of Pontivy. A special battlegroup was created under *Obst.* Heintz, commander of *GR 984 (275. I.D.)*. *GR 984* provided the majority of the forces: its headquarters, the 13th and 14th Companies and the *I./984*. The reserve battalion of the *265. I.D..*, the *II./895*, was attached as well. *Osttruppen* took part: The *1./Ost-Radf.Abt. 285* and a platoon of the Cossack Detachment (*Kosaken-Kommando*) in Pontivy.[232] The battlegroup was later reinforced by two heavy armoured cars from the *21. Pz.Div.*[233] The *II./895* joined *Kampfgruppe Heintz* on **18 April**, going into position along a line southwest of Pontivy — running from Guémené-sur-Scorff to Remungol through Melrand and Pluméliau, while the *1./Radf.Abt. 285* moved to Bubry.[234] On **26 April**, the corps announced that *Ost-Reiter-Abt. 281* would also be attached to the anti-resistance sweep, allowing the *II./895* to return to its original area.[235]

On **13 May**, the battalion returned from its mission, taking up its original positions around Gestel and Pont-Scorff. The *1./Radf.Abt. 285* also returned to its original positions and the battlegroup itself was dissolved on **20 May**.[236] The battalion's deployment under *KG Heintz* was appreciated by *Gen.Lt.* Düvert, as it had provided the men with practical experience.[237] The battalion did not get much time to rest. On **18 May**, it was sent to protect areas considered suitable for airborne landings.[238] This mission was relatively short and the first two companies returned to Gestel on **22-23 May**.[239]

Operation Landgraf

Earlier in the month *Heeresgruppe B* had ordered a deception operation: *Aktion Landgraf*.[240] Elements of the *265.* and the *275. I.D.*, along with some corps troops, would be combined to simulate a new division, the fictitious *101. I.D.* (This designation would be changed to the equally fictitious *506. I.D.* before going "into action"). The operation would run **15-31 May**; following its completion, most of the forces would return to their parent formations.[241] As one of the few reserve forces of the *XXV. A.K.*, the *II./895* was again called upon to participate.[242] It did not, however, take part in the preparatory stages of the operation, which continued until **25 May**, when other elements of the "division" were to arrive.[243] These included the battalion, which was sent to Pluvigner. The 8th Company did not accompany the battalion. Instead, it was sent on a special three-day mission of its own to Locunolé.[244] The battalion returned to the division on **2 June,** going into position around Gestel and Pont-Scorff.[245]

The Kampfgruppe

The battlegroup's mobility meant it was the division's main fighting force for operations in other areas. In early **April**, the battlegroup's deployment was planned for an Allied assault in Normandy (under the *LXXXIV. A.K.*) or on the north Breton coast around St. Malo (*LXXIV. A.K.*). These potential Allied landings were referred to as *Fall 3A* and *3B*. In addition, the battlegroup could be deployed outside of the *AOK 7* area of responsibility as well. This would include operations in southern France under *AOK 1* or *AOK 19*, or to the north under *AOK 15* or the Netherlands. This placed a premium on the value of the battlegroup in comparison to elements such as *KG 275* and *KG 266*, which were restricted to the *7. Armee* sector.[246] For deployment under the *XXV. A.K.*, the battlegroup was a corps reserve and under the *7. Armee*, it was a field-army reserve.[247] As a corps reserve, it could be committed throughout the corps area, including the division's own sector as well as *KVA "B"* and *"C2"*.[248] By **26 May**, however, the battlegroup had been restricted to operations of *AOK 7* in Normandy or Bretagne.[249] The scenario that *KG 265* and *KG 275* might be pulled out together was contemplated; if this were to occur, they could be combined into an ad hoc formation under command of the *275. I.D.*, but this never came to pass.[250]

265. Infanterie-Division

In the months before D-Day, much of the battlegroup was used for coastal defence. This included its artillery, its engineer company, two companies of the *III./894*, as well as the headquarters, headquarters company and the 13th Company of *GR 896*.[251] The *12./894* was in reserve until the end of **May**, when it was sent to Plovan to build beach obstacles.[252] This left just the *11./894*, the *II./895*, the *14./895* and the *14./896* in reserve with the support troops. The detachment of elements from the battlegroup to work on coastal defence makes clear that, despite its significance, it was still subject to more mundane taskings from the division. When needed, the battlegroup could be rapidly assembled and dispatched to the front. For example, the *14./895* conducted several loading exercises in **1943**.[253] Plans for the battlegroup's transfer by rail were prepared under the code name *Bewegung Spargel* (Movement Asparagus) and would require 15 trains.[254]

As commander of *GR 896*, *Obst.* Coep was in charge of the battlegroup, but he would not lead it into action. On **8 June**, *Obstlt.* Jäger, commander of *GR 898* (*343. I.D.*), took command.[255] The reason for the personnel change is not clear. According to *Obstlt.* Jäger, his predecessor had suffered a nervous breakdown. The lieutenant colonel was pleased with his new role and considered his "little division" to be a nice assignment for a simple *Oberstleutnant*.[256] Yet, things would soon turn out to be very difficult.

Combat

At 09:20 on D-Day *AOK 7* ordered the *XXV. A.K.* to prepare *Kampfgruppe 265* and *275* for movement (*Marschbereitschaft*).[257] *KG 265* was second in priority.[258] At 23:30, the *7. Armee* issued a warning order (*Vorbefehl*) regarding the battlegroup's movement. Just after midnight, it ordered the immediate transfer by rail of *KG 265* towards St. Lô. From there, the battlegroup would be directed further by the *LXXXIV. A.K.*, depending on the situation. To prepare for the battlegroup's arrival, an advance party was to be dispatched to the corps immediately.[259] Thanks to months of preparations, the troops were soon ready to move and, upon receiving the code word, *Kampfgruppe-Einsatz* ("Battlegroup Employment"), they moved out quickly.[260]

At 11:15 the next morning, the division reported everything was on schedule despite some enemy interference.[261] At 08:00, the *9./AR 265* had been on its way to the assembly area, when it was attacked by aircraft, but it sustained no losses. By late morning, the *II./895*, the engineer company and elements of the signals battalion had reached their assembly areas.[262] As planned, several stand-by trains were assigned to transport the battlegroup. The first train was scheduled to leave at 12:00, but at 10:00, the trains were reassigned to *KG 275*.[263] Later in the day, the entire — well prepared — *Bewegung Spargel* was cancelled. The cancellation of the rail movement may have been fortuitous, as air attacks and sabotage caused transport difficulties for *KG 275*. Its lead train, carrying the headquarters and the 1st Company of *Pi.Btl. 275*, was completely destroyed near Avranches, with 70-80 men killed and 140 wounded. All vehicles and equipment were lost.[264]

At 17:20, *AOK 7* announced a change of plans. Due to the catastrophic experience of *KG 275*, *KG 265* would move by road instead, either motorised or by bicycle. Motorisation would be provided by motor companies of the *XXV. A.K.*, and a request for additional transportation from the *Kriegsmarine* was placed with *Heeresgruppe B*. The elements suitable for road march were to leave at dark, following the route: Gourin - Gouarec - Uzel - Plouguenast - La Chapelle Blanche - Bécherel - Vieux-Vy-sur-Couesnon - Baillé - 13 km west of Fougères - St. Brice-en-Coglès - St. Georges-de-Reintembault - St. Martin-de-Landelles - St. Hilaire-du-Harcouët - Parigny - Juvigny-le-Tertre - Chérencé-le-Roussel - Gathemo - St. Martin-de-Tallevende - Le Mesnil-Benoist - Le Mesnil-Robert - Beaumesnil - Tessy-sur-Vire - Le Mesnil-Opac - St. Lô.[265] All means of transportation used for this transfer were to be returned to Bretagne as soon as possible.[266] Horse-drawn units, mainly the trains, were not suited to road march and would be sent by rail later.[267]

The battlegroup's composition as it was on its way to Normandy differed from plans made before the invasion. It had been strengthened by a third motorised AT platoon, coming from the *14./894*.[268] This meant that all the division's motorised AT platoons were now assigned to the battlegroup and as a result, all of the division's assigned *7,5 cm Pak 40's*. A more significant reinforcement came from the *353. I.D.* — all of *Pz.Jg.Abt. 353*.[269] This major addition provided the battlegroup with three powerful companies: The 1st Company with 14 *Marders*, the 2nd Company with 10 assault guns and the 3rd Company with 9 3.7 cm SP *Flak*.[270] The *353. I.D.* had already reported the battalion's *Flak* company ready for movement on the morning of **6 June**.[271] The AT battalion would make its way to the front separately from the battlegroup.[272] Its three trains were unloaded at L'Hermitage, Landébia and Dinan

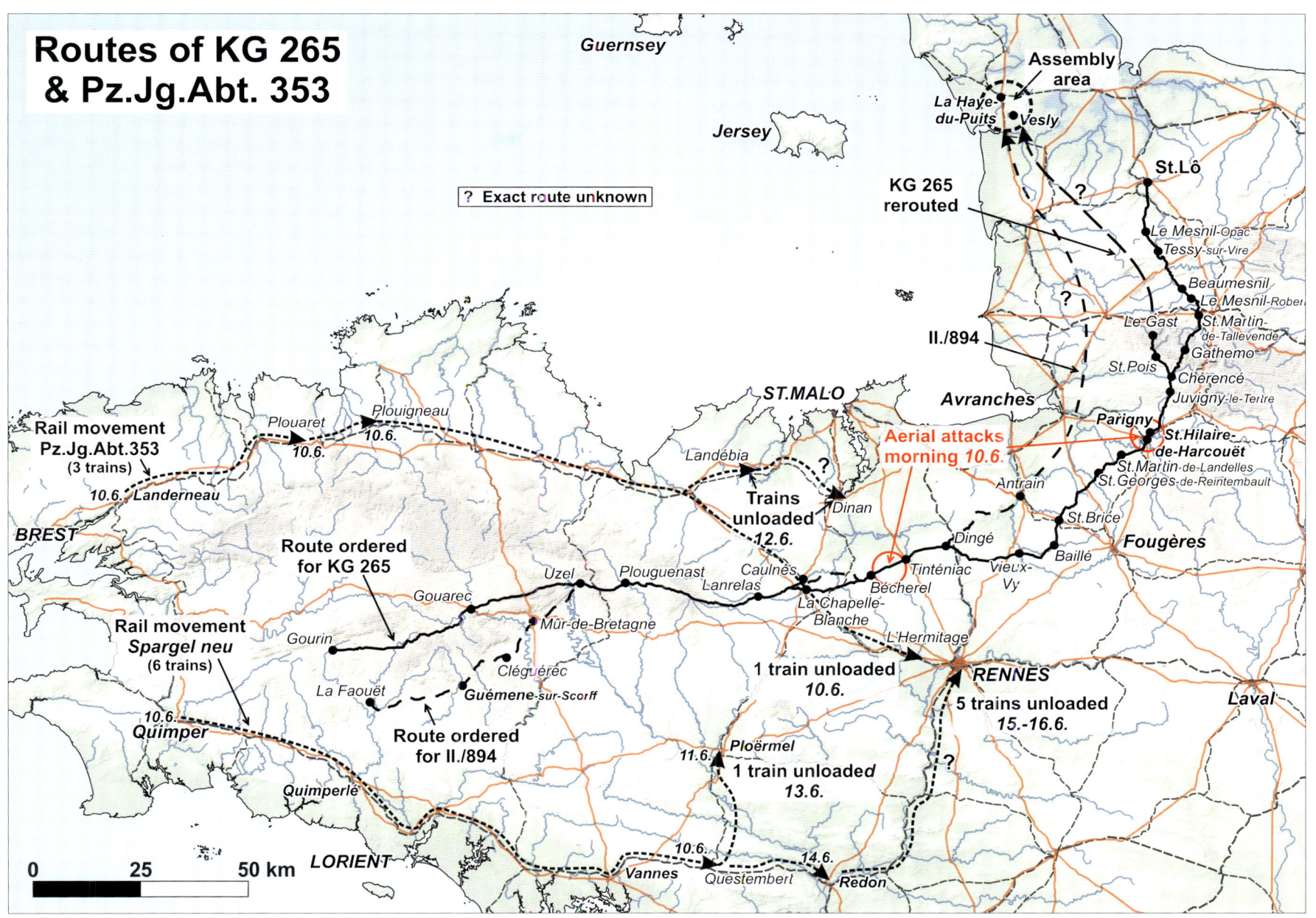

After the planned rail transport had been cancelled, much of KG 265 was ordered to move by road. With St.Lô over 300 km away, it took much time and effort for the reinforced battlegroup to reach the front. The less mobile elements and Pz.Jg.Abt. 352 did travel by rail, but had to be unloaded well before their objectives due to attacks on the railroads.

For a defender the hedgerow country provided excellent camouflage. It, however, also restricted observation and limited fields of fire. This made mutually supporting fire difficult and forced troops to be spread out to cover the front. (Collectie CegeSoma – Rijksarchief (OD4))

on **10** and **12 June**. From there, the troops continued the journey by road.[273] At what point the battalion joined *KG 265* is not clear, but it was listed under the battlegroup on **19 June**; moreover, elements of the battalion were in place to engage the 82nd AB Division at Prétot on the **20th**.[274] It seems the battalion rejoined the *353. I.D.*, when the division arrived at Périers a few days later. It was not listed as part of *KG 265* or *Gruppe König* on **23 June**.[275]

The horse-drawn units of the battlegroup that were in Bretagne did not have long to wait before new trains were available. The operation was called (rather appropriately) *Spargel Neu* (*Asparagus New*) and clearly demonstrated the virtually insurmountable problems caused by unremitting Allied air attacks on the rail network. Simply put, these attacks severely disrupted — and at times paralysed — German rail transportation, seriously delaying the arrival of reinforcements at the front.[276] On the night of **8-9 June**, it was announced that trains would be ready in the morning — two at Quimper and two at Lorient.[277] The trains left on the evening of **9 June**.[278] Specifically, at 20:50, the first train left Quimper with elements of the *III./894* (*Hptm.d.R.* Wild) and the *2./Pi. Btl. 265*. A second train left at 05:25 with elements of the artillery, including the headquarters battery and the 2nd and 3rd Batteries. A third train carried additional elements of the 3rd Battery. This particular train was the last to leave Quimper on the morning of **10 June**. It apparently first made for Lorient to pick up the final elements of the battlegroup. By then, two trains were already en route from Lorient. The first had left at 21:50 with elements of *GR 896*, including the headquarters and the 13th Company, as well as parts of the *9./AR 265*. The second train departed at 05:25, carrying elements of the *II./895* (*Hptm.* Weissenborn). A sixth train had left Rosporden at 02:40; it carried one of the division's transport columns (*3. Kleine Fahrkolonne 265*).[279] By the end of **10 June**, only the train that had moved from Quimper to Lorient had not yet left for the front.[280] The next morning, this train was also on its way.[281]

Aerial attacks on trains posed a serious threat, but they were simple to prevent. During the day, trains generally halted and did not resume movement until after dark. On **10 June**, the lead train reached Questembert. The next day, the trains were forced to take a different route. The first train got as far as Ploërmel and, on **12 June**, all movement stopped due to damaged tracks. On **13 June**, the first train was completely blocked in all directions. Track repairs would take several days, but no manpower was available for this, as all men and equipment were being used to repair the main rail lines. With no other choice, the troops were unloaded and ordered to continue by road. The movement of the other trains was still completely blocked. On **14 June**, these trains were finally able to move again, and their lead train reached Redon. On the **15th**, three trains reached Rennes, where the troops were unloaded and started a road march. The remaining trains reached the area of Rennes on **16 June** and were unloaded. In seven days the trains had covered between 160 and 220 km. Even so, because of the otherwise very limited mobility of these elements of the battlegroup, this was still considered acceptable.[282]

The units of *Kampfgruppe 265* that travelled by road had been split into groups. The bicycle elements and an AT platoon (probably the *14./895*) were the first to leave at 23:30 on **7 June**. Their first destination was Gourin. The other two AT platoons left at 11:10 the next day.[283] Unlike the other companies in its battalion, the *12.(Radf.)/894* moved to the front on its own. Except for the weapons, everything had been packed prior to the invasion, making it possible to move out in just a few hours. The company travelled via Douarnenez to Quimper, arriving in the evening; at noon on **8 June**, it set out for Normandy.[284]

It took some time for sufficient motor transport to arrive for the *III./894(-)*, the headquarters company of *GR 896* and the *13./896*.[285] The first *Kriegsmarine* vehicles only arrived at 06:00 on **8 June** while, at 07:25, some 85 tonnes of lift capacity were still lacking.[286] The last of these elements, the *III./894*, left at 14:10.[287] At 21:40, the division reported that the battlegroup's three artillery batteries had moved out.[288] Although times are less specific, the headquarters battery of the *I./AR 265* and the *2./Pi.Btl. 265* were on their way by evening. The forward elements of *KG 265* had now reached the area of Gouarec.[289] By 23:30, all formations of the battlegroup, except for its horse-drawn units, had left.[290] The last unit to leave was the medical company, which moved out at 23:00.[291]

Thanks to several reports, it is relatively easy to track the battlegroup's progress. On **9 June**, the motorised elements reached a rest area near Tinténiac, then continued to Juvigny-le-Tertre at 00:00. The bicycle units, of course, did not move as rapidly, but they had reached the woods east of Merdrignac; in the evening, they continued to the woods east of Hédé. The battlegroup's headquarters was at Bécherel and relocated to Ste. Hilaire-du-Harcouët during the night.[292]

Up to that point, the battlegroup had not been attacked from the air, but such good fortune could not last.[293] By the morning of **10 June**, the battlegroup had not reached its march objectives for that night, so *Obstlt.* Jäger ordered it to do so even if it meant marching by day — a disastrous decision.[294] The *13./896* had been unable to move during the night, because the available fuel had been used by the *I./AR 265*. The company was forced to wait in an area east of La Baussaine until the fuel lorries arrived between 10:00 and 11:00. As the vehicles were stretched out along the road to refuel, they were strafed. A Russian driver was killed and two men wounded. Two lorries and a bus were destroyed, and another bus lost its transmission. The maintenance section and two fuel lorries from *Kraftfahr-Kompanie XXV* were damaged and no longer roadworthy.[295] After this, horses from the company trains were used to draw the guns.[296]

Further east, the *III./894* and the *I./AR 265* also ran into trouble. This force had been delayed for 30 minutes by an abatis of trees felled by resistance fighters. Around 10:00-11:00, when the force was on the road northeast and southwest of Ste. Hilaire-du-Harcouët, it too came under air attack.[297] A dozen aircraft bombed and strafed the column, inflicting heavy losses.[298] The *I./AR 265* suffered seven killed and six wounded. Two of its buses, seven lorries and five wagons (*Ersatzfeldwagen 40's*) were knocked out. Four lorries incurred mechanical or tyre damage, while two guns were damaged and three limbers destroyed. Casualties in the (reinforced) *III./894* were also significant, with 7 dead and 18 wounded.[299] The battalion headquarters, travelling in one bus, six lorries and two staff cars, lost the bus and two lorries. One man was killed and two were wounded. The 9th Company lost 3 men killed and 12 wounded, as well as all heavy weapons (two mortars and also two light MG's and two heavy MG's) and ammunition. Of the three busses transporting the 10th Company, two were destroyed, while three men were killed and four were wounded. The company also lost heavy weapons and ammunition. The *14./896* suffered three dead and six wounded. In total, 10 men were killed and 25 wounded in the *III./894* (including the *14./894* and the *14./896*). Vehicle losses initially reported were nonetheless lower, amounting to three buses, two lorries, two field kitchens and a mortar cart.[300] The *II./895* was more fortunate, escaping with just one man dead.[301]

It took some time for *KG 265's* exact losses on **10 June** to become clear. They were finally reported as 19 NCO's and men killed and 31 wounded; 32 vehicles and six trailers destroyed; two guns damaged; one AT gun put out of action; and six limbers destroyed. A total of 10 tonnes of artillery ammunition had been lost and several companies had partially lost their basic load of ammunition (*Erstausstatung*).[302] In addition, most of the signals munitions, mines and other unspecified weapons were lost.[303] Much of this was later confirmed by *Obstlt.* Jäger, although he gave slightly different numbers.[304] The 14./896 was in a particularly bad state, having lost all of its vehicles.[305]

The rest area for bicycle units on **10 June** had been the Forêt de Tanouarn, south of Combourg, while the rest-area for **11 June** was Hamelin, some 50 km away. The bulk of the motorised elements were around Juvigny-le-Tertre on **10 June** and would move to the Forêt de St. Sever that night. The battlegroup's headquarters was moved to Le Gast, southwest of the forest. The advance of these elements had been limited to just 30 km, perhaps due to a lack of fuel. This issue was expected to delay the battlegroup's arrival in St. Lô until the night of **11 June**.[306]

The battlegroup had apparently learned from its previous experiences and suffered no losses on **11 June**.[307] That day, it was designated as the corps reserve of the *LXXXIV. A.K.*, while *KG 275* was subordinated to the battered 352. I.D.[308] The corps planned on committing *KG 265* at Pont-l'Abbé to crush the Merderet bridgehead and push the enemy back to the east of the river.[309] However, developments on the front thwarted these plans. On the night of **12-13 June**, the 508th PIR crossed the Douve River and advanced towards Baupte.[310] This created a hole in the German lines that was cause for concern at the *LXXXIV. A.K.* and *AOK 7*. The corps had no reserves to stabilise the situation, and *KG 265* had not yet arrived.[311] The first formation to be moved in was the II./1049 (77. I.D.), which was brought up by motor transport.[312] In the afternoon, *KG 265* was finally located and would be committed that evening. The intention was to hold Baupte and Les Moitiers-en-Bauptois and push the enemy back. Yet it apparently took until **14 June** before the battlegroup was in position, while Baupte fell to the paratroopers the day before.[313] The Baupte bridgehead was a serious setback to the defence of the Cotentin, for it had forced the battlegroup into action. This meant it was immediately committed and could not be used for the planned counterattack north of the Douve or as a relief force.

Shortly after the battlegroup's arrival, *Gen.* Hellmich placed it tactically under *Maj.* Eitner, the former commander of the I./1057 (91. LL.D.). This command change must have taken place sometime between its arrival on **13 June** and **15 June**, when *Maj.* Eitner was in command. The major had already

German footage from the Cotentin peninsula is rare, but a cameraman filmed an infantry unit cycling through Vesly. The shots were included in Wochenschau #723 (released 13 July 1944), but this does not narrow down the period enough to identify the formation these men belonged; bicycles were used by multiple divisions traveling to the front. Based on the location they nonetheless should be members of either KG 265, the 77. or 353. I.D.

been in the sector south of the Douve before the invasion and was thus familiar with the area. Measures taken by *Obstlt.* Jäger were assessed as having been too slow and partly incorrect.[314] Jäger later gave his version of events:[315]

Marcks of course scolded me, since I wasn't there [yet]. I said: "Herr General, we have everything loaded, the heavy weapons on lorries. When they give me fuel, I'll get there!" For three days... I sent them off to Le Mans, to Rennes, to [get] fuel. The lorries didn't come back. It was a disaster.

As they [the troops] arrived, in platoons and companies, that's how they were sent in! I never got my battlegroup together, it was with the 77th Division [...] the devil knows with whom, and with the 91st. That's what happened. Terrible.

Orders from *KG Eitner* for **15 June** have been preserved and reveal the organisation of the battlegroup and its tactical employment. The infantry

Upon arrival, KG 265 was immediately used to seal off the Baupte bridgehead. Most troops were placed under KG Eitner which was further reinforced by II./1049 (77.I.D.). Obstlt. Jäger was later given command of a battlegroup blocking the St.Sauveur-le-Vicomte - La Haye-du-Puits highway. Elements of the 265. I.D, would continue to hold the right wing of the front south of the Douve up to the July offensive by VIII Corps. Suffering heavy casualties, the remnants were then absorbed by other formations.

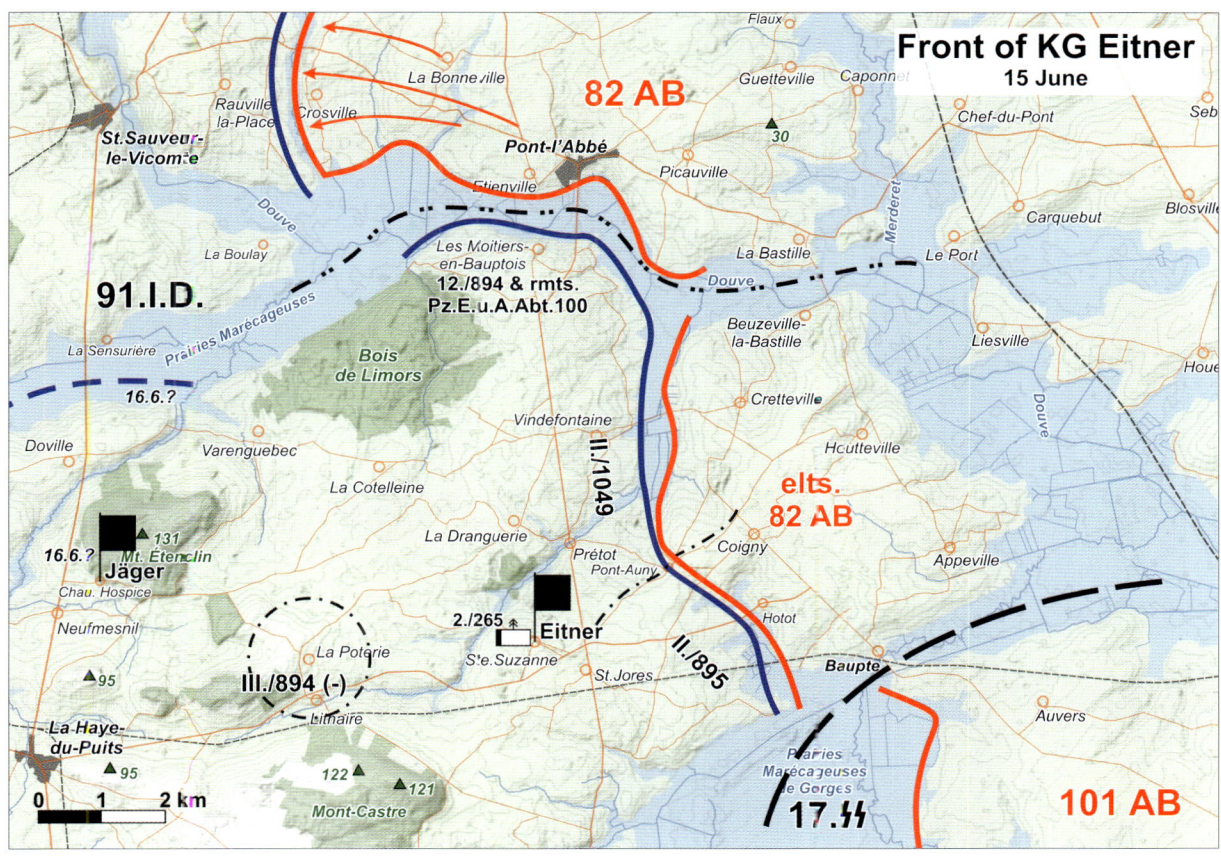

consisted of the *III./894*, the *II./895* and the *II./1049* (*77. I.D.*); smaller units were the *14./895*, the *2./Pi.Btl. 265* and remnants of *Pz.Ers.u.Ausb. Abt. 100*. Artillery support was from the *I./AR 265* and the *II./AR 177* (*77. I.D.*). The battlegroup held an area running east along the Douve, beginning at Longerac, then south along the Senelle River, then across the low ground around Pont-Auny, to the Praires Marécageuses de Gorges. The northern sector, around Le Moitiers-en-Bauptois, faced the Douve and was held by the *12./894* and remnants of the tank-training battalion. In contrast the main front of the battlegroup faced east. The *II./1049* was committed north of the Carrefour-St. Jores - Coigny road (D138) and the *II./895* was to the south. These battalions were supported by artillery from their own division. The bulk of the *III./894* was in reserve around La Poterie and the *2./Pi.Btl. 265* was at St. Suzanne, as was the battlegroup's command post.[316]

There were no real changes along the front over the next few days, although a platoon from the *11./894* was attached to the 12th Company. The two units were to be relieved by the *9./894* on the night of **18-19 June**.[317] It is possible that other elements of the *III./894* were elsewhere on the front by **19 June**. The 82nd AB identified the *II./895* east of Vindefontaine, north of an unspecified road, possibly the D67 to Cretteville. The *II./1049* was in position south of this road.[318] When comparing this to the orders of **15 June**, it means that the *II./895* was brought up from the right (southern) flank of *KG Eitner*. This southern sector may have been taken over by elements of the *III./894*.

265. Infanterie-Division

After the Cotentin had been cut by American forces on **17-18 June**, a new defensive line was established across the base of the peninsula as the new *Nordfront* of the *LXXXIV. A.K.* To defend the new line, a new force was formed: *Gruppe König* (Commander of the *91. LL.Div.*). This included, among other elements, *KG Eitner* (which became *Untergruppe Eitner* under the superior battlegroup). Records of the *91. LL.Div.* (*Gruppe König*) provide additional information on the condition of *KG Eitner*; among them is an organisational document for the situation on **18 June**. It shows that the force was joined by the headquarters company of *GR 896* and the *14./894* which, like the *14./895*, had two AT guns. The third AT platoon, the *14./896*, which had been mauled by Allied air attacks, was in Granville. The fourth heavy weapons company, the *13./896*, had also arrived with five infantry guns. The signals troops were also listed under the battlegroup, while engineers and medical elements were listed alongside similar elements of the *91. LL.D.* The artillery was subordinated to *AR 191*. Each of the batteries still had four guns, while the 3rd and 9th Batteries were both listed with a single 2 cm *Flak*.[319] But this organisation of the battlegroup didn't last for long. At 14:00 on **19 June**, the corps reported the latest organisation of the *Nordfront*. It was divided into three sub-sectors: On the right was *U.Gr. Eitner*, in the centre *U.Gr. Jäger* and, on the left, *U.Gr. Klosterkemper* (*243. I.D.*).[320] To form *U.Gr. Jäger*, troops had again been removed from *KG Eitner*. To the rear of *Gruppe König* a new defensive line (the *Mahlmann-Linie*) was being established and would be held by the *77.* and *353. I.D.*[321]

Although *U.Gr. Jäger*'s front was relatively quiet until early **July**, this was not the case for *U.Gr. Eitner*. On the night of **18-19 June**, the 325th GIR (82nd AB) crossed the Douve River south of Pont-l'Abbé and established a bridgehead at Les Moitiers-en-Bauptois. The area was defended by the reinforced *12./894* and *Pz.Ers.u.Ausb.Abt. 100*, which lost several tanks in the fighting. The bridge across the river was quickly repaired, allowing American reinforcements to be brought up. From the Baupte bridgehead (to the east), the 1/507th PIR (82nd AB) attacked westwards to Vindefontaine and the two bridgeheads were united.[322] On **20 June**, the Americans continued their advance. The 3/508th PIR (82nd AB) captured Prétot and came under heavy German fire from the high ground south and east of the town. It was here that *Pz.Jg.Abt. 353* had its baptism of fire and deployed its assault guns. Having suffered heavy losses, the paratroopers withdrew from the town. To the northwest, the 3/505th PIR had better luck in occupying the Bois de Limors.[323] On **19** and **20 June**, the 82nd AB had made considerable advances and captured men from *KG 265*, among them 52 from the *III./894*, 13 from the *II./895* and one from the *II./894*.[324] On **21 June**, having been pushed back to the southern edge of the Bois de Limors, *Gruppe König* withdrew to a line 200 metres southwest of the forest to establish better fields of fire.[325]

The Americans paused their operations south of the Douve as they now focused on the capture of Cherbourg. As a result, the frontline established by *U.Gr. Eitner* and *U.Gr. Jäger* would change little until the VIII Corps offensive in **July**. A portion of the front was now taken over by *U.Gr. Lewandowski*, which was inserted between the other two *Untergruppen*. *Gruppe König* continued to evolve during this period of relative calm. New developments included the arrival of additional elements and forces assigned to different commands. These events were not all correctly reported and, as a result, some of the information for this period conflicts and some dates are unclear. There is no doubt, however, that most of the forces of *KG 265* remained under *U.Gr. Eitner*.[326]

It is noteworthy that the organisational document for the reinforced *91. LL.D.* on **20 June** (primarily showing formations and no weapons) included *KG 265* as, for all practical purposes, organic to the division. This suggests that the division considered it more than a temporary reinforcement. Considering the absence of the *265. I.D.* as a whole, such a view would be understandable. On this document, the infantry elements and parts of *Nachr. Abt. 265* were listed together under the headquarters of *GR 896*. Oddly, the three infantry battalions under this headquarters also included the *II./894*. This may indicate an intention to move the battalion from Bretagne. Most of the rest of *KG 265* was listed. The artillery battalion was under *AR 191* and had two 2 cm *Flak*, while its three batteries still had four guns each. The *2./Pi. Btl. 265* was listed next to *Pi.Btl. 191* and, in similar fashion, the medical personnel were listed next to that of the *91. LL.D.*[327]

Although the *II./894* (*Major* Mecklenburg) was still in Bretagne, the *7. Armee* ordered the *XXV. A.K.* to put the battalion on the road to join the battlegroup in Normandy on **21 June**.[328] The battalion moved out at 22:30 on **22 June**.[329] On the first night, it would travel through Le Faouët, Guémené-sur-Scorff and Cléguérec to Mûr-de-Bretagne; on the second night it was to move through Uzel, Plouguenast and Lanrelas to Caulnes; and, on the third night, the battalion would advance to Antrain via Bécherel, Tinténiac and Dingé. The rest of the route would be decided by the *LXXXIV. A.K.*[330] The battalion arrived at *Gruppe König* on **28-29 June** and joined *U.Gr. Eitner*.³³¹ On **29 June**, the *LXXXIV. A.K.* issued orders for the battalion to relieve the *II./1049*.³³²

On the *AOK 7* order of battle for **23 June**, *U.Gr. Eitner* was listed with the *III./894* (minus its 11th and 12th Companies and plus the *5./895*), the *II./1049*, the *II./895* (minus the 5th Company) and the *12./894*. Support was from *Stu.Gesch.Brig. 902*, alongside remnants of the *91. LL.D.* This list may appear erratic, but it does show the organisation and order of the different areas, with the *III./894* on the right and the *12./894* on the left flank. It should also be noted that *Pz.Ers.u.Ausb.Abt. 100* was not listed.³³³ This organisation was still reported on **29 June**, but its accuracy is uncertain given that the left flank had been taken over by *U.Gr. Lewandowski*; moreover, the *II./1049* appears to have returned to its division towards the end of **June** and the *III./894* may have already arrived.³³⁴ In fact, many of these changes are covered by the organisational document for *Gruppe König* on **28 June**. Here, *U.Gr. Eitner* was listed with signals units (from *KG 265*), the *II.* and the *III./894* and the AT platoons of *GR 894, 895* and *896*. The latter were equipped with one, three and three AT guns, respectively.³³⁵

U.Gr. Lewandowski was first included in the *AOK 7* order of battle for **29 June**, but without subordinated forces.³³⁶ On the *AOK 7* situation maps, it had been in the line since **22 June**.³³⁷ The battlegroup had been built around *GR 1058* (*91. LL.D.*) and taken over by *Maj. Lewandowksi*. The organisational document for *Gruppe König* around **28 June** shows that the *II./895* was also attached. Other elements in the *Untergruppe* were the *II./1057* and the *III./1058*, with support from the *14./1057*, the *14./1058* and a number of infantry guns, most likely from the *13./1057* and the *13./1058*.

Obstlt. Jäger had a much smaller force — *U.Gr. Jäger*, which blocked the highway from St. Sauveur-le-Vicomte to La Haye-du-Puits. Its front ran along the southern edge of the wetlands south of St. Sauveur-le-Vicomte and across the Prairies Marécageuses; its headquarters was at Château Hospice, 2 km south of Doville.³³⁸ The same order of battle for **23 June** also included *U.Gr. Jäger*, which comprised the *11./894* (minus one platoon), the engineer platoon of *GR 896* and *SS-Pz.Aufkl.Abt. 17* (minus its 2nd Company).³³⁹ It is also likely that the *13./896* provided support. The AT platoons of the *14./894* and *14./896* have also been linked to *U.Gr. Jäger*, although it seems more likely they were with *U.Gr. Eitner*.³⁴⁰ On the evening of **16 June**, *SS-Pz.Aufkl.Abt. 17* was reported to be on its way to the high ground on either side of the highway — Hills 121 and 131.³⁴¹ This battalion apparently remained with the *Untergruppe* until relieved by *Ost-Btl. Huber* around **28 June**. On that date, *U.Gr. Jäger* was listed on the organisational document for *Gruppe König* with the headquarters company of *GR 896*, *Ost-Btl. Huber* and the *13./896* with

After the 91.LL.D.'s losses in the first week of the invasion, KG 265 provided a significant part of the division's combat power.

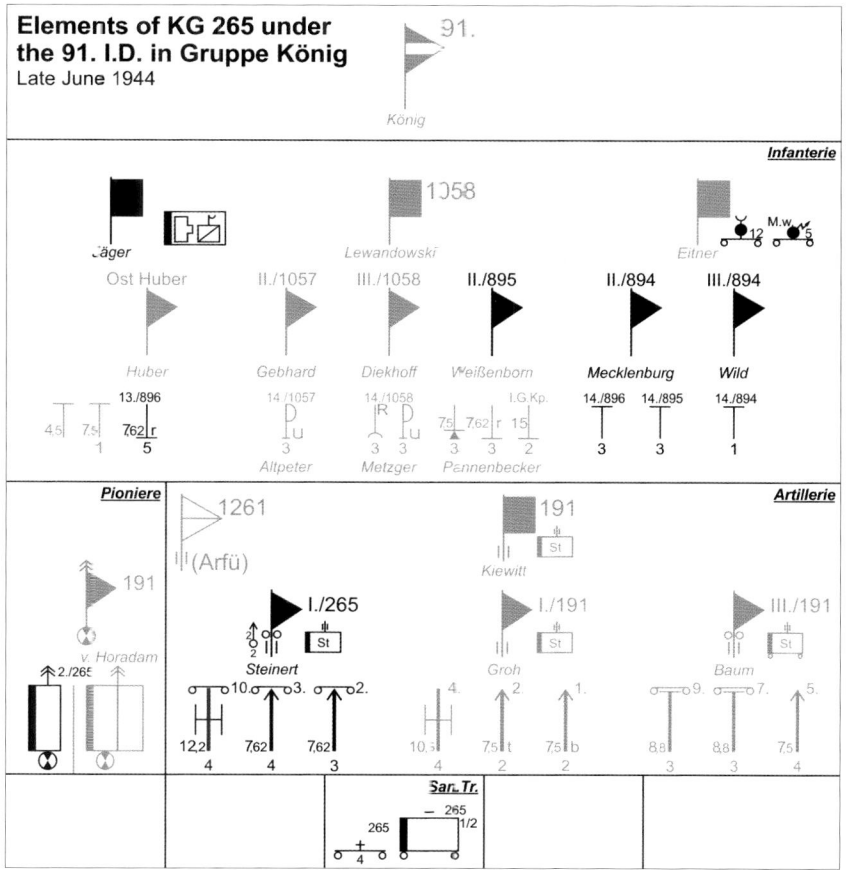

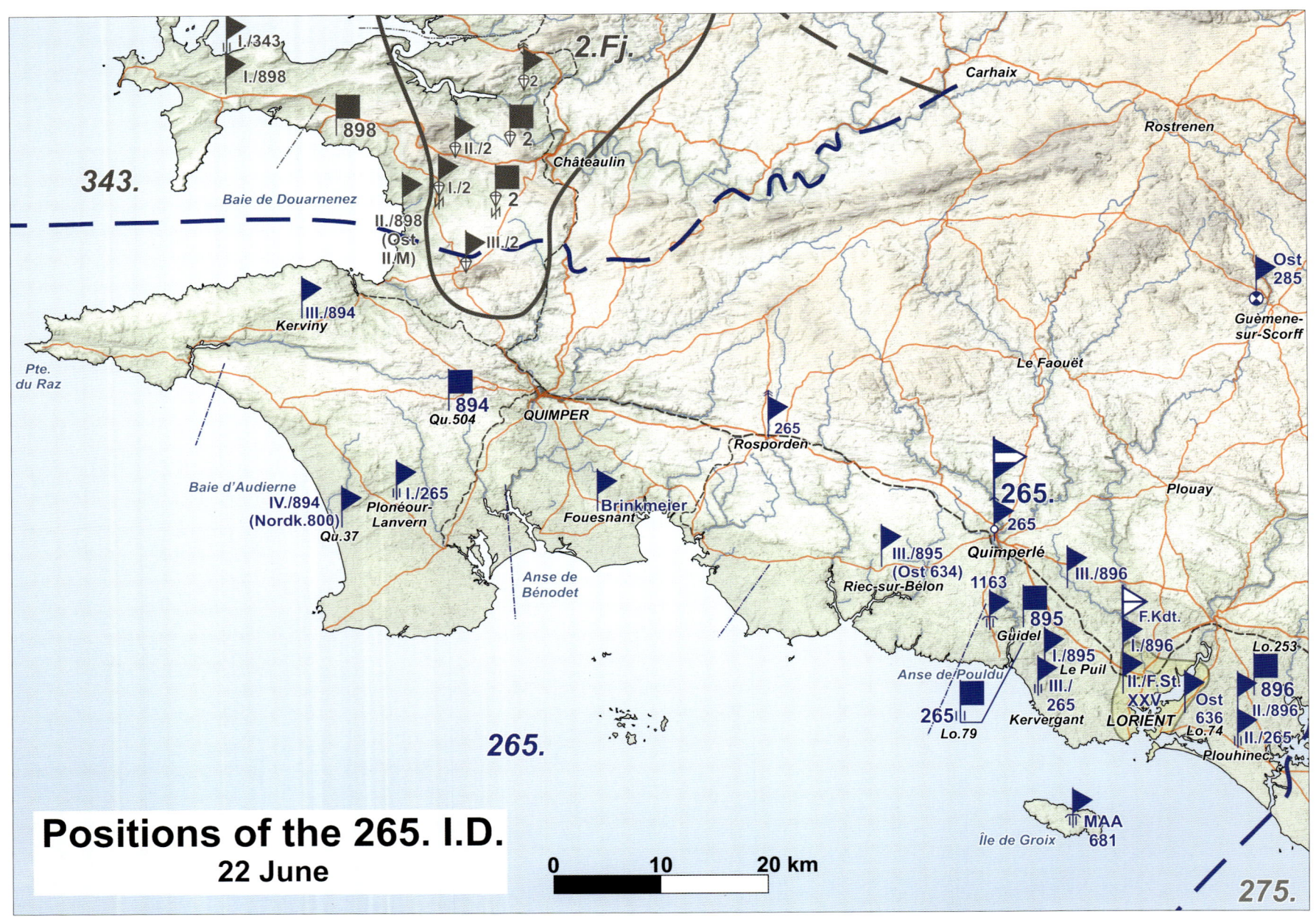

After the departure of KG 265, the division's sector was reorganised. The 343.I.D. was still the right neighbour, but the 2.Fj.D. moved into areas previously held by the 3.Fj.D. and 353.I.D.

five 7.62 cm Russian infantry guns. The *Untergruppe* also had one 7.5 cm AT gun and an unidentified number of 4.5 cm AT guns, probably from the eastern battalion.[342] The order of battle for *AOK 7* still shows the *SS* battalion with *U.Gr. Jäger* on the **29th**, but this appears to be outdated information.[343]

The final elements of *KG 265* were also listed on the **28 June** organisational document. The artillery battalion of *KG 265* was under *AR 191*. The 2nd Battery was down to three pieces, but the 3rd and 9th Batteries still had four guns each, and there were still two *Flak*. The *2./Pi.Btl. 265* was apparently linked to *Pi.Btl. 191*, but it was not necessarily subordinated to it.[344]

The locations of elements of *265. I.D.* with *Gruppe König* are not clear after **19 June**, but they can be partially reconstructed using Allied records. The 82nd AB, which fought the *Untergruppe* during this period, identified its areas of operation on **20 June**. The right (south) flank of *U.Gr. Eitner* (*III./894*) was thought to run from the Praires Marécageuses-de-Gorges to Pont-Auny. The next sector (*II./1049*) ran northwest from Pont-Auny to north of Prétot. The third sector (*II./895*) continued to west of Les Margueries. The fourth, a line towards the Douve that was held by the reinforced *12./894*, stretched to north of Le Bequeret, and thus partially through the Bois de Limors.[345] These locations appear credible. Situation maps from late **June** put the *III./894* on the far right, making contact with the Praires de Marécageuses de Gorges.[346] If the American observations were accurate, they also point to a number of changes made to *U.Gr. Eitner* and its orders from **15 June**. The main difference was the shift of the *II./895* and the *II./1049* to the northwest, making room for the *III./894*. As the American advance had lengthened the front, the insertion of another battalion was necessary.

The two northernmost sectors, around the Bois de Limors, were soon taken from *U.Gr. Eitner*. The area south of the forest came under the command of *U.Gr. Lewandowski*. It seems this battlegroup had been inserted to fill the lines that had been lengthened by the 82nd AB's advance into the forest.[347] As noted, the *II./895* was subordinated to Lewandowski, probably when its sector was taken over by the new *Untergruppe*. The extreme left wing of *U.Gr. Eitner* appears to have been taken over by *U.Gr. Jäger*, specifically by elements of *Ost-Btl. Huber*.[348]

The order of the formations was confirmed in late **June** and early **July**. On **29 June**, the 90th ID captured a member of the *9./894*, who stated that his battalion was in position north of the Baupte marshland (Les Sablons area).[349]

Another prisoner, taken by the 82nd AB on **2 July**, stated that his battalion (*II./894*) was west of Prétot, with the *II./895* on its left.[350] Further west, south of the Bois de Limors, the two *91. LL.D.* battalions under *U.Gr. Lewandowski* were identified on **4 July**. This lends credence to the *II./895* being in the area around Les Margueries.[351]

In late **June** and early **July**, there were also a number of command initiatives affecting the centre and right flank of the *Nordfront*. One was the arrival

The so-called Essenbehalter was used to carry hot meals forward. Its carrier and the man to his left have camouflaged their helmets with pieces of cloth cut from American parachutes. (Collectie CegeSoma – Rijksarchief (OD4))

of *U.Gr. Lewandowski*, but others should be addressed as well. On **28 June**, following the arrival of the *II./894*, the *LXXXIV. A.K.* urged the *7. Armee* to send the regimental headquarters of *GR 894* to the corps.[352] Apparently, the corps saw an opportunity to rebuild the regiment and put its elements back under their original commander. Pulling the headquarters from Bretagne, however, was easier said than done, as it still had responsibilities there. As a result, *AOK 7* ordered the *XXV. A.K.* to form a small staff from the regiment, which would include the regimental adjutant and a signals officer. The corps, however, soon informed the *7. Armee* that this order could not be carried out either. Instead, personnel had to be gleaned from the headquarters of other regiments.[353] The newly formed headquarters included men, equipment and vehicles from the *265.*, the *275.*, and the *343. I.D.* along with corps troops. Transport was provided by one German lorry, a staff car and two bicycles. The headquarters consisted of the adjutant, 2 other officers and 10 enlisted personnel.[354] This ad hoc headquarters finally left for Normandy at 19:00 on **29 June**.[355]

The same day, the *II./894* was ordered to relieve the *II./1049*, which was to return to its division. The decision was also made to disband *Gruppe König* as of **1 July** and divide the *Nordfront* between the *243. I.D.* (left) and the *91. LL.D.* Most of *KG 265* would remain with the *91. LL.D.* For a brief period *U.Gr. Jäger* would be under the command of the *243. I.D.*, but its sector would soon be taken over by *Ost-Regiments-Gruppe Bunjatschenko*, which formed an ad hoc regiment out of available *Ostsoldaten*. *U.Gr. Jäger*'s headquarters would then return to the *91. LL.D.*[356]

The future of *Obstlt.* Jäger became increasingly uncertain as criticism of his performance at the front continued. On **30 June**, the adjutant of the *Untergruppe* informed the *91. LL.D.* that the tactical leadership of *Obstlt.* Jäger, even of the meagre forces at his disposal, was questionable. After this complaint was investigated and confirmed by the divisional commander, *Obstlt.* Jäger — now labelled as *"unfit to lead troops in a major operation"* — was transferred to the *LXXXIV. A.K.* officer manpower reserve (*Führer-Reserve*).[357]

On **1 July**, the sector held by *U.Gr. Jäger* was taken over by *Ost-Regiments-Gruppe Bunjatschenko*. This formation took command of *Ost-Btl. Huber* and elements of the headquarters company of *GR 896*. Further east, *Maj.* Eitner was relieved by *Maj.* Mecklenburg, most likely upon arrival of the ad hoc regimental headquarters.[358] This put the infantry of *GR 894* back under their own officers. It does not appear that the *II./895* joined *U.Gr. Mecklenburg*.[359]

As always, the losses sustained by elements of the *265. I.D.* are difficult to determine with any precision without official reports. An indication of those losses can be constructed by looking at the number of prisoners. By the evening of **5 July**, just 77 soldiers of the division had been counted in the POW cages in the UK. Of these, 56 were from *GR 894*, 17 from *GR 895* and 4 from *GR 896*.[360] Based on the numbers, most of them had already been captured by the 82nd AB on 19-20 June.

The US VIII Corps launched its offensive against the *Nordfront* on **3 July**. The initial objective of the offensive was to capture the line Lessay - Gorges, before pushing on to the final objective: The high ground at Coutances. Generally speaking, the sector held by *KG 265* (under the *91. LL.D.*) came under attack by the 90th ID from the east (*GR 894*) and the 82nd AB from the northeast (the *II./895* and elements of the *II./894*).[361] Having relieved the *II./1049*, the fresh *II./894* occupied most of the forward line of *KG Mecklenburg*, while the *III./894* defended the eastern portion of the *Mahlmann-Linie*, which itself appears to have been partially on the frontline.[362] The *II./895*, which held the line northwest of Prétot, faced the full weight of the American attack; it was cut off and virtually annihilated, with only 40 men making it back to German lines.[363] These stragglers likely joined the forces under *Maj.* Mecklenburg. Another unit sent into action that day was the *2./Pi.Btl. 265*; it was reportedly employed as an infantry escort for four assault guns, suffering heavy casualties.[364]

On **4 July**, the forward lines were withdrawn to the *Mahlmann-Linie*. *KG Mecklenburg* thus joined the sector of the *77. I.D.* and came under its command. The *91. LL.Div.* was no longer operational.[365] On **5 July**, the *Kampfgruppe's* headquarters was in Pierrepont and from **7 July** in La Moulinerie. By early **July**, mounting losses had reduced *KG 265* to 200 men (presumably its infantry strength). Because such a small force no longer required much of a headquarters, what remained of the battlegroup was taken over by *Hauptmann* Wild (*III./894*). After he was wounded, command passed to *Oberleutnant* Risch (*11./894*).[366] The exact operations of the badly attenuated *Kampfgruppe* under the *77. I.D.* are not known. Along with the rest of the *Nordfront*, the troops were ultimately pulled back to the *Wasserlinie* on the night of **13 July**.[367]

While *KG 265* losses against the VIII Corps offensive had been enormous, German sources do not offer precise figures. POW's, however, do provide some information. Most of these men were captured early in the offensive, when *KG 265* had been holding much of the frontline. American forces in the field on **3 July** — mainly the 82nd AB and the 90th ID — had captured 60 men;[368] another 38 were recorded by the 82nd AB the next day.[369] On the **5th**, new prisoners taken by the 82nd AB amounted to just 12.[370] By this time, the remnants of *KG 265* had joined the *77. I.D.*, which was facing the American 90th ID. For the period of **4-5 July**, the 90th ID accounted for 55 men from *GR 894* and 110 from *GR 895*.[371] Combined, they total 275 prisoners, but for the period of **3-6 July** the numbers for VIII Corps as a whole were even higher at 416. Most of the POW's came from the *II./895* (160), the *II./894* (159) and the *III./894* (78). The headquarters company of *GR 896*, *Nachr.Abt 265* and *Pi.Btl. 265* had eight, six and five men captured, respectively.[372]

No new POW numbers were reported for the next period, but another 18 men from *GR 894* were captured on **13 July**.[373] By the evening of **14 July**, the POW cages in the UK held 371 men of the division. Of these, 254 (+198) belonged to *GR 894*, 99 (+82) to *GR 895* and 9 (+5) to *GR 896*. The others were: From *AR 265* one (+1); *Pi.Btl. 265* seven (+7) and the support troops one (+1).[374] These figures illustrate that a large number of prisoners from the **July** offensive had been transported to the UK; on **5 July** there had been just 77 prisoners of the division there.

By **17 July**, little remained of *Kampfgruppe 265*. The remnants of the two battalions of *GR 894* were merged into a single company, although the heavy weapons companies of *GR 896* still existed. All these elements were placed under the headquarters of *GR 1050* (*77. I.D.*). There were also two battalions of *GR 1049*, making seven companies in total; one of these was what remained of the *II./1049*. The two heavy companies from *GR 1050* and the infantry gun company of *GR 1049* were also part of this force.[375] On **17 July**, the *77. I.D.*'s combat troops, including *GR 1050*, were taken over by the *91. LL.D.* In summary: *Kampfgruppe 265*'s infantry had been reduced to about a company and attached to a battalion of *GR 1049* (*77. I.D.*), which was under the command of *GR 1050* (*77. I.D.*), which was subordinated to the *91. LL.Div.*[376] So much for keeping things simple! The *2./Pi.Btl. 265* was still attached to *Pi.Btl. 191*, where it essentially operated as its 3rd Company The artillery battalion was now subordinated to *AR 177*. It still had three batteries, although their strength is unknown. The elements of *Nachr.Abt. 265* and the signals platoon of *GR 896* joined *Nachr.Abt. 191*.[377] Since *KG 265* effectively no longer existed, the staff of *Maj.* Mecklenburg was available for other assignments. It was put in charge of the combined trains of the *91. LL.D.* and *KG 265*, which were assembled around Grimesnil, on either side of the highway to Coutances (D7).[378]

On **19 July** the (infantry) remnants of the *Kampfgruppe* were in reserve under *GR 1050*. They had a combat strength of 77 all ranks.[379] Compared to **17 July**, the composition of elements under the *91. LL.D.* had changed again by **20 July**. *GR 1049* had been reassembled, leaving the combined remnants of *GR 894* (a company in strength) under the headquarters of *GR 1050*. In addition to this company, the "regiment" consisted of just two infantry companies (*II./1049* and *I./1050*) plus two heavy weapons companies. An AT company from *FJR 15* was present and the *14./895* had reappeared. The remaining two AT platoons were assigned to *GR 1049*. Finally, the *13./896* supported the *I./AR 265*. The situation of the engineer company was unchanged.[380] A report from the *LXXXIV. A.K.* (**23 July**) provides numbers and details about *KG 265*. The infantry was down to one worn-out battalion (*abgekämpft*). This was the aforementioned company formed by the remnants of *GR 894*. There were five heavy AT guns and the artillery still consisted of three batteries.[381] Three days later, the infantry company had moved again, to *GR 1049*. The heavy weapons companies were no longer listed, except the *13./896*, which was still supporting the artillery. The *2./Pi.Btl. 265* remained attached to *Pi.Btl. 191*.[382]

In the chaos following *Operation Cobra*, what little remained of the *265. I.D.* suffered further losses, the extent of which has been impossible to ascertain. On **30 July**, *Major* Eitner was able to assemble a force from troops escaping to the south, including survivors from *KG 265*. Instead of heading to Avranches, this force moved southeast and reached Reffuveille (10 km east of Avranches); it was then redirected to Le Mans where the *91. LL.D.* was assembling.[383] Acutely aware of the threat posed by *Operation Cobra*, the *91. LL.D.* had already sent its trains to the south. Around Gavray, large numbers of vehicles were lost in traffic jams and to air attacks on **27-28 July**. What remained of the trains assembled in the area of Le Luot - Chavoy (northeast of Avranches) on **28-29 July** and moved to the Ducey area over the next two days. When American armoured units broke out of Normandy, they scattered the trains of the *91. LL.D.* and *KG 265*. The majority of the vehicles and horses were lost to enemy armour and aircraft, while the troops suffered heavy casualties. On **1 August**, efforts to assemble the trains in the area of Fougères - Mayenne - Laval failed, as US armour advanced on Rennes.[384] The remnants of *KG 265* were to return to their division, but the American advance into Bretagne thwarted

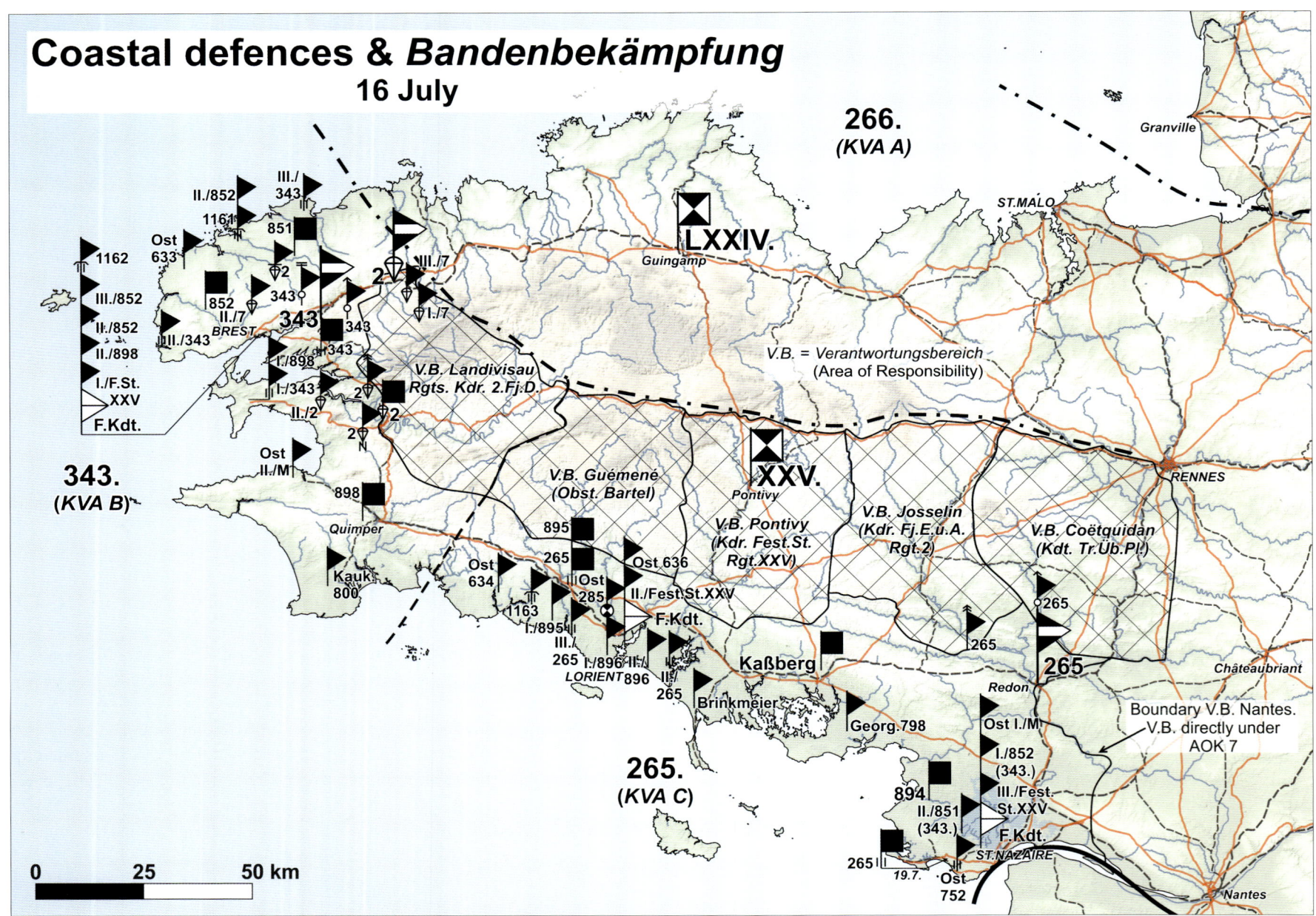

In Bretagne XXV. A.K. faced growing difficulties in defending the coast with decreasing numbers of troops, and an increase in resistance activity inland. On 22 June, as part of its Bandenbekämpfung (anti-partisan operations), the corps' rear area was divided into "areas of responsibility" and assigned to a variety of formations and commands to secure. On 15 July an additional area was added, stretching all the way to Rennes. In the meantime, the 265.I.D. had already taken over the 275.I.D.'s sector around St.Nazaire.

this intent.[385] The majority of the trains of *AOK 7* were assembled at Le Mans by Collection Staff Mecklenburg (*Auffangsstab Mecklenburg*). From there, they withdrew, ultimately reaching Aachen. **On 21 August**, the men who arrived in Germany (including elements of the *265. I.D.*) were assigned to the *18. Luftwaffen-Feld-Division* along with their vehicles.[386]

Bretagne: Facing the Résistance and the Allied Breakout

Despite the battlegroup's transfer to Normandy, the main body of the *265. I.D.* remained in Bretagne throughout **June** and **July**. Although most of the forces were stationed on the coast, some were inland. With the start of the invasion, the resistance in Bretagne became much more active, prompting a robust German response.[387] Before the invasion, the *Résistance* had primarily targeted messengers and sentries, but now large numbers of Free French paratroopers (along with weapons and supplies) were dropped to organise resistance fighters. The daily logs of the *XXV. A.K.* recorded:[388]

In recent days there have again been parachute landings by Frenchmen, dressed in English uniforms. Simultaneously, it has been determined that there has been a general increase in terrorist activity in certain areas, as well as the formation of larger resistance groups, to a level that has not been experienced before.

It is therefore expected that the enemy, in addition to a general increase in subversive activities, will provide certain groups with military-trained leaders and equipment. This will allow them to fight against us in the rear areas with forces that are both organised and led militarily. This must be prevented by all possible means.

The transfer of forces to Normandy — the *II. Fs.K.*, the *77. I.D.*, the *353. I.D.*, the *3. Fj.D.*, as well as *KG 265, 266, 275* and *343* — had seriously weakened the German presence in Bretagne. On **12 June**, the *XXV. A.K.* conceded that the forces on the coast were only sufficient to guard it, not defend it; moreover, the mobile reserves were insufficient for any kind of defensive operation, although they might be effective against resistance fighters. It was thus decided that all remaining mobile units should be assembled — without weakening the fortresses — into reinforced battalions.[389]

The *265. I.D.* was ordered to provide two bicycle companies and, for fire support, the *6./AR 265*. The infantry would be sent to the Pont-Scorff area and combined into an ad hoc battalion that included a company from the *275. I.D.*

If possible, both divisions would make additional units available for operations against the *Résistance*.[390] The divisions promptly reported those units that were available. The *265. I D.* could provide the headquarters of the *I./895* and two bicycle companies (*3./895* and *5./896*), as well as the *5./AR 265*. The battalion commander, *Major* Brinkmeier, was put in command, thus the force was called *Bataillon Brinkmeier*.[391] The *275. I.D.* would send the *3./985* to the *265. ID* to join the battalion.[392] The additional (local) reserves of the *265. ID* consisted of the *5.* and the *7./894*, the *7./896*, the *4./Nordkauk.Inf.Btl. 800* and the *1./Ost-Btl. 634*. Of these, only the *7./895* had bicycles.[393] For now, these particular units remained in reserve. On **14 June**, *Btl. Brinkmeier* assembled around Pont-Scorff - Gestel, with its headquarters in Gestel. Further west, the *5./894* was temporarily moved to St. Yvi to combat the *Résistance* in the area.[394]

The corps orders for **12 June** included instructions to mobilise the elements intended for redeployment, as far as vehicles and bicycles could be obtained from the sector held by the divisions. As the corps itself could not provide more transport, this task largely fell to Field Administrative Command 752 (*Feldkommandantur 752*) (Quimper).[395] On **15 June**, it informed the corps that it would cover the shortages of the *265. I.D.*[396] In fact, that day it issued 1,000 confiscated bicycles and a large number of vehicles to the division.[397] As noted, the bicycles were used to turn the *II./894* into a bicycle-mobile battalion. The corps informed *AOK 7* on **18 June** that the mobile role of *Btl. Brinkmeier* had been assumed by this battalion. The majority of the trains were horse-drawn, with only a fraction motorised.[398]

On **19 June**, the headquarters of *Btl. Brinkmeier* moved to Fouesnant and took over *KVU Fouesnant* with the *3./895* and the *5./896*.[399] In turn, the *II./894* and the *3./985* assembled around Scaër.[400] On **20 June**, this battalion and company were taken over by *Obst.* Hett (commander of *AR 265*) and became known as *Kampfgruppe Hett*. Command of *AR 265* was assumed by *Major* Offergold, most likely one of its battalion commanders.[401] The headquarters of *Kampfgruppe Hett* was located at Le Faouët and that of the *II./894* at Scaër. Its four companies were at Lanvénégen, Penquer-Coadigou (today Coadigou), Meslan and Kerandreau (today Kerandréo), respectively. The *3./985* was in Berné and the *4./Ost-Radfahr-Abteilung 285* in Pont-Croix, although only its 2nd Platoon was deployed. The 1st and 3rd Platoons were in reserve in *KVU Douarnenez*.[402] The following day, *AOK 7* ordered the *II./894* to Normandy, the battalion departing on the evening of the **22nd**.[403]

265. Infanterie-Division

On **22 June**, the *XXV. A.K.* reorganised its anti-resistance operations. Due to the stepped-up activity of the *Résistance*, the Administrative Commander in Southwest France (*Befehlshaber Südwestfrankreich*) (Angers) furnished extra forces to support the corps and to help coordinate operations. The rear area was divided into five so-called areas of responsibility. The coastal divisions were still responsible for anti-resistance operations near the coast, but rear areas were assigned to other forces. *Obst.* Borst, an officer from the over-all command responsible for the administration of (most of) occupied France (*Militärbefehlshaber Frankreich*), who was responsible for combatting the *Résistance*, was put in charge of the entire rear area. The boundary between the front and rear was the line Landivisiau - Châteaulin - Briec - Scaër - Plouay - St. Jean-Brévelay - Malestroit - La Gacilly. Individual sectors were under command of a regimental commander from the *2. Fj.Div.* and the commanders of *Sich.Rgt.* 195 (*Obstlt.* Bartel), *Fest.Stamm-Rgt. XXV* (*Obst.* Witt), *Fj. Ers.u.Ausb.Rgt. 2* (*Obst.* Deffner) and *Hptm.* Brüggemann (*275. I.D.*) These officers were generally in charge of their own formations.[404]

The unrest in Bretagne intensified and, on **26 June**, *AOK 7* asked *Heeresgruppe B* to designate everything west of the line Nantes - Rennes – Avranches (essentially the entire Brittany peninsula) as a combat zone (*Kampfzone*).[405] This was approved by *Ob.West* the next day.[406] Up to then, the combat zone had been restricted to the invasion area up to the Seine.[407]

On **1 July**, *KG Hett* took over Guémené sector. This force consisted of the *1./896*, *1./Ost-Btl. 634* and the 2nd and 3rd Companies of *Ost-Radf.Abt. 285*.[408] Most of these companies had arrived on **23 June**, when they relieved the *II./894*.[409] The *4./Ost-Radf.Abt. 285* joined *KG Hett* on **5 July**.[410] The anti-resistance sectors were altered again on **15 July**; one sector was dissolved and two new ones established. *KG Hett* was relieved and put at the disposal of the *265. I.D.*[411]

Early **July** marked the beginning of an important change in Bretagne. Up to that point, the *265.* and *275. I.D.* had each dispatched a *Kampfgruppe* to Normandy but were still in control of their coastal sectors in Bretagne. On **3 July**, *Heeresgruppe B* decided it was time to send the rest of the *275. I.D.* to Normandy.[412] The relief of the division was to begin on **6 July**.[413] This meant that its coastal sector, *KVA "C2"*, would have to be defended by other elements.

The *XXV. A.K.* already had insufficient forces to defend the coast, and the problem was now worsened. The corps had to limit itself to defending the fortresses and guarding only the coast in between. It was also to continue operations against resistance fighters and secure the supply lines to the fortresses.[414] It was decided that the *265. I.D.* would take over *KVA "C2"* from the *275. I.D.*, making the former division responsible for the entire *KVA "C"*.[415] To ease the strain on the division, the right flank of *"C1"* was reassigned to *KVA "B"*, with the new boundary formed by the bay northwest of Concarneau and continuing via Rosporden to Coray. On **6 July**, elements of the *343. I.D.* took over *KVG Quimper*.[416] *Btl. Brinkmeier* and the *3./895* were relieved by the *4./Kauk.Inf. Btl. 800*, and the *5./896* by the *1./Ost-Btl. 634* (the day before).[417] The *343. I.D.* was not restricted to its own sector. Some of its men were transferred to serve in *KVA "C"* under the *265. I.D.* These included the *I./852*, which would take over *KVG Guérande*, northwest of St. Nazaire, and the *II./851*, which was deployed in *Festung St. Nazaire*.[418] In practice, the two battalions essentially swapped missions.[419] St. Nazaire was further reinforced by the *1./AR 265*, which would be brought up from Pont-l'Abbé. The relief plans called for *GR 894* to take over part of the *275. I.D's* sector, and the regiment was given command of *Btl. Brinkmeier*, which was still with the *3./895* and the *5./896* in the Plouharnel area. The *2./Ost-Btl. 636* was subordinated to *Btl. Brinkmeier*, and it was expected to arrive early on **7 July**. *Georg.Inf.Btl. 798* was also put under the regiment, as was the *5./AR 265*.[420]

On **7 July**, responsibility for *KVG Michel* (the area of *KVA "C2"* south of the Loire) was taken over by *Festung St. Nazaire*. Further north, the commander of *GR 894* took charge of *KVG Vannes*.[421] The sector's new right boundary was the line Auray – Plouharnel. On **9 July** (18:00), the *265. I.D.* finally took command of *KVA "C2"*.[422] The next day, the commander of the *15./894* took over *KVU Plouharnel*. As planned, the *1./AR 265* arrived in St. Nazaire.[423] More changes took place and, on **13 July**, *Obst.* Schlee (commander of *GR 985*) took over *KVG Michel*.[424] The headquarters of the *265. I.D.* moved to Redon on **14 July**, joined by *Nachr.Abt. 265* the next day; *Pi.Btl. 265* (-1st Company) moved to St. Gavré, also on **15 July**.[425]

On **15 July**, the *XXV. A.K.* issued orders regarding the reinforcement of *Festung Lorient* and *St. Nazaire*. One company from the *II./896* would remain in *KVG Plouhinec*, while the battalion itself and two of its companies would move to *Festung Lorient*, where the battalion would be subordinated to the *Festungs-Kommandant*. The *II./851* would be deployed in *Festung St.*

Nazaire in its entirety, while *KVG Guérande* would be taken over by *GR 894* with its 13th and 15th Companies and parts of 14th Company. *Stab Käßberg* (commander of *GR 983, 275. I.D.*) would take over *KVG Vannes*. *Stab Esser* (*15./894*) would remain in command of *KVU Plouharnel* with the *2./Ost-Btl. 636* and a company from *Georg.Inf.Btl. 798*; these two companies would be extracted from *KVU Sarzeau*. Two other companies from *Georg.Inf.Btl. 798* would remain in that sector. The artillery in the fortresses was also reorganised, with the headquarters of the *III./AR 265* and the 8th Battery moving to Lorient and the *II./AR 265* with two batteries to St. Nazaire.[426]

Much of this plan was carried out over the next few days. At 12:00 on **16 July**, *Stab Käßberg* took over *KVG Vannes*. The same day, *GR 895* established its headquarters at Quimperlé and *Pi.Btl. 265* at La Touch.[427] The next day, *GR 894* assumed command of *KVG Guérande*. That evening, the left flank of *KVG Plouhinec* (up to the Étel) was taken over by *KVU Plouharnel* (*4./Georg. Inf.Btl. 798*).[428] On **19 July**, the headquarters of *AR 265* was relocated to La Baule, west of St. Nazaire.[429]

On **20 July**, the inland sector around Guémené was assumed by the commander of *Sicherungs-Bataillon 1221 (O)*, a battalion with many suffering from hearing loss or ear ailments. (*O = Ohrenkranken*). *Ost-Radf.Abt. 285* moved to Lorient with two troops. In the fortress, the eastern portion was taken over by the *II./896* (-5th Company), assisted by the *4./Ost-Btl. 636*. To the southeast, the *16./Fest.Stamm-Rgt. XXV* took command of *KVG Plouhinec*, which was tactically subordinated to the fortress. The same day, the *II./AR 265* (-6th Battery) arrived in *Festung St. Nazaire*.[430] These units had been transferred from Hennebont by rail.[431] The following day, the *I./852* and the *II./851*, both in *Festung St. Nazaire*, were placed under the operational control of the *265. I.D.*[432] Essentially, this detached them permanently from the *343. I.D.*[433] Another change involved the remaining elements of the *275. I.D.* (*Obst. Käßberg*). The *265. I.D.* was ordered to return them to their division immediately.[434]

The transfer of artillery to the fortresses required careful organisation and the *XXV.A.K.* issued corresponding orders on **25 July**. The headquarters of the *III./AR 265* in *Festung Lorient* was in command of 6th, 7th, 8th and 10th Batteries, as well as the *3./H.K.A.A. 1162*. The latter was to be brought up by the *343. I.D. H.K.A.A. 1163*, with its three batteries, was directed to coordinate closely with the fortress as well.[435] The artillery in *Festung St. Nazaire* was led by the headquarters of *AR 265* and consisted of three battalions. The *II./AR 265* had its own 4th and 5th Batteries, as well as control of the *3./Ost-Art.Abt. 752*. Three batteries were assembled under *Artillerie-Stab Bald*: The *4./H.K.A.A. 1162*, the *1./AR 265*, and *Geräte-Batterie St. Nazaire*. Finally, *Ost-Art.Abt. 752* (2nd and 4th Batteries) was in the area of La Baule - Escoublac, west of St. Nazaire.[436]

Although the redeployment of the *265. I.D.* throughout *KVA "C1"* and *"C2"* was largely completed by the end of **July**, not all of its units would remain in that sector. In early **August** the *II./896(-)* and the mobile *10./ AR 265* were brought up to Dinan and sent into action. On **2 July**, the battery had been part of the security forces in *Festung Lorient*, and its commitment elsewhere forbidden.[437] The American breakout dramatically altered the situation and, on **2 August**, the battalion and battery were assigned to *Kampfgruppe Spang*, a battlegroup under the command of the *266. I.D.* This battlegroup fought on the Rance around Dinan, where the battalion held the right wing.[438] *Kampfgruppe Spang* issued new orders on **4 August**. Elements of the battlegroup were assigned specific sectors to delay the enemy's ability to reach the various fortresses in Bretagne. The *II./896* and its 6th and 8th Companies were to cover the approaches to Lorient and withdraw towards the city if under enemy pressure.[439] The plan was changed the next day, and the battalion formally attached to the *266. I.D.*, its commander becoming local area commander for Belle-Isle-en-Terre. This put the battalion directly on the route to Brest, rather than to Lorient.[440] It appears the battalion withdrew towards Brest with the remnants of the *266. I.D.*, and it was destroyed when the Americans captured the town in **September**.

Substantial elements of the *265. I.D.* survived the fighting in Bretagne, either because they had remained in *Festung Lorient* and *St. Nazaire* or because they were able to withdraw to these fortresses in time. On **3 August**, the commander of the *265. I.D.* was given responsibility for opposing the American advance on the two fortresses.[441] Lorient was selected as the withdrawal location for the troops between the boundary with *343. I.D.* and the line Port Navallo - Vannes – St. Jean-Brévelay, as well as for the Guémené and Pontivy areas of responsibility. St. Nazaire was the destination for the troops in the rest of the *265. I.D.* sector, including the Josselin and Coëtquidan areas of responsibility.[442] This meant that the surviving elements of the division were trapped in *Festung Lorient* and *St. Nazaire*.[443] As a result, the division was considered lost by the Army High Command on **28 August**, and it was formally disbanded on **2 October**.[444]

353. Infanterie-Division

The *353. Infanterie-Division* was typical of a 21st Wave division. It was a sister formation to the *352. I.D.*, which defended Omaha Beach on D-Day. Both divisions were raised in the autumn of **1943** under *AOK 7*, in Bretagne and Normandy, respectively. The *353. I.D.* was established with elements from several different divisions, including the *306. I.D.*, the *328. I.D.*, the *334. I.D.* and the *371. I.D.* Since it took time to forge these elements into a proper division, the force was known as *Kampfgruppe Bretagne* until late **November**.

The *353. I.D.* was still in Bretagne when the invasion began and was sent to Normandy a few days later. A battlegroup fought around St. Lô under the *II. Fs.K.*, while the bulk of the division was moved to the *Nordfront* of the *LXXXIV. A.K.* in late **June**. Towards the end of **July**, the division was transferred to the corps' east flank, where it was pushed back and cut off by *Operation Cobra*. It managed to break out, but it was trapped once more, this time in the Falaise Pocket in **August**. Again, it escaped and reached the German border, albeit with significant losses. In the autumn, it returned to action in the Hürtgenwald.

On D-Day, the division was led by *Gen.Maj.* Paul Mahlmann, who was in command throughout the Normandy fighting. After the war, he wrote a series of monographs for the Foreign Military Studies. Although these accounts contain some errors and sometimes lack precision, they provide an interesting day-to-day overview of the division's operations in Normandy.

With additional sources, it is possible to get a relatively complete picture of the division in the Normandy fighting. The division's history in the summer of **1944** is also inextricably linked to that of the *LXXXIV. A.K.*, because it was attached to the corps almost until the latter's destruction in the Falaise Pocket. For this reason, the division's history will also be examined for the period after **15 July**.

Organisation and Equipment

The condition of the *353. I.D.* at the time of the invasion is well documented in surviving records. The division is interesting as it was part of the 21st Wave, making it a prime example of both the *Inf.Div. n.A*, which had been standardised in **October 1943**, and the subsequent shift to the *Inf.Div. 44* in

Gen.Lt. Paul Mahlmann was appointed division commander on 20 November 1943. He remained in active command until mid-December 1944. Previously, the General had been in command of the 137. I.D., 147. Res.Div. and the 39. I.D. (BArch, PERS 6/300176)

early **1944**. In organisation and equipment, the division was very close to the base organisational document (*Grundgliederung*) on **1 June 1944**. In discussing the division, the **September 1943** authorisation document will only be used to illustrate the development of those elements that changed before the invasion.[1]

The authorised organisation of an *Inf.Div. 44* called for three infantry regiments, each with two battalions and two heavy weapons companies. Additional infantry was provided by a fusilier battalion. The artillery regiment consisted of three light and one heavy battalion, each with three batteries of four guns. The organisational document also included an engineer battalion, a field-replacement battalion and several options for the organisation of the divisional AT elements.[2]

The shift to an *Inf.Div. 44* organisation meant that some equipment and men became superfluous. The authorised end strength for the personnel dropped from 14,058 on **1 February** (not counting the AT battalion) to 13,486 on **1 June**. The authorised number of MG's decreased from 779 to 723 in the same period.[3] By **1 May**, the division's excess personnel had been reported to higher headquarters, and the extra equipment was ready to be picked up.[4]

The division closely adhered to the authorisation document and was near its authorised strength on **1 June 1944**. Against an authorisation of 340 officers, 2,230 NCO's, 9,124 men and 1,792 *Hiwi's*, it was short 13 officers, 137 NCO's and 6 *Hiwi's*, an aggregate shortage of just 156 (1.2%).[5]

Official records on the age build-up of the division have not been found. It was not included in the overviews of **December 1943**, likely because it was still in its formation process. The division was, however, covered in the MIRS

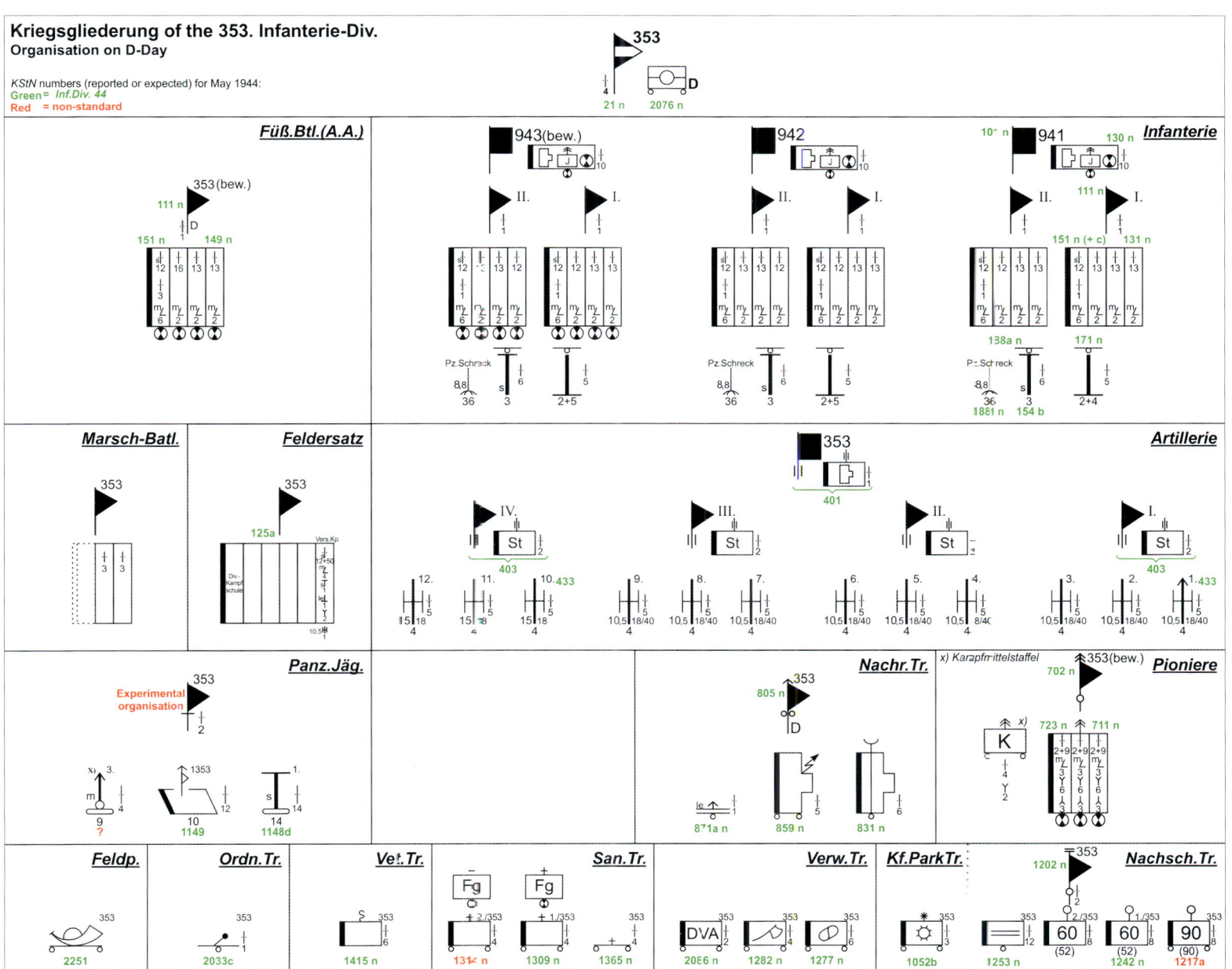

On D-Day, the 353.I.D. was a good example of a Type 44 infantry division and close to authorised strength. Its mobility had been further improved by the 'Beweglungsmachung' programme (bew.) and it had begun with the formation of its own Marschbataillon.

353. Infanterie-Division

paybook study in the summer of **1944**.[6] Based on 720 paybooks, it found that 6% of the men were born in 1909 or earlier, 44% in 1910-24, 12% in 1925, and 34% in 1926.

	Sample size	≤1909	1910-24	1925	≥1926
MIRS	720	5.7%	44.0%	11.8%	33.5%
KIA/MIA	464	11.2%	55.6%	6.7%	26.5%
Difference	256	5.5%	6.6%	-5.1%	-7%

Table 1: Comparison of age groups in the *353. I.D.* between MIRS and KIA/MIA numbers.

Analysing a sample of 464 KIA/MIA,[7] including losses in non-frontline units, provides lower percentages for the youngest two age groups and higher numbers for the oldest two. This suggests a stronger bias in the MIRS study. The KIA/MIA numbers show that 19% of the men were 30-40 years old (born 1904-13), 27% were 20-30 (1914-23) and 52% were 20 or younger (born 1924 at the earliest). Less than 2% were older than 40 (born 1903 or earlier). The division was remarkable in having both a large contingent of men born in 1924 (19%) and 1926 (27%). The importance of 1924 also illustrates why the MIRS age group 1910-1924 is too large to be used without more context. Among the KIA/MIA, those of the preferred age 20-35 (born 1909-23) amounted to 39%. The spread within this age group was quite even, unlike in some of the other divisions. Overall, the division's almost 80% aged 30 or younger sets it apart from all other divisions covered in this book.

Still, as always, it is difficult to identify the sample's bias, but some two-thirds were assigned to the three infantry regiment or the fusilier battalion. In a *Inf.Div. 44*, these units should only amount to some 50%. This shows a bias towards frontline infantry, but the exact effect is difficult to determine.

	≤1903	1904-1908	1909-1913	1914-1918	1919-1923	1924	1925	1926
Kia/MIA	1.9%	7.1%	12.3%	11.9%	14.7%	19.0%	6.7%	26.5%

Table 2: Age distribution in the *353. I.D.* (Based on 464 KIA/MIA)

On **1 June**, the division was fully equipped with MG's, artillery pieces and AT guns; the AT battalion was fully equipped as well. The division's weapons were entirely of German design and only 10 of the MG's were *MG 34's*, the other 713 were *MG 42's*.[8] Small arms included 9,477 rifles, 813 *G41* self-loading rifles, 200 sniper rifles, 445 grenade launchers, 898 machine pistols and 3,341 pistols.[9]

The divisional headquarters was protected by four MG's, two more than the authorisation. Although not listed on the order of battle, the *KStN* allowed for a divisional band, which was present. To support the staff's activities, the division included a motorised mapping section.[10]

The division had three infantry regiments: *Grenadier-Regiment 941, 942*, and *943* (*Obst*. Schmitz, Cordes and Boehm), all three consisting of two battalions, an infantry-gun company (13th) and an AT company (14th). There was also a headquarters company.[11] In **October 1943**, formation of the regiments began around three battalions transferred from other divisions. The *II./754* and the *III./755* arrived from the *334. I.D.*, while the *III./671* was provided by the *371. I.D.*[12] On **20 November**, these battalions were redesignated as the *II./941, I./942*, and *I./943*, respectively.[13] During this period, there were no regimental headquarters and no headquarters formed for the three battalions. Both types of headquarters arrived in **December**, drawn from recently disbanded divisions.[14] The regimental headquarters of *GR 548* and *569* (both *328. I.D.*) and *581* (*306. I.D.*) were used for *GR 941, 943* and *942*, respectively.[15] Three infantry battalion headquarters also arrived in December: The *III./569*, as well as the *I.* and *II./581*.[16] The arrival of another headquarters, the *II./548*, has not been found in the records, but it was apparently used to form the *I./941*.[17] There is some confusion as to which headquarters were used for the remaining two battalions. The *III./569* was apparently used for the *II./943*, and the headquarters of the *II./942* was probably formed from the *I.* or *II./581*.[18] One of these may have formed the division's field-replacement battalion.[19]

By **1 January 1944**, formation of the regiments was well under way, and, on **1 June**, all three were close to authorised strength.[20] The headquarters company of all three regiments embraced the usual signals, bicycle, and engineer platoons, for a total of 10 MG's per company.[21]

Each infantry battalion had the typical organisation of three rifle and one MG Company. On **1 June**, the companies were almost fully equipped. Each rifle company had 12 (*7./941, 3. & 5./942* and *1. & 5./943*) or 13 light MG's and 2 medium mortars. Each MG Company had 12 heavy MG's, 1 light MG and 6 medium mortars. One more machine gun was available to each battalion headquarters, except for the *I./941* which did not have one.[22] This organisation differed from the official *Inf.Div. 44*, which concentrated the mortars in the MG Company and provided two heavy MG's for each rifle company.[23] Reportedly, on **13 June**, each rifle company of (at least) the *II./943* did receive a heavy machine gun from the battalion's MG Company.[24]

The organisation of the companies was straightforward; they consisted of three rifle platoons and a mortar section. The company headquarters comprised an officer, a junior NCO and five messengers. The platoons were led by a senior NCO (an officer authorised in the case of the 1st Platoon), who was assisted by two messengers. The rifle platoons were organised into three sections which typically consisted of an NCO and about eight men; their weaponry was standard with a light *MG 42*, a machine pistol, a sniper rifle, a grenade launcher, a self-loading rifle, plus *K98k* rifles and pistols. Additional weapons were available at platoon level, including a variety of handheld anti-tank weapons and self-loading rifles. The company mortar section consisted of a junior NCO and six men. Three men crewed each of the two medium mortars.[25] The *2./942* reportedly included an AT section (*Panzervernichtungstrupp*), consisting of two NCO's and five men. They were armed with *Faustpatronen*, *Hafthohlladungen* and some smoke pots.[26]

Few reports are available on the MG companies, but the *4./942* had three MG platoons (each with two sections with two heavy MG's) and one mortar platoon (three sections with two medium mortars each), matching the strength report of **1 June**.[27] After the invasion, around **19-20 July,** three NCO's and 12 men were transferred from *F.E.B. 353* to form an AT platoon with three sections for the *4./943*. They were given 1½ days of instruction to operate *Puppchen* AT rocket launchers, of which the platoon received three. Each section consisted of one NCO and four men. They were equipped with one launcher, 15 rounds, one cart and one horse. Three men manned the weapon, while the fourth brought up ammo and the fifth was a driver.[28]

Reports on the strength of the companies are rare, but some information is available for *GR 942*. According to prisoners, there were 117 men in the *1./942*, 110 in the *2./942* and the *6./942* and 120 men in the *4./942*.[29] The men were mostly from year groups 1925-1926.[30] The majority were Germans, but there were also foreigners. Between 10 and 22 foreigners were reported in several companies, some identified as Turkestanis, others simply as Russians.[31] The *I./942* reportedly had 20% *Volksdeutsche* — some 20 per company — and 10% Caucasians.[32] This would be in line with *GR 943*, which reportedly had 20% Poles. At some point, the *7./943* had 22 Poles, but the regiment transferred some to units manning the coast in **February 1944**. Instead, Russians were assigned, of which the company received 20 in **March**.[33]

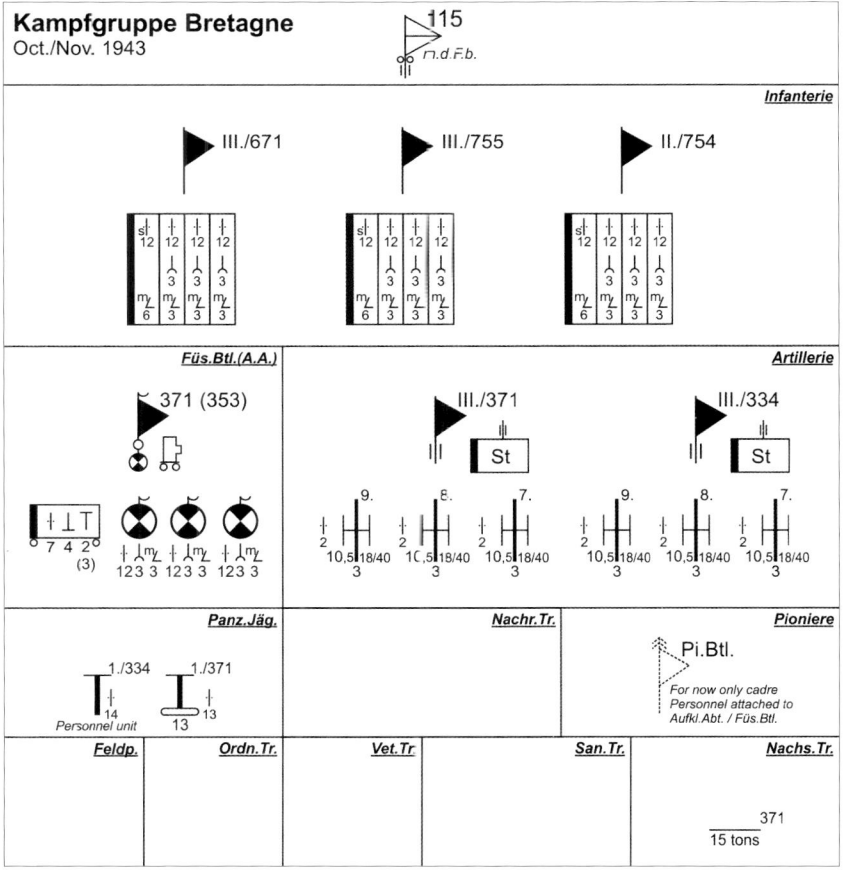

Initially, KG Bretagne was under the command of Arko 115. It consisted of three infantry battalions, a (former) reconnaissance battalion, two artillery battalions and two anti-tank companies.

Information on transportation of the infantry battalions varies. In the 6./942, the company trains were led by a *Hauptfeldwebel*, who oversaw 2 junior NCO's (both for administration, with one also attending to supply matters) and 9 or 10 drivers. Mobility in this company was provided by nine horse-drawn wagons.[34] Much higher numbers are provided for two companies in the *II./943*. Reportedly, each section had its own wagon, one to three more were at platoon level and two to five more at company level.[35] This would allow for 14 to 25 wagons per company. All figures are hard to match to the *KStN* of a rifle company, which called for 15 horse-drawn wagons/carts and 11 infantry carts.[36]

GR 943 was a recipient of mobility enhancement efforts and, thus, had increased mobility, to include bicycles for its infantry companies.[37] It is not clear how far the battalion headquarters and trains were motorised, but 15 lorries were reportedly available for the regimental headquarters, mostly Renault.[38]

The regimental heavy weapons companies were partially motorised, with *RSO's* to tow the guns.[39] The 13th Company in each regiment was to have two heavy and six light infantry guns.[40] Six *15 cm s.I.G. 33's* and 14 *7,5 cm le.I.G.18's* arrived in **December** and **January**.[41] The authorised number of light guns had not been met by **1 June**. The 13th Companies of *GR 942* and *GR 943* had five each, and the *13./941* had just four, although each company had the authorised five MG's and two heavy infantry guns.[42]

Each 14th Company was at authorised strength with 3 *7,5 cm Pak 40's*, 36 *Ofenrohre* and 6 MG's, all of which arrived by **1 May**.[43] According to a soldier in the *14./941*, his company consisted of one AT gun platoon and two tank-destroyer platoons, matching the requirements for a *Inf.Div. 44*.[44] The AT gun platoon was equipped with three *Pak 40's*, three light *MG 42's* and some *Faustpatronen*; personnel consisted of an officer, three NCO's, and 21 men. The second and third platoon reportedly had three sections each. The platoons were led by a *Feldwebel* and the sections consisted of an NCO and nine men. They were armed with three *Ofenrohre*, one light *MG 42*, some *Faustpatronen* and the standard rifles and pistols.[45] This only accounts for 18 of the 36 *Ofenrohre* in the company, meaning it is possible that the rest were held in reserve. *Ofenrohre* have also been reported in the rifle companies, as many as one per platoon, but it may be that these were simply provided by detachments of the 14th Company.[46] No information is available for the companies of *GR 942* and *943*, however, the *14./941* reportedly had a strength of 2 officers and 115 other ranks, including 15-20 Turkestanis.[47]

Résistance activities dealt a serious blow to *GR 942* even before the invasion. In the weeks prior, attacks were primarily aimed at messengers and individual soldiers. On **5 June**, however, the divisional commander's staff car was fired on with machine pistols. The commander of *GR 942*, *Obst*. Cordes, was killed, and the division's intelligence officer, *Hptm*. Starcke, was wounded. *Gen. Mahlmann* survived the ambush unscathed.[48] *Maj.d.R*. Görtmüller, the division's National Socialist Leadership Officer (*National-Sozialistischer Führungs-Offizier / NSFO*), became the new regimental commander on 15 June.[49]

As a good example of an *Inf.Div. 44*, the division boasted a seventh infantry battalion: *Füsilier-Bataillon (A.A.) 353* (*Rittmeister* Theuerkauf).[50] The battalion began its existence as *Aufkl.Abt. 371* and was transferred from the *371. I.D.* to *KG Bretagne* as *Div.Füs.Btl.(A.A.) 371* in the autumn of **1943**. The fusilier battalions introduced with the *Inf.Div. n.A.* were similar to a regular infantry battalion; in fact, the grenadier battalions and the fusilier battalion of the division used the same *KStN's*, except for a single bicycle Schwadron,* which was only present in the fusilier battalion.[51]

The infantry-gun companies of GR 941, 942, and 943 were all armed with a number of 7.5 cm le.I.G.18, the standard German light infantry gun. This particular piece was photographed by members of the 101st AB, and most likely belonged to 14./914 (352.I.D.) which opposed the division northeast of Carentan. (Mark A. Bando Collection)

---

* Schwadron: A cavalry term used instead of Kompanie, with "troop" being the equivalent in US and "squadron" in British reconnaissance units.

To meet this new standard, the battalion was redesignated as *Füs.Btl. 353*, a transition completed on **22 January**.[52] Its origins as a reconnaissance battalion is apparent from the *(A.A.)* in its designation and in continued use of the branch-of-service colours *(Waffenfarben)* of the cavalry and cavalry terminology. Examples of this are *Rittmeister* instead of *Hauptmann*, and *Schwadron* in lieu of *Kompanie*.[53] In fusilier battalions without such a lineage, the companies were simply called *(Füsilier-) Kompanie*.[54]

On **1 June 1944**, the battalion had three bicycle troops and a heavy troop. The battalion was listed as mobile because of the enhanced mobility efforts it received. This enabled all rifle troops to be outfitted with bicycles rather than just one, as called for in the *Inf.Div. 44*. The 1st and 2nd Troops both had 13 light MG's, and the 3rd Troop had 16. All three rifle troops had two medium mortars; the heavy troop had 12 heavy MG's, 1 light MG and 6 medium mortars. Another light MG was with the battalion headquarters.[55]

According to men from the battalion, the rifle troops had three rifle platoons and one heavy platoon. The troops were led by an officer, with the headquarters including the commander, three medical orderlies and three messengers. About 20% of the personnel were non-German, including Poles *(Volksliste III)*. It is claimed that the 3rd Troop had a strength of just 70-100 men. Although this seems low, the rifle sections were apparently only seven or eight men strong. As usual, the rifle platoons consisted of three sections, each armed with a light MG, a self-loading rifle, a machine pistol, a grenade launcher, a sniper rifle and regular rifles. The sections had a strength of one NCO and six or seven men. At platoon level were the platoon leader, two messengers and a stretcher bearer. The 4th Platoon was equipped with two medium mortars and may also have had a number of heavy MG's, although (some of) those may have been assigned from the 4th Troop. In addition to bicycles, the rifle troops had one *Volkswagen*, a field kitchen and three French buses. Communications equipment was provided by the battalion's signals platoon, with one *"Bertha"* wireless set for each company.[56]

The heavy troop was organised into three MG platoons and a mortar platoon (4th). It was armed with 12 heavy MG's and 6 medium mortars. The headquarters was composed of the company commander, the headquarters section leader, three messengers, a medic (NCO) and a signals section with telephones. According to a soldier, the commander had a *Volkswagen* and two *Kettenkräder* were with the headquarters section. The MG platoons were led by a platoon leader with two messengers. Their four machine guns were divided into two sections, each consisting of a section leader and 12 men, 6 per MG. The mortars were assigned to the 4th Platoon and distributed among three sections with two mortars each. As in the other platoons, the platoon leader was assisted by two messengers. Each MG crew had a horse and two infantry carts to transport weapon and ammunition; this arrangement was the same for the mortars. The men were allocated bicycles, and the trains were horse-drawn. Although few details are available about the troop's personnel, it reportedly had a strength of 170-180 men, including 20 Turkestanis in the trains.[57]

Four or five buses were allocated to the troop during its march to the front. These were used to carry the heavy MG's, mortars, ammunition, field kitchen and rations, along with men whose bicycle tyres had been punctured. When the company arrived in the battle area, the buses were withdrawn, leaving just one for the kitchen and rations.[58]

Divisions of the 21st Wave had an impressive amount of artillery and *Artillerie-Regiment 353* (*Obstlt.* Köhler) was no exception. The authorisation document shows that *AR 353* was organised into three light battalions and one heavy battalion; the regiment and each battalion had a headquarters battery. The four battalions each had three batteries, and each of them were issued four artillery pieces. Although divisions of the 21st Wave were intended to have four guns per battery, some were temporarily limited to three. Since the *353. I.D.* was a regular infantry division, the artillery regiment was fully mobile, meaning it was horse-drawn.[59]

The foundations of the regiment had been laid by the *III./AR 371* and the *III./AR 334*, both of which had been transferred to *KG Bretagne* in **October**. Both arrived with three batteries of three *10,5 cm le.F.H.18/40's*.[60] The regimental headquarters was provided by *AR 328*, which arrived on **6 December** along with the headquarters of the *III./AR 328*.[61] With a cadre of such quality, the formation of a full regiment should have been straightforward, but this was not the case. It started with the transfer of *III./AR 371*, which left on **26 December** to become the *I./AR 272*.[62] As a result, three battalions needed to be formed, rather than two. About the same time, *Feldpost* numbers were assigned or modified, with this being confusing in itself. Somehow, the number for the new heavy 4th Battalion ended up with what became a light (1st Battalion) battalion and vice versa. This confusion did not apply to the *III./AR 328* or the *III./AR 334*, which became the *II.* and the *III./AR 353*, respectively.[63]

353. Infanterie-Division

On **1 January 1944**, the 4th Battalion was already operational and fully equipped, albeit issued mostly with light field howitzers. The 1st Battalion was also well equipped, but still forming. The 3rd Battalion was forming with one battery, and the only heavy battery in the regiment was assigned to the 4th Battalion.[64] The formation of the heavy battalion and a third light battalion was impeded by the shortage of cadre personnel.[65]

The improper equipping of the 4th Battalion with light guns was corrected on **11 January**, when the battalion was redesignated as the 3rd Battalion and the 10th through 12th Batteries were redesignated as the 7th through 9th. In a similar fashion, the 3rd Battalion was redesignated as the 4th Battalion, with corresponding battery numbers.[66] These changes demonstrate that the mix-up of *Feldpost* numbers had exceeded that of just the 1st and 4th Battalions. The entries of these two battalions in the official lists were duly changed by flipping the battalion numbers.[67]

The regiment's formation made good progress throughout **January**. On **9-10 January**, more troops arrived for the regiment, including the headquarters and headquarters battery of *AR 137* and personnel for three light and three heavy batteries.[68] It is not clear how the personnel of *AR 137* were used, but they may have been used to augment other elements of *AR 353* or to form another battalion headquarters.

On **13 January**, locations were reported for all headquarters (and their headquarters batteries) and the batteries of the 3rd and 4th Battalions.[69] This shows that all the battalions at least had a headquarters. Over the next few days, the 1st through 3rd Batteries were listed as being formed.[70] The same was reported for the 2nd Battalion's batteries on **26 January**.[71] The order of battle of **30 January** illustrates that all four battalions, along with their batteries, had been established. Yet only the 3rd Battalion was fully equipped at this time. The 1st Battalion had two batteries with two guns and one with three guns. The condition of the 2nd Battalion was slightly better, with three guns per battery. There were still only four heavy guns in the 4th Battalion, and these were divided among its batteries. One of these had two guns, the others just one.[72]

The arrival of the regiment's artillery pieces occurred incrementally over a four-month period; the nine guns that had arrived with the *III./AR 334* being the exception. Six *le. F.H.18's* were delivered on **22 November** and 13 more on **18 December**.[73] The division received its first three *15 cm s.F.H.18's* on **19 December** and another piece three days later.[74] Four more *s.F.H.18's* and four *le. F.H.18/40's* arrived on **6 February** and, on **24 February**, the final five *le. F.H.18/40's* arrived.[75] These weapons were enough to fully equip the nine light batteries and assign a spare gun to *F.E.B. 353*.[76] Although the time of the arrival of the last four of the authorised 12 *s.F.H.18's* has not been found, this must have happened in **February** as well; the regiment was fully equipped on **1 March**, having been short of eight heavy howitzers a month earlier.[77]

There were no changes in the months immediately preceding the invasion. On **1 June**, the batteries in the three light battalions each fielded four *10,5 cm le. F.H.18/40's* and the 4th Battalion had four *15 cm s.F.H.18's*. Each battery also had five MG's.[78] Although *AOK 7* records still show a headquarters battery with each battalion, the corps records, beginning on **1 May**, only list a signals platoon and a surveying section. In each battalion, this combination of the headquarters, surveying section and signals platoon was equipped with two MG's.[79] The regimental headquarters also had a single MG.[80]

Little information has been gleaned from prisoner records. A prisoner of the headquarters battery of the 3rd Battalion stated that about half the men in his battalion were between 30-35 years old and the rest between 17-19 years. Most of the older men had experience from the Eastern Front. The headquarters battery included about 20 Russian drivers. It had 43 wagons and about 80 horses. The wagons were used for various purposes: Telephonic communications, field mess, equipment, straw and hay, and ammunition (eight wagons). There were also four infantry carts. For communications, the battery was equipped with *"Bertha"* (*Torn.Fu.b1*) and *"Konrad"* (*Torn.Fu.K*) wireless sets and field telephones.[81]

According to a soldier from the 9th Battery, the personnel were mainly Germans, with only eight Russians and six Poles. The headquarters section included the commander, a battery officer,* two NCO's, two messengers, a driver and two horsemen. The personnel in the signals section encompassed two NCO's and nine telephone and wireless operators. The gun crews consisted of one NCO and six men, armed with rifles or a pistol. Ammunition remained in short supply, as it had been before the invasion, with only 90 rounds per gun. The trains were fairly extensive. It was led by a senior NCO (*Hauptwachtmeister*) and included a clerk, a fitter, 2 men for the field kitchen, a shoemaker, a tailor, a saddler, a stable NCO, 4 blacksmiths and 29 drivers. As

---

* *Similar to the Gun Position Officer in the British artillery.*

Even a fully mobile infantry division like the 353. I.D. largely depended on horse-drawn mobility for its artillery. Here we see a light artillery battery on the move in Normandy. To pull just one 10,5 cm le.F.H.18/40 and its limber, four heavy and two light draught horses were required. (Archives du Calvados, 10Fi/4, photo 312, Agence Fama)

expected, transport was by horse and comprised 12 ammunition wagons and five wagons for the headquarters, signals equipment and baggage. Another 25 wagons were requisitioned and driven by French civilians, who primarily transported ammunition; the civilians were released upon arrival at the gun positions. In total, there were 96 horses in the battery.[82]

When serving on the front in **July**, the forward observation posts from the batteries of the 3rd Battalion were reportedly 200 metres from the frontline and manned by one lieutenant, two wireless operators and two telephone operators. They were equipped with two *Konrad II* radios and a field telephone. The battalion's observation post was 2 km to the rear and manned by another lieutenant, a *Wachtmeister*, seven NCO's, four wireless operators and six telephone operators. Their weapons and equipment consisted of four *Bertha I's*, four field telephones, one telescope and one light *MG 42*. The information from the forward observers was processed there and firing data transmitted to the gun batteries and headquarters battery, which were some 4 km further to the rear.[83]

Since the regiment was largely horse-drawn, it was vulnerable to related problems. The 1st and 2nd Batteries were immobile on **1 June**, as their horses were suffering from respiratory infections. This was an improvement from previous months, when the problem had affected the entire regiment. The horses of the 2nd and 3rd Battalions had recovered since **April** and, by **1 May**, 25% of the horses in the 4th Battalion had been reported as ill.[84]

As was typical for an *Inf.Div. 44*, *Pionier-Bataillon 353* (*Hauptmann* Pillmann) had three companies. By **1 June**, its mobility had improved through enhance mobility measures and, as a result, it possessed three bicycle companies instead of one. The companies were well equipped with two heavy MG's, nine light MG's, two medium mortars and six flamethrowers. There were also three or four *Granatbüchse* (obsolete anti-tank rifles converted to grenade launchers).[85] All of the companies were provided with bicycles, and the battalion headquarters was partially motorised. Attached to the headquarters was the motorised combat equipment supply section (*Kampfmittelstaffel*), which had an additional four light MG's and two flamethrowers.[86] The companies were comprised of three regular platoons and one heavy platoon. The regular platoons had three sections with 1 junior NCO and 10-12 men each; they were equipped with one light MG and two *Hafthohlladungen*.[87] The heavy platoon had a section with medium mortars and a section with two heavy *MG 42's*. Most of the personnel used bicycles, while others relied on horse-drawn transportation, with 32 horses per company. The battalion and company commanders had *Schwimmwagen*.[88] Mobility of the 3rd Company — the original bicycle company — may have been better than that of the other companies. It is said to have had three lorries, four motorcycles and two *Schwimmwagen*.[89]

Reports on the personnel strength and composition of the battalion are unusual. The 1st and 3rd Companies are said to have had a strength of 90 to 100 men.[90] These company strengths are low compared to an authorised strength of 179 all ranks.[91] The 1st Company reportedly included 30 Russians and six Poles. Twelve men in the company were older, while the rest were 18-year-olds.[92] The "Russians" may well have been Azerbaijanis. One such legionary was attached to battalion headquarters as an interpreter and visited the companies in that capacity.[93] This suggest that such personnel was present in all companies, and their numbers appear to have been significant. A legionary in the 1st Company claimed there were about 40 Azerbaijanis in his company.[94] This number would be high compared to the authorised number of 15 *Hiwi's*. The *KStN* did allow for the creation of a *Hiwi* construction platoon with up to 30 men, but this does not appear to explain the number of foreigners in the battalion.[95] Instead, there are indications that legionaries were used as regular soldiers, fighting alongside the German personnel.[96]

The division's replacement battalion was fairly strong on **1 June**. *Feldersatz-Bataillon 353* (*Hauptmann* Creuz) consisted of four regular (personnel) companies, a supply company (*Versorgungs-Kompanie*) and the divisional combat school (attached as the 5th Company).[97] This organisation was in compliance with the organisational document for such a battalion in the *Inf.Div. 44* template.[98] On paper, the heavy weaponry was in the weapons section of the supply company, which had four medium mortars, two flamethrowers, one heavy AT gun and one 10.5 cm howitzer; there were also 12 heavy MG's and 50 light MG's.[99] These numbers may seem high, but they accurately reflect the authorised numbers for the battalion. In fact, the battalion was short of equipment, since it lacked eight mortars and a medium AT gun.[100]

Based on statements of a soldier of the battalion, it seems the equipment was distributed among the battalion's four regular companies which, when the invasion began, each had a strength of about 150 NCO's and men. The supply company was used for administrative tasks.[101] Other prisoners from the battalion state that the battalion's companies were organised into three platoons with four sections each. The sections were armed with a light *MG 42*, one *Hafthohlladung* and *K98k* rifles. They estimate the strength of the battalion as about 600. About 50% of the men were artillery personnel.[102] The 4th Company apparently acted as the MG company, and its organisation has also been reported. The company had four platoons. The 12 heavy MG's were part of an MG platoon, and the four mortars were in the mortar platoon. The AT platoon had one *7,5 cm Pak 40*, towed by an *RSO*. There was also an infantry-gun platoon with light guns, but the 10.5 cm howitzer is not mentioned. Like most of the division, the battalion relied on horse-drawn transport. There were, however, only four wagons in the battalion, thus vehicles and drivers had to be requisitioned when the battalion moved to Normandy. After a certain distance, these were released and new vehicles and drivers were requisitioned and the whole process was repeated.[103]

The combat school, also known as the 5th Company, was led by an *Oberleutnant* and used to train NCO's. Courses typically lasted six weeks and either trained platoon or section leaders. The combat school was reportedly dissolved before the division moved to the front, with the men rejoining their companies.[104]

On orders of *Ob.West*, the division established another battalion: *Marschbataillon 353* (Replacements Transfer Bataillon 353). *Gen*. Mahlmann's monograph suggests that this battalion was formed after D-Day, but the order of battle of **1 June** includes it.[105] The battalion was to be used to help replace the division's anticipated losses at the outset of the invasion.[106] Usually a replacements-transfer battalion would be sent by the Replacement Army, but in this case it formed an additional personnel reserve within the division.

The records of the *XXV. A.K.* confirm the battalion's existence as of **19 May**.[107] It consisted of a headquarters and two companies, while a third company was being formed. The 1st and 2nd Companies both had three light MG's.[108] The personnel were drawn from regular units within the division and thus reduced the strength of those units;[109] however, this affected the combat units less than might be expected, since the 1st Company conducted infantry-courses for the trains and supply units.[110] It appears that at least some of the MG's in the battalion were taken from the infantry battalions, explaining why some were understrength despite the division receiving its full allotment.

Two members of the battalion have provided some information. A *Stabsfeldwebel*, who joined the 1st Company on **6 June**, states his company consisted of an officer and 80 men. There were three Russians. Weapons consisted of nine light *MG 34's*, with the men carrying rifles.[111]

An enlisted man of the 2nd Company states that he joined the battalion on **28 May**, when one section from each of the division's infantry companies was transferred to the battalion. The 2nd Company was larger than the 1st and had about 240 men in eight platoons, each with three sections. His section was armed with a light MG and a grenade-launcher, while the men carried *K98k* rifles. There were two *Ofenrohre* in his company. For transport to Normandy, about 21 horse carts were requisitioned from French civilians. After the battalion's arrival at Canisy, a 3rd Company was formed by taking men from the 2nd Company and new arrivals from the Division Replacement Centre at Schwerin-Mecklenburg. This brought the battalion up to 500 men in strength.[112]

There is a wealth of information concerning the divisional AT battalion, *Panzerjäger-Abteilung 353* (*Major* Kampf). The division's authorised organisation of **September 1943** had only a towed AT company with 12 heavy AT guns and 13 MG's.[113] While this was the weakest of the *Inf.Div. n.A.* options, expansion of the divisional AT troops to a full battalion was already under consideration. If it were decided to establish a full battalion, a headquarters, a self-propelled company and a *Flak* company could be added (instead of the SP company, an assault-gun battery could be substituted).[114]

When the division (*KG Bretagne*) was formed, it received AT personnel from the *1./Pz.Jg.Abt. 371* and the *1./Pz.Jg.Abt. 334*. The latter was only a cadre unit, but the former was equipped with 13 SP guns.[115] The division, however, was only authorised to have one company of towed guns.[116] As a result, it had to give up these vehicles and the company was reorganised into a unit with towed guns.[117] In **November**, 10 of the SP guns, identified as heavy AT guns on armoured Lorraine tractors (aka "*7,5 cm PaK 40 auf Sfl. Lorraine Schlepper 'Marder I' (Sd.Kfz.135)*) were transferred to the *709. I.D.* and the other three to the *708. I.D.* The personnel not involved in this were exchanged with towed AT personnel from the Replacement Army.[118]

The division was joined by the headquarters of *Pz.Jg.Abt. 328* in early **December**, but there was no need for it in the *353. I.D.* As a result, it was subsequently disbanded.[119] This decision was premature, however, since *Ob.West* ordered the formation of *Pz.Jg.Abt. 353* on **13 January 1944**. The order was forwarded by AOK 7 to the *XXV. A.K.* two days later. The battalion would be formed with a headquarters, an AT SP company (1st), an AT assault-gun company (2nd) and a *Flak* company (3rd). Replacements would come from *Pz.Jg.Ers.Abt. 2* in *Wehrkreis II*. Orders for the formation of the headquarters would be issued later.[120] No organisational details were provided for the 3rd Company, as it would be formed elsewhere and sent to the division as a complete unit.

The 1st Company would use *KStN 1148d*, authorising 14 SP 7.5 cm AT guns (*Marder*): four vehicles in each platoon and two with the headquarters section leader. Personnel would be drawn from *Pz.Jg.Ers.u.Ausb.Abt. 20* in *Wehrkreis X*. The company would be created by using the existing divisional towed AT company.[121] Personnel no longer required — due to arrival of personnel for the self-propelled company — were to be sent to the AT replacement battalion of *Wehrkreis X*. The transfer was carried out on **12 February**.[122] The 12 motorised AT guns were handed over to the 275. I.D. (7) and 276. I.D. (5).[123]

The 2nd Company initially followed *KStN* 446a, which called for three platoons of three guns and one platoon with the *Gruppe Führer*.[124] It is possible that the company changed to *KStN* 1149 when that *KStN* was introduced on **1 February** and became standard for the *Inf.Div. 44*.[125] *Pz.Jg.Ers.Abt. 2* from *Wehrkreis II* provided the personnel.[126] Officially, the *Pz.Jg.Stu.Gesch. Kp.* became *Sturmgeschütz-Abteilung 1353* when *Sturmgeschütz* units were redesignated in **February 1944**.[127] For clarity, this work will continue to refer to the 2./*Pz.Jg.Abt.* 353, since it remained part of the battalion.

The transformation into a full AT battalion required considerable time, and the process is well documented. On **1 January 1944**, the division only

Kriegsberichter Umbach took a series of photographs on the Cotentin Peninsula, which would narrow down the owner of this Marder III down to just the 243. or 353. I.D. Based on the heavy camouflage pattern, the latter seems to be the best candidate. Collectie CegeSoma – Rijksarchief (OD4))

* *H.Pz.N.Za.: Heeres-Panzer-Nebenzeugamt, or Army Armour Ordnance Supply Office.*

had *Pz.Jg.Kp. 353*, which was armed with 5 towed AT guns and 14 MG's; its personnel strength was at 91%.[128] The missing seven heavy AT guns arrived soon after and were listed on **30 January**.[129]

On **24 January**, a train arrived with personnel for the new 1st Company, consisting of 3 officers and 140 NCO's and men.[130] The *1./Pz.Jg.Abt. 334* had been located at Berrien since late **October**, and the new units were apparently assembled there, too.[131] On **25 January**, a *Leutnant* arrived from the east — the advance party from the headquarters of *Pz.Jg.Abt. 238*.[132] This is peculiar because the order to use that headquarters for *Pz.Jg.Abt. 353* was not officially issued until **28 January**.[133] On **31 January**, another train arrived in Morlaix with personnel for the assault-gun company: 3 officers, 42 NCO's and 98 men.[134] The actual headquarters of *Pz.Jg.Abt. 238* arrived on **8 February**.[135] On **23 February**, a train arrived at Morlaix with the entire the 3rd Company. It had 3 officers, 21 NCO's and 123 men.[136]

On **1 March**, the battalion was finally listed with its three companies on the order of battle for *AOK 7*. There were four *Marders* but none of the assault guns had yet arrived. During this transition period, the (eight remaining) towed AT guns and four *Marders* were temporarily combined into the 1st Company[137] The *Flak* company was equipped with nine 3.7 cm *Flak* on tracked chassis, presumably *Sd.Kfz.6/2* or *7/2* halftracks.[138] This equipment is of interest, since the *Inf.Div. n.A.* only showed 12 self-propelled 2 cm *Flak*, while the later *Inf.Div. 44* increased the options to include towed guns, either 12 2 cm or 9 3.7 cm.[139] Nonetheless, there must have been a logic behind this, since its sister formation (*Pz.Jg.Abt. 352*) had the same self-propelled weaponry.[140]

It took some time for the armour of the 1st and 2nd Companies to arrive. The first four *Marders* reached Berrien on **21 February**.[141] By **15 March**, five more guns arrived, although it is possible they had arrived some days earlier.[142] The appearance of the final five *Marders* was reported on **30 March**.[143] Although the 10 assault guns reached Brest on **31 March** (from the ordnance depot at Breslau-Masselwitz)* their arrival was not recorded by *AOK 7* until **4 April**.[144] On **1 April**, the division listed the battalion as fully equipped with combat vehicles.[145] Since an order of battle only outlines the weaponry and overall organisation, some of the battalion's heaviest equipment is not addressed. On **16 April**, the battalion was assigned a heavy trailer for the assault-gun company, a 22-tonne lowboy trailer (*Tieflade-Anhänger - Sd.Ah.116*).[146] The 18-tonne halftrack-tractor, *Sd.Kfz. 9*, needed to tow it followed on **4 May**.[147]

Being well equipped, of course, does not make a unit fully operational and the report of **1 April** specifically reported problems with the training of the tracked elements of the battalion due to a shortage of fuel.[148] This was not easily solved. Although *Gen.* Mahlmann considered the division ready for offensive and defensive operations on **1 May**, this status did not yet apply to the AT battalion. It was only deemed ready for defence. This was due in part at least to the condition of the assault-gun company. Because of fuel shortages and technical problems with the vehicles, the company had yet to reach the required level of training. This was particularly true for the drivers.[149]

The division's repeated reports on the shortage of fuel for training purposes were apparently noticed, because the battalion was issued a special fuel allowance of 15,000 litres on **4 May** for training purposes from the logistics command in the west.[150] This was in addition to the 31,000 litres of fuel and 2,000 litres of diesel issued to the entire division for training in **May**.[151] On **1 June**, *Gen.* Mahlmann observed that although the training of the assault-gun company had improved, it was not yet complete. The battalion as a whole still required unit-level training (*Verbandausbildung*). As a result, he concluded that the battalion was ready for defensive operations but only for limited offensive action.[152]

Little information is available for the division's non-combat units. An exception is *Feldgendarmerie-Trupp 353*. The section was led by *Leutnant* Winter and had a strength of 32 men; it was armed with pistols and rifles and some senior NCO's carried machine pistols. The section was motorised with a lorry, a *Kfz. 15*, three *Volkswagens*, and a motorcycle.[153]

Mobility and Beweglichmachung

By **1 June**, the division's organic mobility was about at its authorised level. It was considered fully mobile, although many units would move on foot or rely on horse-drawn transport.[154] Motorisation only suffered from minor shortages. There was a slight shortage of motorcycles, with an on-hand inventory of 13 (authorised 12) *Kettenkräder*, 32 (34) motorcycle-combinations and 97 (105) regular motorcycles. The number of light cars was actually above authorised strength. The on-hand numbers of cross-country vehicles was 171 (141) and that of the others was 36 (34). With two light (one to five

tonne) and six medium or heavy (8 to 18 tonne) halftracks, all authorised prime movers were available and the number of *RSO's* was one above the authorisation at 29. The available lorries covered the authorised lift capacity of 680 tonnes, although 3% were in short-term repair. The shortage of *Maultiere* (authorised 17, on-hand 11) and cross-country lorries (authorised 65, on-hand 4) was more serious, but it had been somewhat compensated for with regular lorries (authorised 295, on-hand 307). The division had also had 4,562 horses, 126 above authorised strength; of these, 83 were *Panje* horses and 56 were mules.[155]

It was a while before the division was included in the enhanced mobility effort. On **20 February**, *Ob.West* ordered that large elements of 21st to 25th Wave divisions were to become bicycle formations. This embraced a full infantry regiment, the fusilier battalion, the engineer battalion and a platoon from the supply company.[156] Under the *7. Armee*, priority was given to three divisions, including the *353. I.D.* On **14 March**, *AOK 7* ordered the division to start preparations and conduct the mobility efforts as far as the available bicycles and motor vehicles allowed. Missing transportation was to be requested from *AOK 7*.[157]

The orders were clarified on **4 April**. While few changes were made, the trains of the infantry regiment and the other battalions were to be motorised. The 13th and 14th Companies would be motorised, too.[158] Further details were provided on **5 May**, when it was clarified that motorisation would also include the mortar platoons. Only the trains of the fusilier battalion would be motorised, and it would give up its horse-drawn transportation. For the other bicycle units, some motor vehicles were allocated to transport heavy weapons and ammunition and for command purposes.[159] For example, a bicycle-equipped grenadier company with motorised trains would have five motorcycles, one light wheeled vehicle, two special-purpose vehicles (not specified) and five lorries. The same number of vehicles was available for a company with horse-drawn trains, but with only one lorry instead of five. In similar fashion, four fewer lorries were available for the bicycle-equipped MG company and bicycle-equipped battalion headquarters with horse-drawn trains (compared to units with motorised trains).[160]

Over time, the motor vehicles for the enhanced mobility efforts started to arrive. By **1 May**, the division had received just 50% of these vehicles and, although the situation improved throughout the month, some vehicles were still lacking on **1 June**.¹⁶¹ As a result, the exact level of mobility is unclear. On **12 May**, the enhanced lift capacity amounted to only 76 tonnes. In contrast, the *352. I.D.* had 347 tonnes of lift available, although much of this was to motorise one regiment.¹⁶² The bicycle units in the *353. I.D.* appear to have been fully equipped with bicycles.¹⁶³

Kampfgruppe

Unlike many other divisions under *AOK 7*, the *353. I.D.* did not have a *Kampfgruppe* on D-Day. In late **December 1943**, orders had been given to prepare the division's combat-ready elements for possible deployment against landings in Normandy and on the north coast of Bretagne (*LXXIV. AK*). These elements, in field-army reserve, were referred to as *"Kampfgruppe 353. I.D."* This term was simply used to denote the division's combat-ready formations, and no formal structure was ever provided for a battlegroup.¹⁶⁴ This may be explained by the fact that the division would be fully mobile (unlike the static divisions) and could be expected to be fully combat-ready by the time of the invasion (unlike divisions that were raised shortly before the invasion, such as the *77. I.D.*).

When the division moved to Normandy, most of the mobile elements simply moved ahead. Upon arrival, some were combined into *Kampfgruppe Boehm*, named for the commander of *GR 943*. This battlegroup was formed by combining his regiment (minus its 1ˢᵗ Battalion) and the fusilier battalion (the advance guard). Unlike many other battlegroups, it did not include any artillery, which makes clear that it had not been planned as a standard *Kampfgruppe*.

History

According to Tessin, the *353. I.D.* was raised on **5 November 1943**, using the various headquarters and cadres of the disbanded *328. I.D.* and elements of the *306. I.D.*¹⁶⁵ While this may be technically correct, it also simplifies the division's formation. In fact, the foundations for the division had been laid down on **22 September 1943**, when establishment of five new divisions in the *Heeresgruppe D* sector was ordered by the General Staff of the Army. Three received priority and the other two (*357. and 359. I.D.*) were ultimately formed in Radom. The *349.*, the *352.* and the *353. I.D.* were to be ready for action by **1 February 1944**.¹⁶⁶

The forces would come from a variety of sources. The German Army in the East would provide a divisional headquarters, some lower-level headquarters, the signals battalion and the supply elements for each of the divisions. Infantry divisions in the *Ob.West* area of operations would furnish each division with four infantry battalions (including some reconnaissance battalions), two light artillery battalions, an AT company and cadre for the engineer battalion. To make this possible, the (regular) infantry divisions would be reorganised as *Inf.Div. n.A.* This affected the *334.*, the *356.*, the *371.*, the *376.*, the *384.* and the *389. I.D.*, although it was not yet clear which elements would be assigned to the new divisions.¹⁶⁷ Ultimately, the *334.* and *371. I.D.* contributed to the formation of the *353. I.D.*

Following the German practice of making forces available for commitment before the complete divisions were ready, they would initially be organised as *Kampfgruppen*.¹⁶⁸ The divisions were raised in specific regions of France and, as a consequence, were initially known as *Kampfgruppe Kanalküste* (Channel Coast), *Kampfgruppe Normandie* and *Kampfgruppe Bretagne*. The battlegroups would then gradually expand into full-fledged divisions. During this process, *KG Bretagne* became the *353. I.D.* and *KG Normandie* the *352. I.D.*¹⁶⁹

The significance of the *328. I.D.*, as suggested by Tessin, is somewhat overrated as it overlooks the fact that *KG Bretagne* was mainly formed using the *334. I.D.* and the *371. I.D.* It was not until later that the *328. I.D.* was able to provide some of the requisite headquarters elements which allowed the *Kampfgruppe* to become a division. Even then, most of the infantry and artillery battalions of the *353. I.D.* and the support troops originated from divisions other than the *328. I.D.* or were newly formed. Following the disasters at Stalingrad and in North Africa, the *334. I.D.* and *371. I.D.* were being rebuilt in France, with the latter in the sector of *AOK 7* and the former under *AOK 1*.¹⁷⁰ This allowed the two divisions to transfer troops, rather than merely a cadre, to *KG Bretagne*.

The *371. I.D.* was reconstituted in Bretagne along the lines of a traditional infantry division, with three battalions in each of its three infantry regiments and a divisional reconnaissance battalion.¹⁷¹ In **September 1943**, with the division approaching full strength, the decision was made to reorganise it as an *Inf. Div. n.A* for the Eastern Front. This meant it would have to relinquish some units, which could then be used for other formations.¹⁷² The bulk of the *371. I.D.* was actually transferred to Italy in early **October**, and its final elements left the sector of the *XXV. A.K.* on **13 October**.[173] Prior to its departure, the division was directed to hand over a number of elements to support the formation of *KG Bretagne*; these included the *III./671*, *Aufkl.Abt. 371*, the *III./AR 371* and the *1./Pz.Jg.Abt. 371*. Other elements were gleaned from the *334. I.D.* These were: The *II./754*, the *III./755*, the *III./AR 334* and the *1./Pz.Jg.Abt. 334*.[174]

On **5 October 1943**, the *Kampfgruppe* was formally assembled. The reinforced headquarters of *Arko 115*, under *Generalleutnant* Dihm, assumed temporary command of the battlegroup.[175] The three battalions of the *334. I.D.* arrived on **6 October** and the *1./Pz.Jg.Abt. 334* the next day.[176] The formations that arrived for the *Kampfgruppe* were generally combat-ready, but this was not the case for the *III./755* and the *III./AR 334*, as about half their horses were ill. The *1./Pz.Jg.Abt. 334* could not be used, because it was a cadre unit with no equipment.[177]

Most of the elements from the **September** orders were listed on the order of battle of **1 November 1943**.[178] It was not until **9 November** that *AOK 7* informed the *XXV. A.K.* that *KG Bretagne* would be assigned the headquarters of the *328. I.D.* In addition, the battlegroup was to receive other elements from the division. These included the headquarters and headquarters companies of two infantry regiments, two infantry battalion headquarters, the headquarters and headquarters battery of the artillery regiment, a headquarters for the 3rd Battalion of the artillery regiment and headquarters for the AT and engineer battalions. The numerical designations of the three infantry regiments were also announced: *GR 941*, *GR 942* and *GR 943*. The other elements would simply use the divisional number.[179]

Effective **21 November**, *KG Bretagne* was redesignated as the *353. I.D.*[180] The same day, elements from the *328. I.D.* began their transfer from the east, arriving in Bretagne in early **December**. *Gen.Maj.* Mahlmann, transferred from the *39. I.D.* and arrived on **1 December**, while the *328. I.D.* divisional headquarters followed the next day.[181] On **4 December**, they relieved *Arko 115* of command of the division.[182]

The headquarters and headquarters company of *GR 548* and *Nachr.Abt. 328* also arrived on **2 December**, and the headquarters and headquarters company of *GR 569* joined them the next day.[183] A large number of headquarters reached the division on **6 December**. Among them were those of the *III./569*, *AR 328*, the *III./AR 328*, *Pi.Btl. 328* and *Pz.Jg.Abt. 328*, although the latter headquarters was later disbanded.[184] Other headquarters were provided by the *306. I.D.*, which had absorbed the dissolved *328. I.D.* in November. This included the headquarters and headquarters company of *GR 581* and the *I.* and the *II./581*. These three headquarters arrived on **20 December**.[185]

In the months leading up to D-Day, the *353. I.D.*, originally a collection of elements from the *306.*, the *328.*, the *334.* and the *371. I.D.* (and several newly raised formations), developed into a proper division. The division's deployment during this period was complicated by the fact that it was not assigned a coastal defence sector. Instead, it was stationed inland, mainly to the rear of the *343. I.D.*, which occupied the tip of the Brittany Peninsula. Some elements of the *353. I.D.* already supported other forces defending the coast.

When the *3. Fj.Div.* arrived in late **February 1944**, it was also deployed near the tip of the Brittany Peninsula. To make room for both divisions, the area was divided into new sectors. The airborne division was assigned an area that roughly covered a large triangle east of Brest, including Pencran, Doualas, Courin and Lanvellec. Most of its strength (its three airborne regiments) was to be positioned along the northern boundary. These sector changes meant that most of the *353. I.D.* had to move. More importantly, the division was divided across two sectors. The first lay north of Brest and covered the area of Landivisiau - Plouvorn - Trézilidé - Lesneven - Plouvien - Gouesnou - Landerneau - Ploudiry - Locmélar. Combat formations for this sector included *GR 941* and *GR 943*, the *IV./AR 353*, *Pz.Jg.Abt. 353* and *Nachr.Abt. 353*. The divisional headquarters was established in Landivisiau, on the eastern boundary. The second sector was the southernmost area of the *343. I.D.*: Briec - Pleyben - Le Faou - Quéménéven. Elements selected to cover this region included *GR 942*, *Füs.Btl. 353* and the *I./AR 353*.[186]

Positions on D-Day

Ironically, the areas held by the combat formations on D-Day lay almost entirely outside of these two planned sectors. The troops had been gradually pulled closer to the coast. This is best illustrated by examining the individual formations and their positions at the time of the invasion.

The divisional headquarters was located at a crossroads northeast of Lampaul-Guimiliau (southeast of Landivisiau).[187] The headquarters of *Nachr. Abt. 353* was nearby at Lézarazien, while its 1st Company was 2.5 km north of Lampaul-Guimiliau and the 2nd Company 2 km west-northwest of Kermat.[188]

When the *3. Fj.Div.* started to arrive, *GR 941* was southeast of Morlaix, an area that had been reassigned to the new division. A delay for the regiment to move to Brest was anticipated, because it would take some time before the *3. Fj.Div.* would be ready to relieve the regiment. On **10 March**, the delay was expected to be 6-8 weeks.[189] By mid-**April**, however, the regiment was able to take up positions in an arc around Brest. The headquarters was located in the northern part of the city, while the headquarters company and the 13th and 14th Companies were likewise in *Festung Brest*. The 1st Battalion was spread over an area east and northeast of the city; its headquarters was at Kerouhant and its 1st through 4th Companies were at Créac'h Burguy, Keroumen, Kergroas and the crossroads 700 metres northwest of Lambézellec, respectively. The 2nd Battalion was in position west and northwest of the city, with its headquarters at Fort du Questel; the battalion's 5th Company was at La Trinité (west of Brest), the 6th at Fort de Penfeld, the 7th at St. Pierre-Quilbignon (west of Brest) and the 8th at the northern outskirts of Brest.[190]

GR 942 was in the sector south of the *3. Fj.Div.* Like the other regiments, it had moved closer to the coast; it was positioned in the southernmost sector of the *343. I.D.*, roughly between the Baie de Douarnenez and Châteaulin. On **10 May**, the headquarters, headquarters company and the 14th Company were moved west of Châteaulin.[191] The 13th Company was about 12 km to the southwest, at Lanzent.[192] The 1st Battalion also moved during **May**, but it stayed in the area around Plonévez-Porzay; on **10 May**, its headquarters moved to Locronan.[193] A week earlier, the 2nd Company had relocated to Coz Quinguis and the 4th Company to Landerrien;[194] the 1st and 3rd Companies remained in the positions they had occupied on **12 April** (Cosquer and Kervelguet).[195] The same day, the 2nd Battalion took up new positions around the Ménez Hom, a large hill north of Plomodiern; on **7 May**, the battalion headquarters moved 2 km northeast of Plomodiern, but its four companies remained in place:[196] The 5th Company was in Cosquer, the 6th 6 km northwest of Châteaulin; the 7th 3 km northeast of Trégarvan and the 8th in Liaven.[197]

GR 943 conducted a major movement shortly before the invasion. On **14 May**, the corps ordered the regiment to move to the coast to reinforce *KVG Lesneven* by taking up positions to the left of *Füs.Btl. 353*.[198] On **23 May**, new locations were reported for the entire regiment. The command post was in Le Lescoat (today Manoir du Lescoat) and the headquarters company at Lanarvily. The 13th Company was in Lampaul-Ploudalmézeau and the 14th in Kernilis. The 1st Battalion headquarters was in Cosquer, and its four companies (1st through 4th) in Keriber, Kerhabo, Keremma and Kervaro, respectively. The 2nd Battalion was in the Lannilis area with its headquarters in Fontaine Rouge. Three of its companies were around Lannilis. The 5th Company command post was 1.5 km to the south-southeast; the 6th 2.8 km to the southwest and the 7th 2 km to the southeast. The 8th Company was 600 metres southeast of Lampaul-Ploudalmézeau.[199]

With the arrival of the *3. Fj.Div.*, *Füs.Btl. (A.A.) 353* was moved to the division's southern sector. In late **March**, it was ordered to relieve *Ost-Radf. Abt. 285* around Goulven on the north coast of Bretagne.[200] On **2-3 April**, the battalion moved from Châteaulin to Tréflez (*343. I.D.* sector) and relieved *Ost-Radf.Abt. 285* on the morning of **4 April**.[201] The fusilier battalion headquarters was at Plounévez-Lochrist along with the 4th (Heavy) Troop. The 1st Troop was at Resistance Nest Avenal 500 (*Wn.Av.500*) and the 2nd at Resistance Nest Caesar (*Wn. Cäsar*) (400 metres northeast of Plouider); the 3rd was in Keriber.[202] Troopers of the units provided details about locations at the time of the invasion. The headquarters and the 4th (Heavy) Troop were still at Plounévez-Lochrist, although the combat sections of the latter troop were spread among the squadron's other troops; each of those units had received two heavy MG sections and two mortars. The command post of the 2nd Troop was on the hill west of Tréflez and that of the 3rd on the high ground south-southeast of Plouider. The location of the command post of the 1st Troop was not specified, but it was in the area between Plounévez-Lochrist and Plouescat.[203]

Since the division was split up, it is no surprise that *AR 353* was also distributed among other divisions. In **February**, two battalions (1st and 4th) were still not yet ready; when their formation and training were completed, they would be deployed in the field (*feldmäßig*) to reinforce the coastal defences. The *XXV. A.K.* planned to use one of these battalions around Plouescat and the other around Cast.[204] By **25 February**, the regimental headquarters and headquarters battery had moved from Landivisiau to Plouvorn.[205] On **4 May**, the headquarters relocated to Château les Isles (2.5 km north of Lesneven).[206] The regimental headquarters supported the *343. I.D.* rather than its own division; on **24 April**, it was tactically attached in direct support of the *343. I.D.* and took command of *Artillerie-Gruppe Goulven*. At its disposal were the *III./AR 343*, the *IV./AR 353* and the *1./H.K.A.A. 1161*.[207]

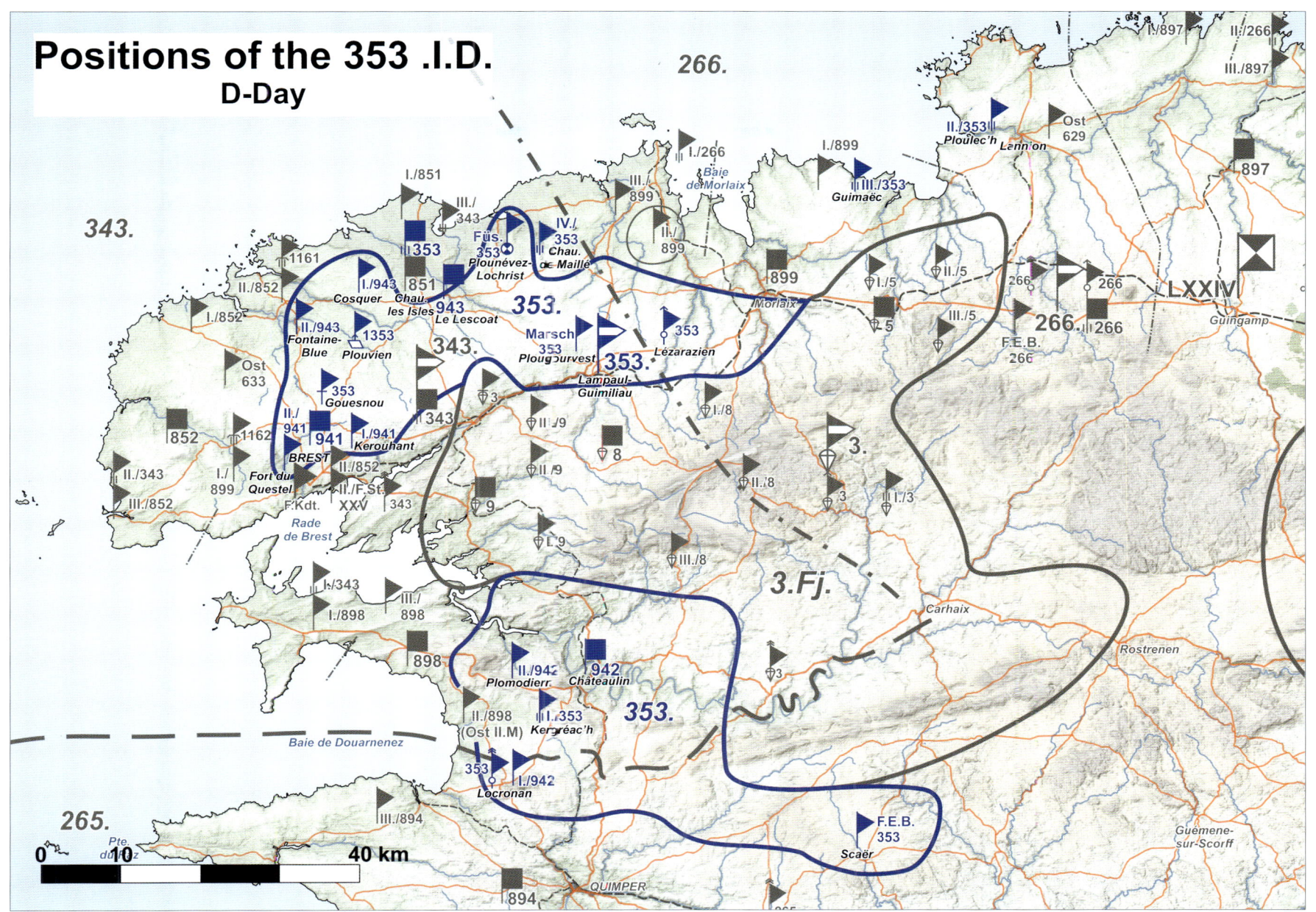

The arrival of the 3.Fj.Div. cut the 353.I.D.'s area into two separate sectors. Its main force was located northeast of Brest. The remaining reinforced infantry regiment provided depth to the defenses of the Baie de Douarnenez. Two artillery battalions were well away from the division, supporting the 266. I.D. on the north coast of Bretagne.

The first two battalions ready for action (*II.* and *III./AR 353*) did not directly support their own division, either. In early **February**, both were transferred to the sector of the *266. I.D. (LXXIV. A.K.)* and remained there until D-Day. The 2nd Battalion was near the coast west of Lannion. The headquarters was at Ploulec'h, the 6th Battery at Ploumilliau, the 5th in Servel and the 4th in Pleumeur-Bodou.[208] The 3rd Battalion was further to the southwest, in the area northeast of Morlaix. The headquarters was fairly close to the coast at Guimaëc, the 7th Battery in Lanmeur, the 8th in Plouégat-Guérand and the 9th in Plouezoc'h, where it could cover the Baie de Morlaix.[209] The 2nd Battalion was moved on **29 May**, but it remained in the same general area. The 4th Battery was 2.5 km east-southeast of Pleumeur-Bodou, the 5th 1.5 km north-northwest of Servel, and the 6th 1 km north-northeast of Ploumilliau. New locations were also reported for the 3rd Battalion: The 7th Battery 2.7 km east of Lanmeur, the 8th 1.5 km northwest of Guimaëc, and the 9th 3 km north-northeast of Plouezoc'h.[210]

Following their formation, the 1st and 4th Battalions were finally deployed in **March**. At the start of the month, the 1st Battalion was sent to the area west of Cast, the southernmost sector of the *343. I.D.*, where it was deployed to defend the Baie de Douarnenez. At the same time, the 4th Battalion was transferred to the Plouescat area, on the north coast of Bretagne. (This sector also belonged to the *343. I.D.*)[211] As noted, it operated as part of *Artillerie-Gruppe Goulven* under the headquarters of *AR 353*. In **March**, there were a number of moves for both battalions. On **14 March**, the final positions for the entire 4th Battalion were reported. The headquarters had its command post in the Château de Maillé (south of Plouescat), while the 10th Battery was 1 km east of Plounévez-Lochrist. The remaining two batteries were in position east of the headquarters, 4.5 km south and 3.5 km southeast of Plouescat. The same day, the headquarters of the 1st Battalion moved to Kergréac'h (east of Ploéven).[212] On the **23rd**, all three of its batteries were reported to have occupied new positions, about 1-2 km west of their previous locations: The 1st Battery was east of Plomodiern, the 2nd east of Ploéven,, and the 3rd east of Plonévez-Porzay.[213]

Pi.Btl. 353 also spent time subordinated to other divisions. In **February**, it was transferred to the northern coast of Bretagne (*KVA "A2"*) under the *LXXIV. A.K.*[214] The battalion headquarters was in Le Vieux-Marché (east of Plouaret) with its three companies in Morlaix, Tréguier and Étables.[215] On **10 March**, the 3rd Company was moved to Lourgat.[216] On **18 May**, the battalion rejoined the division, arriving in the area of Châteaulin.[217] The headquarters was located at St. Coulitz, the 1st Company at Pont-de-Buis, the 2nd at Cast and the 3rd at Port Launay.[218] By **19 May**, the decision was made to subordinate the battalion to two other divisions; the headquarters and two companies were placed under the *265. I.D.* and one company under the *343. I.D.* The companies attached to the *265. I.D.* were to work on the construction of the coastal defences west of Quimper. The company under the *343. I.D.* was to build air-landing obstacles and lay minefields in the Ménez Hom area; it would also take part in the construction of beach obstacles in the Douarnenez Bight.[219] It took some time for the battalion to leave Châteaulin, with its units reportedly arriving in their new sectors on **26-27 May**.[220] On **27 May**, the new positions were reported. The headquarters was at Locronan, the 2nd Company at Kerlaz and the 3rd at Pont-Croix. The 1st Company had arrived in the sector of the *343. I.D.* on **26 May** and was located in Trégarvan.[221]

When the *3. Fj.Div.* arrived in late **February**, *Pz.Jäg.Abt. 353* was moved to make room for the new division. Hitherto, the battalion was in the area northwest of Huelgoat, while the battalion headquarters had been forming at Scrignac since **19 January**.[222] On **31 January**, the headquarters moved to La Feuillée (northwest Huelgoat) and, on **26 February**, to Gouesnou (northwest of the Brest airfield), where it remained until D-Day.[223] The 1st Company only conducted one significant relocation: From Berrien to Plabennec on **26 February**.[224] On **31 January**, the 2nd Company arrived in Scrignac, apparently taking over the billets from the battalion headquarters.[225] The company moved to Plouvien on **27 February**.[226] The 3rd Company had arrived as a complete unit on **23 February** and was sent to Brennilis;[227] three days later, it was split up — into platoons it appears — and sent to St. Thégonnec, Landivisiau, and Plabennec.[228] Its command post was in Plabennec as well.[229] The company was transferred to Landerneau and reported to be combat-ready on **2 May**.[230]

Few reports are available on *F.E.B. 353*. On **28 February**, it moved near Scaër (*265. I.D.*); the headquarters and the 4th and 5th Companies moved into the town itself. The new positions of the 1st Company were in Tourch, while the 2nd was in Coray and the 3rd in Guiscriff.[231] Prisoners from the battalion confirm the locations of the 3rd and 4th Companies and link the headquarters to a Château on the road between Guiscriff and Scaër.[232]

On **19 May**, the headquarters of *Marschbtl. 353* was in Plougourvest, with the 2nd Company in Plougar;[233] The 1st Company assembled a week later in Plougourvest.[234]

Combat

In the first hours of D-Day, the division was notified that Alert Level II (*Alarmstufe II*) had been declared, which initially had few consequences.[235] Shortly after 09:00, *AOK 7* issued new orders to the *XXV. A.K.*: *Kampfgruppe 275* and *265* were to prepare for action. The priority was with the AT units of the two divisions and the *353. I.D. Pz.Jg.Abt. 353* would be sent forward when the time came.[236] The division reported that the *1./Pz.Jg.Abt. 353* was prepared to move, but the rest of the division would need up to 10 hours to get moving after receiving its orders. Indeed, the division required orders as soon as possible, since current deployments needed to be cancelled and the engineer battalion, artillery battalions and the fusilier battalion would have to first be returned to the division.[237]

Later that morning, most of the division was ready to move. Exceptions were the artillery and engineers, as well as companies of both *GR 942* and *943*, which were digging trenches in the area of the *343. I.D.*[238] At 13:00, the *XXV. A.K.* ordered *Pi.Btl. 353* to return to its division. It was to assemble in the area of Pont-de-Buis - Châteaulin. The *265.* and the *343. I.D.* were to dispatch elements of the battalion to that area as rapidly as possible.[239] By 14:30, the battalion was en route to the assembly area and its headquarters had already arrived at Pont-de-Buis. Although, the last company was expected to arrive around midnight, a small detachment on the Île-de-Sein could not be picked up because water transportation had been forbidden.[240]

7 June was a relatively quiet day for the division. At 19:10, the *XXV. A.K.* informed the *265.* and the *353. I.D.* that *Pz.Jg.Abt. 353* would be attached to *Kampfgruppe 265*. The AT battalion would be sent to the battlegroup by rail towards St. Lô.[241]

At 18:55 on **8 June**, the *353. I.D.* reported the latest developments to the corps. The *3./943* and an ad hoc company of *GR 942* had again been returned to the division after their deployment under the *343. I.D. Pz.Jg.Abt. 353* had assembled around Landerneau and was ready to be loaded on the trains. *Stu.Gesch.Abt. 1353* (the official designation of the *2./Pz.Jg.Abt. 353*) and a platoon from the 3rd Company had already started loading. *F.E.B. 353* was planning to start moving to its new area, the Monts-d'Arrée, that evening.[242]

At midnight, the division reported that *Pi.Btl. 353* had arrived in its entirety south of Pont-de-Buis during the day. The movement of *F.E.B. 353* had started at 22:00 and it was expected to reach Plonévez-du-Faou early on **9 June**; the battalion was projected to arrive at the Monts-d'Arrée on the morning of **10 June**. Meanwhile, the first train transporting *Pz.Jg.Abt. 353* departed at 23:20.[243]

At 15:48 on **9 June**, the division updated the corps on the status of *Pz.Jg.Abt. 353*: The first train had reached St. Brieuc and would continue on to Normandy at 23:00. A second train was loaded and had been ready to move since 14:00, but it was still missing its locomotive. The third train had not yet arrived and was still in Morlaix.[244] On the night of **9-10 June**, the last two trains carrying *Pz.Jg.Abt. 353* departed.[245] The first train unloaded on **10 June** at L'Hermitage, only halfway to the front. The other two trains, hindered by air attacks on the railroad network, halted around Plouigneau and Plouaret.[246] The next day, air attacks and sabotage again disrupted movements of the two trains still underway. On **12 June**, they eventually made it to Dinan and Landébia, where they were unloaded, the men and vehicles continuing their advance to the front by road.[247]

Is not clear when the battalion joined *KG 265*, but elements were in place to engage the 82nd Airborne Division at Prétot on **20 June**.[248] It seems the battalion rejoined the division near Périers a few days later. This might explain why it was not listed as part of *KG 265* or *Gruppe König* on **23 June**.[249]

The rest of the division began its move to Normandy a few days after the departure of the battalion. On the evening of **9 June**, *AOK 7* informed the corps and the division that it (the division) should prepare for deployment on the Cotentin Peninsula. Detailed orders would follow.[250] Later that evening, the *XXV. A.K.* petitioned *AOK 7* to keep *F.E.B. 353* in Bretagne, because it was needed to secure the Monts-d'Arrée and engage in anti-partisan operations.[251]

By 07:00 on **10 June**, *F.E.B. 353* had arrived at the Monts-d'Arrée. In other sectors, *GR 941*, *GR 943* and the fusilier battalion had assembled their forces.[252] Because time was of the essence, the corps proposed to transfer the division by road instead of rail. The bicycle units and heavy weapons (motorised) would be sent ahead. These more mobile elements were *GR 943*, *Füs.Btl. 353* and the headquarters and one company from the engineer battalion. The rest of division would move on foot. To expedite the transfer, any transport returning from bringing *Kampfgruppe 265* to Normandy could be used for the division.²⁵³

Late that afternoon, *AOK 7* issued orders for the immediate transfer of the division to Normandy, *F.E.B. 353* included. The division would be attached to the *II. Fs.K.* and assemble southwest of St. Lô. In line with the proposal of the *XXV. A.K.*, the bicycle elements would move ahead. The foot elements, depending on the situation, might receive motor transport, if it became available.²⁵⁴

The division itself received formal orders to move to Normandy early in the evening.²⁵⁵ In preparation for the transfer, a number of changes were made in the sector of the *XXV. A.K.* The 6., the 8. and the 13./943 left the *343. I.D.* and rejoined their parent division. In similar fashion, *Pi.Btl. 353* was returned to the division, and its 1ˢᵗ and 2ⁿᵈ Companies attached to *GR 942*, most likely for geographic reasons. The battalion headquarters and the 3ʳᵈ Company assembled near Lampaul-Ploudalmézeau and were attached to *GR 943* for the move to Normandy. The regiment's infantry battalions were readied for action, as were those of *GR 941* and the fusilier battalion. To protect the *IV./AR 353* on its march to the front, the *1./941* was moved to Château de Maillé.²⁵⁶

The division was ordered to follow prepared routes and bypass Avranches to the east. Troops were only to march after dark and use secondary roads. The transfer was to be conducted with all possible speed and daily objectives absolutely had to be reached.²⁵⁷ According to *Gen.* Mahlmann, priority was likewise given to seeking cover during daylight.²⁵⁸ The orders also stated that the division was to contact the corps several times a day to make it possible to bring up motor transport for the foot troops.²⁵⁹

The division was organised into seven march groups: A and C-H. The composition of these groups has been recorded: Column A with the *II.* and *III./AR 353* and two troops of *Füs.Btl. 353*; Column C with *GR 943*, *Füs. Btl. 353 (-)* and the headquarters and the *3./Pi.Btl. 353*; Column D with the *IV./AR 353* and one company of *GR 941*; Column E with *GR 941 (-)*, the headquarters battery of *AR 353*, the 2. and the *3./Fahrschwadron 353*, *Nachschub-Kompanie 353*, horse-drawn elements of *Nachr.Abt. 353*, *GR 943* and *Füs.Btl. 353*; Column F with *GR 942*, the *I./AR 353*, the 1. and *2./Pi.Btl. 353*, the *1. Sanitäts-Kompanie 353*; Column G with the headquarters of the division's logistics command, the *2. Sanitäts-Kompanie 353*, *Krankenkraftwagen-Kompanie 353 (-)* and the *Werkstatt-Kompanie 353*; and finally Column H with *F.E.B. 353*, the divisional headquarters (-), *Feldgendarmerie-Trupp 353*

and the signals battalion (-).²⁶⁰ There was no March Group B, but this serial had probably been planned for *Pz.Jg.Abt. 353*. The remaining supply troops would move on their own, depending on their intended employment. The divisional headquarters would be in Quentin from early on the **12ᵗʰ** until the evening of the **13ᵗʰ**. The next day it would move to Combourg.²⁶¹

On the second or third day of the march, the *II. Fs.K.* ordered the division to be brought up with extreme urgency. This meant moving by day despite the risks. *Gen.* Mahlmann ordered the march groups to spread out further and march eight hours on, eight hours off.²⁶²

In Bretagne, the division's transfer seriously weakened the areas where it had been located. For one, *GR 941* and *943* had departed the coastal sector held by the *343. I.D.*²⁶³ In response, *AOK 7* ordered the *XXV. A.K.* to immediately transfer the *2. Fj.Div.* to the sectors previously held by the division.²⁶⁴

Limited information is available regarding the beginning the division's journey to the front. Generally, the formations managed to reach their daily objectives between **11-13 June**.²⁶⁵ An exception was the *IV./AR 353*, which experienced delays on **11 June**.²⁶⁶ The next day, the division's advance elements reached the area southeast of St. Brieuc.²⁶⁷ On the **13ᵗʰ**, the mobile *Kampfgruppe* was reported 30 km northwest of Rennes.²⁶⁸ The division continued to make good progress on **14 June**, once again attaining its daily objectives, the battlegroup reaching a point 13 km west of Fougères. The other groups were coming up from southwest of Jugon - Quintin – Gurunhuel.²⁶⁹

The division's deployment was a point of contention. *AOK 7* was concerned about the condition of the *352. I.D.* It was now badly weakened and would be unable to defend against serious enemy attacks; hence, *AOK 7* requested permission from *Heeresgruppe B* to commit the *353. I.D.* to relieve the *352. I.D.* in the sector of the *II. Fs.K.* Yet, the *LXXXIV. A.K.* emphasised that the situation in its own area would deteriorate without the division; the corps wanted to commit it in the sector of the *709. I.D.* The *7. Armee*'s rebuttal, however, was that it had to consider the situation along the entire front.²⁷⁰

By the next morning, *AOK 7* had reevaluated its position and was now prepared to dispatch the *353. I.D.* to the *LXXXIV. A.K.*, but the field army's decision first needed the approval of *Heeresgruppe B*, which had planned using the division elsewhere. For his part, *Gen.* Dollmann (commander-in-chief of the *7. Armee*) was now convinced the division was needed to reinforce the corps, which was stretched to the breaking point, while the *352. I.D.* was a shell of its former self and in need of withdrawal from the front. Thus, *AOK 7* requested that *Heeresgruppe B* transfer the *353. I.D.* to the *LXXXIV. A.K.* and replace the *352. I.D.* with another infantry division.[271] As sound as this plan was, the lack of reinforcements ultimately forced the *7. Armee* to reconsider. The front northeast of St. Lô, defended by the battered *352. I.D.*, was deemed to be the weakest point of the field army's defences.[272] After D-Day, the division's front stretched from east of Carentan to east of St. Lô. During the fighting, it was initially reinforced by *Schnelle Brigade 30* on the right flank and later by *Kampfgruppe 275* (Heintz) on the left flank (west of the Vire River). The *17. SS-Pz.Gren.Div.* "Götz von Berlichingen" and the *3. Fj.Div.* were committed on the left (*17.*) and right (*3.*) of the reinforced division, reducing its defensive front. The weak *352. I.D.* remained responsible for the front around St. Lô.[273] Yet an American breakthrough at St. Lô was the worst possible scenario for the German defenders, for it could result in cutting off and isolating the Cotentin Peninsula and the entire western region of Normandy. Holding the southwest corner of the Calvados front was thus of vital significance for the defence of the Cotentin, too. For this reason, *AOK 7* decided that the *353. I.D.* was most urgently needed at St. Lô after all. To secure the Cotentin, *Gruppe Hellmich* would need to provide the forces himself, as there were no reinforcements available from other sectors.[274]

While the corps, *AOK 7* and *Heeresgruppe B* were busy deciding how to commit the *353. I.D.*, the division continued its march to Normandy. March Group D reached its objective, but some of the others were delayed. March Group E was near Cohiniac, F near Plémy, G near Pleyber-Christ and H near Bourbirac. No reports are available for March Group A.[275] March Group C, the mobile battlegroup, reached an area west of Sourdeval. It would resume its advance after dark from there; it was expected to reach the deployment area east of St. Lô early on **16 June**. Around the same time, the division's foot elements reached Jugon and Quessoy.[276]

On **16 June**, the divisional headquarters was established at the base of the Cotentin, near Millières, west of Périers.[277] Later that morning, *AOK 7* informed the *LXXXIV. A.K.* that the recently arrived mobile regiment could be sent to Montmartin-en-Graignes to support the front. The corps was to keep in mind that, when the whole division had arrived, it would be at the disposal of *Heeresgruppe B*.[278]

Shortly thereafter, *AOK 7* was contacted by *Heeresgruppe B*. As Hitler had forbidden a withdrawal to Cherbourg, the situation for the *LXXXIV. A.K.* became serious; as a result, *Heeresgruppe B* agreed to commit the division with the corps.[279] The *7. Armee* immediately informed the corps that the division had been put at its disposal and could be employed on the *Nordfront*. Yet the corps was now acutely aware this would still not prevent the impending collapse of the front. Even the mobile element in the division, *KG Boehm*, were unavailable to shore up the *Nordfront*. In the early afternoon, they stood at La Luzerne (northeast of St. Lô) in the sector of the *II. Fs.K.* Here, east of St. Lô, there was heavy fighting in the area of the *3. Fj.D.*, which still had not yet fully arrived. North of the town, the battered *352. I.D.* was also under heavy pressure and close to collapse. *KG Boehm* — headquarters and heavy weapons companies of *GR 943*, the *II./943* (*Maj.* Moll), *Füs.Btl. 353* and the *3./Pi.Btl. 353* — was ordered to counterattack and restore the situation.[280] According to *Obstlt.* Ziegelmann, the operations officer of the *352. I.D.*, *Obst.* Boehm arrived at the divisional headquarters around 16:00, but the *Kampfgruppe* did not arrive in full until late that evening. Boehm was instructed to assemble his forces, after dark, for a counterattack towards Villiers-Fossard. The objective was simple: Recapture as much ground to the north as possible.[281]

The original after-action report from the division, however, paints a different picture. At 19:00 on the **16th**, American forces attacked east of the main Moon-sur-Elle - St. Lô road (D6). Supported by tanks, they took the Bois de Bretel. To stop their advance, the *II./943*, reinforced by the remnants of *F.E.B. 352*, established a front from St. André-de-l'Épine to the crossroads at La Forge. Another threat developed further to the northwest, where the Americans crossed the D6 at Le Repas, heading west towards Villiers-Fossard. *Füs.Btl. 353* was brought up from the area of Les Romains and, at 20:00, counterattacked towards Villiers-Fossard. The town was secured and the situation was back under control by 22:00. *Obst.* Boehm was now given responsibility for the right wing of the *352. I.D.* front. The division's centre was held by *GR 916* (*Obst.* Goth); the situation on the left wing was more worrisome, but that night two companies from the *17. SS-Pz.Gren.Div.* were brought up to help stabilise the situation.[282]

While the mobile elements of the *353. I.D.* had now arrived northeast of St. Lô, most of the division was still in Bretagne. Artillery elements, most likely March Group A, had reached the area south of Pontorson, while the bulk of the division had reached the area of Lamballe (excl.) - Quessoy - Montcontour

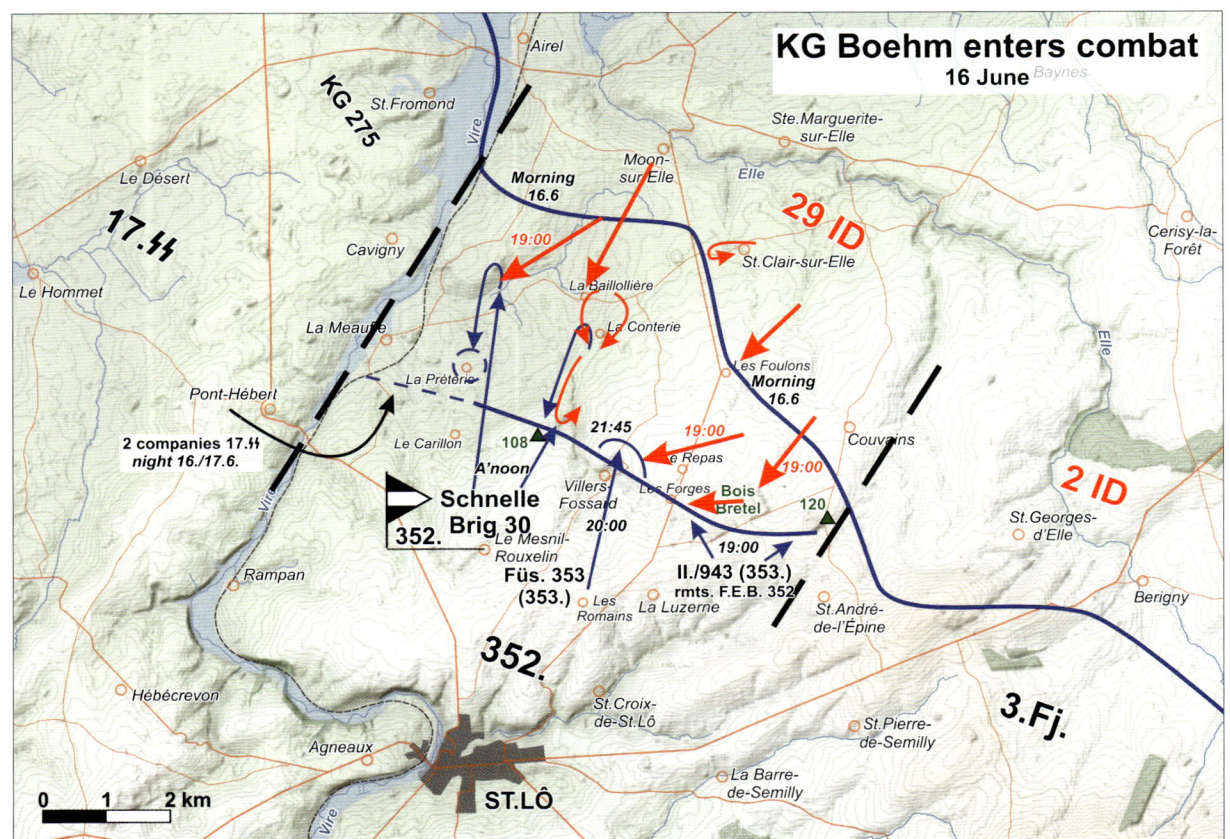

KG Boehm entered the fighting on the evening of 16 June when the battered 352.I.D. was under heavy pressure. The arrival of the battlegroup helped to stabilise the front, which remained mostly stationary until the American launched a new offensive on 7 July.

- west of Merdrignac - southwest Jugon.[283] March Groups A, D and H had reached their daily objectives; March Group E was near Bréhand, F near Caulnes and G near Pleyber-Christ.[284]

Ziegelmann's post-war account states that the counterattack by *KG 353* only began at 06:00 on **17 June** — rather than during the evening of the **16th** — and gained significant ground;[285] yet, the day's after-action report does not support this. Instead, the **17th** was spent in defence against numerous American attacks. Beginning at 12:00, *KG Boehm* repulsed some seven attacks.[286] By 14:30, the *LXXXIV. A.K.* reported that the American advance towards St. Lô had been stopped. In the course of the day, the German main line of resistance north-northeast of St. Lô, along the line St. André-de-l'Épine - Villiers-Fossard -

La Meauffe, was re-established and the battlegroup's timely arrival was recognised as the main reason for the defensive successes.[287] *AOK 7* now intended to deploy the entire *353. I.D.* in the sector when it arrived.[288]

Behind the front, March groups D, E and H reached their daily objectives. The artillery arrived in the area south of Avranches. Two groups were near Combourg, and a third east of Jugon (March Group F). No data is available for Groups A and G.[289]

On **18 June**, the intended commitment of *353. I.D.* changed again. Dollmann instructed the *LXXXIV. A.K.* not to commit too much at the front east of St. Lô. The division had to be kept together.[290] The assembly area was the area around Périers, where the division was to prepare to counterattack to the east and northeast. If possible, the battlegroup at St. Lô was to be relieved as well.[291]

Four march groups were reported in the areas of Avranches, St. James, south of Antrain and Combourg. *F.E.B. 353* (March Group H) was further west, around Jugon.[292]

On **19 June**, the march groups moved to Villedieu-les-Poêles, Avranches and Pontorson, while the field-replacement battalion was southeast of Dinan.[293] The next day, most of the division had arrived in the St. Lô area. Only the field-replacement battalion was still in Bretagne, moving up from Combourg.[294] On **21 June**, the bulk of the division moved to its deployment area on the Cotentin while the field-replacement battalion reached St. James.[295] The next day, the battalion was northeast of Avranches, and it reached the area southeast of Coutances on **23 June**.[296] It finally rejoined the division on **24 June**, completing the transfer to Normandy.[297]

The division's move to the front had resulted in losses of both men and matériel from ground and air attacks. Yet despite moving by day, these losses were relatively minor. *Gen.* Mahlmann attributed this to marching in groups with adequate distancing and moving through terrain that largely prevented aerial observation. Among the more serious equipment losses were two guns of a heavy infantry-gun platoon, possibly the *13./942*. Personnel losses included the commander of *Füs.Btl. 353*, *Rittmeister* Theuerkauf, who was wounded in an air attack.[298]

On **17** and **18 June**, the American breakthrough to the west coast of the Cotentin Peninsula breached the German lines, not only towards Cherbourg but also towards the south. In the following days, *AOK 7* and the *LXXXIV. A.K.* took measures to re-establish the *Nordfront*.[299] Early on the **19th**, the Germans decided to strengthen the base of the Cotentin by bringing up the *353. I.D.* and reorganising forces already in the area (*Gruppe König*).[300] The division would be deployed along a second defence line, which has already been introduced by this author as the *Waldbergstellung* or *Mahlmann-Linie*. The line stretched from the northwest corner of the Praires Marécageuses de Gorges (Le Plessis), via the Forêt de Mont-Castre, to St. Germain-sur-Ay. Additionally, a blocking position would be established, stretching northwest from the Praires Marécageuses de Gorges (Le Plessis) to Hill 131. These lines would cover the high ground north of the La Haye-du-Puits - Lithaire road, run past La-Haye-du-Puits, then run southwest along the high ground to St. Germain-sur-Ay. *Gen.* von Choltitz

(commanding general of the *LXXXIV. A.K.*) described a slightly different route, which matches the *AOK 7* situation maps. According to him, the line followed the route: La Rivière on the northern edge of the Baupte Marshland - southern edge of St. Jores - southern edge of Ste. Suzanne - northern edge of La Poterie - Hill 95 (northeast of La Haye-du-Puits) - northern edge of La Haye-du-Puits - southwest to the northern edge of Montgardon - northern edge of La Graverie - Bretteville-sur-Ay (on the coast). The dominating Mont-Castre was also incorporated into the defence, providing depth and artillery observation posts. The centre of gravity would lay on the right wing, where the D24 offered the most direct route to Périers. The *353. I.D.* would be used to defend the right wing, while the *77. I.D.* covered the left wing. The boundary between the two divisions ran west of La Haye-du-Puits, from Bolleville (*353. I.D.*) to Biémont (*77. I.D.*). If under too much pressure, the forward defensive line, held by *Gruppe König* with the *243. I.D.* on the left and the *91. LL.D.* on the right, could be pulled back to the *Mahlmann-Linie*.[301]

On **19-20 June**, US forces advanced in the Prétot - Bois de Limors sector. Here, in the sector of *U.Gr. Eitner*, the fighting continued on **20 June**. At 09:00, the *LXXXIV. A.K.* reported renewed attacks against the right wing of the *Nordfront*. Prétot had already been captured by the Americans (3/508th PIR, 82 AB) and it would be difficult to restore the situation as reserves were non-existent. The front around the town was held only by elements from the *353. I.D.*, with the headquarters and a company of *Pi.Btl. 353*, a number of assault guns and two platoons of *Pz.Jg.Abt. 353*.[302] *AOK 7* ordered the lines to be held at all cost and directed the corps to bring up *Ost-Btl. Huber* and the *353. I.D.*[303]

Faced by the advancing Americans, elements of the division were deployed in the second line as soon as they arrived. The first arriving units were committed on the line Le Plessis - Mont-Castre on the **20th**, while the next group to arrive was sent to the Montgardon Ridge.[304] *GR 941* was positioned on the division's left flank while *GR 942* held the right flank down to the Praires Marécageuses de Gorges.[305]

Although the division was being deployed on the *Nordfront*, *KG Boehm* was still with the *II. Fs.K.* Plans were made to return it to the division. On the **20th**, the decision was taken to commit *Kampfgruppe Kentner* (*266. I.D.*) in the sector of the *352. I.D.* around St. Lô and relieve *KG Boehm*.[306] Instead, when it arrived, the battlegroup was used to relieve *GR 914* (*352. I.D.*).[307] *AOK 7* remained determined to relieve *KG Boehm* on the St. Lô front.[308] On **25 June**, it informed

Heeresgruppe B of its intent to use *FJR 15* for this purpose.[309] OKW, however, had designated the regiment a Western Front reserve (*Ob.West Reserve*) and the *II. Fs.K.* was ordered to transfer it to the *LXXXIV. A.K.* Once again, the relief of *KG Boehm* had been stymied, and the battlegroup remained with the *352. I.D.*[310] At St. Lô, the front had nonetheless stabilised. The US V Corps had halted its offensive, after its attacks on **16-18 June** had failed to break through the German defences. Only a minor operation was carried out by the US 3rd Armored Division (3 AD) on **29** and **30 June**, aimed at eliminating the Villiers-Fossard salient, which was held by *KG Boehm*.[311] On the first day, facing repeated attacks with tank support, *Füs.Btl. 353* and the *II./943* suffered serious losses and the battlegroup was forced to give up Villiers-Fossard. A new line was established south of the town.[312] The fighting continued throughout the next day. That evening, the Americans achieved a 1 km wide and 1.5 km deep penetration before their advance could be sealed off.[313] Having accomplished its main objectives, the 3 AD halted its advance. After this, the wider St. Lô front remained stationary until **7 July**, when the US V and XIX Corps began a new offensive, which ultimately led to the fall of the town on **18 July**.[314] Throughout this period, *KG Boehm* remained with the *352. I.D.* It was not until **2-3 August** that its remnants finally made it back to the *353. I.D.*[315]

AOK 7 assessed the situation of the *LXXXIV. A.K.* on **29 June**. *Gruppe König* held a 27 km area of the front. Later that day, it was decided to disband König's battlegroup and split the front between the *243. I.D.* on the left and the *91. LL.D.* on the right (as of **1 July**). Behind this tenuous front line, the *353. I.D.* and the battered *77. I.D.* occupied a 23 km long defence line (*Mahlmann-Linie*).[316]

To free up the *17. SS-Pz.Gren.Div.* for mobile operations, *AOK 7* proposed relieving it with the *353. I.D.* and *FJR 15*. The SS division would then assemble as a field-army reserve northeast of Périers. From that location, it could counterattack to the north, northeast or east. To make this possible, the *353. I.D.* would first be relieved by the *77. I.D.* Again, priority was given to securing the right wing of the line.[317]

Corresponding orders were given that day. First, the *353. I.D.* was to be withdrawn from the line Le Plessis - St. Germain-sur-Ay (*Mahlmann-Linie*) and assemble northeast of Périers, where it was to prepare for counter-attacks to the northeast and east. The *77. I.D.* would take over the eastern stretch of the *Mahlmann-Linie*, with the centre of gravity on the Forêt de Mont-Castre.[318] According to *Gen.* Mahlmann, some elements remained on the second line: The *I./942* (*Maj.* Ibe) and artillery on the right supporting the *77. I.D.* and *Pi. Btl. 353* (*Hptm.* Pillmann); the *II./942* (*Hptm.* Rosenow) and artillery on the left. The rest of the division, less *KG Boehm*, was assembled around Périers.[319]

The extraction of the *353. I.D.* was the first step in relieving the *17. SS-Pz.*

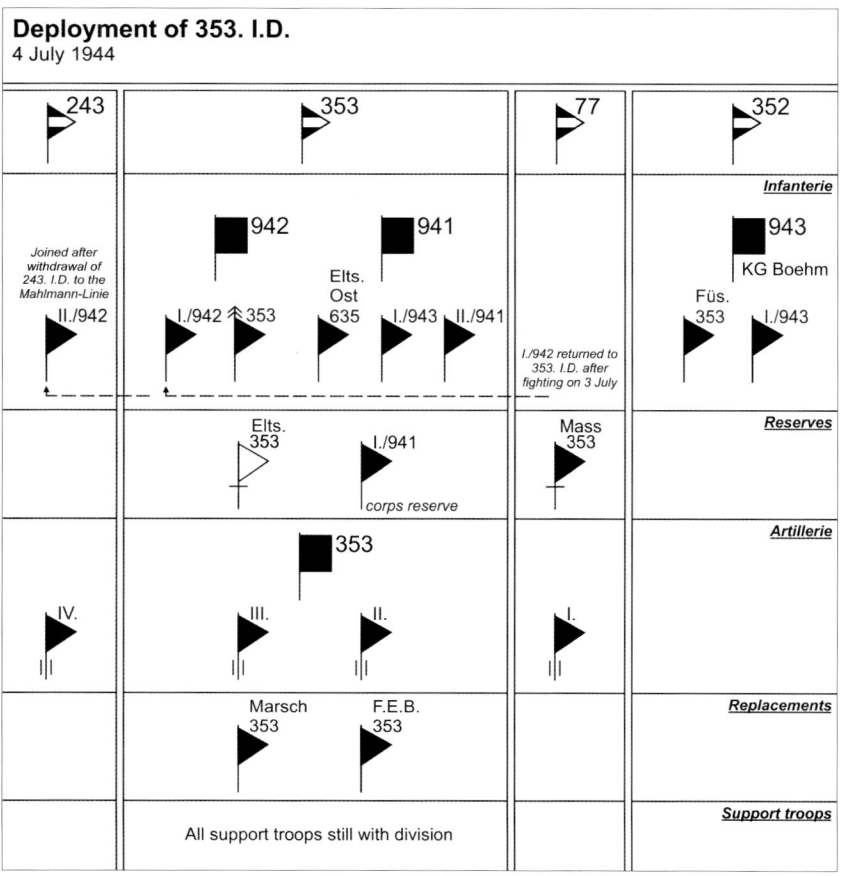

When the division entered combat on 4 July it did not do so as a complete division. KG Boehm was still in action around St.Lô and on the Nordfront several infantry and artillery battalions as well as parts of the anti-tank troops were in support of other divisions.

Gr.Div. While moving the *353. I.D.* weakened the *Nordfront*, the corps' task of holding the frontline did not change.[320] Because of its major new mission, the weakened *77. I.D.* was a high priority for replacements;[321] the division could also call on two-thirds of *Pz.Jg.Abt. 353*, with eight assault guns, six *Marders* and four 3.7 cm *Flak* to support its eastern flank. This force is said to have been located around "St. Germain", presumably St. Germain-sur-Sèves. The remainder of the battalion was either in reserve or attached to other elements.

The *I./AR 353* also supported the *77. I.D.*[322] The *I./942* held the left flank of *KG Lausberg* (*77. I.D.*), which covered the area east of the road from Ste. Suzanne along the east of the Forêt de Mont-Castre to Lastelle. The lines here ran along the Carentan - La Haye-du-Puits railway.[323]

The US VIII Corps launched its attack on the *Nordfront* on **3 July**, with three divisions abreast: 90th ID on the left (east), 82nd AB in the centre, and 79th ID on the right.[324] It soon became apparent that the front was in serious trouble; the *353. I.D.* was rushed back to the *Mahlmann-Linie* and inserted into the line between the *77. I.D.* and the *243. I.D.*[325] *Gen.* Mahlmann later estimated the division's combat strength at 4,500, not counting roughly 1,500 men in the field-replacement battalion and the replacements-transfer batatalion or the infantry and artillery attached to other divisions.[326] The *I./943* (*Maj.* Dickertmann) was hurried forward to strengthen the centre of the *Nordfront*, where *Ost-Btl. Huber* had suffered grievous losses and the ensuing counterattack by *Ost-Btl. 635* had been unsuccessful. The new battalion, however, managed to halt the American advance along the line La Champellerie – Neufmesnil.[327]

The boundary between the *77. I.D.* and the *353. I.D.* ran roughly north-south from Varenguebec to Mobecq. This put the Forêt de Mont-Castre and La Poterie in the area of operations of the *77. I.D.*, and Lithaire and the Bois de la Poterie in that of the *353. I.D.*[328] The division's left boundary ran from Lessay through Montgardon to St. Sauveur-le-Vicomte. The *I./941* was held as a corps reserve northwest of Périers. That night, the *77. I.D.* took over the area and the forces of the *91. LL.D.* The *I./942* was released from the *77. I.D.* and returned to its division, where it was deployed west of La Haye-du-Puits. The elements already committed (*I./943*, *Pi.Btl. 353*, *Pz.Jg.Abt. 353* and artillery), along with the *I./942*, were freed up to allow the employment of the division as a whole. The batalion would form a reserve with the intention of counterattacking to the east and northeast.[329]

The bulk of the *353. I.D.* went into action on **4 July**. In the divisional sector, the *I./942* held the front north of Montgardon, *Pi.Btl. 353* (still minus its 3rd Company) defended La Haye-du-Puits and the *I./943* (reinforced by *Ost-Btl. 635*) held the high ground north of the La Haye-du-Puits - Lithaire road, while the *II./941* (*Hptm.* Vogel) was northeast of Lithaire. *Pz.Jg.Abt. 353* was in reserve southwest of Mobecq, and the artillery regiment was spread from Angoville-sur-Ay to Gerville-la-Forêt. The divisional headquarters was in Renneville. To the division's left, the *II./942* and the *IV./AR 353* were attached to the *243. I.D.* It is likely that the *II./942* had supported the *243. I.D.* since before the fighting began on **3 July**, just as the *I./AR 353*, which was on the right of the *Nordfront*, had supported the *77. I.D.*[330] This left very few forces for the division itself.

Few details are available concerning the division's actions on **4 July**. It was credited with repulsing three attacks and managed to hold Hill 95 (northeast of La Haye-du-Puits).[331] For the most part, the front in its sector held firm.[332] To the east, the situation around La Poterie (*77. I.D.*) was more troublesome, because the Americans had made progress there.[333] The *77. I.D.* had sustained further setbacks, which also affected the *353. I.D.* In the sector of *KG Lausberg*, the assault guns of *Pz.Jg.Abt. 353* had suffered serious losses due to artillery fire, and they were no longer able to support the battlegroup.[334]

By **5 July**, the gap at La Poterie had still not been closed, although the Bois de la Poterie was in German hands. The day would see more bitter and costly fighting. In the sector of the *77. I.D.*, the Americans were able to push past Le Fry. The only corps reserve, the *I./941*, launched an immediate counterattack, but it was hit in the flank by an Allied attack from St. Jores and brought to a halt. Further west, US troops broke into the Bois de la Poterie, captured the forest and reached Château Brocboeufs. Here, the *II./941* was sent in for an immediate counterattack. On the division's left flank, the American troops were also advancing. The forward German positions around Bolleville were pushed back, and the attackers seized both St. Symphorien and La Haye-du-Puits; both towns, however, were recaptured by successful German counterattacks. By evening, the division's front ran from south of the Bois de la Poterie, via "Hill 34" (a point west of the Bois de Brocboeufs) and St. Symphorien to Biémont.[335] *Pi.Btl. 353* continued to defended La Haye-du-Puits against repeated enemy attacks. Not until **7 July** did American forces succeed in reaching the southern edge of the town, while isolated groups from the battalion still held out in the town.[336]

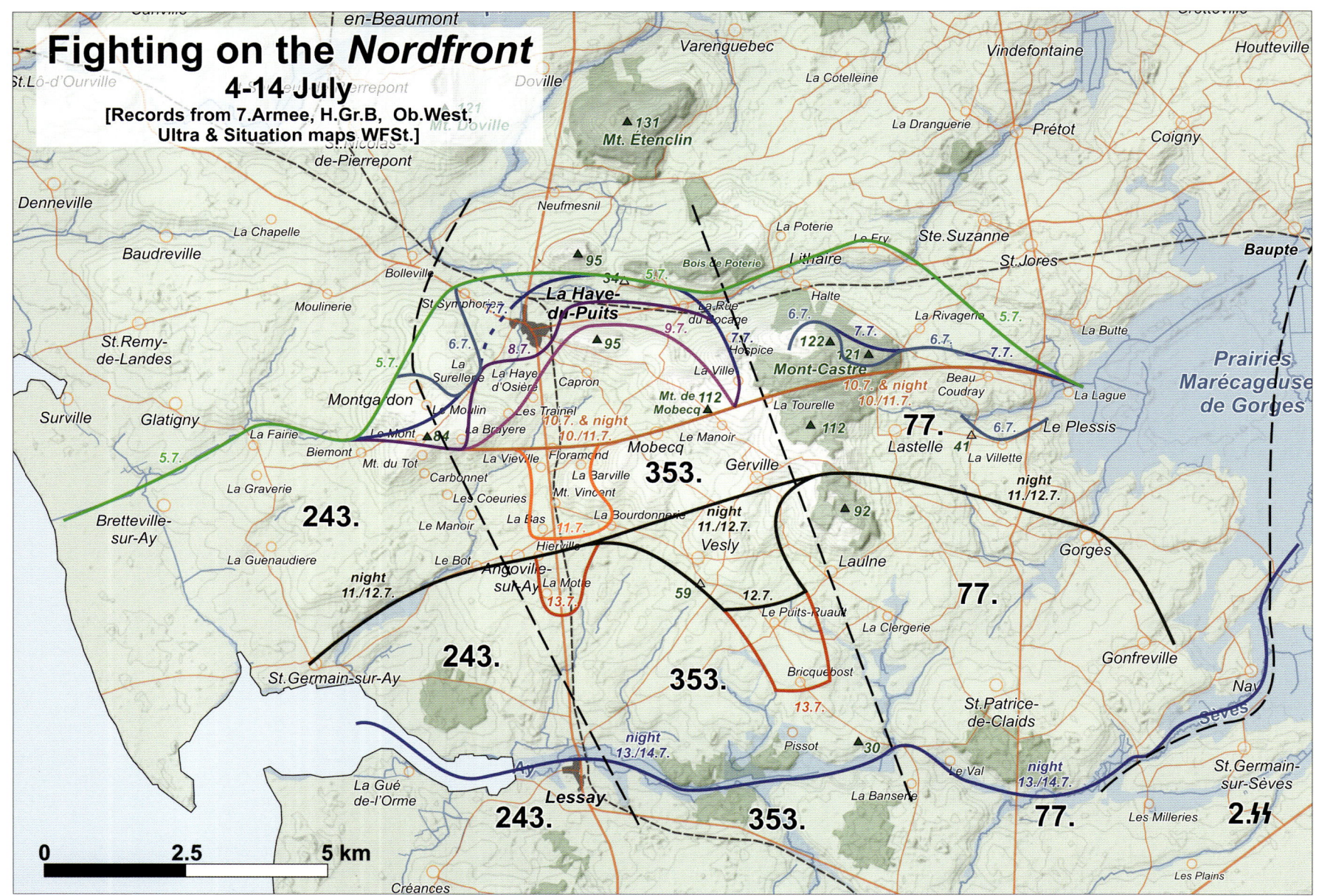

The fighting on the Nordfront was very costly for both sides, but the Americans managed to push back the German defenders. With the capture of the high ground around La Haye-du-Puits and Mont-Castre, the attackers finally broke the Mahlmannlinie. Unable to hold their ground, the German withdrawal accelerated and on the night of 13/14 July the frontline was taken back to the Wasserlinie.

Reinforcements were on their way to help restore the situation on the *Nordfront*. To the right of the division, in the area held by the *77. I.D.*, American forces had reached Mont-Castre. To address this situation, *FJR 15* was brought up and took over the left flank of the *77. I.D.* the next day.[337] The regiment relieved the *I./941*. Nonetheless, it was unable to return to its division until days later.[338] Losses in this battalion had been enormous. In one-and-a-half days of fighting, it had lost roughly 50% of its men.[339]

The *353. I.D.* would at least receive direct support. On the evening of the **5th**, the *2. SS-Pz.Div. "Das Reich"* was attached to the *LXXXIV. A.K.* and established a battlegroup.[340] The *Kampfgruppe* was formed around *SS-Pz.Gren.Rgt. 4 "Der Führer"*, with its 3rd Battalion and some regimental companies. It was augmented by *SS-Pz.Aufkl.Abt. 2*, *SS-Stu.Gesch.Abt. 2*, and the *II./SS-Pz.Art. Rgt. 2*. As a third infantry battalion, the *III./SS-Pz.Gren.Rgt. 3 "Deutschland"*, was later added. The *Kampfgruppe* was subordinated to the *353. I.D.*, and its mission was to prevent La Haye-du-Puits from being encircled. The battlegroup was not committed as a single force, but rather as individual, battalion-sized battlegroups. The *III./D* was dispatched to the Forêt de Mont-Castre (*77. I.D.*), while the reconnaissance battalion was positioned on the high ground between the forest and La Haye-du-Puits. The *III./DF* deployed southwest of La Haye-du-Puits up to Montgardon.[341] In this manner, the *SS* battlegroup would support the left and right flanks, as well as the centre of the division.

Yet it would take time before the *Kampfgruppe* was ready to fight. For much of **6 July**, the *353. I.D.* would still be on its own. That morning, the division recaptured Le Vieux Château, Hospice and La Rue du Bocage on the northwest corner of the Forêt de Mont-Castre.[342] Further west, American troops made an advance east of Montgardon, which was sealed off in the area of La Surellerie - Le Mont. Another attack at Le Moulin was repulsed, while fighting southwest of La Haye-du-Puits continued into the evening.[343] Although the *SS-Kampfgruppe* had been tasked with counterattacking Hill 112, the attack was delayed due to enemy air activity and heavy artillery fire. Its start was postponed until after dark.[344] When it finally got underway, it was able to reach the area northeast of Mobecq.[345]

The attack continued on the **7th** and the battlegroup moved past the western edge of the forest and reached the old German main line of resistance south of Halte La Guillaumerie. That morning, the lines of the *353. I.D.* ran roughly along the northern edge of Mont-Castre (actually the sector of the *77. I.D.*) - north of La Ville - northern edge of La Rue du Bocage - Château la Haye du Puits - La Surellerie - Le Moulin.[346] Contact was made with *FJR 15* at Hospice.[347] On the left wing of the *353. I.D.*, US troops took St. Symphorien and pushed into La Haye-du-Puits, where they reached the southern outskirts of the town but were unable to secure it. The American advance opened up a gap in the German lines that stretched from the northern outskirts of the town (where the Château was still in German hands) to La Surellerie. In response, elements of the *SS-Kampfgruppe* were sent south and southwest of the town.[348]

While the fighting on the *Nordfront* went on, the situation for the *LXXXIV. A.K.* as a whole had deteriorated. The US XIX Corps had established a bridgehead between the Vire and Taute Rivers, on the corps' right flank. To deal with this, *Das Reich* would be transferred to support the *17. SS-Pz.Gren.Div.*[349] The extraction of all elements of the *SS-Kampfgruppe* soon proved impossible, because the *Nordfront* had not yet stabilised and the fighting was ongoing.[350]

On the morning of the **8th**, the penetration southwest of La Haye-du-Puits was sealed off at La Sullerie, while another attack on La Haye-du-Puits was beaten back on the town's western outskirts.[351] Although in German hands, it was far from secure. That evening, American troops were reported moving into the town. With no reserves to counter them, it had to be abandoned. To the southwest, the fighting continued throughout the day with American forces reaching La Bruyère.[352] In this area, the *III./DF* fought off between 9 and 11 attacks.[353] Little has been reported about the fighting in the centre of the division, but there were attacks on Hill 95 in the evening. (Hill 95 just east of La Haye-du-Puits, not Hill 95 northeast of the town.) During the morning, a gap opened up on the division's right, west of the Forêt de Mont-Castre, which the *SS-Kampfgruppe* was unable to close.[354] Attempts to seal the gap continued in the afternoon, but they were thwarted by American attacks to the southwest, out of the forest.[355] That evening, American attacks were also reported near La Rue du Bocage.[356] Despite the intention to pull the *SS-Kampfgruppe* out of the front, the situation on the *Nordfront* was so serious that it had to remain in position, helping to hold a line that now ran south of the railway and south of La Haye-du-Puits.[357]

The gap at La Ville had still not been closed by the morning of the **9 July**. The division had withdrawn here to just west of La Tourelle. Due to

After days of heavy fighting, La Haye-du-Puits was finally liberated by the 79th ID on 8 July. Although the town had suffered significant damage, the extend was was still limited compared to towns like Saint-Lô. (NARA)

a lack of forces, the gap remained open throughout the day and could only be covered by reconnaissance elements. There was little activity in the gap itself, although an American attack was launched from La Rue du Bocage that was soon repulsed.[358] In the centre of the division, Hill 95 was attacked in the morning — from the west, north and east and was captured by the Americans. The Germans counterattacked and, by 16:30 that afternoon, had recaptured the hill.[359] On the division's left flank, assaults out of La Haye-du-Puits were sealed off on the eastern and southern outskirts of the town by the last reserves.[360] There was fighting southwest of the town, where German forces repulsed several attacks and mopped up local incursions.[361]

By afternoon, the division's front ran along the following line: 0.5 km northeast of the Mont de Mobecq - 1 km west of Capron - La Haye-d'Osière (on the highway) - Les Trainel - south of La Bruyère.[362] This was the situation prior to Hill 95 being recaptured, which would have put the line about 1 km north of Capron. In general, *AOK 7* and *Heeresgruppe B* assessed the day on the *Nordfront* as having been without serious fighting, with the exception of Hill 95. German attempts to recapture La Haye-du-Puits had failed and would not be resumed.[363]

Early on **10 July**, the division pulled back to a new line due to losses sustained at Hill 95 and in an effort to conserve forces. The line ran southwest from La Tourelle, via the crossroads at Mobecq and Floranond to Mont du Tot. The new position shortened the division's lines, closed the gap and

Men of the 79th ID move out of La Haye-du-Puits. The division is easily identified by the unusually large mesh helmet nets used by its personnel in Normandy. Together with Mont-Castre, the town formed the key objectives for the US VIII Corps to force the Germans south. Pi.Btl. 353 was at the heart of the towns defense and suffered heavy losses in the battle. (NARA)

enabled *Das Reich* to finally withdraw.[364] The right boundary now followed the line: Le Val - Laulne - La Tourelle - Abbaye de Blanchelande. The left boundary was now: Lessay - along the railway line to Beauvais - the church at Angoville-sur-Ay - La Haye-du-Puits.[365] The Americans achieved a local penetration at La Tourelle, on the division's right flank, that was cleaned up by German countermeasures. To the west, prisoners were taken when an penetration at Barville was eliminated. A third American attack, this one on La Vieville, was also stopped.[366]

That night the Americans unsuccessfully attacked the area of Barville - La Bruyère.[367] The German lines were then pushed back to Mont-Vincent (today Hau. Vindi) on the **11th**.[368] From here, the Americans advanced eastward towards La Bourdonnerie and west towards Le Bas. A German counterattack failed to recapture the lost ground. Facing an American counterattack, Hierville was abandoned.[369]

On the night of **11-12 July**, the *Nordfront* was again moved back, this time to the line Gorges - the hills south of Gerville-la-Forêt - Angoville-sur-Ay - St. Germain-sur-Ay. The shortened line allowed the *I./941* and the *II./942* to return to the division. Both battalions became divisional reserves, the former around Pissot, the latter near Beauvais.[370] On **12 July**, US troops advanced through Vesly to Laulne. *GR 941*, including the *I./941*, launched a counterattack that was stopped 500 metres south of Vesly in front of Hill 59. The lines of *GR 942*, astride the Lessay highway, managed to hold, but only by committing the

353. Infanterie-Division

II./942.[371] The division's eastern flank, near the boundary with the *77. I.D.*, was now a particularly weak spot. At 22:00, a 1 km gap was reported, stretching east from Vesly. Enemy troops were advancing through it. Late that evening, reserves were deployed northwest of Le Puits Ruaule to seal the gap.[372]

Enemy attacks were launched along the entire *Nordfront* the next day (**13**th). The situation was serious enough for the corps commanding general (*Gen. von Choltitz*) to begin to contemplate a withdrawal to the *Wasserlinie*. During the day, American forces breached German positions south and southeast of Vesly and south of Hierville; the front could only be restored by committing the final reserves. All of the *77. I.D.'s* troops had to be used to support the *353. I.D.* By evening, it was reported that the enemy had reached Bricquebost, north of the Rivière de Claids. Once again, the division had suffered heavy casualties.[373]

While *AOK 7* had not yet considered a withdrawal to the *Wasserline* to be necessary, a visit by *Gen.* von Choltitz to the front convinced the German leadership otherwise. At 18:00, *Heeresgruppe B* authorised the move for the coming night.[374] That night, **13-14 July**, the *Nordfront* was indeed pulled back to the third prepared line, the *Wasserlinie*, although outposts were maintained north of the river.[375] The division held the line from La Val (west of the D24) in the east to the railway crossing southeast of Lessay.[376] Once again, *GR 942* was committed on the left and *GR 941* on the right.[377] The division's neighbours remained the *243. I.D.* to the left and the *77. I.D.* to the right. The latter was relieved by the *91. LL.D.* on the **17**th, although this was little more than a change of headquarters.[378]

From the start of the VIII Corps offensive on **3 July** to the withdrawal to the *Wasserlinie* on the night of the **13**th, the division had sustained heavy losses and some figures exist to show this. When *Pi.Btl. 353* was pulled out of La Haye-du-Puits, it was down to 30-40 men, effectively having lost 90% of its personnel strength. Its commander, *Hptm.* Pillmann, was missing. In another example, most of the field-replacement battalion had to be assigned to *GR 942* to compensate for the regiment's losses.[379]

On **10 July**, when the frontage of the *353. I.D.* had stretched more than 8 km, its combat strength was no more than 1,250 men, including the remnants of the *91. LL.D.*[380] The next day, replacements in the form of *Marschbtl. zbV 353* — not to be confused with the division's own replacements-transfer batatalion battalion — arrived 4 km southeast of Villedieu-les-Poêles. The battalion, which had been formed at Dresden in mid-June (presumably to provide replacements for the division), reportedly consisted of about 600 men, all from *Wehrkreis IV*. It travelled by train to Paris and then continued by lorry. Two-hundred seventy men were transferred to *Pz.Gr. West* and another 130 to the *Pz.Lehr-Div.*. The remainder joined the *353. I.D.* after reaching Muneville-le-Bingard on **13 July**. The fate of the division's organic cadre battalion is not entirely clear. It may have been absorbed by *GR 941* at the same time its sister element arrived. Personnel of *Marschbtl. zbV 353* have been linked to *GR 942*.[381]

Gen. Mahlmann estimated the current combat strength of the division at about 2,000 men.[382] Official records show that, on **14 July**, infantry strength was down to 34 officers, 69 NCO's and 585 men. This figure encompassed personnel that had been assigned to the infantry from the headquarters and the trains as well as the cadre of the field-replacement and replacements-transfer

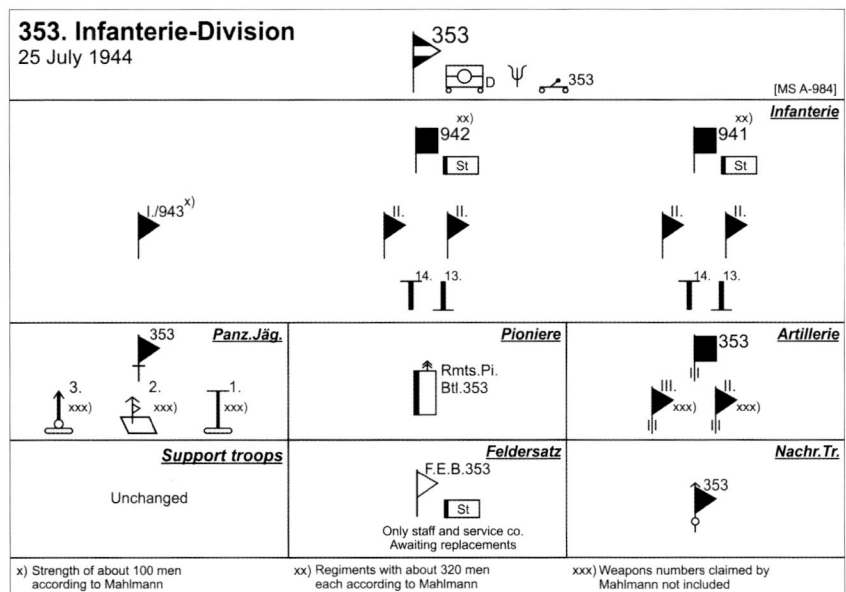

By the time of Operation Cobra, the division's strength had been greatly reduced. KG Boehm was still not available and two of its artillery battalions had been left on the Nordfront to support the 91.LL.D. and 243.I.D.

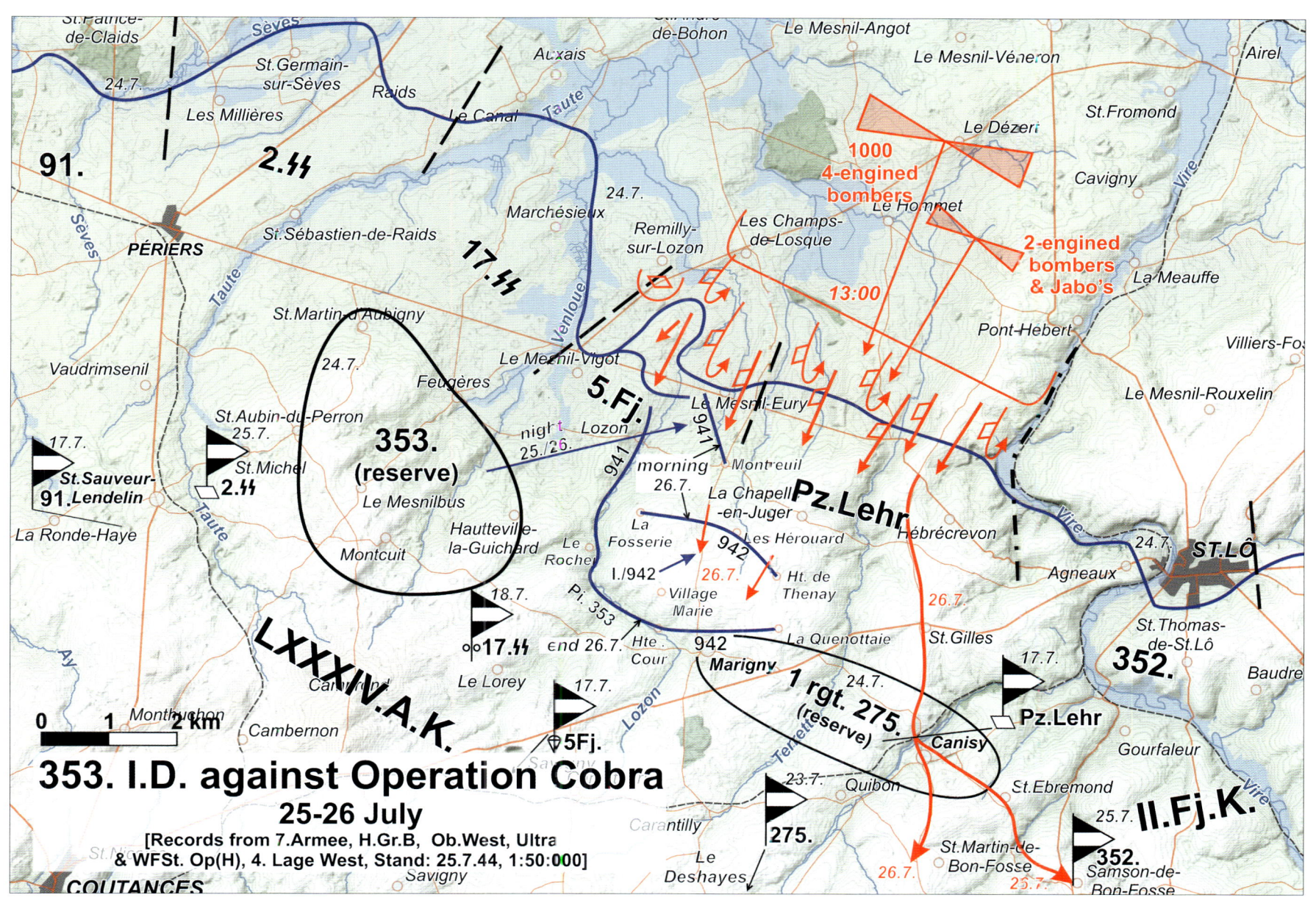

When Operation Cobra was launched on 25 July, the 353.I.D. was in reserve behind the 17.SS-Pz.Gr.Div. and 5.Fj.Div. That evening the GR 941 counterattacked and GR 942 went into action the next morning. By the end of the 26th, the division held positions along the Lozon River and continued to block the approaches to Marigny. It would be of little consequence: the division was already being outflanked by US forces advancing over St. Gilles and Canisy.

Like so many other divisions, the 353.I.D. suffered considerably equipment losses in the Roncey pocket. Three Marders were lost (two visible here) in the centre of the town. Although these could also have belonged the 243.I.D., the tactical numbers and camouflage patterns do not match that division. These two self-propelled guns are numbered 121 and 122, indicating that they were the first and second vehicle in the 2nd Platoon of their battalion's 1st Company. (NARA)

batatalion battalions.[383] Further east, on the St. Lô front, *Kampfgruppe Boehm* had also suffered serious losses.[384] On **11 July**, the infantry strength of this battlegroup was reported as about 180 men. Its casualties to date had been 480 men.[385] On **19 July** the division held a sector 3.9 km wide. On the left was the GR 942, fielding a single battalion: *II./942*. The battalion had a strength of 204 men. The rest of the division's front was held by the *GR 941*; The *I./941* was committed on the left (west), followed by the *II./941* and *I./943*. From left (west) to right the three battalions had a strength of 204, 184, 169, and 147, respectively. The divisional reserve was formed by the *I./942* and *Pi.Btl. 353*. Together those could field 344 men. The division's overall combat strength was 1,565; an increase compared to **16 July** when it had been 704.[386]

Although the *Nordfront* had become relatively quiet after reaching the *Wasserlinie*, the situation in the corps sector as a whole continued to deteriorate. This was especially true for the right wing of the corps, between the Taute and Vire Rivers. Here, the *17. SS-Pz.Gren.Div.*, the *5. Fj.Div.* and the *Pz.Lehr-Div.* had been unable to halt the advance of the XIX Corps, which reached the Périers - St. Lô road. To the east, in the sector of the *II. Fs.K.*, St. Lô itself had been lost, increasing the threat to the right flank of the *LXXXIV. A.K.*. There was little hope of stabilising the front as the three divisions deployed on the right wing had already been severely weakened by the fighting.[387] The *Pz. Lehr-Div.* was rated at Combat Status III (*Kampfwert III*) and the *17. SS-Pz. Gren.Div.* at Combat Status IV (*Kampfwert IV*), while the poor performance of the *5. Fj.Div.* had already become all too apparent.[388]

Reserves were urgently needed to shore up the right wing of the *LXXXIV.*

A.K., thus, on **21 July**, the corps was ordered to pull the entire *353. I.D.* out of the *Nordfront*, starting the next day.[389] That day (**22ⁿᵈ**), more detailed orders were issued, instructing the corps to move the division (minus two light artillery battalions) to its new assembly area.[390] The relief appears to have been carried out in phases. During the day, the *I./941* was relieved by the *I./943*. That night, *GR 941*, on the division's right wing, was relieved by the *II./1050* (*77. I.D.* but operating under the *91. LL.D.*). On the left wing, the *243. I.D.* relieved *GR 1058* (*91. LL.D.*), which had been subordinated to it. This regiment was then transferred to the *353. I.D.* and used to relieve *GR 942*, which then moved to the division's assembly area.[391] The relief of the division was thus achieved by lengthening the defensive frontages of the *91. LL.D.* and the *243. I.D.* Two battalions of *AR 353* remained behind to support these divisions: The 1ˢᵗ Battalion with the *91. LL.D.* and the 4ᵗʰ Battalion with the *243. I.D.*[392] This meant that, contrary to earlier plans, one light and one heavy battalion remained on the *Nordfront*. *Pz.Jg.Abt. 353* also remained on the *Nordfront*, where it was attached to *GR 1050*.[393] Meanwhile, the mass of the division assembled behind the *17. SS-Pz.Gren.Div.* and the *5. Fj.Div.* in the area of St. Martin-d'Aubigny - Montcuit - Hautteville-la-Guichard. In similar fashion, elements of the *275. I.D.* formed a reserve force behind the *Pz.Lehr-Div.* in the area of Marigny-Quibou.[394]

Relatively precise information is available on the condition and organisation of the division during this period. *AR 353* was still close to full strength; its 2ⁿᵈ Battery and the three batteries of the 2ⁿᵈ Battalion were down to three guns each, but the other batteries still had the authorised four.[395] The state of the infantry was much worse. The division (minus *KG Boehm*) was down to one average and four weak infantry battalions.* *F.E.B. 353* only consisted of cadre personnel and was staged around Mortain awaiting replacements. *KG Boehm*, with its two battalions, was still with the *II. Fs.K.*[396] In his post-war monograph, *Gen.* Mahlmann estimated that *GR 941* and *942* both possessed a strength of 320 men and the *I./943* is said to have had about 100 men. *Pi. Btl. 353* no longer existed as such, having been reduced to a single company of about 30-40 men.[397] Available heavy AT weapons consisted of 13 AT guns (including *Marder* SP guns) and eight assault guns. Three more heavy AT guns were with *KG Boehm*, most likely from the *14./943*.[398] Mobility in the division was 100% for both the horse-drawn and motorised elements. Despite its shortcomings, the division was still rated at Combat Status II (*Kampfwert II*), making it the strongest division of the *LXXXIV. A.K.* after *Das Reich*.[399]

On **24 July**, Allied air forces struck the *5. Fj.Div.* and the *Pz.Lehr-Div.*, but the attacks were eventually suspended due to poor weather. The air attacks resumed the next day (**25ᵗʰ**) with the start of *Operation Cobra*. US troops crossed the St. Lô - Périers highway and advanced against the already badly weakened German defensive lines.[400] In response, the *353. I.D.* was sent in to help restore the front. That evening, supported by *AR 353* (2ⁿᵈ and 3ʳᵈ Battalions) and remnants of *Pz.Jg.Abt. 353*, *GR 941* counterattacked, although *GR 942* was still held in reserve.[401]

By the morning of **26 July**, *GR 941* reached a line just west of Le Mesnil-Eury - Montreuil. Another attack was planned with the reinforced *GR 942* (including the *I./943*), striking north from positions north of Marigny. The objective was to link up with *GR 941* on the left and *Pz.Gr.Rgt. 901* (*Pz.Lehr. Div.*) on the right. The remnants of *Pi.Btl.* 353 were in reserve 3 km northwest of Marigny.[402] The division was reinforced by elements of the *5. Fj.Div.* consisting of *KG Trimborn* and the remnants of the *II./Fs.Jg.Rgt.14*. In addition to these troops, a SS AT company was attached to the division.[403] The attack of *GR 942* reached a line running from Haut-de-Thenay (today L'Hôtel d'Arthenay) via Les Hérouard (today Village Hérouard) to east of La Fosserie (today La Fossairie). This new line effectively blocked the two main roads (D29 and D89) leading to Marigny. The line, however, was breached by American forces along both roads that afternoon. The reserve battalion (*I./942*) launched an immediate counterattack towards the east from north of Village Marie, but the results are unclear. The regiment was ordered to take up positions in a line north of Marigny, running from La Questnottae to Haute Cour (west of the town). From there, *Pi.Btl. 353* held the line along the Lozon River to Le Rocher (today L'Hôtel Rauline), where the lines of *GR 941* continued to Lozon. On the division's left flank, *KG Trimborn* launched an attack to establish contact with the left-hand neighbour of the division. It reached the St. Lô - Périers highway and apparently made contact there with forces from "*Götz von Berlichingen*", which had been assigned a similar mission.[404] Marigny remained in German hands during the night but, to the east, US armour had advanced through St. Gilles and Canisy to St. Samson-de-Bonfossé. The Americans had thus made a decisive breakthrough that they would soon exploit.[405]

---

* Weak: Combat strength (Kampfstärke) between 100-200; Average: Combat strength between 200-300.

The next day (**27ᵗʰ**), US armour — Combat Command B (CCB) of the 3ʳᵈ AD operating under the 1ˢᵗ ID — bypassed Marigny and, by advancing across the St. Lô - Coutances road, moved into the rear of the *353. I.D.* (around its right flank).⁴⁰⁶ The corps ordered a general withdrawal across the Soulles River, and the division began to withdraw to the area of Roncey (10 km southeast of Coutances). By next morning, it had established a new defence line east of the town and then south past St. Martin-de-Cenilly (excl.). Enemy armour again moved around the right flank of the division — over the road from St. Martin-de-Cenilly to Lengronne (D38) — and captured Lengronne, Grimesnil, Cambry and Trelly behind the division's front. The division was now cut off and a breakout was ordered from the "Roncey Pocket."⁴⁰⁷ The corps intended to take up new positions along the line: Percy - Sourdeval - west of Sourdeval - La Baleine - Gavray - Cérences - Bréhal - coast. The division was intended for the sector of Gavray – Cérences.⁴⁰⁸

That night (**28-29 July**), as *GR 942* covered the rear, *GR 941* secured the flanks and punched a hole in the American lines, enabling the division to move via St. Denis-le-Gast to La Baleine (7 km south of Roncey), where it crossed the Sienne River and escaped from the pocket. On the southern bank of the river, it took up positions between the *91. LL.D.* at Gavray (on the left) and *KG 275* (*KG Heintz* formed around *GR 984*) on the right (the latter element holding the area just east of La Baleine). The line was consolidated with *GR 942* on the left, *GR 941* in the centre and *KG 275* on the right wing. (*KG Heintz* was now subordinated to the division.) Elements of the *243. I.D.* formed the right-hand neighbour, and the *91. LL.D.* was still on the left. *Pz.Jg.Abt. 353* was to the rear at Sourdeval-les-Bois, while the engineer company was at Les Monts; both elements were in reserve and a battalion formed from stragglers was located around Montaigu. The artillery had taken up position in the area around Le Mesnil-Bonant and Le Mesnil-Hue.⁴⁰⁹

On the **30ᵗʰ**, continued enemy attacks forced *KG 275* back from the river and reached the AT battalion and engineer company, which now formed the new right wing of the division.⁴¹⁰ For **31 July**, the *LXXXIV. A.K.* ordered a withdrawal of its troops to the lines Villedieu-les-Poêles - Avranches.⁴¹¹ In response, the *353. I.D.* pulled back to Villedieu-les-Poêles (11 km southeast of La Baleine). It then received a temporary reinforcement in the form of *GR 957* (*Obst.* Freiherr von Gall) of the *363. I.D.* This regiment was the spearhead of its division and would return to its parent division, when it arrived at the front. Since the new division would be committed to the right of the *353. I.D.*, it was determined that the regiment should be deployed on the right wing of the *353. I.D.* to enable it to easily rejoin its parent formation, which it did around **7-8 August**.⁴¹² The regiment went into position to the northeast of the town, which was held by *GR 941*. To the southwest of the town was *KG 275*, while *GR 942* made up the left wing of the division. To the rear, as usual, were *Pz.Jg.Abt. 353*, *Pi.Btl. 353* and *AR 353*.⁴¹³ During the day, the division was joined by the remnants of *Fj.Rgt. 6* (*Maj.* von der Heydte); it was several companies in strength and had become separated from the *2. SS-Pz.Div.*, to which it had been attached.⁴¹⁴

On **31 July**, an enemy attack on the town during the day was repulsed but, to the left, American armoured forces broke through the lines of *GR 942*. The *I./943*, which had been in regimental reserve, was shattered and lost as a coherent fighting force. The Americans pressed their advance and did great damage to the trains, reaching as far as the gun positions of *AR 353* and divisional headquarters. To secure the division's rear area, key roads were blocked by *Pz.Jg.Abt. 353* and the division headquarters. Another enemy attack split the remnants of *FJR 6* in two, leaving only the commander and a company-sized formation with the division to be used as a small reserve force to seal off penetrations. The paratroopers finally departed the division on **14-15 August**.⁴¹⁵

On **31 July**, *AOK 7* reported the strength of the division. *GR 941* was but a shadow of its former self, consisting of 11 officers, 31 NCO's and 164 men; this figure included the headquarters and regimental elements. The situation of *GR 942* was no better: 14 officers, 40 NCO's and 162 men. *AR 353* had eight guns left in each of its two battalions. The 1ˢᵗ and 4ᵗʰ Battalions were now with the *2. SS.Pz.Div.*, as were the engineers. The supply troops still had 50 tonnes of motor and 120 tonnes of horse-drawn lift capacity.⁴¹⁶

According to *Gen.* Mahlmann, the division withdrew to the west edge of the Forêt de St. Sever on the night of **1 August**.⁴¹⁷ This, however, is at odds with period records, which show that the division still occupied the area between the forest and Villedieu-les-Poêles on **2 August**. In this position, it secured the left flank of the *XXXXVII. Pz.K.*, while the left the wing of the *LXXXIV. A.K.* was exposed.⁴¹⁸

Further to the right (northeast), the front of *AOK 7* was also not continuous. To remedy this, and to free up troops for other missions, the *7. Armee* pulled back its front. This action primarily affected the right wing of the *II. Fs.K.* in an effort to make contact with *Pz.Gr. West*, while the corps' left wing would attempt to make

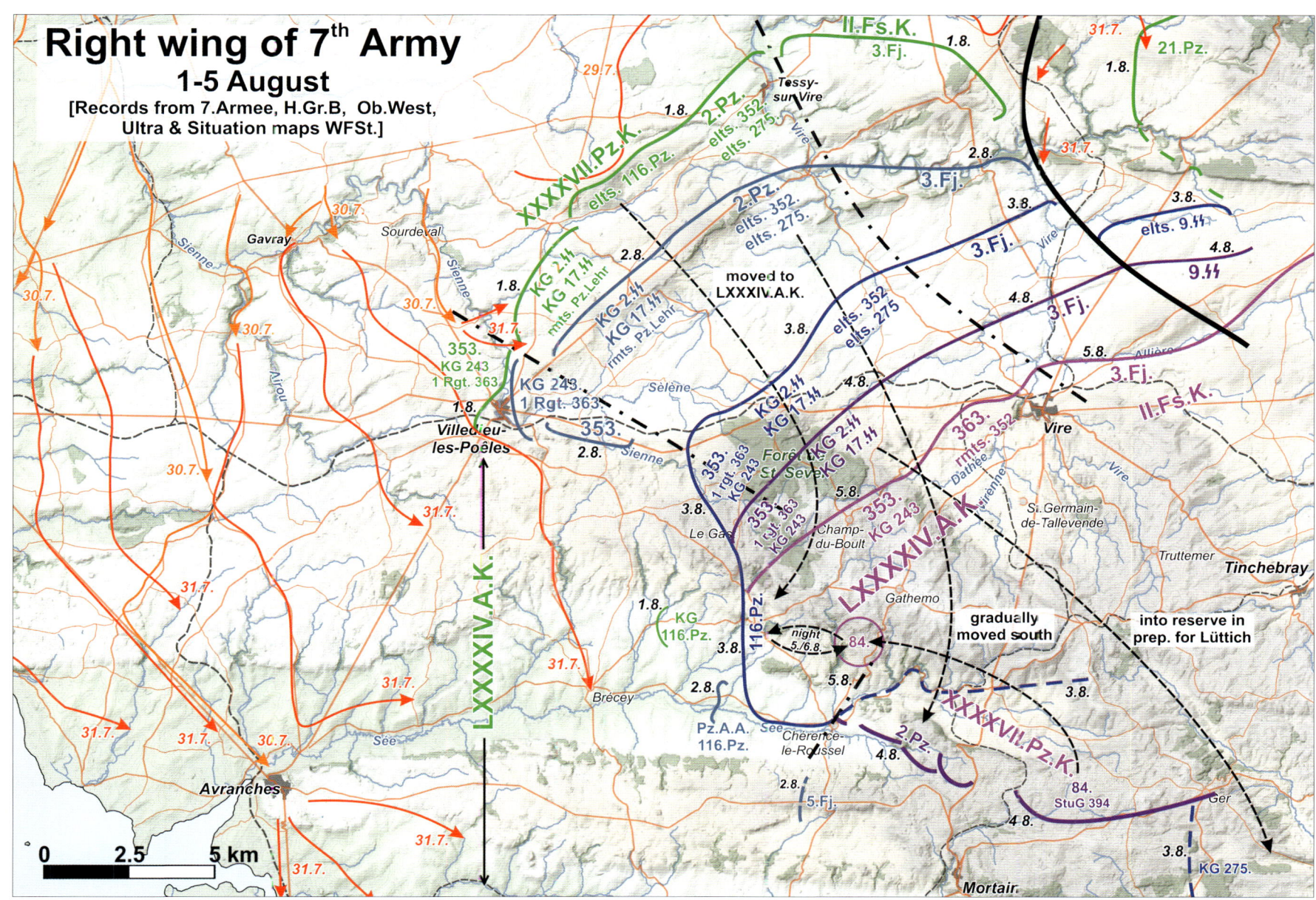

About 1 August, having escaped from the Roncey Pocket, LXXXIV. A.K. attempted to reestablish control of the situation at Villedieu-les-Poêles. Supported by elements of other divisions, the 353.I.D. defended the town, but to the south the rest of the corps sector was wide open. Over the next days, the right wing of 7th Army withdrew to the southeast to shorten the lines and free the XXXXVII. Pz.K. for Operation Lüttich, the armoured counterattack towards Avranches.

contact with the *XXXXVII. Pz.K.*, which was also moving back. Conducted on the night of **2-3 August**, the withdrawal enabled the *2. Pz.Div.* to be pulled from the front and assembled for further operations. The *353. I.D.* was temporarily attached to the *XXXXVII. Pz.K.* for operations on its left wing.[419] The front of the *7. Armee* was withdrawn to the Forêt de St. Sever, where the *353. I.D.* was committed in the southern sector (Bois de la Vierge and Bois du Gast), around Le Gast (12 km south-southeast of Villedieu-les-Poêles). Once again, *GR 957* occupied the right (north) wing, followed by *GR 941, 984* and *942*.[420]

On **3 August**, *AOK 7* noted that the strength of the *353. I.D.* had dwindled to such a point that it could no longer be committed as a closed formation. As a result, the right boundary of the corps was moved south and the *LXXXIV. A.K.* was ordered to reorganise what remained of the division.[421] A reorganisation of the division was indeed carried out during this period. On **2-3 August**, what remained of *KG Boehm* finally returned to the division.[422] Replacements allowed *GR 943* to be brought up to "battalion strength" (there were still only about 120 men), while *Füs.Btl. 353* was partially reconstituted with 60-80 men. After the reorganisation, the division consisted of four infantry forces under regimental headquarters staffs. *GR 941* consisted of its headquarters and 13th and 14th Companies, as well as the remnants of *Füs.Btl. 353, GR 941* and *GR 942*. *GR 984* comprised the remnants of *Kampfgruppe 275* and the *243. I.D.*, as well as those of *GR 943*. Its headquarters and heavy weapons companies were part of this force as well. The third regiment was *GR 957*, which still had its original organisation of two battalions, a headquarters company and heavy weapons companies. The remnants of *FJR 6* formed a final combat unit (under a regimental headquarters), but this was, at best, of only company strength. The headquarters of *GR 942* and *943* were still available, but they were used for other missions.[423] According to Mahlmann, the *1.* and the *3./Pz. Jg.Abt. 353* were armed with two AT guns and three *Flak*, respectively. The 2nd Company no longer had any assault guns. He also stated that the two artillery battalions still possessed six howitzers each. Since his numbers are apparently based on memory, their value is questionable.[424] Indeed, it is doubtful that four howitzers had been lost since **31 July**.

3 August was a significant day in the fighting, since it marked the start of preparations for a major counteroffensive to recapture Avranches and restore the situation in Normandy. This operation, *Unternehmen Lüttich*, would be carried out by *AOK 7* with armoured formations of the *XXXXVII. Pz.K.* spearheading the attack. At this time, the planned area for the offensive was still assigned to the *LXXXIV. A.K.*, which meant the two corps would have to swap positions. The *LXXXIV. A.K.* would first have to hold the line of departure for the planned offensive and then secure the right flank of the offensive.[425]

Pressure on the corps was unremitting. On **4 August**, the Americans attacked Le Gast on the southern edge of the Forêt de St. Sever and reached the forest.[426] German forces withdrew during the night of **4-5 August** to the area of Champ-du-Boult. The *353. I.D.* took up positions between the high ground at Le Barbot and the bend in the road (D150) 400 metres northeast of the Champ-du-Boult church.[427] In effect, the division joined the rearward line established by the *363. I.D.* and the *84. I.D.*, the two divisions becoming its right and left neighbour, respectively, with the *363. I.D.* attached to the *II. Fs.K.*[428] These moves also completed the relief of the *XXXXVII. Pz.K.* by the *LXXXIV. A.K.*[429] The *Panzer-Korps* assembled to the south in preparation for *Operation Lüttich*. In the sector of the *353. I.D.*, *GR 957* held the right wing and *GR 941* the left wing, while *KG 275* was just to the rear in the centre of the division.[430]

On **6 August**, US troops entered the Bois de la Haye (6 km southwest of Vire) and also penetrated German lines south of Champ-du-Boult. Under threat from the north and south, the village was evacuated and a new line established between L'Euderie and La Jeulière (*363. I.D.*).[431] The next day, an enemy attack on the boundary between the two divisions made progress towards St. Germain-de-Tallevende.[432] To the left, the *84. I.D.* was thrown back, threatening the left flank of the *353. I.D.*, which was in a hedgehog-position for all-round defence at La Moinerie (north of Gathemo).[433]

While the *353. I.D.* relinquished its ground gradually, its right neighbour (*363. I.D.*) was forced back in the area south of Vire, placing the right flank of the *353. I.D.* in jeopardy. On **8 August**, *Feldm.* von Kluge considered the situation with the *LXXXIV. A.K.* so critical that *Unternehmen Lüttich* would have to be called off unless the corps could somehow manage to restore its tottering front.[434] The enemy breach in the sector of the *363. I.D.* was expanded even further on the **9th**, making a crisis situation even worse.[435] In an effort to re-establish its lines south of Vire, the *LXXXIV. A.K.* organised a counterattack. To support the *363. I.D.*, elements of the *331. I.D.*, the *Pz.Lehr.Div.*, and the *1. SS-Pz.Div.* were brought up to strike from the east and southeast, while the *353. I.D.* and elements of the *84. I.D.* would attack from the south.[436] The headquarters of the *353. I.D.* was moved from La Moinerie to La Huberdière.[437]

The fighting south of Vire was particularly heavy and the pressure on LXXXIV. A.K. was also a threat to any plans to restart Operation Lüttich. On 10 August, a counter attack was launched to eliminated a dangerous penetration south of Vire. Despite support from elements of the Pz.Lehr and 1. SS-Pz.Div., the frontline could not be reestablished and 7th Army was forced to begin its withdrawal towards the east.

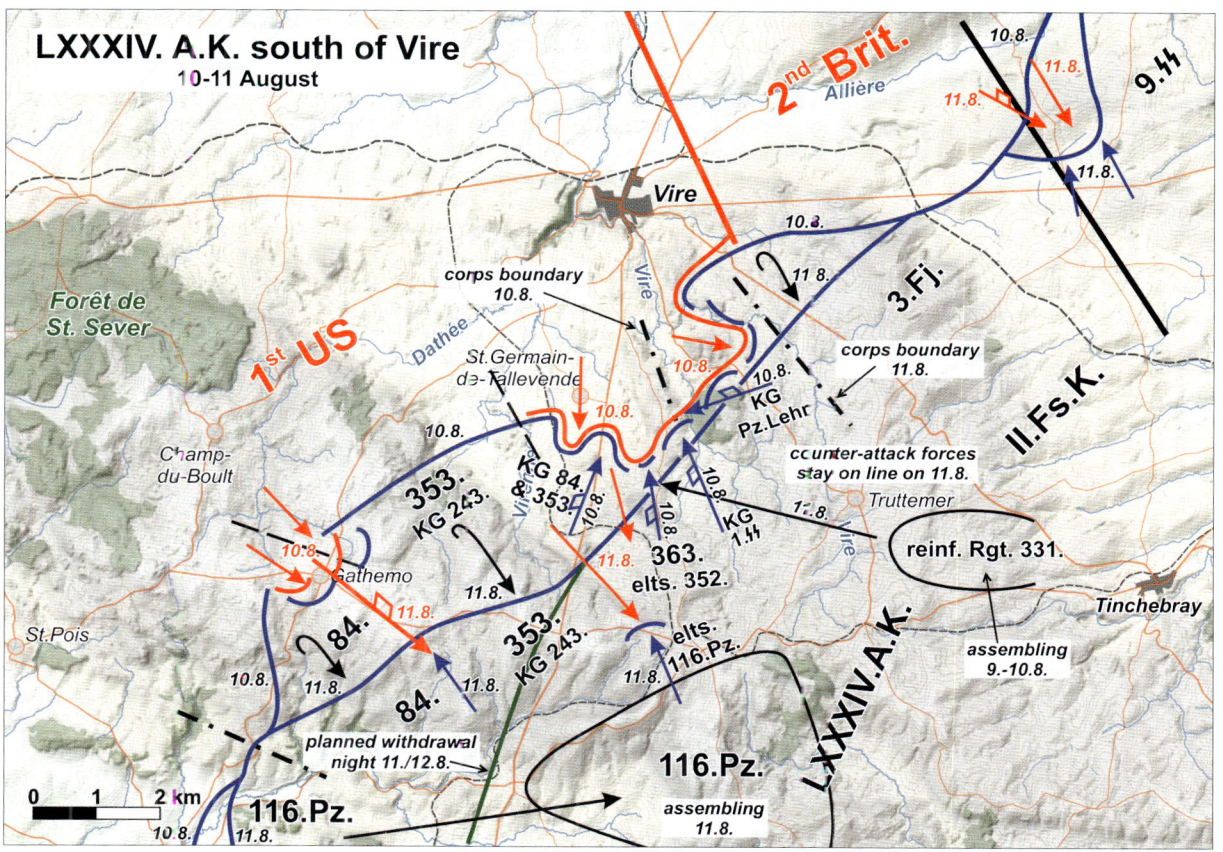

The attack was launched on the morning of **10 August** and succeeded in recapturing some of the lost ground. On the right wing of the *353. I.D.*, *KG Heintz* launched a successful attack, as did *GR 943* along the Sourdeval - Vire road (D577). *GR 941*, however, was unable to cross the flat creek country to the northwest.[438] What appeared to have been a modest success for the division was suddenly rendered moot when US troops counterattacked the *363. I.D.* and pushed it back, forcing its own attack to be cancelled.[439] Once again, the front was withdrawn during the night, and a new line established from La Lande-Vaumont (approximate corps boundary) to Perriers-en-Beauficel.[440] On the morning of the **11th**, the division occupied a defensive front between La Bercendière (*363. I.D.*) and La Béchellerie.[441]

Additional replacements now reached the division, enabling *GR 942* to be partially reconstituted. The regiment was brought up to the strength of two weak battalions and regimental units (headquarters company and heavy weapons companies). Other elements of the division were also reinforced. By **11 August**, as a result of the reorganisations, its composition had changed considerably compared to **5 August**. *GR 957* had returned to the *363. I.D.*, while *GR 941* was unchanged, except for the departure of elements of *GR 942*. Instead, the remnant of *GR 941* were now joined by the remnants of *GR 943* and together formed a battlegroup. This transfer of elements of *GR 943* to *GR 941* meant that the infantry under *GR 984* had been reduced to two groups, formed by the remnants of *Kampfgruppe*

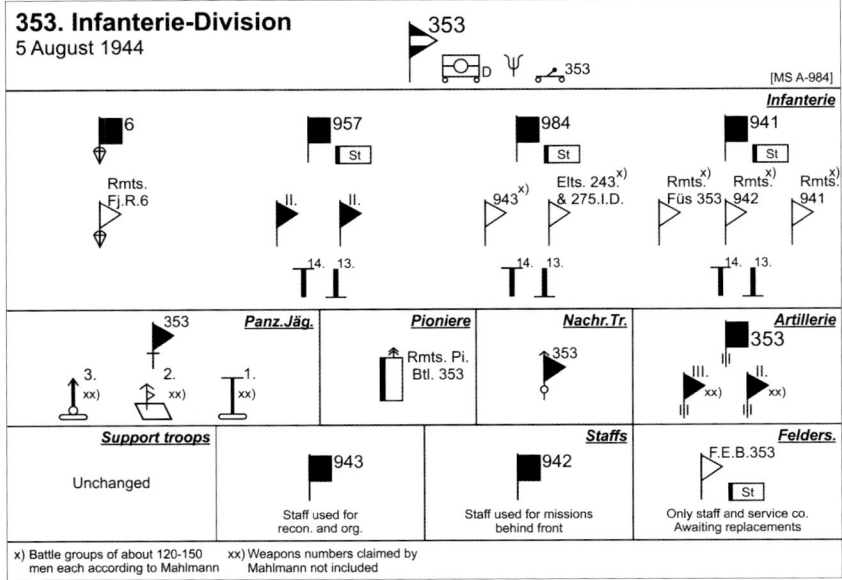

In the sector southwest of Vire, the division was again reorganised and able to field three regimental battlegroups. Most of its remaining infantry was gathered under the HQ of GR 941, while GR 984 (275.I.D.) and GR 957 (363.I.D.) provided additional troops to the division.

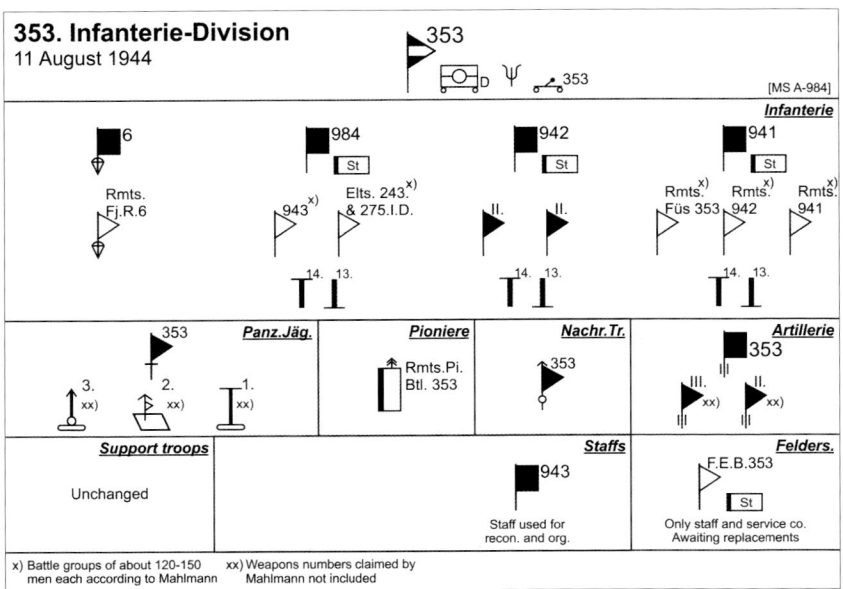

As the division joined in the general German withdrawal, its organisation had changed once more. GR 957 left the division, but GR 942 was reactivated with two battalions and formed the strongest force within the division.

275 and the *243. I.D.*, respectively. The situation of *FJR 6* remained unchanged.[442]

The slow but inexorable withdrawal continued on the night of **11 August**. The *LXXXIV. A.K.* pulled back to the line La Lande-Vaumont - high ground west of Vengeons and Sourdeval (all south of Vire). During the day (**12th**), an enemy attack reached Le Petit-Bourg and Gillotière. The former town was then recaptured.[443] For the most part, the German front remained intact, but it was taken back once again during the night (**12-13 August**). A shorter line was established at La Lande-Vaumont - Rancoudray. The division was reinforced by the advance guard of the *331. I.D., Rgt. von Dobeneck*.[444] In the early hours of **14 August**, the sector of the division was reported to be between Truttemer and St. Sauveur-de-Chaulieu.[445] In the following night (**14-15 August**), the division withdrew to the area east and southeast of Tinchebray, between La Rivière and Les Hardouinières.[446]

The division moved to the area south of Flers on the night of **15-16 August**, although the exact boundaries of the corps and division have not been found. The next day, after the *363. I.D.* had been put under control of the *II. Fs.K.*, the division held the right wing of the corps.[447] It was decided that the front of *AOK 7* would be taken back that night to the general line Breél, Notre-Dame-du-Rocher, Ste. Opportune, Briouze.[448] Plans were also made to extract the *84. I.D.* and transfer it to *Pz.AOK 5*. This division, however, left a regiment behind that was attached to the *353. I.D.* On the morning of the **17th**, the division held a sector that stretched north from Briouze (incl.) to near the Bois de la Mousse (excl.), where the corps boundary ran. The force from the *84. I.D.* was committed at Briouze and, during the day, a threat developed south of the town on the exposed left flank of the division, but an encirclement was ultimately avoided. That evening the battlegroup from the *84. I.D.* returned to its division.[449]

Orders were given for *AOK 7* to pull back across the Orne River during the coming night. The transfer of the *84. I.D.* left the *353. I.D.* as the only division in the corps. On the morning of the **18th**, having successfully crossed the river, the division took up position on the east bank, roughly from St. Croix-sur-Orne to Giel.⁴⁵⁰ During the day, there was only mild enemy pressure on the western front of *AOK 7*.⁴⁵¹ The division now pulled back from the river and occupied a position along the Argentan - Nécy railway, approximately between Clinchamps and Occagnes. The division was placed under the *II. Fs.K.*, stripping the *LXXXIV. A.K.* of its last formation. During the night, the bulk of the division was ordered back to the western edge of the Bois de Feuillet and the Forêt de Gouffern.⁴⁵²

On **19 August**, the *II. Fs.K.* informed the division of the planned withdrawal across the Dives River and the breakout from the Falaise Pocket. This move would be carried out during the night. *Gen.* Mahlmann decided that the main body of the division, including *KG Schmitz* (941) and *KG Dobeneck*, would break out via Chambois, while *KG Heintz* (984) and *GR 942* (the rearguard) would break out via St. Lambert-sur-Dives. The objective of the division was the western slope of Mont-Ormel.⁴⁵³

In the chaos that followed, *KG Dobeneck* went in a different direction and another division assumed control over it. The *353. I.D.* also lost contact with *KG Heintz* and *GR 942*. Contact with *KG Heintz* was re-established some days later, but *GR 942* was still missing. Nearly all the division's vehicles, equipment and guns were lost in the escape. Only two or three *Volkswagens* got through. The troops arriving on Mont-Ormel, among them stragglers from many different units and service branches, were organised into three groups: *Heer* (*KG Schmitz*), *Fallschirmjäger* and *SS*. They withdrew to the Vie River some kilometres to the east.⁴⁵⁴

Over the next few days, the division (including elements of the *275. I.D.*) pulled back to the areas of Le Sap (**21st**) and Ecardenville (**22nd** and **23rd**), arriving at Tostes (southeast of Elbeuf) near the Seine River on the **24th**. There, it successfully crossed the Seine.⁴⁵⁵

Since its escape from the Falaise Pocket, an almost indescribable cataclysm, the division had been reporting directly to *AOK 7*, as no corps headquarters were available to take command.⁴⁵⁶ This finally changed on the **27th**, when the division was assigned to the *LXXXI. A.K.* under *5. Pz.Armee*.⁴⁵⁷ The retreat continued, and so did the losses. On the night of **30 August**, a battlegroup

Fighting on the western end of the Falaise pocket, the 353. I.D. found itself in an increasingly difficult position. It was among the last divisions to try and break out. Many of its troops did not succeed. Those lucky enough to survive, ended up among the tens of thousands of prisoners taken. (NARA)

was formed under *Obst.* Schmitz. It consisted of about 30 infantrymen and engineers, some 20 men from the divisional band, 10-12 men from the division's military police, some 40 men from *Nachr.Abt. 353* and one howitzer with crew from *AR 353*. The supply elements had withdrawn in time and most had been saved.⁴⁵⁸

The division retreated across northern France and Belgium to the area around Hasselt near the Dutch border.⁴⁵⁹ From there, it moved to Maastricht, where it first had to hand over its non-organic troops and later its own combat troops. This left the division with only its trains and headquarters elements. The "division" was then used to prepare the defence of the *Westwall* around Aachen until relieved. It was then transferred to Schevenhütte in the Hürtgenwald to prepare the defence of the second line of the *Westwall*.⁴⁶⁰ In **November**, the division was significantly reconstituted and remained committed until finally meeting its end in **April 1945** in the Ruhr Pocket.⁴⁶¹

709. Infanterie-Division

The *709. Infanterie-Division* was raised on **1 May 1941** in *Wehrkreis IX* as part of the 15th Wave, which included the *702.*, the *704.* and the *707.-719. Inf.Div.* Preparations for these divisions had begun months earlier and the *709. I.D.* was to be ready for deployment as soon as **15 May**.[1] Indeed, by early **June** the division was already assigned to the *XXV. A.K.* in Bretagne.[2]

Starting late **November 1942**, the division was transferred to the Cotentin Peninsula and subordinated to the *LXXXIV. A.K.*[3] It remained there until D-Day and, for much of this period, was almost solely responsible for coastal defence of the peninsula and most of the west coast of Manche. This was a monumental task. In fact, on **1 May 1944**, the division, together with *Gren.Rgt. zbV 752*, defended a coastline 220 km in length![4]

On D-Day, the division defended against the amphibious landings on Utah Beach and airborne landings further inland. Soon after, along with many subordinated formations, it became responsible for the northern front of the beachhead. In mid-**June**, all troops on the northern part of the Cotentin were subordinated to the division as *Gruppe von Schlieben*. Following the American breakthrough to the west coast of the peninsula, this force withdrew into *Festung Cherbourg*. After the fall of the fortress, a battlegroup, *KG Keil*, continued to defend the Jobourg Peninsula until the surviving elements surrendered on **1 July**. The division was formally disbanded on **24 July**.[5]

The division went through a series of commanders. It was first commanded by *Gen.Maj.* von Bessel.[6] On **15 July 1941**, *Gen.Maj.* Albin Nake took over the division until succeeded by *Gen.Lt.* Kurt Jahn on **21 March 1943**.[7] A few months later, on **11 July**, *Gen.Maj.* Eckhard von Geyso became the new division commander.[8] Finally, it was *Gen.Maj.* Karl-Wilhelm von Schlieben, who assumed command on **19 December 1943**.[9] Von Schlieben remained in command (promoted to *Gen.Lt.* as of **1 May 1944**) until his surrender at Cherbourg on **26 June**.

This chapter will address the history of the division in detail. Its arrival on the Cotentin Peninsula in late **1942** means that its history is intimately related to that of the peninsula in the one-and-a-half years prior to the invasion. This period is well covered by corps and field army records. The arrival and departure of many other formations during this period affected the division and will thus be examined here as well.

After D-Day, the division held a key position in the fighting for the beachhead and later in the battle for Cherbourg. As a result, it is impossible to examine the division's role in the fighting without discussing the many other

Left: Gen.Maj. Arnold von Bessel commanded the 709.I.D. from 1 June 1941 to 15 July 1942. On 31 January 1944 he was released from active duty.

Centre: Gen.Maj. Albin Nake (shown here as Oberstleutnant in 1938) was given command of the division on 15 July 1942. He held that position until 15 March 1943 and thus was its commander when the division moved to Normandy. (BArch, PERS 6/770)

Right: Gen.Lt. Kurt Jahn only commanded the division for some three months, from 15 March to 23 June 1943. (BArch, PERS 6/299934)

Left: Gen.Maj. Eckhard von Geyso was in charge of the 709.I.D. from 23 June to 12 December 1943. (BArch, PERS 6/299709)

Right: Gen.Lt. Karl-Wilhelm von Schlieben would be the division's final commander. Having been in charge from 12 December 1943 onwards, he was taken prisoner at Cherbourg on 26 June 1944. (BArch, PERS 6/300785)

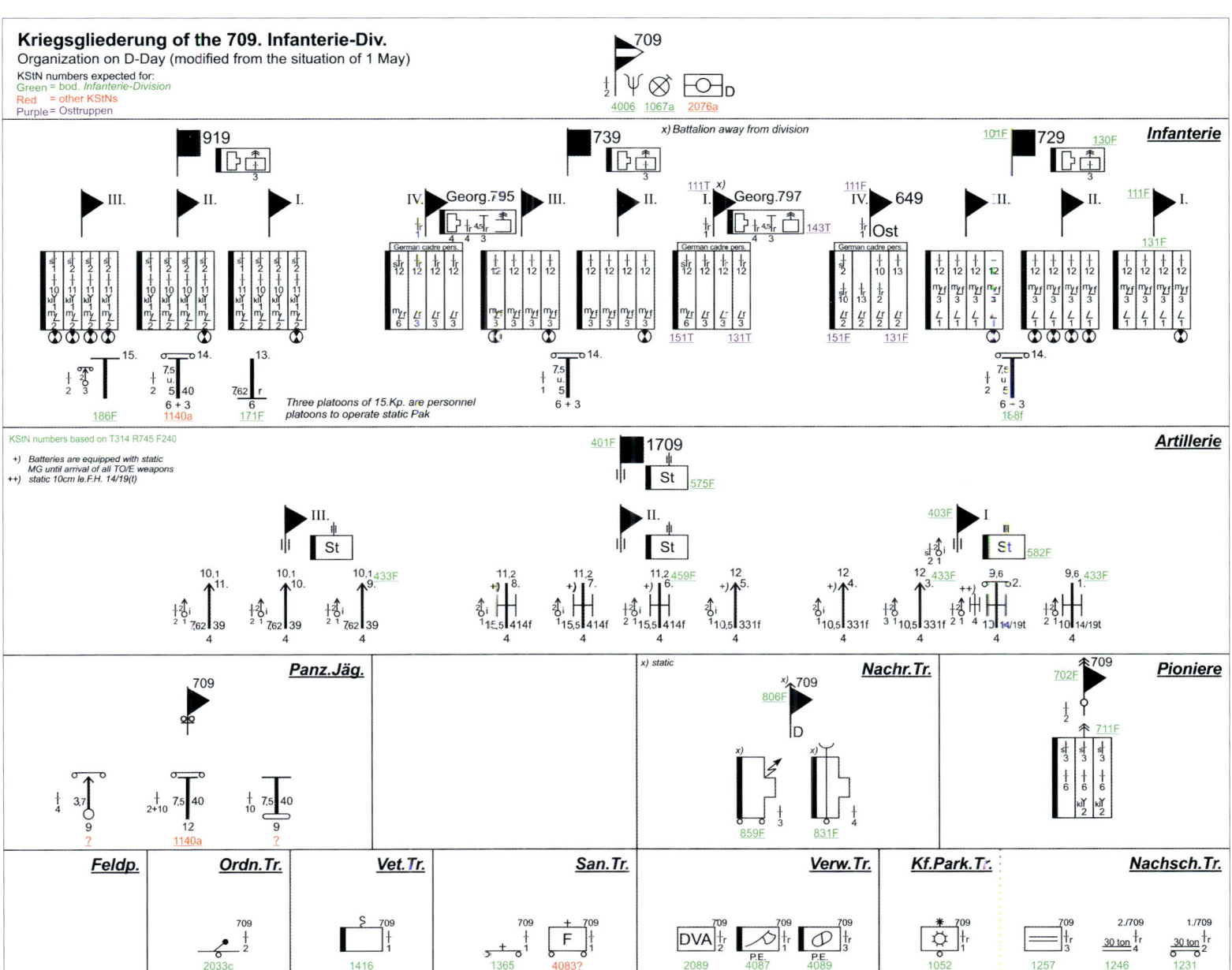

On D-Day the 709.I.D. was exceptionally large with eight German and three eastern battalions, although one was away from the division. The artillery was also significant in number with no less than eleven batteries.

formations that fought under it. Examining the division's combat history is unfortunately complicated by the paucity of credible sources. Establishing its record during this period requires extensive reconstruction.

Useful, if limited, information can be found in the records of *AOK 7*, as well as in Allied documents and intelligence files. Many more details are available in the Foreign Military Studies, which include extensive monographs from *Gen.Lt.* von Schlieben and *Obstlt.* Keil (a regimental commander and later commander of *KG Keil*). Yet these studies raise several serious problems. For example, the account of the division commander often lacks detail and typically quotes records of *AOK 7* and *Heeresgruppe B* to explain the difficulties the division faced, rather than providing local details on the fighting itself.

Keil's contribution is much more detailed. Not only does he cover the activities of his regiment on D-Day, but also the later operations of his battlegroup, which remained in action until the end of **June**. The principal shortcoming of his work is the timeline: dates often conflict with other sources and his chronology of events is sometimes demonstrably incorrect.[10] To his credit, Keil readily admitted that his dates and certain locations might be wrong, however, he insisted that the events themselves happened just as he described them.[11] Certain events, of course, can be checked against other sources, and Keil's descriptions do indeed appear to be largely reliable, varying only in minor details. Due to the significance of his account, an attempt will be made here to correct the timeline and to provide more context. The framework for this effort is found in the Allied records and publications that furnish dates and locations in more detail than do existing German sources.

It should also be noted that the accounts of Von Schlieben and Keil do not cover all of the division's elements or sectors. This is especially true for the fighting on the eastern wing and — to a lesser extent — the eastern part of the *Cherbourg Landfront*. Fortunately, wartime reports are available from several key officers, including battalion commanders, and these reports, while still incomplete, help to fill in some of the blanks. Many of these accounts are found in official German records from **1944**. In certain cases they conflict with the accounts of Von Schlieben and Keil. In such cases, priority will generally be given to battalion commanders over higher ranking officers, since the former were more familiar with the operations of their own troops.

Organisation and Equipment

Although the *709. I.D.* was classed as a static formation on D-Day, it had not started out as such in **1941**. The divisions of the 15th Wave demonstrated a somewhat different organisation compared to earlier organisational waves. This is understandable, since these divisions were envisaged for occupation and security duties, rather than regular frontline service.[12] The division initially had just two infantry regiments (*IR 729* and *739*) with the typical three battalions, but without regimental heavy weapons companies. The artillery consisted of just one battalion (*Art.Abt. 669*) with three batteries. The final combat element was a single engineer company. The divisional support troops were also weak.[13]

Most of the earlier regular infantry divisions had three infantry regiments along with several heavy weapons companies. Their artillery typically consisted of a regiment with three battalions, each with two or three batteries. These divisions normally possessed an engineer battalion with three companies and numerous support troops. Many divisions combined their anti-tank and reconnaissance elements in a single battalion, although these could also be organised as separate battalions.[14]

On **9 September 1942**, the *OKH* decided that divisions of the "700" group (15th Wave) were to be reorganised as coastal defence divisions.[15] As a result, the *709. I.D.* was reclassified as a static division. The reorganisation of the division, which encompassed the formation of several new elements, was to be completed by **1 December**. Changes included establishment of a self-propelled AT company, a signals battalion and an engineer battalion with two companies. The infantry was now characterised as "fortress infantry" (*Festungs-Infanterie*) and the artillery as static.[16] In **1943**, the former was described as "fortress troops" (*Festungstruppen*).[17]

Although another authorisation document was introduced in **September 1943**, several of the most important changes before the invasion were not covered by it.[18] It still offers a good place to start to illustrate developments that took place later, however.

The authorisation document called for two infantry regiments, each consisting of a headquarters company, three battalions and an AT platoon. The headquarters company had a signals platoon and an engineer platoon with three MG's. As was standard for a static division, the infantry battalions had no MG companies. Instead, there were four rifle (*Schützen*) companies. Each company was authorised 12 MG's and 3 medium mortars. The first company in each battalion was to be equipped with bicycles. Both regiments had an AT platoon with three heavy AT guns and three MG's, but without motorisation.[19] The division had been formed without such platoons, which were not included on the authorisations document of **October 1941**, but finally appeared on the organisational document of **October 1942**.[20]

The divisional artillery was particularly weak. Until mid-**1943**, it consisted of just *Art.Abt. 669*. During that summer, the battalion was reorganised into a regiment by adding a regimental headquarters and a second battalion.[21] The authorisation document, however, still shows the 2nd Battalion as just a headquarters. On paper, the 1st Battalion had a headquarters battery and three gun batteries. These batteries each had four light field guns, one light *Flak* and two MG's. The guns in the 1st Battery were of Czechoslovakian origin.[22]

The division was also earmarked to receive an AT company with nine self-propelled heavy AT guns and nine MG's. In addition, the authorisation document directed *Pi.Btl. 709* to consist of three companies; the headquarters would have two MG's and each of the companies another nine MG's. The 1st and 2nd Companies both had a flamethrower.[23]

Apart from the changes outlined in the **September** authorisation document, the division experienced additional changes in its makeup before the invasion: The artillery was expanded to three battalions; the regimental AT troops were strengthened; and a full AT battalion was formed. There were also changes to the infantry: A third infantry regiment arrived in **October**.[24] An infantry battalion left in **November**, and several battalions of *Osttruppen* were incorporated into, or attached to, the division.

The last known order of battle of the division is dated **1 May 1944**. Although some changes between that date and the invasion are certainly possible, these would most likely have been minor (in some cases, handwritten corrections or clarifications were added to the document). It should be noted that there are two versions of this order of battle and they conflict on some points. One significant difference pertains to the use of bicycles in certain infantry battalions.[25] This discrepancy can probably be explained by one version (that of the division itself) following the authorisation document and the other (from *AOK 7* records) portraying the actual organisation, which included non-organic bicycles that had been supplied as part of enhanced mobility efforts. To assess the mobility of the infantry, the latter document will be used in this narrative.

A second noteworthy difference is the absence of an eastern battalion in the organisational document of the division itself, while it was listed in the records of *AOK 7*. The battalion was still officially part of the division, but no longer under its direct command. This has an effect on how eastern

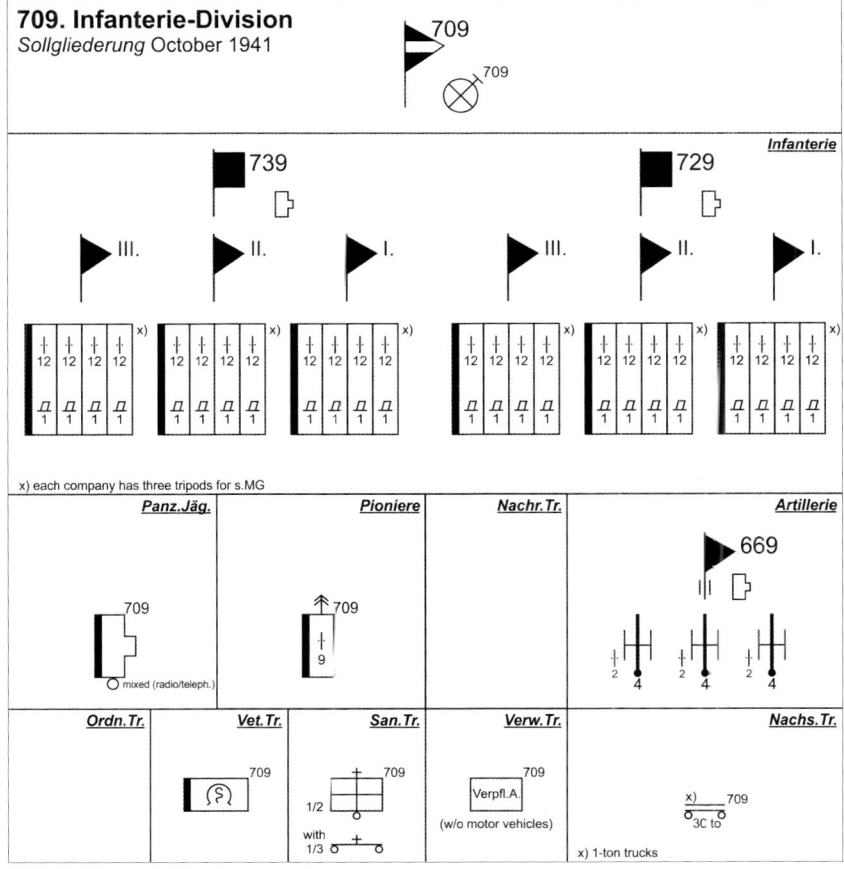

In early 1941 the division was raised with two regiments, a single artillery battalion and an individual engineer, and signals company.

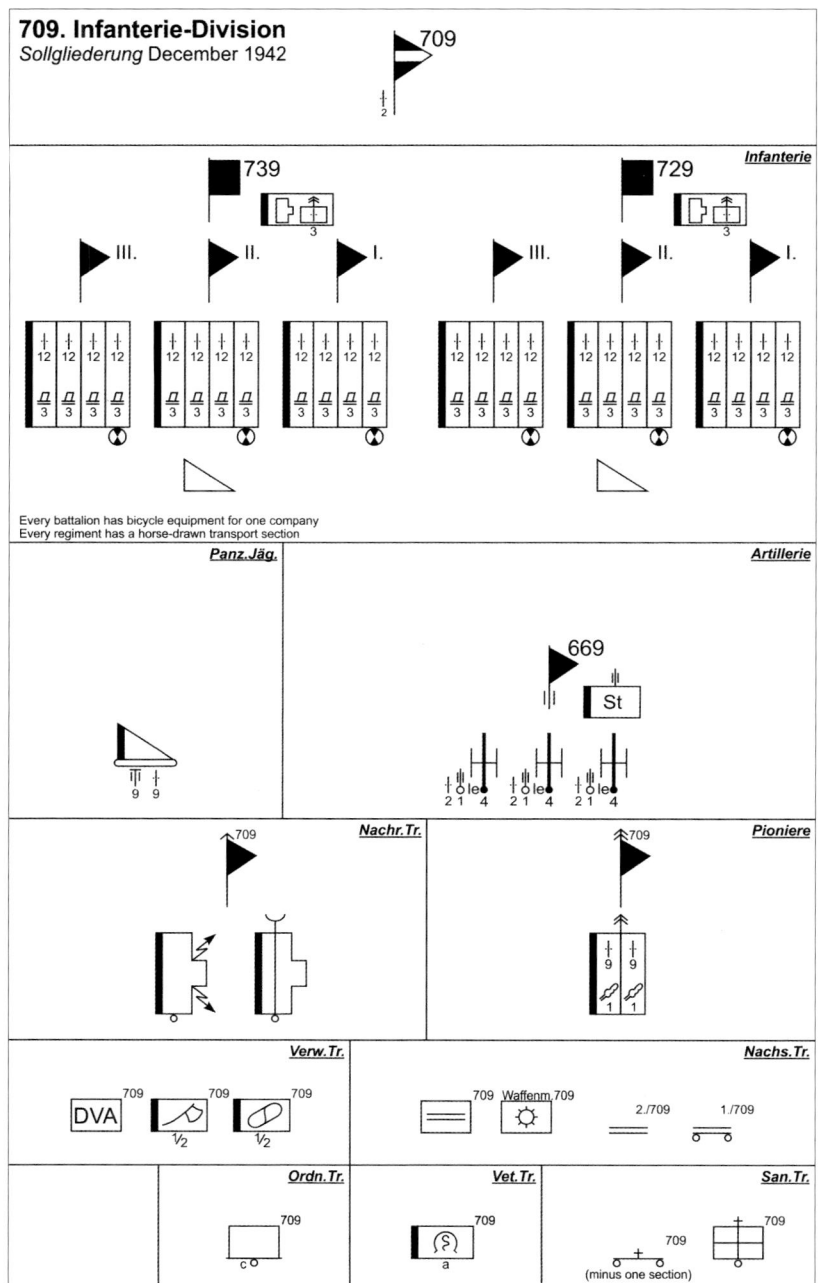
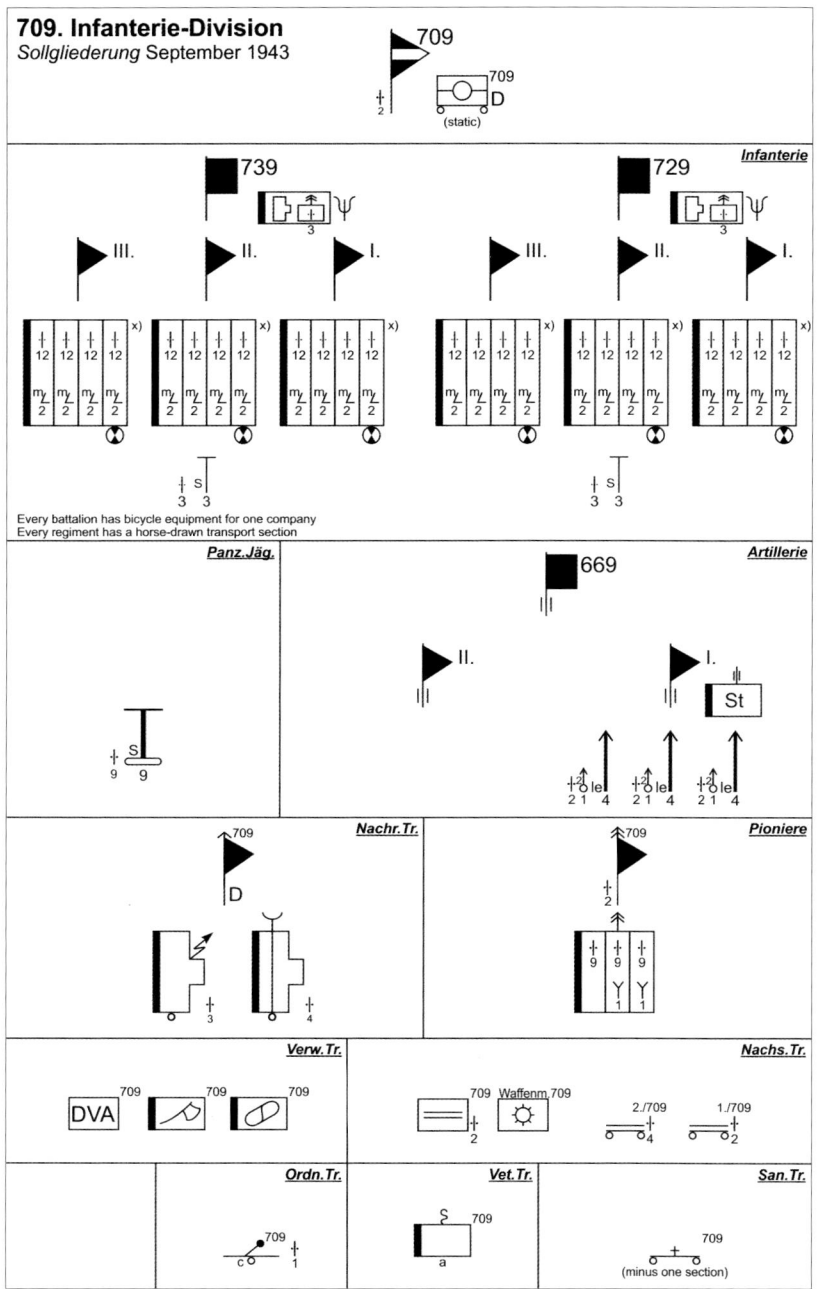

personnel numbers, which are identical on both documents, should be interpreted: Does the number of *Ostsoldaten* represent two or three battalions?

On **1 May**, the divisional headquarters was protected by two light MG's and supported by a mapping detachment and a motorcycle dispatch rider platoon. There was even a division band. *Nachr.Abt. 709* consisted of a headquarters and wireless and telephone companies. The battalion's personnel shortage was 8%. No such shortages were shown for the division's support troops, which suggests they were at 100%.[26]

On D-Day, the division had three infantry regiments, *Grenadier-Regiment 729, 739* and *919*, commanded by *Obst.* Rohrbach, *Obst.* Köhn and *Obstlt.* Keil, respectively. Rohrbach had held his position since **16 June 1942**, while Köhn had only taken over his regiment on **14 May 1944**, succeeding *Obst.* Manussi, who had been in command since **1941** but was no longer fit to lead a regiment due to health issues. Although a late replacement, *Obst.* Köhn was quite familiar with the sector, having served with *AOK 7* from **August 1942** to **21 January 1944**.[27] He also acted as a liaison officer between the Commanding Admiral for the Channel Coast (*Kommandierender Admiral Kanalküste*, stationed in Rouen) and *AOK 7* and *AOK 15*.[28]

The three regiments differed on several points, but *GR 729* and *739* demonstrate enough similarities to be discussed together. Both regiments consisted of a headquarters, headquarters company, two (*739*) or three (*729*) German battalions and an AT company. Each was also reinforced by *Osttruppen*; for *GR 729* this was *Ost-Btl. 649*, which was officially renamed the *IV. (Ost)/Fest.Gren.Rgt. 729* on **19 April**.[29] *GR 739* included two Georgian battalions, one of which replaced a German battalion. The *I./739* had been sent to the Eastern Front in late **1943**.[30] A new 1st Battalion was formed by assigning and redesignating *Georg.Inf.Btl. 797* as the *I. (Georg.)/Fest.Gren.*

Previous page, left: By late 1942 the division was being expanded. The signals troops and engineers received an additional company and were turned into battalions. The division also received divisional and regimental anti-tank elements and the infantry regiments changed their light mortars for medium ones.

Previous page, right: The division's authorised strength was again updated in September 1943. The changes were relatively minor, but they do reflect the development of its artillery towards a full regiment.

Rgt. 739. The same happened with *Georg.Inf.Btl. 795*, which became the *IV. (Georg.)/Fest.Gren.Rgt. 739*.[31] On D-Day, neither of these battalions was available to the regiment, as both were located in other sectors. Together with *Ost-Btl. 649*, these battalions will be discussed separately in a future volume.

On **1 May 1944**, the two regiments were close to authorised strength. *GR 729* had a personnel shortage of 4% in its infantry battalions and *GR 739* a shortage of 4.5%.[32] In *GR 729*, the 2nd Battalion was fully equipped with bicycles, as were the first companies of both the 1st Battalion (1st Company) and the 3rd Battalion (9th Company).[33] *GR 739* had bicycles in the 5th and 9th Companies, while 12th Company may have also had bicycles.[34]

The headquarters company of both *GR 729* and *739* included a signals and an engineer platoon, the latter armed with three light MG's.[35] In *GR 729*, the company reportedly also included a dispatch rider section equipped with motorcycles. While most of the transportation of the company was horse-drawn, there were six lorries as well. The company had a strength of 78 officers and about 240 other ranks, including 10 Russian *Hiwi's*.[36]

On **1 May**, the 20 rifle companies in the two regiments were each equipped with 11 (*4./729*) or 12 light MG's and a single 5 cm mortar (*Gr.W. 36*). Each company also had three *8,14 cm Gr.W. 278(f)* — even though these medium mortars were not shown on the order of battle — and three tripods to allow machine guns to be used as heavy weapons.[37] This differed from the *KStN*, which called for a command section, three platoons (each with four rifle sections and a light mortar section), a heavy MG section (with two heavy MG's) and the trains, for a combined strength of 3 officers, 25-28 NCO's and 155 men.

Few prisoner accounts are available, but the companies in *GR 729* were most likely organised in three rifle platoons. According to a soldier who had served in the 8th Company, the rifle platoons had three rifle sections, each consisting of an NCO and eight men. Each section was equipped with a light *MG 42*. Each platoon also had two sections with heavier weapons: One heavy MG section and one mortar section. The heavy MG section was led by an NCO with six or seven men, and the mortar section consisted of a commander and five men. This particular company is said to have had just two medium mortars instead of three.[38] Although this organisation deviates from the *KStN*, it almost matches that of the authorisation document in numbers of MG's and medium mortars.[39]

Although there are not enough accounts to confirm them, the reports for *GR 739* are quite different. Two soldiers of the *5.* and the *12./739* both stated that their companies consisted of only two rifle platoons and a heavy platoon. The rifle platoons had four sections, each armed with one light *MG 34* and a machine pistol. In 5th Company the platoons also had received two *Faustpatronen* each. In this company, section strength was just one NCO and six men: it had been in reserve around Urville-Hague when it was hit hard by air attacks on the night of **31 May - 1 June**; The majority of the 17 killed, 14 missing, and 32 wounded in the bombings were suffered by the company, which also lost its commander (MIA).[40]

The equipment and organisation of the heavy platoon in the *5./739* is more confusing. When compared to other records, it seems that it was armed with four MG's, three of which were heavy MG's, made possible by the tripods in each company. The platoon supposedly had four (French) medium mortars, but it is more likely there were only three and perhaps a light mortar. The organisation of these platoons is not clear, but it appears there were two MG sections and a mortar section.[41] After the bombings, the combined strength of the 5th Company is said to have been about 90 men, including replacements from the 6th Company. The company had about 20 Poles in its ranks. A similar number of Poles, 15-20, was reported for 12th Company, but it had a strength of 120 men.[42]

The two POW's have indeed confirmed the presence of bicycles, but little is known about other means of transportation in these companies. The 5th Company reportedly had six horse-drawn wagons, one lorry and a field kitchen. The horse vehicles were lost in air attacks around **1 June**. The 12th Company relied entirely on bicycles with the exception of two horse-drawn vehicles for the mortars.[43]

Both *GR 729* and *739* had an AT company: The 14th.[44] These were formed in 1944 by strengthening and expanding the existing regimental AT platoons.[45] According to *Gen.* von Schlieben, the AT companies were formed by taking men from other units in the regiments.[46] The personnel of the company even retained their original *Feldpost* number.[47]

For most of **1943**, the AT platoons were (officially) armed with three 7.5 cm AT guns, almost certainly *Pak 97/38's*.[48] By **1 November**, the guns of *Pz.Jg. Zug 729* were deployed in resistance nests, thus the platoon was armed with three *5 cm Pak 38's* borrowed from *Pz.Jg.Kp. 709* and motorised in an ad hoc fashion using sector-limited ("static") prime movers.[49] The guns of *Pz.Jg.Zug 739* were first used by *Pz.Jg.Kp. 709*. Nonetheless, by **1 December**, these were deployed on the coast as well. During this period, the platoon was outfitted with three *5 cm Pak 38's*, also borrowed from *Pz.Jg.Kp. 709*.[50] In **December**, there were plans to re-equip the platoons with *Pak 97/38's* and provide each battalion with an AT platoon with three *Pak 38's*, but it is unclear if this was carried out. The orders of battle never show such platoons with the battalions.[51]

In both regiments, the AT companies finally made their appearance on the order of battle of **1 March 1944** with identical weaponry. Each company had a single light MG, six 7.5 cm AT guns and three 5 cm AT guns.[52] This was still the same on **1 May**.[53] Although the exact type of 7.5 cm guns is not listed, this can be determined from other sources. In **May**, the division had 15 medium AT guns, nine of which were *5 cm Pak 38's*.[54] By default, the other six were *Pak 97/38's*, as no other medium AT guns are associated with the division. The division also had 33 assigned heavy AT guns, of which 21 were part of the AT battalion. This leaves 12 heavy AT guns for the AT companies in the three infantry regiments. Six of those can be linked to *GR 919*.[55] As a result, the 7.5 cm AT guns of both the *14./729* and the *14./739* were almost certainly three Pak 40's and three *Pak 97/38's*.

These companies were organised in three platoons armed with a single type of AT gun. The *14./729* was motorised and had lorries and halftracks at its disposal.[56] The *14./739* used different vehicles to draw the guns: French two-man tankettes. These presumably were Renault UE prime movers, which also carried ammunition.[57] In addition, the trains had two lorries and two horse-drawn vehicles, while the company headquarters section included two messengers with motorcycles. It has been reported that the AT company also had two 8.8 cm guns, although this has not been confirmed.[58] These may have been among the six *8,8 cm Pak 43/41's* that had seen service with *Pz.Jg.Kp. 709* in **1943**.[59] Another possibility is that they were some of the 8.35 cm *Flak* that had arrived with the division in **February 1944**.[60]

GR 919 (*Obstlt.* Keil) arrived around **5-6 October 1943**, having been detached from the *242. I.D.* Together with a battalion of *AR 242*, it was transported by seven trains from Gent (Belgium) to the area of Carentan-Cherbourg.[61] Its organisation differed from the other two regiments and, on **1 May 1944**, it consisted of a headquarters, headquarters company, three line battalions and three heavy weapons companies. The 13th Company was an infantry-gun company, while 14th and 15th Companies were both

AT companies. Little can be said about the headquarters company but, like the other regiments, it included a signals and an engineer platoon with three MG's. Together, the battalions had a personnel shortage of 3.5% and, in the heavy weapons companies, this was 4%.[62]

The three infantry battalions were organised similarly to the other regiments with four rifle companies each, however, there was a difference in weaponry, with the companies in *GR 919* possessing two medium mortars, a light flamethrower and varying numbers of MG's. Each company had 1 or 2 heavy MG's and 10 or 11 light MG's.[63] These numbers probably indicate a shortage of machine guns. The authorised strength of the companies should have been 2 heavy and 12 light MG's. The companies had three platoons with four rifle sections each. All sections were armed with one light *MG 34* or *MG 42* and had a strength of 9 or 10 men. The mortars and heavy MG's were collected in separate mortar and MG sections.[64]

The heavy weapons companies were reasonably well equipped. The 13th Company had six Russian 7.62 cm infantry guns.[65] Although the guns are not identified, photographic evidence shows these to be *7,62 cm I.K.H. 290(r)'s*.[66]

Unlike the AT companies in *GR 729* and *739*, the *14./919* already existed when the regiment joined the division; it was listed as a partially motorised company with three 7.5 cm AT guns on the original authorisation document.[67] In **October 1943**, the company was indeed listed with three 7.5 cm AT guns and two MG's. The company had four platoons, three of which operated "static" AT guns.[68] In **January**, its issued AT guns were identified as *Pak 40's*.[69] This organisation and equipment remained identical until the order of battle of **1 May 1944**, when the company no longer had responsibility for "static" weapons. It was listed with six 7.5 cm and three 5 cm AT guns and two MG's.[70] These additional AT guns had arrived towards the end of **April** and were used to form another heavy AT platoon and a medium AT platoon.[71] Thus, it appears that all six 7.5 cm guns were *Pak 40's*, while the three 5 cm guns were *Pak 38's*.[72]

When the regiment joined the division, the 15th Company had no organic heavy weapons.[73] In **October**, it was listed as having three platoons manning nine "static" AT guns, just like 14th Company. The company then received a 4th Platoon, which had hitherto been attached to the headquarters company. This platoon was armed with three light *Flak*,[74] which were reportedly 2 cm *Flak 30's*. The platoon consisted of 2 NCO's and 12 men.[75] After the platoon joined the 15th Company, the latter was listed with two MG's, yet their origin and position within the company are not clear.[76] Initially, the *Flak* were towed by French *chenillettes*, but these were later replaced by Opel *Admiral* and *Horch* prime movers. Although the platoon should have had a fourth gun, it never arrived.[77]

Whereas some motorisation was available for several heavy weapons companies, this was not the case for the regiment as a whole. For the most part, the regiment had to rely on horses and bicycles. The regiment's level of mobility is actually somewhat confusing. According to Keil, one company in each battalion was equipped with bicycles: The 1st, the 5th and the 9th Companies.[78] This is less certain when it comes to the 3rd Battalion. According to the

This 7.62 cm I.K.H.290 (r) was photographed in its firing position. It almost certainly belonged to 13./919 which was equipped with six of these weapons. (Mark A. Bando Collection)

orders of battle of **1 March** and **1 May**, it had four bicycle companies, which is in line with official plans (enhanced mobility efforts) and also supported by statements of soldiers from the 11ᵗʰ Company.⁷⁹ No clear evidence is available for the 10ᵗʰ and the 12ᵗʰ Companies.

The discrepancy between the sources is difficult to explain, but for some time the entire regiment had been a bicycle formation — before having to hand over most of its bicycles.⁸⁰ The 3ʳᵈ Battalion may have been the exception, for it had clearly been intended to be a bicycle battalion, just like the *II./729*.⁸¹

It is clear that the regiment relied on horses for much of its transport. The regimental headquarters had 5 riding horses; 3 more were in the headquarters company, along with 10 light and 4 heavy draught horses. Information also exists for the horse column (*Bespannungsstaffel*) of the regiment, a type of unit also present in the other infantry regiments. In *GR 919*, it was part of the headquarters company. It had 2 riding horses and 44 light draught horses for transport purposes. These were paired with 22 wagons, which were distributed among the companies as a general rule.⁸²

Each battalion headquarters had 4 riding horses, 15 light and 2 heavy draught horses. The rifle companies only had one riding horse for the commander and two heavy draught horses for the field kitchen. Horses were also used in the heavy weapons companies. The largest numbers were in 13ᵗʰ Company, which was not motorised; it had a single riding horse, eight light and two heavy draught horses. The 14ᵗʰ and 15ᵗʰ Companies had no riding horses, but they did have six light and two heavy draught horses.⁸³

Similar figures are given by soldiers of various companies, although the figures differ slightly. The 8ᵗʰ Company allegedly had two horse-drawn wagons.⁸⁴ In the reserve battalion (3ʳᵈ), transport for the 9ᵗʰ Company consisted of one lorry, a light car and two two-horse wagons; bicycles were available for the men.⁸⁵ The transport for the 12ᵗʰ Company was slightly different; it included a field kitchen, ammunition cart and a supply wagon. Each vehicle was drawn by two horses. There were also three infantry lorries used as trailers.⁸⁶

On D-Day, the division had an engineer battalion, *Pionier-Bataillon 709* (*Major* Hornung). The division had been formed with just a single engineer company but, as noted, it was decided in the autumn of **1942** to establish a proper battalion with a headquarters and two companies.⁸⁷ The addition of a third company was ordered in **August 1943**, and the company arrived by the end of that month.⁸⁸

On **1 May 1944**, each company was equipped with three heavy and six light MG's. The first two companies both boasted two light flamethrowers. The battalion headquarters had two MG's and was the only element that was partially motorised. The battalion was slightly understrength, with its personnel at 94%.⁸⁹

A detailed list of the vehicles with the battalion command post has been provided by the NCO in charge of the transportation. There were a number of four-seater civilian cars of many types. Apart from a single Peugeot and Fiat, there were two Citroën's and two Austin's, along with a six-seater Dodge that ran on wood gas. The lorries included three Opel *Blitz* and a 1-tonne Renault; four 3-tonne GMC's were used for transport. Finally, there were four motorcycles: One *DKW*, one BSA, and two Gillet's. Horse transport was available in the form of and 20 horses for 10 carts.⁹⁰

On **1 May 1944**, the division had a full artillery regiment, *Artillerie-Regiment 1709* (*Obst.* Reiter). The regiment consisted of a headquarters battery and three gun battalions. The first two battalions had four batteries each, while the 3ʳᵈ Battalion had only three.⁹¹

The regiment was now organised much differently than it had been in **1941**. At that time, it had only had a single artillery battalion (*Art.Abt. 669*).⁹² The division's organic artillery remained limited to this battalion throughout **1942** and early **1943**.⁹³ It was not until **May 1943** that the artillery began to resemble an actual regiment. On orders of the *OKH*, the *LXXXVII. A.K.* in Bretagne was instructed to raise the headquarters of the *II./AR 709* for the *709. I.D.* This order was peculiar, since the division was stationed in a different sector and its only artillery battalion carried the number *669*. In any case, the new battalion was temporarily subordinated to the *343. I.D.*⁹⁴ In mid-**June**, the battalions were redesignated. The original battalion became the *I./AR 669*; the new battalion the *II./AR 669*.⁹⁵ Later that month, the *OKH* ordered *Ob.West* to establish a regimental headquarters for the division's artillery.⁹⁶ This headquarters was first listed on the order of battle in **August**. The *II./AR 669* was still with the *LXXXVII. A.K.*⁹⁷ Since this battalion was never physically with the division, it is no surprise it was no longer listed on **1 October**.⁹⁸ It became the *III./AR 266* of the *266. I.D.*, which had arrived in Bretagne near the end of **July**.⁹⁹

The official transfer of the battalion meant that a new 2ⁿᵈ Battalion had to be formed for the *709. I.D.*¹⁰⁰ This was done with separate batteries already located on the Cotentin.[101] Another reinforcement during the month was the *II./AR 242*, which joined the regiment as the *III./AR 669* and, like *GR 919*, was drawn from the *242. I.D.*[102] The regiment was redesignated as *AR 1709* in **December 1943**.[103]

Because of the gradual development of the regiment, each headquarters and battalion has its own unique history and characteristics. To understand their conditions on D-Day, it is thus easier to examine the sub-units individually.

As a component of a static division, the regimental headquarters was to follow *KStN 401F* and the headquarters battery *KStN 575F* (both **1 November 1943**).[104] A member of the regimental headquarters provided details about its composition and that of the headquarters battery on D-Day, which suggest there were some deviations. According to him, the headquarters proper consisted of the commander, an adjutant and an officer assistant; it was supported by a signals section of one officer, eight telephone operators and six wireless operators. In addition, there was a technical officer with three assistants.[105]

The headquarters battery consisted of several platoons and sections. The signals platoon allegedly had a strength of 12-16 men (including two senior NCO's) and was outfitted with bicycles. Roughly half the men operated wireless sets, the others telephones. The battery commander was also the commander of this platoon and the regimental signals officer. The surveying section consisted of an NCO and seven men; other sections were that of the armourer/artificer (an NCO with an assistant) and the administrative section, which consisted of a paymaster (NCO) and two men. Personnel in the battery also included the *Hauptwachtmeister* (in charge of the trains), a medical NCO and a field kitchen with two cooks. In addition, there was a light artillery column of six to eight horse-drawn wagons;[106] it appears to have had about 20 drivers.[107] This was not a unit listed in the *KStN* and may have been formed by gathering the horses of the headquarters and battery; it can be considered part of the trains.

The regimental headquarters had a strength of about 12 officers and men and there were about 70 in the headquarters battery, figures close to the *KStN's*. Both elements are a good illustration of the poor motorisation of the regiment. Their combined mobility was provided by a lorry, some horse-drawn wagons with 40-45 horses, two light cars and three motorcycles.[108] Motorisation was nonetheless better than the *KStN*, which only allowed for two light cars and two motorcycles with the headquarters.

When the division was raised in **1941**, *Art.Abt. 669* had been formed with a headquarters, a signals platoon and three batteries. Each of the batteries was initially armed with four *10,5 cm le.F.H.16's* and two MG's, but this changed in early 1942.[109] Following the invasion of the Soviet Union, the production of artillery pieces fell below the needs of the Army in the East (*Ostheer*). As such, the *OKH* ordered divisions in the west to hand over their German guns and be re-equipped with lower calibre and/or captured guns in **December 1941**. This order also affected several divisions of the 15th Wave, including the *709. I.D.* All of these divisions would be rearmed with two batteries of *7,5 cm F.K.16 nA's* and one battery with *10,5 cm le.F.H. 325(f)'s*. Orders for the exchange were issued in early **January 1942**.[110]

The authorisation document for the division was updated in **October 1942**, and this also affected the battalion. Instead of a simple signals platoon, it now called for a headquarters battery and each battery would have a light *Flak*. The artillery pieces would be German 10.5 cm light field howitzers.[111] When the division joined the *LXXXIV. A.K.* in **December 1942**, the battalion did not yet fully match this organisation. The headquarters battery had been formed, but the *Flak* had not arrived and the artillery pieces had not been exchanged. The first battery still had four French 10.5 cm howitzers, while the other batteries still operated *F.K.16 nA's*.[112] It was noted that an issuance with Czechoslovakian field pieces was underway, although this was apparently delayed.[113] On **1 February 1943**, the 1st through 3rd Batteries were armed with 10.5 cm French light howitzers, 10 cm Czech light howitzers and *7,5 cm F.K.16 nA's*, respectively.[114] In **April**, cannon were listed in all batteries. The 1st Battery was equipped with four *8 cm F.K.17(t)'s*; the 2nd and 3rd Batteries both with four *7,5 cm F.K.16 nA's*.[115]

Officially, nothing had changed as of **1 June**, but the guns of the 1st and 2nd Batteries were now committed elsewhere, most likely in resistance nests. Both batteries now fielded four "10.5 cm howitzers". The battalion also had eight 8 cm Czech guns, which were at the disposal of the *OKH* to be reassigned.[116] Three 2 cm *Flak* 38's arrived on **13 August**, and they were first listed on the order of battle of **1 September**. By then, the eight guns requisitioned by the *OKH* and the 10.5 cm howitzers were no longer mentioned.[117] In early **November**, the 1st and 2nd Batteries were both listed with four "static" *10 cm le.F.H. 14/19(t)'s*.[118] It is not clear if these were the same weapons as the "10.5 cm howitzers" they had used earlier. It appears the *le.F.H.14/19(t)'s* were assigned to the battalion during **December**. Although the order of battle of **1 December** still listed them as "static" replacements for the authorised guns, they were listed as standard equipment in records dated **19 December**. These orders also called for the *F.K.16 nA's* of the 3rd Battery to be replaced by *10,5 cm K.331(f)'s*. The battalion was joined by *Geräte-Batterie Westmark* (aka *Westeck*), which was already equipped with the same type of guns and became the battalion's 4th Battery. This latter development was part of a general reorganisation of the artillery on the Cotentin, which included the reorganisation of *Art.Abt. 669* into a regiment with three battalions.[119] In this period, the *KStN's* were specified as *KStN 403F* for the headquarters, *KStN 582F* for the headquarters battery and *KStN 433F* for the light batteries. All were dated **1 November 1943**.[120]

On **1 January 1944**, the battalion headquarters was armed with two heavy MG's. Both the 1st and 2nd Batteries still had four Czech 10 cm howitzers, but each also had two 2 cm *Flak* and two light MG's. The 3rd Battery had the same number of MG's and *Flak*, but it had not yet turned in its guns and still had four *7,5 cm F.K.16 nA's*. The newly assigned 4th Battery had four French *10,5 cm K.331(f)'s*; it also had two French MG's but there were no *Flak* with the battery. Its MG's were actually "static" since its authorised weapons had not yet arrived.[121] The orders of battle for early **1944** are generally difficult to read, but it appears that the 3rd Battery had indeed been reequipped with four *K. 331(f)'s* by **1 March**.[122]

The last known organisational document, dated **1 May**, lists the battalion headquarters with two heavy MG's and two light *Flak*. Prisoners from the battalion identify the machine guns as an *MG 34* and an *MG 08*. The 1st and 2nd Batteries were still equipped with four *10 cm le.F.H. 14/19(t)'s*. The 2nd Battery was motorised and also had two "static" *le.F.H.14/19(t)'s* at its disposal. The remaining two batteries in the battalion were both equipped with four *10,5 cm K.331(f)'s* All batteries now had a single 2 cm *Flak*, rather than two. The *Flak* in 1st through 3rd Batteries were German, while the 10 guns in the other batteries (and with the 1st Battalion headquarters) were Italian and most likely came from the batch of 10 *2 cm Scotti(i)'s* the division had received in **March**. Machine guns were still in short supply. The 1st through 3rd Batteries each had two light MG's, but the 4th Battery did not have any. Instead it used "static" machine guns, but these were not listed.[123]

The battalion's headquarters battery reportedly included a signals section, a survey section (one NCO and two men) and a light artillery supply column with four or five horse-drawn wagons.[124] Other reports claim there were about 10 such wagons in the battery and 60 to 74 horses, as well as three lorries and two or three light cars. The battery strength was about 60 men, including 20 Poles. The men were primarily armed with *K98k* rifles, but there were also some *M98* and Polish rifles.[125] The battalion commander provided some additional information, giving the combined strength of his battalion as 400-500 men. This number is close to the *KStN's* which called for some 433 men: 77 per gun battery, 111 in the headquarters battery and 14 with the headquarters. According to the commander's statements, the battalion had about 140 horses and a small number of motor vehicles. All batteries were horse-drawn, which would mean the 2nd Battery was not actually motorised, as it was shown to be on the order of battle.[126]

Prisoners from the battalion, however, provide some additional details and different numbers. The strength of the 1st Battery was about 60 men, including 10 Poles. The 2nd Battery was weaker with about 50 men, including 5 Poles. The 3rd and 4th Batteries were similar in strength to the 1st Battery, but both included a Yugoslav, while the 4th Battery only had five Poles in its ranks. Reportedly all soldiers of about 25 years old were transferred to the east in October 1943 and had been replaced by 18-19 year olds. Some details are available for the weapons in the 3rd Battery. The two light MG's were Polish. In addition, there was a 5 cm mortar and the men were armed with *K98k* and some Czech rifles. The mobility in the 1st Battalion relied on horse-drawn vehicles, but there were not enough to provide organic mobility to the batteries. To move the batteries, horses needed to be borrowed from the headquarters battery. There are indications that the batteries had four horse-drawn wagons, but the enhanced mobility efforts may have increased this. The 3rd Battery reportedly had eight riding horses and 12 draught horses for supply. The 2nd Battery had some 18 draught horses, but also some motorisation. Some state there were prime movers to move the guns, while others only mention four to seven lorries for both that purpose and to transport supplies. There was also a car for the battery commander.[127]

All these mobility numbers can be compared to the *KStN* of a light static artillery battery, which allowed for eight bicycles, eight riding horses and four heavy draught horses for two wagons and the field kitchen.[128] Per the *KStN*, the headquarters battery should have 18 or 19 riding horses, 7 light, 34 heavy and 24 very heavy draught horses. Together, they moved the battery's two carts, the field kitchen and 21 wagons. The heavy and very heavy draught horses could also be used to move the guns and limbers, and wagons and carts of the gun batteries. In addition to horses, the headquarters would have 12 bicycles, while motorisation was limited to two 2-tonne lorries.[129]

Even before it was officially reassigned to the *266. I.D.*, the original *II./AR 709* (later the *II./AR 669*) had never contributed much to the *709. I.D.* Instead, a new *II./AR 669* was established and this time it stayed with the division until its demise in the summer of **1944**. The battalion was formed from a newly built battalion headquarters and headquarters battery. Its batteries were formed by assigning four batteries already on the peninsula: *Geräte-Batterie Ostmark* (also known as *Osteck*),* *Stellungs-Batterie (Küste) 317*, *Batterie Thüringen* (Thuringia) and the self-propelled *Batterie Reichenau*. These became the battalion's 5th through 8th Batteries.[130]

All four batteries had different weaponry, but in **November** orders were received to change this. The 7th Battery would relinquish its *le.F.H.14/19(t)'s* and the 8th Battery its self-propelled *s.F.H.13/1's*. Both batteries were to be re-equipped with four *15,5 cm s.F.H.414(f)'s*. This type of gun was already present in the 6th Battery, while the 5th Battery could keep its *10,5 cm K.331(f)'s*.[131] The *KStN's* used by the 1st Battalion were also suitable for the 2nd Battalion, except for its heavy batteries, which would use *KStN 459F*.[132]

It would take some time for the new guns to arrive. On **1 January 1944**, the 7th Battery still had four *le.F.H.14/19(t)'s*, while 8th Battery still had not turned in its three self-propelled *15 cm s.F.H.13/1's* mounted on French armoured Lorraine tractors. All four batteries of the battalion were armed with "static" machine guns since sufficient authorised weapons had not yet arrived. The 5th Battery had two French MG's; the 6th three French heavy MG's, two German light MG's and two *2 cm Kw.K. 38's*; the 7th was outfitted with five French MG's; the 8th had only two Czech MG's.[133] The 7th Battery reportedly received its 15.5 cm howitzers in early **February**, and it appears that all batteries had been equipped with their planned artillery by **1 March**. The full complement of authorised MG's had still not been received.[134]

The situation on **1 May** is quite clear and presumably reflects much of the situation as it existed on D-Day. At that time, the battalion's headquarters battery was identical to that of the 1st Battalion and included a signals section, a light artillery column with four or five horse-drawn wagons and a survey section of one NCO and two other ranks.[135] The battalion did not have two 2 cm *Flak* outside of the gun batteries, however. The battalion thus had a *KStN* strength of 371 men (Headquarters battery with 101 personnel and heavy gun batteries with 85 men each).[136]

All batteries were fully equipped with artillery pieces, but a shortfall of MG's remained a problem. The 6th Battery was the only one listed with two authorised MG's, but this may have changed in the other batteries before the invasion. Each battery did possess an Italian (Scotti) 2 cm *Flak*.[137]

Prisoners have provided some additional details about the individual batteries. The 5th Battery is said to have had a strength of some 90 men, including 30 *Volksdeutsche*. Yet this number seems high compared to the identically armed 3rd and 4th Batteries. Although horses are not mentioned, the 5th Battery had 10 carts and one car.[138] The 7th Battery reportedly had 16 horses, which would be above the *KStN*, and similar numbers were claimed for the other batteries: 16-20 horses. When the 7th Battery needed to change positions, 30 horses had to be borrowed from the headquarters battery.[139]

The 8th Battery reportedly had a strength of only about 50 men, 12 of whom were *Volksdeutsche*. Another prisoner states that the battery had 1 officer, 60 German and 10 Italian personnel. These numbers can be compared to the *KStN* of 85 all ranks. Each gun was to have a crew of one NCO and eight men, but typically only five or six men were available. Such small crews were possible because the battery was immobile. The guns had been taken off their wheels and mounted on platforms with 360 degree traverse. In addition to its 15.5 cm howitzers, the battery had a single *MG 34*, a Czech MG and rifles. This may indicate that the authorised machine guns had begun to arrive before the invasion. There were four two-horse vehicles in the battery, but the exact number of horses is unknown.[140]

While the development of the 1st Battalion took place over several years and the background of the 2nd Battalion was rather complex, the story of the *III./AR 1709* is more straightforward. It joined the *709. I.D.* in **October 1943** as the *II./AR 242*. Upon its arrival, the battalion was immediately redesignated as the *III./AR 669*, and its batteries were renumbered from 7 to 9. The battalion had been raised with a headquarters, headquarters battery and three gun batteries, an organisation that did not change either before or after joining the division.

---

* *Geräte-Batterie: Battery with equipment but without assigned personnel. Stellungs-Batterie (K): A separate static coastal (Küste) battery.*

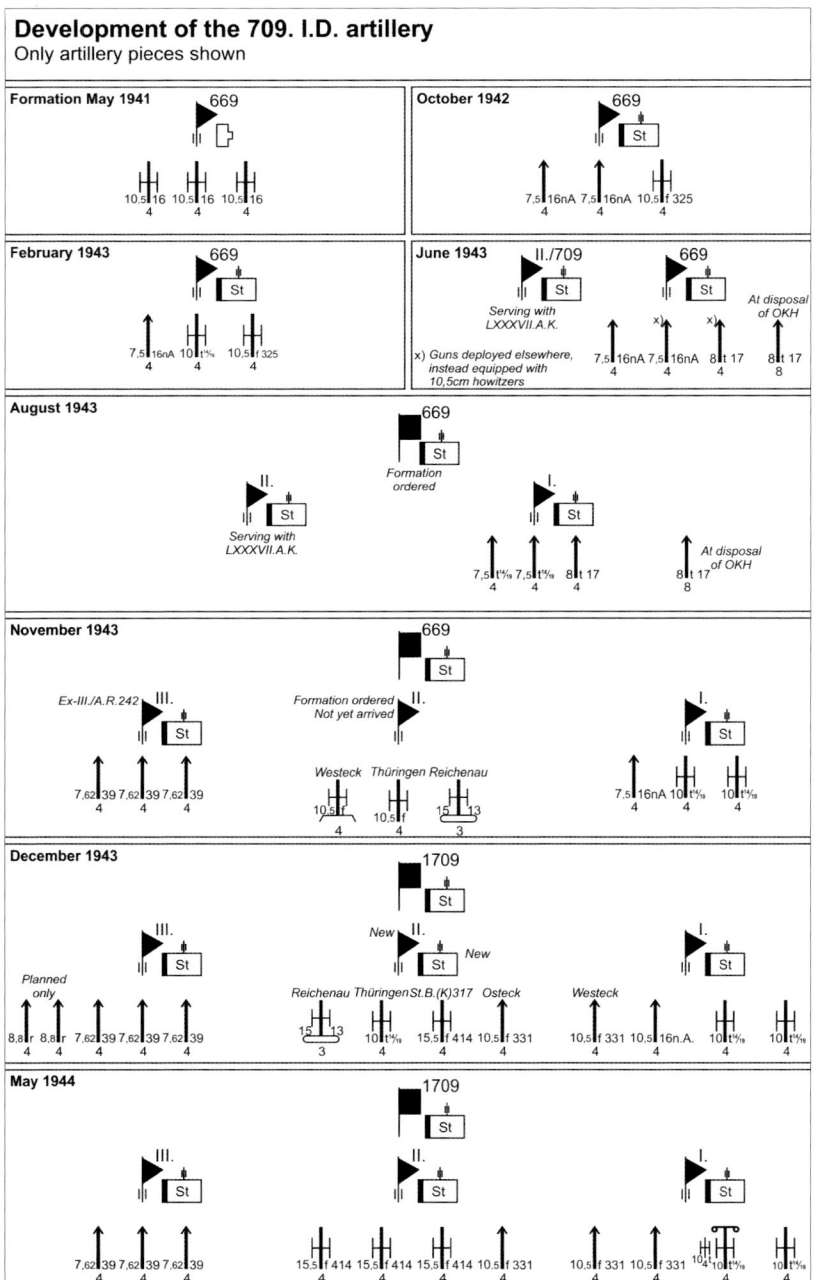

At that time, all three batteries were armed with three *7,62 cm F.K. 39(r)'s* and two machine guns.[141] When the reorganisation of the artillery of the *LXXXIV. A.K.* began in **November**, it was decided that the batteries would each receive a fourth gun. As part of the reorganisation, the batteries needed to be renumbered, given that 1st and 2nd Battalions would have four batteries each. Thus, the batteries in the 3rd Battalion were redesignated 9 through 11.[142] The requisite three Russian 7.62 cm pieces arrived on **28 December**.[143] Considering its weaponry, the battalion must have used the same *KStN's* as the 1st Battalion.

On D-Day, all three batteries of the *III./AR 669* where still armed with four *F.K. 39(r)'s* and two MG's. Each battery had also received an Italian 2 cm (Scotti) light *Flak*.[144] Limited information is available about the individual batteries, but the 11th reportedly had a strength of about 65 officers and men. Its two MG's were *MG 42's*.[145]

A senior signals NCO from the battalion was able to furnish some details on the organisation and equipment of the signals troops in his battalion and the regiment as a whole. The signals section at the battalion headquarters consisted of a signals officer and a senior NCO section leader. It appears there were three junior NCO's to operate telephones and another three for radio communication. In line with the *KStN*, there were three field telephone sections (each with one NCO and four men) and four wireless sections (each with one NCO and two men).[146]

The same prisoner also identified the equipment used. At battalion level, there were four *Bertha* radio sets (*Torn.Fu.b*), while the 11th Battery had two. The 9th and 10th Batteries were equipped with *Konrad* sets (*Torn.Fu.k*). The batteries in the other battalions reportedly all had *Fritz* sets (*Torn.Fu.f*). The regiment and the first two battalions are said to have used "type 6" wireless sets, but this type has not been identified.[147]

The 3rd Battalion reportedly used two 10-line switchboards for its telephones. Lines ran as follows: Each battery (sometimes two); the regiment; the infantry regiment in the area; the battalion's headquarters battery; the battalion commander; and the adjutant. All of this activity could be managed

---

The division's artillery had started out with just a single battalion with three batteries in 1941. By the time of the invasion it had grown into a full regiment with 11 batteries armed with a wide variety of guns.

by a single switchboard, but having two allowed for additional capacity if required. The battalion itself had 30 km of telephone cable and the batteries each had 20 km. The battalion's signals troops had three telephone wagons and one radio wagon. All were drawn by two horses.[148]

Although this information covers much of *AR 1709*, there were also a number of interesting developments that cannot readily be listed under a specific sub-element. Four of these are of particular interest.

In **December 1943**, plans were afoot to add two more batteries to *AR 1709*: The 12th and the 13th. Both would be armed with four *8,8 cm Flak M31(r)'s* and a third, identical battery would be formed for *AR 1716* (*716. I.D.*).[149] Eight guns reached the *709. I.D.* on **19 December** and the *716. I.D.* reported its guns six days later (**25th**). The two batteries in *AR 1709* were in fact listed on the order of battle of **1 January 1944**, although it was noted that the personnel were not yet ready.[150] By **1 February**, these batteries were no longer listed on the order of battle.[151] The guns, and perhaps the batteries in their entirety, were transferred to *H.K.A.R. 1262*. Together with the battery from the *716. I.D.* They became the *6.-8./H.K.A.R. 1262* and were committed along the west coast of the Cotentin.[152]

The transfer of these guns to *H.K.A.R. 1262* may explain why the division received another eight heavy *Flak* on **29 February 1944**. These were *8,35 cm Flak 22(t)'s*.[153] It seems doubtful, however, if the plan to establish two more batteries was still in place, making it unclear why the division received the guns. By **1 April 1944**, six of them were committed as ground-defence weapons (*Landesabwehrgeschütze* / *LAG*) and two were reported as a divisional reserve.[154] *Gen.* von Schlieben, in his Foreign Military Study, provided some information about the latter two. The guns had been found quite useful, given their range of 16 km and 360 degree traverse (most guns in the fortress were trained strictly on the sea and not on land targets). Thus, the division had gone to great effort to position two of them so they were capable of supporting the *Landfront*. Yet it was all for naught. In **May**, much to von Schlieben's frustration, orders arrived for the guns to be pulled out and handed over to the *243. I.D.* to be deployed on the west coast.[155]

Other changes affected the light *Flak* of the regiment itself. The situation regarding the *Flak* as reported on **1 May** was quite different compared to earlier reports. On **1 April**, the 1st Battalion had one *Flak 30* and three *Flak 38's*, while the 2nd Battalion had three *Flak 30's* and the 3rd Battalion two *Flak 30's*.[156] The regiment thus went from 6 *Flak 30's* and 3 *Flak 38's* on **1 April**, to 10 Italian and 3 German guns on **1 May**. The reason for this change, and the fate of the German guns no longer being listed is unknown. It is possible that the latter had only been static pieces and were replaced as soon as the authorised Italian guns arrived.

A final interesting change in the regiment in the period prior to the invasion pertained to the self-propelled guns of the former *Batterie Reichenau*. Redesignated the *8./AR 1709*, that battery was rearmed with *15,5 cm s.F.H.414(f)'s* in **January 1944**. The SP guns were last listed on the order of battle of **1 January**.[157] They initially stayed with the battery and later were held in reserve by the division.[158] Sometime after **1 April**, the guns were transferred to the *716. I.D.*, and integrated into that division's self-propelled battery. As a result, the *11./AR 1716* had six self-propelled guns on D-Day.[159] The only SP guns that remained in the *709. I.D.* were in the AT battalion.

Although raised without divisional AT elements, the division did have a dedicated AT battalion on D-Day: *Panzerjäger-Abteilung 709* (*Hauptmann* Hümmerich).[160] The battalion was a rather recent addition to the division, and it is not clear when its establishment was ordered. Orders related to the AT formations of static divisions under *Ob.West* were apparently issued in late **March 1944**, but such orders have not been found.[161]

Be that as it may, in **1943** there had only been a single AT company (*Pz.Jg.Kp. 709*) in the division; yet in **November 1943**, it received orders to form two more companies.[162] This seems to have led to the formation of the battalion in early **1944**, and both the battalion headquarters and the 2nd Company were formed through "command channels" (*auf dem Kommandowege*).[163] The associated *Feldpost* number was changed from *Pz.Jg.Kp. 709* to *Pz.Jg.Abt. 709* with a 1st and a 2nd Company on **31 March**. On **31 May**, this was altered again to include a 3rd Company as well.[164]

As a result, on D-Day, the AT battalion consisted of a headquarters and three companies as did many infantry divisions in Normandy. The 1st Company fielded self-propelled guns, the 2nd was armed with towed AT guns and the 3rd was equipped with *Flak*.[165] The weaponry of the 2nd Company differed significantly from divisions such as the *243.*, the *346.*, the *352.*, and the *353. I.D.*, which were equipped with assault guns rather than towed guns. The *716. I.D.*, however, also had towed guns in its 2nd Company. Another difference was the type of SP guns in the 1st Company. Because the order of battle does not specify the actual type, there has been some speculation about the guns. Unable to find them in the allocation records, Niklas Zetterling suggested that the vehicles were either "delivered before **May 1943** or some kind of locally made conversion, possibly using captured French vehicles."[166] Both assumptions, however, are incorrect.

In **1941**, the division had been formed without organic AT forces.[167] The authorisation document of **October 1942** was the first to call for a divisional AT company. The company was to be equipped with nine self-propelled 7.5 cm AT guns and nine MG's. This initiative was supposed to be finished by **1 December 1942**, but there was a major delay in the arrival of the vehicles.[168] In fact, the delivery of the self-propelled guns did not take place until **November 1943**.[169] During this waiting period, the company was equipped with a series of other guns.

On **1 February 1943**, the company possessed no AT guns, just four MG's, half of them heavy.[170] The heavy machine guns were later listed as French and, by **1 May**, the number of light MG's had increased to 12.[171] On **1 June**, the company was listed with five self-propelled 4.7 cm AT guns on Renault R35 chassis: The *4,7 cm Pak(t) auf Panzerkampfwagen 35R(f) ohne Turm*. These were officially static weapons but were used by the company in absence of the 10 intended self-propelled heavy AT guns. The number of MG's had not changed.[172] A month later, the company also had six *8,8 cm Pak 43/41's* at its disposal.[173] Again, these weapons were label as static, but they were used in a similar fashion as the self-propelled AT guns.[174] The guns had been motorised through the use of Laffly prime movers.[175]

On **8 July**, the division was informed it would receive four *7,5 cm Pak 41's*, while the *716. I.D.* would be getting two. Both divisions were given a week to make plans for their deployment and report these to the corps.[176] It was decided that the guns in the division would be deployed as battalion reserves, with two guns in *KVU Barfleur* (*III./729*) and two in *KVU St. Vaast* (*II./729*). Mobility would be provided by four 2.8-tonne Laffly tractors that belonged to the corps and four lorries to transport ammunition.[177]

On **26 July**, the corps informed both divisions that they would each receive 10 *5 cm Pak 38's* to temporarily fill the gap of the missing SP AT guns. In addition, the divisions were to continue to use six of the 8.8 cm AT guns as a mobile reserve with the AT company.[178]

On **8 August**, the corps gave the two divisions new instructions on the

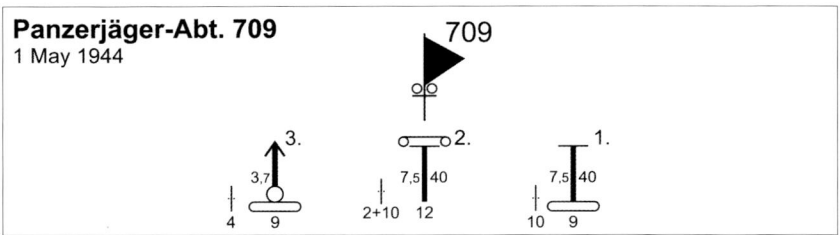

Pz.Jg.Abt.709 was only created in the spring of 1944 and partially through command channels. Despite knowing the battalion's weaponry, some questions remain regarding its vehicles and the organisation of the HQ.

organisation of their AT companies. Instead of four *7,5 cm Pak 41's*, the *709. I.D.* would receive only three and the other would go to the *716. I.D.* Rather than being assigned to infantry battalions (as previously planned), the guns would be allotted to the AT companies until the *Pak 38's* and *Pak 41's* had arrived. Meanwhile, the company was to retain its current organisation and only reorganise after the AT guns arrived. In addition to the three *Pak 41's*, the companies would continue to deploy two *8,8 cm Pak 43/41's* in a mobile role. The remaining six 8.8 cm AT guns were to be deployed in a static manner.[179]

Since it was deemed undesirable to have more than three types of guns in a company, it would have to field either the 5 cm or the self-propelled *4,7 cm Pak(t)* and turn in the other type. The guns that were freed up would be considered for employment as mobile platoons with infantry elements, although the role had yet to be determined. The orders also included some practical considerations. Based on experience, it was concluded that the heavy Laffly prime movers did not provide enough off-road mobility for the *8,8 cm Pak 43/41's*. Instead, these guns were to be towed by halftracks. The Laffly prime movers were still deemed the appropriate means of transportation for the *Pak 41's*, and light Laffly prime movers would be used for the *5 cm Pak 38's*. The self-propelled 4.7 cm AT guns, of course, already had their own transportation.[180]

The preparations for arrival of *Pak 41's* ultimately proved to be in vain. The plan was for AOK 7 to receive 24 pieces, which were to be transferred from the Eastern Front (*Heeresgruppe Mitte*) in **July**, but this date was not met. It soon (**August**) became clear that a schedule for arrival of the guns could not be determined due to the situation in the east.[181] In any case, it appears the *Pak 41's* were never delivered to *7. Armee*, let alone the division.

The promised *Pak 38's*, however, did arrive and were reported in both the *709.* and the *716. I.D.* on **31 August**.[182] In addition, four tow vehicles were transferred from *Pz.Jg.Abt. 93*, which was exchanging its *Pak 38's* for *Hornisse*.*[183]

The 10 *Pak 38's* were already included on the organisation document of **1 September**. The company also had 10 MG's and the 5 self-propelled guns, along with the 6 8.8 cm AT guns still listed.[184] The company's own situation report (**1 September**), however, paints a rather different picture. In addition to the self-propelled guns, the company actually had only three newly arrived *7,5 cm Pak 97/38's* (borrowed from the AT platoon of *GR 739*), while the *Pak 43/41's* had left.[185] Despite the intent to have two of the 8.8 cm AT guns towed by prime movers, they were actually employed in fixed positions, because no tow vehicles were available, making them quite useless to the company.[186] The company's **September** report does agree with the order of battle on the presence of the 10 MG's, while also specifying the small arms as 59 rifles, 14 machine pistols and 69 pistols. At this time the company, under *Leutnant* Ogroske, had a strength of three officers, 38 NCO's (a shortfall of 17 compared to the authorised numbers) and 83 men (+17).[187] The report also reveals that the 10 *Pak 38's* had not actually been assigned to the company, despite what the orders of battle suggest. The orders of battle for **October** are also inaccurate, showing just the 10 medium AT guns and 10 MG's.[188]

These discrepancies appear to have been corrected in **November**, when the divisional AT forces were again listed with the five self-propelled 4.7 cm AT guns. They now also showed the three 7.5 cm AT guns, thus matching the company's own report from early **September**. As noted, these three guns were *7,5 cm Pak 97/38's* from the AT platoon of *GR 739*, which, in turn, used three *5 cm Pak 38's* that belonged to *Pz.Jg.Kp. 709*. Three more of the 10 *Pak 38's* were now operating with the AT platoon of *GR 729*, while the last four were deployed on the coast.[189] The company thus still did not control any of the 10 *Pak 38's* that it — in theory at least — had received in **August**. Although the company had thus far been poorly equipped, the division's AT capabilities were about to take a turn for the better.

On **19 November**, *AOK 7* informed the *LXXXIV. A.K.* that the field army would receive 18 *Pak 40's*, which would be assigned to the corps. These guns would be used to form three AT companies through "command channels".

The *709. I.D.* would receive 12 of the guns and the other 6 would go to the *716. I.D.*[190] Four days later (**23rd**), *AOK 7* informed the corps that it would be receiving even more AT guns, although no numbers were mentioned. More importantly, it was announced that 16 Somua prime movers would be provided to tow the guns. The corps decided to use the equipment to establish three companies with six guns each, rather than two with nine. On its request, 12 of the 7.5 cm AT guns and 12 Somua (halftrack) prime movers would be sent to Valognes (*709. I.D.*) and the other 6 AT guns and 4 prime movers to Caen (*716. I.D.*). The corps also asked the field army for an AT company as a cadre unit.[191] Two days later (**25th**), the corps informed the two divisions of these developments. The *709. I.D.* was instructed to use the *14.* and the *15./919* to build the two new AT companies. As a guide, they would follow *KStN 1140* (**1 April 1943**), with three guns per platoon.[192]

In addition to the new AT companies, the original *Pz.Jg.Kp. 709* finally received its long awaited self-propelled heavy guns. On **30 November**, the arrival of 10 *7,5 cm Pak 40's* (SP) on Lorraine chassis was reported. These were commonly known as the "*Marder I*" rather than by their official designation: *Sd.Kfz. 135, Selbstfahrlafette für 7,5 cm Pak 40/1 auf Fahrgestell Lorraine Schlepper*.[193] The 10 vehicles were transferred from another division, which explains why Zetterling was unable to find them. In **November 1943**, three divisions of the 21st Wave were still in the process of being established: The *349.*, the *352.*, and the *353. I.D.* To form the divisions, they had been assigned elements from many other formations. In some cases, these included companies equipped with self-propelled AT guns. Yet the authorisation documents of these divisions did not authorise such companies, which meant they had to be replaced with towed AT guns.

This was the case with the *353. I.D.* which had received the *1./Pz.Jg.Abt. 371 (371. I.D.)*. This company was armed with 13 *Marder I's*.[194] Around mid-**November**, orders were given to the division to transfer 10 of these vehicles and their personnel to the *709. I.D.* This involved 3 platoon leaders, 10 vehicle commanders, 10 gunners, 10 drivers, 3 mechanics and an assistant armourer. Another three vehicles and their personnel were transferred to the *708. I.D.* The remaining personnel were then returned to the Replacement Army.[195]

The order of battle of **1 December** already listed the 10 *Marder I's* and 10 MG's with *Pz.Jg.Kp. 709*. No other AT guns were still listed with the com-

---

* The 8,8 cm PaK 43/1 auf Fgst. Pz.Kpfw. III/IV (SF) (Sd.Kfz. 164). It was initially called the Hornisse (hornet); later, this was changed to Nashorn (rhinoceros).

pany. The AT platoons of *GR 729* and *739* were listed with three "static" *5 cm Pak 38's*, while their three authorised 7.5 cm AT guns were deployed on the coast. The *14./919* did have three 7.5 cm AT guns.[196] The self-propelled *4,7 cm(t)'s* were no longer listed, nor were four of the 5 cm AT guns. All five self-propelled guns were handed over to *Schnelle Brigade 30* in **February 1944**.[197]

The formation of the two new AT companies continued during **December 1943** and a detailed report was made to *AOK 7* on the **13th**. The companies were designated as the *2.* and the *3.Pz.Jg.Kp. 709*. For the time being, they were both organised with two platoons with three *Pak 40's* each. It was intended that both would later form a third platoon, but this elicited concern, given that serious shortages of personnel and vehicles already existed for the companies with two platoons, let alone three. The corps' requirement for additional prime movers (*RSO's*) would at least be reduced if 12 more Somua prime movers became available from *s.Art.Abt. 456* and *457*.[198] Some changes were made the next day (**14th**). It was decided there would not be a *3. Pz.Jg.Kp. 709*, but it would simply be the *14./919*. The new *2. Pz.Jg.Kp. 709* was formed from

The Marder I was a small size tankhunter, but for the occasion five men have managed to cram themselves into the fighting compartment (4 April 1944. Archives du Calvados, 10Fi/2, Photo 110. Agance Fama, France et Atlantic, Berlin)

Aufklärungs-Schwadron 84. The troop not only provided the personnel but also a number of AT guns, as its two *Pak 97/38's* were exchanged for two static *Pak 40's*. In turn, the new *14./919* was formed using elements of the *14.* and the *15./919*. The AT and *Flak* platoons of the regiment, as well as the crews who were operating static weapons, were to be gathered in the 15th Company. The remaining personnel were to be used to build the new 14th Company[199]

AOK 7 had announced that the *LXXXIV. A.K.* would be receiving another 27-30 *Pak 40's*. When these arrived, the *14./919* would form another platoon and the *2. Pz.Jg.Kp. 709* one or two more platoons.[200] Transport, however, remained a concern. Although the *7. Armee* would provide tow vehicles for the guns, the divisions would have to provide the other vehicles wherever possible. A number of lorries would be provided by a platoon of *Kraftfahr-Kompanie 84*, which had been attached to *GR 919*, but it was no longer fully needed as the regiment transitioned to bicycle transportation for its heavy weapons and ammunition. The vehicles it no longer required could be used for the *14./919* and also for the new AT company of the *716. I.D.* Transport for the *2. Pz.Jg.Kp. 709* would be provided by *Aufklärungs-Schwadron 84*.[201]

The two divisional AT companies were first listed together on the order of battle of **1 January 1944**. The 1st Company had 10 *Marder I's* and the 2nd Company had three towed 7.5 cm AT guns that were static.[202] The orders of battle up to **May** are difficult to decipher. This not only makes it difficult to determine when the 2nd Company received its guns but also to ascertain the weaponry of the AT companies in the infantry regiments. It is quite possible that the formation of the *2. Pz.Jg.Kp. 709* took place at *Aufklärungs-Schwadron 84* during **February**, because the reconnaissance troop was listed with 10 *Pak 40's* on the **1st**.[203] These must have been recent arrivals, since no such guns had been with the troop on **1 December**.

Despite the paucity of data from the orders of battle, *Pz.Jg.Abt. 709* took shape as a battalion in **March**, although the 3rd Company did not arrive until early **April**.[204] Fortunately, the situation on **1 May** and around D-Day is quite clear.

The organisation document of **1 May** was the first to list the battalion headquarters.[205] This may be explained by the fact that it had also been formed through "command channels".[206] No orders for its establishment have been found, and its organisation may well have been ad hoc in nature. This is illustrated by its commander, *Hptm*. Hümmerich. The captain was the former commander of *Aufklärungs-Schwadron 84*, part of which had been absorbed by the battalion. This officer lacked a background in the *Panzertruppen*, but he still became battalion commander, an appointment most likely based on convenience.[207] It is not clear when the reconnaissance troop was dissolved, but the orders of battle suggest it happened sometime between **1 February** and **1 April**. During this time, it may have been preoccupied with the formation of the 2./*Pz.Jg.Abt. 709* and a company for the *716. I.D.* It is quite possible the battalion headquarters was only formed after the other units had been completely established.

Insufficient information is available about the battalion headquarters, but according to a POW, the battalion had a small headquarters company. This apparently consisted of a *Hauptfeldwebel*, two clerks, a paymaster, two messengers and a signals section of 14 men — a combined strength of about 30 men. The company had three ammunition lorries, one petrol lorry, and one lorry for the administration, along with four light cars and three motorcycles.[208] When *Hptm.* Hümmerich was interviewed after the war by Cornelius Ryan (author of the famous book *The Longest Day*), he reported the presence of three armoured cars and six motorcycles. The armoured cars were four-wheeled, armed with a single machine gun in a turret and crewed by two men in the front, one in the middle, and a radio operator in the rear. Apart from the turret, this description seems closest to the rare *Sd.Kfz. 247*.[209] Alternatively, the turret suggests that the vehicles may have been one of several more common types of armoured car, but that would require a different internal layout than what was described by Hümmeric. Either way, the presence of armoured cars is highly unexpected, since such vehicles were typically reserved for reconnaissance units. In this particular case, they may have been left over from *Aufklärungs-Schwadron 84*. That duly noted, the presence of armoured cars in the troop or the battalion is not supported by any other period records, photos or other German accounts. This makes it difficult to confirm Hümmerich's claims, but his description of fighting in such a vehicle on D-Day does lend some credibility to his account.[210]

On **1 May**, the 1st Company (*Lt.* Ogroske) was equipped with nine self-propelled 7.5 cm *Pak 40's* and 10 light MG's.[211] The company reportedly consisted of a headquarters section and three platoons with three *Marder I's* each. Each platoon is said to have had two MG's, but this may be a reference to the standard armament of the vehicles.[212] The fate of the 10th SP gun is unknown.

Unlike *Pz.Jg.Abt. 243* and *353*, the 2nd Company (*Leutnant* Seidel, acting commander) was not equipped with assault guns. Instead, it had 12 *7,5 cm Pak 40's*, all of which were motorised. In addition to the AT guns, there were 2 heavy MG's and 10 light ones.[213] In light of the *KStN* that had been used as a guide, it is highly likely that the company had four platoons with three guns each. The vehicles used to tow the guns are not clear, but it would make sense if the 12 Somua prime movers ended up in the company, although the regimental AT companies may have received these instead.

The 3rd Company (*Leutnant* Mosebach) was the last addition to the battalion. On **1 May**, it was equipped with nine 3.7 cm *Flak* and four light MG's and was listed as motorised.[214] The company had been raised at Gotha in **February 1944**, receiving its *Feldpost* number on **3 February** as an unnumbered and motorised 3.7 cm *Flak* company.[215] On **1 March**, its designation was changed to *Fla-Kompanie 709*.[216] The company joined the division on **4 April**.[217]

Because former soldiers in the company have provided conflicting information, its precise equipment remains unclear. According to one prisoner, all guns were mounted on halftracks.[218] Others stated that only two platoons were self-propelled — one using halftracks and the other Büssing-NAG lorries — while a third platoon had guns towed by *Maultier* halftrack lorries.[219] This latter description appears to be the most accurate; indeed, it is supported by most of the men and by another (albeit less specific) account, which also states there were just two self-propelled platoons.[220] The type of halftracks is not clear, but it has been asserted that these were *Sd.Kfz. 6's*, mounting *3,7 cm Flak 36's*. Each platoon leader reportedly had a car and a motorcycle at his disposal.[221]

The company headquarters consisted of just the company commander, a *Feldwebel*, a signalman and a dispatch rider. The signals section was led by a senior enlisted man, nine wireless operators with three *Bertha* radio sets (*Torn.Fu.b*) and three switchboard operators.[222] Another man stated the signals section was actually only seven men strong. According to that witness, the company trains consisted of a *Hauptfeldwebel*, two clerks, three cooks, a quartermaster section of three men (a gun fitter and two vehicle mechanics), a cobbler and a tailor.[223]

The trains were reportedly equipped with three four-wheel Mercedes lorries to carry ammunition. A car was available to the fitter/mechanics and another to the *Hauptfeldwebel*. In addition, there was a lorry for the field kitchen and one for quartermaster supplies along with a motorcycle. Another soldier stated that there was one car for orderly-room equipment and, apparently, a lorry with spare vehicle and gun parts.[224] The company had a combined strength of 100 officers and men, all German.[225]

Weaponry

Since the records of the *LXXXIV. A.K.* for **1944** are largely missing, there are no known status reports for that period. This makes it difficult to determine the exact state of the division with regard to specific shortages in weaponry, mobility or personnel. Because the division's makeup is somewhat unique, no attempt has been made to calculate its authorisations. However, it is possible to gain more insight by examining the records of other sources, such as *AOK 7*.

It appears the division was close to authorised strength on D-Day as far as its heavy weapons were concerned. The presence of foreign weapons in the division, outside the eastern battalions, suggests there was still a shortage of machine guns.[226] This was also the conclusion of *Heeresgruppe B* on **27 April**. Having assessed the **March** status reports of the divisions in its theatre of operations, the army group noted a shortage of AT guns and MG's in the division; yet it considered this a minor issue given the overall armament situation.[227] This assessment marked a change from the previous month, when *Heeresgruppe B* made an urgent call for one *Pak 40*, two medium mortars, 60 light MG's, two heavy MG's, 191 rifles, and 132 machine pistols to strengthen the division.[228]

On **1 May**, the German small arms encompassed 7,800 rifles, 45 self-loading rifles (*G41's*), 451 grenade launchers, 720 machine pistols and 1,301 pistols, but there were no sniper rifles. Some of the foreign weapons were Russian: 3 pistols, 81 self-loading rifles, 42 machine pistols and 19 MG's. Other weapons included 634 French and 322 Czech rifles and 1,183 Polish and 160 Belgian pistols. The presence of French 8.14 cm mortars has been noted, and the division had a total of 72 tubes. In addition, 19 Russian light MG's were deployed by support units.[229]

Clearly, the overwhelming majority of the small arms of the division were of German manufacture. The "conventional wisdom" that static divisions were primarily outfitted with outdated captured weaponry is an exaggeration, particularly when it comes to small arms. This can also be illustrated by looking at the types of MG's. Although the data for **1 May** do not specify the types and numbers of automatic weapons, this information is available for **1 March**.

At that time, the division had 287 light *MG 34's*, six heavy *MG 34's*, 145 light *MG 42's* and 25 heavy *MG 42's*. Moreover, there were 72 tripods that enabled light MG's to be turned into heavy ones. Older models of machine guns included just 2 *MG 08's*, 20 *MG 08/15's* and 2 *MG 13's*.[230] Another four *MG 34's* arrived on **25 April**.[231]

The assumption that static divisions on the *Atlantikwall* used foreign or outdated machine guns is only accurate when looking at the static weapons of the wall's fixed defences, not when examining the issued inventory of the divisions themselves. On **1 March**, static (sector bound) weaponry in the sector of the division included 6 *MG 26(t)'s*, 129 light *MG 116(f)'s*, 7 heavy *MG 08's*, 2 light *MG 156(f)'s*, 4 heavy *MG 30(p)'s*, 19 *MG 311(f)'s* in tank turrets, 18 *MG 14(p)'s*, 52 *MG 257(f)'s*, 71 *MG 311(f)'s*, 2 *MG 34's* and 20 *MG 42's*. All told, this made for an aggregate of 330 static MG's. There were also 11 AT rifles and 24 *Ofenrohre*. The mortars included 9 *5 cm Gr.W. 201(b)'s*, 8 *5 cm Gr.W. 203(f)'s*, 8 *5 cm Gr.W. 36's*, 40 *8.14 cm Gr.W. 278(f)'s* and 5 *5 cm M19* automatic mortars.[232] Just how many of these weapons were positioned along Utah Beach on D-Day is not clear. Nor is it clear how many of them remained in the division's sector after it gave up the western coast of Manche to the *243. I.D.* and *Gren.Rgt. zbV 752*.

Mobility, Enhanced Mobility Efforts and Battlegroups

Of course, as a static formation, the *709. I.D.* had quite limited mobility, and whatever mobility it did have was further reduced by the vehicles themselves. In **July 1943**, the division possessed 320 motor vehicles of no less than 180 different types. Considering the *KStN's*, they must have been mostly substitutes for authorised items.[233] Regardless of their age or type, efforts to maintain so many different vehicles in operation must have been a logistical nightmare.

The initial attempt to improve the division's mobility was made in early **1943**. As in other divisions, this called for establishment of a mobile *Kampfgruppe*, although the *709. I.D.* would no longer have one at the time of the invasion. In **January 1943**, the recent departure of field-army reserves increased the importance of both divisional and corps reserves possessing the mobility to be moved about rapidly as reinforcements, both within and outside the corps sector.[234] Both the *709.* and the *716. I.D.* established reinforced regiments that would be motorised in a ad hoc fashion; this can be

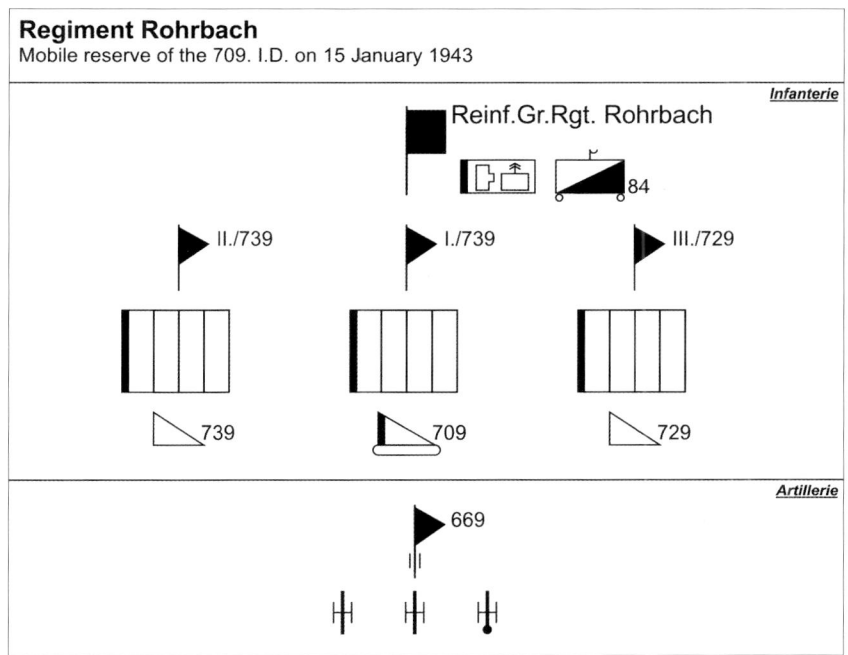

The division's ability to intervene in other sectors relied largely on its battlegroup (shown here with early war symbols). The composition of the Kampfgruppe depended on the reserves available, which continuously changed as infantry battalions were rotated to and from the coast. The anti-tank elements (triangles) and artillery battalion were a constant in the battlegroup.

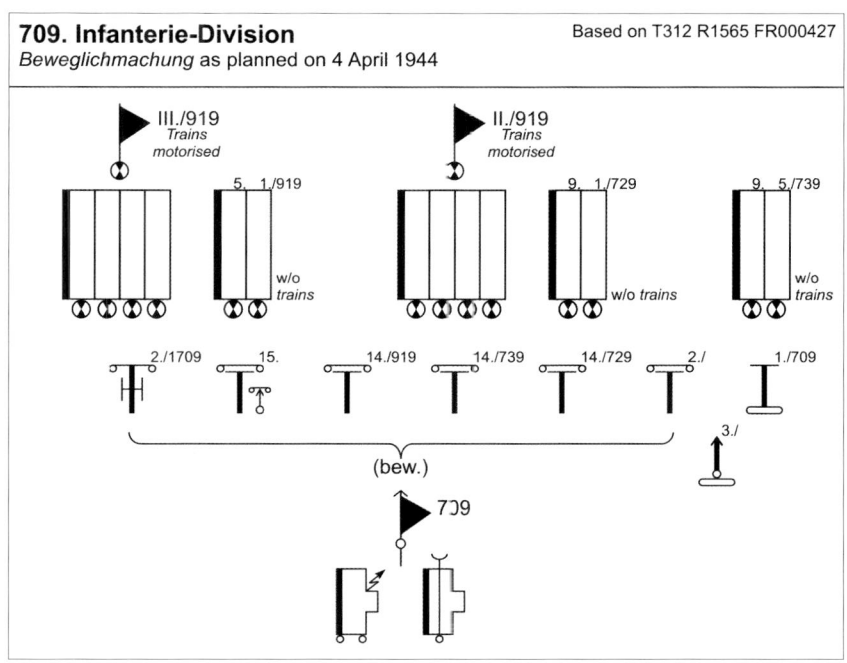

Being classified as static, the 709.I.D. possessed only limited mobility. Starting late 1943, this was somewhat improved by the 7th Army's mobility programme, but it affected mainly infantry elements and their heavy weapons companies.

understood as the original enhanced mobility measure of the division. The regiment of the *709. I.D.* (*Regiment Rohrbach*) was led by the headquarters of *GR 729* (*Obst.* Rohrbach). Combat troops initially included the *III./729*, the *I.* and the *III./739* and the AT platoons of the two regiments. Other troops attached to the regiment were *Pz.Jg.Kp. 709, Aufkl.Schw. 84* and *Art.Abt. 669*.[235]

The composition of this reserve regiment depended on those battalions that were in reserve at any given moment. For example, on **31 January**, the three battalions were the *I./729*, the *II./739*, and *MG-Btl. 17*.[236] Motor transport was provided by *OT* vehicles, assigned vehicles, transportation columns and vehicles from Naval transport forces (*Marine-Kraftfahrstaffel*). Assembling these vehicles was no small feat, since it required 99 light cars and 267 lorries for a total of 680 tonnes.[237] In **February**, the regimental headquarters was replaced by that of *GR 739* (*Obst.* Manussi), which was due to move south from the *Cherbourg* defensive sector to relieve the *165. Div. Aufkl.Schw. 84* was no longer part of the reinforced regiment.[238]

In **June**, however, the plans for a reinforced regiment were again cancelled. The division itself would no longer provide an ad hoc regiment. Instead, one would be formed by combining elements of the *709.* and the *716. I.D.* The regiment would still be under *Obst.* Manussi, but the division would only provide two infantry battalions (one from each regiment), the AT platoon

German forces used a wide variety of vehicles including captured lorries. This Morris-Commercial C8 had likely been captured in the summer of 1940. It finally met its end on the on the Rue Paul Lecacheux in Montebourg four years later. (NARA)

of *GR 739*, and the *2./AR 669*. The *716. I.D.* would furnish a third infantry battalion, an engineer company and the divisional AT company. Most of the artillery would also come from that division: A battalion headquarters and two batteries.[239]

In **October**, the arrival of *GR 919* provided the corps with a standing reserve regiment (minus the 15th Company), which could be used for Contingency Measure II. The composition of the artillery battalion and support companies did not change. The infantry battalion of the *716. I.D.* would provide another reserve force, unrelated to the regiment. This battalion and the reserve battalion (*709. I.D.*) at La Haye-du-Puits, could also be committed under Contingency Measure III. The regiment used improvised motorisation.[240]

Much of this arrangement was again cancelled in **November**, when it was decided that Contingency Measure I and II no longer concerned the corps.[241] A few days later, Contingency Measure III was further restricted to just elements of the *716. I.D.*[242] These modifications to defence planning did not mean that the enhanced mobility efforts for the *709. I.D.* were cancelled altogether. Of course, *Führer* Directive No. 51 also supported the objective of increased mobility. For example, the *I./729*, the *I./739* and the *14./739*, the *13.* and the *15./919* and the *2./AR 669* were still listed among the motorised formations using *OT* vehicles. Moreover, there were other sources from which to obtain vehicles, although the *OT* vehicles that had been used to mobilise *GR 919* would mostly be returned to the *243. I.D.* Bicycles were also considered as a way to enhance the mobility of the reserves, although their allocation was not yet specified.²⁴³ Towards the end of the month, it was reported that for the intended enhanced mobility measures the division was still short 300 horse-drawn vehicles and 400 horses — 300 to pull one-horse vehicles, 80 for multi-horse vehicles and 20 riding horses — which at least indicates that horse transport would play a part in the increased mobility of the division.²⁴⁴

In early **February 1944**, *AOK 7* reassessed the situation concerning motor vehicle availability in the corps as well as the strength of the transport companies and platoons (*OT*). Because of the limited number of vehicles and the requirements of the planned enhanced mobility efforts for the tactical and operational reserves, *AOK 7* decided to make significant changes. As a result, it issued new orders that affected the division. Motorisation beyond the *KStN's* was cancelled for the entire division. The *OT* vehicles that had been used for the reinforced *III./739 (mot)* and the reinforced *GR 919 (Radf.)* were to be gathered in the transportation company of the corps. They were intended to transport the *352. I.D.* to either Caen or Bretagne, if required.²⁴⁵

The delivery of vehicles to the division remained rather limited but, on **15 March**, it was lorries with a lift capacity of 90 tonnes.²⁴⁶ This is, in fact, the only significant allotment found in the records and the reason for the shipment is unclear. On **4 April**, new plans were introduced. Bicycles became the main means of mobility for 14 infantry companies. In *GR 729* these were the 1ˢᵗ and 9ᵗʰ Companies and the entire 2ⁿᵈ Battalion. The situation of *GR 919* was similar: Its 3ʳᵈ Battalion being fully equipped with bicycles, along with the 1ˢᵗ and 5ᵗʰ Companies. In *GR 739*, only two companies were outfitted with bicycles: the 5ᵗʰ and the 9ᵗʰ.²⁴⁷ Motorisation remained limited among the infantry. Only the trains of the two bicycle battalions were motorised (*II./729* and *III./919*). In addition, elements of the heavy weapons companies were also motorised, including the 14ᵗʰ Company of the three regiments and the *Flak* platoon in the *15./919*. *Pz.Jg.Abt. 709* was fully motorised by definition. *Nachr. Abt. 709* and the *2./AR 1709* would be motorised, although some parts of the former would only be partially motorised. This was all in line with the authorisation document and apparently was extended to include the *III./739*.²⁴⁸

On **7 May**, *AOK 7* once more issued new orders regarding enhanced mobility measures for its formations. These called for a reduction in the number of elements with vehicles provided under the measures. Many units that had so far been equipped with vehicles by the programme were again to relinquish their motorisation in favour of other units and the formation of transportation companies.²⁴⁹ This initiative also affected the *709. I.D.* Simply put, it meant that, since the mobility measures had been limited for the division, its two bicycle battalions would lose the motorisation of their trains. A single artillery battery in the division, undoubtedly the *2./AR 1709*, was the only element which could keep the motorisation it had received from the mobility efforts.²⁵⁰ Yet, on **12 May 1944**, the division still had an enhanced lift capacity of 144 tonnes.²⁵¹ How this pertains to the order of **7 May** is not entirely clear. Nor is it clear whether this figure concerned motor vehicles or horses.

Personnel

Although there were admittedly shortcomings in the armament and mobility of *709. I.D.*, the division has often been cited by military historians as a prime example of the poor quality of personnel in the static divisions. This "fact" is usually attributed to the age of the men and/or the high percentage of non-German personnel. Since typically no evidence is offered to support such assertions, they are worth examining in more detail.

On **1 May**, the division had a total strength (*Gesamtkopfstärke*) of 10,536 German troops, 1,784 Eastern soldiers and 333 *Hiwi's*.²⁵² Without an authorised end-strength level for the division, it is difficult to fully appreciate these numbers, but the number of Eastern soldiers would appear to be too low for three non-German battalions. This indicates that only *Ost-Btl. 649* and *Georg. Inf.Btl. 795* were counted, because *Georg.Inf.Btl. 797* was no longer under divisional control, with the exception of one of its companies (that may have been included in the count). The inclusion of just two battalions would also match the division's own organisational document which, in any case, was almost certainly the source of the numbers. The number of Germans and *Hiwi's* is even more difficult to interpret, but on **1 April** the division had been short 416 *Hiwi's*, while having a surplus of 375 Germans.²⁵³ It is not clear how these numbers changed before the invasion.

The characteristics of the personnel remain unclear as well. Little data exists concerning age groups or the number of *Volksdeutsche*. Yet despite a lack of source materials, many authors have averred that the average age in the division was 36 — the evidence for which is hardly compelling. This claim can be traced back to a single report made in late **June 1944** to *Heeresgruppe B* by an officer of the division, explaining its failure to prevent the loss of Cherbourg.[254] His statement was first picked up by Harrison in the book *Cross-Channel Attack* (1951) and repeated by authors in every decade since.[255] Although there are other German documents that might appear to support the claim, these were likely based on the very same anecdotal evidence travelling up the chain-of-command.[256]

In itself, an average age is not a particularly relevant statistic, yet its continued popularity in relation to the division demands a closer examination. It should be realised that, without context, an average age can be misleading, as it tells us nothing about how large the different age groups were. Were most men in the division around 36? Or were there also much younger and much older men? This is also exactly where the number does become relevant: To compensate for young personnel, older personnel must be very high in number and/or much older. The higher the percentage of younger soldiers, the more compensation is required and increasingly so. This means that getting the average wrong by several years can have a profound impact on how the age build-up of the division is perceived. For that reason it is better to examine what is actually known about the division's personnel and only use averages to illustrate general trends in a specific period.

Although reliable age-related data for the time of the invasion could not be located, numbers do exist for earlier periods. In **July 1943**, the average age of the division's regimental and battalion commanders was 49, while for company commanders, lower-ranking company officers, NCO's and men, it was 40, 31 and 33, respectively. Only 15% of personnel had served on the Eastern Front.[257]

The data for **October** is less specific, but on average officers were 35 years of age. Of the 137 officers in the division (2.2% of all manpower), 42 had experience in the East. Not all of the officers were suitable for combat employment (*kriegsverwendungsfähig* or "*k.v.*"): 11 were classified as fit for garrison duties outside of the home front (*garnisonsfähig Feld / g.v.F.*) and 6 were only classified for garrison duty in the homeland (*garnisonsfähig Heimat / g.v.H.*). At this time, the division had a strength of 6,089 NCO's and men; of these, just 24 (0.4%) were classified as *g.v.H.* and 312 (5.1%) belonged to *Volksliste III*. The rest of the men were classed as *k.v.* or *g.v.F.* A small cohort was born in 1905 or earlier (7.4%), most between 1906-1924 (78%) and the youngest in 1925 (9.1%). The combined average age of the oldest two age groups was 30.8 years.[258] Combined with the data for the 1925 age group, the numbers manifest an average age of NCO's and men of about 29-30, revealing a clear drop in age since the summer. Still, it should be noted that this does not include men under *Volksliste III* or the *g.v.H.*, as their ages are not known (together 5.4% of the division). Adding the limited number of officers is, on its own, not enough to raise the average age in the division to over 30 but, together with the unknown categories, it might just have.

The final known reports on the division's personnel come from **December 1943**. On the **2nd**, the average age of the combat troops was 31 and 35 among the support troops. Depending on how these numbers were rounded up or down, this would give an average age of about 30.8-31.8. A week later, the overall strength of the division was reported as 9,359 men, a significant increase since October. 92.6% of the men were part of the combat troops, the remaining 7.4% belonged to the support troops. Among the former group, 0.1% was born in or before 1899, 10% in 1900-05, 53% in 1906-13, 17% in 1914-22 and 19% in 1923 or later. For the support troops, these numbers were 3%, 40%, 45%, 10%, and 2%, respectively.[259] These **December** numbers seriously undermine the possibility of the average age of the division being 36 at the time of the invasion. They illustrate that even with the arrival of *GR 919* and departure of the *I./739*, the average age remained well below 36. Although no reliable numbers are available for **1944**, this makes it statistically highly unlikely that later replacements and reinforcements would have raised the average by four or five years in just five months.

Since the **October** numbers were incomplete, albeit not enough to raise the average by much, it remains difficult to assess the influence of the two aforementioned organisational changes. Still, it is quite possible that they were largely responsible for the increase in average age which appears to have occurred between **October** and **December**. According to *Obstlt.* Keil, his *GR 919* was made up of NCO's and men of whom about 75% ranged in age from 35-45. Even without data for the rest of the regiment, its average age was at least somewhat higher than in other units of the *709. I.D.* 25% of the NCO's and men in the regiment had been transferred from the Eastern Front and, although most were more than 35 years old, nearly all of them had combat experience. After arriving in Normandy, the regiment began receiving 18-19 year old soldiers to replace experienced and physically able personnel being returned to the Eastern Front. The regiment also received additional *Volksdeutsche*, who already made up 10% of the formation.[260] The soldiers sent to the East were of course able-bodied, many in their 20's. They were replaced with younger men, but this did not lower the average age in the division as much as it would have, if men in their 30's had been replaced. The pattern described by Keil is supported by a member of the headquarters company of *GR 729*, who stated that about 30% of *GR 729* and *739* was transferred to the East in late **February** or early **March**, their average age just 21. They were replaced by 18-19 year olds, thus reducing the average age in the regiments, albeit just slightly.[261]

As mentioned, there are no available records that show the division's age build-up at the time of the invasion, nor are there many alternatives to obtain such information. For one, the division was not covered in the MIRS paybook study. Secondly, the destruction of the division, and its records, in **June 1944** is reflected in a low number of death cards and only somewhat compensated by the lists of MIA. As a result, only a sample of 169 KIA/MIA could be obtained (excluding the three eastern battalions).[262] A comparison with the **December 1943** numbers shows an increase in personnel born in 1923 or later, which could reflect the intended change to 20% born in 1925 but also a bias towards frontline troops. The latter also applies to the slightly higher percentage of men born in 1914-22. The values for the older age groups are all lower than in December which may reflect bias but also actual personnel changes. About 80% of the sample concerns members of the three infantry regiments, which is clearly an over-representation. Due to the complexity of the division's organisation, it is hard to establish exactly how much of the division's manpower was gathered in its eight German infantry battalions. The difference in the sample between the average age in the infantry regiments and the other elements is, nonetheless, only about one year, which suggests that the bias towards the former has less effect than might be feared.

	≤1899	1900-1905	1906-1913	1914-1922	≥1923
Dec. 1943	0.3%	12.3%	52.5%	16.7%	18.1%
KIA/MIA	0.0%	10.1%	47.9%	17.8%	24.3%
Difference	-0.3%	-2.3%	-4.6%	1.1%	6.1%

Table 1: Comparison of age groups in the *709. I.D.* in December 1943 and 169 KIA/MIA in the summer of 1944.

The KIA/MIA sample shows that 22% were aged 20 or younger (born 1924 or later), 20% were 20-30 (born 1914-23), 53% were 30-40 and 5% were more than 45. The preferred 1909-23 age group (20-35 years old) amounted to 47% of the division's manpower, while 31% was older. A closer look at the numbers reveals some interesting details. For one, the important 1909-1923 age group was clearly leaning towards older personnel, with almost 60% of it aged 30-35. This was also the largest group in the division, followed by 1904-08. The group born in or after 1924 was the third largest group, with 1925 accounting for the vast majority and seemingly matching the intended 20%. 1924 was only of minor importance, and personnel born in 1926 have not been found at all. As with the *265. I.D.*, these numbers show that the personnel of the static *709. I.D.* included a significant percentage of both older and younger personnel. Compared to regular infantry divisions, the division clearly contained much more personnel over 30. Even though the sample is limited, it does illustrate the age build-up of the division much better than the falsely claimed 36-years-old average age.

	≤1903	1904-1908	1909-1913	1914-1918	1919-1923	1924	1925	1926
KIA/MIA	5.3%	25.4%	27.2%	10.1%	9.5%	1.8%	20.7%	0.0%

Table 2: Age distribution in the *709. I.D.* (Based on KIA/MIA numbers)

Like the age build-up of the division, the percentage of *Volksdeutsche* is not easy to ascertain. However, unless the division received exceedingly high numbers of men from *Volksliste III* in the months prior to the invasion, it is hard to see how it could have approached anywhere near 40% as has sometimes been suggested.[263] Such a situation is unlikely to begin with: In late **1943** there was a policy to increase the amount of *DVL III* in the static divisions from 5% to 8%, but nothing higher.[264] Even if this number were raised in **1944** — and there are no indications that it was — the extent cannot be determined from a few statements. As this author has made clear, the numbers of *Volksdeutsche* serving in particular units is always difficult to determine.[265] With certain exceptions, the lack of information illustrates that they were not considered a serious issue to begin with.

History

The division was formed in *Wehrkreis IX* (Kassel, Frankfurt am Main, Weimar) and officially raised on **1 May 1941**. Because of preparations preceding formation of the division, it was to be ready for deployment by **15 May**, along with the 12 other divisions of the 15th Wave.[266] On **27 May 1941**, the division was still listed as part of the Replacement Army.[267] Eight days later (**4 June**), it was already listed under the *XXV. A.K.* in France. This corps was responsible for the defence of Bretagne. Other divisions under the corps at the time were the *205.*, the *211.* and the *332. I.D.*[268]

The *709. I.D.* was deployed on the northern coast of Bretagne. Initially, its sector stretched from west of Lannion to east of Fougères;[269] this area was then reduced in size and, in late **August 1942**, the division covered the area from Tréguier in the west to Pontorson in the east.[270] The headquarters was at Lamballe. Although elements of the *161.* and the *343. I.D.* were deployed in the same region, these were not committed on the coast.[271]

On **20 November**, *AOK 7* announced that the newly formed *Gen.Kdo. LXXXVII* would take over three divisions currently operating under the *XXV. A.K.* These were the *161.*, the *343.* and the *709. I.D.* As a consequence, the new corps assumed command of much of the northern coast of the Brittany Peninsula three days later (**23 November**).[272]

The *709. I.D.* would not remain assigned to the new corps for long. On **22 November**, the *LXXXIV. A.K.* in Normandy was informed that the *320. I.D.* would soon be replaced by the *709. I.D.*[273] The original division was responsible for the defence of Manche, including the Cotentin Peninsula; it was supported by elements of the *165. Div.* (primarily *GR Reithinger* and *Art.Abt. Römer*) that were committed in the Cherbourg Defensive Zone (Verteidigungsbereich Cherbourg). [274] The commander of the *165. Div.*, *Gen.Lt.* von Schacky auf Schönfeld, was also the commander of the Defensive Zone.[275]

The *709. I.D.* would relieve both of these divisions around Cherbourg. The division was expected to arrive between **27-30 November**, but due to transport problems, it did not fully reach its destination until early **December**.[276] Both the Defensive Zone and the Jobourg Peninsula were taken over by *GR 739*, while *GR 729* assumed command of the east coast of the Cotentin.[277] The *165. Div.* left the Defensive Zone but remained in Manche; it took over the west coast of Manche (Vauville - Bréhal) from the *320. I.D.*, which left the *7. Armee* in **January 1943**.[278] The boundary between the *709. I.D.* and the *165. Div.* ran southeast from Biville on the west coast, through Bricquebec (*709. I.D.*), St. Sauveur-le-Vicomte and Baupte (*709. I.D.*) to Carentan (*709. I.D.*). The sector of the *165. Div.* then continued to St. Clair-sur-l'Elle – Torigni-sur-Vire – Villedieu-les-Poêles – Gavray – to Bricqueville-sur-Mer (excl.) on the west coast.[279] This also reflects another change: Since the *709. I.D.* was a weaker division than the *320. I.D.*, the decision was made to move the left boundary of the corps north, to the line Bréhal - Cérences. On **3 December**, the coast south of Bréhal (*KVG Granville*) was taken over by the *346. I.D.* This division had already assumed command of the coastal sector held by the *709. I.D.* in Bretagne two days earlier.[280]

When orders were given for transfer of the *709. I.D.* to the Cotentin, two battalions of the *165. Div.* (*GR Reithinger*) were committed on the *Cherbourg Landfront*. The 1st Battalion was at Digosville and the 3rd Battalion at Sideville; the 2nd Battalion was in reserve at Tourlaville.[281] The latter battalion was quickly dispatched to the west coast, without being replaced, while the *I.* and *III./Reithinger* were to be relieved by the *I.* and the *III./739*, respectively.[282] The three batteries of *Art.Abt. Römer* were in position in the eastern sector of the Cherbourg Defensive Zone and two of them were earmarked for support of the *709. I.D.* The 1st Battery remained at Digosville and the 2nd was to relocate to the Montebourg area to support *GR 729*.[283] The *II./739* was expected to arrive on **28 November** to take over the *Seefront* from *GR 587* (*320. I.D.*) at noon on the **30th**.[284] The battalions of *GR 729* would relieve the *III./586*, the *III./587* and the current corps reserve, the *II./585*.[285] Although *Art.Abt. 669* was intended to relieve the *I./AR 320* on the east coast, the arrival of *H.K.A.A. 755* (a coastal artillery battalion) in that sector between **8-12 December** allowed it to relieve the *II./AR 320* on the Jobourg Peninsula instead.[286]

Other formations on the Cotentin at this time were *MG-Btl. 17* and *Pz. Abt. 223*. The latter, later redesignated as the *I./Pz.Rgt. 100*, was positioned in the southeast corner of the peninsula, the area around Carentan.[287] The battalion remained in that general area until it was transferred in **November 1943**.[288] *MG-Btl. 17* stayed on the Cotentin and was subordinated to the new division.[289] On **29 November 1942**, the battalion relieved the *II./585* (*320. I.D.*) on the Jobourg Peninsula. That same day, the arrival of the *II./739* at Cherbourg was reported, the battalion probably taking over the *Seefront* shortly after that.[290] The precise arrival times of most of the division's other units are unknown but, at 18:00 on **1 December**, *Gen.Maj.* Nake took command of the coastal sector of the *320. I.D.*, including elements of that division that were still deployed there.[291] Two days later (**3rd**), the headquarters of the *709. I.D.* was reported at Valognes.[292]

After arriving in Bretagne in June 1941, the 709.I.D. held the northeast coast of the peninsula. It would remain there until late 1942 when it moved to Normandy instead.

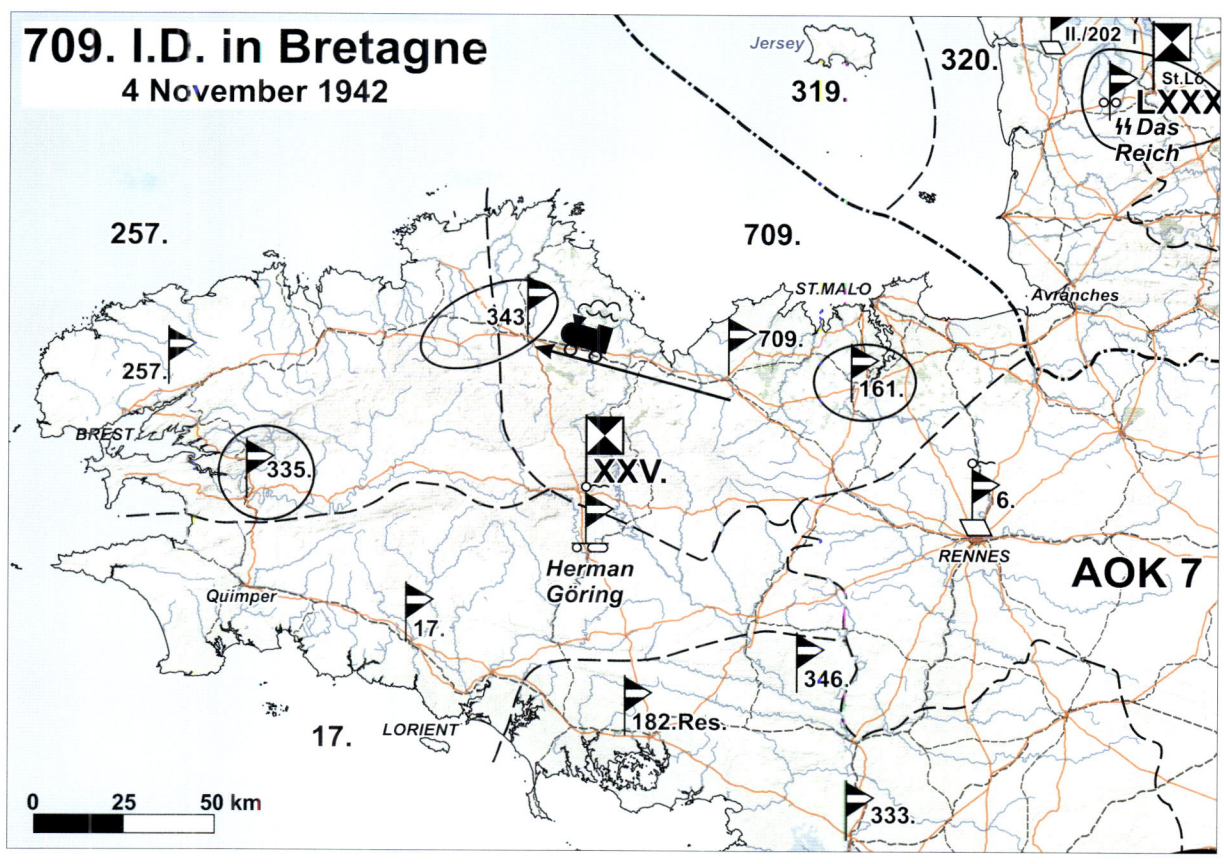

On **4 December**, the *I./729* relieved the *III./586* and, the next day, the *III./729* relieved the *III./587* in the area of Tocqueville. That same day, the commander of *GR 739*, *Obst.* Manussi, took command of the Cherbourg Defensive Zone from the *165. Div.*[293] Five days later (**10th**), he was formally installed as the commander of the zone.[294] The transfer of the *709. I.D.* to Cherbourg was completed on **6 December**, with both the *165. Div.* and the *709. I.D.* assuming full command of their new sectors.[295]

From then until the invasion the infantry regiments of the *709. I.D.* typically held one battalion in reserve, although this could vary from none to two. The battalions were rotated on a regular basis; the reserve elements relieved one of the battalions on the coast which, in turn, would become the reserve battalion. *MG-Btl. 17* also took part in these rotations, essentially functioning as an extra battalion for the division.[296] In the sector of *GR 739*, the reserve battalion was typically located in the area of St. Croix-Hague and Le Bigard, while in the sector of *GR 729* the area of Montebourg served that purpose.

To appreciate the activities in the division's sector during **1943**, it is important to know that the departure of the *320. I.D.* in late **1942** resulted in a major loss of manpower for the *LXXXIV. A.K.* That division had three infantry regiments compared to just two in the *709. I.D.* The bulk of the *709. I.D.* was committed in the most important sectors: the east and north coast — including the Cherbourg Defensive Zone — of the Cotentin. The manpower problem

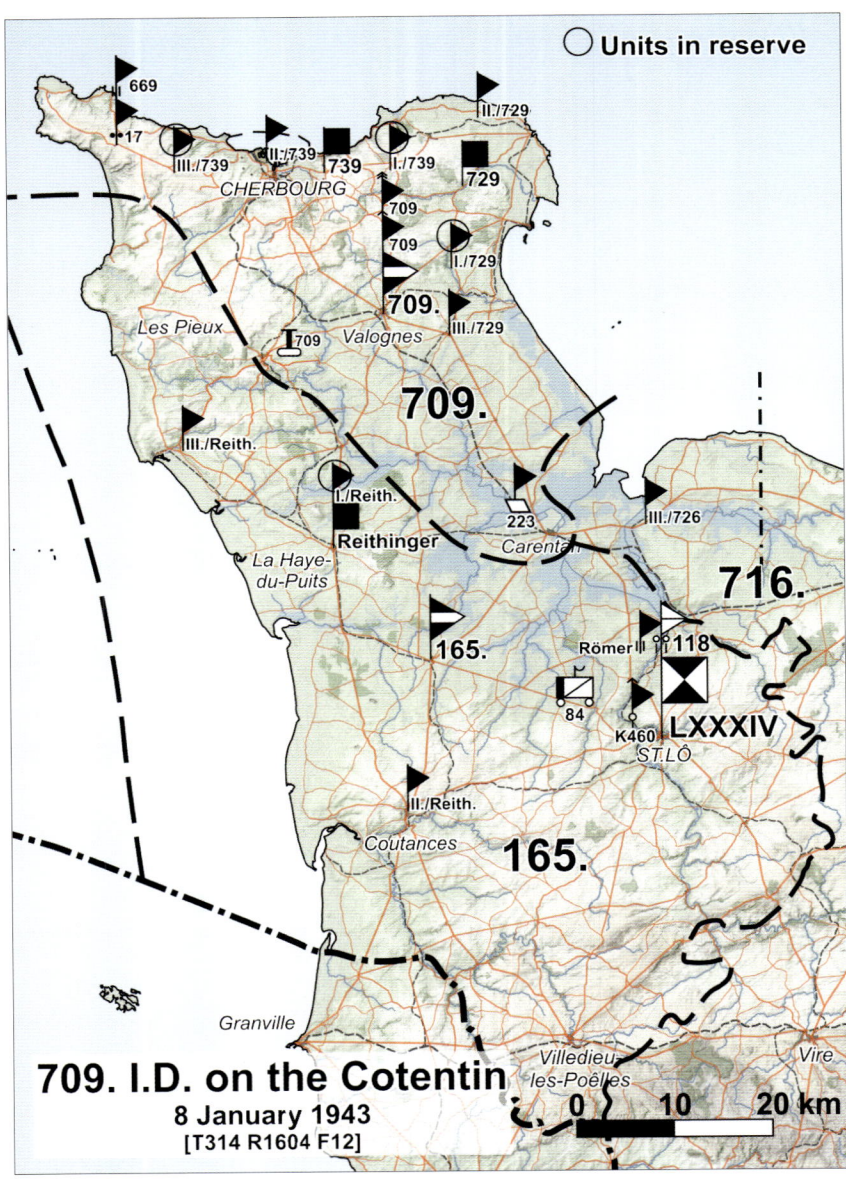

When it arrived in December 1942, the 709.I.D. was given responsibility for the northeast half of the Cotentin, including Cherbourg. During 1943 its sector was expanded to include the entire peninsula and much of Manche.

worsened in **February 1943**, when the *165. Div.* was transferred without being replaced. This reduced the number of infantry battalions in the sector from 12 in late **1942** to just 6. Moreover, taking over the coastal sector of the *165. Div.* meant that the *709. I.D.* now covered 212 km of coast![297]

The division's priority remained the north and east coast, with the result that it had no choice but to leave the rest of its sector exposed. To address this problem, a series of measures was taken, which can be divided into three main categories:

- The reserves of the division were reorganised and motorised.
- Some forces were sent to the sector as semi-permanent reinforcements; some were separate formations, while others joined the division.
- Divisions temporarily took over certain sectors, primarily at the base of the peninsula.

Since all reinforcements helped to relieve the pressure on the division's sector, these will be briefly discussed below.

By the beginning of **1943**, the division had established its headquarters at Valognes, as had *Pi.Btl. 709* and *Nachr.Abt. 709*; *Pz.Jg.Kp. 709* was at Bricquebec. As noted, *GR 739* had taken over the Cherbourg Defensive Zone; its headquarters was at Tourlaville and the 2nd Battalion in Cherbourg itself. Both the 1st and 3rd Battalions were divisional reserves, at Digosville and Sideville, respectively. *MG-Btl. 17* and *Art.Abt. 669* were in position at Beaumont-Hague, west of the *Landfront*. *GR 729* defended the east and northeast coast of the Cotentin; its regimental headquarters was at Montebourg with its three battalions located at Tocqueville and Le Ham.[298]

On **3 January**, the headquarters of *GR 729* moved from Montebourg to Château de Pépinvast (near Le Vast) and four days later to Le Vast (**7th**).[299] Several of its battalions also changed their positions. On **4 January**, the *I./729* moved to Octeville-l'Avenel and the *III./729* to Montebourg.[300] On the **17th**, these battalions again swapped positions.[301] The battalions of *GR 739* also moved during the month. On **5 January**, the *III./739* relocated from Sideville to St. Croix-Hague.[302] On **27 January**, the *I.* and *II./739* swapped positions, with the 1st Battalion going to Cherbourg and the 2nd Battalion to Digosville, where it became a divisional reserve.[303]

On **31 January**, the *LXXXIV. A.K.* was informed that it would receive a

Turkic battalion, which was to be committed on the west coast of Manche.[304] Although this development was not yet relevant to the *709. I.D.* — that sector was still held by the *165. Div.* — this would change when the *165. Div.* departed.

On **2 February**, *MG-Btl. 17* moved to the area around St. Croix-Hague and became a divisional reserve, while the *III./739* took over the Jobourg Peninsula.[305] On **19 February**, *Pi.Btl. 709* (divisional reserve) moved to Château de l'Ermitage (northwest of Ruffosses) and four days later (**23rd**) the *I./729* was relieved as a corps reserve at Montebourg by the *II./729*.[306] The 1st Battalion was relocated to the northeast corner of the peninsula to take over the former positions of the 2nd Battalion around Tocqueville.[307]

On **11 February**, *Ob.West* ordered the transfer of the *165. Div.* to *AOK 15* before the **25th**.[308] The corps decided to relieve the division with the regimental headquarters of *GR 739* and one of its battalions.[309] This battalion would move to La Haye-du-Puits and await the arrival of the Turkic battalion, which would then move to that town, while the German battalion relocated to nearby Blanchelande.[310]

On the **16th**, the *II./739* returned to the area of Cherbourg and the 1st Battalion moved to the sector of the *165. Div.* to take over the coast.[311] The next day, the headquarters of *GR 739* and the 1st Battalion relieved *GR. Reithinger* (*165. Div.*).[312] The regimental headquarters moved to Périers and the battalion to La Haye-du-Puits.[313] *GR 739* was ordered to disguise itself as "*Division 739*", with the battalion at La Haye-du-Puits posing as a regiment.[314] The Turkic battalion (*Georg.Inf.Btl. 797*) arrived on **17 February** and was first divided between Bricquebec and Périers.[315] It had been earmarked to take over much of the west coast from the *165. Div.*, but it arrived too late to carry out that mission immediately.[316] Six days later (**23rd**), the battalion moved to its future deployment area around La Haye-du-Puits, although it was not yet committed on the coast.[317]

On **20 February**, the *165. Div.* relinquished command of its coastal sectors to *GR 739*.[318] The division left the corps area two days later.[319] *Art. Abt. Römer* remained behind with the corps;[320] the battalion was reorganised and redesignated as *s.Art.Abt. 450*.[321] It continued to support the division and work on the *Landfront* until transferred in early **August**.[322]

The relocation of the headquarters of *GR 739* to Périers also had consequences for the Cherbourg Defensive Zone, which had been under the regimental commander. *AOK 7* assigned a new officer to command it and

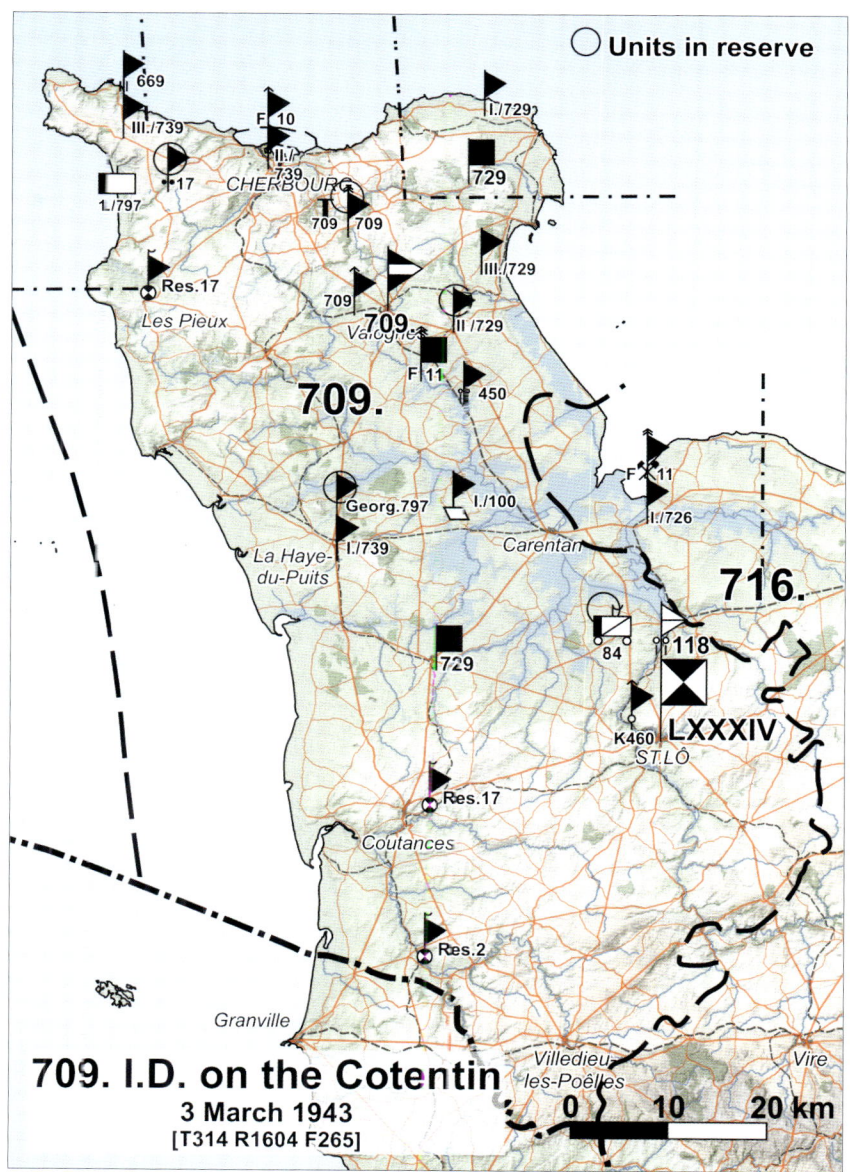

When the 165.Div. left the LXXXIV. A.K. in early 1943, its sector was taken over by the 709.I.D. The Vire Estuary remained under the 716.I.D.

directed the *709. I.D.* to provide him with a headquarters. The field army also proposed that the commandant position and headquarters be classified as static, which would prevent this problem from arising again.[323] In **May**, this sector was further strengthened by establishment of a static garrison battalion: *Festungs-Stamm-Abt. LXXXIV*.[324] It was permanently stationed in the Cherbourg Defensive Zone.

In **February**, the corps was assigned three reserve bicycle battalions (*Reserve-Radfahr-Abteilungen*) for reconnaissance and security missions along the west coast and the boundary with the *LXXXVII. A.K.*[325] This meant they would be located in the division's sector. The battalions were placed under a headquarters and consolidated as *Schnelle Brigade 30*.[326] The battalions were *Schnelle Abt. 513, 517* and *518*.[327] The three battalions arrived on the **24th** and **25th**, with *513* moved to Lessay, *517* to Les Pieux and *518* to Cérences.[328] The headquarters was being established and would initially be located in Argentan;[329] on **12 March**, it moved from there to Coutances.[330] Two of the battalions generally maintained their positions, but *Schnelle Abteilung 517* moved repeatedly. On **3 March**, it transferred to the area around Les Pieux - Rauville-la-Bigot and, on **12 April**, to Bricquebec.[331] It remained there until **27 September**, when it moved to Périers.[332] On **9 January 1944**, its headquarters moved to Bréhal, where it remained until D-Day. By then the entire brigade was outside the sector of the *709. I.D.*, which had given up control of the southwest coast of Manche to *Gren.Rgt. zbV 752*.[333]

On **22 March 1943**, *Stu.Gesch.Abt. 905* arrived on the Cotentin. Its headquarters was at Valognes, while its batteries were well spread out.[334] On **10 April**, however, the battalion again left the corps area.[335] No relocations of the *709. I.D.* were reported during **March 1943**, but **April** was quite a different matter. On **9 April**, the *II.* and the *III./729* swapped positions. The 3rd Battalion moved to Montebourg (as a reserve), while the 2nd Battalion covered the coast between Réville and Ravenoville. Its headquarters was at Octeville-l'Avenel.[336]

Since its arrival in **February**, *Georg.Inf.Btl. 797* had been unable to relieve the *I./739* on the west coast of the Cotentin. The relief finally took place on **23 April**, and the German battalion became a corps reserve in the area of La Haye-du-Puits.[337] Further north, *MG-Btl. 17* and *Pi.Btl. 709* swapped positions on **29 April**. This meant that the former was relocated to the area north of Valognes and *Pi.Btl. 709* in the area of Sideville - St. Croix-Hague. Both battalions remained a divisional reserve.[338]

May was a relatively quiet month. On the **23rd**, the *III./729*, which was in reserve, was selected as a labour force to assist with construction of the *Landfront*. On **29 May**, its companies were transported to the area of Teurthéville-Hague – Tollevast.[339] During the month, the sector of the *389. I.D.*, which was being reconstituted in the Calvados, was expanded. This was done to accommodate its growth from a *Kampfgruppe* into a proper division. Its new area overlapped part of the sectors of the *709.* and the *716. I.D.* The three combat-ready infantry battalions of the *389. I.D.* were positioned closest to the coast. The *I./544* was at Ste. Mère-Église and the regimental headquarters at Carentan; the other two battalions were in the Calvados, to the rear of the *716. I.D.* Elements in the sector of the *709. I.D.* were limited to the division headquarters (Canisy), the signals battalion (Marigny) and units of *GR 546* (approximate area of St. Jean-de-Daye).[340] As the division formed new battalions during the summer, the *III./544* went into position northwest of Pont-Hébert and *Aufkl.Abt. 389* at Cerisy-la-Salle.[341] The *389. I.D.* departed Normandy in the second half of **September**, although some elements remained behind to help build the future *352. I.D.* This included *Aufkl.Abt. 389*, which became *Füs.Btl. (A.A.) 352*.[342]

On **5 June**, the *709. I.D.* received news that *Ob.West* had requested the Replacement Army to assign an additional infantry regiment and a light artillery battalion to the division, although this information did not, as yet, affect the division. The option of creating a regimental headquarters for the artillery and strengthening the supply elements was still under consideration.[343] Other changes in its sector were relatively minor. On the **17th**, the *I./729* was moved to Montebourg as a corps reserve and the *III./729* to Tocqueville.[344]

July was also relatively uneventful, but on the final day of the month *Art. Abt. 450* was ordered to be ready for transfer at 20:00. To compensate for the expected departure of the artillery battalion, the self-propelled batteries of the *709.* and the *716. I.D.* (*gepanzerte Geräte-Batterie 709* and *716*) were directed to move to Bolleville and Flottemanville (near Valognes).[345]

In late **August**, the motorised *Artillerie-Regiment zbV 621* arrived in the division's sector with one of its battalions, *s.Art.Abt. 457*, as a field-army group reserve.[346] This allowed *gepanzerte Geräte-Batterie 716* to return to its division.[347] In mid-**September**, the regiment's other battalion arrived, *s.Art. Abt. 456*.[348] Between **November 1943** and **April 1944**, the regiment was committed behind the east coast of the Cotentin.[349] In **April 1944**, it was relocated to Bricquebec (regimental headquarters), Négreville (*s.Art Abt. 456*) and Quettetot (*s.Art.Abt.* 457).³⁵⁰ It was thus in the sector of the *91. LL.D.* on D-Day, and still a field-army group reserve.³⁵¹

In **August 1943**, the sector of the *709. I.D.* was not only strengthened by the arrival of artillery units but by the arrival of a reinforced regiment from the *384. I.D.* that had been destroyed at Stalingrad but would be reconstituted. The ad hoc regiment was formed by the headquarters of *GR 535* and included one battalion from each of the division's three regiments along with an ad hoc regimental AT company. Further elements included the *II./AR 384* (initially misidentified as the *I./AR 384*), an engineer company and a divisional AT company.³⁵² The regiment arrived between **23-26 August** and became a field-army reserve.³⁵³ It was deployed at the base of the peninsula, and it took over part of the mission of the *389. I.D.* north of Carentan. This enabled the *I./544* (*389. I.D.*) to move to Sainteny. The headquarters of *GR 535* was at Ste. Mère-Église and the *II./535* nearby, in the area east and south of the town. The *III./534* was located around La Haye-du-Puits; the *II./536* northeast of St. Sauveur-le-Vicomte. The *II./AR 384* was further north, in the area between Cherbourg and Canteloup.³⁵⁴ The reinforced regiment remained in the area until mid-**October**.³⁵⁵

The arrival of *GR 535* allowed the *709. I.D.* to make some changes. On **23 August**, *I./739* was relieved around La Haye-du-Puits and moved to the area of St. Croix-Hague as a divisional reserve. That same day, *Pi.Btl. 709* moved from St. Croix-Hague to Les Pieux.³⁵⁶ With all of its forces once again stationed around Cherbourg, the headquarters of *GR 739* relocated from Périers to Bricquebec on **25 September**.³⁵⁷

On **3 October**, the division was informed of the anticipated arrival of a reinforced regiment from the *242. I.D.* — the forces that had been requested by *Ob.West* in **June** and announced on **4 September**. These formations were now identified as *GR 919* and the *II./AR 242*. Both would be incorporated into the division, and the artillery battalion redesignated as the *III./AR 669*.³⁵⁸ The battalion was committed in the area of Les Pieux to defend the coast north and south of Cap de Flamanville.³⁵⁹ On **7 October**, its headquarters was reported to be at Flamanville.³⁶⁰

To make room for the new infantry regiment, the *I./729* moved from Montebourg to St. Martin-d'Audouville on **6 October**. The reinforced *GR 919* arrived the same day, and its headquarters was at Ste. Mère-Église.³⁶¹

Three days later (**9ᵗʰ**), the regiment's three battalions were reported to be at Fauville (south of Ste. Mère-Église) (1ˢᵗ), in Montebourg (2ⁿᵈ) and La Haye-du-Puits (3ʳᵈ).³⁶² The regiment was made a corps reserve.³⁶³ On the **17ᵗʰ**, the *II./919* moved to Flottemanville (near Valognes) and, a week later (**24ᵗʰ**), it relocated to St. Germain-de-Tournebut (northeast of Valognes).³⁶⁴

The arrival of the regiment allowed for a number of changes. It was decided to change the boundary between the *709.* and the *716. I.D.* Everything north of the Canal du Port de Carentan was transferred to the *709. I.D.* To make this possible, a third battalion from the division would be deployed in *KVG Cotentin-Ost*;³⁶⁵ this was the *I./729*, which moved to the area of Beuzeville-au-Plain - Ste. Marie-du-Mont on **17 October**.³⁶⁶ On **19 October**, the boundary between the *709.* and the *716. I.D.* was officially changed; as a result, the entire east coast of the Cotentin was now controlled by *GR 729*. Its headquarters moved from Le Vast to Montebourg to be closer to the centre of the regiment. The 1ˢᵗ Battalion assumed command of the new *KVU Marcouf* and its headquarters was located at Beuzeville-au-Plain. The 2ⁿᵈ Battalion was in command of *KVU St. Vaast* with the headquarters at Octeville-l'Avenel, while the 3ʳᵈ Battalion was responsible for *KVU Barfleur* with its command post at Tocqueville.³⁶⁷

The headquarters of *AR 669* was first listed on the situation map of **8 October**. At that time it was at Tourlaville.³⁶⁸ When it had become active is not clear. On **22 October**, the headquarters of the *I./AR 669* and *Eisenbahn-Artillerie-Abteilung 681* swapped positions. The former was now at Équeurdreville and the latter at Beaumont-Hague.³⁶⁹

The division was further reinforced by *Georg.Inf.Btl. 795*, which arrived on **13 October**.³⁷⁰ It was committed on the *Cherbourg Landfront* as a divisional reserve, except for one company that was deployed on the coast.³⁷¹ On **14 October**, the battalion was in the area of St. Croix-Hague - Beaumont-Hague, with the headquarters at Nacqueville.³⁷² In **April 1944**, the battalion was formally incorporated into the division as *IV.(Georg.)/Fest.Gren.Rgt.739*.³⁷³

On **17 October**, the division was ordered to prepare the *I./739* for transfer to the east. The battalion would be relieved by *MG-Btl. 17* as a divisional reserve in the area west of Cherbourg.³⁷⁴ The *I./739* moved to Bricquebec on the **23ʳᵈ** and, three days later (**26ᵗʰ**), *MG-Btl. 17* was reported in the area around St. Croix-Hague with its headquarters at Le Bigard.³⁷⁵ The *I./739* departed on **12 November**.³⁷⁶

While the reinforced *GR 535* left in **October**, another regiment joined

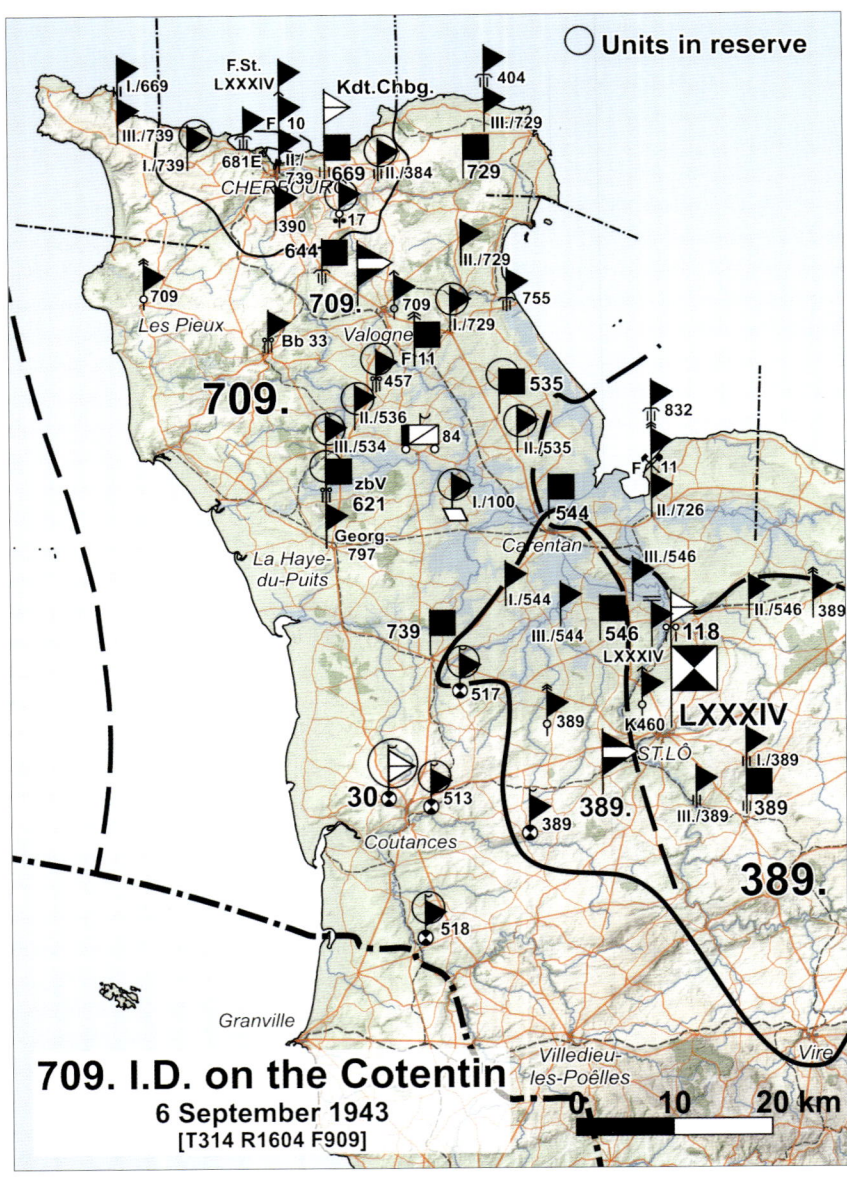

709. I.D. on the Cotentin
6 September 1943
[T314 R1604 F909]

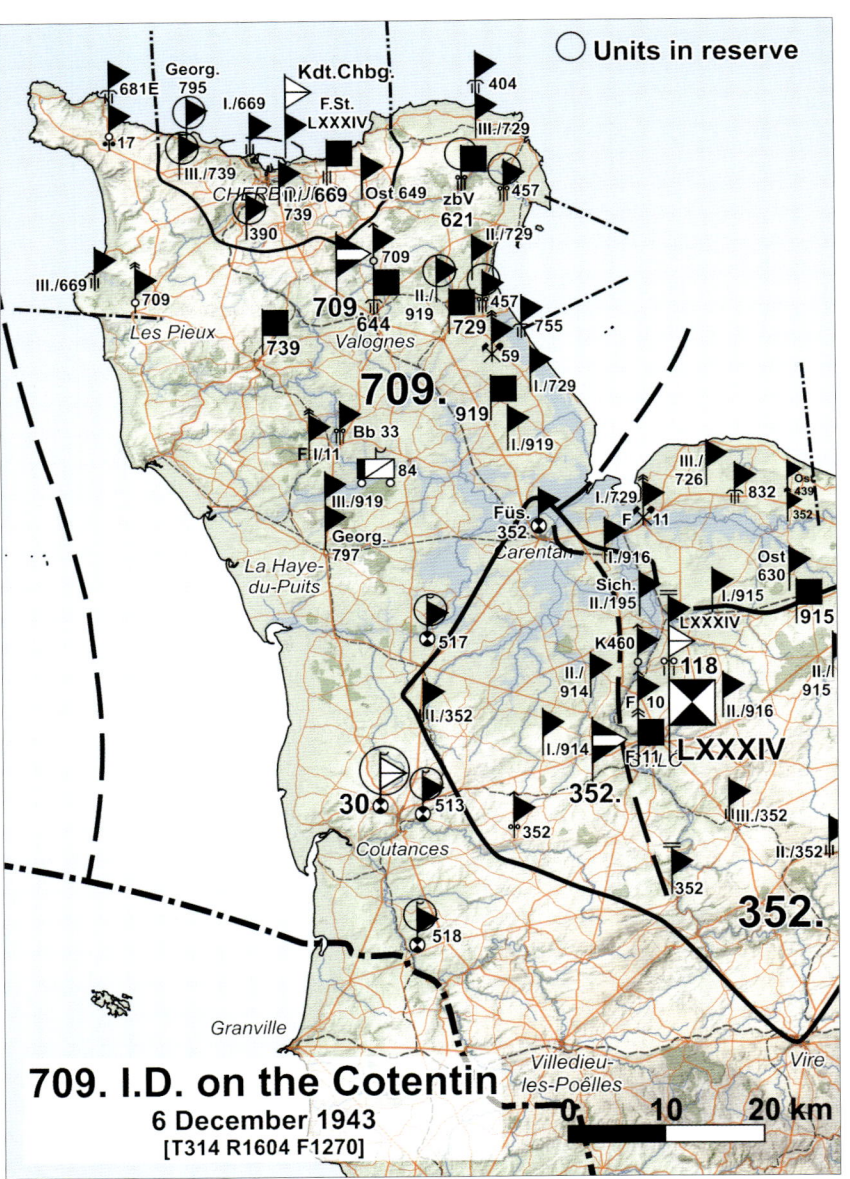

709. I.D. on the Cotentin
6 December 1943
[T314 R1604 F1270]

While the 389.I.D. was being rebuilt in Normandy, it provided both the corps and 709.I.D. with welcome reinforcements. The 389.I.D. later gave up its northern most positions on the Cotentin and instead the reinforced GR 535 arrived, providing the peninsula with a dedicated reserve.

The arrival of GR 919 changed the situation on the Cotentin. The division's right boundary was moved to Carentan, relieving the 716.I.D. on the coast north of the Douve.

the division's sector. On **1 October**, *GR 922* (*243. I.D.*) arrived in the area of Carentan. It consisted of the headquarters and headquarters company of *GR 922*, the *IV./920* and the *IV./922*.³⁷⁷ The next day, the regimental headquarters and that of the *IV./922* were at Carentan, while the headquarters of the *IV./920* was at Sainteny.³⁷⁸ The regiment left again in late **November**-early **December**.³⁷⁹ To help relieve it, *Füs.Btl. 352* moved to Carentan on **2 December**.³⁸⁰

In **November**, the division was joined by *Ost-Btl. 649*. It arrived at Cherbourg on the **18ᵗʰ** and the next day its headquarters was located at Château Digosville. The battalion remained deployed in the eastern sector of the *Landfront* and was ultimately incorporated into the division as the *IV.(Ost)/Fest.Gren.Rgt. 729*.³⁸¹ The rotation of battalions continued and, on **5 December**, *MG-Btl. 17* relieved the *III./739* on coast. The former was now at Beaumont-Hague, while the *III./739* became divisional reserve in the area around Le Bigard.³⁸²

The positions of the division changed significantly in **January 1944**, as *GR 919* took over much of the east coast of the peninsula from *GR 729*. On **6-7 January**, the *I./919* moved to the southern sector of the coast (*KVU Marcouf*) and established its command post at Beuzeville-au-Plain. This relieved the *I./729*, which assembled as a reserve force around Le Ham.³⁸³ It soon left to join the rest of its regiment.³⁸⁴ On **19 January**, the headquarters of *GR 919* moved to Montebourg, while the headquarters of *GR 729* moved from that town to Le Vast. At the same time, the headquarters of the *II./919* moved to Octeville-l'Avenel and assumed command of the southern part of *KVU St. Vaast*. The *III./919* relocated to Le Ham as a reserve.³⁸⁵ The arrival of the *II./919* in its new sector allowed the *II./729* to move north. On **9 February**, the headquarters moved to the area around Tocqueville.³⁸⁶ The division received an interesting reinforcement on **8 January**, when *Arko 118* moved from the corps headquarters at St. Lô to Valognes. There, it joined the headquarters of the *709. I.D.* and also served as the artillery command of the division.³⁸⁷

Another noteworthy development in the sector of *LXXXIV. A.K.* was the arrival of the *243. I.D.*, which assembled at the base of the Cotentin in early **January**. It occupied a sector west of the *352. I.D.*, covering the area of Carentan - Ste. Mère-Église (excl.) - Montsurvent - Coutances - Colombières.³⁸⁸ Later that month, a regiment and an artillery battalion moved north, expanding the divisional sector to include Orglandes, St. Jacques-de-Néhou, and La Haye-du-Puits.³⁸⁹ In **February**, elements moved even further north, with troops at Colomby and artillery battalions around Ste. Marie-du-Mont and Hattainville.³⁹⁰ With these troop transfers, the division gave up its presence east of the Taute River. Following these movements, the sector of the division did not change significantly until **May**, when it relieved the *709. I.D.* on the west coast of Manche, including the Jobourg Peninsula.

Apart from the *243. I.D.*, few combat units arrived in the area of the *709. I.D.* during **January**. An exception was *s.Stellungs-Werfer-Abt. 103* — later redesignated as the *III./s.St.W.Rgt. 101* — which was transferred to the Cotentin early in the month as a field-army reserve. It was located around Vindefontaine and left in **February**.³⁹¹

At the end of **January**, *Feldm.* Rommel visited the *LXXXIV. A.K.* and his inspection resulted in a number of changes. For one, the field marshal insisted on committing as many forces as possible on the coast, rather than maintaining sizeable reserves. As a result, two of the division's reserve battalions (*Georg.Inf.Btl. 795* and the *III./739*) were repositioned on the coast. Moreover, elements of the *13.* and the *14./919* that were not yet committed were deployed directly on the coast.³⁹² On **8 February**, *Georg.Inf.Btl. 795* took over *KVU Jobourg* and the *III./739* assumed command of the newly formed *KVU Vauville*; their headquarters were located at Beaumont-Hague and Vasteville, respectively.³⁹³ The day before, *MG-Btl. 17* had moved to the reserve area around Le Bigard.³⁹⁴ On **27 February**, apparently unrelated to Rommel's visit, the *III./AR 1709* was transferred from the west coast to the northeast corner of the Cotentin. It was positioned around St. Pierre-Église, where its headquarters was located.³⁹⁵

March and **April** were relatively quiet months. In a positive development, the division's sector along the west coast was significantly reduced by the arrival of *Gren.Rgts.Stab zbV 752*, which took over the southern half of Manche as *KVA "J2"*, which covered the area south of the line St. Sauveur-le-Vicomte - Barneville - Cap de Carteret.³⁹⁶ Since much of *Georg.Inf.Btl. 797* was in that sector, it was subordinated to the new headquarters.

The sector of the *709. I.D.*, now called *KVA "J1"*, was reinforced by the arrival of yet more *Osttruppen*: *Ost-Btl. 561*. This battalion arrived on **8 March** and was briefly in the area of Querqueville - St. Croix-Hague - Les Pieux.³⁹⁷ In the second half of the month, it was committed in the Flamanville area, where the headquarters established its command post. It held a coastal sector that stretched from approximately Flamanville to Barneville.³⁹⁸

On **24 March**, the fortress itself was strengthened by the arrival of two battalions of the *243. I.D.*: The *II./921* (Hainneville) and the *I./922* (Tourlaville).[399] Both battalions were deployed on the *Landfront*, where they remained under the *709. I.D.* until after D-Day. The former battalion moved to Sideville on **8 April**, and the latter to Le Mesnil-au-Val on **17 May**.[400] They were better known as the *Landfront* battalions.

A new arrival in **April** was the *3./Pz.Jg.Abt. 709*, which arrived at Pépinvast (near Le Vast) on the **4th**.[401] A week later (**11th**) it was relocated to the high ground at La Pernelle.[402]

On Hitler's orders, a final attempt to strengthen the Cotentin Peninsula was carried out in **May**. The *243. I.D.* was shifted to the west coast of the Cotentin, taking over *KVA "J1"* in the area west of *Festung Cherbourg*. As a result, *Ost-Btl. 561* was subordinated to the *243. I.D.*, as was *MG-Btl. 17*, which relieved *Georg.Inf.Btl. 795* on the Jobourg Peninsula on **13 May**. The Georgian battalion, however, remained with the *709. I.D.* It first moved to Le Bigard, before transferring to the southeast corner of the peninsula, where it was attached to *GR 919*.[403]

Earlier (**6 May**), the headquarters of *GR 739* had moved from Bricquebec to Sotteville, but this still put it in the new sector of the *243. I.D.*[404] The *III./739* was still at Vasteville, and it was also briefly subordinated to that division.[405] In **mid-May**, *Heeresgruppe B* intended to use the elements of *GR 739* still with the *243. I.D.* to gradually relieve the *Landfront* battalions, but this did not occur.[406] Instead, on **22 May**, the headquarters of *GR 739* moved to Hainneville, inside the fortress.[407] On **5 June**, it relocated once more to just south of the village.[408] The *III./739* was relieved from its coastal defence sector under the *243. I.D.* (**26 May**). It was staged with the *14./739* in the area around St. Croix-Hague as a corps reserve. The battalion headquarters was stationed at Château du Bigard.[409]

Another formation affected by the changes was *Pz.Jg.Abt. 709*. The *2./Pz.Jg.Abt. 709* moved to Bricquebec on **18 February** and then to Fleury (near Jobourg) on **3 May**; yet it would still have to move once more to return to its division's sector. The headquarters of *Pz.Jg.Abt. 709*, located at Bricquebec, moved only once — to Câtelet (east of Valognes) on **18 May**.[410]

Most of the other elements of the *709. I.D.* remained where they were throughout **May** and into the first days of **June**. An exception was the *III./919*, which had first moved to Tocqueville on **3 May** but returned to its regimental sector (Octeville-l'Avenel) on the **17th**.[411] The headquarters of *Georg.Inf.Btl. 795* moved to Brucheville on the **17th**, then to Beuzeville-au-Plain the next day (**18th**), and finally to Turqueville on the **19th**.[412]

The *91. LL.D.* also arrived on the Cotentin in **May**, where it took over the centre of the peninsula. This further reduced the sector of the *709. I.D.*, which became limited to *Festung Cherbourg* and the east and northeast coast of the peninsula. The boundary between the divisions ran generally east of the N13 highway from Carentan (*91.*) to northwest of Montebourg (*91.*), Valognes (*709.*) and Brix (*91.*).[413]

Although reduced in size, the sector of the *709. I.D.* was reinforced by additional arrivals. On **16 May**, the headquarters of the *I./s.St.W.Rgt. 101* (field-army-group reserve) was reported to be at Aumeville-Lestre, north of Quinéville, while *Sturm-Bataillon AOK 7* (field-army reserve) moved to the area of Le Vast, where its headquarters would be located.[414] A very late arrival was the *II./Fj.Ers.u.Ausb.Rgt. 1*, which reached the area on **2 June**. Although its companies were spread out over the peninsula, the battalion headquarters and three companies were within the sector of the division.[415]

Positions on D-Day

On **6 June 1944**, the divisional headquarters was at Chiffrevast (*Wn. 543*) along with *Arko 118* (*Obst.* Hamann). The colonel was the acting artillery officer of the division, rather than *Obst.* Reiter, who was in *Festung Cherbourg*. The command post of *Nachr.Abt. 709* was a few kilometres to the east of division headquarters.[416]

Festung Cherbourg was under the command of the *Festungs-Kommandant*, *Gen.Maj.* Sattler. The fortress had the status of a brigade headquarters. The troops of *GR 739* were committed in this sector. The regimental headquarters was at Hainneville, while the 2nd Battalion was in Cherbourg itself and holding resistance nests along the coast. Likewise, *Festungs-Stamm-Abt. LXXXIV* was in Cherbourg, but its companies were spread out. The *III./739* was at Château du Bigard as a corps reserve and *Ost-Btl. 649* was at La Brasserie.[417] On the Seefront, the *II./739* was supported by elements of the fortress garrison battalion, the *Luftwaffe* and the *Kriegsmarine*. Other elements of the fortress garrison battalion were deployed on the *Landfront*, as was *Ost-Btl. 649*.[418] Additional reinforcements for this front included the two *Landfront* battalions

(*243. I.D.*). The first battalion (*II./921*) was at Les Courts, near Sideville;[419] the second (*I./922*) at Brucan in the wider La Glacerie - Le Mesnil-au-Val area.[420] The *II./Fj.Ers.u.Ausb.Rgt. 1* had two companies at "Lager La Boulée" (Le Boulay, near Martinvast) and a third at La Glacerie.[421]

The fortress was also defended by divisional artillery. *AR 1709* had its command post at Hameau de la Planque, within the fortress; its commander, *Obst.* Reiter, was the artillery officer of the fortress.[422] He had two of his battalions at his disposal: The *I.* and the *II./AR 1709*. These battalions had their command posts at Équeurdreville and Le Becquet, respectively.[423] Three batteries of the 1st Battalion (2nd through 4th) were at Tonneville, Branville and *Wn. 481* (La Fosse du Gast), respectively.[424] The 1st Battery was not available to the battalion, as it had left its sector on **5 June**. However, the 7th Battery had arrived in the area and was in position 1 km northeast of the St. Croix-Hague church.[425] The remaining three batteries of the 2nd Battalion (5th, 6th and 8th) were at Fermanville (La Judée), Digosville (*Wn. 243*), and just west of west of Hau. Pinabel.[426]

The northeast corner of the peninsula, east of *Festung Cherbourg*, was held by *GR 729*. It was thus responsible for *KVU Barfleur* and parts of *KVU St. Vaast*.[427] The command post of the regiment was at Le Vicel. The north coast was held by the 3rd Battalion; its command post was near the coast, most likely near Gouberville, together with the headquarters of the *III./H.K.A.R. 1261*.[428] New locations were reported for 10th and 12th Companies in early **May**, when they moved to Néville-sur-Mer and Gatteville, respectively.[429]

The 1st Battalion was responsible for the right (eastern) coastal sector of the regiment. The headquarters was at Quettehou.[430] *AOK 7* records do not provide the positions of its companies.[431]

The bicycle battalion (2nd Battalion) was a divisional reserve around Tocqueville.[432] For most companies, no relocations were reported after arriving in that sector. An exception is the 5th Company, which moved to Réthoville in early **May**.[433] It appears that the 6th Company had remained southwest of Barfleur (at Montfarville), while the 8th Company was still near Gouberville and the 7th Company most likely still at Denneville.[434] According to the battalion commander, his companies were distributed to the rear of the other two battalions in early **May**.[435]

The artillery in the sector was reinforced by the *III./AR 1709*; its headquarters was at St. Pierre-Église. The 9th Battery was just south of Varouville (*Wn.* 157) and the 11th Battery at Maurepas (*Wn.* 165). The 10th Battery was about 2 km southwest of St. Pierre-Église.[436] The day before the invasion, the *1./AR 1709* also arrived in the area and went into position 1 km north of the town's church.[437] The headquarters of the *II./H.K.A.R. 1261* was at Morsalines.[438]

The final and southernmost coastal sector of the division embraced Utah Beach. This area was held by *GR 919*. Thanks to the post-war monograph of *Obstlt.* Keil, it is possible to examine the deployment of his regiment in detail. The regiment held the area from the Carentan-Canal (*352. I.D.*) in the south to a line in the north running from La Belle Croix (*GR 919*), via Crasville (*GR 729*), to the intersection of the Quettehou - Valognes road (D902) with Montaigu - St. Germain-de-Tournebut road (D63) (*GR 729*).[439]

The regimental headquarters and the engineer platoon were at the stone quarry on Hill 69, located at the road triangle north of the Montebourg – Quinéville road, halfway between the two towns. The forward command post was in a signals bunker next to the headquarters of *H.K.A.R. 1261*.[440]

The I./919 held the coast from the Carentan-Canal to the roads leading east to the coast from Ravenoville (incl.) and west to Cibrantot (incl.), the D15 and D420, respectively. The headquarters of the 1st Battalion was north of Foucarville, as was the headquarters of the *I./H.K.A.R. 1261*. The headquarters held positions on both sides of the Foucarville - Quettehou road (D14). The bicycle company (1st Company) was in reserve at Ste. Marie-du-Mont, but it only had a reinforced platoon at its disposal. The rest of the company had been committed on the coast. The southernmost sector of the coast was held by the 2nd Company, which occupied *Wn. 1, 2, 2a, 3, 4* and *6* (company command post). The 3rd Company held the centre of the battalion's front with *Wn. 5, 7* (command post) and *8* and *St.P. 9*. The 4th Company was on the left wing of the battalion; its sector included *Wn. 10, 10a, 11, 11a* (command post) and *13*, as well as *St.P. 12*.[441]

Georg.Inf.Btl. 795 was inland as regimental reserve and covered the area of Écoquenéauville, Audouville-la-Hubert and St. Martin.[442] The battalion headquarters was at Turqueville.[443]

The command post of the *II./919.* was in a stone quarry northwest of Quinéville (near La Michauderie). The 5th Company (bicycle) was in reserve on the so-called *Ginsterhöhe*, the hill northwest of the intersection west of Quinéville (today the area of Le Poteau). The other companies were on the coast. On the right (south) was the 6th Company, which held *Wn. 14, 14a* and

15 and *St.P. 16*; its command post was located at *Wn. 15*, near Dangueville. To its left was the 8th Company, holding *Wn. 17, 19 and 20* and *St.P. 18*, where the command post was located. The left wing was held by the 7th Company, which was at Aumeville-Lestre; *Wn. 21-24* were in this sector.[444]

Towards the end of **May**, the 3rd Battalion was deployed on the high ground around Lestre and Aumeville-Lestre, where it dug in. It is no surprise that this bicycle battalion was used as a divisional reserve. The battalion headquarters was at Octeville-l'Avenel. The 9th Company was in that same area and the 10th through 12th Companies (south to north) were on the high ground between the town and the beach.[445]

The regimental infantry gun company (13th Company) was deployed in the sector of the 1st Battalion. Its command post and four guns were in position near Hébert (today Hameau Hubert). One of its platoons was deployed at Cauvin, near Ste. Marie-du-Mont, to defend the plains north of Carentan; this platoon was supported by a section from the 1st Company, which provided observation and security.[446]

When the regiment received more AT guns in **April**, it was possible to add a heavy AT platoon and a medium AT platoon to 14th Company. These platoons were committed to defend the causeways leading inland from the beaches. The most threatened areas were covered by a both a medium and heavy AT gun and, on Rommel's orders, the heavy AT guns were moved forward in early **June** and deployed on the coast. Behind Utah Beach, only the medium AT platoon, reinforced with a French 4.7 cm AT gun, remained inland; these guns were committed on the hill at the Hébert crossroad and on the two roads from St. Germain-de-Varreville and Ravenoville to the coast. Further north, the other AT platoon was deployed on the high ground between Lestre and Aumeville-Lestre. The company commander and the trains stayed at Les Mézières, west of St. Martin-de-Varreville.[447]

The light *Flak* platoon of the 15th Company was on the hill northwest of the crossroads of D42 and D14. The company command post and trains were at Couhière, northeast of Montebourg. The regiment, it seems, had a number of static light *Flak* its disposal. Personnel from the 1st Battalion manned a light *Flak* platoon protecting the battalion's command post near Foucarville. Another *Flak* platoon was in position northwest of that of the 15th Company. It was manned by soldiers of the 2nd Battalion[448]

The rear of the *I./919* was protected by elements of the *91. LL.D.* The *III./1058* was located at St. Côme-du-Mont, while a battlegroup built around the *14./1058* and the combat school held the high ground south of Ste. Mère-Église (Hill 20) and the crossroads of N13 and D70 at Les Forges.[449] The transport battery of *Flak-Rgt. 30*, which was not a combat formation, was located at Ste. Mère-Église. Further south, a *Flak* platoon of the *Luftwaffe* defended the bridges of the N13 across the Jourdan and Douve Rivers northwest of Carentan; this almost certainly was the platoon from the *4./le.Flak-Abt. 996* that was at Carentan.[450]

On D-Day, the headquarters and equipment of *Pi.Btl. 709* were located at La Préfontainerie (east of St. Joseph). The 1st and 2nd Companies were deployed in mine laying on the east and north coast of the peninsula. The command post of the 1st Company was at Émondeville along with one of its platoons; the other two platoons were at Pouppeville (near Ste. Marie-du-Mont) and Barfleur. The 2nd Company was at Château Montvason, east of Ruffosses; the locations of its platoons are not clear. The 3rd Company had also been used for mine laying and conducted this mission in the northwest part of the peninsula until the *243. I.D.* arrived and the sectors were redrawn. The company transferred responsibility for the minefields to the new division and was redeployed in the area of Saussemesnil - Le Vast to construct airlanding obstacles. It was intended to have the complete battalion available for the division, when the fighting got underway. Once Alert Level II (*Alarmstufe II*) was declared, the platoons were to stop their activities and assemble at their company command posts.[451]

The locations of *Pz.Jg.Abt. 709* have been difficult to determine. On the situation map of **5 June**, the battalion headquarters was still at Câtelet, just east of Valognes.[452] According to *Hptm.* Hümmerich, his headquarters was in a barn some 3 km from Valognes. Although he mentioned La Croix-du-Bois (1 km northwest of Valognes) as the location, he may have confused it with St. Croix-Verte (3 km southeast of Valognes and close to Câtelet).[453] In any case, the positions of the companies have not been well recorded. The exception is the 3rd Company, which was between Le Vast and La Pernelle, where it had arrived in **April**;[454] it held the high ground that overlooked the Morsalines Bight and commanded the surrounding area.[455]

The 1st Company had been positioned around the southeast sector of the *Landfront* since early **1943** and had moved to Teurthéville-Bocage on **1 February 1944**.[456] On D-Day, it was in the area of Lieusaint and Flottemanville (south of Valognes).[457] The 2nd Company had been at Fleury on **3 May**.[458]

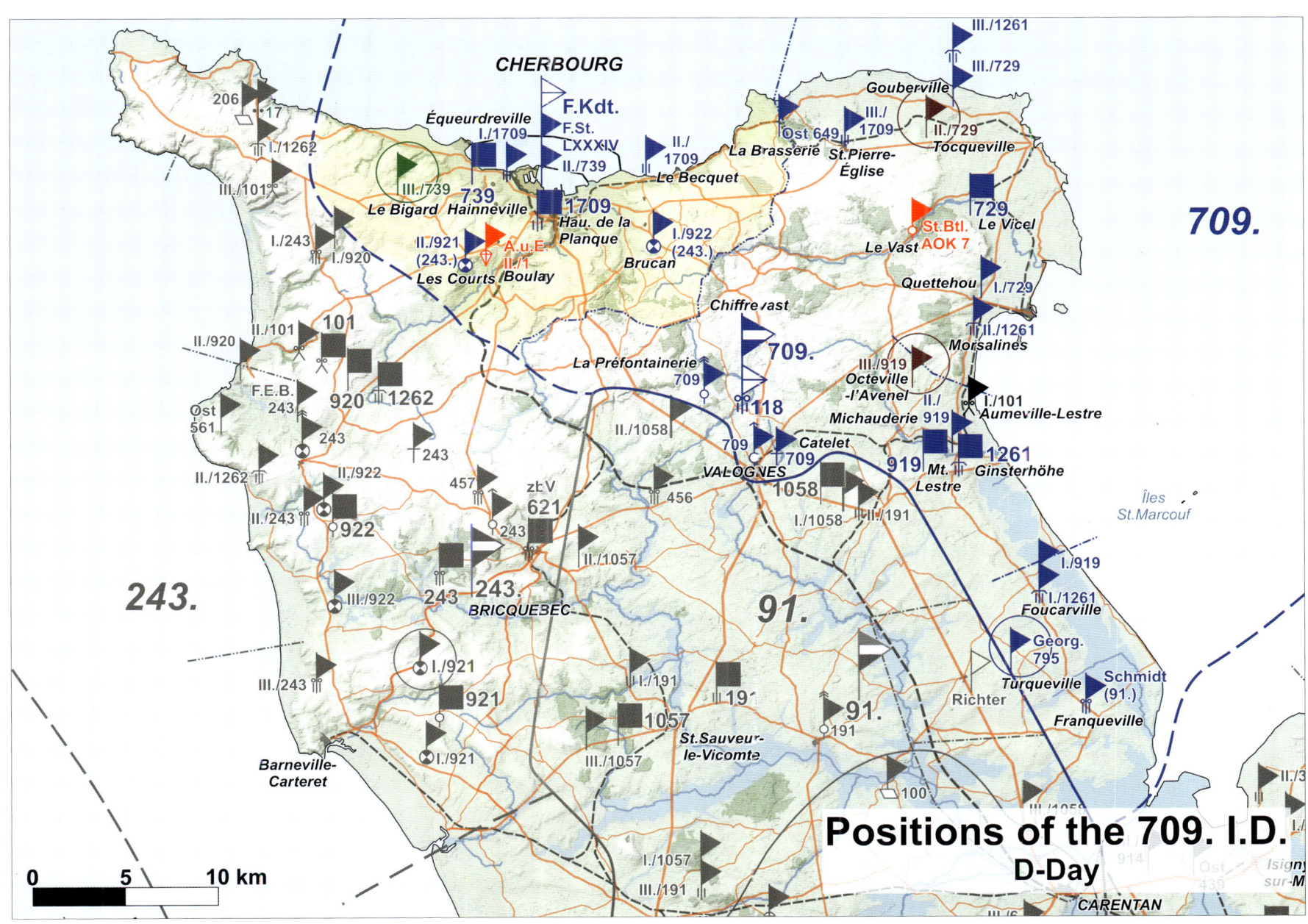

In the course of May, the 709.I.D. was relieved on the west coast of the Cotentin by the 243.I.D. and in the centre of the peninsula by the 91.LL.D. On D-Day it was thus only responsible for the east and northeast coast of the Cotentin peninsula. This still meant it was responsible for both Festung Cherbourg and Utah Beach.

After the arrival of the *243. I.D.*, the company can be expected to have been moved to a more central location in the sector of the *709. I.D.* Indeed, according to the battalion commander, it was in the woods near Huberville (just north of Câtelet) on D-Day.[459]

Obstlt. Keil, however, reported that on D-Day an AT company from the battalion was in position northwest of Sortosville — more specifically, southeast of the crossroads of the D42 (Montebourg – Quinéville) and the D14 (Fontenay-sur-Mer – Quettehou).[460] There is indeed evidence to support this. For example, an officer of the battalion stated that only one company was in reserve in the Valognes area, while the other two were deployed along the Morsalines Bight.[461] Moreover, a prisoner of the 2nd Company reported that his unit had moved from Valognes to the Quinéville area in **May**.[462] This suggests that *Hptm.* Hümmerich had simply forgotten about the late change when his account was recorded in 1958. This is even more plausible, when one considers that he went into action with his 1st Company on D-Day, making the 2nd Company less prominent in his memory. Another possibility is that the company may have been split up, but there is no evidence to confirm that.

It was quite standard for coastal divisions to integrate their artillery into the coastal defences, but *AR 1709* took this one step further. Arguably, it was more part of the coastal defences than a supporting element of the division; it did not even cover the division's entire sector but only the north coast, and many of its guns were in fixed positions with work underway to place them in fortified emplacements (casemates). The 1st to 2nd, 4th through 6th, 8th to 9th and 11th Batteries have been linked to such positions.[463] It is clear there was no mobile role intended for most of the regiment.

The entire regiment was committed along the north coast of the peninsula. Its positions stretched from the western flank of the *Cherbourg Landfront* to beyond St. Pierre-Église in the east. This meant that the regiment played no part in the defence of Utah Beach.[464] Instead, the artillery defence of Utah Beach was in the hands of the coastal batteries of the Army (*H.K.A.R. 1261*) and *Kriegsmarine* (*Batterie Marcouf*). Additional artillery was provided by an ad hoc headquarters from the *91. LL.D.*, with the *3./AR 191* at Holdy, the *6./AR 191* at Brécourt, the battery of *Sturm-Btl. AOK 7* near Cibrantot and the *1./s.St.W.Rgt. 101* at Brucheville. The *709. I.D.* contributed the six infantry guns of the *13./919* to these batteries. To contest the American landing in this area, the division would have to rely largely on artillery provided by the motorised firepower of *Art.Rgt. zbV 621* and *s.St.W.Rgt. 101* (both field-army-group reserves) or the motorised artillery of the neighbouring *243. I.D.*

Combat

Like so many other key officers, *Gen.Lt.* von Schlieben was not at his command post on the eve of D-Day. He spent the night in Rennes, where war games had been planned for the 6th. In his absence, *Obst.* Hamann (*Arko 118*) was left in charge of the division. The general himself was accompanied to Rennes by two other commanders: *Obst.* Köhn (*GR 739*) and *Maj.* Messerschmidt (*Sturm-Btl. AOK 7*). Around 06:30 on 6 June, a messenger informed *von Schlieben* that the war games had been cancelled and that he was to return to his division immediately. Since no explanation was given, *Maj.* Messerschmidt sought more information. He finally learned of the invasion at the Rennes military administrative command. The officers headed back to Normandy at once and, at Avranches, the general placed a call to *Obst.* Kessler (*Gren.Rgt. zbV 752*), who furnished more details and proposed driving along the west coast and over Bricquebec to Valognes to avoid the enemy.[465]

Absent from his command post, *von Schlieben* had missed the final Allied preparations for the invasion and the landings. Around 23:30 on **5 June**, heavy bombing raids had struck the east coast of the Cotentin and airborne forces began landing around 01:00 (**6th**).[466]

As the paratroopers landed behind the coast, the *I./919* (*Hptm.* Fink) was quickly cut off. Further north and in the rest of the division sector, contact with the enemy was limited to encounters with scattered American airborne troops; some of the enemy had even landed as far north as the fortress area.[467] Because of its location, the *I./919* bore the brunt of the Allied attack and had little hope of surviving D-Day. For much of the day, the battalion headquarters and that of the *I./H.K.A.R. 1261* defended their command posts, reinforced by men from the *4./919* and about 25 unarmed construction personnel, who had been freed from their American captors. As evening approached, the remaining personnel of these reinforced headquarters were driven into an area west of the road (D14) and the battalion commander handed over leadership to the commander of the artillery battalion. Shortly thereafter, the fighting came to an end and the troops surrendered.[468]

On the coast, the 2nd Company was hit hard in its resistance nests, which fell methodically to the attacking American forces. The 3rd Company experienced a similar unhappy fate. Further north, the 4th Company withstood an attack on *Wn. 10* and, after dark, the company commander withdrew to *Wn. 10a*.[469] Behind the coast, elements of the 1st Company had attempted to come to the aid of one of the batteries of the *91. LL.D.* but — unaware that the battery had been relocated the day before — were unsuccessful. The company later linked up with the platoon of 13th Company at Cauvin. Eventually, the infantry guns were blown up and the remnants of the company fought their way south, crossing the waterways north of Carentan and ultimately reaching positions of the *352. I.D.*[470]

The main body of 13th Company did not survive D-Day. Its positions behind the beach came under heavy fire and, at 18:00, they were overrun by tanks.[471] Much of 14th Company was also lost. The command post and rear elements of the company fought at Les Mézières for much of the day, reinforced by some 40 construction personnel and about 10 men of the *1./H.K.A.R. 1261*, which had been largely annihilated by the previous night's bombing. Around noon, the area was hit by artillery and the farm buildings caught fire. The men fought their way to St. Martin, but they were pushed back again to Les Mézières.[472] The group surrendered between 18:00-19:00.[473]

Although *Obstlt.* Keil was out of contact with his 1st Battalion, much of the fighting took place in his battalion's sector. He was an active participant in, and witness to, the countermeasures that were organised by the division and the *LXXXIV. A.K.* At 02:35, the *91. LL.D.* was released from being a field-army reserve and subordinated to the *LXXXIV. A.K.*, which made its troops available for a counterattack.[474] By then, *Obstlt.* Keil had proposed to his division that it request release of a battalion of *GR 1058* (*91. LL.D.*) for a counterattack on Ste. Mère-Église, which had been identified as the main American objective. The order for the attack followed soon after and Keil expected the battalion to reach the town by 07:00 at the latest. He would be disappointed, however, since the battalion had not advanced beyond Montebourg by that time.[475]

At 10:00, *Hptm.* Hümmerich (*Pz.Jg.Abt. 709*) received orders to support the regiment's attack with his 1st Company. The AT personnel were to link up with the regiment at Fresville, where the infantry was assembling for the attack. Leading the advance to Fresville with his headquarters, the captain encountered robust enemy resistance outside of Écausseville; as a result, he bypassed the town to the left (east) and made contact with *GR 1058* at Magneville. The 1st Company arrived there as well around 11:00. It then continued onto the highway north of Neuville-au-Plain.[476] At that village, however, German hopes of advancing rapidly on Ste. Mère-Église were frustrated by tenacious American resistance that continued for several hours.[477] Ste. Mère-Église would remain out of reach to the Germans on D-Day.

Sturm-Btl. AOK 7 was also brought up to attack the invasion forces. *Obstlt.* Keil was informed that it would be arriving around noon, and it was ordered to move the battalion via St. Floxel and Joganville to Beuzeville-au-Plain. Its attack was to be supported by half of the *2./Pz.Jg.Abt. 709*, which was in position near Quinéville. The battalion arrived between 12:00-13:00, but the AT forces, which were to link up with the battalion at Azeville, did not wait for their infantry support. Instead, they foolishly advanced on their own and were wiped out accordingly. The assault battalion, however, was able to make contact with *Georg.Inf.Btl. 795* before being pushed back again.[478] *Hptm.* Hümmerich confirms the destruction of the AT forces, but his version mentions different locations.[479]

A further reinforcement, a battalion from *GR 739*, was promised to Keil. He was informed it would arrive towards the evening and establish contact with the St. Marcouf naval battery. Indeed, the *III./739* (*Maj.* Elbrecht), which had been a corps reserve, arrived in the late afternoon and was deployed on the southern edge of the park of Château de Fontenay with its left wing on the battery.[480]

After *Gen.Lt.* von Schlieben rejoined his division, he was at once briefed on the situation and the countermeasures so far taken. The attacks of *GR 1058* and the assault battalion had gone in without artillery support, and von Schlieben considered this a critical factor in the failure to reach Ste. Mère-Église. The general informed the corps of his return and requested release of *Art.Rgt. zbV 621* to support *GR 1058*; his request was granted. He then left for the front to confer with the commander of *GR 1058* (*Obst.* Beigang) and put him in contact with *Obstlt.* Seidel (*AR zbV 621*), whose two battalions were still in position at Négreville and Quettetot.[481]

By 18:00, it was clear to von Schlieben that the attack on Ste. Mère-Église had failed to reach the town and had not even secured Neuville-au-Plain.[482] However, under growing German pressure, the village was eventually evacuated by the Americans and duly occupied.[483] Von Schlieben ordered Beigang to reorganise his forces and resume the attack early on **7 June**. Support would be provided by *AR 621* and the self-propelled company of *Pz.Jg.Abt. 709*.⁴⁸⁴

Except for the battalions already noted, few forces were available to secure the area between the coast and the N13. The *1./Pi.Btl. 709*, at Émondeville, was one of the few units in that sector; it was ordered to hold the village and prevent the enemy from reaching the highway via Azeville.⁴⁸⁵

Late in the evening, *Gen.Lt.* von Schlieben received notification that a battlegroup of the *243. I.D.* would be brought up during the night. Formed around the headquarters of *GR 922* (*Obstlt.* Müller) and including the *III./922*, the *II./920* and *Pi.Btl. 243*, it would be committed with its left wing on the St. Floxel - Fontenay-sur-Mer road. These battalions were presumably used to cover the area up to the highway. The heavy artillery battalion of the *243. I.D.*, the *III./AR 243* (minus its 10th Battery), was also to support the counterattack. During the night, it went into position near Écausseville and was subordinated to *AR 621*.⁴⁸⁶

Although outdated by 1944, the French 4.7cm anti-tank gun (aka the 4.7 cm Pak 181 (f)) remained in German service. A considerable number was used on the Atlantic Wall, including on Utah Beach. In the spring of 1944 one gun was in reserve with 14./919 in the area behind the beach, which is where this one was photographed by a member of the 101st AB. (Mark A. Bando Collection)

The counterattacks from the north being organised by the division were part of a larger scheme to destroy the enemy beachhead. From the west, the *91. LL.D.* (*GR 1057*) was to resume its attack across the Merderet River towards Ste. Mère-Église, while *FJR 6* would resume its attack against the beachhead from the south.⁴⁸⁷ These attacks would be decisive: The final opportunity to defeat the Cotentin beachhead without reinforcements.

German operations on the left wing of the division (east of the N13) on **7 June** are not clearly mentioned by German sources. According to Keil, Müller's forces attacked early that day and recaptured the village of St. Marcouf before being driven back by naval artillery. Elsewhere, the attack made no progress.⁴⁸⁸ Later that morning, the 22nd IR (4th ID) launched battalion-sized attacks against both *Batterie Azeville* and *Marcouf*. These were repulsed and, in the afternoon, German counterattacks pushed the Americans back to their line of departure.⁴⁸⁹ After the fighting, German lines in this sector ran roughly from Les Maisons de Haut (northeast of Émondeville) to *Batterie Marcouf*. *Obstlt.* Keil ordered these lines to be held.⁴⁹⁰ The positions around *Batterie Azeville* became an outpost that was reinforced by *Pi.Btl. 243*.⁴⁹¹

The resistance nests on the coast continued to hold out, but *Wn. 13* finally surrendered during the night. To its south *Wn. 10a* and *Wn. 11* and *St.P. 12* remained in German hands.⁴⁹² Further west, the 12th IR (4th ID) attacked in the morning and took Beuzeville-au-Plain and Baudienville. It continued north until stopped by German positions on the line Azeville - Bisson.⁴⁹³ These positions were presumably held by elements of Müller's forces.

The main German effort on **7 June** took place along the N13 highway, where the reinforced *GR 1058* (minus the 3rd Battalion) sought to recapture Ste. Mère-Église. In addition to the reinforcements already noted, further support arrived in the form of *Pz.Jg.Abt. 243* and the assault battalion.⁴⁹⁴ During the night, facing a flanking movement from the enemy, *Maj.* Messerschmidt moved his battalion west to the N13 highway between Montebourg and Neuville-au-Plain; it took part in the attack of *GR 1058* along the N13.⁴⁹⁵

Although the assault made good progress, it was stopped just short of Ste. Mère-Église. In the afternoon, American forces counterattacked with tank support and drove the Germans back with heavy losses.⁴⁹⁶ A total collapse was only prevented by the personal intervention of von Schlieben, who established an expedient defence line about 1,200 metres north of Neuville-au-Plain.⁴⁹⁷ *Sturm-Bataillon AOK 7* was committed west of the highway, possibly with elements on the other side.⁴⁹⁸ Where and how the remnants of *GR 1058* were deployed remains unclear but, in the evening, it was ordered to assemble for an attack west of Montebourg.⁴⁹⁹ The remnants were gathered in the *II./1058*, which was deployed west of the highway.⁵⁰⁰ The division's lines were reported to run from Fresville via Azeville and south of Marcouf to the coast.⁵⁰¹

7 June had proven to von Schlieben that the beachhead could no longer be destroyed with locally available forces. Thus, the decision was taken to go over to defensive operations and await reinforcements.⁵⁰² In the evening, German forces on the northern front (*Nordfront*) of the beachhead were reorganised. The troops were placed under the unified command of *Obst.* Rohrbach (*GR 729*) as *KG Rohrbach*. *Obstlt.* Keil could also have been selected for this position, since he was closer to the action, but additional landings were expected in his sector between Quinéville and St. Vaast-la-Hougue.⁵⁰³ Since the other regimental sectors still needed to be defended, an ad hoc headquarters was formed around Rohrbach, who was only able to take his assistant with him. The rest of the headquarters was formed by members of *GR 739*, which Rohrbach later accused of providing little more than the adjutant and an officer assistant.⁵⁰⁴

The weakness and ad hoc nature of this headquarters may have limited its effectiveness. Rohrbach complained that he initially had neither wireless nor telephones to communicate with his troops.⁵⁰⁵ Keil suggests that this problem was further exacerbated because Rohrbach's command post constantly changed position, making communication and coordination impossible.⁵⁰⁶ Other officers also reported serious communications difficulties.⁵⁰⁷

Poor communications was also the reason that elements of the *Nordfront* were not placed under Rohrbach's direct control after all. Because the signals communications of Müller's forces (*Kampfgruppe Müller*) already ran through Keil's command post, he (Keil) was given control of the left wing. As a result, *KG Keil* formed a battlegroup next to that of Rohrbach, who was in direct command of the centre and right wing of the *Nordfront*.⁵⁰⁸

To reinforce the front, more troops were brought up or relocated. These included the two battalions that had been in divisional reserve: The *II./729* (*Hptm.d.R.* Schwellenbach) and the *III./919*. The former, positioned around Tocqueville on the northeast corner of the peninsula, had already assembled in the woods at Montaigu on the morning of **7 June** (although it appears the 7ᵗʰ Company was not present). That afternoon, it moved to Hill 117, northwest of Montebourg, to protect against airlandings. It was not there for long and, during the evening, it was ordered to join the front west of the N13 highway.⁵⁰⁹

The division's final reserve battalion (the *III./919*, under *Hptm.* Berg) was also dispatched towards the front. It was attached to *KG Rohrbach* and went into position around St. Floxel, where it remained in reserve for the time being.⁵¹⁰ While the exact deployment of Rohrbach's forces east of the highway up to *KG Müller* is somewhat obscure, it did include the *II./920* and *Pi.Btl. 243*, which were no longer under Müller's control.

The *1./Pi.Btl. 709* was still east of the highway. It was ordered to remain at Émondeville, which had become part of the front. The available elements of the battalion's 2ⁿᵈ and 3ʳᵈ Companies were ordered to assemble around Montebourg the next day, with the battalion command post to be located in that area as well.⁵¹¹

KG Müller's sector stretched east from the western fringe of the park belonging to Château de Fontenay, with the front running along the southern edge of the park and including *Batterie Marcouf*. The *III./739* was committed on the left (east) wing and covered the battery and the St. Marcouf - Quettehou road (D14). The right wing of the *Kampfgruppe* was held by the *III./922*.⁵¹²

Possession of Montebourg was crucial, since it controlled the road to Cherbourg. On D-Day, it was held by troops of the headquarters company of *GR 919* and the division's combat school.⁵¹³ Its importance is illustrated by the appointment of a local area commander (*Kampfkommandant*)* to handle its defence. This mission was given to *Hptm.* Simoneit,⁵¹⁴ the company commander. Over the next few days, the town's defences were slowly reinforced. The troops that took part in its defence included several heavy anti-aircraft guns, one or two airborne training companies, *Pz.Abt. 206* and the *III./919*.⁵¹⁵

Pi.Btl. 709 was now called into action. Except for its 1ˢᵗ Company, which was already engaged at the front, the battalion was ordered to lay minefields and blow up key crossroads and bridges. This task was complicated by the fact that almost the entire inventory of mines had been installed on the coast (on Rommel's orders), leaving the battalion with just 300 *Teller* mines.⁵¹⁶

To find additional troops for the front, von Schlieben decided to reduce the manning of the resistance nests that had not been attacked, although it is not clear when this order was carried out or if it involved all coastal sectors at

---

* Kampfkommandant: The highest military authority of a specific locality that is surrounded and/or being contested but has to be held at all costs. The *Kommandant* controlled all forces in that specific area.

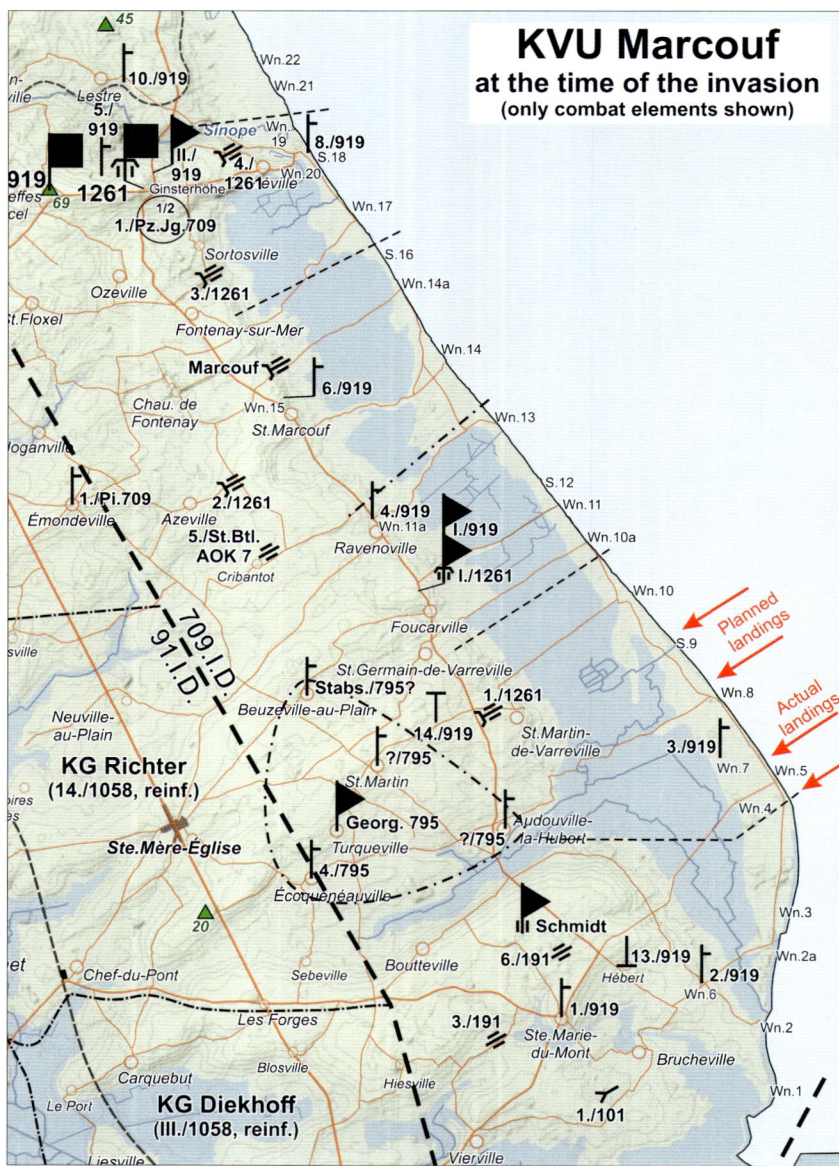

Utah Beach was defended by I./919. The artillery positions were west of the inundated area behind the coast, as was Georg.Inf.Btl. 795 which was in reserve. Further to the rear was the 91.LL.D. with a series of battlegroups along the N13 highway and Merderet and Douve rivers.

the same time. The reduction left only skeleton crews, the so-called emergency or essential manpower (*Not-* or *Kernbesatzung*).[517] The rest of the personnel were assembled inland. Since no transport was available, the men would have to walk to the front. As a result, it would take some time before these reinforcements became available. The withdrawal of these men from the coast also increased the supply problems, since the field kitchens were left behind to supply the resistance nests, leaving the companies at the front without the means to feed their troops.[518]

At 03:00 on **8 June** the lines of the division ran from Le Port Bréhay (west of Fresville), north of Fresville to Azeville and then St. Marcouf.[519] In the early morning, the *II./729* arrived at the front west of the N13 and went into position along a line about 2.5 km south of Écausseville. The railway formed its right (west) boundary and *Sturm-Btl. AOK 7* was to the left.[520]

The division's front now faced the entire 4th ID. The 8th IR was deployed west of the N13, while the 12th IR held the centre and the 22nd IR was committed on the right wing. In addition, the reinforced 505th PIR (82nd AB) was deployed on the left flank of the 8th IR to shield it from German troops across the Merderet River. In this sector, the 8th IR advanced on Magneville, west of the highway.[521] The *II./729* yielded some ground, but generally held its position. At midnight, it was ordered to withdraw to Écausseville and take up positions west of the village.[522] East of the highway, the 12th IR advanced on Émondeville.[523] The *III./919*, which had been in reserve at St. Floxel, was moved up and inserted between *Sturm-Btl. AOK 7* and *Pi.Btl. 243*, with its right flank resting on the highway.[524]

Facing heavy resistance, the 12th IR fought its way through and past Émondeville during the day. Information about the ferocious fighting is confusing, but a surprise attack by *Sturm-Btl. AOK 7* and elements of *Pz. Jg.Abt. 709* appears to have recaptured the village at 14:00 before these forces, fearing encirclement, abandoned it some hours later. After the fighting, the Americans recovered about 300 bicycles, an indication that German units, possibly the *III./919*, had rushed forward and brought their bicycles too close to the front.[525] Behind the coast and on the beach little progress was made by the 22nd IR against *KG Müller*. The two main strongpoints in this sector, *Batterie Azeville* and *Marcouf*, continued to resist.[526] On the coast, *Wn. 14* and *14a* were abandoned, and the personnel transferred to *Batterie Marcouf*.[527]

During the evening, Montebourg was reinforced by the arrival of *Pz.Abt.*

206 with its captured French tanks. The battalion went into position to the east and southeast of the town.⁵²⁸

The day (**8 June**) marked an important change: *Gen.* Marcks ordered a permanent switch to defensive operations as significant reinforcements were no longer expected to arrive any time soon. The main defence line would be established on the high ground along the Montebourg - Quinéville road. The existing positions in front of this line would still be held as long as possible. It was also decided that *Batterie Azeville*, already beyond the German frontline, would be held to gain time.⁵²⁹ That evening, the corps placed *Gen.Lt.* Hellmich in charge of the forces on the Cotentin, meaning the *91. LL.D.*, the *243.* and the *709. I.D.* fell under his command as elements of *Gruppe Hellmich*.⁵³⁰

In line with its orders, *Pi.Btl. 709* prepared to set up roadblocks and/or conduct demolitions at key bridges, culverts and on roads between the N13 and the east coast. These activities compelled the battalion to use all available men to bring up ammunition and protect the demolition sites; as a result, it only had two platoons at its disposal for special operations around Montebourg. Since each demolition site needed to be guarded by at least two men — who would set off the explosives when the time came — the operational strength of the battalion soon dwindled. Serious losses were also suffered by enemy attacks on these key locations.⁵³¹

By mid-morning on **9 June**, the lines of the *Nordfront* were reported to run from southeast of Le Haut-du-Ham, past Écausseville, along the northern edge of Joganville, south of Château de Fontenay, along the northern edge of St. Marcouf to east of Crisbecq. The boundary between *KG Keil* and *KG Rohrbach* ran from east of Joganville to the Ozeville church.⁵³² On Rohrbach's right, the *II./729* held a sector that stretched from the railway, via the Écausseville airfield (with its airship hangar) to the southwest edge of Écausseville.⁵³³ *Sturm-Btl. AOK 7* was still committed on the left, followed by the *III./919* and the *II./920*. An AT battalion was attached to *KG Rohrbach*, but it is unclear if this was *Pz.Jg.Abt. 243* or *709*. The right wing of Müller's forces continued to be formed by the *III./922* and the left wing by the *III./739*. *Batterie Azeville* remained in German hands and *Pi.Btl. 243* was deployed in that sector, although it is not fully clear where and how.⁵³⁴ About mid-day, the German lines were still holding firm, but this was about to change.⁵³⁵

After heavy fighting, *Batterie Azeville* fell during the afternoon; elements of the 22ⁿᵈ IR advanced to Château de Fontenay, but they were stopped at the

As the reinforced 4ᵗʰ Infantry Division fought its way north along the coast, it had to overcome a series of coastal resistqance nests. Some were evacuated by the Germans, while others did offer resistance but could nor etneless only delay the American advance for a short period. (NARA)

crossroads west of the castle park (D63, D69 and D214). *Batterie Marcouf* remained in German hands, which meant that the main defensive positions of *KG Müller* were still intact. On the coast, *Wn. 10a* was seized by the Americans;⁵³⁶ this only left *Wn. 11* and *St.P. 12* in German hands on the coast south of Fort de Ravenoville.

The developments to the west, on the left wing of *KG Rohrbach*, were considerably more worrisome. Early in the morning, *Obstlt.* Keil had been ordered to send emergency forces to support *KG Rohrbach*. In response, elements of the *II./919* were assembled in an ad hoc company (*Alarmeinheit Grabbe*). It was formed by taking 50 men each from the 6ᵗʰ through 8ᵗʰ Companies and 20 from the 5ᵗʰ Company. At 08:00, this force was sent to *KG Rohrbach* and committed to an attack on both sides of St. Floxel, north of the Montebourg - Fontenay-sur-Mer road (D71); the objective was the high ground east of Joganville. Also supporting the attack was the divisional combat

Pz.Jg.Abt.709 lost half of its towed anti-tank gun on D-Day. 1st Company also saw action with its self-propelled guns. Although the date of this loss is unknown, this particular example was left on the N13 highway near Le Rôti. (NARA)

school with 50 men. The attack was launched at 12:00 and managed to cross the Coisel River, before it was stopped.[537]

Grabbe's force appears to have run into 12th IR. That afternoon, this regiment moved through Émondeville and continued on to Joganville. Following an intense engagement, German opposition was overcome and the regiment pushed on to the north.[538] On orders of Rohrbach, the *III./919* carried out a withdrawal towards Montebourg. In the process, it lost contact with its 9th Company. The *III./919* was then deployed at Montebourg, while the company was attached to the *II./920. Pi.Btl. 243* was pushed northeast by the American advance, opening up a gap east of the *III./919*.[539] The two assault battalions of the 12th IR finally halted along a line running from just south of St. Floxel to a position about 1 km northwest of Joganville. The reserve battalion (3/12) was inserted between the battalions, but it did not remain in that position. Instead, it made a long advance to the north that lasted well into the evening. It crossed the Montebourg - St. Floxel road (D71) before pressing on to the Montebourg - Quinéville highway (D42).[540]

The *LXXXIV. A.K.*, of course, was keeping a close eye on these developments; at 17:25, the corps informed *AOK 7* that it appeared the feared penetration near Montebourg had now occurred. In light of this development, *Gen.* Marcks requested the release of the *Landfront* battalions for the front south of Montebourg. This was approved by *AOK 7* and later by Rommel.[541]

At 20:00, the German lines were reported to run from St. Marcouf (excl.) in the east via Joganville (excl.) to beyond Écausseville.[542] West of the highway, the *II./729* had successfully held its ground against the 8th IR throughout the day; that evening, the battalion, out of ammunition and without contact on either flank, withdrew to Éroudeville, where a new line was being established.[543] It is quite possible that *Sturm-Btl. AOK 7* had also withdrawn in response to the advance of the 12th IR on its left flank on the opposite side of the N13.

The American advance east of the highway had not gone unnoticed, although the daily report of *AOK 7* still listed the German frontline as running from east and northeast of Urville - Écausseville - Émondeville - Azeville (incl.) - St. Marcouf (excl.).[544] At midnight, *Gen.* Marcks reported that the Americans had crossed the Montebourg - Quinéville road, adding that he expected **10 June** to be decisive.[545] The situation, however, was less critical than it appeared to be. Up to that point, only a single US battalion had managed to reach the highway to Quinéville, and it was isolated since the main body of the 12th IR was still to the rear with its flanks unprotected. On the left (west) and right of this salient, the 8th and the 22nd IR were facing stiff German opposition. Nonetheless, the swift advance of the 12th IR through the centre of the *Nordfront* was in itself cause for concern. The arrival of the *I./922*, one of the *Landfront* battalions, must have helped to shore up the situation, since it was inserted into the gap east of the *III./919* (*Pi.Btl. 243* was its left neighbour).[546] While the exact moment of the battalion's arrival is not clear, it most likely joined the lines during the night.

At 02:00 on **10 June**, von Schlieben arrived at the command post of *Pi. Btl. 709*. Concerned about the enemy crossing the main road to Quinéville, he ordered an armed reconnaissance to assess the situation and strength of the enemy. The mission was carried out by a heavily armed force, about platoon sized, that advanced from Montebourg along the highway towards Gouhière. Against expectations, the village was already in American hands, and the patrol came under assault from all sides, suffering serious losses.[547] This patrol may well have been the reason why, at 04:45, *AOK 7* reported that a breakthrough to the northwest had taken place east of Montebourg.[548]

The 12th IR resumed its advance towards its objective just north of the Montebourg - Quinéville highway. The 2/12th IR ran into the defences of Montebourg and, after an unsuccessful attack on its outskirts, swung north to bypass the town. Orders were given to seal off the town but not to enter it. In the meantime, the 1/12th IR reached the hilltop northeast of Montebourg, with elements north of the road. Late that evening, German counterattacks struck the battalion and it had to pull back. By the end of the day, the three US battalions held positions south of the highway, north and northwest of St. Floxel.[549]

To the east, *Kampfgruppe Müller* managed to hold on to its main positions, but the 3/22nd IR broke through the German defences at the crossroads. The battalion moved north, bypassed German positions to its right, and advanced to Ozeville - Vaudival, where it encountered a German strongpoint. After two frontal attacks had failed to breach its defences, the battalion withdrew to the road junction about 1 km to the south; it remained there for the rest of day. The 1/22nd IR had followed in its wake. Rather than moving on Ozeville, however, it turned right to contain Fontenay-sur-Mer. To the rear, the 2/22nd IR attempted to capture Château de Fontenay, albeit without success.[550]

The German troops west of Montebourg — remnants of *GR 1058*, *Sturm-Btl. AOK 7* and the *II./729* — which had been operating for days without much direction from *KG Rohrbach*, were organised into a proper battlegroup under *Obstlt.* Hoffmann. *Kampfgruppe Hoffmann* appears to have operated semi-independently from *KG Rohrbach*; its main defence line was organised along the (today no longer existing) railway that branched off from the main Carentan - Cherbourg line north of the Le Ham station and continued via Montebourg to the east coast.[551] During the day, the *II./729* withdrew to this line and took up positions between Le Ham (station) and Éroudeville.[552] The remnants of the assault battalion were apparently still deployed on its left. The new battlegroup was reinforced by the arrival of the second *Landfront* battalion (*II./921*);[553] it was committed southwest of Montebourg in the area of Éroudeville, with the assault battalion on its left (east) and the *II./729* on its right.[554]

Thus far, the division's right boundary had been formed by the Merderet but, as the line moved north, a gap opened between the railway and the river. Further south, no troops had been needed to hold the ground west of the railway, as it merely consisted of flooded fields along the river. Around Le Ham, however, there was high ground west of the railway that lengthened the front. Elements of *KG Simon* (the *243. I.D.* but operating under the *91. LL.D.*) were inserted into this gap, which placed the left boundary of the *91. LL.D.* east of the river. The Le Ham railway station was lost to the 505th PIR during the day. To the east, the 8th IR fought its way forward and crossed the Le Ham -

Montebourg road (D42); unable to break through the German main line of resistance along the railway, it took up positions south of the road.[555]

At 18:00, the *709. I.D.* reported that its lines ran from the Le Ham railway station - the southern edge of Montebourg - La Fosselerie (south of St. Floxel, today La Josselerie) - Vaudival - Fontenay-sur-Mer - Château de Courcy.[556] This frontline makes clear that both *Batterie Marcouf* and Château de Fontenay had become outposts in front of the main German lines.

That evening, Rohrbach, having been unable to hold the American advance in check, proposed to pull back his left wing to the main defence line on the Quinéville Ridge. Such a move, however, would have lengthened the front and exposed the right flank of *KG Müller*. Because insufficient forces were available to form a continuous frontline, it was decided to organise a counterattack with Rohrbach's battalions east of the highway (*III./919, II./920, I./922* and *Pi.Btl. 243*) to recapture the old frontline. The attack would commence at 07:00, with fire support provided by *AR zbV 621, s.St.Werf.Rgt. 101* and several of the coastal batteries.[557]

The counterattack was launched as intended on the morning of **11 June**; poorly coordinated, it was doomed from the start.[558] The planned artillery support failed to materialise, and not all infantry battalions had been informed of the operation. On the right (west), the *III./919* attacked on schedule and managed to get beyond its original objective. Yet the other battalions had not received the attack order, leaving the *III./919* dangerously exposed. It was counterattacked and thrown back with heavy losses. The *I./922* and the *II./920* also came under assault and, by 10:00, had joined the withdrawal. The bulk of the *III./919* fell back towards Montebourg, while the 9th Company moved to *Obstlt.* Keil's command post on Hill 69.[559]

Unable to contact Rohrbach, Keil took matters into his own hands, managing to stop the withdrawal and establishing a new line 200 metres south of the road from Hill 69 to Les Carrières (D271). *Pi.Btl. 243* was committed to close the gap between the left wing of *KG Rohrbach* and the right wing of *KG Müller*. The 9./919, on the right wing of the newly established front, was positioned on the road from St. Martin-d'Audouville to Montebourg (D25). Yet between the company and the town was a 1 km gap that could not be closed for a lack of troops.[560] Instead of being driven back by the German counterattack, the 12th IR had been able to conduct its own attack. During the morning, it reached its objective, the western half of the Montebourg - Quinéville Ridge. This position, however, put the regiment in an exposed position, with Montebourg on the left rear and Ozeville to the right rear, both strongly held by German troops. At 23:00, the regiment received orders to withdraw to the St. Floxel - Montebourg road and to dig in.[561]

The advance of the 12th IR placed *KG Keil* in an increasingly tenuous position. While Rohrbach's lines were pushed back, those of *KG Keil* continued to hold against the 22nd IR; the result was a gap of almost 1 km on Keil's right flank that was only held by a thin screening front. Under such conditions, holding on to the outposts was no longer prudent. In the morning, *Gen.* Marcks had already ordered *Batterie Marcouf* to be abandoned during the coming night, while instructing Keil to pull back his front to a line running along the southern edge of Fontenay-sur-Mer to Dangueville. This also meant giving up Château de Fontenay. During the night, both outposts were evacuated and the new line occupied without incident.[562]

West of the highway, the *II./729* continued to hold the railway between Le Ham railway station and Montebourg. The town was reinforced by an airborne training company (*8./Fj.Ers.u.Ausb.Rgt. 1*) under *Hptm.* Hallmann.[563] Meanwhile, the 8th IR had not made significant progress, but the 2/325th GIR (82nd AB) took Le Ham and high ground west of the railway and *KG Simon* withdrew across the Merderet to Urville. This again put the boundary of the *709. I.D.* division on the river. The capture of Le Ham meant that all American objectives west of the N13 had been seized. As a result, their advance was halted for the moment.[564]

The troops of *KG Hoffmann* still held their own main line of resistance. The first elements of the *77. I.D.* began to arrive in the evening and began preparations at once to take control of the area from *KG Hoffmann*.[565] The relief of Hoffmann's forces began that very night and continued throughout the day (**12 June**). The *II./1058*, the *II./921* and the *II./729* and a platoon from *Pi.Btl. 709* were pulled from the line. Only the assault battalion remained in place, now subordinated to *KG Brandt* (*77. I.D.*).[566] The *II./729*, which had already sacrificed over half its strength, became a divisional reserve and was moved to the Bois de Montebourg (southwest of Vaudreville) for rest and replenishment.[567]

The abortive counterattack east of the highway and the ensuing withdrawal were cause for a major reorganisation of the *Nordfront*. *Obst.* Rohrbach was relieved of his command and *Obstlt.* Keil took control of the battlegroup. On Keil's request, *KG Müller* was given autonomy and remained

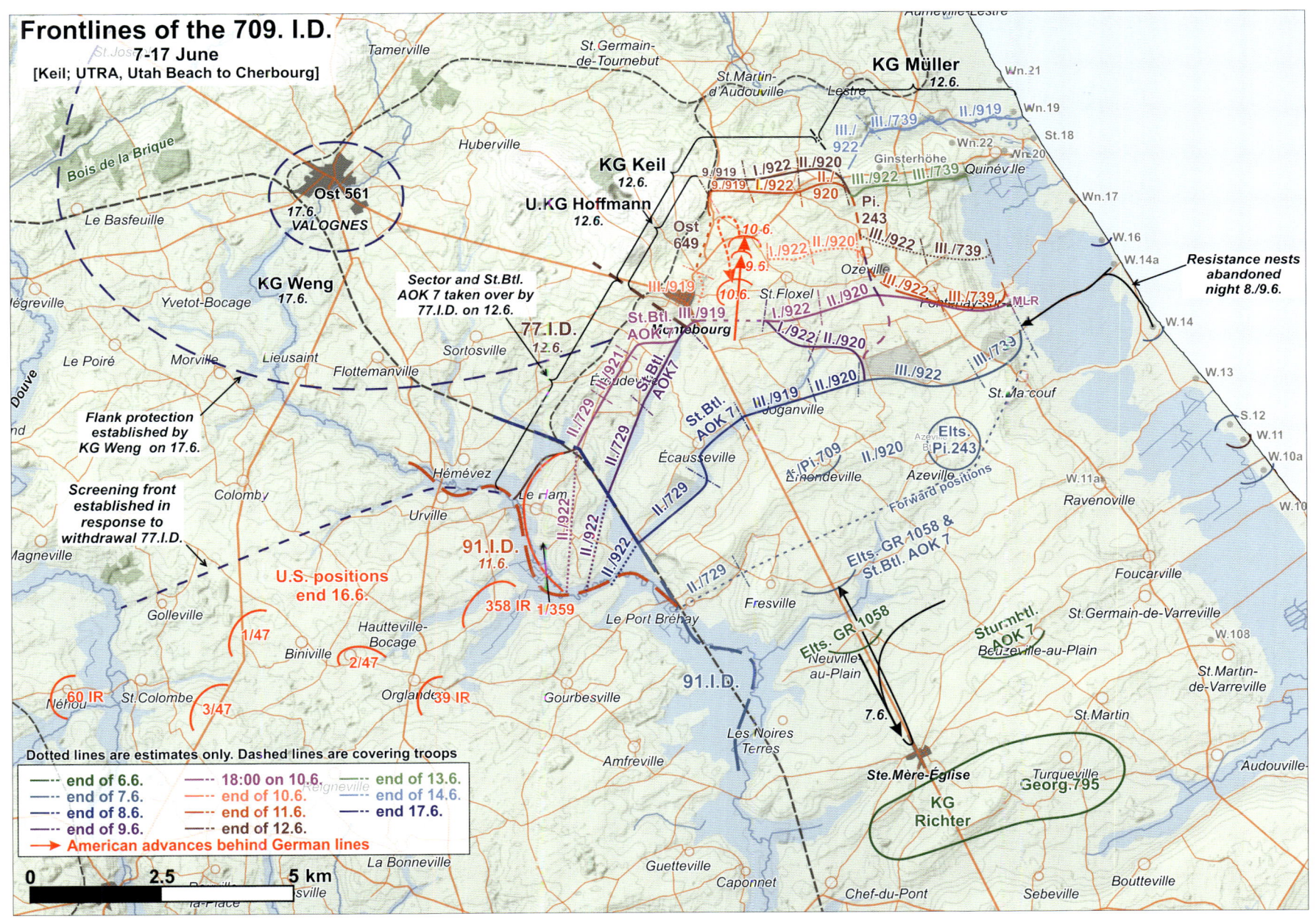

On D-Day the 709.I.D. was given responsibility for the northern front of the Utah Beachhead, between the Merderet River and the coast. After its failure to recapture Ste.Mère-Église on D-Day and D+1, the division went over to the defence. Despite significant reinforcements from the 243.I.D., it was gradually pushed back to the Quinéville Ridge northeast of Montebourg and the railroad southwest of the town.

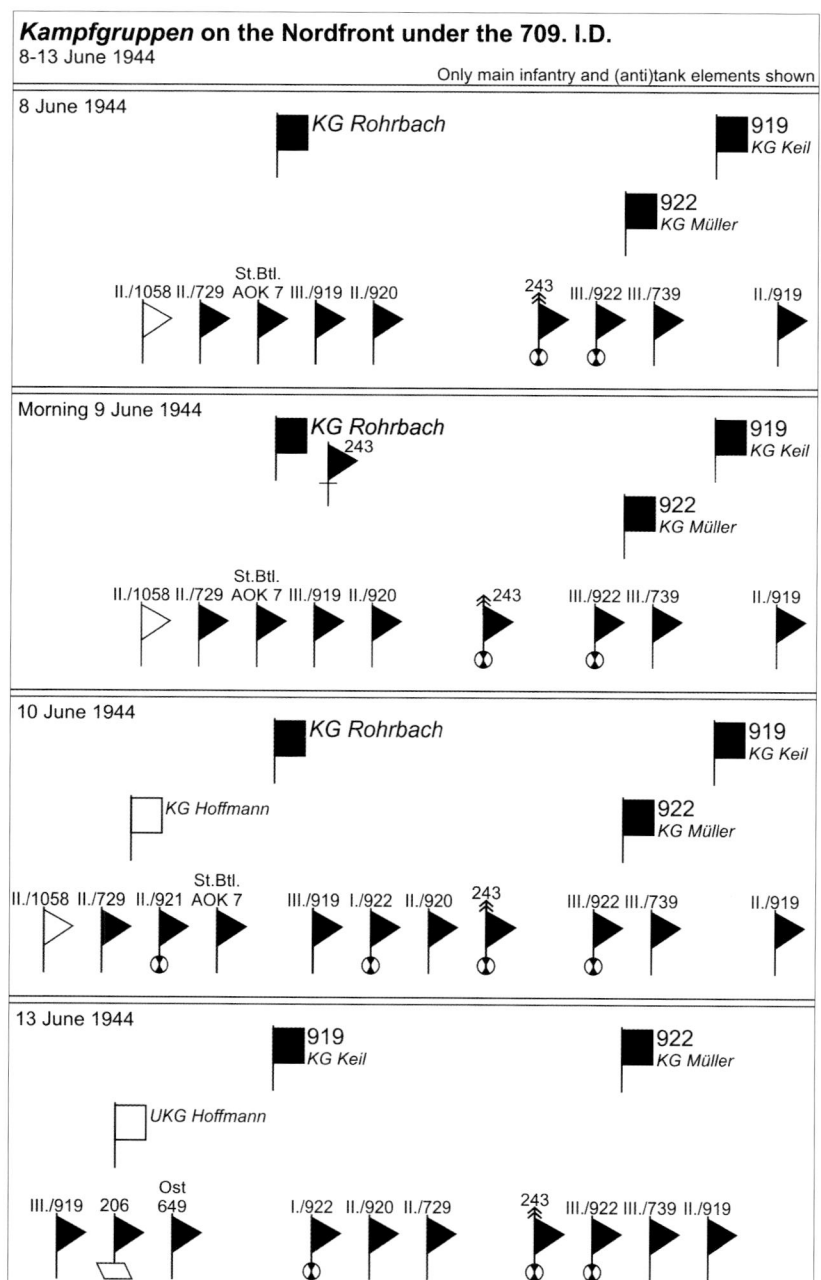

responsible for the left wing.[568] The new *KG Keil* encompassed a large number of elements. On the right wing, *Unterkampfgruppe Hoffmann* was now responsible for Montebourg. *Hptm.* Simoneit was wounded and succeeded as *Kampfkommandant* by *Hptm.* Weng, the commander of *Pz.Abt. 206*. In addition to that battalion, the town was still defended by the company from the *II./Fj.Ers.u.Ausb.Rgt. 1* and by the *III./919* (minus its 9th Company). The combat school was positioned on the hills north of Montebourg. *Obstlt.* Hoffmann took over the headquarters of Rohrbach, including its heavy wireless equipment. The gap north of Montebourg was closed by bringing up *Ost-Btl. 649*, which also became part of Hoffmann's forces.[569]

The left wing of *Kampfgruppe Keil* was directly under Keil's control. The forces on the left wing were the *9./919*, the *II./920* and the *I./922*. Both battalions had sustained grievous casualties during their withdrawals and an alert unit of *GR 729* was attached to the latter as a reinforcement. The *9./919* was deployed on the right (west), the *I./922* in the centre and the *II./920* on the left up to Keil's command post on Hill 69. From there, the line was held by *KG Müller*.[570]

Artillery support for *KG Keil* was provided by *s.Art.Rgt. zbV 621* and *s.Stellungs-Werfer-Rgt. 101*. The command post of *AR 621* was with Hoffmann, while one of its battalions was in position behind *U.KG Hoffmann* and the other behind Keil's own sector. In similar fashion, both sectors had a battalion from the rocket-launcher regiment, while its command post was located near that of Keil's. Additional fire support could be provided by several coastal batteries, and the AT defences were strengthened by guns from *Pz.Jg.Abt. 709* and heavy *Flak* from *Flak-Rgt. 30*.[571]

The reorganisation of the *Nordfront* also affected the now separate *KG Müller*. It was reinforced by *Pi.Btl. 243*. The *II./919* (*Maj.* Hadenfeldt), which had been holding the coast, was also placed under the battlegroup, although this battalion had already lost most of its personnel; *Alarmeinheit Grabbe* and the 5th Company had already been transferred to *KG Rohrbach*, while the 6th Company had been attached to the *III./739*. The 8th Company was still holding the coast and Quinéville, with the result that it was unavailable for other missions. This only left the 7th Company, which had not yet encountered the enemy.[572]

The composition of the battlegroups holding the Nordfront changed repeatedly between 8 and 13 June. Obstlt. Keil and Müller were however a constant.

On the afternoon of **12 June**, the 12ᵗʰ IR resumed its attack and captured its objectives.⁵⁷³ On its extreme right, the regiment targeted Keil's command post with infantry and tanks, but it was repulsed and had several tanks knocked out by the engineer platoon.⁵⁷⁴ The command post was moved to St. Martin-d'Audouville.⁵⁷⁵ On the left (east) wing of the *Nordfront*, the Ozeville strongpoint was lost to the Americans during the day, as were Dangueville and Fontenay-sur-Mer.⁵⁷⁶

On **13 June**, Keil's old command post was captured by the Americans and *Hptm.d.R.* Flockerzi, the commander of the *II./920*, which held the area, was killed. The *II./729*, Keil's reserve, was ordered to launch an immediate counterattack to recapture the old main line of resistance, 100 metres south of the Montebourg - Quinéville road. The attack began at 17:30. In bitter fighting, the battalion lost all its remaining officers killed, wounded or missing. The battalion commander, *Hptm.* Schwellenbach, was wounded (as was his successor).⁵⁷⁷ During the night, two German assault groups — one attacking from the west, the other from the north — attempted to recapture the quarry but were unsuccessful.⁵⁷⁸ The *II./729* was then consolidated with the *II./920*.⁵⁷⁹ Further east, the front of *KG Müller* was withdrawn to the Montebourg - Quinéville road, making contact with the *II./920*. This released *Fi.Btl. 243*, which became *Müller's* reserve.⁵⁸⁰

During the day, *Arko 118* was succeeded as the artillery command of the division by the headquarters of *H.K.A.R. 1261* (*Obst.* Triepel). Although most of the division's assigned artillery was still sitting idle in its positions along the north coast, some elements were now sent to the front. This applied to the *1.*, the *3.* and the *10./AR 1709*, which were made mobile, albeit in a makeshift fashion, by assigning them horses. These batteries were moved to the area of St. Germain-de-Tournebut (5 km north of Montebourg), where they operated under the headquarters of the *III./AR 1709*. The 1ˢᵗ and 3ʳᵈ Batteries apparently made this move on **15 June**, when they were detached from their battalion.⁵⁸¹

14 June witnessed heavy attacks against *KG Müller*. The 22ⁿᵈ IR took the eastern part of the Quinéville Ridge, including the *Ginsterhöhe*. On the coast, Quinéville (Le Havre) (*St.P. 18*) was captured by the 3/39ᵗʰ IR, while *Wn. 19* was surrendered without a fight. Further south, *St.P. 16* was seized by the 1/39ᵗʰ. *Wn. 17*, it seems, was abandoned, given that the two American battalions were able to make contact in the vicinity of the resistance nest.⁵⁸²

In response to these developments, *KG Müller* established a new line north of the Sinope River. (The command post moved to Hill 45.)⁵⁸³ This move finally drew the *II./919* (Hadenfeldt) into the front, although some of its elements had been committed earlier. The *7./919* was deployed north of the river, where it held the line stretching west from *Wn. 21*. The resistance nests north of *Wn. 21* had been abandoned. To the company's right was *Kompanie Schimpf*, an alert unit of *GR 729* that was attached to the *II./919*. This company covered an area that included the St. Marcouf – Quettehou road (D14). The line continued west with the *III./739*, followed by the *III./922*.⁵⁸⁴

The loss of Quinéville and the eastern half of Quinéville Ridge to the Americans meant that the 4ᵗʰ ID had reached its objectives, with the division temporarily suspending its advance.⁵⁸⁵ As a result, the *Nordfront* caught its breath from **15-18 June**. Little changed among the German troops holding the line. *KG Keil* still consisted of *U.KG Hoffmann* and the two battalions under *Obstlt.* Keil's own command. The *II./729* was not mentioned at this time. According to Keil, it had become part of the *II./920*. Total strength of the battlegroup amounted to 34 officers, 1 official, 218 NCO's and just over 1,000 men. The combat strength, of course, was lower: 26 officers, 171 NCO's and 929 men. *KG Müller* was still made up of the same four battalions. His reserve was formed by the *2./729*, the *9./729* and an airborne training company (*Kompanie Kollanowski*). The combined strength of this battlegroup was 19 officers, 2 officials, 145 NCO's and 940 men; its front-line strength was 17 officers, 118 NCO's and 797 men.⁵⁸⁶

On **15 June**, *AOK 7* informed *Heeresgruppe B* that the *709. I.D.* had sustained such heavy losses that its combat effectiveness was now greatly reduced. This was despite the fact that it had not yet committed all its elements to combat. In fact, because of its poor state, the division (with attached elements) was now simply "*Kampfgruppe 709. Inf.Div.*"⁵⁸⁷ The division itself could not even be considered to be a battlegroup anymore.⁵⁸⁸ The next day, it was reported to have suffered 4,000 casualties since the start of the invasion, a figure that likely included attached elements.⁵⁸⁹

While the *Nordfront* remained quiet during this period, the situation was quite different on the *Westfront* of the beachhead. Here, the US VII Corps sought to break through to the west coast to cut off the peninsula. The American objective was obvious and, in response, parts of *Gruppe Hellmich* were split off on **15 June** to form a second force: *Gruppe von Schlieben*.⁵⁹⁰ The reorganisation would enable *Gruppe Hellmich* to focus on the *Westfront*, while *Gruppe von Schlieben* became responsible for operations on the *Nordfront* on both sides of Montebourg;[591] it also placed elements of the *77. I.D.* that had been committed southwest of the town under control of von Schlieben. The boundary between the two groups was initially at Urville, running along the Merderet.[592] This changed the next day (**16th**), with the new boundary running from St. Jacques-de-Néhou - Ste. Colombe (incl.) - Orglandes - Ste. Mère-Église.[593] As a result, areas of the front west of the river were now under *Gruppe von Schlieben*, which should have included additional units of the *77. I.D.*[594]

By 10:35, the division of *Gruppe Hellmich* into *Gruppe von Schlieben* and the new *Gruppe Hellmich* had been completed. The latter battlegroup was in poor condition, and the *LXXXIV. A.K.* considered an American breakthrough to the west coast to be inevitable within a matter of hours. There was no way to prevent a loss of contact between the two groups. Due to this situation, the corps had to look ahead. It deemed the supply level of the fortress insufficient for the intended number of forces. Instead, it suggested having the *709. I.D.* defend only the inner ring of the fortress and sending the *77. I.D.* to the south. *AOK 7* replied that this measure could only be taken on direct orders from it. In the meantime, it stressed that all formations intended for mobile warfare, including artillery not presently in action, should be moved south. At 10:50, *AOK 7* learned that Hitler had forbidden a withdrawal to Cherbourg and ordered the current lines to be held.[595]

During the day, the Americans captured St. Sauveur-le-Vicomte and broke contact between the two groups. Although the right wing of *Gruppe von Schlieben* only faced feeble attacks along the line Le Ham - Urville – Colomby, *AOK 7* informed *Heeresgruppe B* that the American breakthrough to the west coast was imminent. The loss of contact between the groups forced both of them to turn their wings to the west but, with their flanks open, they would be unable to offer effective resistance. The already deteriorating situation was complicated by the fact that new landings were expected on the west coast, which could prevent both groups from reaching the fortress. Since the defence of the fortress was the main priority, the *7. Armee* insisted that *Gruppe von Schlieben* immediately withdraw into the fortress that very night.[596]

That evening, Rommel decided that the *77. I.D.* should move troops to St. Sauveur-le-Vicomte at once to prevent the enemy from advancing towards Cherbourg; at the same time, however, it had to continue to hold its present positions. A withdrawal was out of the question.[597]

At 10:35, **17 June**, a new *Führer* Directive reached *AOK 7*. Hitler ordered *Festung Cherbourg* to be held at any cost. A fighting withdrawal of *Gruppe von Schlieben* — to delay the enemy — was authorised, but a move into the fortress in a single, rapid action remained forbidden. In accordance with Hitler's directive, Rommel issued his orders: The withdrawal of the group from its current positions could only begin under strong enemy pressure. The advance of the enemy had to be delayed by any means possible. The line from Vauville along the *Landfront* to Le Theil to St. Vaast-la-Hougue (on the east coast) was to be defended. The defensive capabilities of the Jobourg Peninsula were to be improved. Only on direct orders of the field-army group were the north-west and northeast corners of the Cotentin to be abandoned.[598]

With the 4th ID quiet for the moment on the Montebourg front, *Gruppe von Schlieben* was not currently under direct pressure and, correspondingly, not allowed to retreat to Cherbourg. On this day, the division commander formally expressed his appreciation of *KG Keil* by recommending it to be mentioned in the Armed Forces Daily Announcement:[599]

A Kampfgruppe of the 709. I.D., led by Oberstlt.d.R. Keil, distinguished itself in exceptional bravery. With outstanding support from artillery and rocket launchers, it prevented, in bitter fighting, the enemy's intention (supported by the heaviest of naval artillery and strong bomber formations) to break through to Cherbourg immediately after landing."

That afternoon, the corps was reminded that all its formations earmarked for mobile warfare were to be withdrawn from the Cotentin Peninsula; among them were *AR zbV 621* and *Sturm-Btl. AOK 7*.[600] The latter formation, which had played a crucial role on the Montebourg front, had already been reduced to barely 100 men and thus would remain in the north.[601] Meanwhile, *AR zbV 621* departed that afternoon. Further to the west, the *77. I.D.* also began to disengage. As a result, the right wing of *U.KG Hoffmann* was left "hanging in the air".[602]

The withdrawal to Cherbourg also had an impact on the division's artillery. Since the headquarters of *AR 1709* was already in the fortress, the headquarters of *H.K.A.R. 1261* would no longer be required as an artillery

Montebourg suffered heavy damage before it was finally liberated on 19 June. By then most of the town lay in ruins. This photo was taken on the Place Jeanne d'Arc, where the N13 highway passed through the town. American soldiers have captured a German wagon, painted an Allied star on it and are using it as additional means to bring up supplies. (NARA)

command and control element; thus, it went south during the night.[603]

Without the troops to hold the front west of the Merderet River, *Gruppe von Schlieben* could only establish a screening front from Le Ham through Urville to Golleville.[604] To cover the deep right flank of the group, major forces were transferred to Valognes. *Ost-Btl. 561* was brought up from Cherbourg and committed around the town, while an airborne training company protected the N13 between Montebourg and Valognes. Additional forces were drawn from *Pz.Abt. 206*, which was extracted from Montebourg during the night and deployed in a wide arc around Valognes, southwest of the N13: Montebourg - Flottemanville (south of Valognes) - Lieusaint - La Basfeuille - St. Joseph. *Hptm.* Weng was put in command of this mixed force.[605]

Pi.Btl. 709 would also play a major role in protecting the right flank of the group. Von Schlieben had already ordered all engineers to be returned to *Pi. Btl. 709*. Of the 1st Company, only the commander with a few men arrived. Due to their serious losses, the 1st and 2nd Companies were consolidated into a single company with a strength of about 80 men. The 3rd Company was not much better off with just 60 men left. The battalion was to block the roads west of the N13 and, once the withdrawal began, to cover the retreat to Cherbourg by carrying out prepared demolitions. The command post was moved from the front to Teurthéville-Hague to oversee the operations.[606]

The remaining construction and engineer elements on the peninsula were also placed under the battalion; these were: *Bau-Pi.Btl. 802*, the 2./*Fest.*

To prevent installations and key infrastructure to fall into Allied hands, Pi.Btl. 709 carried out demolitions. This included the division's signals bunker in the centre of Valognes. (Author's collection)

Pi.Btl. 11 and *Gesteinsbohr-Kp. 28* (Rock Drilling Company 28). These formations also carried out demolitions between the front and the fortress, as well as within Cherbourg itself. In addition, they built another defence line closer to the town that was anchored on the old French forts.[607] During these operations, *Pi.Btl. 709* carried out demolitions at 60-70 sites, using 700-1,000 kg of explosives (French aircraft bombs) per location. Among the key infrastructure destroyed by the battalion and its subordinated units were the railway tunnel just in front of Cherbourg and the railway viaduct east of Fermanville.[608]

The anticipated American breakthrough to the west coast came during the night of **17 June**.[609] The night passed quietly for *Gruppe von Schlieben*, however, except for vigorous artillery fire.[610] At 10:00 on **18 June**, the group was relieved from its attachment to the *LXXXIV. A.K.* and placed directly under *AOK 7* control.[611] In addition, an order from Hitler placed all elements of the armed forces that were both inside and outside the fortress (including the *Festungs-* and *Seekommandant*) under the command of *Gen.Lt.* von Schlieben. He would lead the fighting on the northern part of the Cotentin and the defence of *Festung Cherbourg*. The general was ordered to continue to hold large areas of the coast before conducting a withdrawal to the actual *Landfront*, but to do so only so long as was possible without risk to the fortress itself. The Jobourg Peninsula would also be included in the *Landfront*.[612] These orders actually gave more freedom for the withdrawal, as they implied that the group

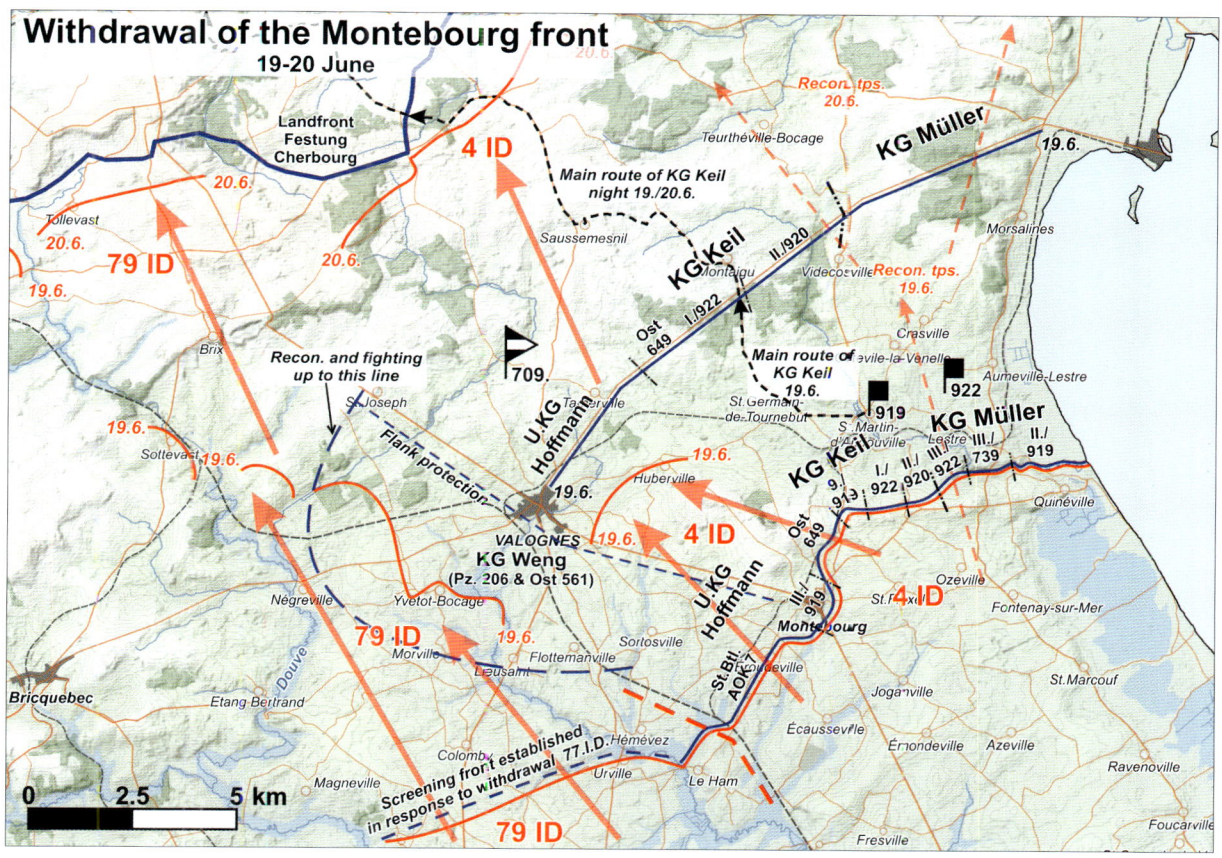

The 709.I.D. became trapped on the Cotentin Peninsula when US forces reached the west coast on 17-18 June. At this time the division still held on to the Montebourg front but its right flank was open. On 19 June the 4th and 79th Infantry Divisions launched their attacks towards Cherbourg and the 709.I.D. began its withdrawal to the fortress where it arrived on 20 June.

should not be outflanked. Either way, the retreat to Cherbourg would only be a matter of time and final preparations for this movement were made during the day.[613]

For the time being and despite the American successes, the group was neither under direct pressure nor under immediate risk of being outflanked. Correspondingly, the conditions for the movement had not yet been met and the group remained in place.[614] At 20:00, it reported that its forces were still defending the line Montebourg - Les Fieffes-Dancel in line with Rommel's orders of the day before. To the west, they had established weak flank protection in the line Montebourg - the bend in the road 2.5 km southeast of Valognes - St. Joseph. Reconnaissance was carried out up to the line St. Joseph - Négreville - Lieusaint - Flottemanville (south of Valognes), basically the frontline of the troops under *Hptm*. Weng, where no enemy forces had yet been encountered. The demolition of roads north of the line Les Pieux - Rauville-la-Bigot - Négreville was now underway.[615]

Although it had been quiet for several days, the Montebourg front was about to erupt. The 4th ID was ordered to conduct a night attack on both sides of the town. The attacks of the 8th and the 12th IR began around 03:00 on **19 June**. Minor US forces managed to cross German lines west of the town, while to the east no real progress was made. After daylight, tanks arrived to provide support, enabling the two regiments to advance to their objectives.[616] Yet the enemy attack also signified that a key condition for the German with-

709. Infanterie-Division

drawal had been met: Withdrawal under enemy pressure. At 12:00, the troops received the code word *Heinrich* to execute *Bewegung Cherbourg*.[617]

The first stage of the withdrawal led the troops to the Valognes - Quettehou road (D902), where a temporary defensive line was set up. *U.KG Hoffmann* held the front west of the bridge across the Franqueterre. *Obstlt.* Keil deployed his *Ost-Btl. 649*, the *I./922* and the *II./920* in the area up to the intersection (excl.) with the road from St. Martin-d'Audouville to St. Pierre-Église (D25). From that point, *KG Müller* held the line all the way to the coast. Rearguards were left in the old positions and, in Keil's sector, they finally disengaged in the early morning of the **20th**.[618]

While the troops were withdrawing from the Montebourg front, those holding the flank around Valognes carried out their mission. Despite a tenacious struggle, they stood their ground against the American 79th ID.[619] Further west, where the 9th ID was advancing on Cherbourg, the situation was more uncertain. The good news was that, by 11:10, German reconnaissance had yet to encounter enemy forces north of the line Les Pieux - Valognes.[620] In the evening, enemy troops were identified at Négreville, Sottevast, Breuville and Grosville, with German opposition merely consisting of screening forces and demolition parties on the main roads.[621]

The mission of *Pi.Btl. 709* was not restricted to the area west of the N13 and securing the withdrawal to the fortress. The battalion also demolished the former division headquarters at Chiffrevast and the signals bunker in Valognes. Similarly, the engineer equipment that had remained at the old command post of the battalion at La Préfontainerie, along with the records of the battalion and of the division operations section, were all destroyed.[622] Just when these facilities were destroyed by the engineers is not clear, but the division headquarters was at its command post until the morning of **20 June**.[623]

Having briefly paused on the Valognes - Quettehou road, the withdrawal towards Cherbourg resumed at 23:00. The withdrawal of Keil's forces took them from the *Nordfront* via St. Martin-d'Audouville, St. Germain-de-Tournebut, Montaigu, Saussemesnil, Mesnil-au-Val and La Glacerie to Cherbourg.[624] The forces of *KG Müller* no doubt used roads to the east, but their exact route is unclear. To the west, the covering force around Valognes was scheduled to follow the movement at 01:00. Because of enemy pressure, however, its departure was moved up to 23:30. The rearguards, however, held their positions for an additional hour.[625]

In general, the withdrawal of *Gruppe von Schlieben* to the fortress took place without interference beyond harassing artillery fire. This success was largely due to adverse weather conditions that had grounded Allied aircraft.[626] At 08:00 on **20 June**, the division reported that the main body of *Gruppe von Schlieben* had reached the fortress.[627] The division moved its headquarters (until then at Chiffrevast) to that of the *Festungs-Kommandant*, which was established in the same tunnels as the *Seekommandant*. The communications equipment at these headquarters was excellent, but the position would be difficult to defend.[628] The location of most support elements is not clear, but the logistics officer was at the Brécourt supply tunnels, just west of Cherbourg.[629] Because the headquarters of the *Seekommandant* became too crowded, *Gen. Maj.* Sattler and his headquarters moved to *Batterie Bastion* at the *Arsenal* on **24 June**.[630]

According to German reports that morning (**20th**), American troops were probing towards Cherbourg along the Bricquebec - Breuville road (D900). The area west of this road was still clear of enemy forces north of the line Héauville - St. Cristophe-du-Foc. The enemy situation was similar in the area north of Brix, just west of the N13.[631] Several hours later, US armoured reconnaissance was reported on the line Grosville - Breuville - Sottevast - 3 km southeast of Sottevast. German screening forces were in action against the enemy, and the demolition of bridges and roads continued. To the east, German rearguards were still deployed southeast of the Valognes - Quettehou road (D902).[632]

The Americans pressed their advance towards Cherbourg. That evening, they began to probe the *Landfront* with armour and motorised infantry in several areas: northwest of St. Croix-Hague, northwest of Flottemanville-Hague, south of Martinvast and southwest and north of Le Theil. While enemy elements were able to infiltrate the German lines, these minor penetrations were, for the most part, rapidly eliminated. Yet some fighting was still ongoing in the early morning hours of **21 June**.[633] By late morning, these actions had come to an end and only minor reconnaissance actions were still underway against the *Landfront*.[634]

Meanwhile, the mass of *Gruppe von Schlieben* had occupied positions in the *Landfront*, while reinforcements from the *Kriegsmarine* and personnel from abandoned fortifications, headquarters and administrative entities were being brought up as well.[635] The centre of Cherbourg was

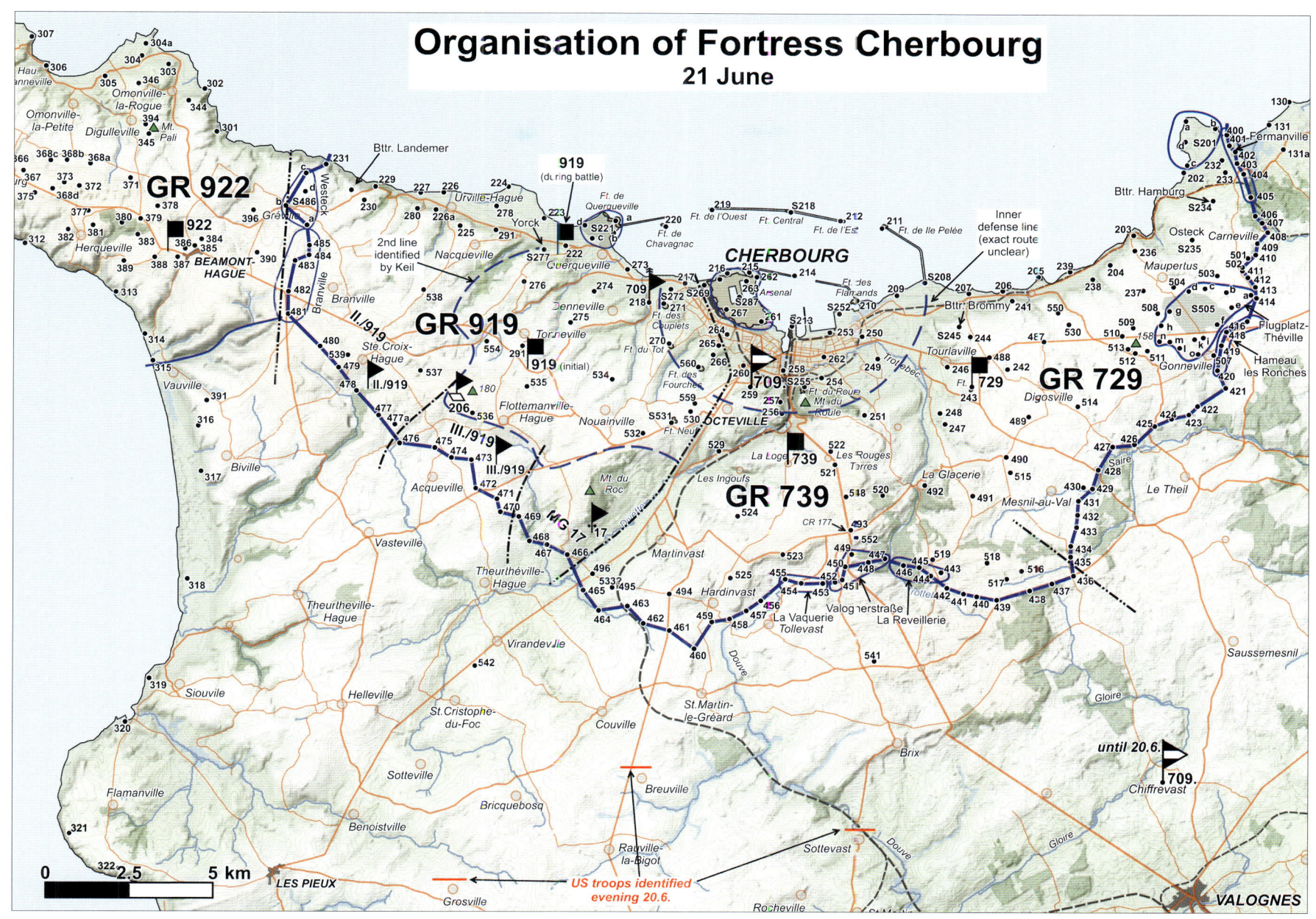

After the move to Cherbourg, the 709.I.D. divided its frontage over four regimental battlegroups. One of these was GR 922 which was formed by 243.I.D. elements which had already seen action on the Montebourg front under the 709.I.D.

occupied by alert* units.⁶³⁶ *Gruppe von Schlieben* was bracing itself for the battle for Cherbourg.

The Battle for Cherbourg

The organisation of the *Landfront* had begun on **20 June**, when *Gen.* von Schlieben ordered all forces that had held the Montebourg front to return to their pre-invasion commanders and sectors (at least as far as that was a realistic possibility). This meant that the battlegroups were to relinquish their non-assigned elements and revert back to being more regular regiments: *GR 729, 739, 919* and *922*. Each of these regiments was given responsibility for a specific sector, an arrangement that went into effect at 03:00 on **21 June**.⁶³⁷ *GR 922* was deployed on the right (west), followed by *919* (southwest), *739* (south) and *729* (southeast).⁶³⁸

GR 922 (*Obstlt.* Müller) was in command of the Jobourg Peninsula. The regiment's frontline ran northeast from Vauville, along a deep valley to the *Landfront* at about *Wn. 481* (excl.); from there, its boundary ran north along the *Landfront* (*Wn. 482-486*). These resistance nests included the strongpoints *Westeck* and *Branville*.⁶³⁹ The regiment was formed from what remained of the *243. I.D.* on the northern part of the Cotentin, with the exception of *Pi.Btl. 243*.⁶⁴⁰ Thus, the regiment included the *I./922*, the *III./922* and the *II./920*. The latter battalion had a strength of 80 men and was commanded by a *Feldwebel*.⁶⁴¹ The strength of the *III./922* was similar, a little more than 80 men. The *I./922* was the strongest battalion with 178 men.⁶⁴²

The next sector was held by *GR 919* under *Obstlt*. Keil. Its left boundary was formed by the Les Pieux - Cherbourg highway (excl.) and continued to the coast along the southwest edge of Cherbourg (excl.).⁶⁴³ The resistance nests in this sector started with *Wn. 481* on the right and ended with *Wn. 466* on the left.⁶⁴⁴ The core of the regiment was its assigned battalions (The 2ⁿᵈ Battalion and the 3ʳᵈ Battalion with company strengths of 30-50 men), the 15ᵗʰ Company and the regimental engineer platoon. The 2ⁿᵈ Battalion consisted of just 5ᵗʰ and the 7ᵗʰ Companies and was assigned an ad hoc company as a reinforcement. This unit, identified as *Troß-Kompanie Schröder*, had absorbed the remnants of the division band and the combat school and served as the battalion reserve.⁶⁴⁵ The "company" was likely formed around *Nachschub-Zug 709*, which was led by *Oblt.* Schröder.

More significant reinforcements were provided by the still fresh *MG-Btl. 17*, which had been holding this sector of the *Landfront* since **13 June**. Reserves were available in the form of the *1./Georg.Inf.Btl. 795*, an airborne training company and *Pz.Abt. 206*, which was deployed on Hill 180 (just northwest of Flottemanville-Hague). Providing fire support were the *I./s. St.W.Rgt. 101* and *Artillerie-Gruppe West* (*Maj.* Quittnat). In addition, the regiment was supported by a company from *Pz.Jg.Abt. 709* with five or six AT guns. To the rear of the regiment was a construction company, responsible for establishing a second defensive line.⁶⁴⁶ Because the resistance nests in the sector were already held by *MG-Btl. 17*, it was decided to keep its companies in place. The infantry would deploy between the resistance nests to form a continuous front. This meant that two of the MG battalion's three companies were placed under control of the *II.* and the *III./919*. In turn, the latter transferred its 9ᵗʰ and 10ᵗʰ Companies to the MG battalion. The *II./919* was deployed on the right (west), the *III./919* in the centre and *MG-Btl. 17* on the left.

That morning, the regiment was assigned *Reich* Work Service (*Reichsarbeitsdienst / RAD*) personnel to bring the companies up to authorised strength, at least numerically. These replacements were young, just 17-18 years old and had previously operated anti-aircraft guns. Alert units from the *Kriegsmarine* also arrived in the course of the day. One alert unit was assigned to both the *III./919* and *MG-Btl. 17* as reserve companies, while another provided infantry for *Pz.Abt. 206*. Unlike the enthusiastic youngsters of the *RAD*, the morale of these troops was low and they would prove to be of little value. The company under *Pz.Abt. 206* abandoned its positions during an attack on Hill 180, while the company with *MG-Btl. 17* simply vanished when the time came to send it into action.⁶⁴⁷

The southern sector of the *Landfront* was the responsibility of *GR 739*; it stretched to the crossroads 2.4 km south of Mesnil-au-Val and consisted of a series of strongpoints — *Wn. 436-465*, with *Wn. 436* on the left (east) protecting the crossroads of the D56 and D87 north of Ruffosses. The sector included three clusters of strongpoints to cover the N13 highway leading into the fortress. From right (west) to left these were: *St.P. La Vaquerie* (two

---

* Also referred to as emergency or alarm units or reaction forces. The author will used the term "alert".

resistance nests), *St.P. Valognerstraße* (six resistance nests) and *St.P. La Reveillerie* (four resistance nests).⁶⁴⁸ The sector was first commanded by *Obstlt.* Hoffmann, until he was replaced by the regimental commander, *Obst.* Köhn, on the **21ˢᵗ**. His forces were thus known as *KG Köhn*. *Obstlt.* Hoffmann joined the headquarters of the *709. I.D.* and then departed Cherbourg by *Schnellboot* late on **23 June** to report in person to *AOK 7* on *Gruppe von Schlieben*.⁶⁴⁹

When *Gruppe von Schlieben* arrived in the fortress this particular sector was held by the *7.* and the *21./Fj.Ers.u.Ausb.Rgt. 1* (both part of the regiment's 2ⁿᵈ Battalion that had arrived on the Cotentin with six companies) and the *2./Fest.Stamm-Abt. LXXXIV*. Although von Schlieben recalled that the headquarters of the latter battalion was committed in this sector, this has not been confirmed.⁶⁵⁰ It was now reinforced by the *7./739* as a reserve company, while the remnants of the *III./739* were committed on the right and *Ost-Btl. 561* on the left.⁶⁵¹ Reportedly, the *III./739* had a strength of just 70 men.⁶⁵² The location of the rest of the *II./739* (*Maj.* Gräfe) remains unclear. Some elements had been attached to the regiment's alert unit but this does not account for the majority of the battalion. Were they still on the *Seefront*?

It is possible to narrow down the sectors of some of the forces by looking at the records of the US 4ᵗʰ ID. The division encountered the *7./739*, *Ost-Btl. 561* and elements of the airborne training battalion (21ˢᵗ Company) south-southeast of La Glacerie. The latter battalion's 7ᵗʰ Company was absent, and probably deployed further west against the 79ᵗʰ ID. The headquarters of the airborne training battalion was reported to be in the triangle Digosville – La Glacerie – Le Mesnil-au-Val, but it does not appear to have been responsible for a sector of the front.⁶⁵³

The final sector, that of *GR 729*, was led by *Obst.* Rohrbach, and it continued to the coast. The front was formed by *Wn. 400-435*. The defences were the strongest in the eastern part of the sector with *St.P. Cap Levy*, *St.P. Fermanville* and *St.P. Hameau les Ronches*. To the rear were two more major strongpoints: *St.P. Osteck* and *St.P. Flugplatz Théville*.⁶⁵⁴

No detailed reports have been found on the strength and composition of Rohrbach's force, but it included the remnants of *GR 729* and *Ost-Btl. 649*.⁶⁵⁵

After the move to Cherbourg, the 709.I.D. divided its frontage over four regimental battlegroups. One of these was GR 922 which was formed by 243.I.D. elements which had already seen action on the Montebourg front under the 709.I.D.

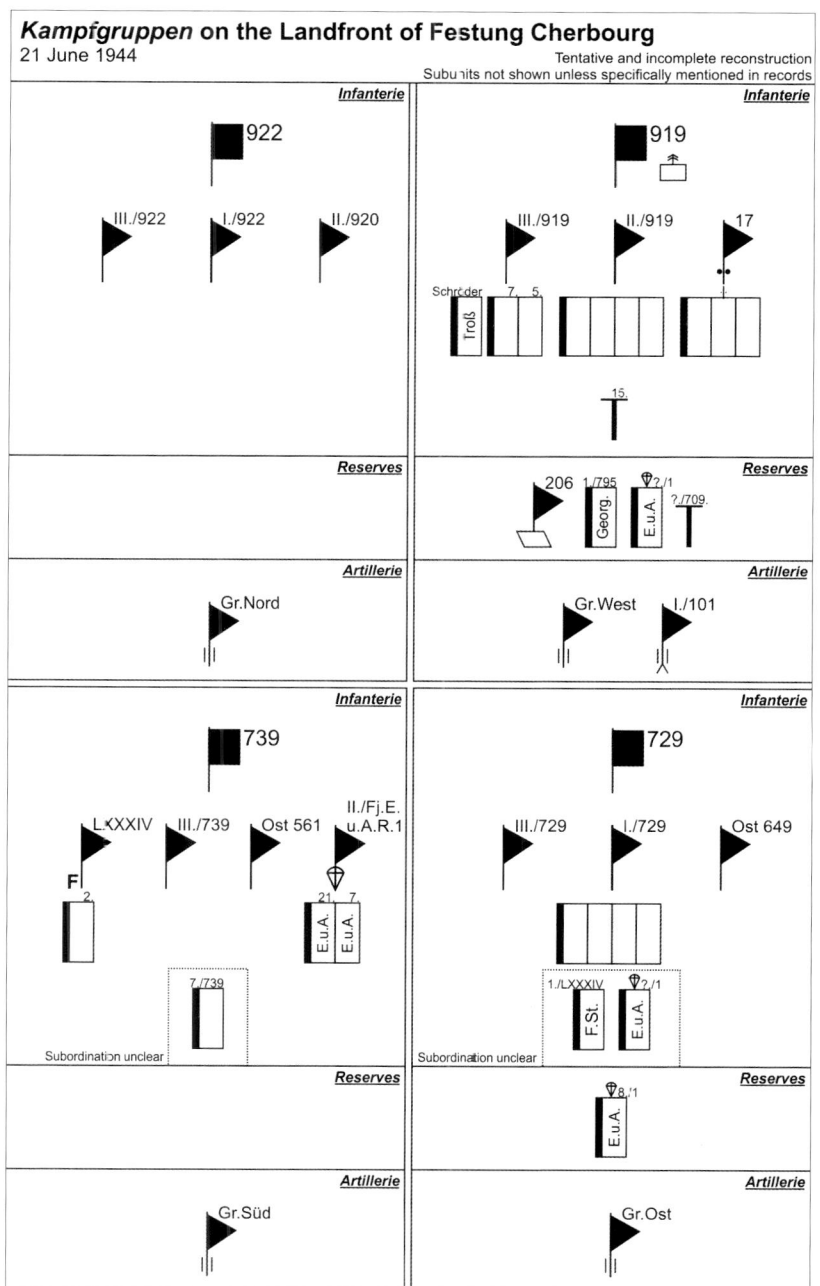

The personnel manning the *Osteck* and the airfield should be added to the German strength in this sector. Again, it is possible to partially reconstruct the deployment of the troops by examining the 4th ID records. They indicate that the 2. and the 4./729 were deployed on the right wing of the regiment, partially intermingled with the *III./729*, which appears to have held the front up to the southwest corner of the airfield. From there, the main body of the *I./729* (*Hptm.* Katzmann) controlled the front with its 1st and the 3rd Companies, supported by *Ost-Btl. 649* and the *1./Fest.St.Abt. LXXXIV*.[656]

Paul Carell states that *Wn. 425* and *426* were held by an airborne training company, but this is not confirmed by the 4th ID records. The division encountered elements of many of the companies of the *II./Fj.Ers.u.Ausb.Rgt. 1*, which gives the impression that they had become scattered or intermixed, making it difficult to draw conclusions. Carell's assertion that *Fallschirmjäger-Ausbildungs-Kompanie Hallmann* (the 8th Company) served as a reserve is also possible but unconfirmed.[657]

The withdrawal of the group to Cherbourg also meant that the division's artillery within the fortress could finally play its part in the fighting on land. The arrival of additional artillery from outside the fortress — including coastal artillery and the weaponry of *Flak-Rgt. 30* — made it necessary to reorganise the artillery ready to face the encroaching threat of the Allied forces. It is unclear, however, how a lot of these batteries were deployed. For example, the *4./AR 1709* was positioned near La Loge and the 17 cm guns of the *4./H.K.A.R. 1262* were 1 km northeast of Les Rouges Terres, which put both in a central position. Despite that, their role remains obscure.[658]

The *I./AR 1709*, which had earlier given up its 1st and 2nd Batteries, now took control over the 3. and the *4./gem.Flak-Abt.152* and the *4./gem.Flak-Abt.153* (each with four 8.8 cm *Flak*) and an unidentified battery of French 15.5 cm howitzers. On **20 June**, the battalion went into action in support of *GR 739*. The *Flak* were only used against ground targets. The battalion was able to concentrate the fire of all batteries, since both radio and telephone communication existed between the command post and the batteries. The battalion commander, *Hptm.* Moritz, was taken prisoner on **26 June** at Les Ingoufs (south of Octeville).[659]

Although the composition of this battalion has been reported, this is not the case for all other artillery in the fortress. Soon after the invasion, artillery groups had been formed. This included an *Artillerie-Gruppe West* and *Artillerie-Gruppe Ost*. The position of *AR 1709* within this structure is not clear. The forces under *Hptm.* Moritz may have been regarded as *Artillerie-Gruppe Süd*.[660] There are also indications that the artillery of *H.K.A.R. 1262* on the Jobourg Peninsula was combined as *Artillerie-Gruppe Nord*.[661]

Art.Gruppe Ost was led by *Maj.* Küppers (commander of the *III./AR 1709*), although it is unknown who had been in charge of the group while he was committed on the Montebourg front.[662] While little is known about the composition of this force, it appears to have included the battalion's three batteries (9.-11.), along with the 5. and the *8./AR 1709* and the *5./H.K.A.R. 1261* on **19 June**.[663] Because of its location, it must have furnished fire support for *GR 729*.

Commanded by *Maj.* Quittnat, *Artillerie-Gruppe West* controlled all artillery west of Cherbourg, except for *H.K.A.R. 1262*.[664] Its composition between D-Day and the withdrawal to the fortress is unclear, but it supported *GR 919* in its defence. Any guns and personnel escaping towards the fortress and arriving in that sector were incorporated into the artillery group. *Maj.* Quittnat provided some details on his forces, but he did not identify his forces or provide precise time periods. His artillery included: A battery of 20.3 cm railway guns (*3./H.K.A.R. 1262* on the Jobourg Peninsula), a battery of "15 cm guns", two batteries of 8.8 cm *Flak* with six guns each, a battery of "Russian 10 cm howitzers", two batteries of "7.5 cm guns" and a number of naval guns.[665] It is possible that some of these batteries only came under his control for the final defence of the Jobourg Peninsula some days later. On **28 June**, *KG Keil* requested the delivery of ammunition for its *10,5 cm K.331(f)'s* and *15,5 cm s.F.H.414(f)'s*, which proves the presence of such guns west of Cherbourg. The 10.5 cm guns were used by seven different batteries on the Cotentin, making it difficult to identify the units involved, but the 3rd Battery was reportedly in position near Jobourg. The 15.5 cm guns were only attached to the *II./AR 1709*, whose 7th Battery had been west of Cherbourg since before D-Day, while the other batteries were east of the town.[666]

According to German reports, **21 June** passed relatively quietly. The Americans probed towards *Wn. 481, 480, 476, 449, 436, 432, 426* and *425* with reconnaissance forces (some in company strength) but were driven back. Most of these resistance nests were tactically significant. *Wn. 449* was one of the resistance nests blocking the N13 highway. *Wn. 476* blocked the D123, north-northeast of Vasteville. *Wn. 425* and *426* covered the D320 crossing the

Saire River northwest of Le Theil. The Americans ratcheted up their artillery fire, which was particularly intense in the areas of Gréville (*Westeck*), *Wn. 481*, *Wn. 436*, *Wn. 426* and *Wn. 425*. Digosville, La Glacerie and Cherbourg itself were also under fire. In Cherbourg, the electricity and water supply were knocked out.[667]

Even though German situation reports were positive, they missed the fact that two battalions of the 22nd IR had actually pierced the southeast *Landfront* and taken Hill 158, just southwest of Théville airfield. The enemy advance had occurred without pushing German troops out of the area. As a result, they slipped in behind the American battalions and the two US battalions were isolated on the hill for the next four days and nights. They had to be resupplied under tank escort.[668] It was not until late in the day that the Germans became aware that American troops had penetrated the area. Even then, it was wrongly assessed as only a minor infiltration.[669]

On **22 June**, the coordinated attack of the US VII Corps on *Festung Cherbourg* finally got underway. The objective of the 9th ID (on the left) was the high ground at Octeville, which meant that the main effort would be made on its right wing. The centre of gravity of the 79th ID would also be on its right wing. The latter division was given the task of capturing the ridge that dominates Cherbourg and ends with Fort du Roule. In the sector of the 4th ID (on the right), the main effort would be made in the centre, where the 12th IR would take Tourlaville and then move to the coast to sever the link between the town and the strongpoints in the eastern part of the fortress.[670]

Following the artillery preparation, heavy air attacks began with fighters and fighter-bombers at 12:40, followed by medium bombers at 14:00.[671] The 9th ID then attacked northeast from the area of Teurthéville-Hague and advanced to within 1 km of Nouainville and Mont du Roc.[672] The front lines of the *11./919* were pushed back and, in the sector of the *9./919*, a resistance nest was lost by *MG-Btl. 17*. As it was already late in the afternoon, *GR 919* postponed its counterattack until the following morning.[673]

In the centre, the 79th ID attacked on both sides of the N13, roughly between the railway and the Trottebec River that formed the boundary with the 4th ID. German reports stated that the attack reached the woods 2 km south of La Glacerie. Similar to the 315th and the 314th IR on the left and in the centre, the 313th IR — which made the main effort on the right wing of the division — encountered tenacious German resistance; however, it soon found a weak spot to the west and rolled up the front from there. By the end of the day, the regiment's three battalions and the 3./314th IR had pushed through the German lines and reached Crossroads 177 (D122 & N13), 2 km southwest of La Glacerie. The 1/314th IR followed during the night. On the division's left wing, the 315th IR concentrated on the Hardinvast area, where stubborn German resistance needed to be contained to protect the flanks of the other regiments.[674]

During the day, *Ost-Btl. 561*, committed in the area of La Glacerie, was reported to be unreliable and no longer under the control of its commander.[675] With no other forces available, alert units of the *Kriegsmarine* were sent to seal off the resulting enemy penetration.[676] In response to the developments southeast of Cherbourg, the *III./922* was taken from *Obstlt.* Müller's control. The division dispatched lorries to pick up the battalion and move it east to address the threat. Two battlegroups were built from the battalion. One of them was to be committed at La Glacerie with *KG Köhn*, the other at an unknown location. The former battlegroup, however, never reached its intended destination. It was ultimately deployed on the railway between Tourlaville and Cherbourg.[677] The transfer of troops to reinforce *GR 739* also affected *GR 919*, since *Pz.Abt. 206* was ordered to transfer a company to *GR 739*. This left just five tanks on Hill 180.[678]

In the sector of the 4th ID, progress was slow. Its 8th IR, located east of the Trottebec River, only managed limited gains, but it was able to breach the *Landfront* and eliminate several strongpoints, including Crossroads 148. While the forces of *GR 729* continued to block the 12th IR at the Bois de Coudray, one of its battalions (3/12th IR) made a flanking movement, crossed the Saire River and advanced along the road to Digosville (D120) to a point 2.5 km southeast of the village.[679] Further east, the fighting against the 22nd IR continued throughout the day, although the Germans remained unaware of the size of the American forces.[680] In the morning, it was reported that countermeasures were being successfully carried out against the infiltration south of the airfield and, that afternoon, it was even reported that the Americans had been driven back beyond the *Landfront*, although fighting was still underway southwest of Théville Airfield. The full extent of the American presence was still apparently underappreciated.[681]

The fortress was rapidly using up its reserves, but there were still some available, including *Pi.Btl. 709*. During the day, the last of the demolition parties returned to the battalion, allowing it to be reorganised one last time. (It had already been given the remnants of *Pi.Btl. 243*, consisting of an officer and about 40 men.) Because its losses had been high, the battalion's trains were dissolved and all available men combined into two companies, one with 60 personnel and the other with 80 (including *Pi.Btl. 243*). One of these companies was again committed to blocking operations in the sector of *Obstlt.* Keil. The other company was a general (engineer) reserve.[682]

In their reserve role, the engineers were called upon repeatedly to help block enemy penetrations, which were reported virtually everywhere. Not all the reports were accurate, however, with the result that the battalion often squandered its energy in futile movements. For example, the entire battalion was assembled near Flottemanville-Hague that night, ready to counterattack, until the battalion's own reconnaissance revealed that the frontline was actually firmly in German hands.[683]

Early on **23 June**, it was reported that all mobile reserves had now been committed.[684] Most of the reserves of *GR 919* were deployed to clear the American penetration of the day before. The counterattack was launched at 05:00 by the airborne company and the *1./Georg.Inf.Btl. 795*.[685] Supported by artillery, the attack initially made good progress along the boundary between the *III./919* and *MG-Btl. 17*. However, it was of little consequence, because the Americans had enlarged their penetration in the west in the sector of the *III./919* towards Flottemanville-Hague, with the 60th IR capturing the village and the nearby road (D123). The headquarters of the 3rd Battalion was surrounded, but it managed to break out after dark. The *II./919* responded to the penetration by sending its reserve company to hold Hill 180, which was of vital tactical importance. Fighting for the hill surged back and forth and went on into the night. Although the hill was mostly held — it appears that the Americans took the eastern part of the hill — the defenders suffered heavy casualties.[686] Further east, the 47th IR continued to advance towards Nouainville, but its penetration was sealed off and the village remained in German hands.[687] Despite the serious enemy breaches, the *III./919* was able to re-establish contact with the battalions on its flanks. The engineer platoon now formed the final reserve of the regiment.[688]

In the sector of *GR 739*, the Americans (79th ID) had reached Crossroads 177. South of La Glacerie, the penetration was widened 1 km to the east. Further east (*GR 729*), the Germans were confident they had restored the *Landfront* between Le Theil and the airfield. Yet now they finally realised that the enemy forces behind their lines were significantly stronger than previously believed.[689]

Throughout the afternoon, the division kept *AOK 7* informed of the situation. The enemy had attacked in four tactical wedges, which had broken through the *Landfront* between Flottemanville-Hague in the west and Le Theil in the east. In the centre, the spearheads had reached the line Les Rouges Terres - La Loge (less than 2 km south of Fort du Roule) - Les Ingoufs (south of Octeville). Breakthroughs were also reported at Flottemanville-Hague and Le Theil, and the Americans had reached the crossroads southeast of Digosville. The seriousness of the advance is illustrated by the fact that elements of the artillery and headquarters had been forced into close combat.[690]

Pi.Btl. 709 received orders to transfer its reserve company via motor transport towards St. Pierre-Église. That evening it was deployed in a successful counterattack. The next morning (**24th**) it came under heavy attack and was wiped out.[691]

A meeting of three commanders in Cherbourg. On the left is the naval commander, Kont. Adm. Walter Hennecke. Gen.Lt. von Schlieben is in the centre and to his left is Gen.Maj. Hennecke, the commander of Festung Cherbourg until 23 June. (Collection Alain Chazette)

With the *Landfront* breached, forces were removed from the *Seefront* to strengthen the Cherbourg perimeter. Several resistance nests were holding out behind American lines, with orders to continue the fight from where they stood. A withdrawal was considered pointless: The inner circle was inadequately fortified, the troops would be overtaken by the motorised enemy and there was no artillery support to cover the retreat.[692]

Despite mounting difficulties, it was noted late in the day that the enemy breaches — at Flottemanville-Hague, 1 km southeast of Nouainville, on both sides of La Loge, and 2 km southeast of Digosville — had not been expanded since the afternoon. The Americans were bringing forward their mortars and artillery for a final assault on Cherbourg itself.[693] If the fortress was to hold out much longer, reinforcements were needed at once.[694] The fortress had already reported possible options: Airborne forces could be dropped east of Cherbourg or aircraft could land on the Querqueville Airfield. Time was running out, and the paratroopers would only make a difference, if they could arrive within a matter of hours. Landings from the sea were still possible at the *Arsenal*, albeit with difficulty.[695]

There was now a change in the command structure. Effective immediately, the *OKW* appointed *Gen.Lt.* von Schlieben as the *Festungs-Kommandant*. *Gen. Maj.* Sattler was relieved of his command and subordinated to von Schlieben.[696] This arrangement made it abundantly clear who was in charge and prevented messages from being directed to the wrong authority.

By early **24 June**, a reorganisation of the forces west of Cherbourg was carried out. Simply put, a new *KG Keil* was formed. It now included (along with Keil's own reinforced regiment) *GR 922* under *Obstlt.* Müller (as *U.KG Müller*), the forces under *Hptm.* Weng, the headquarters and a company of *Pz.Jg.Abt. 709* and *Sturm-Btl. AOK 7*. Its mission was to hold Hill 180 and the Jobourg Peninsula and to draw enemy troops away from Cherbourg through movements and artillery fire from the west. Artillery support was provided by *Art.Gruppe Quittnat*, which still boasted considerable strength.[697]

For the moment, *GR 919* continued to defend the southwest sector of the *Landfront*. During the morning, two worrisome developments were reported: Strong armoured formations were pushing north from Flottemanville-Hague, while at Le Pont (southwest of Octeville) and to its west, enemy reinforcements were being brought up.[698] Indeed, the 9th ID made good progress during the day, albeit without yet reaching Cherbourg proper. The 47th IR advanced some 3 km before one of its battalions was stopped in front of Fort des Fourches and another at Fort du Tot. The 39th IR advanced alongside the latter battalion and entered Octeville, halting there for the remainder of the day.

The day's attacks by the 9th ID had finally broken the defences of *GR 919* in front of Cherbourg. The *9./919* was routed, enabling the Americans to break through the right wing of *MG-Btl. 17* and overrun the line occupied by the battalion headquarters. The *9./919* fell back towards *KG Keil* (northwest), while the battalion headquarters, with its remaining organic elements and the *10./919*, withdrew into Cherbourg.[699]

Following the collapse in the sector of *MG-Btl. 17*, a makeshift front was established near La Traisnellerie in connection to Hill 180. Before dark, however, the left wing was pushed back to Hainneville. Yet the front still held and Hill 180 remained in German hands. Rather than awaiting its destruction in Cherbourg, *GR 919* was to withdraw to the Jobourg Peninsula and defend it

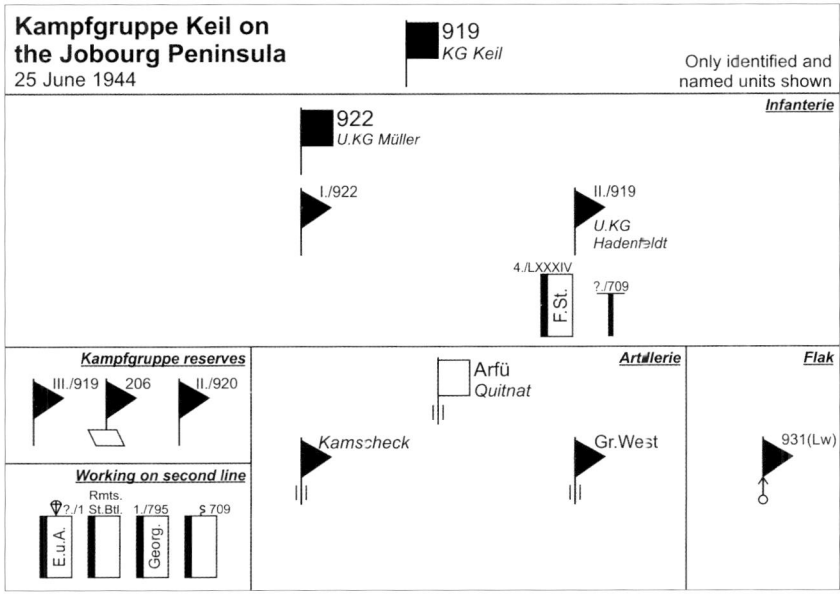

After the withdrawal of GR 919 to the Jobourg peninsula a new KG Keil was formed for the defence of the peninsula. All available troops were put under Keil's command, including those of Obstlt. Müller.

as part of *KG Keil*. This move began at 23:00, although the trains had been sent ahead during daylight hours. The withdrawal was carried out without interference.[700]

While the front lines of *GR 919* were crumbling, the commander of *Pi. Btl. 709* was preparing for his part in the battle for Cherbourg in the rear. *Maj.* Hornung intended to block the valley of the Vaublat River, which runs from Nouainville to Brécourt (east of Hainneville), where it reaches the coast and allows access to Cherbourg from the west. The area was also important for another reason: Dug into the hills at Brécourt were vast underground supply facilities. The staff of the logistics officer of the division and other command posts had also been located there, but they had now pulled back into Cherbourg itself. The only men remaining at the site were the commander of the division's headquarters company, an officer from *Nachr.Abt. 709* and about 60 other men. They were placed under Hornung's control as he received orders to demolish the tunnels and bunkers and destroy the remaining supplies. The preparations were made during the night with the battalion destroying its remaining vehicles and equipment.[701]

While the 79th ID pressed its advance towards Mont-du-Roule, early German reports were still remarkably optimistic, claiming that enemy attacks had been repulsed west of La Glacerie.[702] Les Rouges-Terres had been lost, but *Wn. 449* and *452* continued to hold out in the enemy's rear[703]. The former was part of *St.P. Valognerstraße*, while *Wn. 452* was just to the north.

Despite the early successes claimed by the Germans, advancing American forces continued to hammer their defences. The 314th IR pushed on towards Mont-du-Roule, until fire from the high ground at Octeville forced it to break off its attack for the day. To the right, the 313th IR advanced to Hameau Gringor on the east side of the Mont-du-Roule Ridge and seized the hamlet.[704]

Early German reports from the southeast of the *Landfront* were also unduly positive; it was claimed that a tank attack 2 km south of Digosville had been repulsed.[705] The road from Théville to Tourlaville was reported clear of enemy troops up to Hameau Piquot.[706] Yet the overly optimistic German reports could not alter the situation on the ground, which continued to rapidly deteriorate. The 12th IR continued its drive on Tourlaville and captured the command post of *GR 729* at St. Gabriel, where *Obst.* Rohrbach was also taken prisoner.[707] Here, in the southeast sector of the front, the infantry defences were crumbling.[708] The remnants of two companies of *GR 729* — *Kompanie Schimpf* (known from *Alarmeinheit 729* on the Montebourg front) and *Kompanie Straube* (unidentified) — were in position near the water tower east of Tourlaville, while elements of the *III./922* were located southeast of Cherbourg, near the quarry.[709] The Americans took Digosville and occupied the western part of Tourlaville during the night.[710] The German troops had already pulled back to Cherbourg and established a fragile defensive front on the eastern outskirts of the town. It ran roughly north to south from the (today no longer existing) railway crossing with the main road to Tourlaville.[711] The front was occupied by a colourful mix of officers, Russians, *Luftwaffe* personnel, *RAD* workers, infantry and engineers.[712]

The overall situation in the fortress continued to worsen. Maintaining a cohesive command was growing increasingly difficult as communications with several battalions was disrupted.[713] Moreover, the loss of officers, coupled with heavy losses from enemy artillery fire, had reduced the fighting capabilities of the troops. The morale of the men from *DVL III* and among the *Osttruppen* had now sunk so low that they "had lost their will to oppose the enemy".[714] The last hope of reinforcements vanished as the *OKW* acknowledged the futility of the situation and decided against sending additional resources to Cherbourg. *Gruppe von Schlieben* was finally authorised to close the harbour.[715]

The struggle for Cherbourg continued to rage on **25 June**, while on the Jobourg Peninsula it remained quiet, allowing *KG Keil* to reorganise its defences after its overnight withdrawal. A new frontline was cobbled together — from Vauville, along the valley, then to the north coast — incorporating *Wn. 480-485* and *Westeck*. Yet these defences were less than ideal, since the resistance nests had been built facing northwest, rather than southeast from where the enemy was approaching; as a result, the anti-tank ditch was behind, rather than in front, of the German positions. *Batterie Landemer*, located on the coast northeast of *Westeck*, was also incorporated into the defences.[716]

KG Keil was organised into two sub-battlegroups. The area north of the highway (incl.) was assigned to the *II./919* under its commander *Maj.* Hadenfeldt; *Artillerie-Gruppe West* was instructed to provide fire support. *Maj.* Quittnat became the artillery officer of *KG Keil* and transferred direct control of his batteries to another officer. *U.KG Hadenfeldt* also received the company of *Pz.Jg.Abt. 709* with five AT guns. At the front, *MG-Btl. 17* held *Wn. 480* and *481* on the road to Beaumont-Hague (D901). The positions on their left, including *Westeck*, were held by the *4./Fest.Stamm-Abt. LXXXIV* and, finally,

The VII Corps attack on Cherbourg began on 22 June. It was preceded by heavy aerial attacks, which aimed to soften up the German defences. (NARA)

the front from *Westeck* to *Batterie Landemer* was held by the *7./919*. The other company (*5./919*) was in position at the anti-tank ditch to the rear of *Westeck*. The combat strength of the *5.* and the *7./919* was about 60 men each.⁷¹⁷

The *III./919*, down to 80 men, was deployed behind the front north of Beaumont-Hague, on the boundary between *U.KG Müller* and *U.KG Hadenfeldt*. It would serve as a reserve to support either force depending on the situation.⁷¹⁸

U.KG Müller held the front south of the road to Beaumont-Hague and had not come under attack since taking command of the peninsula on **21 June**. The *I./922* was at the front, while the remnants of the *II./920* were in the woods east of Herqueville.⁷¹⁹ *Obstlt.* Keil placed the latter battalion under his command as the battlegroup reserve along with the remnants of *Pz.Abt. 206*, which were in the woods as well. The artillery battalion (identified only as *Kamscheck*) that had been supporting Müller continued to do so, but, like the artillery force supporting Hadenfeldt, was put under the overall command of *Maj.* Quittnatt to facilitate the concentrated fire of all guns on the peninsula.⁷²⁰

To provide defence in depth on the peninsula, a second defensive line was to be built from Herqueville on the south coast to Mont-Pali in the north. The line would be occupied by any forces that could be scraped together, among them the division veterinary company, remnants of the airborne training company, the *1./Georg.Inf.Btl. 795* and *Sturm-Btl. AOK 7*. A third line was also planned from Laye, south of Auderville, to La Belle-Martins.⁷²¹

Additional forces in the sector included *le.Flak-Abt. 931* under *Maj.* Jürgens; this formation was distributed along the main road with a large number of guns. The railway guns of the *3./H.K.A.R. 1262* were placed under the command of *Maj.* Quittnat. A *Luftwaffe* signals unit occupied the resistance nest on the coast, and it was ordered to reduce the manning to provide men for the companies at the front. The remaining troops consisted of a heterogenous collection of naval and *Luftwaffe* personnel, men from the trains, stragglers and personnel of a hospital east of Herqueville.⁷²²

Around Cherbourg, the fighting picked up again in the morning. At 06:00, *Maj.* Hornung arrived at his command post, located on the high ground opposite the Brécourt tunnels, and gave the order to begin the demolitions. The troops not involved in this operation were gathered in reconnaissance parties that were dispatched in the direction of Tonneville, Nouainville and Équeurdreville. Only a handful of officers and men, armed with a single light MG, remained at the command post.⁷²³

Contrary to the expectations of *Maj.* Hornung, the enemy attack did not come through the valley but across the high ground to the east. Here, the 2/47ᵗʰ IR captured Fort des Couplets after the fort had been subjected to heavy shelling.⁷²⁴ From his command post, the major had a clear view of the fort and watched as the defenders simply gave up without a fight. Enraged by the lack of resistance, he ordered his machine gun to open fire on the Americans and the surrendering Germans, but before his order could be executed, the command post came under intense fire and *Maj.* Hornung was seriously wounded.⁷²⁵

After capturing the fort and nearby gun positions, the American battalion turned east and, early that afternoon, entered Cherbourg and began clearing the area southwest of the *Arsenal*. The other US battalions were stopped by German resistance in front of the Redoute des Fourches (3/47ᵗʰ IR) and from positions north of that strongpoint (1/47ᵗʰ IR). To the east, the 39ᵗʰ IR slowly fought its way through the streets of Octeville.⁷²⁶ It was closing in on the suburb of St. Sauveur, where the underground command posts of *Gruppe von Schlieben* were located.

In the centre of the VII Corps' front, the upper levels of the dominating Fort du Roule were taken by the 79ᵗʰ ID (314ᵗʰ IR) after bitter fighting. To the south, the German pocket between Martinvast and Hardinvast continued to hold out against the 315ᵗʰ IR. The division's other regiment (313ᵗʰ IR) approached Cherbourg from the southeast, but it had yet to enter the town.

In the east, the 4ᵗʰ ID seized the high ground north of Tourlaville and captured *Batterie Brommy*. That evening, the 12ᵗʰ IR moved into Cherbourg and, following its orders, halted in front of the Amiot works.⁷²⁷

As the Americans methodically tightened their grip on the fortress, German reports from Cherbourg began to flicker out. During the day, it was reported that the harbour and other important installations had been demolished. The strength of the defenders was further reduced by the loss of several batteries, which had either expended their ammunition or been eliminated by enemy fire.⁷²⁸

Direct radio contact between *Gruppe von Schlieben* and *AOK 7* was lost at 20:00, shortly after von Schlieben reported that the final fighting for Cherbourg had begun.⁷²⁹ Communications between the general and the 7.

As the 79th Infantry division fought its way deeper into the town, it overran a number of German facilities. This included the tunnel complex dug in the hull below Mont du Roule. (NARA)

Armee now passed through *Obstlt.* Keil, who was still in contact with von Schlieben and kept the field army informed during the evening. There was no significant pressure against his own front, which still ran from Vauville via *Wn. 481-486* to *Batterie Landemer*.[730]

Southwest of Cherbourg, the Americans were in full control of the area around Nouainville. In the evening, they had also taken the high ground between Flottemanville-Hague and St. Croix-Hague (Hill 180 and Hill 176) and were believed to be in Tonneville. Near Querqueville, the coastal road to the Jobourg Peninsula had been mined and blown up, while the Brécourt tunnels had also been demolished.[731]

The reports now coming out of Cherbourg were limited and confused. It was not even clear if the *Arsenal* and Fort du Roule were still in German hands. According to reports, the initial American assault on the *Arsenal* had been repulsed, while the division headquarters was said to be engaged in close quarter fighting at its location. No information was available on the situation further to the east.[732]

26 June witnessed the final defeat of *Festung Cherbourg*. The eastern part of the town was cleared by the 4th and the 79th ID, despite ongoing resistance from the lower levels of Fort du Roule, which was not firmly in American hands until early that evening.[733]

In the western sector of the town, the 9th ID fought its way forward. On the left, the 47th IR faced heavy fire from the *Arsenal* and was unable to reach it. To its right, the 39th IR advanced towards the city centre. In the afternoon, the 2/39th IR reached the German headquarters, which sent out its last radio message at 14:06: "Documents and encryption equipment destroyed".[734] The attack on the headquarters began. The ventilation system was quickly knocked out and gas masks distributed. The many wounded, including the commander of *AR 1709*, were at risk of suffocating from the gas and lack of oxygen. Further resistance was both pointless and irresponsible. *Gen.Lt.* von Schlieben surrendered the headquarters and was taken prisoner along with *Adm.* Hennecke.[735] The general, however, refused to surrender all German troops in the fortress. As a result, the fighting continued. By day's end, only the *Arsenal* and isolated strongpoints remained in German hands. These included the seaplane base, but the port's railway station, Gare Maritime, was reportedly lost.[736]

Some kilometres to the east, the 22nd IR opened its attack on Théville Airfield. The 1/22nd IR took out a number of fortified positions to the south of it, captured Gonneville and reached the east side of the airfield by nightfall. In the centre, the 2/22nd IR captured the west end of the airfield, while the 3/22nd IR took Maupertus (northwest of the airfield) and subdued the defences on the north side of the airport. German resistance at the airfield, however, would continue into the next day.[737]

In the sector of *KG Keil*, the day was mostly quiet. During the night, it had been possible to bring artillery that had deployed at the front onto the peninsula. The road from Cherbourg to Beaumont-Hague was free of the enemy, who continued to advance deliberately towards *U.KG Hadenfeldt*. *Wn. 482* and *483* were subjected to mortar fire.[738]

The last major German stronghold in Cherbourg fell on the morning of **27 June**, when *Gen.Maj.* Sattler surrendered the *Arsenal* around 10:00.[739] Cherbourg was now in American hands with the exception of three minor resistance nests on the outer breakwater and one of the jetties. The latter, Fort l'Ile de Pelée, surrendered after dark.[740]

The breakwater, with Fort l'Ouest, Fort Central and Fort l'Est, was controlled by the harbour commander, *Fregattenkapitän* Witt. During the preceding night, he had sailed to it with some 30 men, including the commander of *s.St.Werf.Rgt. 101*. This group was determined to make a final stand from Fort l'Ouest, which controlled the minefield blocking the western entry to the outer roadstead (the eastern entry was blocked by fixed obstacles). The less enthusiastic occupants of the fort were relieved of their duties and locked up in Fort Central.[741] The forts finally surrendered on **29 June**.[742]

East of Cherbourg, the 22nd IR resumed its attack on the remaining strongpoints around Cap Lévy. *Osteck* was surrendered by *Maj.* Küppers late in the evening, and the defenders went into captivity the next morning (**28th**).[743]

Since *Gruppe von Schlieben* no longer existed, *KG Keil* was directly subordinated to *AOK 7*. Its mission was simple: Hold the Jobourg Peninsula to the last and defend the line Vauville - Westeck - Batterie Landemer.[744] *Obstlt.* Müller remained subordinated to Keil.[745] The day passed quietly, although the Americans probed the entire front of *U.KG Hadenfeldt*. Due to misinterpretation of an order, *Wn. 480* and *481* were evacuated without having been attacked, then hastily reoccupied.[746]

Around 03:00 on **28 June**, *Obstlt.* Keil was informed that he had been

The final stand on the northern part of the Cotentin Peninsula was made by KG Keil. It was however unable to oppose the US 9th ID for long and the front collapsed on 30 June. By the morning of the next day all organised resistance on the Jobourg Peninsula had ceased.

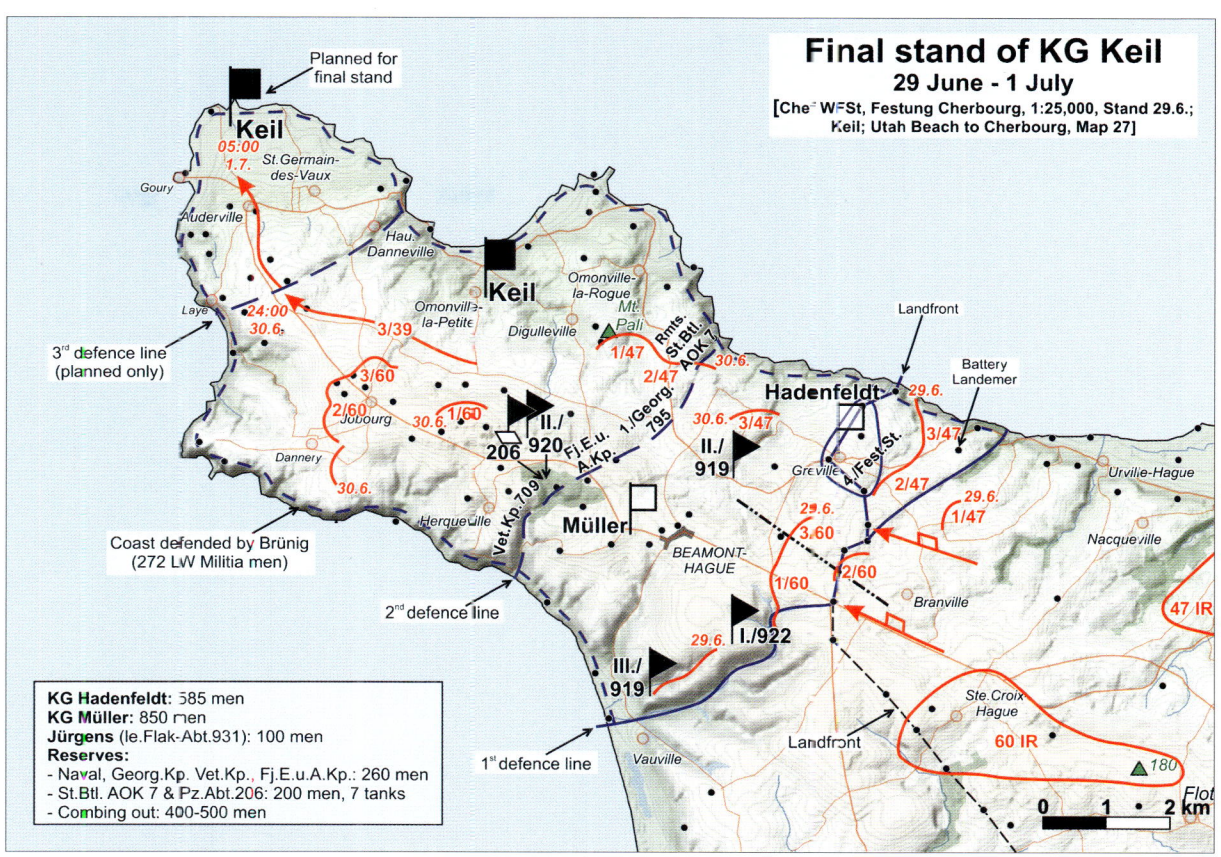

awarded the *Ritterkreuz*. On **24 June**, von Schlieben had recommended him for the honour in recognition of his role in the fighting withdrawal to Cherbourg:[747]

> As the commander of a Kampfgruppe, Obstlt. Keil, through his tireless personal commitment, made a decisive contribution that enabled the 709. I.D. to hold up the enemy in the Ste. Mère-Église bridgehead and to withdraw into the Landfront of Festung Cherbourg.

Keil's command on the Jobourg Peninsula, however, led to friction. *Obstlt.* Müller, unlike Keil, was not a reserve officer and was, in fact, senior to him.

He was unhappy in his role as Keil's subordinate. More serious was the refusal of an artillery commander to obey Keil's orders on account of seniority. This officer was swiftly relieved of his command.[748] Keil felt compelled to issue a bulletin stating that any officer who disobeyed his orders would be relieved and reported. Due to the disobedience he had encountered, he also demanded that the *Kriegsmarine* and *Luftwaffe* refrain from contacting their elements on the peninsula and only communicate with him. He feared that the forces subordinated to him might otherwise attempt to hide behind "special orders". Keil also requested two competent infantry battalion commanders as a reserve and to be given the authority to replace officers as needed.[749]

The day itself was uneventful, with German artillery engaging assembly areas on the road between St. Croix-Hague and Cherbourg and also around Vauville. Except for a reconnaissance against the left wing, there were no attacks, but the Americans were closing in on the main line of resistance along Keil's entire front, and their offensive was expected the next day.[750]

On **29 June**, *KG Keil* still boasted a sizeable number of forces. *U.KG Hadenfeldt* had a strength of 585 men, and its artillery consisted of 13 guns, including seven 8.8 cm *Flak*. *U.KG Müller*, where the *III./919* had been deployed on the right wing, was somewhat stronger with 850 men; 11 artillery pieces were in support, along with what remained of the *13./922*. Among the reserves of *KG Keil* were elements of the *Kriegsmarine*, the *1./Georg.Inf.Btl. 795*, *Veterinär-Kompanie 709* and the airborne training company, for a total of 260 men. Combined, *Sturm-Btl. AOK 7* and *Pz.Abt. 206* had 200 men and 7 tanks. By combing out all remaining elements another 400-500 men had been scraped together. The *Flak* troops of *Maj.* Jürgens amounted to 100 men. The final combat elements on the peninsula were formed by 272 *Luftwaffe* militiamen, who were deployed on the coast under an officer named Brünig.[751]

Meanwhile, Keil had increased his request for officers to four. These men, a battalion commander and three company commanders, were made available by the *319. I.D.*, but the Navy was unable to bring them across to the mainland.[752]

At 10:30 (**29th**), the Americans launched the expected attack along the entire front, with the centre of gravity on both sides of Branville.[753] West of Branville, *Wn. 482-485* were lost, allowing the Americans to achieve a 1 km deep penetration that was sealed off at the anti-tank ditch. Throughout the day, artillery fire in support of the infantry prevented a decisive American breakthrough.[754] But the fleeting success came at a heavy cost, for Keil had been forced to commit his last infantry reserve (*II./920*). Although it was reported that Keil's command post had moved all the way to Cap de la Hague, this appears to have been an advance warning. In reality, it remained in place north of Digulleville.[755]

At 01:00 on **30 June**, Keil submitted a detailed report. He informed *AOK 7* that *U.KG Müller* was under attack and that *U.KG Hadenfeldt* was still in action into the night. The lines now ran from *Batterie Landemer* via the blocking position between the battery and *Wn. 231* to *Westeck* (German), and from there via Lieu Bailly (US) to La Rue de Gréville (German). The objective was to drive the Americans back into the minefields west of *Wn. 482-485* and re-establish contact with *U.KG Müller*. Any intention of recapturing these resistance nests had already been abandoned, since there was no longer enough infantry available. In fact, no reserves were available at all, although it was intended to bring up 60 *Flak* troops to both Müller and Hadenfeldt during the night. To the rear were members of *Veterinär-Kompanie 709*, all 45-50 year olds busy laying minefields but otherwise possessing no combat value. Keil complimented the artillery for their contribution to the fighting. If they were able to repeat their performance, he figured it might just be possible to hold out one more day.[756]

Yet the morale and control of the troops at the front was declining. After dark, young *RAD* personnel deserted along with some soldiers. The lack of officers made it impossible to maintain control. Keil again requested the four officers he had been promised. They were needed for the coming day. Without them, it would no longer be possible to lead the troops at the front.[757]

The 9th ID resumed its advance in the morning and broke through the first German line at 07:30.[758] North of the main road, *Westeck* was surrounded. At 14:40, it reported that it had repulsed an attack but had suffered heavy losses in doing so. For the moment at least, the strongpoint was holding out.[759]

South of the road, the command post of *Obstlt.* Müller was surrounded during the morning. Attempts to extricate him from the command post were unsuccessful. The command post continued to receive direct artillery support, which prevented the Americans from taking the position. At 16:00, the artillery ran out ammunition and, at 17:10, Keil reported that contact with *U.KG Müller* had been lost.[760] Müller himself was subsequently taken prisoner.[761] Aware that time was running out, Keil had already ordered his artillery to expend their ammunition and then spike the guns and for the signals installations to be destroyed.[762]

Now that the first line had been breached, the battlegroup intended to hold the second line in an attempt to halt the American advance.[763] As reinforcements, all remaining 2 cm *Flak* were brought up to the front.[764] Still, without sufficient artillery and AT guns, it was all too clear that the line could not be held against armour. In fact, artillery support was now virtually nonexistent, with just two batteries still in action (the others had already spiked their guns).[765] Attempts were made to send the trains to the front, but this intent was impeded by heavy enemy artillery fire on the main road.

Again, Keil contacted *AOK 7* to inform them of the latest developments. He ended his report with the warning that artillery support would no longer

Towards the end of June, the 101st Airborne Division was relieved on the Carentan front. It was then sent towards Cherbourg for security operations. During that period, some members took the opportunity to inspect German positions and equipment. This is when they photographed this Sd.Kfz. 7/2, although the location is unclear. The vehicle is numbered 313, identifying it as the third vehicle in 1st Platoon of a 3rd Company. If found close to Cherbourg, it probably belonged to 3./Pz.Jg.Abt. 709. If taken close to the Douve river, 3./Pz.Jg.Abt. 352 is a more likely option.
(Mark A. Bando Collection)

be available the next day and that fighting without such support would result in heavy losses to simply gain a few hours. He considered such a scenario to be particularly wasteful, since at least 30% of the men fighting at the front had a special protected status, such as having to provide for large families. Despite his reservations, he declared that he would execute his orders to fight to the last.[766]

The Americans continued their advance to the second line. By 18:00, however, *Veterinär-Kompanie 709*, which held the main road, had not yet come under attack. Further north, the airborne training company was still holding out, but it had lost contact with the *1./Georg.Inf.Btl. 795*. *Sturm-Btl. AOK 7*, on Mont-Pali, was also out of contact with the Georgians and under assault from all sides.[767] It did not take long for the Americans to break through the second line

and capture Jobourg. The last remaining German battery slowed their advance from Jobourg until it had also exhausted its ammunition. Since the Americans had yet to break through to Auderville, the battlegroup attempted to hold the third line with all available personnel, but it was a line in name only.[768]

The battlegroup stayed in contact with *AOK 7* throughout the evening in what were the final hours of organised resistance. Shortly after 20:00, it reported a penetration near its third line, but there was no longer any artillery to counter the threat.[769] The 9th ID pushed on until about midnight, but it did not continue towards the tip of the peninsula that night.[770]

At 21:30, the battlegroup reported that its command post was surrounded and that it was no longer possible to get out.[771] Believing that *Obstlt*. Keil had

Within Cherbourg most of the fighting ended with the surrender of the Arsenal on 27 June. Here some German survivors left the complex through one of its main gates and are having a friendly conversation with a GI from the 9th Infantry Division. [NARA]

been killed outside the headquarters, *Maj*. Quittnat hoisted the white flag and Keil returned too late to stop it.[772] At 21:55, the command post dispatched its final message, stating that the battlegroup would fight to the last round and the men who remained would attempt to make their way south through enemy lines.[773] Not bound by the white flag, Keil tried to move north to the tip of the peninsula for the final fight. Instead, he ran into American troops and was captured around midnight.[774]

With the loss of *Obstlt*. Keil, organised resistance came to an end. When the 9th ID resumed its advance early next morning (**1 July**), it met only scattered German resistance. At 08:00, the Americans captured Auderville and Goury at the tip of the peninsula. The fighting ceased completely around 11:00, when *Maj*. Hadenfeldt surrendered *Westeck*.[775] That day, *Kampfgruppe* Keil was lauded one final time in the Armed Forces Daily Announcement:[776]

On the northwest tip of the Cherbourg Peninsula, our weak forces, crowded together in a narrow area, continued to bitterly resist superior enemy forces. Fighting to the last, they inflicted heavy casualties upon the enemy.

The collapse of all resistance on the Jobourg Peninsula also marked the end of the *709. I.D.* This is evident in the prisoner numbers. As of **5 July**, 6,652 members of the division had been identified in POW cages in the UK.[777] This figure increased to 7,301 by **14 July**, largely through the addition of members of *GR 919*, *AR 1709* and the support troops — essentially matching the elements under *KG Keil*.[778] Having been totally destroyed, the division was formally disbanded on **24 July**.

Leaving the Arsenal, Gen.Maj. Sattler looked considerably more dejected than many of his men. Here he is escorted out by Maj. Gen. Manton S. Eddy, commander of the 9th Infantry Division which liberated most of the western part of Cherbourg. (NARA)

Despite Allied efforts to minimise the damage to Cherbourg's infrastructure, the German forces did their best to achieve the opposite. After its liberation, it took months of effort before the harbour was fully operational again. (NARA)

German demolition work destroyed much of the harbour facilities, its waters were left blocked by mines and scuttled vessels. The damage was particualrly heavy around the Gare Maritime, the main railroad station. Not only had much of the station been demolished, the quays were also left in ruins. (NARA)

APPENDIX

A Timeline of the occupation of Lower Normandy
B Coastal Defence Sectors
C Grundgliederungen

Glossary
German Military Symbols
Comparative Table of Ranks
Terminology and Abbreviations

Appendix A

Timeline of the occupation of Lower Normandy

Département Eure, directly east of Lower Normandy (Calvados, Manche and Orne), is included here since troops often covered parts of both the Calvados and Eure.

1940

June Cherbourg falls to the reinforced 7.Pz.Div. on the 19th. Brig. Senger stays behind to control the area.

AOK 4 follows in the wake of the German advance. Its X.A.K. moves into Basse-Normandie. Here it establishes control with 216.I.D.

To the east it is H.Kdo.XXXII under Militärbefehlshaber Frankreich, which covers the Seine estuary. It moves up 223.I.D. which relieves 216.I.D. east of the Orne around the 25th.

216.I.D. is used to relieve Brig. Senger on the Cotentin on the 27th.

The sector of the division is reduced when 57.I.D., also under X.A.K., takes over its sector in the Calvados.

July The Channel Islands surrender on 1-4 July and are occupied by elements of 216.I.D.

On the 10th 223.I.D. is taken over by X.A.K.

On the 11th 57.I.D. also relieves 223.I.D. on the coast up to the Seine estuary.

On the 12th IX.A.K. takes over the western sector of X.A.K., including 216.I.D. Both corps are put under AOK 6 and H.Gr.A control at this time. The AOK 6 thus relieves AOK 4 in Normandy.

X.A.K. leaves AOK 6 control on the 23rd and is directly placed under H.Gr.A before being taken over by AOK 9 on the 28th. At the same time XXXXIII.A.K. takes over the 57.I.D. and 223.I.D., yet X.A.K. remains in place for other purposes.

IX.A.K. remains under AOK 6 which is taken over by H.Gr.B on the 23rd. 211.I.D. joins the corps on the 20th.

Preparations for for Unternehmen Seelöwe (Operation Sealion) begin towards the end of the month. On the 22nd the boundary between IX.A.K. and X.A.K. is moved to Bayeux – Condé-sur-Noireaux – Carrouges. To make room for the divisions of a new corps, 211.I.D. is relieved on the 23rd by both 216.I.D. and 256.I.D. and leaves on the 28th.

II.A.K. moves into the sector of IX.A.K. with three new divisions. The new corps relieves IX.A.K. on the 27th, taking over 216.I.D. The Avranches sector remains under the old corps, held by the 256.I.D. The new divisions – 12.I.D., 31.I.D., and 32.I.D. – assume command of their sectors on the 29th.

To the east X.A.K. is assigned 30.I.D. for Operation Seelöwe. The division arrives in the rear area of 57.I.D. and 223.I.D. on 31 July - 2 August.

Aug. 223.I.D. takes over part of the coast from 57.I.D. on the 2nd.

Sept. 12.I.D. leaves II.A.K. on the 4th.

IX.A.K. surrenders command to II.A.K. on the 6th, before leaving on the 9th. This puts 6.I.D. and 256.I.D. under II.A.K.

The departure of 31.I.D. begins on the 10th.

H.Gr.C assumes command over AOK 6 on the 10th.

6.I.D. moves into Normandy and assumes command of its sector on the 12th.

32.I.D. leaves on the 18th.

Oct. H.Gr.D relieves H.Gr.C on the 26th.

Nov. 170.I.D. relieves 223.I.D. on the 1st, becoming the right neighbour of II.A.K.

Appendix A

1941

Feb. 225.I.D. relieves 170.I.D. on the 1st, becoming the right neighbour of II.A.K.

March XXVIII.A.K., which is holding much of Brittany's north coast, briefly takes over the sector of II.A.K. on the 1st. II.A.K. then leaves on the 3rd.

The former sector of II.A.K. is again largely taken over by XXXXIII.A.K. on the 15th, except for 256.I.D. which remains with XXVIII.A.K. The change moves the 6.I.D. and 216.I.D. sectors in Normandy from AOK 6 to AOK 9 control.

Separately from these developments, the departure of 6.I.D. from Normandy begins on the 12th. Its sector is taken over by 57.I.D. and 216.I.D.

April The H.Kdo.LX arrives and relieves XXXXIII.A.K. under the cover name XXXXIII.A.K. (T) on the 6th. It thus controls 57.I.D., 216.I.D. and 225.I.D. 323.ID. arrives and relieves 57.I.D. on the 9th, which then leaves the corps. 319.I.D. arrives and assumes command of its sector on the 10th. It essentially replaces 6.I.D.

AOK 9 is relieved by AOK 15 under the cover name AOK 9 (T) on the 14th.

H.Gr.A is relieved by H.Gr.D, which thus takes over AOK 15.

225.I.D. and its sector are transferred from the H.Kdo.LX to H.Kdo.XXXII on the 30th. This permanently moves Département Eure to a different corps with the Dives as the general boundary.

May AOK 7 takes over H.Kdo. LX from AOK 15 on the 21st.

June 83.I.D. arrives and relieves 216.I.D. on the 9th. Both remain with the corps.

322.I.D. joins H.Kdo.XXXII on the 13th and relieves the 225.I.D., becoming the right neighbour of H.Kdo.LX.

July AOK 15 and H.Kdo.LX resume use of their own names on the 5th.

716.I.D. joins the corps and is operational on the 18th.

319.I.D. surrenders its sector on the mainland and establishes its HQ on Guernsey on the 27th.

Nov. 711.I.D. arrives and relieves 716.I.D. on coast on the 28th. 716.I.D. then leaves.

Dec. 320.I.D. arrives and relieves 83.I.D. on the 23rd.

216.I.D. leaves on the 25th.

1942

Jan. 83.I.D. leaves on the 7th.

711.I.D. leaves on the 24th. It joins H.Kdo.XXXII and relieves 332.I.D., becoming the right neighbour of H.Kdo.LX.
319.I.D. takes over Alderney, assuming permanent command of all Channel Islands.

March 716.I.D. returns to LXXXIV.A.K. and relieves 323.I.D. on the 23rd which then leaves the corps by the 28th.

Flieger-Div.7 begins to arrive at LXXXIV.A.K. on the 29th.

May H.Kdo.LX is renamed LXXXIV.A.K. as of the 15th. The corps is taken over by AOK 7 on the 21st. This permanently moves Département Eure to a different Armee. There H.Kdo.XXXII is renamed LXXXI.A.K. on the 28th.

Oct. Flieger-Div.7 leaves on the 1st.

SS-Div. Das Reich arrives at LXXXIV.A.K. on the 11th.

165.Div. arrives at LXXXIV.A.K. on the 17th.

Dec. The Avranches – Granville sector is taken over by LXXXVII.A.K. on the 3rd, using 346.I.D. These become the left neighbours of LXXXIV.A.K.

709.I.D. arrives at LXXXIV.A.K. on the 6th to relieve 165.Div. and 320.I.D., while the 165.Div. relieves part of 320.I.D. All three divisions remain with the corps.

SS-Div. 'Das Reich' leaves on the 14th.

1943

Jan. 320.I.D. leaves on the 8th.

Feb. 165.Div. leaves on the 22nd.

March 389.I.D. gradually arrives at LXXXIV.A.K. to be rebuilt.

April	Flieger-Div.7 returns to LXXXIV.A.K. on the 22nd.	August	American forces break out at Avranches on the 1st.
May	Flieger-Div.7 is renamed 1.Fj.Div. and its departure begins on the 26th.		The battle for the Falaise pocket ends on 21 August.
August	LXXIV.A.K. relieves LXXXVII.A.K. on the 1st, taking over 346.I.D. and becoming the left neighbour of LXXXIV.A.K.		Paris is liberated on the 26th.

1945

March	Channel-Island troops raid Granville on the night of 8-9 March.
May	VE-Day, Germany capitulates on 8 May.
	Guersney and Jersey are liberated on 9 May.
	Alderney is liberated on the 16th as one of the last areas in Europe.

Sept. 389.I.D. leaves on the 26th.
Start of the formation of the 352.I.D. as KG Normandie at LXXXIV.A.K.

1944

Jan. Div. zbV 721 takes over the Avranches – Granville sector from 346.I.D.

243.I.D. arrives at LXXXIV.A.K.

Start of the formation of 77.I.D. at LXXXIV.A.K.

H.Gr.B takes control over AOK 7 and its forces.

April The Avranches – Granville sector returns to LXXXIV.A.K. It is controlled by Gr.Rgt. zbV 752.

21.Pz.Div. arrives on the 30th.

May 77.I.D. leaves on the 5th. It becomes the left neighbour of the corps under LXXIV.A.K.

91.LL.Div. arrives on the 15th.

June D-Day, the Allied landings begin on 6 June.

July Final resistance on the northern Cotentin ceases on 1 July.
St.Lô liberated on 18 July.

Caen fully liberated on the 19th.

Operation Cobra begins on 25 July, breaking through the German lines.

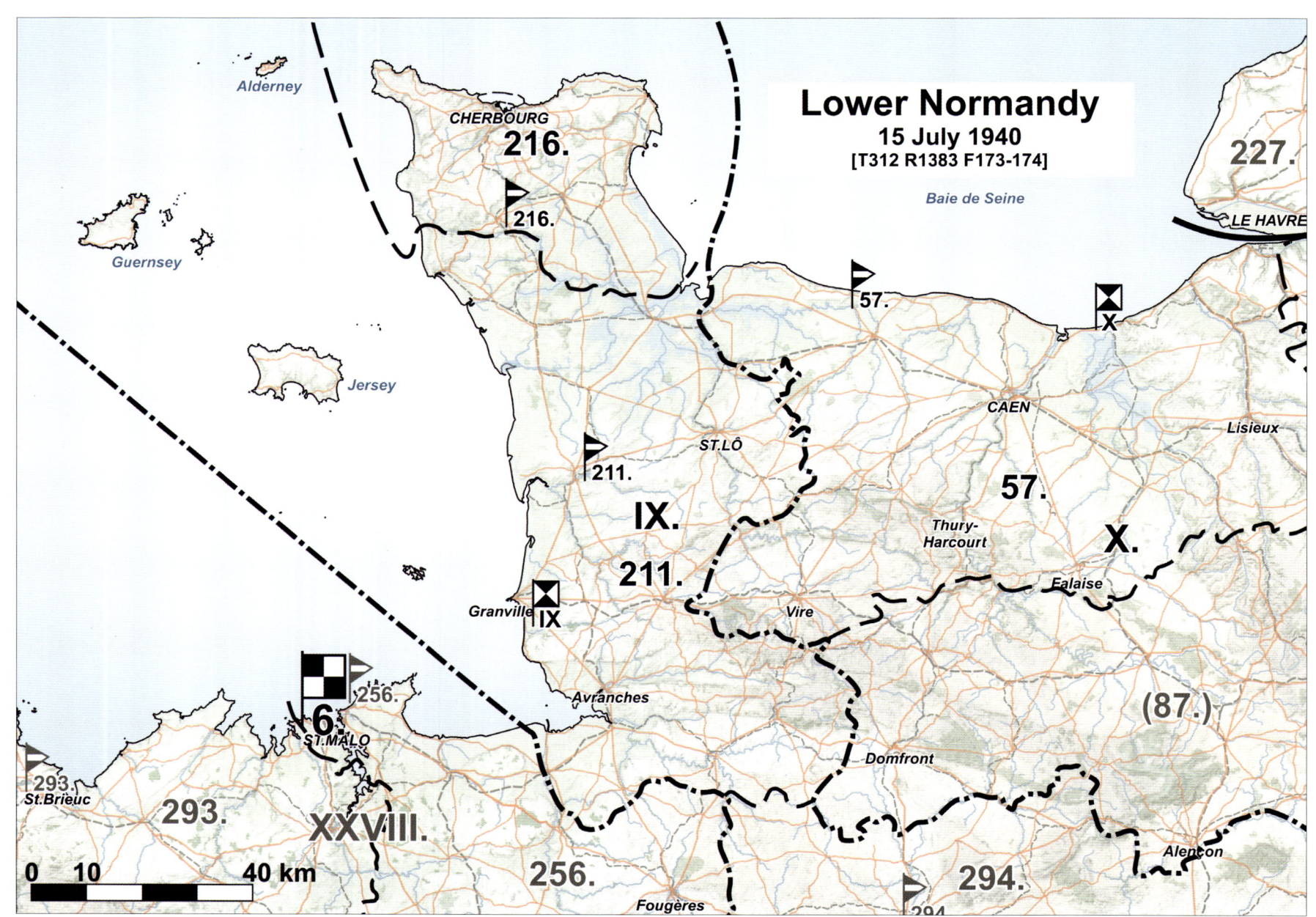

After the Armistice, German troops moved further into France to take control of the Occupation Zone. Lower Normandy became the responsibility of 6th Army and was further divided over two army corps. IX. A.K. was responsible for the western half with the 211. and 216. I.D. To the east was X. A.K. with the 57., 87. and 223. I.D.

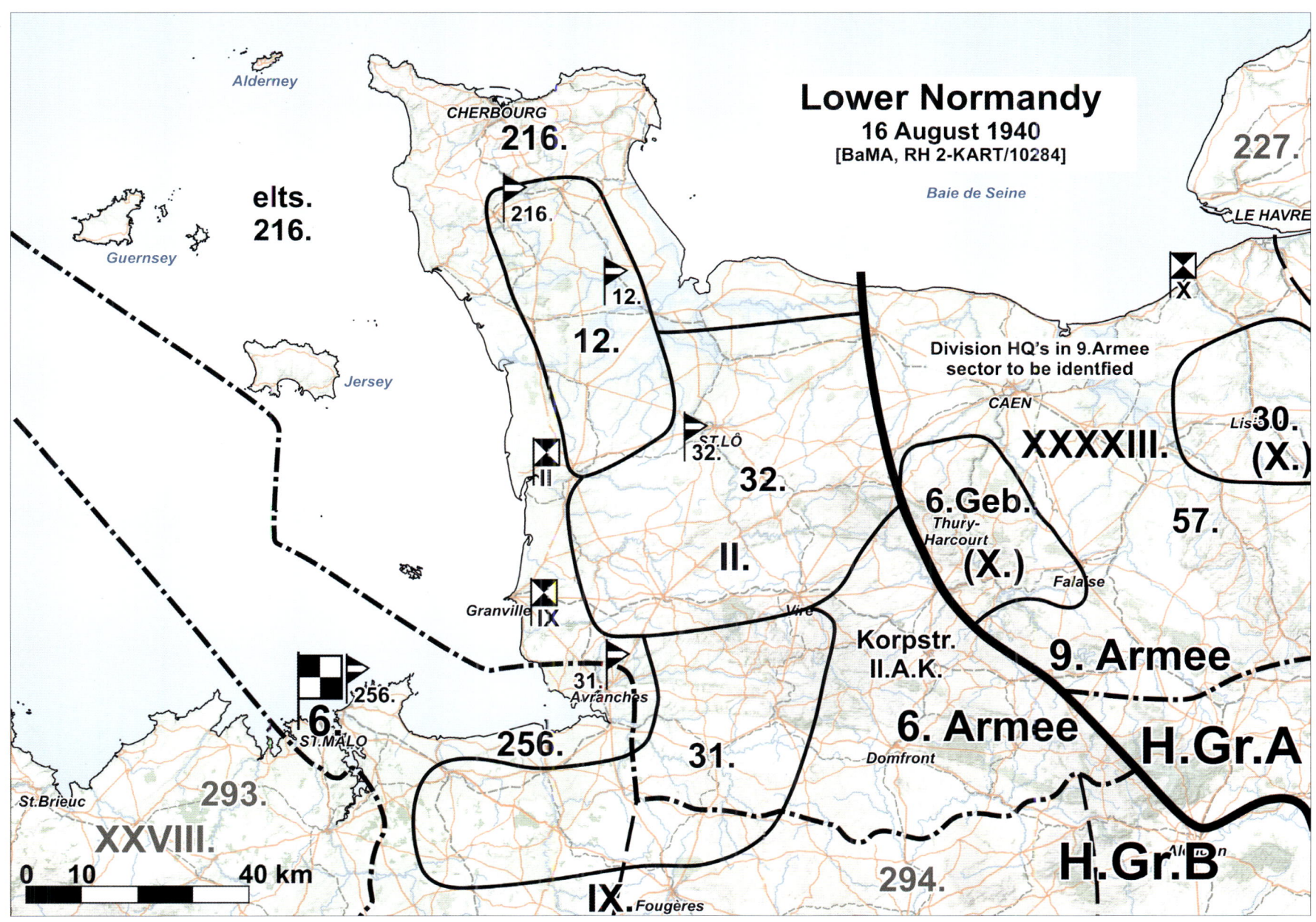

In preparation for Operation Sealion (Seelöwe) there was a massive troop buildup along the Channel Coast. Lower Normandy was divided between Army Group A (with 6th Army) and Army Group B (with 9th Army). This allowed some of the assault force to attack via Cherbourg and the others via Le Havre. The increase in troops brought the number of army corps in the area to four: II., IX., X. and XXXXIII.A.K.

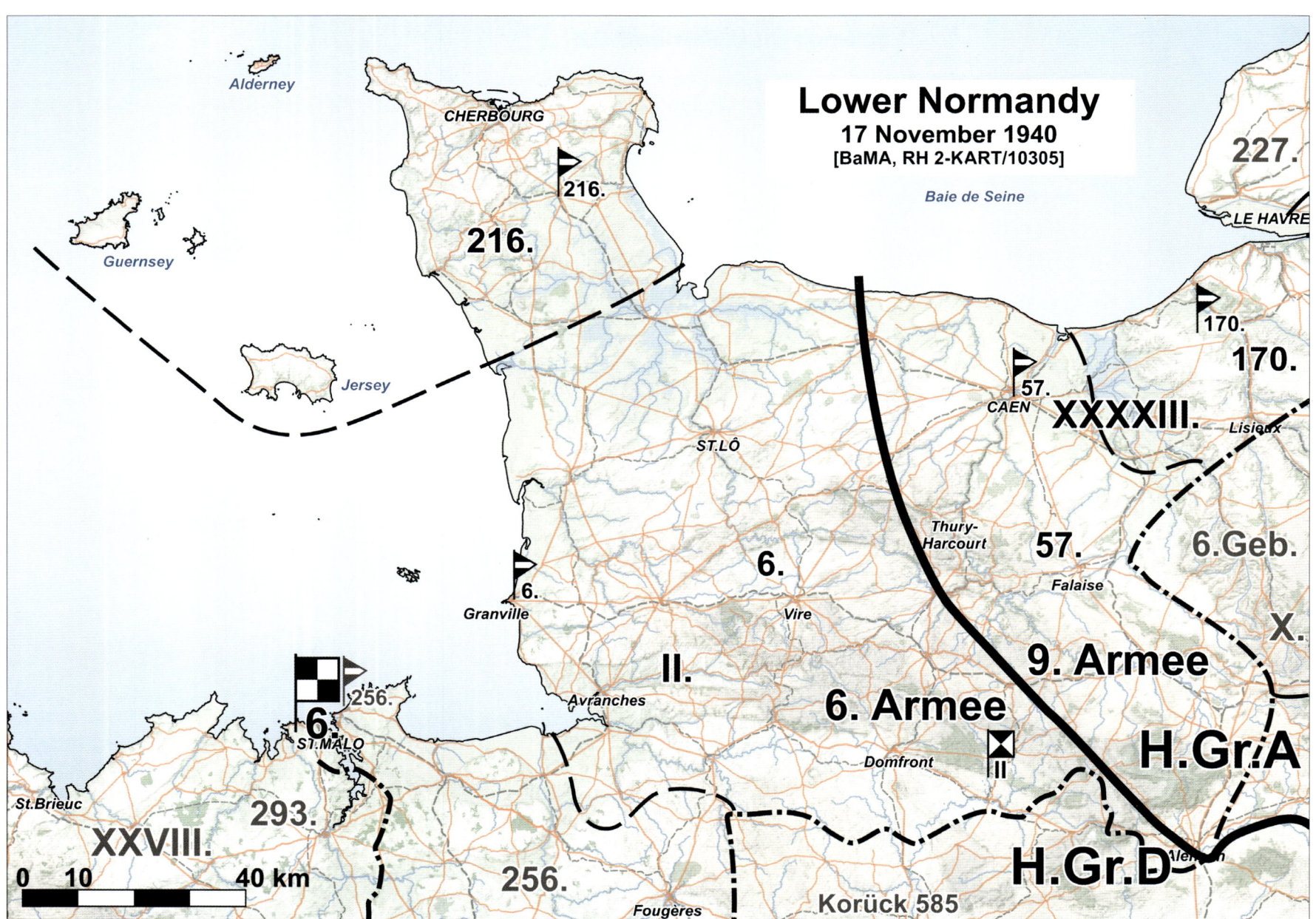

As 1940 progressed, it became increasingly clear that Operation Sealion would not take place. In response many of the invasion forces were again pulled from the Channel Coast and the troops went over to defensive operations. Lower Normandy remained divided between two army groups, but the number of army corps was brought down to two. II. A.K. in the west fielded the 6., 216. and 256. I.D., although the latter was in Bretagne. In the east, XXXXIII. A.K. included the 57. and 170. I.D.

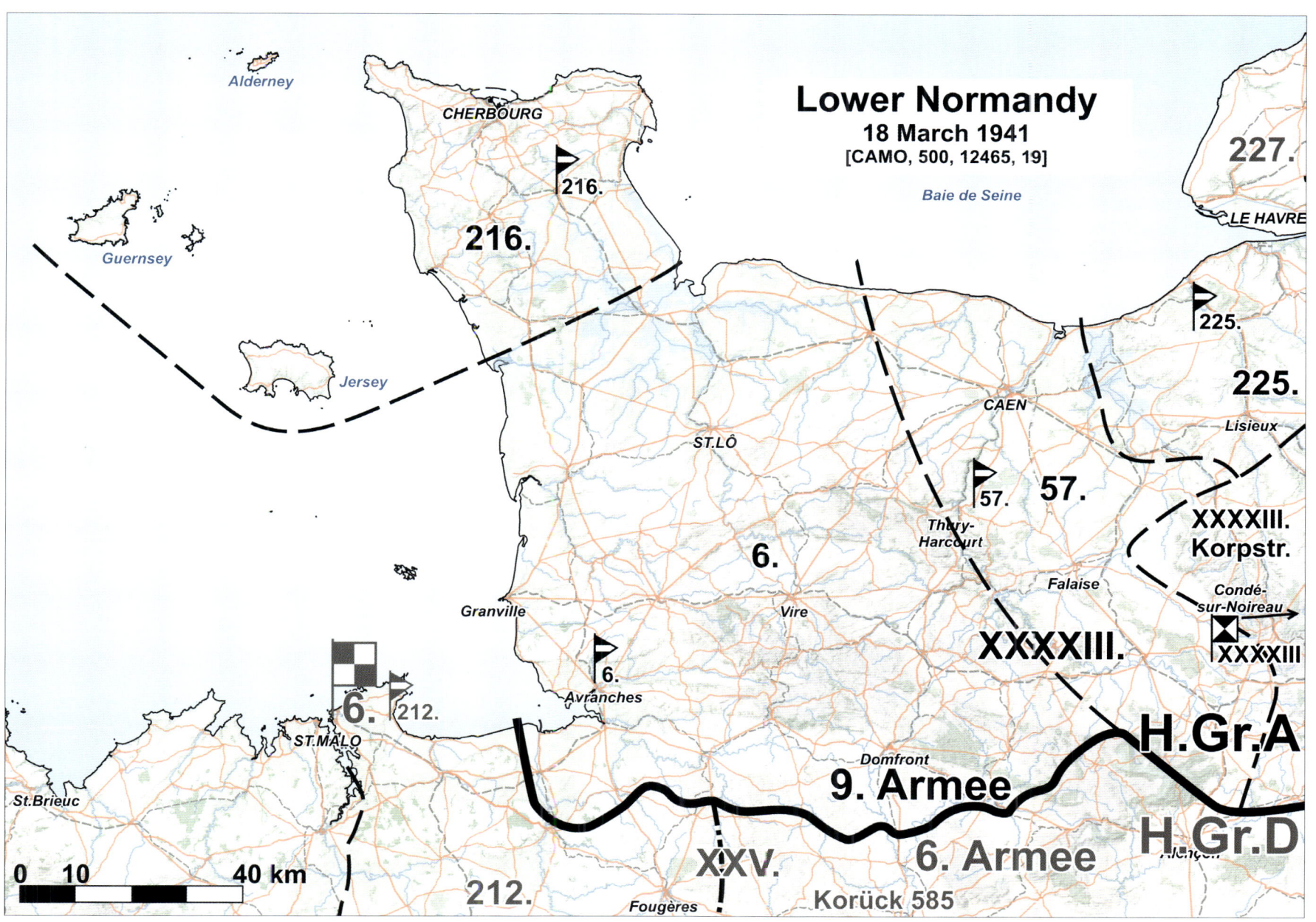

By March 1941, many German formations and commands were moved east in preparation for Operation Barbarossa. The defences in the west were reorganised and by mid March Lower Normandy was fully controlled by H.Gr. A, 9th Army and XXXXIII. A.K. This would however soon change and many of the divisions and commands would be replaced. In April Höhere Kommando zbV LX (the later LXXXIV. A.K.) would arrive to take over the area and focus on its defence.

Appendix B

Coastal Defence Sectors

The coast of occupied Europe was divided into many different sectors at different levels. When combined, these typically corresponded with the boundaries of a regiment, division or corps. In turn, they aligned to field army and/or field-army group boundaries.

Since the individual areas corresponded with the boundaries of specific elements, they typically changed when the sectors of those forces were altered. This was also the case in Normandy, where certain changes were only made in the months preceding the invasion, mostly by adding new formations. This led to shifts at all three levels of the coastal defence sectors.

Sectors

Following Hitler's orders of **December 1941** to transform the west coast of Europe into a new *"Westwall"*, *Ob.West* began its preparations to do so. In **May 1942**, the entire coastline was divided into Coastal Defence Sectors (*Küstenverteidigungsabschnitte*, or simply *KVA's*). The Netherlands were divided into two sectors, *KVA "A"* and *"B"*. South of the Scheldt, *AOK 15* was divided into *KVA "A"* to *"G"*. The area of *AOK 7* continued with *KVA "H"* and *"J"* in Normandy and started over with *KVA "A"* to *"C"* in Bretagne. To its south, *AOK 1* was organised into *KVA "D"* to *"F"*.[1] The peculiar lettering of the *AOK 7* sectors can easily be explained. During the planning phase at *Ob.West*, Basse-Normandy had still been the southernmost sector of *AOK 15* before it was transferred to *AOK 7* later in **May 1942**.[2]

Under *AOK 7*, a corps area generally encompassed two or three *KVA's*, with each *KVA* usually corresponding to the territory held by an individual division. This system was later expanded when larger sectors were subdivided into two or more smaller ones. In the area of *AOK 7*, this first occurred in Bretagne. Here, the northeast coast of Bretagne was called *KVA "A1"*, followed by *KVA "A2"*, *"B"*, *"C1"* and *"C2"*. In Normandy, the Calvados was called *KVA "H"* and the Cotentin (including most of the west coast of Manche) *KVA "J"*. This system remained unchanged well into **1944**. The sectors were also commonly referred to by their geographic locations: *KVA Calvados* and *KVA Cotentin*.

KVA's were divided into smaller geographical units, known as *Küstenverteidigungs-Gruppen* (Coastal Defence Groups), abbreviated as *"KVG"*. These tended to match regimental sectors. The groups were typically named after their locations, which could be major towns in their area or simply the name of the general region.

The final sector level was the *Küstenverteidigungs-Untergruppe* (Coastal Defence Sub-Group), or *"KVU"*. A *KVG* was typically subdivided into a number of these sub-groups, but this was not always the case. Sub-groups were usually defended by a single battalion. Just like the *KVG's*, these sub-groups used geographical designations. In addition to towns and areas, river names were commonly adopted if a a sub-group covered the estuary or mouth of a river.

LXXXIV. A.K.

Although the system of *KVA's*, *KVG's* and *KVU's* was employed in Normandy, it was not regularly noted in corps records until **1943**. The system had a drawback, however, inasmuch as the boundaries were largely determined by the distribution of forces and were thus susceptible to changes, which could make the planning and construction of defences more complicated. To address this problem, the existing sectors of the three divisions of the *LXXXIV. A.K.* received official geographical designations in late **1942**: *Calvados* (716. I.D.), *Cotentin* (320. I.D.), and *Kanalinseln* (319. I.D.). When *KV*-sectors changed, this would not affect these geographical sectors, meaning tactical and geographical boundaries no longer needed to be identical.[3]

For tactical purposes only, the *KV*-designations mattered. In early **1943** — after the 709. I.D. had relieved the 320. I.D. and the 165. Div. on the Cotentin — the area occupied by *LXXXIV. A.K.* on the mainland consisted of two main sectors corresponding with those of the 709. and 716. I.D.[4]

KVA Calvados (716. I.D.) was subdivided into two *KVGs'*, with the boundary at about Asnelles. The right (east) sector was known as *KVG Caen* and was further divided into two sub-sectors. *KVU Orne* was responsible for the mouth of the Orne and the coast on either side of the river; *KVU Seulles* was much larger and stretched west from Lion-sur-Mer. The other group was

KVG Bayeux, which also had two sub-sectors; its right wing was formed by *KVU Bessin* while *KVU Vire* covered the Vire Estuary.[5]

KVA Cotentin (*709. I.D.*) comprised three *KVG's*. The east coast of the peninsula was known as *KVG Cotentin-Ost*. It was organised into *KVU St. Vaast* in the south and *KVU Barfleur*, which covered the northeast corner of the peninsula. To its left was *KVG Cherbourg*, which was responsible for *Verteidigungsbereich Cherbourg*; it consisted of two sub-groups, although only one of these covered the coast: *KVU Cherbourg*-See (sea). The group's other sub-group was *KVU Cherbourg-Land*, the *Landfront*. Responsible for the west coast of the peninsula was *KVG Périers*; this stretched all the way to the southern boundary of the corps but was organised into just two sub-groups. The Jobourg Peninsula and the beaches in the Vauville Bight were part of *KVU Jobourg*, while the rest of the coast belonged to *KVU Cotentin-West*.

Despite several minor changes, this organisation of the *LXXXIV. A.K.* lasted until **October 1943**.[6] At that time, the *709. I.D.* took over the southern portion of the east coast of the Cotentin from the *716. I.D.* This change extended the boundary of the *709. I.D.* to the Carentan Canal and pushed back the western boundary of *KVU Vire* (and with it that of the *KVG* and *KVA*);[7] it also meant that *KVA Cotentin* increased in size. Another battalion was moved in to occupy the new right wing, leading to the establishment of a third sub-group in *KVG Cotentin-Ost*: *KVU Marcouf*.[8]

About this time, it was planned to add an Eastern battalion to both *KVU Bessin* and *KVG Caen*, which would have enabled the existing battalion sectors (*KVU's*) to be reduced in size.[9] This change, however, would not take place until **February 1944**, and there were no additional alterations in the organisation for the remainder of **1943**.[10]

Changes Before the Invasion

Reinforcements and reorganisation in **1944** led to many noteworthy changes in the coastal defence sectors affecting both the Calvados and Manche. In the former sector, *Ost-Btl. 642* and *439* were moved up to reinforce the coast in **February**, adding a third battalion to both *KVG Bayeux* and *KVG Caen*. The left wing of the latter sector was taken over by *Ost-Btl. 642* as *KVU Meuvaines*. In *KVG Bayeux*, a *KVU Percée* was positioned between *KVU Vire* (taken over by *Ost-Btl. 439*) and *KVU Bessin*.[11] On the Cotentin, *Georg.Inf.Btl. 795* took over *KVU Jobourg*, while *KVU Vauville* was established for the *III./739* to its south.[12]

In **March**, the corps sector was changed significantly. The left boundary (with the *LXXIV. A.K.*) would be moved south to run from Pontorson to the bight 3 km west of the mouth of the Canal du Couesnon. This shifted *KVG Granville* to *LXXXIV. A.K.*, where it would join *KVA "J"*. In turn, that sector would be split into *KVA "J1"* (*709. I.D.*) and *KVA "J2"* (*Gren.Rgt. zbV 752*) as the left wing of the corps. The boundary between the two *KVA's* was formed by the line St. Sauveur-le-Vicomte (J1), Barneville (J1) and Cap de Carteret (J1).[13] This meant that almost the entire coastline of the Cotentin Peninsula became part of the new *KVA "J1"*. Here, the sector of the *709. I.D.* along the west coast became *KVG Bricquebec* and consisted of *KVU Jobourg* and *KVU Les Pieux*.[14] The latter apparently replaced *KVU Vauville*.

The changes also signified that the old *KVG Périers* was split up. The northern part became *KVG Bricquebec*, while the southern part joined *"J2"*, which was also known as *KVA Coutances*. Although regimental sectors were typically known as *KVG's*, this did not apply in this case, since a separate regiment was in charge of the *KVA*. The sector was further subdivided into *KVG Lessay* and *KVG Granville*, which were, in fact, battalion sectors.[15] The *LXXXIV. A.K.* assumed command over its new left wing on **2 April**.[16]

In the Calvados, *KVA "H"* also underwent some important changes in the spring of **1944**. In **April**, *KVG Caen* and *KVG Bayeux* were renamed *KVA "H1"* and *KVA "H2"*, respectively.[17] This was a logical initiative, as the *352. I.D.* had already assumed command of *KVG Bayeux* in **March**.[18] The new *KVA "H1"* was subdivided into *KVG Riva Bella* and *KVG Courseulles*. Each of these included two sub-groups; *KVU Orne* and *KVU Luc* (apparently recently established) were part of the former, while *KVU Seulles* and *KVU Meuvaines* belonged to the latter.[19] No new designations have been found for the (sub)sectors of *KVA "H2"*.

The situation on the Cotentin changed significantly when the *243. I.D.* took control of the west coast in **May**. As a result, *KVA "J1"* was held by two divisions (rather than one) at the time of the invasion. It also meant that *KVG Bricquebec* was occupied by quite a few battalions, but it does not appear their sectors received official designations prior to D-Day.[20] To the south, the situation in *KVA "J2"* changed little before the invasion, as the sector remained defended by little more than an ad hoc regiment. As a result, on **6 June 1944**, both the overstrength *KVA "J1"* and the understrength *"J2"* were peculiar anomalies among the German coastal defences.

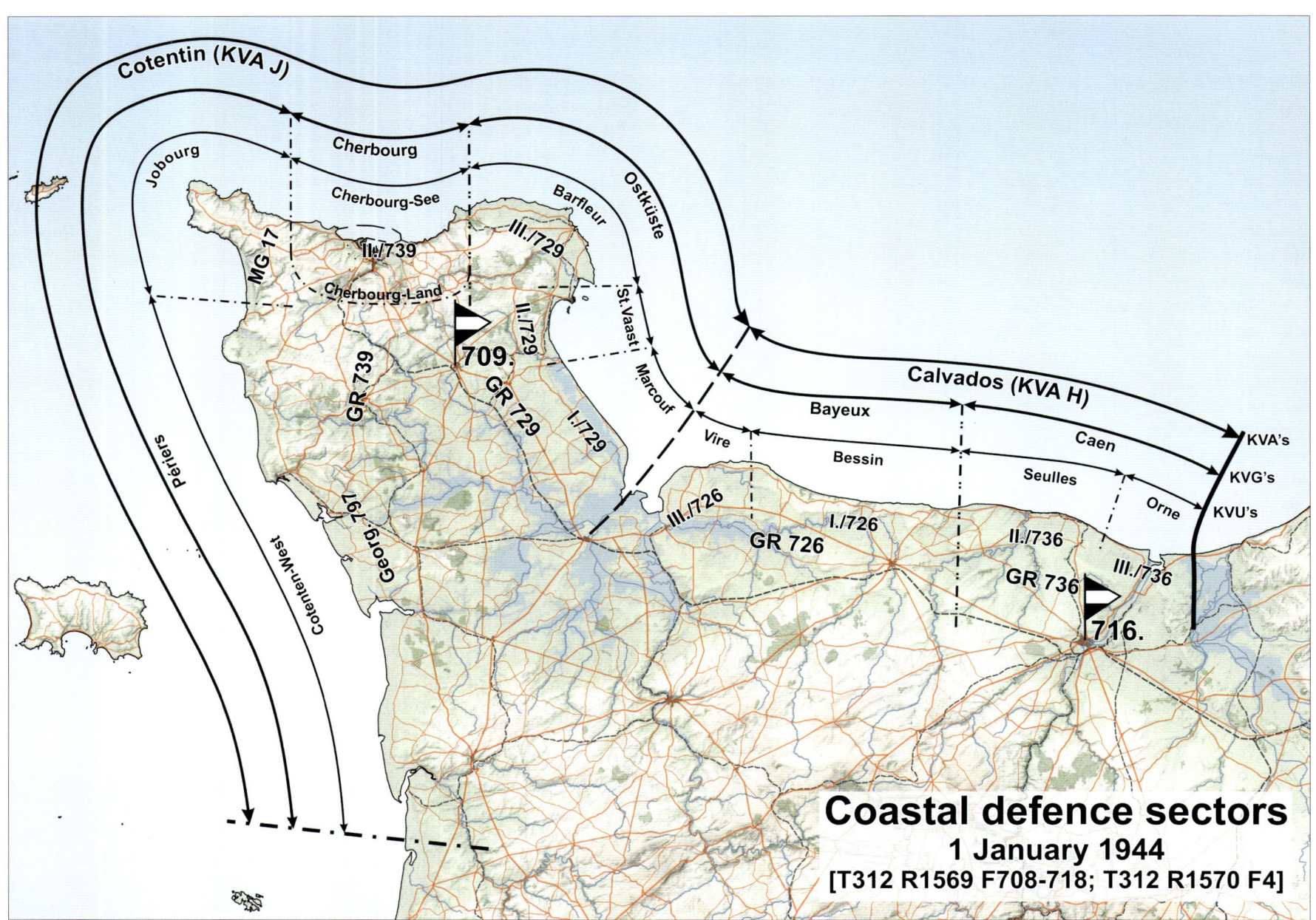

Until early 1944, the organisation of the coastal defence sectors was almost textbook. The main exception was Defence Sector Cherbourg which was a KVG of its own. With just two divisions defending the coast, it was relatively straighforward to divide the regiments and battalions while keeping reserves inland.

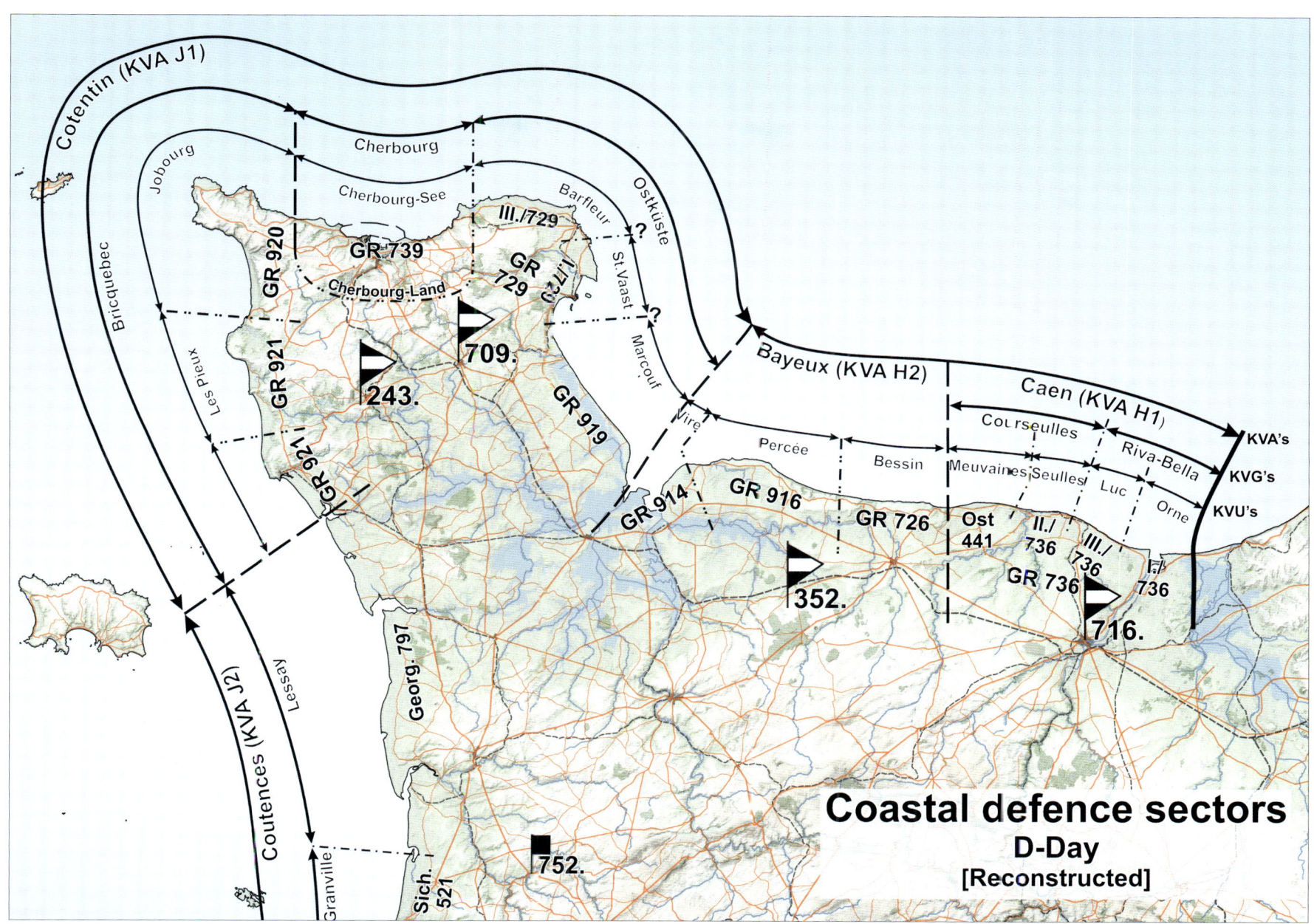

Up to D-Day, the transfer of additional forces to the coast, made the defense sectors in Normandy increasingly complex. Many KVU's became regimental sectors. A lack of reports makes it difficult to establish where exactly boundaries were established and if new (sub)sectors were created.

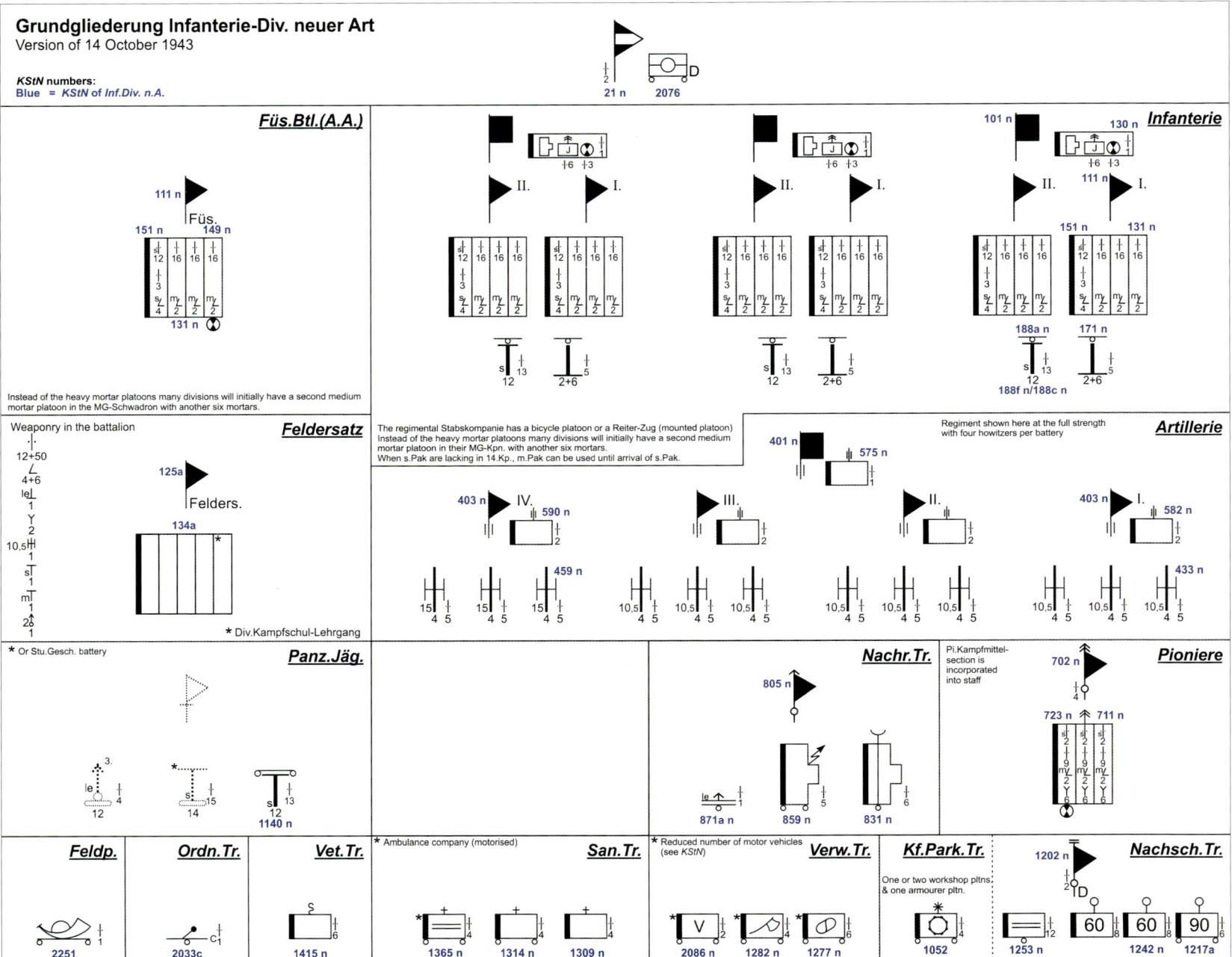

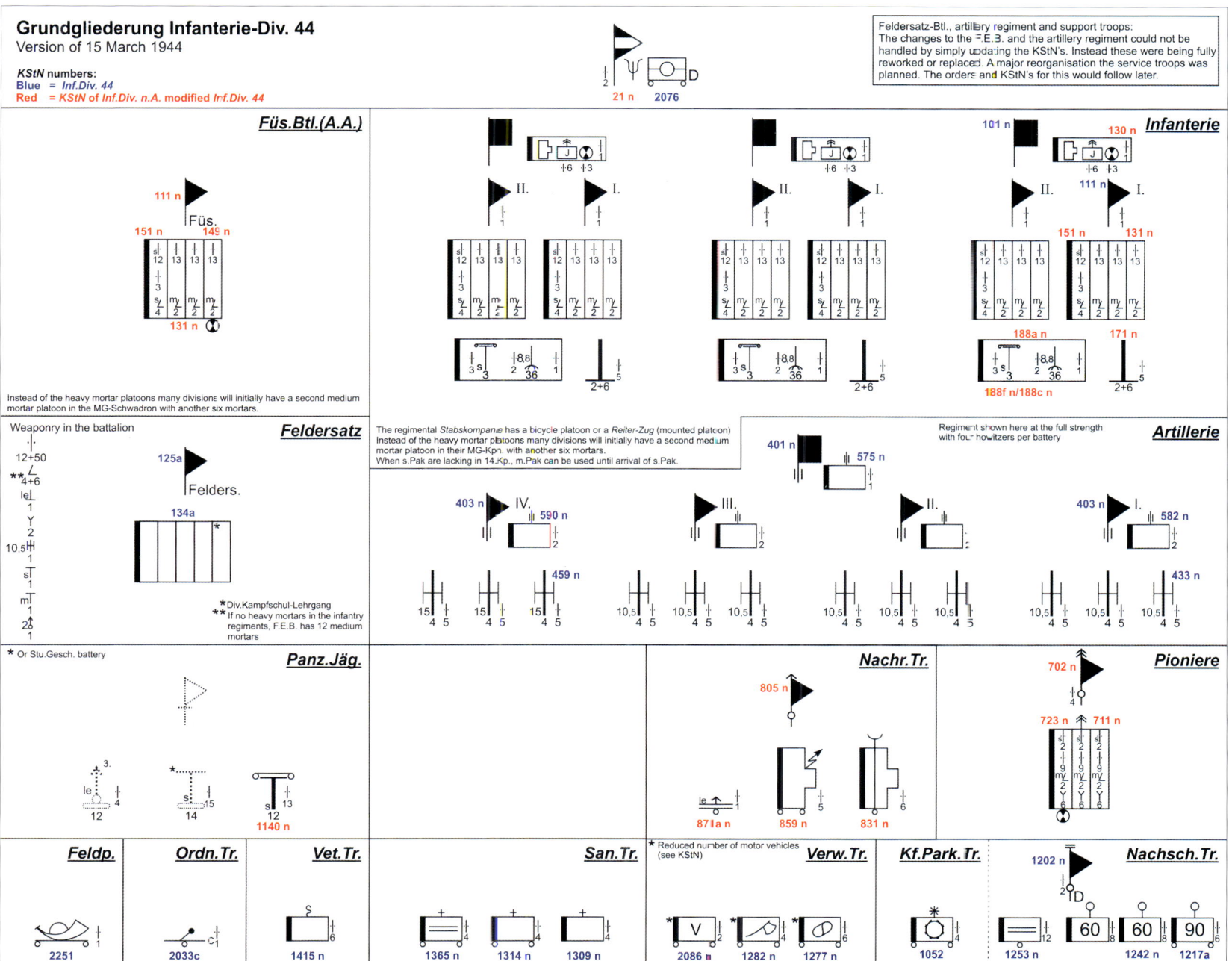

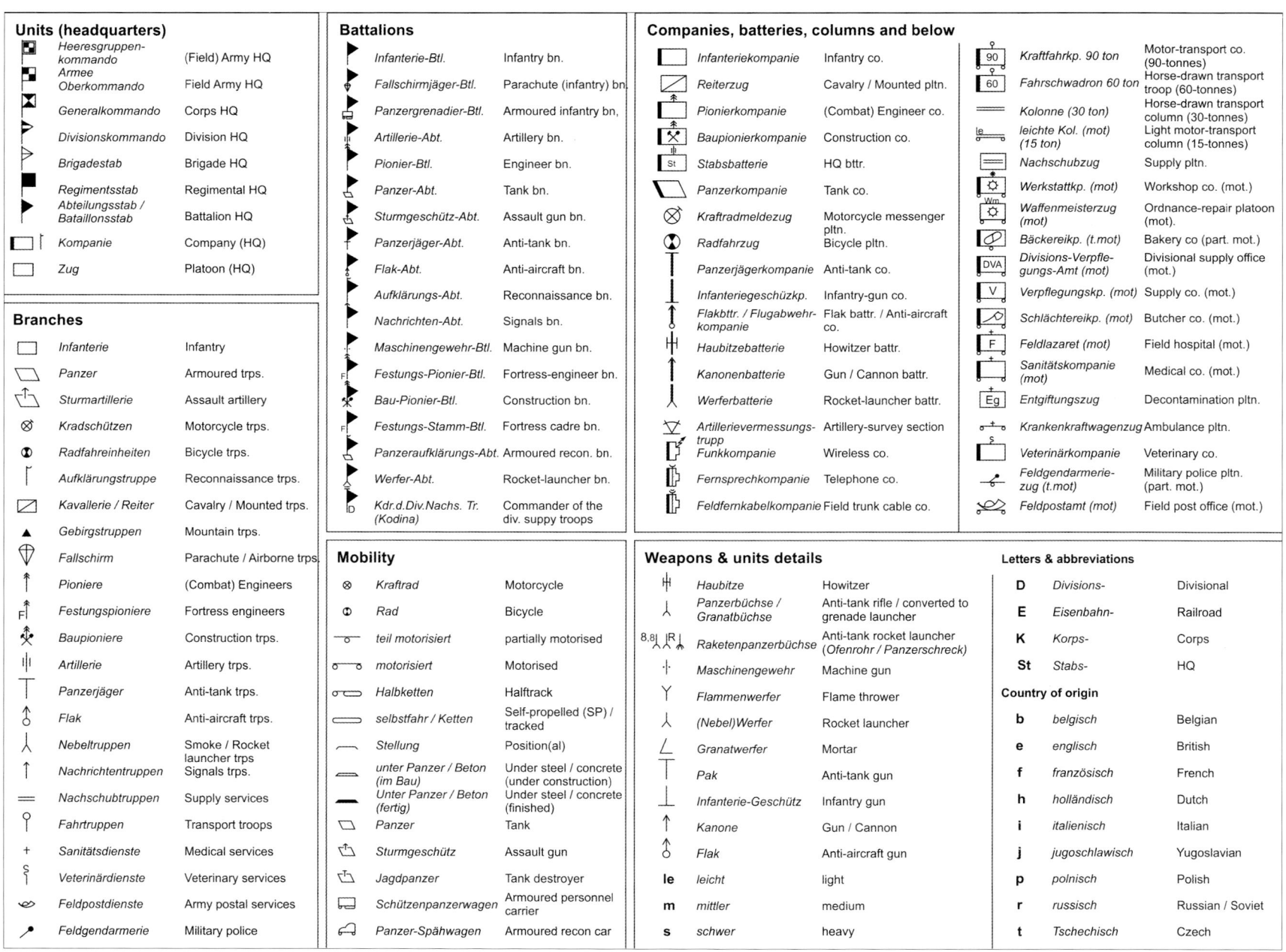

Comparative Table of Ranks

Heer	Waffen-SS	US Equivalent	UK Equivalent
Enlisted men			
*Soldat**	*Mann; Schütze*	Private	Private
*Obersoldat**	*Oberschütze*	Private First Class	Senior Private
Gefreiter	*Sturmmann*	Acting Corporal	Lance Corporal
Obergefreiter	*Rottenführer*	Corporal	Lance Corporal
Stabsgefreiter	-	Administrative Corporal	Lance Corporal
NCOs			
Unteroffizier	*Unterscharführer*	Sergeant	Corporal
Unterfeldwebel; Unterwachtmeister	*Scharführer*	Staff Sergeant	Sergeant
Feldwebel; Wachtmeister	*Oberscharführer*	Technical Sergeant	Staff Sergeant
Oberfeldwebel; Oberwachtmeister	*Hauptscharführer*	Master Sergeant	Sergeant Major
Stabsfeldwebel; Stabswachtmeister	*Sturmscharführer*	Sergeant Major	Regimental Sergeant Major
Officers			
Leutnant; Assistentsarzt; Veterinär	*Untersturmführer*	Second Lieutenant	Second Lieutenant
Oberleutnant; Oberarzt; Oberveterinär	*Obersturmführer*	First Lieutenant	Lieutenant
Hauptmann; Rittmeister; Stabsarzt; Stabsveterinär	*Hauptsturmführer*	Captain	Captain
Major; Oberstabsarzt; Oberstabsveterinär	*Sturmbannführer*	Major	Major
Oberstleutnant; Oberfeldarzt; Oberfeldveterinär	*Obersturmbannführer*	Lieutenant Colonel	Lieutenant Colonel
Oberst; Oberstarzt; Oberstveterinär	*Standartenführer*	Colonel	Colonel
-	*Oberführer*	-	Brigadier
Generalmajor	*Brigadeführer*	Brigadier General	-
Generalleutnant	*Gruppenführer*	Major General	Major-General
General (der Infanterie; der Artillerie; der Kavallerie; der Panzertruppen; der Pioniere)	*Obergruppenführer*	Lieutenant General	Lieutenant-General
Generaloberst	*Oberst-Gruppenführer*	General	General
Generalfeldmarschall	*Reichsführer-SS*	General of the Army	Field Marshal

*The basic private rank carried different names in the branches, e.g.: Infantry: *Schütze, Grenadier, Füsilier*; Engineers: *Pionier*; Cavalry: *Reiter*. Artillery: *Kanonnier*; Signal: *Funker* (wireless operator), *Fernsprecher* (telephonist); Anti-tank: *Panzerjäger*; Military-Police: *Feldgendarm*; Transport & logistics: *Fahrer*.
Specific ranks combine the role and branch, e.g.: Armoured Infantry: *Panzergrenadier*; Motorcycle: *Kradschütze*.

Terminology and Abbrevations

A

A.A.: *Artillerie-Abteilung*: Artillery battalion; *Aufklärungs-Abteilung*: Reconnaissance battalion
AB: Airborne (division)
Abt.: *Abteilung*: Battalion. Term used with artillery, (anti) tank and signals units. Can also refer to a detachment, when referring to training and replacement elements.
AD: Armored Division (US)
A.K.: *Armee-Korps*: Army corps
angegliedert: Semi-permanent attachment of a unit/formation to a larger formation it has no organic organisational ties with
AOK: *Armee-Oberkommando*: Field army headquarters
A.R. (AR): *Artillerie Regiment*: Artillery regiment
Arfü: *Artillerie-Führer*: Headquarters in overall control of all artillery in a sector, typically at division level
ARKO: *Artillerie-Kommandeur*: Headquarters in overall control of all artillery in a sector, typically above division level
Armee-Oberkommando: Field army headquarters
Art., *Artillerie*: Artillery
Arzt: Doctor, medical officer
Auf dem Kommandowege: Creation of a new element in the field (e.g. raised through "command channels")
Aufkl., *Aufklärung*: Reconnaissance
Ausb., *Ausbildung*: Training (e.g., *Pz.Ers.u.Ausb.Abt. 100*)
A.V.T.: *Artillerie-Vermessungstrupp*: Artillery survey section

B

(b), *belgisch*: Belgian
Bäck., *Bäckerei*: Bakery
Bataillon: Battalion. Term used with infantry and engineer formations
Batterie: Battery
Bau(truppen): Construction (troops)
Beamte: Civilian official in the military
Befehlshaber: Commander (general officer commanding above corps level)
Befh.: *Befehlshaber*
beh.: *behelfsmäßig*: Makeshift; ad hoc, field expedient
Beob.: *Beobachtung*: Observation (e.g., *Beobachtungs-Abteilung*)
(bew.): *beweglich*: Mobilised using means from the enhance mobility efforts (*Beweglichmachung*)
Beweglichmachung: Increasing the mobility of units over their TO/E authorisations
Bn: Battalion
bo.: *bodenständig*: Static, as in belonging to a sector. Not to be confused with immobile
Brig.: *Brigade*: Brigade
Brif.: *Brigadeführer*
Brigadeführer: A general officer; see "Comparative Table of Ranks"
Btl. (Btle.): *Bataillon(e)*; Battalion(s)
Bttr.: *Batterie*: Battery

C

Chef H. Rüst u. BdE, *Chef Heeresrüstung und Befehlshaber des Ersatzheeres*: Chief of Army Armaments and Commander-in-Chief of the Replacement Army
Closed formation: *geschlossen*: Commitment of a unit as a whole; in its entirety (not split up)
Co.: Company
CP: Command Post

D

Div.: *Division*: Division
d.R.: *der Reserve*: Used to indicate reserve officers (e.g.: *Maj.d.R.*)
DVL: *Deutsche Volksliste*: System to classify people in occupied territories based on their German descent

E

(E): *Eisenbahn*: Railway
(e): *englisch*: British
E.: *Ersatz*: Replacement
Eingegliedert: Officially incorporated into a larger formation. (e.g., *Ost-Btl. 649* was *eingegliedert* in *GR 729*)
Ers.: *Ersatz*: Replacement (e.g., *Pz.Ers.u.Ausb.Abt. 100*)

F

(f): *französisch*: French
FA: Field Artillery (Battalion)
Fallschirmjäger: Paratroop(er)
Faustpatrone: Single-shot handheld anti-tank weapon (superseded by the *Panzerfaust*)
F.E.B.: *Feldersatz-Bataillon*: Field Replacement Battalion
Feld: Field
Feldg(end).: *Feldgendarmerie*: Military Police
feldmässig: Field type (e.g., field-type fortifications)
Feldw., Feldwebel, Fldw.: A senior NCO; see "Comparative Table of Ranks"

Fernsprech: Telephone
Fest.: *Festung*: Fortress
F.H.: *Feldhaubitze*: Field howitzer
Fhr.: *Führer*: Leader or acting commander (e.g., *Zug-Führer*)
Fj.: *Fallschirmjäger*
FJR: *Fallschirmjäger-Regiment*
F.K.: *Feldkanone*: Field gun
Fla: *Flieger-Abwehr*: Anti-aircraft defence
Flak: *Flieger-* or *Flug-Abwehr-Kanone*: Anti-aircraft gun
FpA: *Feldpostamt*: Army Post Office
FpN: *Feldpostnummer*: Field Post Number
Fs.: *Fallschirm*: Parachute
Fu.: *Funk*: wireless
Führerreserve: Officer manpower reserve
Funk: Wireless
Füs.: *Füsilier*: Type of infantryman or unit (generally referring to light infantry)

G

Geb., Gebirgs-: Mountain (e.g., *Gebirgsgeschütz*)
Gef.Std.: *Gefechtsstand*: Headquarters of a combat formation/staff
Gefr.: *Gefreiter*: A senior enlisted soldier; *see* "Comparative Table of Ranks"
Gen.: *General*: A general officer; *see* "Comparative Table of Ranks"
Gen.Kdo.: *Generalkommando*: Corps headquarters
Gen.Lt.: *Generalleutnant*: A general officer; *see* "Comparative Table of Ranks"
Gen.Maj.: *Generalmajor*: A general officer; *see* "Comparative Table of Ranks"
Gen St.d.H.: *Generalstab des Heeres*: General Staff of the Army
gep.: *gepanzert*: armoured
GIR: Glider Infantry Regiment
Gliederung: (graphic representation of the) Order of Battle, organisation of units
GR: *Grenadier-Regiment*
Gren.: *Grenadier*: Infantry; infantryman (in general); *see also* "Comparative Table of Ranks"
groß: Large
Grundgliederung: Standard organisation (Order of Battle) of a specific type of formation (e.g., *Infanterie-Division 44*)
Gruppe: Group, section, squad
g.v.F.: *garnisonverwendungsfähig Feld*: Personnel suitable for garrison duty in the field
g.v.H.: *Heimat*: Personnel suitable for garrison duty in the homefront
Gruf.: *Gruppenführer*
Gruppenführer: A general officer; *see* "Comparative Table of Ranks"

H

(h): *hollandisch*: Dutch

Hafthohlladung: Magnetic anti-tank grenade
Hau., Haub.: *Haubitze*: Howitzer
Hauptkampffeld: Main Combat Area
Hauptkampflinie: Main Line of Resistance (MLR)
Hauptmann: A company-grade officer; *see* "Comparative Table of Ranks"
Hauptsturmführer: A company-grade officer; *see* "Comparative Table of Ranks"
Heer: Army (as a branch of service)
Heeresgruppe: (Field) Army Group
H.Gr.: *Heeresgruppe*
Hiwi: *Hilfswiliger*: Voluntary non-German personnel in military support service
H.K.A.A. *Heeres-Küsten-Artillerie-Abteilung*: Army Coastal Artillery Battalion
H.K.A.R.: *Heeres-Küsten-Artillerie-Regiment*: Army Coastal Artillery Regiment
H.K.B.: *Heeres-Küsten-Batterie*: Army Coastal Artillery Battery
H.Kdo.: *Höheres Kommando*: Corps headquarters (generally with assigned or attached elements)
HKF: *Hauptkampffeld*
HKL: *Hauptkampflinie*
Hptm.: *Hauptmann*
HQ: Headquarters
Hstuf.: *Hauptsturmführer*

I

(i): *italienisch*: Italian
Ia: Chief of Operations (division or above)
Ib: Supply (Logistics) Officer (division or above)
Ic: Chief Intelligence Officer (division or above)
I.D.: *Infanterie-Division*: Infantry Division
ID: Infantry Division
i.G.: *im Generalstab*: Academy-trained General Staff Officer (e.g.: *Maj.i.G.*)
I.G.: *Infanterie-Geschütz*: Infantry gun
IIa: Officer for personnel matters of officers (division or above)
IIb: Officer for personnel matters of non-commissioned ranks (division or above)
I.K.H.: *Infanterie-Kanone-Haubitze*: Infantry-gun-howitzer
Inf.: *Infanterie*: Infantry
Instandsetzung: Maintenance (repair)
I.R.: *Infanterie-Regiment*: Infantry Regiment (later replaced with *Grenadier-Regiment*)
IR: Infantry Regiment
I-Staffel: *Instandsetzungsstaffel*: Maintenance Section
Ist-Stärke: Actual strength, as opposed to *Soll-Stärke*

J

(j): *jugoslavisch*: Yugoslavian

K

k.: *kurz*: Short
K.: *Kanone*: Cannon
Kampf: Combat
Kampfgruppe: Battlegroup
Kampfmittel-Staffel Section holding combat-related supplies and inventory (including ammunition and demolitions)
Kampfschule: Combat School
Kampfstärke: Combat strength (lit.); trench strength
Kampfzone: Battle zone
Kartenstelle: Mapping detachment
Kdr.: *Kommandeur*: Commander of formations (generally) of battalion through division level
Kdt.: *Kommandant*: Commander of specific entities. Localities such as a *Festung*, camp, road network, etc. Also used for vehicle commanders.
Kettenkrad: *Kettenkraftrad*: Motorcycle halftrack
Kf.: *Kraftfahr*: Motor vehicle (e.g. *Kraftfahrkompanie*)
Kfz.: *Kraftfahrzeug*: Motor vehicle
KG: *Kampfgruppe*
KM: *Kriegsmarine*: Navy
Kodina: *Kommander der Divisions-Nachschubtruppen*: Commander of divisional supply troops
Kompanie: Company
Kopfstärke: "Head-count"; *see Verpflegungsstärke*
Korps: Corps
Kp. (Kpn.): *Kompanie (Kompanien)*
Kps.: *Korps*
Kr.Kw.: *Krankenkraftwagen*: Ambulance
Krad: *Kraftrad*: Motorcycle
Kriegsgliederung: Existing organisation and strength of a formation; actual order of battle
Kriegsmarine: (German) Navy
Kriegstagebuch: War diary (daily logs)
KStN: *Kriegstärkenachweisung*: Table of Organisation and Equipment
KTB: *Kriegstagebuch*
k.v.: *kriegsverwendungsfähig*: Fit for active service
KVA: *Küstenverteidigungsabschnitt*: Coastal Defence Sector (usually defended by a single division)
KVG: *Küstenverteidigungsgruppe*: Coastal Defence Group (level below *KVA*)
KVU: *Küstenverteidigungsuntergruppe*: Coastal Defence Sub-group (level below *KVG*)
Kw.K.: *Kampfwagenkanone*: Main gun of an armoured vehicle

L

L: *Luftwaffe*
l.: *leichte*: Light; *lang*: Long
LAG: *Landesabwehrgeschütz*: Anti (sea) landing gun
landeseigen: Native
Lds.: *Landes*: Regional (e.g., *Landes-Bau-Pi.Btl.*)
le.: *Leichte*: Light
Lehr: Training, doctrine
Leutnant: A company-grade officer; *see* "Comparative Table of Ranks"
LL: *Luftlande*
Lt.: *Leutnant*
Luftlande: Airlanding (e.g., *91. Luftlande-Division*)
Luftwaffe: (German) Air Force
LW: *Luftwaffe*

M

M: *Marine*
m.: *mittler*: Medium
M.A.A.: *Marine-Artillerie-Abteilung*: Naval artillery battalion
m.d.F.b.: *mit der Führung beauftragt*: Temporarily placed in command, acting commander
M.K.B.: *Marine-Küsten-Batterie*: Navy coastal battery
MLR: Main Line of Resistance
Maj.: *Major*: A field-grade officer; *see* "Comparative Table of Ranks"
Marine: (German) Navy; naval
Melder: Messenger
MG: *Maschinen-Gewehr*: Machine gun
mittler: Medium
mot: *motorisiert*: Motorised
motZ: *motorisierter Zug*: Drawn by motor vehicle
MP: *Maschinenpistol*: Machine-pistol or sub-machine gun
MTW: *Mannschafttransportwagen*: Troop (personnel) carrier

N

nA: *neuer Art*: New style, type
Nachr.: *Nachrichten*: Signal's communications
Nachs.: *Nachschub*: Supply, logisitcs (broadest sense)
Nord: North

O

(o): *ortsfest*: Fixed, stationary, immobile
Ob.: *Oberbefehlshaber*: Commander-in-Chief; term used for field army commanders and up
Oberf: *Oberführer*

Oberführer: A general officer; *see* "Comparative Table of Ranks"
Obergruppenführer: A field-grade officer; *see* "Comparative Table of Ranks"
Oberleutnant: A company-grade officer; *see* "Comparative Table of Ranks"
Oberst: A field-grade officer; *see* "Comparative Table of Ranks"
Oberstgruf.: *Oberstgruppenführer*
Oberstgruppenführer: A general officer; *see* "Comparative Table of Ranks"
Oberstleutnant: A field-grade officer; *see* "Comparative Table of Ranks"
Obersturmbannführer: A field-grade officer; *see* "Comparative Table of Ranks"
Obersturmführer: A field-grade officer; *see* "Comparative Table of Ranks"
Obkdo.: *Oberkommando*: High Command (e.g. *AOK*, *OKH* and *OKW*)
Oblt.: *Oberleutnant*; Company-grade officer; *see* "Comparative Table of Ranks"
Obst.: *Oberst*
Obstlt.: *Oberstleutnant*
Ogruf.: *Obergruppenführer*
Ofenrohr: aka *Panzerschreck*: German type "bazooka"
Offz.: *Offizier*: officer
OKH: *Oberkommando des Heeres*: Army High Command
OKW: *Oberkommando der Wehrmacht*: High Command of the Armed Forces
O.Qu.: *Oberquartiermeister*: General staff officer in charge of supply and administration
Ord.Offz., (Ord.O.; O.O.): *Ordonnanzoffizier*: Special missions officer; officer assistant
Ost: East
Ost-Bataillon: Battalion formed using Slavic personnel from the Soviet Union
Osttruppen: Collective term for non-German units and personnel from the Soviet Union (excluding *Hiwi's*)
Ostubaf.: *Obersturmbannfuhrer*
Ostuf.: *Obersturmführer*
OT: *Organisation Todt*
Otrag: *Organisation Todt Transportgruppe*

P

(p): *polnisch*: Polish
Pak: *Panzer-Abwehr-Kanone*: Anti-tank (AT) gun
Panzer: Tank; armour(ed)
Panzerfaust: Single-shot handheld anti-tank weapon
Panzerjäger: Anti-tank, term used for vehicles, units or soldiers
Panzerkampfwagen: Tank
Panzerschreck: aka *Ofenrohr*: German type "bazooka"
Panzer(späh)wagen: Armoured (reconnaissance/scout) car
Panzerzerstörer: Tank-destroyer, term used for units equipped with anti-tank rocket launchers
P.E., Personnal-Einheit: Unit with personnel only (no equipment)
PGR: *Panzer-Grenadier-Regiment*
Pi.: *Pionier*: engineer

PIR: Parachute Infantry Regiment
POL: Petroleum, oil, lubricants
Pz.: *Panzer*
Pz.Gren.: *Panzer-Grenadier*: Armoured (mechanised) infantry
Pz.Kpfw.: *Panzerkampfwagen*
Pz.Jg., Pz.: *Panzerjäger*: Anti-tank vehicle, unit or soldier

Q

Quartiermeister: Quartermaster

R

(r): *russisch*: Russian (actually meaning from the USSR)
Rad: Bicycle
Radf., Radfahr-: Cyclist; bicycle-
Res., Reserve: Reserve
Reiter-: Mounted, cavalry (e.g., *Reiterzug*)
Riegelstellung: (Secondary) blocking position/line to prevent a breakthrough
Rgt.: *Regiment*: regiment
RSO: *Raupenschlepper Ost*: Fully tracked light truck / prime mover

S

s.: *schwer*: Heavy
San., Sanitäts: Medical
Schießbecher: Rifle grenade launcher
Schlächt., Schlächterei: Butcher
Schlepper: Tractor (prime mover)
Schn., Schnelle: Fast (e.g., *Schnelle-Brigade*)
Schule: School
Schw., Schwadron: Company equivalent. Squadron (UK), Troop (US)
Sd.Fhr.: *Sonderführer*: Civilian specialist in a military role (translator, propaganda, etc.)
Sd.Kfz.: *Sonderkraftfahrzeug*
Selbstfahr(lafette): Self-propelled (gun carriage)
Sich., Sicherungs: Security (e.g., *Sicherungs-Rgt.*)
Sollgliederung: Theoretical (authorized) organisation of a formation
Soll-Stärke: Authorised strength, as opposed to *Ist-Stärke*
Sonderkraftfahrzeug: Special-purpose motor vehicle
Sonderstab: Special purpose staff
SP: Self-propelled
SPW: *Schützenpanzerwagen*: armoured halftrack for infantry
St., Stab: Staff
Staf.: *Standartenführer*:

Standartenführer: A field-grade officer; *see* "Comparative Table of Ranks"
Staffel: Section
ständig: Permanent (e.g., permanent fortifications)
St.P.: *Stützpunkt*: organised tactical locality, strong point. Term also used for resistance nests stronger than the *Widerstandsnest* (*Wn.*)
Stubaf.: *Sturmbannführer*
StuG., Stu.Gesch.: *Sturmgeschütz*
StuH., Stu.Haub.: *Sturmhaubitze*
Stu.K.: *Sturmkanone*: Main gun on an assault gun
Sturmbannführer: A field-grade officer; *see* "Comparative Table of Ranks"
Sturmgeschütz: Assault gun unit or vehicle
Sturmhaubitze: Assault gun armed with a howitzer
Süd: South

T

(t): *tschechisch*: Czech
(tmot): *teil motorisiert*: Partially motorised
Torn., Tornister: Backpack, term used for portable-wireless
Tr., Trupp: section, detachment
Tr.Üb.Pl.: *Truppenübungsplatz*: Troop training area/facility/camp
Troß(e): Trains, as in supply/baggage trains of a unit
Trupp: Section, team, squad
Truppen: Troops, forces
Turk-Bataillon: Type of battalion formed using Turcic personnel from the Soviet Union

U

U: *Unter*: Sub (e.g. *UKG, Unterkampfgruppe*)
u., und: and
Uffz., Unteroffizier: NCO or specific rank; *see* "Comparative Table of Ranks"
Untersturmbannführer: A field- grade officer; *see* "Comparative Table of Ranks"
Ustuf.: See *Untersturmführer*
Untersturmführer: A company grade officer; *see* "Comparative Table of Ranks"

V

(v): *verlegefähig*: Moveable, transportable
v.B.: *vordere Beobachter*: Forward observer
V.B.: *Verteidigungsbereich*
Verb.Kdo.: *Verbindungskommando*: Liaison section/ detail
Verpfl., Verpflegung: Supplies (of food)
Verpflegungsstärke: Rations strength
vers.: *Verstärkt*: Reinforced

Verteidigungsbereich: Defence sector (e.g., *V.B. Cherbourg*)
Verwaltungs-: Administrative
Vet., Veterinär: Veterinary-; veterinarian
V-weapons: *Vergeltungswaffen*: Reprisal weapons (*V1, V2*)

W

Wachtm.: *Wachtmeister*: Artillery rank equivalent to *Feldwebel*
Waffenmeisterei: Armoury, ordnance shop
Wehrkreis: Military district
Wehrmacht: German Armed Forces
Welle: Mobilisation wave (group of divisions formed around the same time with a similar organisation)
Werkstatt: Workshop
W.F.St.: *Wehrmachtführungsstab*: Armed Forces Operations Staff
wirtschaftlich: administrative
Wn.: *Wiederstandsnest*: Resistance nest

Z

Z.: *Zug*
z.b.V., zbV: *zur besondere Verwendung*: Special purpose
Zgkw.: *Zugkraftwagen*
Zug: Platoon; train (rail)
Zugkraftwagen: Prime mover, halftrack carrier
Zustandsbericht: Status report of a unit

Bibliography

Materials referenced for this book include, but are not limited to, the following publications and records. Nearly all of these have provided valuable information, but a few of the books have only been used to illustrate historiography.

Archives

Bundesarchiv, Militärarchiv (BaMa)
RH 2/1108; RH 10/20; RH 10/248; RH 12-21/60; RH 19-IV/18; RH 19-IX/2; RH 19-IX/3; RH 20-7/138K.

The Central Archives of the Ministry of Defence of the Russian Federation (CAMO)
Captured documents, Bestand 500
OKW: Findbuch 12450, Akte 115.
OKH: Findbuch 12451, Akte 142 & 418.
Heeresgruppe D: Findbuch 12465, Akte 19 & 44.

The National Archives (UKNA)
HW 5/466, 468, 474, 479, 487, 494, 495, 498-501, 503-512, 514, 515, 519-522, 524-526, 529, 530, 531, 536, 538-540, 544, 546-567, 574, 587.
WO 171/131.
WO 208/3590, 3591, 3622, 3630-3635, 3640, 3645-3647, 4138, 4139, 4154, 4164, 4363, 4367.
WO 219/5229.

National Archives and Records Administration (NARA)
RG 165, Box 659, 660, 661.
RG 242.
RG 407, Box 1396, 3282, 3498.

Microfilm Rolls
OKW: T77 R1421.
OKH: T78 R11, 269, 298, 311, 314, 391-393, 297-399, 401, 404-410, 412, 418-421, 431-432, 526-528, 531, 533, 622, 649, 672, 708-709, 763, 848-851, 885, 887-888, 890-893, 895, 897, 908, 911-913, 917, 937.
Army Groups: T311 R1, 3-4, 16, 20, 24-25, 29.
Armies: T312 R519, 1553, 1558-1559, 1562-1571.
Panzer Armies: T313 R420.
Corps: T314 R742-3, 745-747, 1568, 1603-1604.
Rear Areas: T501 R26, 157, 218.

Articles, Papers, Reports and Theses

Historical Section (G.S.), Army Headquarters (1951), *Report No. 41, The German Defences in the Courseulles St. Auvin Area of the Normandy Coast - Information from German sources* [Available at www.canada.ca/content/dam/themes/defence/caf/militaryhistory/dhh/reports/ahq-reports/ahq041.pdf]

History Section, United States Army, European Theater of Operations (ETO), *Regimental Unit Study Number 3, 506 Parachute Infantry Regiment in Normandy Drop*

O.S.S., Research and Analysis Branch (1945), *Nationality and Age of German Armed Forces Prisoners Captured in Northern France, June to August 1944 (R & A No. 2581.1)*

Books

Ambrose, S.E. (1994), *D-Day - June 6, 1944: The Climactic Battle of World War II*, New York (NY): Simon & Schuster

Andorfer, V., et al (2000), *Nuts & Bolts Vol. 17, Marder III, Part I: Ausführung M*, Nuts & Bolts

Archer L. & Auerbach, W. (2014), *Panzerwrecks 17: Normandy 2*, Heathfield: Panzerwrecks

Balkoski, J. (2006), *Utah Beach: The Amphibious Landing and Airborne Operations on D-Day*, Mechanicsburg, PA: Stackpole Books

Bando, M. (2007), *101st Airborne - The Screaming Eagles in World War II*, St.Paul, MN: Zenith Press

Baret, J. (2014), *Une Tombe en Normandie - Vie et Mort du Sergent Adolph Greter*, Valognes: Imprimerie ICL

Blumenson, M. (1961, 1993 reprint), *Breakout and Pursuit*, Washington D.C.: Center of Military History, United States Army

Caddick-Adams, P. (2019), *Sand & Steel - A new history of D-Day*, London: Arrow Books

Carell, P. (1960, revised edition 1994, reprint 1997), *Sie Kommen! Die Invasion 1944*, Berlin: Ullstein Buchverlage GmbH

Chazette, A. (2012), *Atlantikwall Utah Beach - de la baie des Veys à Quinéville*, Vertou: Editions Histoire & Fortifications

Crookenden, N. (1976), *Dropzone Normandy - The Story of the American and British Airborne Assault on D Day 1944*, New York: Charles Scribner's Sons

DeTrez, M. (2004), *Sainte-Mere-Eglise - Photographs of D-Day*, D-Day Publishing

D'Este, C. (1983, reprint 2001), *Decision in Normandy*, London: Penguin books

Griesser, V. (2007), *Die Löwen von Carentan, Das Fallschirmjäger Regiment 6 1943-45*, Herne: VS-Books

Hubatsch, W. (reprint 2005a), *Kriegstagebuch des Oberkommandos der Wehrmacht (Wehrmachtführungsstab), Band II: 1. Januar 1942-31. Dezember 1942*, Augsburg: Verlagsgruppe Weltbild GmbH

Hubatsch, W. (reprint 2005b), *Kriegstagebuch des Oberkommandos der Wehrmacht (Wehrmachtführungsstab), Band III: 1. Januar 1943-31. Dezember 1943*, Augsburg: Verlagsgruppe Weltbild GmbH

Harrison, G.A. (1951, reprint 1984), *Cross-Channel Attack*, Washington D.C.: Office of the Chief of Military History United States Army

Havers, R.P.W. (2004), *Battle for Cherbourg*, Stroud: Sutton Publishing

Hayn, F. (1954), *Die Invasion - Von Cotentin bis Falaise*, Heidelberg: Scharnhorst Buchkameradschaft der Soldaten

Historical Division, War Dept. (1945), *Omaha Beachhead (6 June-13 June 1944)*, Washington D.C.: US Government Printing Office

Historical Division, War Dept. (1948), *Utah Beach to Cherbourg (6-27 June 1944)*, Washington D.C.: US Government Printing Office

Lefèvre, E. (1983, reprint 1999), *Panzers in Normandy then and Now*, London: Battle of Britain International Ltd.

Leleu, J.L. (1999), *10.SS-Panzer-Division „Frundsberg,"* Bayeux: Editions Heimdal

Leleu, J.L. (2022), *Combattre en Dictature, 1944 – La Wehrmacht Face au Débarquement*, Paris: Perrin

Meyer, H. (1982), *Kriegsgeschichte der 12.SS-Panzerdivision „Hitlerjugend", Band I*, Osnabrück: Munin Verlag GmbH

Morgan, M.K.A. (2004), *Down to Earth: The 507th Parachute Infantry Regiment in Normandy*, Atglen, PA: Schiffer Publishing

Müller, P. & W. Zimmermann, (2007), *Sturmgeschütz III, Rückgrat der Infanterie, Band 1, Geschichte: Entwicklung, Fertigung, Einsatz*, History Facts

Nauroth, H.S. & B. Steinberg (2017), *Die Geschichte der 91.Luftlande-Division - Rekonstruktion eines Großverbändes der Deutschen Wehrmacht*, Hamburg: tredition GmbH

Nordyke, P. (2005), *All American - All the Way*, St.Paul, MN: Zenith Press

Nordyke, P. (2006), *Four Stars of Valor- The Combat History of the 505th Parachute Infantry Regiment in World War II*, St.Paul, MN: Zenith Press

Office of Naval Intelligence (1950), *War Diary - German Naval Staff, Operations Division, Part A, Volume 53, January 1944*, Washington, DC.

Ose, D. (1982), *Entscheidung im Westen 1944, Stuttgart Der Oberbefehlshaber West und die Abwehr der alliierten Invasion*, Stuttgart: Deutsche Verlags-Anstalt

Overmans, R. (1999), *Deutsche militärische Verluste im Zweiten Weltkrieg*, München: Oldenbourg Verlag

Paine, L. (1981), *D-Day*, London: Robert Hale Ltd.

Perrigault, J.C. (2002), *21. Panzer-Division*, Bayeux: Editions Heimdal

Rawson, A. (2004), *Cherbourg - 4th, 9th and 79th Infantry Divisions*, Barnsley: Pen & Sword Military

Rolf, R. (2014), *Atlantikwall - Batteries and Bunkers*, Middelburg: PRAK publishing

Schramm, P.E. (1961), *Kriegstagebuch des Oberkommandos der Wehrmacht (Wehrmachtführungsstab), Band IV: 1.Januar 1944-22. Mai 1945*, Frankfurt am Main: Bernard und Graefe Verlag

Tessin, G (1965-2002), *Verbände und Truppen der deutschen Wehrmacht und Waffen-SS im Zweiten Weltkrieg 1939-1945, 2.-5. Band*, Frankfurt/Main: E.S. Mittler & Sohn, *1. & 6.-17. Band*, Osnabrück: Biblio Verlag

Wind, M. & H. Günther (2004), *Kriegstagebuch 17.SS-Panzer-Grenadier-Division "Götz von Berlichingen" Auswahl von Dokumenten 30. Oktober 1943 bis 6. Mai 1945*, St.Infbert: Dengmerter Heimatverlag

Zaloga, S.J. (2011), *Armored Attack 1944*, Mechanicsburg, PA: Stackpole Books

Zaloga, S.J. (2015), *Cherbourg 1944 - The first Allied victory in Normandy*, Oxford: Osprey Publishing

Zetterling, N. (2000), *Normandy 1944, German Military Organisation, Combat Power and Organisational Effectiveness*, Winnipeg: J.J.Fedorowicz Publishing.

Foreign Military Studies

Blumentritt, G. (1948), MS # D-330 (Engl.), response to questions regarding the artillery around Ste. Marie-du-Mont on D-Day

Choltitz, D. von (1947), MS # B-418 (Germ.), *Kämpfe des LXXXIV. A.K. in der Normandie vom 18.6.144 ab*

Criegern, F. von (1948), MS # B-784 (Germ.), *Teil I, Die Kämpfe des LXXXIV. A.K. in der Normandie von der alliierten Landung bis 17.6.44* and *Teil II, Die Kämpfe des LXXXIV. A.K. in der Normandie vom 30.7.-20.8.44*

Dettling. A. (1946), MS # B-163 (Engl.), *Report on the participation of the 363 Inf Div in the campaign in Northern France*

Elfeldt, O. (1945), MS # A-968 (Engl.), *LXXXIV Inf Corps (28 July-20 August 1944)*

Fahrmbacher, W. (1946), MS # B-371 (Germ.), *Bretagne 6.6.44-10.6.44 und Normandie 12.6.44-25.6.44*

Hausser, P. (1945), MS # A-907 (Germ.), *Seventh Army 29 June-20 August 1944*

Hausser, P. (1946), MS # A-974 (Germ.), *Normandie - 7. Armee vom 29.6.-24.7.1945*

Heydte, F.A. von der (1952), MS # B-839 (Germ.), *Der Einsatz des Fallschirmjäger-regiment 6 in der Normandie*

Keil, G. (1948a), MS # C-018 (Germ.), *Bericht über die Kämpfe des hessisch-thüringischen Grenadier-Regiments 919 unter der Kampfgruppe Keil*

Keil, G. (1948b), MS # B-844, (Germ.), *Bericht zu der Anfrage der Historischen Division über den Einsatz des Inf. Regiments 1058 und der Kampfgruppe Keil*

Keppler, G. (1947), MS # B-623 (Engl.), *Fighting of the I SS-Panzer-Corps in Northern France (from 16 August to 18 October 1944)*

Kogard, R. (1947), MS # B-427 (Engl.), *Brest - 343rd Infantry Division (May-18 September 1944)*

König, E. (1946), MS # B-010 (Germ.), *Kämpfe in der Normandie*

Mahlmann, P. (1946a), MS # A-983 (Germ.), *353.Inf.Division*

Mahlmann, P. (1946b), MS # A-984 (Engl.), *353.Inf.Div. (24 July-10 September 1944), Report of the Commander*

Mahlmann, P. (1946c), MS # A-985 (Engl.), *353.Inf.Div. (11-21 August 1944), Report of the Commander*

Mahlmann, P. (1946d), MS # A-986 (Engl.), *353.Inf.Div. (21 August-7 September 1944), Report of the Commander*

Mahlmann, P. (1946e), MS # A-987 (Engl.), *353.Inf.Div. (8-14 September 1944), Report of the Commander*

Mauer, E. (1946), MS # D-382 (Engl.), *Operations against American Army troops (from 5 June approximately 30 June 1944*

Meindl, E. (1946), MS # A-923, (Engl.), *The part played by the II. Paratroop Corps in Northern France, 20 July-14 September 1944*

Neitzel, H. (1947), MS # B-536 (Engl.), *89th Infantry Division in Engagements on Invasion Front and during Retreat to the Westwall*

Pemsel, M. (1948), MS # B-763, *Die 7. Armee in der Schlacht in der Normandie und in den Kämpfen bis Avranches (6.6.-29.7.44)*

Pemsel, M. (1949a), MS # C-056 (Germ.), *Stellungnahme zur Arbeit über die Schlacht in der Normandie des Gen. v. Choltitz (MS # B-418) (6.6.-15.7.)*

Pemsel, M. (1949b), MS # C-057 (Germ.), *Stellungnahme zur Arbeit über die Schlacht in der Normandie - des Oberstlt. I.G. v. Criegern (MS # B-784) (Vorgeschichte und 6.6.-17.6.44)*

Poppe, W. (1954), MS # P-168, *Einsatz der 77. Infanterie-Division in Nordfrankreich vom 1.2.-15.8.1944*

Schlieben, K.W. von (1948), MS # B-845 (Germ.). *Die deutsche 709. Infanterie-Division vor und während der anglo-amerikanischen Invasion vom 6. Juni 1944*

Straube, E. (1948), MS # B-824 (Engl.), *The LXXIV Infantry Corps in Brittany, May-September 1944*

Stückler, A. (1954), MS # P-159, *2.SS-Panzer-Division "Das Reich," Juni bis September 1944*

Triepel, G. (1946), MS # B-260 (Germ.), *I.Abschnitt, Cotentin (6. Juni-18. Juni 1944)*

Triepel, G. (1947), MS # B-649 (Germ.), *II.Teil, (18.6.-31.7.44), Artillerie-Führer 91.Infanterie-Division*

Viebig, W. (1946), MS # B-610 (Engl.), *Commitment and battles of the 277th I.D. in the time from 13 August-1 September 1944*

Ziegelmann, F. (1946a), MS # B-432 (Germ.), *Die Geschichte der 352.Inf.Div.*

Ziegelmann, F. (1946g), MS # B-438 (Germ.), *Die Geschichte der 352.Inf.Div., Die Kämpfe vom 15.6. bis 17.6.44*

Personal (After Action) Accounts, Reports and Interviews

Hoffmann (1944), *Bericht über Kampfgruppe v. Schlieben* [T312 R1566 57351/13]

Hornung, A. (1944), report on the operations of *Pi.Btl. 709* [T78 R672 H41/61a]

Hümmerich, W. (1958), interviewed on 25 June 1958 [Cornelius Ryan Collection of World War II Papers, Mahn Center for Archives and Special Collections, Ohio University Libraries]

Kreibig (1945), *Ergänzung zu taktischem Bericht für 265. I.D.. des Hauptmann Kastner*

vom 29.10.1944 [T78 R672 H41/61b]

Neugebauer (1944), recording of information provided by Lt. Rösgen regarding certain individuals in the fighting between Ste. Mère-Église and Montebourg [T78 R672 H41/61a]

Rösgen, P.W. (1944), *Bericht über den Heldenkampf der Panzerjäger Abteilung 709 im Raume Cherbourg/Frankreich* [T78 R672 H41/61a]

Schwellenbach (1944), *Erlebnisbericht über Kampfhandlungen des II./GR 729 im Kampfraum Cherbourg (Cotentin-Halbinsel)*, p.2 [T78 R672 H41/61b]

Stadlhofer (1944), *Bericht über den Einsatz der III./AR 243 vom 6.6.1944 bis 25.6.1944* [T78 R672 H41/61b]

Wilbrand (1944), *Gefechtsbericht des Grenadier Regimentes 1050 (77.Infanterie-Division)* [T78 R672 H41/61b]

Websites

The online (re)sources used for this book include, but were not limited to, the following websites:

Ancestry: www.ancestry.com

Axis History Factbook: www.axishistory.com & **Axis History Forum**: https://forum.axishistory.com

Bayonet Strength: www.bayonetstrength.uk

Bunkermuseum Hanstholm: https://bunkermuseumhanstholm.dk

Das Bundesarchiv: www.bundesarchiv.de

Deutsch-russisches Projekt zur Digitalisierung deutscher Dokumente in Archiven der Russischen Föderation: http://wwii.germandocsinrussia.org

Deutschen Digitalen Bibliothek (DDB): www.deutsche-digitale-bibliothek.de

Deutsches Rotes Kreuz, Suchdienst: https://vbl.drk-suchdienst.online/Feldpostnummer/FPN.aspx

Echodelta: www.echodelta.net/mbs/eng-translator.php

Feldgrau: www.feldgrau.net

Fold3: www.fold3.com

First Division History Museum, Col. Robert R. McCormick Research Center, Digital Collection: https://firstdivisionmuseum.nmtvault.com/jsp/searchresults.jsp

Geoportail: www.geoportail.gouv.fr

German History in Documents and Images (GHDI): http://germanhistorydocs.ghi-dc.org

Ibiblio, The Public's Library and Digital Archive: www.ibiblio.org/hyperwar

IGN: Remonter le Temps: https://remonterletemps.ign.fr

Ike Skelton Combined Arms Research Library (CARL) Digital Library: http://cgsc.contentdm.oclc.org/cdm

Kfz. der Wehrmacht: www.kfzderwehrmacht.de

Lexikon der Wehrmacht: www.lexikon-der-wehrmacht.de

Missing-Lynx, Axis WWII AFV Discussion Group: www.tapatalk.com/groups/missinglynx/axis-wwii-afv-discussion-group-f47207/Previously: www.network54.com/Forum/47207

Panzer-Archiv.de: http://panzer-archiv.de (defunct)

Sturmpanzer.com: http://sturmpanzer.com

The 90th Division Association: www.90thdivisionassoc.org

The National Archives: www.nationalarchives.gov.uk

The National Archives and Records Administration: www.archives.gov

The US Army Center of Military History (CMH): https://history.army.mil

Volksbund: www.volksbund.de

WWII Aerial Photos and Maps: www.wwii-photos-maps.com

WWII Day by Day: www.wwiidaybyday.com

Index

M
Military Forces
Allied
US
1st Infantry Division: *113*
3rd Armored Division: *104, 113*
4th Infantry Division: *31, 32, 158, 160, 167, 168, 170, 174, 175, 176, 177, 181*
8th Infantry Regiment (4th Infantry Division): *32, 160, 162, 163, 164, 170, 177*
9th Infantry Division: *37, 171, 176, 179, 181, 184, 185*
12th Infantry Regiment: *158, 160, 161, 162, 163, 164, 166, 170, 176, 177, 180, 181*
22nd Infantry Regiment: *158, 160, 161, 162, 163, 164, 167, 176, 177, 182*
39th Infantry Regiment (9th Infantry Division): *167, 179, 181*
47th Infantry Regiment (9th Infantry Division): *178, 179, 181*
60th Infantry Regiment (9th Infantry Division): *177*
79th Infantry Division: *43, 105, 171, 174, 176, 177, 178, 179, 181*
82nd Airborne Division: *35, 36, 37, 43, 65, 70, 72, 73, 74, 99, 105, 160, 164*
90th Infantry Division: *32, 36, 72, 73, 74, 105*
313th Infantry Regiment (79th Infantry Division): *177, 179, 181*
314th Infantry Regiment (79th Infantry Division): *177, 179, 181*
315th Infantry Regiment (79th Infantry Division): *177, 181*
325th Glider Infantry Regiment (82nd Airborne Division): *35, 70, 164*
359th Infantry Regiment (90th Infantry Division): *32*
505th Parachute Infantry Regiment (82nd Airborne Division): *70, 160, 163*
507th Parachute Infantry Regiment (82nd Airborne Division): *70*
508th Parachute Infantry Regiment (82nd Airborne Division): *68, 70, 103*
Combat Command B (3rd Armored Division): *113*
V Corps: *104*
VII Corps: *40, 43, 70, 73, 74, 105, 110, 167, 176, 181*
XIX Corps: *104, 107, 112*

German
Battalions / Squadrons / Separate Detachments
1. Nordkaukakisches Infanterie-Bataillon: *60.* See also Nordkaukakisches Infanterie-Bataillon 800
Artillerie-Abteilung 450: *148*
Artillerie-Abteilung 669: *122, 123, 128, 129, 130, 139, 144, 146.* See also Artillerie-Regiment 669
Artillerie-Abteilung Kamscheck: *180*
schwere Artillerie-Abteilung Römer: *144, 147*
Aufklärungs-Abteilung 371: *95.* See Füsilier-Bataillon (A.A.) 353
Aufklärungs-Abteilung 389: *148.* See also Füsilier-Abteilung (Aufklärungs-Abteilung) 352
Bataillon Brinkmeier: *75, 77, 78*
Bau-Pionier-Bataillon 802: *168*
Divisions-Füsilier-Bataillon (A.A.) 371. See Füsilier-Bataillon (A.A.) 353
Eisenbahn-Artillerie-Abteilung 681: *149*
Feldersatz-Bataillon 177: *41*
Feldersatz-Bataillon 243: *15, 29, 31, 32, 39*
Feldersatz-Bataillon 265: *55*
Feldersatz-Bataillon 352: *101*
Feldersatz-Bataillon 353: *85, 88, 98, 99, 100, 103, 113*
Festungs-Pionier-Bataillon 11: *168*
Festungs-Stamm-Abteilung LXXXIV: *148, 152, 174, 175, 180*
Füsilier-Bataillon 352: *148, 151*
Füsilier-Bataillon 353: *86, 87, 95, 96, 99, 100, 101, 103, 104, 116*
Füsilier-Bataillon (A.A.) 353: *86, 96, 101, 104*
gemischte Flak-Abteilung 152: *175*
gemischte Flak-Abteilung 153: *175*
Georgisches-Infanterie-Bataillon 795: *29, 125, 141, 149, 151, 152, 153, 157, 174, 177, 180, 183, 184, 191*
Georgisches-Infanterie-Bataillon 797: *29, 40, 125, 141, 147, 148, 151*
Georgisches-Infanterie-Bataillon 798: *24, 78*
Heeres-Küsten-Artillerie-Abteilung 755: *144*
Heeres-Küsten-Artillerie-Abteilung 1161: *96*
Heeres-Küsten-Artillerie-Abteilung 1162: *78*
Heeres-Küsten-Artillerie-Abteilung 1163: *78*
Kaukausisches Infanterie-Bataillon 800: *77*
leichte Flak-Abteilung 931: *180*
leichte Flak-Abteilung 996: *154*
Marine-Artillerie-Abteilung 264: *61*
Marine-Artillerie-Abteilung 681: *61*
Marschbataillon 353: *90, 99*
Marschbataillon zbV 353: *110*
Marschbataillon zbV 364: *43*
Marschbataillon zbV 369: *43*
Maschinengewehr-Bataillon 17: *29, 31, 139, 144, 145, 146, 147, 148, 149, 151, 152, 174, 177, 179, 180*
Nachrichten-Abteilung 191: *74*
Nachrichten-Abteilung 243: *7, 24, 27, 41*
Nachrichten-Abteilung 265: *50, 55, 60, 71, 74, 78*
Nachrichten-Abteilung 328: *95*
Nachrichten-Abteilung 353: *95, 100, 119*
Nachrichten-Abteilung 709: *125, 141, 146, 152, 179*
Nordkaukakisches Infanterie-Bataillon 800: *52, 55, 60, 61, 75*
Ost-Artillerie-Abteilung 752: *45, 78*
Ost-Bataillon 439: *191*
Ost-Bataillon 561: *29, 31, 151, 152, 168, 174, 177*
Ost-Bataillon 634: *52, 56, 60, 61, 75, 77*
Ost-Bataillon 635: *105*
Ost-Bataillon 636: *26, 56, 60, 63, 78*
Ost-Bataillon 642: *191*
Ost-Bataillon 649: *125, 141, 151, 152, 164, 171, 175, 198, 210*
Ost-Bataillon Huber: *40, 43, 72, 73, 103, 105*
Ost-Radfahr-Abteilung 285: *60, 61, 63, 77, 78, 96*
Ost-Reiter-Abteilung 281: *63*
Panzer-Abteilung 206: *29, 38, 159, 160, 164, 168, 174, 177, 180, 183*
Panzer-Abteilung 223: *144.* See Panzer-Regiment 100
Panzer-Ersatz-und-Ausbildungs-Abteilung 100: *70, 71, 198, 210*
Panzerjäger-Abteilung 93: *135*
Panzerjäger-Abteilung 238: *92*
Panzerjäger-Abteilung 243: *17, 27, 29, 32, 39, 40, 41, 42, 47, 137, 158, 161*
Panzerjäger-Abteilung 251: *17*
Panzerjäger-Abteilung 328: *91, 95*
Panzerjäger-Abteilung 334: *91, 92, 95*
Panzerjäger-Abteilung 352: *19, 92*
Panzerjäger-Abteilung 353: *19, 41, 59, 65, 70, 91, 92, 95, 98, 99, 100, 103, 105, 113, 114, 116, 137*
Panzerjäger-Abteilung 371: *91, 95, 135*
Panzerjäger-Abteilung 387: *20*
Panzerjäger-Abteilung 709: *32, 133, 136, 137, 141, 152, 154, 157, 158, 160, 161, 166, 174, 178, 180*
Panzerjäger-Abteilung 1176: *47.* See also Panzerjäger-Abteilung 243
Panzerjäger-Ersatz-Abteilung 2: *91*
Panzerjäger-Ersatz-und-Ausbildungs-Abteilung 17: *17*
Panzerjäger-Ersatz-und-Ausbildungs-Abteilung 18: *17*
Panzerjäger-Ersatz-und-Ausbildungs-Abteilung 20: *91*
Pionier-Bataillon 191: *71, 72, 74, 75*
Pionier-Bataillon 243: *7, 16, 21, 24, 26, 29, 31, 32, 37, 38, 158, 159, 160, 161, 162, 163, 164, 166, 172, 177*

Pionier-Bataillon 265: *26, 50, 54, 58, 59, 60, 63, 67, 70, 71, 72, 74, 75, 78*
Pionier-Bataillon 275: *65*
Pionier-Bataillon 328: *95*
Pionier-Bataillon 346: *26*
Pionier-Bataillon 353: *43, 98, 99, 100, 101, 103, 104, 105, 110, 113, 114*
Pionier-Bataillon 709: *38, 123, 128, 146, 147, 148, 149, 154, 158, 159, 161, 163, 164, 168, 169, 171, 177, 178, 179, 207*
Radfahr-Abteilung 285: *60, 61, 63, 77, 78, 96*
Schnelle Abteilung 513: *148*
Schnelle Abteilung 517: *148*
Schnelle Abteilung 518: *148*
schwere Artillerie-Abteilung 456: *136*
schwere Artillerie-Abteilung 457: *136*
schwere Artillerie-Abteilung 450: *147*. See also Artillerie-Abteilung Römer
schwere Artillerie-Abteilung 456: *136, 148, 149*
schwere Artillerie-Abteilung 457: *148*
schwere Stellungs-Werfer-Abteilung 103: *151*. See also schwere Stellungs-Werfer-Regiment 101
Sicherungs-Bataillon 1221 (O): *78*
SS-Panzer-Aufklärungs-Abteilung 2: *107*
SS-Panzer-Aufklärungs-Abteilung 17: *40, 72*
SS-Sturmgeschütz-Abteilung 2: *107*
Sturm-Bataillon AOK 7: *32, 152, 156, 157, 158, 160, 163, 168, 178, 180, 183*
Sturmgeschütz-Abteilung 905: *148*
Sturmgeschütz-Abteilung 1243: *17*. See Panzerjäger-Abteilung 243; See also Panzerjäger-Abteilung 243
Sturmgeschütz-Abteilung 1353: *99*. See also Panzerjäger-Abteilung 353
Wolga-Tatarisches-Infanterie-Bataillon 627: *40, 41, 42, 43*

Brigades
IV. Marine-Flak-Brigade: *61*
Schnelle Brigade 30: *101, 136, 148*
Sturmgeschütz-Brigade 902: *40, 42, 43, 45, 71*

Companies / Batteries / Troops
1. Sanitäts-Kompanie 353: *100*
2. Sanitäts-Kompanie 353: *100*
Alarmeinheit 729: *180*
Alarmeinheit Grabbe: *161, 166*
Aufklärungs-Schwadron 84: *136, 137, 139*
Batterie Azeville: *158, 160, 161*
Batterie Bastion: *172*
Batterie Brommy: *181*
Batterie Landemer: *180, 181, 182, 184*
Batterie Marcouf: *156, 158, 159, 160, 161, 163, 164*
Batterie Reichenau: *131, 133*
Batterie Thüringen: *131*
Fahrschwadron 353: *100*
Fallschirmjäger-Ausbildungs-Kompanie Hallmann: *175*
Fla-Kompanie 243: *20*
Fla-Kompanie 709: *137*. See also Panzerjäger-Abteilung 709
Geräte-Batterie St. Nazaire: *78*
Geräte-Batterie 716, gepanzert: *148*
Geräte-Batterie Osteck. See Gerate-Batterie Ostmark
Geräte-Batterie Ostmark: *131*
Geräte-Batterie Westeck. See Geräte-Batterie Westmark
Geräte-Batterie Westmark: *130*
Gesteinsbohr-Kompanie 28: *168*
Kompanie Kollanowski: *167*
Kompanie Laumann: *41*. See also Feld-Ersatz-Bataillon 177
Kompanie Schimpf: *167, 180*
Kompanie Straube: *180*
Kraftfahr-Kompanie 84: *136*
Kraftfahr-Kompanie XXV: *67*
Krankenkraftwagen-Kompanie 353: *100*
Nachschub-Kompanie 353: *100*
Panzerjäger-Kompanie 243: *14, 17*. See Panzerjäger-Abteilung 243; See also Panzerjäger-Abteilung 243
Panzerjäger-Kompanie 353: *92*. See also Panzerjäger-Abteilung 353
Panzerjäger-Kompanie 709: *126, 133, 135, 136, 139, 146*. See also Panzerjäger-Abteilung 709
Panzerjäger-Kompanie 1363b: *47*. See also Panzerjäger-Abteilung 243
Sanitäts-Kompanie 243: *41*
Stellungs-Batterie (Küste) 317: *131*
Troß-Kompanie Schröder: *174*
Veterinär-Kompanie 243: *20*
Veterinär-Kompanie 709: *183, 184*
Werkstatt-Kompanie 353: *100*

Corps
Generalkommando LXXXVII. See LXXXVII. Armee-Korps
II. Fallschirm-Korps: *75, 82, 100, 101, 103, 104, 112, 113, 114, 116, 118, 119*
Höheres-Kommando XXXII. See also LXXXI. Armee-Korps
Höheres-Kommando zbV LX. See also LXXXIV. Armee-Korps
LXXIV. Armee-Korps: *64, 98, 191*
LXXXI. Armee-Korps: *119*
LXXXIV. Armee-Korps: *5, 17, 21, 24, 26, 31, 35, 37, 38, 43, 44, 46, 60, 63, 64, 68, 70, 71, 72, 73, 74, 82, 100, 101, 102, 103, 104, 107, 112, 113, 114, 116, 117, 119, 120, 129, 132, 135, 136, 138, 144, 145, 146, 151, 157, 161, 167, 169, 190, 191, 206*
LXXXVII. A.K.: *128, 148*
LXXXVII. Armee-Korpds: *144*
XXV. Armee-Korps: *5, 21, 24, 48, 55, 56, 59, 63, 64, 65, 71, 73, 75, 77, 78, 91, 95, 96, 99, 100, 120, 144*
XXXXVII. Panzer-Korps: *114, 116*

Divisions
1. SS-Panzer-Division "Leibstandarte SS Adolf Hitler": *116*
2. Fallschimjäger-Division: *77, 100*
2. Panzer-Division: *114*
2. SS-Panzer-Division "Das Reich": *46, 107, 108, 113, 114, 207*
3. Fallschimjäger-Division: *75, 95, 96, 98, 101*
5. Fallschirmjäger-Division: *112, 113*
17. SS-Panzergrenadier-Division "Götz von Berlichingen": *29, 39, 46, 101, 104, 107, 112, 113, 206*
18. Luftwaffen-Feld-Division: *75*
21. Panzer-Division: *63*
39. Infanterie-Division: *95*
77. Infanterie-Division: *29, 35, 36, 37, 38, 39, 40, 42, 43, 44, 57, 68, 70, 74, 75, 94, 103, 104, 105, 107, 109, 110, 113, 164, 167, 168*
84. Infanterie-Division: *116, 118*
91. Luftlande-Division (91. Luftlande-Infanterie-Division): *27, 29, 31, 32, 35, 37, 39, 41, 43, 44, 45, 46, 69, 70, 71, 72, 73, 74, 75, 103, 104, 105, 110, 113, 114, 149, 152, 154, 156, 157, 158, 161, 163*
94. Infanterie-Division: *59*
98. Infanterie-Division: *10*
101. Infanterie-Division: *63*
161. Infanterie-Division: *144*
162. Reserve-Infanterie-Division: *46*
165. Reserve-Division: *139, 144, 145, 146, 147, 190*
176. Infanterie-Division: *47*
205. Infanterie-Division: *144*
211. Infanterie-Division: *144*
242. Infanterie-Division: *126, 129, 149*
243. Infanterie-Division: *5, 8, 9, 12, 15, 17, 19, 20, 22, 24, 26, 27, 29, 32, 35, 36, 37, 38, 40, 41, 43, 44, 46, 51, 58, 60, 70, 73, 103, 104, 105, 110, 113, 114, 116, 117, 133, 138, 140, 151, 152, 153, 154, 156, 158, 163, 172, 191*
265. Infanterie-Division: *7, 9, 48, 51, 57, 58, 59, 63, 71, 72, 73, 75, 77, 78, 79, 98, 99, 103, 128, 131, 143, 207*
266. Infanterie-Division: *51*

275. Infanterie-Division: 26, 27, 56, 57, 60, 63, 64, 73, 75, 77, 78, 91, 113, 119
276. Infanterie-Division: 91
306. Infanterie-Division: 82, 84, 94, 95
319. Infanterie-Division: 183, 190
320. Infanterie-Division: 144, 145, 190
328. Infanterie-Division: 82, 84, 94, 95
332. Infanterie-Division: 144
334. Infanterie-Division: 82, 84, 94, 95, 116, 118
343. Infanterie-Division: 57, 60, 64, 73, 77, 78, 79, 95, 96, 98, 99, 100, 128, 144
344. Infanterie-Division: 52
346. Infanterie-Division: 20, 58, 133, 144
349. Infanterie-Division: 94, 135
352. Infanterie-Division: 17, 68, 82, 94, 100, 101, 103, 104, 133, 135, 141, 148, 151, 153, 157, 191
353. Infanterie-Division: 5, 17, 19, 39, 43, 44, 46, 60, 65, 68, 70, 75, 82, 87, 93, 94, 95, 99, 100, 101, 102, 103, 104, 105, 107, 110, 112, 113, 114, 116, 118, 119, 133, 135, 141, 148, 151, 153, 157, 191
356. Infanterie-Division: 94
357. Infanterie-Division: 94
359. Infanterie-Division: 94
363. Infanterie-Division: 46, 114, 116, 117, 118
363. Volks-Grenadier-Division: 47
371. Infanterie-Division: 82, 84, 86, 94, 95, 135
376. Infanterie-Division: 94
384. Infanterie-Division: 24, 60, 94, 149
387. Infanterie-Division: 7, 24
389. Infanterie-Division: 24, 94, 148, 149
403. Sicherungs-Division: 59. *See also* 265. Infanterie-Division
506. Infanterie-Division: 63. *See* 101. Infanterie-Division
702. Infanterie-Division: 120
704. Infanterie-Division: 120
707. Infanterie-Division: 120
708. Infanterie-Division: 91, 120, 135
709. Infanterie-Division: 9, 27, 29, 31, 32, 35, 37, 38, 40, 51, 91, 100, 120, 122, 128, 129, 131, 133, 134, 135, 138, 139, 140, 141, 142, 144, 145, 146, 147, 148, 149, 151, 152, 156, 161, 163, 167, 168, 174, 182, 185, 190, 191
710. Infanterie-Division: 120
711. Infanterie-Division: 120
712. Infanterie-Division: 120
713. Infanterie-Division: 120
714. Infanterie-Division: 120
715. Infanterie-Division: 120
716. Infanterie-Division: 40, 133, 134, 135, 136, 137, 138, 139, 140, 148, 149, 190, 191
717. Infanterie-Division: 120
718. Infanterie-Division: 120
719. Infanterie-Division: 120
Division B: 24. *See* 243. Infanterie-Division
Panzer-Lehr-Division: 110, 112, 113, 116

Field Armies
5. Panzer-Armee: 119
7. Armee: 19, 22, 26, 41, 60, 64, 71, 72, 73, 93, 100, 101, 114, 134, 136, 144, 168, 181, 206, 207
15. Armee: 24
Armee-Oberkommando 1: 64, 94, 190
Armee-Oberkommando 7: 5, 11, 14, 17, 18, 20, 22, 24, 26, 27, 32, 37, 46, 48, 55, 56, 57, 58, 59, 64, 65, 68, 71, 72, 75, 77, 82, 88, 91, 92, 93, 94, 95, 99, 100, 101, 102, 103, 104, 108, 110, 114, 116, 118, 119, 122, 123, 125, 134, 135, 136, 138, 141, 144, 147, 153, 161, 162, 163, 167, 168, 169, 174, 178, 181, 182, 184, 190
Armee-Oberkommando 15: 64, 125, 147, 190
Armee-Oberkommando 19: 64
Panzer-Armee-Oberkommando 5: 118. *See also* 5. Panzer-Armee
Panzergruppe West: 110, 114

High Commands
Befehlshaber Südwestfrankreich: 77
Heeresgruppe B: 47, 63, 65, 77, 100, 101, 104, 108, 110, 122, 138, 142, 152, 167, 168
Heeresgruppe D: 94, 204
Heeresgruppe Mitte: 7, 134
Oberbefehlshaber West: 9, 21, 22, 24, 27, 46, 47, 51, 55, 60, 77, 90, 91, 93, 94, 128, 133, 147, 148, 149, 190
Oberkommando der Wehrmacht (OKW): 25, 104, 178, 180, 201, 204, 205, 214
Oberkommando des Heeres (OKH): 5, 17, 18, 19, 20, 24, 48, 122, 128, 129, 201, 204, 205, 214
Replacement Army: 7, 59, 91, 135, 144, 148, 198, 210
Wehrkreis I: 59
Wehrkreis II: 91
Wehrkreis III: 59
Wehrkreis IV (Dresden): 7, 110
Wehrkreis IX: 120, 143
Wehrkreis VI: 59
Wehrkreis VII (Munich): 7
Wehrkreis X: 59, 91
Wehrkreis XI: 59
Wehrkreis XVIII (Salzburg): 7, 17
Wehrkreis XVII (Vienna): 5, 7, 17, 20, 24

Kampfgruppen (Battlegroups)
Artillerie-Gruppe Goulven: 96, 98
Gruppe Hellmich: 29, 37, 101, 161, 167
Gruppe König: 37, 38, 39, 40, 41, 42, 43, 65, 70, 71, 72, 73, 99, 103, 104
Gruppe von Schlieben: 37, 120, 167, 168, 169, 172, 174, 180, 181, 182
Kampfgruppe 243. I.D.: 37, 41, 44. *See also* 243. Infanterie-Division; *See also* Untergruppe Klosterkemper
Kampfgruppe 265: 54, 65, 67, 68, 70, 71, 72, 73, 74, 75, 99, 100
Kampfgruppe 266: 64, 75
Kampfgruppe 275: 64, 65, 68, 99, 101, 114, 116, 117
Kampfgruppe 353. I.D.: 102. *See* 353. Infanterie-Division
Kampfgruppe 709. Infanterie-Division: 167. *See also* 709. Infanterie-Division
Kampfgruppe Bacherer: 37
Kampfgruppe Bayer: 35, 39
Kampfgruppe Boehm: 94, 101, 102, 103, 104, 110, 113, 116
Kampfgruppe Brandt: 164
Kampfgruppe Bretagne: 82, 86, 87, 91, 94, 95
Kampfgruppe Dobeneck: 119
Kampfgruppe Eitner: 70
Kampfgruppe Heintz: 63, 114, 116, 119
Kampfgruppe Hett: 77
Kampfgruppe Hoffmann: 32, 35, 36, 163, 164, 167, 168, 170
Kampfgruppe Kanalküste: 94
Kampfgruppe Keil: 32, 120, 122, 159, 161, 164, 167, 168, 176, 178, 179, 180, 182, 183, 185, 206
Kampfgruppe Kentner: 103
Kampfgruppe Klosterkemper: 36, 39
Kampfgruppe Köhn: 174, 177
Kampfgruppe Lausberg: 105
Kampfgruppe Mecklenburg: 74
Kampfgruppe Müller: 31, 32, 35, 37, 38, 40, 46, 159, 160, 161, 163, 164, 166, 167, 171, 172
Kampfgruppe Normandie: 94. *See also* 352. Infanterie-Division
Kampfgruppe Rohrbach: 32, 35, 159, 161, 163, 164, 166
Kampfgruppe Schmitz: 119
Kampfgruppe Simon: 35, 36, 37, 39, 163, 164
Kampfgruppe Spang: 78
Kampfgruppe Trimborn: 113
Kampfgruppe von Saldern: 35, 37, 39
Ost-Regiments-Gruppe Bunjatschenko: 73
Regiment Rohrbach. *See* Grenadier-Regiment 729
Untergruppe Eitner: 70, 71, 72, 103
Untergruppe Jäger: 43, 70, 72, 73

Untergruppe Klosterkemper: *40, 41, 70*
Untergruppe Lewandowski: *43, 70, 71, 72*
Untergruppe Mecklenburg: *73*
Unterkampfgruppe Hadenfeldt: *38, 180, 182, 184*
Unterkampfgruppe Hoffmann: *164*
Unterkampfgruppe Müller: *38, 178, 180, 183, 184*

Miscellaneous

Artillerie-Gruppe Nord. *See* Heeres-Küsten-Artillerie-Regiment 1262
Artillerie-Gruppe Ost: *176*
Artillerie-Gruppe Quittnat: *179*
Artillerie-Gruppe Süd. *See* Artillerie-Regiment 1709
Artillerie-Gruppe West: *174, 176, 180*
Artillerie-Kommandeur 115 (Arko 115): *95*
Artillerie Kommandeur 118 (Arko 118): *151, 152, 156, 166*
Aufstellungsstab West: *19*
Feldgendarmerie-Trupp 243: *7, 20*
Feldkommandantur 752: *57, 77*
Feldlazarett 243: *7*
Festungs-Kommandant Lorient: *60*
Festungs-Pionier-Abschnitts-Gruppe Beger: *26*
Festungs-Stamm-Regiment XXV: *24, 60, 61, 77, 78*
Kosaken-Kommando: *63*
Sonderstab Beger. *See* Festungs-Pionier-Abschnitts-Gruppe Beger
Stab Esser: *78*
Stab Käßberg: *78*
Verteidigungsbereich Cherbourg: *191*

Regiments

Artillerie-Regiment 137: *88*
Artillerie-Regiment 177: *35, 70, 74*
Artillerie-Regiment 191: *27, 29, 35, 39, 70, 71, 72, 156*
Artillerie-Regiment 242: *126, 129, 131, 149*
Artillerie-Regiment 243: *16, 17, 21, 26, 27, 29, 31, 32, 35, 37, 39, 40, 41, 45, 46, 158, 207*
Artillerie-Regiment 265: *50, 54, 58, 59, 60, 61, 63, 64, 67, 68, 70, 74, 75, 77, 78*
Artillerie-Regiment 266. *See* Artillerie-Regiment 669
Artillerie-Regiment 272: *87*
Artillerie-Regiment 320: *144*
Artillerie-Regiment 328: *87, 95*
Artillerie-Regiment 334: *87, 88, 95. See* Artillerie-Regiment 353
Artillerie-Regiment 343: *96*
Artillerie-Regiment 353: *43, 87, 88, 95, 96, 98, 100, 105, 113, 114, 119*
Artillerie-Regiment 371: *95. See* Artillerie-Regiment 353
Artillerie-Regiment 384: *149*
Artillerie-Regiment 621: *158, 164*
Artillerie-Regiment 669: *128, 129, 131, 132, 140, 149. See also* Artillerie-Regiment 1709
Artillerie-Regiment 709: *128*
Artillerie-Regiment 1709: *128, 129, 131, 133, 141, 151, 153, 167, 168, 175, 176, 181, 185*
Artillerie-Regiment 1716: *133*
Artillerie-Regiment zbV 621: *148, 156, 157, 163, 164, 168*
Fallschirmjäger-Ersatz-und-Ausbildungs-Regiment 1: *152, 153, 164*
Fallschirm-Ersatz- und Ausbildungs-Regiment 2: *77*
Fallschirmjäger-Regiment 6: *20, 29, 32, 46, 114, 116, 117, 158*
Fallschirmjäger-Regiment 14: *113*
Fallschirmjäger-Regiment 15: *74, 104, 107*
Festungs-Grenadier-Regiment 729. *See* Grenadier-Regiment 729
Festungs-Grenadier-Regiment 739. *See* Grenadier-Regiment 739
Flak-Regiment 30: *154, 166, 175*
Grenadier-Regiment 290: *10*
Grenadier-Regiment 534: *149*
Grenadier-Regiment 535: *149*
Grenadier-Regiment 536: *141, 149, 204, 207*
Grenadier-Regiment 544: *148, 149, 204*
Grenadier-Regiment 546: *148*
Grenadier-Regiment 548: *84, 95*
Grenadier-Regiment 569: *84, 95*
Grenadier-Regiment 581: *84, 95*
Grenadier-Regiment 585: *110, 144, 182*
Grenadier-Regiment 586: *144, 145*
Grenadier-Regiment 587: *144, 145, 204*
Grenadier-Regiment 671: *95*
Grenadier-Regiment 729: *32, 38, 122, 125, 126, 127, 128, 134, 135, 136, 139, 140, 141, 143, 144, 145, 146, 147, 148, 149, 151, 153, 159, 160, 161, 162, 163, 164, 166, 167, 172, 174, 175, 176, 177, 178, 180, 207*
Grenadier-Regiment 739: *29, 32, 38, 122, 125, 126, 127, 135, 136, 139, 140, 141, 142, 143, 144, 145, 146, 147, 148, 149, 151, 152, 156, 157, 159, 161, 166, 167, 172, 174, 176, 177, 178, 191*
Grenadier-Regiment 754: *95*
Grenadier-Regiment 755: *84, 95*
Grenadier-Regiment 851: *77, 78, 205*
Grenadier-Regiment 852: *77, 78*
Grenadier-Regiment 854: *52*
Grenadier-Regiment 894: *48, 52, 53, 54, 57, 58, 59, 60, 61, 64, 65, 67, 68, 70, 71, 72, 73, 74, 75, 77, 78*
Grenadier-Regiment 895: *48, 52, 53, 54, 57, 58, 59, 60, 61, 63, 64, 67, 68, 70, 71, 72, 73, 74, 75, 77, 78, 205*
Grenadier-Regiment 896: *48, 52, 53, 54, 57, 58, 59, 60, 61, 63, 64, 67, 68, 70, 71, 72, 73, 74, 75, 77, 78, 79*
Grenadier-Regiment 898: *64*
Grenadier-Regiment 914: *32, 103*
Grenadier-Regiment 916: *101*
Grenadier-Regiment 919: *32, 38, 125, 126, 127, 128, 129, 135, 136, 140, 141, 142, 149, 151, 152, 153, 154, 156, 159, 160, 161, 162, 163, 164, 166, 167, 172, 174, 176, 177, 178, 179, 180, 183, 185, 206*
Grenadier-Regiment 920: *9, 10, 11, 13, 14, 15, 20, 22, 24, 26, 27, 29, 31, 32, 35, 36, 37, 38, 39, 40, 41, 42, 43, 45, 46, 151, 158, 159, 161, 163, 164, 166, 167, 171, 172, 180, 183*
Grenadier-Regiment 921: *9, 10, 11, 12, 13, 14, 15, 20, 22, 24, 26, 27, 29, 31, 32, 35, 36, 37, 39, 40, 41, 42, 44, 45, 46, 152, 153, 163, 164*
Grenadier-Regiment 922: *9, 10, 11, 12, 13, 14, 15, 20, 21, 22, 24, 26, 27, 29, 31, 32, 35, 36, 37, 38, 39, 40, 41, 42, 45, 46, 151, 152, 153, 158, 159, 161, 162, 163, 164, 167, 171, 172, 177, 178, 180, 183*
Grenadier-Regiment 941: *84, 85, 86, 95, 96, 99, 100, 103, 105, 107, 109, 110, 112, 113, 114, 116, 117, 119*
Grenadier-Regiment 942: *43, 44, 84, 85, 86, 95, 96, 99, 100, 103, 104, 105, 109, 110, 113, 114, 116, 117, 119*
Grenadier-Regiment 943: *84, 85, 86, 94, 95, 96, 99, 100, 101, 104, 105, 112, 113, 114, 116, 117*
Grenadier-Regiment 957: *114, 116, 117*
Grenadier-Regiment 983: *78, 207*
Grenadier-Regiment 984: *63, 116, 119, 207*
Grenadier-Regiment 985: *75, 77, 78, 207*
Grenadier-Regiment 1049: *68, 70, 71, 72, 73, 74, 75*
Grenadier-Regiment 1050: *38, 40, 41, 42, 74, 113*
Grenadier-Regiment 1057: *35, 37, 39, 41, 69, 72, 158*
Grenadier-Regiment 1058: *32, 44, 72, 113, 154, 157, 158, 159, 163, 164, 206*
Grenadier-Regiment Reithinger: *144, 147*
Grenadier-Regiment zbV 752: *120, 138, 148, 151, 156, 191*
Heeres-Küsten-Artillerie-Regiment 1261: *153, 156, 157, 166, 168, 176*
Heeres-Küsten-Artillerie-Regiment 1262: *29, 31, 133, 175, 176, 180*
Infanterie-Regiment 729: *122*
Infanterie-Regiment 739: *122. See also* Grenadier-Regiment 739
Panzer-Grenadier-Regiment 901: *113*
Panzer-Regiment 100: *144*
Regiments-Gruppe Bunjatschenko: *43*
Regiment von Dobeneck: *118*
schweres Stellungs-Werfer-Regiment 101: *29, 31, 151, 152, 156, 163, 164, 174, 182*
Sicherungs-Regiment 195: *77*
SS-Panzer-Artillerie-Regiment 2: *107*

SS-Panzer-Grenadier-Regiment 3 "Deutschland": *107*
SS-Panzer-Grenadier-Regiment 4 "Der Führer": *44, 107*

Military Operations, Placed and Lines
Cherbourg Landfront: *27*
Festung Brest: *96*
Festung Cherbourg: *27, 36, 120, 152, 153, 168, 169, 176, 181, 182*
Festung Lorient: *48, 60, 61, 78, 79*
Festung St. Nazaire: *48, 77, 78, 79*
Küstenverteidigungsabschnitt "A2": *98*
Küstenverteidigungsabschnitt "B": *64, 77*
Küstenverteidigungsabschnitt "C": *77*
Küstenverteidigungsabschnitt "C1": *58, 60, 61, 78*
Küstenverteidigungsabschnitt "C2": *24, 64, 77, 78*
Küstenverteidigungsabschnitt Calvados: *190*
Küstenverteidigungsabschnitt Cotentin: *190, 191*
Küstenverteidigungsabschnitt Coutances: *191*
Küstenverteidigungsabschnitt "J": *59. See also* Küstenverteidigungsabschnitt "C1"
Küstenverteidigungsabschnitt "J1": *151, 152, 191*
Küstenverteidigungsabschnitt "J2": *151*
Küstenverteidigungsabschnitt Kanalinseln (Channel Islands): *190*
Küstenverteidigungsgruppe Anse de Pouldu: *61*
Küstenverteidigungsgruppe Bricquebec: *191*
Küstenverteidigungsgruppe Caen: *190, 191*
Küstenverteidigungsgruppe Cherbourg: *191*
Küstenverteidigungsgruppe Cotentin-Ost: *149, 191*
Küstenverteidigungsgruppe Courseulles: *191*
Küstenverteidigungsgruppe Granville: *144, 191*
Küstenverteidigungsgruppe Guérande: *77, 78*
Küstenverteidigungsgruppe Lesneven: *96*
Küstenverteidigungsgruppe Lessay: *191*
Küstenverteidigungsgruppe Michel: *78*
Küstenverteidigungsgruppe Périers: *151*
Küstenverteidigungsgruppe Plouhinec: *61, 63, 78*
Küstenverteidigungsgruppe Quimper: *61, 77*
Küstenverteidigungsgruppe Riva Bella: *191*
Küstenverteidigungsgruppe Vannes: *78*
Küstenverteidigungsuntergruppe Barfleur: *134, 149, 153, 191*
Küstenverteidigungsuntergruppe Bayeux: *191*
Küstenverteidigungsuntergruppe Bessin: *191*
Küstenverteidigungsuntergruppe Cherbourg-Land: *191. See also* Landfront (Cherbourg)
Küstenverteidigungsuntergruppe Cherbourg-See: *191*
Küstenverteidigungsuntergruppe Clohars: *61*
Küstenverteidigungsuntergruppe Cotentin-West: *191*
Küstenverteidigungsuntergruppe Douarnenez: *77*
Küstenverteidigungsuntergruppe Fouesnant: *77*
Küstenverteidigungsuntergruppe Jobourg: *151, 191*
Küstenverteidigungsuntergruppe Les Pieux: *191*
Küstenverteidigungsuntergruppe Luc: *191*
Küstenverteidigungsuntergruppe Marcouf: *149, 151, 191*
Küstenverteidigungsuntergruppe Meuvaines: *191*
Küstenverteidigungsuntergruppe Orne: *190, 191*
Küstenverteidigungsuntergruppe Percée: *191*
Küstenverteidigungsuntergruppe Plouharnel: *63, 78*
Küstenverteidigungsuntergruppe Sarzeau: *78*
Küstenverteidigungsuntergruppe Seulles: *190, 191*
Küstenverteidigungsuntergruppe St. Vaast: *134, 149, 151, 153, 191*
Küstenverteidigungsuntergruppe Vauville: *29, 151, 191*
Küstenverteidigungsuntergruppe Vire: *191*
Landfront (Cherbourg): *22, 27, 29, 32, 37, 122, 143, 144, 146, 147, 148, 149, 151, 152, 154, 156, 161, 162, 163, 168, 169, 172, 174, 176, 177, 178, 179, 182, 191. See also* Küstenverteidigungs-Untergruppe Cherbourg-Land
Organisation Todt: *21, 52, 139, 201, 214*
Nordfront: *5, 29, 32, 35, 36, 37, 38, 40, 42, 43, 44, 45, 70, 72, 73, 74, 82, 101, 103, 105, 107, 108, 109, 110, 112, 113, 159, 161, 162, 164, 166, 167, 172*
Bewegung Cherbourg: *170*
Bewegung Spargel: *64*
Falaise Pocket: *46, 82, 119*
Operation Cobra: *5, 45, 46, 75, 82, 113*
Operation Landgraf: *3, 61, 63*
Operation Landgraf (Aktion Landgraf): *3, 61, 63*
Operation Lüttich. *See* Unternehmen Lüttich
Operation Sealion. *See* Unternehmen Sealion
Operation Seelöwe. *See* Unternehmen Seelöwe
Spargel Neu: *65*
Unternehmen Lüttich: *116*
Waldbergstellung. *See* Mahlmann-Linie
Wasserlinie: *44, 74, 110, 112*
Westfront: *29*
Westwall: *119, 190, 207*

Miscellaneous
Armed Forces Daily Announcement (Wehrmachtsbericht): *37, 44, 168, 185*
Knight's Cross: *37*
Knight's Cross (Ritterkreuz): *182*
Nationalsozialistischer-Führungsoffizier (NSFO): *86*
Résistance: *3, 63, 75, 77, 86*
Ritterkreuz. *See* Knight's Cross

U-Boot: *60*
ULTRA: *17*
Volksliste III: *7, 87, 142, 143*
Wehrmachtsbericht. *See* Armed Forces Daily Announcement

P

Place Names
Aachen: *75, 119*
Abbaye de Blanchelande: *109*
Agon: *27*
Amfreville: *35*
Angers: *77*
Angoville-sur-Ay: *38, 40, 43, 44, 105, 109*
Antrain: *71, 103*
Argentan: *119, 148*
Arradon: *26*
Arsenal: *181, 182*
Asnelles: *190*
Auderville: *180, 184, 185*
Audierne Bight: *61*
Audouville-la-Hubert: *153*
Aumeville-Lestre: *152, 154*
Auray: *24, 78*
Avranches: *65, 75, 77, 100, 102, 103, 114, 116, 156, 207*
Azeville: *31, 32, 157, 158, 159, 160, 162*
Bactol: *44*
Baie d'Audierne: *61, 63*
Baie de Douarnenez: *96, 98*
Baie de Morlaix: *98*
Baillé: *65*
Balleroy: *26*
Barfleur: *134, 149, 153, 154*
Barneville: *20, 29, 151, 191*
Barville: *109*
Baudienville: *158*
Baudreville: *43*
Baupte: *68, 69, 70, 72, 103, 144*
Bayeux: *191, 205, 206*
Beaumesnil: *65*
Beaumont-Hague: *29, 37, 146, 149, 151, 180, 182*
Beauvais: *44, 109*
Bécherel: *65, 67, 71*
Belle-Isle-en-Terre: *79*
Benodet: *61*
Bergen Training Area: *59*
Berné: *77*

221

Berrien: *92, 98*
Besné: *26*
Besneville: *29, 38*
Beuzeg. See Chau. Le Beuzec
Beuzeville-au-Plain: *149, 151, 152, 157, 158*
Beuzeville-la-Bastille: *37*
Biémont: *43, 44, 103, 105*
Bisson: *158*
Biville: *144*
Blainville-sur-Mer: *27*
Blanchelande: *109, 147*
Blavet River: *60, 63*
Bois de Bretel: *101*
Bois de Brocboeufs: *105*
Bois de Coudray: *177*
Bois de Feuillet: *119*
Bois de la Haye: *116*
Bois de la Mousse: *118*
Bois de la Poterie: *105*
Bois de la Vierge: *116*
Bois de Limors: *40, 70, 72, 103*
Bois de Montebourg: *164*
Bois du Gast: *116*
Bolleville: *43, 103, 105, 148*
Bourbirac: *101*
Branville: *153, 172, 183*
Brécourt: *156, 172, 179, 181*
Breél: *118*
Bréhal: *114, 144, 148*
Bréhand: *102*
Brenn. See Le Bren
Brennilis: *98*
Breslau-Masselwitz: *92*
Brest: *48, 79, 92, 95, 96, 98, 206*
Bretagne: *3, 5, 24, 26, 27, 42, 46, 48, 57, 59, 60, 63, 64, 65, 71, 72, 75, 77, 79, 82, 94, 95, 96, 98, 99, 100, 101, 103, 120, 128, 141, 144, 190, 206*
Bretteville-sur-Ay: *43, 44, 103*
Breuville: *171, 172*
Bricquebec: *27, 29, 144, 146, 147, 148, 149, 152, 156, 172*
Bricquebost: *110*
Bricqueville-sur-Mer: *144*
Briec: *77, 95*
Briouze: *118*
Brittany Peninsula: *95, 144*
Brix: *152, 172*
Brucan: *153*

Brucheville: *152, 156*
Bubry: *63*
Caen: *24, 60, 135, 141*
Calvados: *26, 101, 148, 190, 191*
Cambry: *114*
Campbon: *26*
Canal du Couesnon: *191*
Canal du Port de Carentan: *149*
Canisy: *91, 113, 148*
Canteloup: *149*
Cap Coz: *61*
Cap de Carteret: *151, 191*
Cap de Flamanville: *149*
Cap de la Hague: *183*
Cap Lévy: *182*
Capron: *108*
Carbonnet: *44*
Carentan: *24, 27, 29, 32, 35, 101, 105, 126, 144, 148, 149, 151, 152, 153, 154, 157, 163, 191, 205*
Carhaix: *60*
Carnac: *24, 60*
Carrefour de la Croix. See Le Mont
Carrefour-St.Jores: *70*
Cast: *96, 98*
Câtelet: *152, 154, 156*
Caudard: *29*
Caulnes: *71, 102*
Cauvin: *154, 157*
Cérences: *114, 144, 148*
Cerisy-la-Salle: *148*
Chambert: *27*
Chambois: *119*
Champ-du-Boult: *116*
Champ Moqtet: *29*
Château Brocboeufs: *105*
Château d'Amfreville: *35*
Château de Courcy: *163*
Château de Fontenay: *157, 159, 161, 163, 164*
Château de l'Ermitage: *147*
Château de Maillé: *98, 100*
Château de Pépinvast: *146*
Château Digosville: *151*
Château du Bigard: *152*
Château Duprey: *40*
Château du Talhouët: *60*
Château Hospice: *72*
Château la Haye du Puits: *107*

Château Lanroz: *60*
Château le Perron: *27*
Château les Isles: *96*
Châteaulin: *60, 77, 96, 98, 99*
Château Malassis: *27*
Château Montvason: *154*
Château Rupalet: *27*
Château Le Beuzec: *61*
Chavoy: *75*
Cherbourg: *3, 5, 22, 27, 32, 35, 36, 37, 38, 70, 101, 103, 120, 122, 126, 142, 144, 145, 146, 147, 149, 151, 152, 156, 159, 163, 167, 168, 169, 171, 172, 174, 175, 176, 177, 178, 179, 180, 181, 182, 185, 202, 205, 206, 207, 215*
Chérencé-le-Roussel: *65*
Chiffrevast: *152, 171, 172*
Cibrantot: *153, 156*
Cléden-Cap Sizun: *61*
Cléguérec: *71*
Clinchamps: *119*
Clohars: *61*
Clohars-Carnoët: *60, 61*
Coadigou. See Penquer-Coadigou
Coëtquidan: *79*
Cohiniac: *101*
Coigny: *70*
Colombières: *27, 151*
Colomby: *151, 168*
Combourg: *68, 100, 102, 103*
Concarneau: *61, 77*
Coray: *77, 98*
Cosniam: *29*
Cosquer: *96*
Cotentin: *5, 24, 26, 27, 29, 36, 37, 38, 40, 44, 69, 70, 99, 101, 103, 120, 129, 130, 133, 144, 145, 146, 148, 149, 151, 152, 156, 158, 161, 168, 169, 172, 174, 176, 190, 191, 205, 207*
Couhière: *154*
Courin: *95*
Coutances: *27, 46, 73, 74, 103, 113, 148, 151*
Coz Quinguis: *96*
Crasville: *153*
Créac'h Burguy: *96*
Créances: *44*
Cretteville: *70*
Crisbecq: *161*
Crossroads 148: *177*
Crossroads 177: *177, 178*
Crozon: *60*

Dangueville: *154, 164, 166*
Denneville: *153*
Digosville: *144, 146, 153, 174, 176, 177, 178, 180*
Digulleville: *184*
Dinan: *48, 65, 78, 99, 103*
Dingé: *71*
Dives River: *119*
Döllersheim: *5, 7*
Donville-les-Bains: *27*
Doualas: *95*
Douarnenez: *60, 61, 67, 98*
Douve River: *27, 37, 39, 68, 69, 70, 72, 154*
Doville: *72*
Dresden: *7, 110*
Ducey: *75*
Ecardenville: *119*
Écoquenéauville: *153*
Elbeuf: *119*
Elven: *26*
Émondeville: *32, 154, 158, 159, 160, 161, 162*
Équeurdreville: *149, 153, 181*
Éroudeville: *32, 162, 163*
Escoublac: *78*
Étables: *98*
Étel River: *26, 60, 61, 63, 78*
Étienville: *37*
Étoupeville: *29*
Falaise Pocket: *46*
Fallingbostel Training Area. *See* Bergen Training Area
Fauville: *149*
Fermanville: *153, 169*
Flamanville: *29, 149, 151*
Flers: *118*
Fleury: *152, 154*
Floranond: *108*
Flottemanville: *148, 149, 154, 168, 170, 172, 174, 177, 178, 179, 181*
Fluguffan: *61*
Fontain du Bienheureux Thomas: *29*
Fontaine Rouge: *96*
Fontenay-sur-Mer: *156, 158, 161, 163, 164, 166*
Forêt de Gouffern: *119*
Forêt de Mont-Castre: *103, 104, 105, 107*
Forêt de St. Sever: *68, 114, 116*
Forêt de Tanouarn: *68*
Fort Central: *182*
Fort de Ravenoville: *161*
Fort des Couplets: *181*

Fort des Fourches: *179*
Fort du Questel: *96*
Fort du Roule: *176, 178, 181*
Fort du Tot: *179*
Fort l'Est: *182*
Fort l'Ile de Pelée: *182*
Fort l'Ouest: *182*
Foucarville: *153, 154*
Fouesnant: *60, 61, 77*
Fougères: *65, 75, 100, 144*
Franqueterre River: *171*
Freistadt: *18*
Fresville: *157, 159, 160*
Frimot: *29*
Gathemo: *65, 116*
Gatteville: *153*
Gavray: *46, 75, 114, 144*
Geffosses: *44*
Gent: *126*
Gerville-la-Forêt: *105, 109*
Gestel: *60, 61, 63, 64, 75*
Giel: *118*
Gillotière: *118*
Ginsterhöhe: *153, 167*
Glatigny: *43*
Golleville: *27, 168*
Gonneville: *182*
Gorges: *27, 73, 103, 109*
Gotha: *137*
Gouarec: *55, 67*
Gouberville: *153*
Gouesnou: *95, 98*
Gouhière: *163*
Goulven: *96*
Gourbesville: *36*
Gourin: *65, 67*
Goury: *185*
Granville: *27, 70*
Gréville: *176*
Grey Castle, the. *See* Château d'Amfreville
Grimesnil: *74, 114*
Grosville: *29, 171, 172*
Guémené: *63, 71, 77, 78, 79*
Guenrouet: *26*
Guérande: *24*
Guidel: *60, 61*
Guimaëc: *98*

Guiscriff: *98*
Gurunhuel: *100*
Hainneville: *152, 179*
Halte La Guillaumerie: *107*
Hambye: *46*
Hameau de la Planque: *153*
Hameau Duval. *See* Hamel Duval
Hameau Gringor: *179*
Hameau Hubert. *See* Hébert
Hameau le Haguais: *29*
Hameau Piquot: *180*
Hamel Duval: *29*
Hamelin: *68*
Hardinvast: *177, 181*
Hasselt: *119*
Hatainville: *27, 29, 151*
Hameau aux Petits: *29*
Hameau Couvert: *29*
Hameau Pinabel: *153*
Haut-de-Thenay: *113*
Haute Cour: *113*
Hautteville-la-Guichard: *113*
Hameau Vindi. *See* Mont-Vincent
Héauville: *172*
Hébert: *148, 154*
Hédé: *67*
Hennebont: *60, 61, 78*
Herbignac: *24, 26*
Herqueville: *38, 180, 181*
Hierville: *44, 109, 110*
Hill 20: *154*
Hill 34: *105*
Hill 45: *167*
Hill 46: *61*
Hill 59: *109*
Hill 69: *153, 164*
Hill 95: *103, 105, 107, 108*
Hill 112: *107*
Hill 117: *159*
Hill 121: *72*
Hill 131: *72, 103*
Hill 158: *176*
Hill 176: *181*
Hill 180: *174, 177, 178, 179, 181*
Holdy: *156*
Hospice: *72, 107*
Hôtel Mauger. *See* Mauger

Huberville: *156*
Huelgoat: *98*
Hürtgenwald: *82, 119*
Île de Groix: *61*
Île-de-Sein: *99*
Isigny-sur-Mer: *27*
Jobourg: *152, 184*
Jobourg Peninsula: *5, 29, 31, 37, 38, 46, 120, 144, 147, 151, 152, 168, 169, 172, 176, 178, 179, 180, 181, 182, 185, 191*
Joganville: *32, 157, 161, 162*
Josselin: *60, 79*
Jourdan River: *154*
Jugon: *100, 101, 102, 103*
Jullouville: *27*
Juvigny-le-Tertre: *65, 67, 68*
Kairon. *See* Queron
Kerandreau: *77*
Kerandréo. *See* Kerandreau
Kéraval: *61*
Kerbascol: *61*
Kerdavy: *26*
Keremma: *96*
Kerfélice. *See* Kerflis
Kerflis: *26*
Kerfoular: *61*
Kergatorne: *63*
Kergréac'h: *98*
Kergroas: *96*
Kerhabo: *96*
Kerhouel: *61*
Keriber: *96*
Kermalvezin: *24*
Kermat: *95*
Kernilis: *96*
Kerouhant: *96*
Keroumen: *96*
Kervaro: *96*
Kervelguet: *96*
Kervergant: *60, 63*
Kerviny: *61*
La Baleine: *46, 114*
La Basfeuille: *168*
La Basseour: *37*
La Baule: *26, 78*
La Baussaine: *67*
La Béchellerie: *117*
La Belle Croix: *153*

La Belle-Martins: *180*
La Bercendière: *117*
La Bourdonnerie: *109*
La Brasserie: *152*
La Bruyère: *107, 108, 109*
La Champellerie: *105*
La Chapelle: *40, 43, 65*
La Charlerie. *See* Champ Moqtet
La Commanderie: *29*
La Coquerie: *27*
La Croix-du-Bois: *154*
La Cuiroterie: *40*
La Fairie: *43*
La Feuillée: *98*
La Forge: *101*
La Fossairie. *See* La Fosserie
La Fosse du Gast: *153*
La Fosselerie: *163*
La Fosserie: *113*
La Gacilly: *77*
La Glacerie: *38, 153, 172, 174, 176, 177, 178, 179*
La Graverie: *103*
La Gravière: *26*
La Groudiere: *40*
La Groudière Château: *38*
La Haye-d'Osière: *108*
La Haye-du-Puits: *27, 37, 42, 43, 44, 72, 103, 105, 107, 108, 109, 110, 140, 147, 148, 149, 151*
La Huberdière: *116*
La Jeulière: *116*
La Josselerie. *See* La Fosselerie
La Judée: *153*
La Laisnerie: *44*
La Lande-Vaumont: *117, 118*
La Loge: *175, 178*
La Luzerne: *101*
La Maison Quoniam. *See* Cosniam
Lamballe: *101, 144*
Lambézellec: *96*
La Meauffe: *102*
La Moinerie: *116*
La Motte: *44*
La Mouinerie: *43*
La Moulinerie: *74*
Lampaul-Guimiliau: *95*
Lampaul-Ploudalmézeau: *96, 100*
Lanarvily: *96*

Landébia: *65, 99*
Landerneau: *60, 95, 98, 99*
Landerrien: *96*
Landivisiau: *77, 95, 96, 98*
Languivoa: *61*
Lanmeur: *98*
Lannilis: *96*
Lannion: *98, 144*
Lanrelas: *71*
Lanroz: *60, 61*
Lanvellec: *95*
Lanvénégen: *77*
Lanzent: *96*
La Pernelle: *152, 154*
La Poterie: *70, 103, 105*
La Préfontainerie: *154, 171*
La Questnottaie: *113*
La Rivière: *40, 103, 118*
La Roche à Coucou: *29*
La Roche-Bernard: *24, 26*
La Ronde-Haye: *43*
La Rue de Gréville: *184*
La Rue du Bocage: *107, 108*
Lastelle: *105*
La Sullerie: *107*
La Surellerie: *44, 107*
La Touch: *78*
La Tourelle: *107, 108, 109*
La Traisnellerie: *179*
La Tringale: *44*
La Trinité: *26, 96*
La Trinité-sur-Mer: *26*
Laulne: *109*
Laval: *75*
La Val: *110*
La Vieville: *109*
La Ville: *107*
Laye: *180*
Le Barbot: *116*
Le Bas: *109*
Le Becquet: *153*
Le Bequeret: *72*
Le Bigard: *145, 149, 151, 152*
Le Bot: *44*
Le Boulay: *153*
Le Bren: *61*
Le Courégant: *61*

Le Cressonnière: 27
Le Dézert: 27
Le Faou: 95
Le Faouët: 71, 77
Le Fry: 105
Le Gast: 68, 116
Le Ham: 32, 35, 146, 151, 163, 164, 168
Le Haut-du-Ham: 161
Le Haut du Neuf Clos: 27
Le Havre: 167
Le Lescoat: 96
Le Luot: 75
Le Mans: 69, 75
Le Mesnil-au-Val: 152, 153, 174
Le Mesnil-Benoist: 65
Le Mesnil-Bonant: 114
Le Mesnil-Eury: 113
Le Mesnil-Hue: 114
Le Mesnil-Opac: 65
Le Mesnil-Robert: 65
Le Moitiers-en-Bauptois: 70
Le Molay: 26
Le Mont: 44, 107
Le Mouinerie: 43
Le Moulin: 44, 107
Lengronne: 114
Le Petit-Bourg: 118
Le Plessis: 103, 104
Le Pont: 29, 179
Le Pont aux Moines: 29
Le Port Bréhay: 160
Le Poteau: 153
Le Pouldu: 61
Le Puil: 60, 61
Le Puits Ruaule: 110
Le Repas: 101
Le Rocher: 113
Le Sap: 119
Les Carrières: 164
Les Coeuries: 44
Les Courts: 153
Les Fieffes-Dancel: 170
Les Forges: 154
Les Hardouinières: 118
Les Hérouard: 113
Les Ingoufs: 176, 178
Les Kerdes: 40

Les Landes: 35
Les Maisons de Haut: 158
Les Margueries: 72
Les Mézières: 154, 157
Les Moitiers-en-Bauptois: 69, 70
Les Monts: 114
Lesneven: 95, 96
Les Noires Terres: 35
Les Oubeaux: 27
Les Perques: 29
Les Pieux: 29, 148, 149, 151, 170, 171, 174
Les Quatre Vents: 26
Les Romains: 101
Les Rouges Terres: 175, 178
Les Rouges-Terres: 179
Les Sablons: 72
Lessay: 5, 27, 43, 44, 73, 105, 109, 110, 148
Les Trainel: 168
Lestre: 152, 154
Lestréminou: 61
Le Theil: 168, 172, 176, 178
Le Tot: 37, 40
L'Euderie: 116
Le Val: 109
Le Vast: 146, 149, 151, 152, 154
Le Vicel: 153
Le Vieux Château: 107
Le Vieux-Marché: 98
Le Vrétot: 29
Lézarazien: 95
L'Hermitage: 65, 99
L'Hôtel d'Arthenay. See Haut-de-Thenay
L'Hôtel Rauline. See Le Rocher
Liaven: 96
Lieu Bailly: 184
Lieusaint: 154, 168, 170
l'Immaculée: 26
Lion-sur-Mer: 190
Lisieux: 24
Lithaire: 103, 105
Locmélar: 95
Locminé: 60, 63
Locronan: 60, 96, 98
Locunolé: 64
Loire River: 24, 78
Longerac: 70
Lorient: 48, 60, 61, 63, 67, 78, 79

Lourgat: 98
Lozon: 113
Lozon River: 113
Maastricht: 119
Magdeburg: 18
Magneville: 157, 160
Mahlmann-Linie: 39, 43, 70, 74, 103, 104, 105
Malestroit: 77
Manche: 27, 46, 120, 138, 144, 147, 148, 151, 190, 191
Manoir du Lescoat. See Le Lescoat
Marcanville: 40
Marcouf: 159
Marigny: 113, 148
Martinvast: 153, 172, 181
Mauger: 29
Maupertus: 182
Maurepas: 153
Mayenne: 75
Melgven: 63
Melrand: 63
Ménez Hom: 96, 98
Merderet River: 29, 31, 32, 35, 37, 68, 158, 160, 163, 164, 167, 168
Merdrignac: 67, 102
Merlevenez: 60, 61
Meslan: 77
Mesnil-au-Val: 152, 153, 172, 174
Millières: 43, 46, 101
Missillac: 26
Mobecq: 105, 107, 108
Moëlan-sur-Mer: 61
Monetebourg: 144
Montaigu: 114, 153, 159, 172
Mont-Castre: 43, 103, 105, 107
Montcontour: 101
Montcuit: 113
Mont de Mobecq: 108
Mont du Roc: 176
Mont du Roule: 179
Mont du Tot: 108
Montebourg: 32, 35, 145, 146, 147, 148, 149, 151, 152, 153, 154, 156, 157, 158, 159, 160, 161, 162, 163, 164, 166, 167, 168, 170, 171, 172, 176, 180, 207
Montfarville: 153
Montgardon: 43, 44, 103, 105, 107
Montmartin-en-Graignes: 101
Montmartin-sur-Mer: 27
Montoir-de-Bretagne: 26

Mont-Ormel: *119*
Mont-Pali: *180, 184*
Montpinchon: *46*
Montreuil: *113*
Monts-d'Arrée: *99*
Montsurvent: *27, 151*
Mont-Vincent: *109*
Moon-sur-Elle: *101*
Morlaix: *92, 96, 98, 99*
Mortain: *113*
Muneville-le-Bingard: *110*
Mûr-de-Bretagne: *71*
Muzillac: *24, 26*
N13 Highway: *32, 152, 154, 158, 159, 160, 161, 162, 164, 168, 171, 172, 174, 176, 177*
Nacqueville: *149*
Nantes: *77*
Nécy: *119*
Négreville: *149, 157, 170, 171*
Néhou: *37*
Neufmesnil: *105*
Neuville-au-Plain: *32, 42, 157, 158*
Neuville-en-Beaumont: *38*
Néville-sur-Mer: *153*
Normandy: *3, 5, 22, 24, 26, 27, 48, 55, 57, 60, 63, 64, 65, 67, 71, 73, 75, 77, 82, 90, 94, 99, 100, 101, 103, 116, 133, 142, 144, 148, 156, 190, 205, 206, 209*
Notre-Dame-du-Rocher: *118*
Nouainville: *176, 178, 179, 181*
Occagnes: *119*
Octeville: *146, 148, 149, 151, 152, 154, 176, 178, 179, 181*
Octeville-l'Avenel: *146, 148, 149, 151, 152, 154*
Ollonde River: *38*
Olmnitz: *18*
Omonville: *40*
Orglandes: *16, 37, 151, 167*
Orne River: *118, 190*
Orval: *44*
Ozeville: *32, 161, 163, 164, 166*
Parigny: *65*
Paris: *110*
Péaule: *26*
Penchâteau: *24*
Pencran: *95*
Penquer-Coadigou: *77*
Pépinvast: *146, 152*
Percy: *46, 114*

Périers: *27, 44, 65, 99, 101, 102, 103, 104, 105, 112, 113, 147, 148, 149*
Perriers-en-Beauficel: *117*
Pierrepont: *38, 40, 74*
Pierreville: *29*
Pirou: *46*
Pissot: *43, 109*
Plabennec: *98*
Plémy: *101*
Pleumeur-Bodou: *98*
Pleyben: *95*
Pleyber-Christ: *101, 102*
Ploaré: *61*
Plobannalec: *61*
Ploemeur: *60, 61*
Ploërmel: *67*
Ploéven: *98*
Plogastel: *60*
Plomodiern: *96, 98*
Plonévez-du-Faou: *99*
Plonévez-Porzay: *96, 98*
Plouaret: *98, 99*
Plouay: *77*
Ploudiry: *95*
Plouégat-Guérand: *98*
Plouescat: *96, 98*
Plouezoc'h: *98*
Plougar: *99*
Plougourvest: *99*
Plouguenast: *65, 71*
Plouharnel: *63, 78*
Plouhinec: *60, 61, 63*
Plouider: *96*
Plouigneau: *99*
Ploulec'h: *98*
Ploumilliau: *98*
Plounévez-Lochrist: *96, 98*
Plouvien: *95, 98*
Plouvorn: *95, 96*
Plovan: *61, 64*
Pluméliau: *63*
Pluvigner: *64*
Pont-Auny: *70, 72*
Pontchâteau: *24, 26*
Pont-Croix: *61, 77, 98*
Pont-de-Buis: *98, 99*
Pont-Hébert: *148*
Pontivy: *63, 79*

Pont-l'Abbé: *27, 35, 37, 61, 68, 70, 78*
Pontorson: *101, 103, 144, 191*
Pont-Scorff: *60, 61, 63, 64, 75*
Portbail: *29, 37*
Port Launay: *98*
Port Louis: *60*
Port Navallo: *79*
Pouldergat: *61*
Pouldreuzic: *61*
Pouppeville: *154*
Prairies de Marécageuses de Gorges: *72*
Prairies Marécageuses: *38, 44, 70, 72, 103*
Prairies Marécageuses: *72*
Prétot: *65, 70, 72, 74, 99, 103*
Quéménéven: *95*
Quentin: *100*
Queron: *27*
Querqueville: *151, 178, 181*
Quessoy: *101*
Questembert: *67*
Quettehou: *153, 156, 159, 167, 170, 172*
Quettetot: *27, 149, 157*
Quiberon Peninsula: *26*
Quibou: *113*
Quimper: *57, 60, 61, 63, 67, 77, 98*
Quimperlé: *56, 59, 60, 61, 63, 78*
Quinéville: *152, 153, 156, 157, 159, 161, 162, 163, 164, 166, 167, 205*
Quintin: *100*
Rade de Pen Mané: *60*
Rade de Port Louis: *60*
Radom: *94*
Rance River: *78*
Rancoudray: *118*
Rauville-la-Bigot: *148, 170*
Rauville-la-Place: *43*
Ravenoville: *148, 153, 154*
Redon: *24, 27, 67, 78*
Redoute des Fourches: *181*
Reffuveille: *75*
Reigneville-Bocage: *36*
Remungol: *63*
Rennes: *67, 69, 75, 77, 100, 156*
Renneville: *105*
Réthoville: *153*
Réville: *148*
Riec-sur-Bélon: *61*
Rivière de Claids: *110*

226

Roncey: *46, 113, 114*
Rosporden: *60, 63, 67, 77*
Rue Batôn: *40*
Rue Bouillie: *38*
Ruffosses: *147, 154, 174*
Ruhr Pocket: *47, 119*
Ruisseau de la Grande Vallée: *37*
Sainteny: *27, 29, 149, 151*
Saire River: *176, 177*
Saussemesnil: *154, 172*
Savenay: *26*
Scaër: *77, 98*
Scheldt Estuary: *190*
Schevenhütte: *119*
Scrignac: *98*
Seefront: *144, 178*
Seine River: *77, 119*
Senelle River: *70*
Servel: *98*
Sideville: *144, 146, 148, 152, 153*
Sienne River: *46, 114*
Sinope River: *167*
Siouville-Hague: *29*
Sortosville: *156*
Sottevast: *35, 171, 172*
Sotteville: *29, 152*
Soulles River: *46, 113*
Sourdeval: *46, 101, 114, 116, 117*
St. André-de-l'Épine: *101, 102*
St. Brice-en-Coglès: *65*
St. Brieuc: *99, 100*
St. Clair: *37, 144*
St. Côme-du-Mont: *27, 154*
St. Coulitz: *98*
St. Cristophe-du-Foc: *172*
St. Croix-Hague: *145, 146, 147, 148, 149, 151, 152, 153, 172, 181, 182*
St. Croix-sur-Orne: *118*
St. Croix-Verte: *154*
St. Cyr: *35*
St. Denis-le-Gast: *46, 114*
St. Dolay: *26*
Ste. Colombe: *37, 167*
Ste. Hilaire-du-Harcouët: *67, 68*
Ste. Marie-du-Mont: *27, 149, 151, 153, 154, 206*
Ste. Mère-Église: *27, 31, 32, 35, 37, 148, 149, 151, 154, 157, 158, 167, 182, 207*
Ste. Opportune: *118*

Ste. Suzanne: *103, 105*
St. Floxel: *32, 157, 158, 159, 160, 161, 163, 164*
St. Gabriel: *189*
St. Gavré: *78*
St. Georges-de-Reintembault: *65*
St. Germain-de-Tallevende: *116*
St. Germain-de-Tournebut: *149, 153, 167, 172*
St. Germain-de-Varreville: *154*
St. Germain-le-Gaillard: *29*
St. Germain-sur-Ay: *27, 44, 103, 104, 109*
St. Germain-sur-Sèves: *105*
St. Gilles: *113*
St. Hilaire-du-Harcouët: *65*
St. Jacques-de-Néhou: *37, 151, 167*
St. James: *103*
St. Jean-Brévelay: *77, 79*
St. Jean-de-Daye: *27, 148*
St. Jean-de-la-Rivière: *29*
St. Jores: *103, 105*
St. Joseph: *154, 168, 170*
St. Lambert-sur-Dives: *119*
St. Lô: *24, 29, 38, 44, 64, 65, 68, 82, 100, 101, 102, 103, 110, 112, 113, 151*
St. Malo: *64*
St. Marcouf: *31, 32, 157, 158, 159, 160, 161, 162, 167*
St. Martin: *65, 113, 114, 149, 153, 154, 157, 164, 166, 171, 172*
St. Martin-d'Aubigny: *113*
St. Martin-d'Audouville: *149*
St. Martin-de-Cenilly: *114*
St. Martin-de-Tallevende: *65*
St. Michel-Chef-Chef: *26*
St. Nazaire: *24, 26, 77, 78, 79*
St. Pierre-Église: *151, 153, 156, 171, 178*
St. Pierre-Quilbignon: *96*
St. Rémy-des-Landes: *40, 42, 43*
St. Samson-de-Bonfossé: *113*
St. Sauveur: *181*
St. Sauveur-de-Chaulieu: *118*
St. Sauveur-de-Pierrepont: *38, 40*
St. Sauveur-Lendelin: *27*
St. Sauveur-le-Vicomte: *27, 36, 37, 43, 71, 73, 105, 144, 149, 151, 167, 168, 195*
St. Sebastian-de-Raids: *46*
St. Suzanne: *70*
St. Symphorien: *43, 105, 107*
St. Thégonnec: *98*
St. Vaast-la-Hougue: *159, 168*

St. Yvi: *75*
Surville: *43*
Surzur: *24*
Taute River: *107, 112, 151*
Tessy-sur-Vire: *65*
Teurthéville-Bocage: *154*
Teurthéville-Hague: *148, 168, 176*
Theix: *26*
Théville: *180*
Théville airfield: *175, 176, 177, 182*
Tinchebray: *118*
Tocqueville: *145, 146, 147, 148, 149, 151, 152, 153, 159*
Tollevast: *148*
Tonneville: *153, 181*
Torigni-sur-Vire: *144*
Tostes: *119*
Tourch: *98*
Tourlaville: *38, 144, 146, 149, 152, 176, 177, 180, 181*
Tréauville: *29*
Tréflez: *96*
Trégounour: *61*
Tréguier: *98, 144*
Trégunc: *61*
Trelly: *114*
Trémeac: *26*
Trescalan: *24*
Trévéré: *26*
Trézilidé: *95*
Tribehou: *18*
Trottebec River: *177*
Truttemer: *118*
Turqueville: *152, 153*
Urville: *35, 162, 164, 167, 168*
Utah Beach: *27, 31, 120, 138, 153, 154, 156, 205*
Uzel: *65, 71*
Valognes: *36, 135, 144, 146, 148, 149, 151, 152, 153, 154, 156, 168, 170, 171, 172, 205*
Vannes: *24, 26, 79*
Varenguebec: *40, 43, 105*
Varouville: *153*
Varreville: *40, 154*
Vasteville: *151, 152, 176*
Vaublat River: *179*
Vaudival: *163*
Vaudreville: *164*
Vauville: *29, 37, 144, 168, 172, 180, 181, 182*
Vauville Bight: *27, 195*

Vengeons: *117*
Vesly: *43, 109, 110*
Vienna: *5*
Vie River: *119*
Vieux-Vy-sur-Couesnon: *65*
Village ès Noels: *44*
Village Hérouard. *See* Les Hérouard
Village Marie: *113*
Villedieu-les-Poêles: *46, 103, 110, 114, 116, 144*
Villiers-Fossard: *101, 102, 104*
Vindefontaine: *70, 151*
Virandeville: *17, 29*
Vire: *116, 117*
Vire Estuary: *191*
Vire River: *101, 107, 112*

PROPER NAMES

Bacherer, Rudolf: *37, 38*
Bartel: *80*
Bayer von Bayersburg: *31, 35*
Beigang: *157*
Berg: *159*
Bessel, Arnold von: *120*
Bethge: *20*
Boehm: *84, 101*
Borst: *80*
Brinkmeier: *79*
Brüggemann: *80*
Choltitz, Dietrich von: *103, 110, 206, 207*
Coep: *52, 66*
Combosch: *31*
Cordes: *84, 86*
Creuz: *90*
Deffner: *80*
Dickertmann: *105*
Dihm, Friedrich: *95*
Dollmann, Friedrich: *10, 17, 100, 102*
Düvert, Walter: *48, 57, 59, 63*
Eitner: *70, 76, 77*
Elbrecht: *157*
Fahrmbacher, Wilhelm: *10, 63, 206*
Falley, Wilhelm: *5, 29*
Fink: *156*
Flockerzi: *31, 167*
Gall, Freiherr von: *114*
Geyso, Eckhard von: *120*
Gimmler, Wilhelm: *55*

Görtmüller: *86*
Goth: *101*
Gräfe: *175*
Habersang: *52*
Hadenfeldt: *166, 167, 180, 182, 186, 188*
Hallmann: *164*
Hallmayer: *35*
Hamann: *152, 156*
Heimbach: *20*
Hellwig: *16*
Hellmich, Heinz: *5, 15, 29, 36, 37, 69, 161, 167*
Hett: *54, 79*
Heydte, von der: *114*
Hoffmann: *32, 163, 165, 175*
Hornung: *128, 180, 182*
Hümmerich: *133, 136, 137, 154, 156, 157*
Ibe: *104*
Jäger: *66, 69, 70, 71, 73, 76*
Jahn, Kurt: *120*
Junck, Hans: *48*
Jürgens: *182, 186*
Kampf: *91*
Käßberg: *81*
Katzmann: *176*
Keil: *122, 125, 126, 127, 142, 143, 153, 156, 157, 158, 159, 161, 166, 167, 168, 172, 174, 178, 179, 184, 185, 186, 187, 188*
Kessler: *156*
Klein: *16*
Klostermper, Bernhard: *5, 10, 29, 31, 35, 37, 38, 44, 46*
Köhler: *87*
Köhn: *125, 156, 175*
König, Eugen: *31, 37, 46*
Küppers: *176, 184*
Lewandowski: *75*
Mahlmann, Paul: *39, 43, 70, 74, 82, 86, 90, 93, 95, 100, 103, 104, 105, 110, 113, 114, 116, 119, 207*
Manussi: *120, 139, 145*
Marcks, Erich: *32, 161, 162, 164*
Maurer: *15*
Mecklenburg: *72, 76, 77, 79, 91*
Mehner: *55*
Messerschmidt: *156, 158*
Moll: *101*
Moritz: *176*
Mosebach: *137*
Müller: *10, 31, 32, 37, 38, 158, 159, 161, 174, 177, 179, 182, 184, 185, 186*
Nake, Albin: *120, 144*

Nesselhauf: *20*
Offergold: *79*
Ogroske: *135, 137*
Pillmann: *89, 104, 110*
Quittnat: *174, 176, 179, 180, 182, 188*
Reese: *52*
Reicherzer: *16*
Reiter: *128, 152*
Rentsch: *32*
Riess: *40*
Risch: *76*
Rohrbach: *32, 125, 139, 162, 164, 166, 175, 180*
Rommel, Erwin: *32, 151, 154, 159, 161, 168, 170*
Rosenow: *104*
Rundstedt, Gerd von: *22*
Sabotha: *54*
Sattler, Robert: *152, 172, 179, 184, 189*
Schacky auf Schönfeld, Sigmund von: *144*
Schlee: *80*
Schlieben, Karl-Wilhelm von: *120, 122*
Schmitz: *84, 119*
Schwellenbach: *159, 167*
Seidel (Obstlt.): *157*
Seidel (Lt.): *137*
Siepmann: *35, 40*
Simon: *10, 40, 41*
Simoneit: *159, 166*
Sörensen: *41*
Starcke: *86*
Theuerkauf: *86, 103*
Triepel: *167*
Vogel: *105*
Weindl: *32, 36*
Weissenborn: *68*
Weng: *166, 169, 171, 179*
Wild: *68, 76*
Winter: *93*
Witt (Obst.): *80*
Witt (Freg. Kptn.): *184*
Witzleben, Hermann von: *5, 10*
Ziegelmann: *101, 102*
Zwanzig: *15*

V

VEHICLES

Combat Support Vehicles
Sd.Kfz. 247: *137*

Prime Movers
Sd.Kfz. 7 (mittlerer Zugkraftwagen 8t / medium prime mover, 8-tonne): *16, 17, 21, 50*
Sd.Kfz. 8 (schwerer Zugkraftwagen 12t / heavy prime mover, 12-tonne): *19*
Sd.Kfz. 9 (Schwerer Zugkraftwagen 18 t) / heavy prime mover, 18-tonne): *93*
Sonder-Anhänger 116 (Tieflade-Anhänger 22t): *93*

Self-propelled Anti-tank Guns
Sd.Kfz. 135 7,5 cm PaK 40 auf Sfl. Lorraine Schlepper 'Marder I': *91, 131, 135*
Sd.Kfz. 138 Marder III (Ausführung M): *18, 19, 20, 41, 42, 91, 113, 135, 136, 137, 205*
4,7 cm Pak(t) auf Panzerkampfwagen 35R(f) ohne Turm: *134*
Sd.Kfz. 164 8,8 cm PaK 43/1 auf Fgst. Pz.Kpfw. III/IV (SF) (Nashorn or Hornisse): *135*
Sd.Kfz. 138 Marder III (Ausführung M): *32, 39, 41, 65, 92, 105*

Self-Propelled Artillery
15 cm sFH 13/1 (Sf.) auf Geschützwagen Lorraine Schlepper(f): *131*

Self-propelled Flak
Sd.Kfz. 6/2 (37 mm FlaK 36 auf Fahrgestell Zugkraftwagen 5t): *92*
Sd.Kfz. 7/2 (Fahrgestell des m. Zgkw. 8t mit 3,7 cm Flak 36/37/43): *92*
Sd.Kfz. 10/5 (für 2 cm Flak 38): *18*

Support Vehicles
Kfz. 12 (medium cross-country personnel vehicle): *22*
Kfz. 15 (medium staff car): *93*
Kfz. 17 (signals support vehicle): *19, 55*
Raupenschlepper Ost (RSO): *17, 21, 41, 86, 90, 93, 136, 201, 214*
Sd.Kfz. 2 (Kettenkraftkrad / Kettenkrad / halftrack motor-cycle): *14, 87, 93*
Sd.Kfz. 3 (Maultier / "mule" halftrack vehicle): *20, 93, 137*
Volkswagen Schwimmwagen, Typ 166: *90*

W

WEAPONS

GERMAN

Anti-aircraft Weapons
2 cm Flak 30: *54, 127, 133*
2 cm Flak 38: *16, 18, 54, 129, 133*
2 cm Scotti(i): *130, 131*
3,7cm Flak (18 / 36/ 37 / 43): *137*
8,8 cm Flak M31(r): *133*
8,35 cm Flak 22(t): *133*

Anti-tank Guns
4,5 cm Pak 184/1(r): *56*
4,7 cm Pak(t): *134, 136*
5 cm Pak 38: *126, 127, 134, 135, 136*
7,5 cm Pak 40: *14, 17, 20, 54, 59, 65, 86, 90, 126, 127, 135, 136, 137, 138*
7,5 cm Pak 41: *134*
7,5 cm Pak 97/38: *126, 135, 136*
8,8 cm Pak 43/41: *126, 134, 135*

Anti-tank Weapons
8,8 cm Raketenwerfer 43 Puppchen: *85*
Raketenpanzerbüchse 54 (Ofenrohr): *11, 12, 14, 15, 53, 86, 91, 138*

Artillery
7,5cm Feldkanone 16 neuer Art (7,5cm FK 16 nA): *129*
7,62 cm Feld-Kanone 39 (r) (7,62 cm FK 39(r)): *16, 54, 132*
7,62 cm leichte Kanonen-Haubitze 290 (r) (L.K.H. 290 (r)): *14, 54, 127*
8 cm Feld-Kanone 17(t) (8 cm F.K.17(t)): *129*
10,5 cm Kanone 331(f) (10,5 cm K. 331(f)): *130, 131, 176*
10,5 cm leichte Feld-Haubitze 16 (le.F.H. 16): *129*
10,5 cm leichte Feld-Haubitze 18 (le.F.H. 18): *87, 88*
10,5cm leichte Feld-Haubitze 325(f) (10,5 cm le.F.H. 325 (f)): *129*
10 cm leichte Feld-Haubitze 14/19(t) (10 cm le.F.H. 14/19(t)): *129, 130*
12,2 cm Kanone 390/2(r) (12,2 cm K 390/2(r)): *16, 54*
12,2 cm schwere Feld-Haubitze 396(r) (12,2 cm sFH 396(r)): *16, 54*
15,5 cm schwere Feld-Haubitze 41(f) (15,5 cm s.F.H. 414(f)): *131, 133, 176*
15,5 cm schwere Feld-Haubitze 414(f) (15,5 cm s.F.H.414(f)): *131*
15cm schwere Feld-Haubitze 13 (s.F.H. 13): *131*
15cm schwere Feld-Haubitze 18 (s.F.H. 18): *88*
leichtes Infanterie-Geschütz 18 (le.I.G. 18): *86*
schweres Infanterie-Geschütz 33 (s.I.G. 33): *86*

Combat Engineer
Flammenwerfer 39: *16*
Flammenwerfer 41: *16*
S-Mine 35: *16*
Tellermine 42: *16*

Machine Guns
Maschinengewehr 08/15 (MG 08/15): *138*
Maschinengewehr 08 (MG 08): *130, 138*
Maschinengewehr 13 (MG 13): *9, 52, 138*
Maschinengewehr 14(p) (MG 14(p)): *138*
Maschinengewehr 26(t) (MG 26(t) 26): *138*
Maschinengewehr 30(p) (MG 30(p)): *138*
Maschinengewehr 34 (MG 34): *9, 20, 84, 91, 126, 127, 130, 131, 138*
Maschinengewehr 42 (MG 42): *9, 11, 12, 15, 16, 20, 51, 52, 53, 54, 55, 84, 85, 86, 89, 90, 127, 132, 138*
Maschinengewehr 116(f) (MG 116(f)): *138*
Maschinengewehr 156(f) (MG 156(f)): *138*
Maschinengewehr 311(f) (MG 311(f)): *138*
Maschinengewehr 257(f): *138*
Maschinengewehr 311(f): *138*

Miscellaneous
2 cm Kampfwagen-Kanone 38: *131*

Mortars
5 cm Granat-Werfer 36: *125, 138*
5 cm Granat-Werfer 201(b): *138*
5 cm Granat-Werfer 203(f): *138*
5 cm M19: *138*
8,1 cm Granat-Werfer 34: *52*
8,14 cm Granat-Werfer 278(f): *125, 138*
12 cm Granat-Werfer 42 (Gr.W. 42): *11*

Rifles
Karabiner 98k (K98k): *9, 12, 16, 52, 53, 55, 85, 90, 91, 130*
Selbstladegewehr 41 (G41): *9, 52, 84, 138*
Gewehr 98 (G98): *9*

Endnotes

Part 2 (continued): Heer Infantry Divisions

243. Infanterie-Division

1 *Div. Verbände, II. Teil, 243.Inf.Div.* [T78 R412 F6380328]; Anl.4 zu OKH/GenStdH/Org Abt Nr.I/2271/43 g.K., 2.5.1943 [T78 R406 F6376013]; **Tessin, G.** (1977), *1. Band*, p.67; **Tessin, G.** (1973), *8. Band*, p.186]
2. *Div. Verbände, II. Teil, 243.Inf.Div.* [T78 R412 F6380328]; **Tessin, G. (1977)**, *1.Band*, p.105; **Tessin, G. (1973)**, *8.Band*, p.186] *"Division C"* never materialised, but the others were redesignated as well. *"Division A"*, *"D"* and *"E"* respectively became the *242.*, the *245.* and the *244. Inf.Div.* [**Tessin G. (1977)**, *1.Band*, p.105; Index cards showing the most basic background of Division A-E in T78 R412 F6380327-6380330]
3. Tessin, G. (1973), *8.Band*, p.186; Overview of the organisational history of the *243. I.D.* [T78 R412 F6380328]
4. OKH/Chef H Rüst u.Bde AHA Ia(I) Nr.3932/43 g.K., 4.8.43 [T78 R850 frame number not known]; Gen St d H Op.Abt. III/Prüf-Nr.: 38243, *Schematische Kriegsgliederug - Stand: 5.8.43.* [T78 R708]; Gen St d H Op.Abt.III/Prüf-Nr.: 39616, *Schematisch Kriegsgliederung - Stand: 14.8.43.* [T78 R708]; AOK 7, *Kriegstagebuch der Führungsabteilung* AOK 7 *für die Zeit vom 1.7.3.44- 31.12.43* [T312 R1558 F29, 45 & 72]; AOK 7, Ia Nr.4968/43 g., 30.9.43 [T312 R1558 F942]
5. AOK 7, Ia Nr.124/43 g.K.Chefs., 11.11.1943, p.1 [T312 R1563 F1004]; AOK 7 BvTO, *Tatigkeitsbericht für die Zeit vom 1. Januar bis 31. März 1944*, p.1 [T312 R1571 F877]
6. AOK 7, Ia Nr.2454/44 g.K., 13.5.44, p.2 [T312 R1565 F696]
7. AOK 7, Kriegsgliederung 7. Armee, Stand 18.5.44, *243. I.D., Stand 1.5.1944* [T312 R1566 F220]
8. German general staff officers files, index cards of *Gen.Maj.* von Witzleben [T78 R895 H6/26] From the start of the war until February 1943, *Gen.Maj.* von Witzleben led a number of schools or courses and was on the staff of several field commands, including being the chief-of-staff of *AOK 2* and serving as the German general with the 2nd Royal Hungarian Army. In his various roles, he received good performance reviews, although his health issues hindered him. *Gen.* Fahrmbacher (*XXV. A.K.*) and *Gen.* Dollmann (AOK 7) mostly shared these views. The latter considered his transfer in January 1944 a great loss.
9. Kartei von Inf.-Kommandeuren, index card of *Gen.Lt.* Hellmich [T78 R908 H6/354]; AOK 7 Ia, *Kriegstagebuch der Führungsabteilung AOK 7 für die Zeit vom 1.Jan. - 30.Juni 1944* [T312 R1564 F33] — Hereafter referred to as: AOK 7 Ia, KTB 1.1.-30.6.1944. At the outbreak of WWII, *Gen.Lt.* Hellmich was on the staff of AOK 7, before being transferred to that of *Heeresgruppe B*. After this, he commanded the *23. I.D.* and the *141. Res.Div.* In December 1942, he was appointed *General der Osttruppen*, which he remained until the end of 1943. Although his initial performance reviews had been excellent, this changed in early 1942 when he was accused of not being tough enough. *Feldm.* von Kluge blamed the general's issues on the impact of having lost both sons on the battlefield in 1940 and 1941 and suggested an extended leave to regain his original performance. [German general staff officers files, index cards of *Gen.Lt.* Hellmich in T78 R887 H6/26]
10. AOK 7 Ia, KTB 1.1.-30.6.1944 [T312 R1564 F330]; Communication between AOK 7 and other commands in the period of 3.-16.8.44, p.12-14 & 27 [T312 R1568 F660]; AOK 7, Ia Nr.3192/44 g., 25.8.44, p.2-3 [T312 R1568 F406-7]
11. PWIS(H)/LF/189, 28 Jun 44, p.1 [UKNA, WO 208/3630]; C.S.D.I.C. (UK) S.I.R. 485, 3 Jul 44, p.3 [NARA, RG 165, Box 659, Folder 2]; PWIS(H)/LF/271, 9 Jul 44, p.1 [UKNA, WO 208/3631] Some authors have claimed that the division used a logo in the form of a capital H with two small vertical bars on the cross bar, making a second H. This supposedly stood for the initials of its commander: Heinz Hellmich. If this existed, it is more likely it was used as a road sign.
12. OKH/GenStdH/Org.Abt.I 16692/44 g.K., 25.4.44, p.1 [T78 R420 F6389709]
13. OKH Chef H Rüst u. BdE, AHA/Ia(I) Nr.3059/43 g.K., 19.6.43, p.1-2 [T78 R849 H36/156]; OKH Chef H Rüst u. BdE, AHA Ia(I) Nr.2529/43 g.K., 20.5.43, p.1 & Anl.2 & 3 [T78 R849 H36/156]
14. OKW Chef H Rüst u. BdE, AHA/Ia(I) Nr.3414/32 g.K., 9.7.43, p.1, Anl. 2 & 3 [T78 R850 H36/157]
15. OKW Chef H Rüst u. BdE, AHA/Ia(I) Nr.3414/32 g.K., 9.7.43, p.1-3 [T78 R850 H36/157]
16. *Ibid.*, p.4-5
17. Anl. zu OKH/GenStdH/Org.Abt. Nr.I/4500/43 g.K., 4.10.43, *Kriegsgliederung des Feldheeres (Sollgliederung), Band I, Stand: September 1943*, p.96 [T78 R409 F637795–] — Hereafter referred to as: OKH, *Kriegsgliederung des Feldheeres September 1943*
18. WFSt/Op. (H) West, Nr.004662/44 g.K., 3.5.44, *Fehlstellen der Divisionen im Bereich Ob.West, Stand 1.4.44*, p.1 [T77 R1421 F237] Referred to in **Zetterling, N. (2000)**, p.242-3
19. Anl.2 zu Ob.West (Obkdo.H.Gr.D) Ia Nr.7183/44 g.K., 9.12.32 [BaMa, RH 19-IV/18]
20. Ob.West (Obkdo.H.Gr.D) Ia Nr.7058/43 g.K., 2.12.43, p.2 [BaMa, RH 19-IV/18]
21. Leleu, J.L. (2022), *Combattre en Dictature*, Paris: Perrin, Appendix 13 (based on MIRS (b), *Various age groups studies*, 12.8.1944)
22. Data obtained from the *DRK Vermisstenbildliste* and death cards in the Ancestry "Germany, Military Killed in Action, 1939-1948" collection.
23. AOK 7, Kriegsgliederung 7. Armee, Stand 10.4.44, *243. I.D., Stand 1.3.1944* [T312 R1566 F192]; AOK 7, Kriegsgliederung 7. Armee, Stand 18.5.44, *243. I.D., Stand 1.5.1944* [T312 R1566 F220]
24. Anl.7 zu 243.Inf.Div., Ia Nr.16/44 g.K., (Zustandsbericht), 1.1.44 [T314 R745 F651]
25. Anl.7 zu 243.Inf.Div., Ia Nr.16/44 g.K., Kriegsgliederung, 1.1.44 [T314 R745 F653]
26. AOK 7/O.Qu., *Kriegstagebuch der Oberquartiermeisterabteilung AOK 7 für die Zeit vom 1.Febr.1944 - 29.Febr.1944* [T312 R1570 F878]; AOK 7/O.Qu., *Kriegstagebuch der Oberquartiermeisterabteilung AOK 7 für die Zeit vom 1.3.44 - 31.3.44* [T312 R1570 F1005 & 8]; AOK 7/O.Qu., *Kriegstagebuch der Oberquartiermeisterabteilung AOK 7 für die Zeit vom 1.3.–4 - 31.3.44* [T312 R1570 F1014 & 22]; AOK 7/O.Qu., *Kriegstagebuch der Oberquartiermeisterabteilung AOK 7 für die Zeit vom 1.5.44 - 31.5.44* [T312 R1571 F306 & 9]
27. PWIS(H)/LDC/98, 11 Jul 44, p.3 [UKNA, WO 208/3646]
28. OKH, *Kriegsgliederung des Feldheeres September 1943*, p.96 [T78 R409 F6377954]; *K.St.N. (Heer) Nr.4006, Kommando einer Infanteriedivision (Besatzung)*, 1.4.42 [T78 R394 F6363028-32]; *K.St.N. (Heer) Nr.1067a, Kraftrad-Meldezug*, 1.1.43 [BaMa, RH 11/10] This called for 26 light motorcycles and 5 heavy motorcycle-combinations, along with 6 NCO's and 25 men.
29. AOK 7, Kriegsgliederung 7. Armee, Stand 18.5.44, *243. I.D., Stand 1.5.1944* [T312 R1566 F220]
30. OKH, *Kriegsgliederung des Feldheeres September 1943*, p.96 [T78 R409 F6377954]; *KStN 101F, 130F* and *131F* can be found in T78 R397_H1/28. The MG company used *KStN 131F* (1.12.42), minus the light mortars and the parts concerning the 8 cm mortars in *KStN 170* (20.5.43).
31. OKH, *Kriegsgliederung des Feldheeres September 1943*, p.96 [T78 R409 F6377954]; *KStN 171F* (4.5.43) and *KStN 186F* (1.12.42) can be found in T78 R397_H1/28
32. *K.St.N. (Heer) Nr.211 F, Teileinheit, Bespannungsstaffel eines Infanterieregiments (bodenständig)*, 1.12.42 [T78 R897 F6366332-3] Authorised strength: 4 NCO's, 30 men, 2 riding horses and 44 light draught horses.
33. OKH/Abwicklungsstab - Sachgebiet 243 (**Schoch, H.**), *Vorläufiger Bericht über den Kampf der 243. I.D. auf the Halbinsel Cotentin v. 6.6 bis 7.8 1944.* 22.12.44 [T78 R672 H41/61b]
34. Ob.West Okdo.d.H.Gr.D, *II. Ausfertigung Ia, K.T.B. vom 1.10 - 31.10.43*, p.86 [T311 R20 F7023303]; Anlage 2 zu OKH/Chef H Rüst u.Bde AHA/ZASt, Nr.7000/43 gK., p.154 [T78 R401 F6371592]
35. AOK 7, Kriegsgliederung 7. Armee, Stand 18.5.44, *243. I.D., Stand 1.5.1944* [T312 R1566 F220]
36. *Ibid.*
37. Gen.Kdo.XXV. A.K., *Kriegstagebuch Nr.11 Gen.Kdo.XXV. A.K. Führungsabteilung (Ia) 1.10.43 - 31.12.43* [T314 R745 F36] — Hereafter referred to as Gen.Kdo.XXV. A.K. Ia, *KTB Nr.11*
38. Anlage zu *243. I.D.*, Ia Nr.16/44 g.K., (Kriegsgliederung) *243.Inf.Dlv., Stand vom 1.1.44* [T314 R745 F653]; AOK 7, Kriegsgliederung 7. Armee, Stand 12.1.44, *243. Infanterie-Div., Stand: 13.1.44* [T312 R1566 F50]
39. Gen.Kdo.XXV. A.K. Ia, KTB Nr.11 [T314 R745 F36]; AOK 7, Kriegsgliederung 7. Armee, Stand 18.5.44, *243. I.D., Stand 1.5.1944* [T312 R1566 F220]

40. PWIS(H)/LF/185, 27 Jun 44, p.1 [UKNA, WO 208/3630]; PWIS(H)/156, 15 Jun 44 [UKNA, WO 208/3622]; PWIS(H)/LF/167, 28 Jun 44 [UKNA, WO 208/3630]
41. PWIS(H)/LDC/98, 11 Jul 44, p.2 [UKNA, WO 208/3646]
42. PWIS(H)/LDC/103, 11 Jul 44 [UKNA, WO 208/3646]
43. AOK 7, Kriegsgliederung 7. Armee, Stand 18.5.44, *243. I.D., Stand 1.5.1944* [T312 R1566 F220]; AOK 7, Ia Nr.724/44 g.K., p.1-2 [T312 R1565 F24-5]
44. AOK 7, Kriegsgliederung 7. Armee, Stand 18.5.44, *243. I.D., Stand 1.5.1944* [T312 R1566 F220]; AOK 7/O.Qu., *Kriegstagebuch der Oberquartiermeisterabteilung AOK 7 für die Zeit vom 1.4.44 – 30.4.44* [T312 R1571 F12]
45. C.S.D.I.C. (UK) S.I.R. 485, 3 Jul 44, App.1 [NARA, RG 165, Box 659, Folder 2]; PWIS(H)/LDC/98, 11 Jul 44, p.2 [UKNA, WO 208/3646]
46. The information about the headquarters company of *GR 921* gives the total strength of the signals, bicycle and engineer platoons as 60, 40 and 40 men respectively. [S.I.R. 485, 3 Jul 44, App.1 in NARA, RG 165, Box 659, Folder 2]
47. PWIS(H)/LDC/98, 11 Jul 44, p.2 [UKNA, WO 208/3646]
48. AOK 7, Kriegsgliederung 7. Armee, Stand 18.5.44, *243. I.D., Stand 1.5.1944* [T312 R1566 F221]; PWIS(H)/LF/271, 9 Jul 44, p.1 [UKNA, WO 208/3631]
49. PWIS(H)/LF/271, 9 Jul 44, p.1 [UKNA, WO 208/3631]; PWIS(H)/LDC/98, 11 Jul 44, p.2 [UKNA, WO 208/3646]
50. PWIS(H)/LDC/98, 11 Jul 44, p.2 [UKNA, WO 208/3646]
51. PWIS(H)/LF/271, 9 Jul 44, p.1 [UKNA, WO 208/3631]
52. C.S.D.I.C. (UK) S.I.R. 485, 3 Jul 44, App. 1 [NARA, RG 165, Box 659, Folder 2]
53. AOK 7, Kriegsgliederung 7. Armee, Stand 18.5.44, *243. I.D., Stand 1.5.1944* [T312 R1566 F220]
54. PWIS(H)/LDC/98, 11 Jul 44, p.2 [UKNA, WO 208/3646]
55. C.S.D.I.C. (UK) S.I.R. 406, 22 Jun 44, p.1 [NARA, RG 165, Box 659, Folder 2]
56. C.S.D.I.C. (UK) S.I.R. 485, 3 Jul 44, App.2 [NARA, RG 165, Box 659, Folder 2]
57. OKH, *Kriegsgliederung des Feldheeres September 1943*, p.96 [T78 R409 F6377954]; *K.St.N. (Heer) Nr.131F, Notetat, Schützenkompanie (bodenständig)*, 1.12.1942 [T78 R397 F6366295-8]
58. AOK 7, Kriegsgliederung 7. Armee, Stand 18.5.44, *243. I.D., Stand 1.5.1944* [T312 R1566 F220]
59. PWIS(H)/181, POW taken on 10 Jun 44 [UKNA, 208/3622]; PWIS(H)/156, 15 Jun 44 [UKNA, WO 208/3622]; PWIS(H)/LF/151, PWs taken on 10 Jun 44) [UKNA, WO 208/3630]; PWIS(H)/LF/167, 28 Jun 44 [UKNA, WO 208/3630]; PWIS(H)/LF/185, 27 Jun 44 [UKNA, WO 208/3630]; PWIS(H)/LDC/70, 3 Jul 44 [UKNA, WO 208/3646]; PWIS(H)/LDC/98, 11 Jul 44 [UKNA, WO 208/3646]; C.S.D.I.C. (UK) S.I.R. 485, 3 Jul 44, App. 3-5 [NARA, RG 165, Box 659, Folder 2]
60. PWIS(H)/181, POW taken on 10 Jun 44 [UKNA, 208/3622]; PWIS(H)/LF/185, 27 Jun 44 [UKNA, WO 208/3630]; PWIS(H)/LDC/70, 3 Jul 44 [UKNA, WO 208/3646]; C.S.D.I.C. (UK), S.I.R. 410, 21 Jun 44, p.1 [NARA, RG 165, Box 659, Folder 2]
61. C.S.D.I.C. (UK) S.I.R. 485, 3 Jul 44, App.3 [NARA, RG 165, Box 659, Folder 2]
62. PWIS(H)/LDC/98, 11 Jul 44, p.2 [UKNA, WO 208/3646]
63. PWIS(H)/156, 15 Jun 44 [UKNA, WO 208/3622]; PWIS(H)/LDC/70, 3 Jul 44 [UKNA, WO 208/3646]; PWIS(H)/LF/151, POW's taken on 10 Jun 44) [UKNA, WO 208/3630]; PWIS(H)/LF/167, 28 Jun 44 [UKNA, WO 208/3630]; PWIS(H)/LDC/98, 11 Jul 44, p.1 [UKNA, WO 208/3646]; C.S.D.I.C. (UK) S.I.R. 485, 3 Jul 44, App.4, & 6 [NARA, RG 165, Box 659, Folder 2]
64. PWIS(H)/LF/151, PW's taken on 10 Jun 44) [UKNA, WO 208/3630]
65. PWIS(H)/LDC/70, 3 Jul 44 [UKNA, WO 208/3646]
66. C.S.D.I.C. (UK) S.I.R. 485, 3 Jul 44, App.4, 5 & 6 [NARA, RG 165, Box 659, Folder 2]
67. *Ibid.*, App.4 [NARA, RG 165, Box 659, Folder 2]
68. OKH, *Kriegsgliederung des Feldheeres September 1943*, p.96 [T78 R409 F6377954]
69. PWIS(H)/181, POW taken on 10 Jun 44) [UKNA 208/3622] The information from this prisoner appears to have been largely outdated for D-Day. Its content is not confirmed by officers from the regiment either.
70. OKH/GenStcH/Org.Abt. Nr.I/15461/44 g.K., 25 3.44, p.2 [T78 R398 H1/39]
71. PWIS(H)/LDC/70, 3 Jul 44 [UKNA, WO 208/3645]; PWIS(H)/LDC/98, 11 Jul 44, p.3 [UKNA, WO 208/3646]; C.S.D.I.C. (UK) S.I.R. 410, 21 Jun 44, p.1 [NARA, RG 165, Box 659, Folder 2]
72. PWIS(H)/LDC/98, 11 Jul 44, p.3 [UKNA, WO 208/3646]
73. PWIS(H)/181, POW taken on 10 Jun 44) [UKNA, 208/3622]; C.S.D.I.C. (UK) S.I.R. 426, 22 Jun 44, p.1 [UKNA, WO 208/3591]; C.S.D.I.C. (UK) S.I.R. 410, 21 Jun 44, p.1 [NARA, RG 165, Box 659, Folder 2]
74. PWIS(H)/LDC/70, 3 Jul 44 [UKNA, WO 208/3646]
75. *Ibid.*
76. C.S.D.I.C. (UK) S.I.R. 485, 3 Jul 44, App.7 [NARA, RG 165, Box 659, Folder 2]
77. PWIS(H)/156, 15 Jun 44 [UKNA, WO 208/3622]; PWIS(H)/LDC/70, 3 Jul 44 [UKNA, WO 208/3646]; C.S.D.I.C. (UK) S.I.R. 410, 21 Jun 44, p.1 [NARA, RG 165, Box 659, Folder 2]
78. C.S.D.I.C. (UK) S.I.R. 485, 3 Jul 44, App.7 [NARA, RG 165, Box 659, Folder 2]
79. PWIS(H)/LF/185, 27 Jun 44, p.2 [UKNA, WO 208/3630]
80. PWIS(H)/LF/167, 28 Jun 44 [UKNA, WO 208/3630]
81. PWIS(H)/LF/151, POW's taken on 10 Jun 44) [UKNA, WO 208/3630]
82. C.S.D.I.C. (UK) S.I.R. 485, 3 Jul 44, p.2 [NARA, RG 165, Box 659, Folder 2]
83. C.S.D.I.C. (UK) S.I.R. 410, 21 Jun 44, p.1 [NARA RG 165, Box 659, Folder 2]; PWIS(H)/126, 13 Jun 44 [UKNA, WO 208/3622]
84. C.S.D.I.C. (UK) S.I.R. 485, 3 Jul 44, p.2 [NARA, RG 165, Box 659, Folder 2]
85. PWIS(H)/126, 13 Jun 44 [UKNA, WO 208/3622]
86. PWIS(H)/LF/167, 28 Jun 44 [UKNA, WO 208/3630]
87. AOK 7, Kriegsgliederung 7. Armee, Stand 18.5.44, *243. I.D., Stand 1.5.1944* [T312 R1566 F220]
88. PWIS(H)/LF/151, POW's taken on 10 Jun 44) [UKNA, WO 208/3630]; PWIS(H)/LF/167, 28 Jun 44 [UKNA, WO 208/3630]
89. PWIS(H)/126, 13 Jun 44 [UKNA, WO 208/3622]
90. PWIS(H)/LDC/103, 11 Jul 44 [UKNA, WO 208/3646]
91. C.S.D.I.C. (UK) S.I.R. 485, 3 Jul 44, p.1 [NARA, RG 165, Box 659, Folder 2]
92. AOK 7, Kriegsgliederung 7. Armee, Stand 18.5.44, *243. I.D., Stand 1.5.1944* [T312 R1566 F220]
93. PWIS(H)/156, 15 Jun 44 [UKNA, WO 208/3622]; PWIS(H)/LDC/98, 11 Jul 44, p.1 & 3 [UKNA, WO 208/3646]; PWIS(H)/LF/167, 28 Jun 44 [UKNA, WO 208/3630]; PWIS(H)/LF/185, 27 Jun 44, p.1 [UKNA, WO 208/3630]
94. PWIS(H)/121, PCW taken on 9 Jun 44 [UKNA, WO 208/3622]; PWIS(H)/LF/151, POW's taken on 10 Jun 44) [UKNA, WO 208/3630] Conflicting reports state that the 8./921 had six or eight heavy MG's. The former matches the order of battle, but of course changes may have happened before the invasion. If so, this may also apply to other companies. [UKNA, WO 208/3622, PWIS(H)/156]
95. PWIS(H)/LF/151, POW's taken on 10 Jun 44) [UKNA, WO 208/3630]; PWIS(H)/LDC/98, 11 Jul 44, p.1 [UKNA, WO 208/3646]
96. PWIS(H)/121, POW taken on 9 Jun 44 [UKNA, WO 208/3622]; PWIS(H)/156, 15 Jun 44 [UKNA, WO 208/3622]; PWIS(H)/LF/151, PWs taken on 10 Jun 44) [UKNA, WO 208/3630]; PWIS(H)/LF/167, 28 Jun 44 [UKNA, WO 208/3630]; PWIS(H)/LF/185, 27 Jun 44, p.1 [UKNA, WO 208/3630]
97. C.S.D.I.C. (UK) S.I.R. 461, 28 Jun 44, p.1 [NARA, RG 165, Box 659, Folder 2]
98. PWIS(H)/LF/185, 27 Jun 44, p.1 [UKNA, WO 208/3630]
99. PWIS(H)/LDC/98, 11 Jul 44, p.1 & 3 [UKNA, WO 208/3646]
100. PWIS(H)/121, POW taken on 9 Jun 44 [UKNA, WO 208/3622]
101. PWIS(H)/LF/167, 28 Jun 44 [UKNA, WO 208/3630]
102. C.S.D.I.C. (UK) S.I.R. 406, 22 Jun 44, p.1 [NARA, RG 165, Box 659, Folder 2]; PWIS(H)/LF/185, 27 Jun 44, p.2 [UKNA, WO 208/3630]
103. PWIS(H)/LF/185, 27 Jun 44, p.1-2 [UKNA, WO 208/3630]
104. PWIS(H)/156, 15 Jun 44 [UKNA, WO 208/3622]; PWIS(H)/LDC/70, 3 Jul 44 [UKNA, WO 208/3646]; C.S.D.I.C. (UK) S.I.R. 485, 3 Jul 44, App.7 [NARA, RG 165, Box 659, Folder 2]
105. C.S.D.I.C. (UK) S.I.R. 485, 3 Jul 44, App.7 [NARA, RG 165, Box 659, Folder 2]
106. C.S.D.I.C. (UK) S.I.R. 406, 22 Jun 44, p.2 [NARA, RG 165, Box 659, Folder 2]
107. *(K.St.N.) 171F, Infanteriegeschützkompanie (zu 6 leichte Infanterie-Geschützen) (bodenständig)*, 4.5.43 [T78 R397 F6366318-90]
108. Anlage zu *243. I.D.*, Ia Nr.16/44 g.K., (Kriegsgliederung) *243. Inf.Div., Stand vom 1.1.44* [T314 R745 F653]
109. PWIS(H)/LDC/25, 26 Jun 44, p.2 [UKNA, WO 208/3645]
110. AOK 7, Kriegsgliederung 7. Armee, Stand 18.5.44, *243. I.D.,*

Stand 1.5.1944 [T312 R1566 F220]
111. PWIS(H)/LF/189, 28 Jun 44, p.1 [UKNA, WO 208/3630]
112. *Ibid.*
113. *Ibid.*
114. PWIS(H)/LDC/25, 26 Jun 44, p.2 [UKNA, WO 208/3645]
115. PWIS(H)/LF/189, 28 Jun 44, p.1 [UKNA, WO 208/3630]
116. PWIS(H)/LDC/98, 11 Jul 44, p.4 [UKNA, WO 208/3630] He claims that there were eight guns, which would have required a fourth platoon. The officer may have been confused with a standard 13th Company which would have had an extra two heavy infantry guns. The number of Personnel would nonetheless still seem fairly close to that of *KStN 171n* (-*s.I.G*.platoon). *KStN 171F*, however, only called for a combined strength of 107 officers and men. If the company really had 143 men, this may have included the heavy AT platoon from the 14th Company
117. AOK 7, Kriegsgliederung 7. Armee, Stand 18.5.44, *243. I.D., Stand 1.5.1944* [T312 R1566 F220]
118. Anl.5 zu *243. I.D.*, Ia Nr.333/43 g.K., (Kriegsgliederung) *243. Inf.Div.), Stand vom 1.12.43*, 4.12.1943 [T314 R745 F211]; AOK 7, Kriegsgliederung 7. Armee, Stand 12.1.44, *243. Infanterie-Div., Stand: 13.1.44* [T312 R1566 F50]
119. AOK 7, Kriegsgliederung 7. Armee, Stand 12.1.44, *243. Infanterie-Div., Stand: 13.1.44* [T312 R1566 F50]
120. This will be discussed under *Pz.Jg.Abt. 243*
121. AOK 7, Kriegsgliederung 7. Armee, Stand 14.2.44, *243. Infanterie-Div., Stand: 1.2.44* [T312 R1566 F118]
122. AOK 7, Kriegsgliederung 7. Armee, Stand 18.5.44, *243. I.D., Stand 1.5.1944* [T312 R1566 F220]
123. PWIS(H)/LDC/98, 11 Jul 44, p.1 [UKNA, WO 208/3646]; PWIS(H)/LDC/25, 26 Jun 44 [UKNA, WO 208/3645]; C.S.D.I.C. (UK) S.I.R. 410, 21 Jun 44, p.1 [NARA, RG 165, Box 659, Folder 2]
124. PWIS(H)/LDC/25, 26 Jun 44, p.2 [UKNA, WO 208/3645]; PWIS(H)/LDC/98, 11 Jul 44, p.4 [UKNA, WO 208/3630]
125. AOK 7, Kriegsgliederung 7. Armee, Stand 18.5.44, *243. I.D., Stand 1.5.1944* [T312 R1566 F220]; Anlage zu *243. I.D.*, Ia Nr.242/43 g.K., (Kriegsgliederung) *243.Inf.Div., Stand vom 1.11.43*, 4.11.1943 [T314 R745 F180]
126. The possible reactivation of these companies remained on the mind of some people, creating some confusion about whether the companies were still intended to exist. [UKNA, WO 208/3646, PWIS(H)/LDC/98]
127. Gen.Kdo.XXV. A.K. Ia, *KTB Nr.11* [T314 R745 F36]
128. AOK 7, Kriegsgliederung 7. Armee, Stand 12.1.44, *Ost u. Georg. Btl. LXXXIV. A.K., Stand: 12.1.44* [T312 R1566 F51]
129. Feldpostübersicht
130. AOK 7, Kriegsgliederung 7. Armee, Stand 18.5.44, *243. I.D., Stand 1.5.1944* [T312 R1566 F220]
131. Alph. Kartei von Allen Inf. Offiziere einschliesslich Oberst, index card of *Maj.d.R.* Maurer [T78 R912 H6/355] In the „*Alph. Kartei von Allen Inf. Offizieren*" his name is spelled as Maurer. His own translated account gives it as "Mauer", although a typographical error is likely.

132. Mauer, E. (1946), MS # D-382 (Engl.), *Operations against American Army troops (from 5 June approximately 30 June 1944*, p.3
133. PWIS(H)/182, POW taken on 6 Jun 44 [UKNA, WO 208/3622]; C.S.D.I.C. (UK) S.I.R. 357, 12 Jun 44 [NARA, RG 165, Box 660, Folder 4]; C.S.D.I.C. (UK) S.I.R. 382, 17 Jun 44, p.3 [NARA, RG 165, Box 660, Folder 4]
134. Mauer, E. (1946), MS # D-382 (Engl.), p.13-14 & 19
135. AOK 7, Kriegsgliederung 7. Armee, Stand 18.5.44, *243. I.D., Stand 1.5.1944* [T312 R1566 F220]
136. PWIS(H)/182, POW taken on 6 Jun 44 [UKNA, WO 208/3622]; C.S.D.I.C. (UK) S.I.R. 375, 19 Jun 44, p.1 [NARA, RG 165, Box 660, Folder 4]
137. C.S.D.I.C. (UK) S.I.R. 357, 12 Jun 44 [NARA, RG 165, Box 660, Folder 4]; C.S.D.I.C. (UK) S.I.R. 375, 19 Jun 44, p.1 [NARA, RG 165, Box 660, Folder 4]; C.S.D.I.C. (UK) S.I.R. 382, 17 Jun 44, p.1 [NARA, RG 165, Box 660, Folder 4]
138. PWIS(H)/182, POW taken on 6 Jun 44 [UKNA, WO 208/3622]; PWIS(H)/126, 13 Jun 44 [UKNA, WO 208/3622]; PWIS(H)/LF/174, 23 Jun 44 [UKNA, WO 208/3630]; C.S.D.I.C. (UK) S.I.R. 382, 17 Jun 44, p.1 [NARA, RG 165, Box 660, Folder 4]; C.S.D.I.C. (UK) S.I.R. 357, 12 Jun 44 [NARA, RG 165, Box 660, Folder 4]
139. PWIS(H)/182, POW taken on 6 Jun 44 [UKNA, WO 208/3622]
140. PWIS(H)/LF/174, 23 Jun 44 [UKNA, WO 208/3630]
141. C.S.D.I.C. (UK) S.I.R. 357, 12 Jun 44 [NARA, RG 165, Box 660, Folder 4]
142. OKH, *Kriegsgliederung des Feldheeres September 1943*, p.96 [T78 R409 F6377954]; *KStN 702F* (1.1.43) and *KStN 711F* (1.1.43) can be found in T78 R397_H1/28
143. Anl.1 zu AOK 7 Ia Nr.6299/43 g.K., *Vorgesehene Kriegsgliederung 243. I.D. für beweglichen Einsatz, Stand: 18.1.44* [T312 R1564 F517]
144. AOK 7, Ia Nr.724/44 g.K., p.1 [T312 R1565 F24]; Anl.1 zu AOK 7 O.Qu./Ia Nr.2500/44 g.K., *Art der Beweglichmachung 243. I.D., 7.5.1944* [T312 R1565 F648]
145. *Volksbund* records list him as a *Major*, indicating he may have been promoted shortly before his death or posthumously.
146. AOK 7, Kriegsgliederung 7. Armee, Stand 18.5.44, *243. I.D., Stand 1.5.1944* [T312 R1566 F220] Using the same document Zetterling states that the battalion as a whole had 19 machineguns, one less than authorised.
147. C.S.D.I.C. (UK) S.I.R. 375, 19 Jun 44, p.1 [NARA, RG 165, Box 660, Folder 4]
148. PWIS(H)/LF/149, POW taken 9 Jun 44) [UKNA, WO 208/3630]; C.S.D.I.C. (UK) S.I.R. 419, 22 Jun 44, p.1 [NARA, RG 165, Box 659, Folder 2]
149. C.S.D.I.C. (UK) S.I.R. 375, 19 Jun 44, p.1 [NARA, RG 165, Box 660, Folder 4]; C.S.D.I.C. (UK) S.I.R. 419, 22 Jun 44, p.1 [NARA, RG 165, Box 659, Folder 2]
150. PWIS(H)/LF/149, POW taken 9 Jun 44) [UKNA, WO 208/3630]; C.S.D.I.C. (UK) S.I.R. 419, 22 Jun 44, p.1 [NARA, RG 165, Box 659, Folder 2]
151. *Ibid.*
152. PWIS(H)/LF/149, POW taken 9 Jun 44) [UKNA, WO 208/3630]; C.S.D.I.C. (UK) S.I.R. 375, 19 Jun 44, p.1 [NARA, RG 165, Box 660, Folder 4]
153. Volksbund
154. PWIS(H)/LF/575, 24 Aug 44 [UKNA, WO 208/575]
155. OKH, *Kriegsgliederung des Feldheeres September 1943*, p.96 [T78 R409 F6377954]
156. OKW Chef H Rüst u. BdE, AHA/Ia(I) Nr.3414/32 g.K., 9.7.43, Anl. 3 [T78 R850 H36/157]
157. AOK 7, Kriegsgliederung 7. Armee, Stand 18.5.44, *243. I.D., Stand 1.5.1944* [T312 R1566 F220]
158. OKH, *Kriegsgliederung des Feldheeres September 1943*, p.96 [T78 R409 F6377954]
159. OKH GenStdH/Org.Abt. Nr.I/5700/43 g.K., 19.12.43, Anl.4 [T78 R528 F890]; AOK 7/O.Qu., *Kriegstagebuch Nr.46, 1.Dez.1943 - 31.Dez.1943* [T312 R1562 F977]; Anlage zu *243. I.D.*, Ia Nr.16/44 g.K., (Kriegsgliederung) *243.Inf.Div., Stand vom 1.1.44* [T314 R745 F653] The three *12,2 cm s.F.H. 396(r)'s* for the 3rd Battalion (7th to 9th Batteries) arrived on 18 December. The arrival of six *7,62 cm F.K.39's* has not been found, but the 1st and 2nd Battalions were at full strength on 1 January 1944.
160. Gen.Kdo.XXV. A.K., Abt. Ia Nr.1359/43 g.K., 15.12.1943 [T314 R745 F249-50]; Gen.Kdo.XXV. A.K., Abt. Ia Nr.18/44 g., 3.1.1944 [T314 R745 F1014]
161. Anlage 2 zu AOK 7 Ia/Stoart Nr.318/43 g.K., 2.12.1943, Blatt 2 [T314 R745 F240]; AOK 7, Kriegsgliederung 7. Armee, Stand 18.5.44, *243. I.D., Stand 1.5.1944* [T312 R1566 F220]
162. AOK 7, Kriegsgliederung 7. Armee, Stand 18.5.44, *243. I.D., Stand 1.5.1944* [T312 R1566 F220]
163. PWIS(H)/LF/150, POW taken 9 Jun 44) [UKNA, WO 208/3630]
164. Anlage zu 243.I.D Ia Nr.242/43 g.K., (Kriegsgliederung) *243. Inf.Div.), Stand vom 1.11.43*, 4.11.43 [T314 R745 F180]; Anl.5 zu *243. I.D.*, Ia Nr.333/43 g.K., (Kriegsgliederung) *243.Inf.Div.), Stand vom 1.12.43*, 4.12.1943 [T314 R745 F211]
165. Gen.Kdo.XXV. A.K. Ia, *KTB Nr.11* [T314 R745 F36-37]
166. PWIS(H)/LF/150, POW taken 9 Jun 44) [UKNA, WO 208/3630]; **Stadlhofer (1944)**, p.8 [T78 R672]
167. (Unknown origin) Nr.1591/44, 24.5.44 [UKNA, HW 5/587 CX/MSS/T194/10] The file actually mentions the number "245" and not "243". It is assumed this number is a simple error, because there was no unit numbered "245" in the area.
168. PWIS(H)/KP/129, 10 Jul 44 [UKNA, WO 208/3624]; Stadlhofer (1944), *Bericht über den Einsatz der III./AR 243 vom 6.6.1944 bis 25.6.1944*, p.6 & 8 [T78 R672 H41/61b]
169. PWIS(H)/KP/129, 10 Jul 44 [UKNA, WO 208/3624]; PWIS(H)/LF/150, PW taken 9 Jun 44) [UKNA, WO 208/3630]
170. PWIS(H)/LF/187, 28 Jun 44 [UKNA, WO 208/3630]
171. PWIS(H)/KP/129, 10 Jul 44 [UKNA, WO 208/3624]
172. FID-DZ No.183, 8 July 1944 [NARA, RG 498, Box 1326]

173. PWIS(H)/LF/150, POW taken 9 Jun 44) [UKNA, WO 208/3630]
174. OKH, *Kriegsgliederung des Feldheeres September 1943*, p.96 [T78 R409 F6377954]
175. AOK 7, Kriegsgliederung 7. Armee, Stand 12.1.44, *243. Infanterie-Div., Stand: 13.1.44* [T312 R1566 F50]; AOK 7, Kriegsgliederung 7. Armee, Stand 9.2.44, (Kriegsgliederung) *243. Infanterie-Div., Stand: 13.1.44* [T312 R1566 F82] This document was used to report the situation on 9 February 1944; Anlage zu *243. I.D.*, Ia Nr.242/43 g.K., (Kriegsgliederung) *243.Inf.Div., Stand vom 1.11.43*, 4.11.1943 [T314 R745 F180]; Anl.3 zu *243. I.D.*, Ia Nr.2325/43 g.K., (Kriegsgliederung) *243.Inf.Div., Stand vom 1.12.43* [T314 R745 F154]; AOK 7, Kriegsgliederung 7. Armee, Stand: 15.11.43, (Kriegsgliederung) *243.Infanterie-Division, Stand: 10.10.43* [T312 R1559 F679] In AOK 7 records, the company was first listed on 10 October, although this document was actually used to report the situation on 15 November. The division's own status report first included the company on 1 December. On 8 November, the division had been listed with 9 assigned *7,5 cm Pak 40's*, while the AT companies in the infantry regiments remained without any assigned AT guns. [AOK 7, Anl.1 zu AOK 7, O.Qu./Qu.1 Nr.1271/43 g.K.v.8.11.43, *Übersicht über vorhandene s.Pak* in T312 R1562 F830; Anl.5 zu *243. I.D.*, Ia Nr.333/43 g.K., (Kriegsgliederung) *243.Inf.Div.), Stand vom 1.12.43*, 4.12.1943 [T314 R745 F211]
176. OKH/ Ch H Rüst u BdE/AHA Ia (I) Nr.493/44 g.K., 11.1.44 [T78 R848 H36/153]
177. AOK 7, Ia Nr.273/44 g.K., 15.1.44 [T312 R1564 F455-8]
178. OKH/ Ch H Rüst u BdE/AHA Ia (I) Nr.609/44 g.K., 28.1.44 [T78 R848 H36/153]; Feldpostübersicht
179. K.St.N. (Heer) Nr.1148 d, schnelle Panzerjägerkompanie (14 Gesch. 7.5 oder 7.62cm Pak (Sf)), 1.11.1943 [T78 R393 F6361806-9]
180. K.St.N. (Heer) Nr.1149, Sturmgeschützabteilung (in Panzer-Jager-Abteilung) (10 oder 14 Geschütze), 1.2.44 [T78 R393 F6361812-7]
181. See the chapter *"Heer Infantry Formations: An Introduction"*.
182. AOK 7, Kriegsgliederung 7. Armee, Stand 12.3.44, *243. Infanterie-Div., Stand: 1.2.44* [T312 R1566 F154] This frame is actually an updated version of the situation on 1st February is included in the *"Kriegsgliederung 7. Armee - Stand: 12.3.1944"*.
183. Anl.2 zu Gen.Insp.d.Pz.Tr./GenStdH/Org.Abt. Nr.I/16030/44 g.K., 18.3.44 [T78 R398 H1/39]
184. C.S.D.I.C. (UK) S.I.R. 356, 15 Jun 44, p.1 [NARA, RG 165, Box 659, Folder 2] The account refers to "Tribon", which has not been found. It is assumed Tribehou is meant.
185. AOK 7, Kriegsgliederung 7. Armee, Stand 14.2.44, *243. Infanterie-Div., Stand: 1.2.44* [T312 R1566 F118]
186. The division had a habit of first listing the arrivals under the heading "Weapons and Equipment" and some days later again under "Motor vehicles". Both types of reports refer to the same vehicles. [Day-to-day reports by the AOK 7 O.Qu. in T312 R1570 and R1571]
187. AOK 7/O.Qu., *Kriegstagebuch der Oberquartiermeisterabteilung AOK 7 für die Zeit vom 1.Febr.1944 - 29.Febr.1944* [T312 R1570 F878]; AOK 7/O.Qu., *Kriegstagebuch der Oberquartiermeisterabteilung AOK 7 für die Zeit vom 1.4.44 - 30.4.44* [T312 R1571 F17]
188. AOK 7/O.Qu., *Kriegstagebuch der Oberquartiermeisterabteilung AOK 7 für die Zeit vom 1.3.44 - 31.3.44* [T312 R1570 F1008]
189. Ibid. [T312 R1570 F1018 & 22]
190. Ibid. [T312 R1570 F1005]; AOK 7, Kriegsgliederung 7. Armee, Stand 12.3.44, *243. Infanterie-Div., Stand: 1.2.44* [T312 R1566 F154] This frame is actually an updated version of the situation on 1st February but is included in the *"Kriegsgliederung 7. Armee - Stand: 12.3.1944"*; AOK 7, Kriegsgliederung 7. Armee, Stand 10.4.44, *243. I.D., Stand 1.3.1944* [T312 R1566 F192] This Gliederung is included in the *'Kriegsgliederung 7. Armee - Stand: 10.4.1944'*; AOK 7, Kriegsgliederung 7. Armee, Stand 18.5.44, *243. I.D., Stand 1.5.1944* [T312 R1566 F220]
191. AOK 7, Kriegsgliederung 7. Armee, Stand 12.3.44, *243. Infanterie-Div., Stand: 1.2.44* [T312 R1566 F154]
192. PWIS(H)/LF/186, 28 Jun 44 [UKNA, WO 208/575]
193. AOK 7/O.Qu., *Kriegstagebuch der Oberquartiermeisterabteilung AOK 7 für die Zeit vom 1.Febr.1944 - 29.Febr.1944* [T312 R1570 F882 & 886] [T312 R1570 F886]
194. AOK 7/O.Qu., *Kriegstagebuch der Oberquartiermeisterabteilung AOK 7 für die Zeit vom 1.3.44 - 31.3.44* [T312 R1570 F1007 & 1017]
195. AOK 7/O.Qu., *Kriegstagebuch der Oberquartiermeisterabteilung AOK 7 für die Zeit vom 1.4.44 - 30.4.44* [T312 R1571 F7 & 10]
196. AOK 7/O.Qu., *Kriegstagebuch der Oberquartiermeisterabteilung AOK 7 für die Zeit vom 1.3.44 - 31.3.44* [T312 R1570 F1020]
197. AOK 7/O.Qu., *Kriegstagebuch der Oberquartiermeisterabteilung AOK 7 für die Zeit vom 1.5.44 - 31.5.44* [T312 R1571 F298]
198. C.S.D.I.C. (UK) S.I.R. 356, 15 Jun 44, p.1-3 [NARA, RG 165, Box 659, Folder 2]
199. Ibid.
200. Ibid.
201. Ibid.
202. Ibid. According to the *KStN*, a crew should have both a loader and a radio operator. It appears it was actually far more common to combine these roles.
203. Ibid.; **Andorfer, V., et al (2000)**, *Nuts & Bolts Vol. 17, Marder III, Part I: Ausführung M*, Nuts & Bolts, p.8. If the number of 58 is correct, additional rounds must have been stored in other places such as on or under the floor of the fighting compartment. Even so, the number seems unlikely.
204. C.S.D.I.C. (UK) S.I.R. 356, 15 Jun 44, p.1-3 [NARA, RG 165, Box 659, Folder 2]
205. Ibid.
206. Verwendungskartei von Offizieren der Pz.Truppen, index card of Major d.R. Bethge [T78 R937 H6/402]; C.S.D.I.C. (UK) S.I.R. 356, p.3 [NARA, RG 165, Box 659, Folder 2]; Volksbund
207. Verwendungskartei von Offizieren der Pz.Truppen, index card of *Hptm.* Nesse fhauf [T78 R937 H6/402]; Volksbund
208. OKH/AHA/Abwicklungsstab, Anl. z. Sachgeb. 91 Nr.6.44 g., *Kriegsgliederung Kampfgruppe König, Stand: 18.6.44 - 28.6.44* [T78 R672 H41/61b]
209. CX/MSS/R.222 (C) 22.6.44, p.19 [UKNA, HW 5/508]
210. Ultra records suggest that the request to return *Oblt.* Stratmann was fulfilled in the 15-20 June period. The name of the other officer may be found among officer casualties in that period.
211. C.S.D.I.C. (UK) S.I.R. 742, 14 Aug 44, p.4 [NARA, RG 165, Box 659, Folder 2]
212. AOK 7, Ia Nr.124/43 g.K.Chefs., 11.11.1943, p.1 [T312 R1563 F1004]
213. AOK 7, Ia Nr.6400/43 g.K., 15.12.43, Anl.1 *Vorgesehene Kriegsgliederung 243. I.D. für bewegl. Einsatz* [T312 R1559 F377]
214. Anl.2 zu AOK 7, Ia Nr.6200/43 g.K. II.Ang. 24.12.43, *Vorgesehene Kriegsgliederung 243. I.D. für bewegl. Einsatz* [T312 R1559 F444]
215. Anl.1 zu AOK 7, Ia Nr.397/44 g.K., *Vorgesehene Kriegsgliederung 243. I.D. für beweglichen Einsatz, Stand 18.1.1944*, 23.1.44 [T312 R1564 F506]
216. Anl.7 zu 243.Inf.Div., Ia Nr.16/44 g.K., (Zustandsbericht), 1.1.44 [T314 R745 F651]
217. Ibid. [T314 R745 F652]
218. AOK 7, Ia Nr.724/44 g.K., p.1 [T312 R1565 F24]; AOK 7, Ia Nr.900/44 g.K., *Befehl für Beweglichmachung und Verlastung von Reserven.*, 6.2.44, p.1 [T312 R1565 F46]
219. Armee-Oberkommando Ia Nr.900/44 g.K., *Befehl für Beweglichmachung und Verlastung von Reserven.*, 6.2.44, p.2 [T312 R1565 F46]
220. AOK 7, Ia Nr.724/44 g.K., p.1 [T312 R1565 F24]
221. AOK 7, Kriegsgliederung 7. Armee, Stand 12.3.44, *243. Infanterie-Div., Stand: 1.2.44* [T312 R1566 F154]
222. A.Pi.Fü. /AOK 7, *Kriegsgliederung der Pioniere des AOK 7, Nr.20, Stand vom: 15.3.1944* [T312 R1566 F204]
223. AOK 7, Kriegsgliederung 7. Armee, Stand 18.5.44, *243. I.D., Stand 1.5.1944* [T312 R1566 F220]
224. AOK 7, Ia Nr.1000/44 g.K., 16.2.44 [T312 R1565 F124]
225. AOK 7, Ia Nr.1542/44 g.K., 14.3.44, p.1-2 [T312 R1565 F283-284]
226. AOK 7 O.Qu./A.C.Kraft/Ia Nr.2500/44 g.K., 7.5.44, p.3 [T312 R1565 F640]
227. Ibid., p.1-8 & Anl.1 [T312 R1565 F638-000650]
228. Kriegstagebuch A.O.K.7/O.Qu., Nr.51, *Besprechungspunkte O.Qu. bei O.Qu.West.*, 12.5.44, p.2 [T312 R1571 F390]
229. Anl.7 zu 243.Inf.Div., Ia Nr.16/44 g.K., (Zustandsbericht), 1.1.44 [T314 R745 F651]
230. AOK 7, Ia Nr.2568/44 g.K., 19.5.44, p.1-2 [T312 R1565 F734-5]
231. PWIS(H)/LDC/98, 11 Jul 44, p.4 [UKNA, WO 208/3630]
232. C.S.D.I.C. (UK) S.I.R. 485, 3 Jul 44, p.2 [NARA, RG 165, Box 659, Folder 2]

233. *Div. Verbände, II. Teil, 243.Inf.Div.* [T78 R412 F6380328]; Anl.4 zu OKH/GenStdH/Org Abt Nr.I/2271/43 g.K., 2.5.1943 [T78 R406 F6376013]; **Tessin, G. (1977)**, *1.Band*, p.67; **Tessin, G. (1973)**, *8.Band*, p.186
234. OKH Chef H Rüst u. BdE, AHA/Ia(I) Nr.3059/43 g.K., 19.6.43, p.1-2 [T78 R849 H36/156]
235. OKH/Chef H Rüst u.BdE AHA Ia(I) Nr.3932/43 g.K., 4.8.43 [T78 R849 H3/157]; Gen St d H Op.Abt.III/Prüf-Nr.: 39616, *Schematische Kriegsgliederung - Stand: 14.8.43.* [T78 R708]
236. AOK 7, *Kriegstagebuch der Führungsabteilung AOK 7 für die Zeit vom 1.7.–3 - 31.12.43* [T312 R1558 F29]
237. AOK 7, Ia Nr.4320/43 g.K., 1.9.43 [T312 R1558 F696]; AOK 7, Ia Nr.4320/43 g.K., 1.9.43 [T312 R1558 F698]; AOK 7, *Kriegstagebuch der Führungsabteilung AOK 7 für die Zeit vom 1.7.43 - 31.12.43* [T312 R1558 F45]; AOK 7/O.Qu., *Kriegstagebuch Nr.43, 1.Sept-1943-30.Sept.1943* [T312 R1562 F405]; AOK 7, *Termine für Ablösung 384. I.D. durch 243.Inf.Div.*, 1.9.43 [T312 R1558 F702]
238. AOK 7 Ia Nr.4621/43 g.K., 13.9.43 [T314 R1604 F920]; AOK 7, Ia Nr.462/43 g.K., 13.9.43 [T312 R1558 F816] *KVA "C2"* was also referred to as *KVA "C"*, whereas *KVA "C1"* was also known as *"J"*. For examples see T314 R745.
239. BvTO b. AOK 7, Bv.T.O. Nr.13/44 g.K., *Tätigkeitsbericht für die Zeit vom 1.Jul bis 31. Dezember 1943.*, 2.1.44, p.7 [T312 R1563 F9]; Gen.Kdo.LXXXIV. A.K., *Kriegstagebuch vom 1.Juli bis 31. Dez. 43 des* Gen.Kdo.LXXXIV. A.K., *Ia* [T314 R1603 F989]
240. Gen.Kdo.LXXXIV. A.K., *Kriegstagebuch vom 1.Juli bis 31. Dez. 43 des* Gen.Kdo.LXXXIV. A.K., *Ia* [T314 R1603 F989]; Anl. zu Gen.Kdo.LXXXIV. A.K., Ia Nr.1831/43 g.K., *Heeresgruppen-, Armee- und Korpsreserven im Bereich de* LXXXIV. A.K., 8.10.43 [T314 R1604 F1038]
241. Anlage zu *243. I.D.*, Ia Nr.242/43 g.K., (Kriegsgliederung) *243.Inf.Div., Stand vom 1.11.43*, 4.11.1943 [T314 R745 F180]
242. Anl.5 zu *243. I.D.*, Ia Nr.333/43 g.K., (Kriegsgliederung) *243. Inf.Div.), Stand vom 1.12.43*, 4.12.1943 [T314 R745 F211]
243. Anlage zu *243. I.D.*, Ia Nr.16/44 g.K., (Kriegsgliederung) *243.Inf.Div., Stand vom 1.1.44* [T314 R745 F653]; AOK 7, Kriegsgliederung 7. Armee, Stand 12.1.44, *243. Infanterie-Div., Stand: 13.1.44* [T312 R1566 F50]
244. BvTO b. AOK 7, Bv.T.O. Nr.13/44 g.K., *Tätigkeitsbericht für die Zeit vom 1.Jul bis 31. Dezember 1943.*, 2.1.44, p.7 [T312 R1563 F9]; Gen.Kdo.LXXXIV. A.K., Ia Nr.2848/43 g.K., 1.10.43 [T314 R745 F294]; Gen.Kdo.LXXXIV. A.K., Ia Nr.2854/43 g.K., 2.10.43 [T314 R745 F297]
245. Ob.West Okdo.d.H.Gr.D, *II. Ausfertigung Ia, K.T.B. vom 1.10 - 31.10.43*, p.5 [T311 R20 F7023221]; Gen.Kdo.XXV. A.K. Ia, *KTB Nr.11* [T314 R745 F6]
246. AOK 7 Ia, Karten u. Kriegsgliederung zum Kriegstagebuch AOK 7 Ia vom 1.7.43 bis 31.12.43, *Lage 7. Armee, Stand: 24.10.43* [T312 R1559 F507]; Gen.Kdo.XXV. A.K., Abt. Ia Nr.3254/43 g., 6.11.43 [T314 R745 F400]
247. AOK 7 Ia, Karten u. Kriegsgliederung zum Kriegstagebuch AOK 7 Ia vom 1.7.43 bis 31.12.43, *Lage 7. Armee, Stand: 24.10.43* [T312 R1559 F507]
248. *Ibid.*
249. *Ibid.*
250. Gen.Kdo.XXV. A.K. Nr.2939/43 g., 11.10.43 [T314 R745 F326]; Gen.Kdo.XXV. A.K. Nr.3061/43 g., 21.10.43 [T314 R745 F355]
251. AOK 7 O.Qu., *Qu.1-Besprechung am 26.9.43, 10.00 Uhr*, 26.9.43 [T312 R1562 F547]; Gen.Kdo. XXV. A.K., Abt. Ia Nr.3126/43 g., 27.10.43 [T314 R745 F372]; Gen.Kdo.XXV. A.K., Abt. Ia Nr.3143/43 g., 28.10.43 [T314 R745 F375]; On 13 October, it was decided that the *III./920* would join the *286. Sich.Div.* [OKH/GenStdH/Org.Abt., Nr.II/12855/43 g.K., 13.10.43, p.1 in T78 R527 F270; Gen.Kdo.XXV. A.K. Ia, *KTB Nr.11* in T314 R745 F12]
252. Anl. zu *243. I.D.*, Abt. Ia Br.B. Nr.242/43 g.K., 4.11.43, Zustandsbericht (with Kriegsgliederung), Stand: 1.1.43 [T314 R745 F179-180]; Gen.Kdo.XXV. A.K. Nr.3061/43 g., 21.10.43 [T314 R745 F355]; Gen.Kdo.XXV. A.K. Nr.3429/43 g., 21.11.43 [T314 R745 F445]
253. AOK 7, Ia Nr.5921/43 g.K., 19.11.43 [T312 R1559 F187]
254. For an overview of the development of Measure I-III, see BvTO b. AOK 7, *Tätigkeitsbericht für die zeit vom 1. Juli bis 31. Dezember 1943*, 2.1.44, p.13 [T312 R1563 F15]
255. AOK 7, Ia Nr.5670/43 g.K., 7.11.43, p.1-7 & Anl. [T312 R1559 F35-42]
256. Telehpone conversation between Ia Ob.West and Ia AOK 7 on 18.11.43 [T312 R1559 F184]; AOK 7, Ia Nr.5953/43 g.K., 20.11.43 [T312 R1559 F192]; AOK 7, Ia Nr.5990/43 g.K., 23.11.43, p.1-2 [T312 R1559 F204-5]
257. Gen.Kdo.XXV. A.K., Abt. Ia Nr.3533/43 g., p.1 [T314 R745 F474]; Gen.Kdo.XXV. A.K. Nr.3548/43 g., p.1 [T314 R745 F479]; Gen.Kdo.XXV. A.K., Abt. Ia Nr.3562/43 g., p.1 [T314 R745 F483]; Gen.Kdo.XXV. A.K., Abt. Ia Nr.3574/43 g., 4.12.43 [T314 R745 F486]
258. Gen.Kdo.XXV. A.K., Abt. Ia Nr.3533/43 g., p.1 [T314 R745 F474]; Gen.Kdo.XXV. A.K. Nr.3562/43 g., p.1 [T314 R745 F483]
259. Gen.Kdo.XXV. A.K., Abt. Ia Nr.3603/43 g., Taktische Tagesmeldung, 6.12.43 [T314 R745 F492]
260. *XXV. A.K.*, Abt. Ia Nr.3639/43 g., 9.12.43 [T314 R745 F500]; AOK 7 Ia, Karten u. Kriegsgliederung zum Kriegstagebuch AOK 7 Ia vom 1.7.43 bis 31.12.43, *Lage 7. Armee, Stand: 30.12.43* [T312 R1559 F509]
261. AOK 7, Ia Nr.6250/43 g.K., 10.12.43 [T312 R1563 F973]
262. Gen.Kdo.XXV. A.K., Abt. Ia Nr.1373/43 g., 19.12.43 [T314 R745 F264]
263. Der Oberbefehlshaber West (Oberkommando H.Gr.D) Ia Nr.832/43 g.K Ch., 28.12.1943, p.1-8 [T312 R1563 F711-718]
264. AOK 7, Ia Nr.6574/43 g.K., 23.12.43 [T312 R1559 F433]
265. AOK 7, Ia Nr.66/44 g., 4.1.44 [T312 R1564 F403]
266. AOK 7, Ia Nr.106/44 g., 6.1.44 [T312 R1564 F410]
267. AOK 7, Ia Nr.6574/43 g.K., 23.12.43 [T312 R1559 F433]; AOK 7 Ia, KTB 1.1.-30.6.1944 [T312 R1564 F199]; AOK 7, *Ferngespräche Oberst i.G. Helmdach*, 3.2.44, p.2 [T312 R1565 F27]
268. AOK 7, Ia Nr.389/44 g., 20.4.44 [T312 R1565 F516]
269. AOK 7, Ia Nr.454/44 g., 25.4.44 [T312 R1565 F539]; AOK 7, Ia Nr.473/44 g., 26.4.44 [T312 R1565 F546]
270. AOK 7, Ia Nr.641/44 g., 8.5.44, p.1 [T312 R1565 F658]
271. BvTO beim AOK 7, *Tätigkeitsbericht für die Zeit vom 1.Januar bis 31. März 1944*, p.1 [T312 R1571 F877]
272. Gen.Kdo.XXV. A.K. Ia, *KTB Nr.11* [T314 R745 F40]; *Kriegstagebuch Nr.12* Gen.Kdo.XXV. A.K. Führungsabteilung (Ia) 1.1.1944 - 31.3.1944 [T314 R745 F597]
273. AOK 7, Ia Nr.642/44 g., 1.2.44, p.1 [T312 R1565 F4]
274. Gen.Kdo.XXV. A.K. Ia, *KTB Nr.11* [T314 R745 F40]
275. AOK 7, Ia Nr.1850/44 g., 20.3.44 [T312 R1565 F310]
276. AOK 7, Ia Nr.1926/44 g., 24.3.44 [T312 R1565 F335]; AOK 7 Ia, Anlage zum K.T.B. Führungsabtl. AOK 7 Ia, Lage-Karten A.O.K.7 vom 6.1.-5.6.44, Stand: 5.6.44 [T312 R1570 F9-10, original in BaMa RH 20-7/138K] — Hereafter referred to as AOK 7, Situation map, 5.6.44; AOK 7, Kriegsgliederung 7. Armee, Stand 18.5.44, *243. I.D., Stand 1.5.1944* [T312 R1566 F220]
277. AOK 7, Ia Nr.642/44 g., 1.2.44, p.1 [T312 R1565 F4]; Gen. Kdo.XXV. A.K., Abt Ia Nr.2214/44 g., *27.6.1944*, 27.6.44 [T314 R746 F1050]
278. AOK 7, Ia Nr.194/44 g.K., 10.1.44 [T312 R1564 F429]
279. *Ibid.*; AOK 7, Ia Nr.365/44 g., 18.1.44 [T312 R1564 F472]
280. AOK 7, Ia Nr.194/44 g.K., 10.1.44 [T312 R1564 F429]
281. AOK 7, Ia Nr.9854/44 g., p.1-2 [T312 R1565 F114-5]
282. AOK 7, Ia Nr.194/44 g.K., 10.1.44 [T312 R1564 F429]; AOK 7, Ia Nr.985/44, Ia-Abendmeldung, p.2 [T312 R1565 F115]
283. *Ibid.*; AOK 7, Ia Nr.453/44 g., 22.1.44 [T312 R1564 F496]
284. AOK 7, Ia Nr.194/44 g.K., 10.1.44 [T312 R1564 F429]; AOK 7, Ia Nr.985/44, 15.2.44, p.2 [T312 R1565 F115]
285. AOK 7, Ia Nr.692/44 g., 2.2.44 [T312 R1565 F10]
286. Gen.Kdo.LXXXIV. A.K., Ia Nr.1168/44, 12.5.44 (incorrectly dated 12.4.44) [T312 R1565 F682]; Daily reports of AOK 7 in T312 R1565, as an example see AOK 7, Ia Nr.2538/44, 13.5.44, p.2 [T312 R1565 F694]
287. AOK 7, Ia Nr.2430/44 g.K., 7.5.44, p.1 [T312 R1565 F634]; AOK 7, Ia Nr.2431/44 g.K., 8.5.44, p.1 [T312 R1565 F662]
288. AOK 7, Situation map, 5.6.44
289. AOK 7, Ia Nr.2431/44 g., 8.5.44, p.1 [T312 R1565 F662]
290. AOK 7, Situation map, 5.6.44
291. Ob.West (H.Gr.D) Ia, 13.5.44 [UKNA, HW 5/489, CX/MSS/T197/31, KV 5416]
292. Anlage zu AOK 7, Ia Nr.2710/44 g.K., p.1, 28.5.44 [T312 R1565 F794]
293. Ob.West, Ia Nr.3819/44, 15.5.44 [UKNA, HW 5/487, CX/MSS/T194/80, KV 5081 & KV 5102]
294. AOK 7, Ia Nr.2538/44 g., 13.5.44, p.2 [T312 R1565 F694]; AOK 7, Ia Nr.809/44 g., 18.5.44 [T312 R1565 F723]
295. AOK 7, Ia Nr.2538/44 g., 13.5.44, p.2 [T312 R1565 F694]; AOK 7, Ia Nr.773/44 g., 15.51944 [T312 R1565 F705]
296. C.S.D.I.C. (UK) S.I.R. 382, 17 Jun 44, p.2 [NARA, RG 165, Box 660, Folder 4]; AOK 7, Ia Nr.2538/44 g., 13.5.44, p.2 [T312 R1565 F694]; AOK 7, Ia Nr.885/44 g., 22.5.44 [T312 R1565 F744]
297. AOK 7, Ia Nr.834/44 g., 19.5.44 [T312 R1565 F731]; AOK 7,

Situation map, 5.6.44
298. AOK 7, Ia Nr.2538/44 g., 13.5.44, p.2 [T312 R1565 F694]; C.S.D.I.C. (UK) S.I.R. 406, 22 Jun 44, Annex, Fig.2 [NARA, RG 165, Box 659, Folder 2]
299. AOK 7, Situation map, 5.6.44; AOK 7, Ia Nr.2538/44 g., 13.5.1941944, p.2 [T312 R1565 F694]
300. C.S.D.I.C. (UK) S.I.R. 485, 3 Jul 44, p.2 [NARA, RG 165, Box 659, Folder 2]
301. AOK 7, Situation map, 5.6.44
302. AOK 7, Ia Nr.696/44 g., 11.5.44 [T312 R1565 F687]
303. AOK 7, Ia Nr.2538/44 g., 13.5.44, p.2 [T312 R1565 F694]
304. Anl. zu OKH/AHA/Abwicklungsstab, Anl. z. Sachgeb. 91 Nr.6.44 g., *Kriegsgliederung (91. LL.Div.), Unterstellungen Stand: 10.6.44* [T78 R672 H41/61b]; 17.SS-Panz.Gren.Division "Götz von Berlichingen" Ia Tgb.Nr.1103/44 g., 21.6.44. [Published in **Wind, M. & H. Günther (2004)**, *Kriegstagebuch 17.SS-Panzer-Grenadier-Division „Götz von Berlichingen" - Auswahl von Dokumenten - 30. Oktober 1943 bis 6. Mai 1945*, St.Ingbert: Dengmerter Heimatverlag]
305. AOK 7, Situation map, 5.6.44; AOK 7 Ia, Kriegsgliederung 7. Armee, Stand 18.5.44, *Kriegsgliederung AOK 7, Stand: 18.5.1944* [T312 R1566 F208]
306. AOK 7, Ia Nr.971/44 g., 26.5.44 [T312 R1565 F773]
307. AOK 7, Situation map, 5.6.44
308. Ibid.; AOK 7 Ia, Kriegsgliederung 7. Armee, Stand 18.5.44, *Kriegsgliederung AOK 7, Stand: 18.5.1944* [T312 R1566 F208]
309. AOK 7, Ia Nr.641/44 g., 8.5.44, p.1 [T312 R1565 F658]; AOK 7 Ia, Kriegsgliederung 7. Armee, Stand 18.5.44, *Kriegsgliederung AOK 7, Stand: 18.5.1944* [T312 R1566 F208]
310. This will be addressed in the chapter *"Georgisches-Infanterie-Btl. 797"* in a future volume.
311. AOK 7 Ia, Nr.832/44 g., 8.2.44 [T312 R1565 F63]
312. Keil, G. (1948a), MS # C-018 (Germ.), *Bericht über die Kämpfe des hessisch-thüringischen Grenadier-Regiments 919 unter der Kampfgruppe Keil*, p.76
313. AOK 7, Situation map, 5.6.44
314. AOK 7 Ia, *AOK 7 Kriegstagebuch Ia - 6 Jun 1944 - 25 Jul 1944*, p.6 [T312 R1569 F224] — Hereafter referred to as: AOK 7 Ia, *KTB 6.6.-25.7.44*
315. Gen.Kdo.LXXXIV. A.K., Ia Nr.1273/44 g.K., 8.6.44, p.3 [T312 R1565 F939]; see chapter *"German command structure in Normandy"* for information about the preparations; **Criegern, F. von (1948)**, MS # B-784, p.21
316. AOK 7, Ia Nr.2949/44 g.K., 10.6.44 [T312 R1565 F925]
317. Information from *Adm. Kanalküste* on 9.6.44 [UKNA, HW 5/498, CX/MSS/T212/92, KV 7550]; *Seekommandant Normandie* at 22:00 on 16.6.44 [UKNA, HW 5/503, CX/MSS/T217/158, KV 8450]; *Gen.* Hellmich early 9.6.44 [UKNA, HW 55/498, CX/MSS/T212/115, KV 7566]
318. Flivo LXXXIV. A.K., 12.6.44 at 10:00 [UKNA, HW 5/499, CX/MSS/T213/43, KV 7678]; also see the situation maps in T312 R1570
319. Pickert, *Reisebericht*, 10.6.44, p.5 in Ob.West, *Anlage zum K.T.B., Befehle Meldungen, 6.6.-18.6.44* [T311 R25 85434.1 F7029433]
320. AOK 7, Ia Nr.2949/44 g.K., 10.6.44 [T312 R1565 F925]; **König, E. (1946)**, p.1
321. Stadlhofer (1944), p.5 [T78 R672 H41/61b]; **Keil, G. (1948a)**, p.20; **Schlieben, K.W. v. (1948)**, MS # B-345 (Germ.), *Die deutsche 709.Infanterie-Division vor und während der anglo-amerikanischen Invasion vom 6. Juni 1944*, p.34-35
322. Stadlhofer (1944), p.5 [T78 R672 H41/61b]; 90th I.D., *IPW Report*, 24 Jun 44 [NARA, RG 407, Box 3498, File 208-7.2]
323. HQ 325th Glider Infantry, *S-2 Journal - Operation Neptune, Cotentin Peninsula, France*, p.5 & HQ 82nd Airborne Div., G-2, *Interrogation Report No.7*, 14 Jun. 44 & HQ 82nd Airborne Div., G-2, Annex No.1 to G-2 Report No.66, *Interrogation Report No.9 (Correct)*, 15 Jun. 44 [all NARA, via Egbert van de Schootbrugge] On several occasions, members of the company were captured just north of the Douve River, away from the main body of the battalion.
324. AOK 7 Ia, Anlage zum KTB Führungsabteilung, Lagekarten A.O.K.7 vom 6.6.44-30.6.44, *Stand: 8.6.44, 22 Uhr* [T312 R1570 F17]
325. Anl. zu OKH/AHA/Abwicklungsstab, Anl. z. Sachgeb. 91 Nr.6.44 g., *Kriegsgliederung (91. LL.Div.), Unterstellungen Stand: 10.6.44* [T78 R672 H41/61b]; AOK 7 Ia, Anlage zum KTB Führungsabteilung, Lagekarten A.O.K.7 vom 6.6.44-30.6.44, *Stand: 12.6.44, 22 Uhr.* [T312 R1570 F20]
326. Conversations of the Ia AOK 7 on the evening of 6.6.44 with the LXXXIV. A.K. [T312 R1565 F866]
327. Keil, G. (1948a), p.51; C.S.D.I.C. (UK) S.I.R. 382, 17 Jun 44, p.2 [NARA, RG 165, Box 660, Folder 4]
328. Stadlhofer (1944), *Bericht über den Einsatz der III./AR 243 vom 6.6.1944 bis 25.6.1944*, p.1-4 [T78 R672 H41/61b]
329. Keil, G. (1948a), p.52
330. For a description of this period see **Keil G. (1948a)**
331. Stadlhofer (1944), p.1 [T78 R672 H41/61b]; for photographic evidence see **Nordyke, P. (2006)** *The All Americans in World War II*, St.Paul MN: Zenith Press, p.72, 73 & 76; **Archer L. & Auerbach, W. (2014)**, *Panzerwrecks 17: Normandy 2*, Panzerwrecks, Heathfield, p.85; PWIS(H)/LF/136, 28 Jun 44 [UKNA, WO 208/575]; **Rösgen, P.W. (1944)**, *Bericht über den Heldenkampf der Panzerjäger Abteilung 709 im Raume Cherbourg / Frankreich*, p.2 [T78 R672 H41/61a]; for photographic evidence see **Nordyke, P. (2006)**, p.72
332. C.S.D.I.C. (UK) S.I.R. 356, 15 Jun 44, p.3 [NARA, RG 165, Box 659, Folder 2]
333. Photos of these vehicles can be found in **Nordyke, P. (2006)**, p.73 & 76; and also in **Zaloga, S.J. (2011)**, *Armored Attack 1944*, Stackpoole Books, Mechanicsburg, PA, p.65, 81 and 85.
334. Keil, G. (1948a), p.53-54 & Anl.10
335. Stadlhofer (1944), *Bericht über den Einsatz der III./AR 243 vom 6.6.1944 bis 25.6.1944*, p.1-4 [T78 R672 H41/61b]
336. Gruppe Hellmich, Ia, 9.6.44 at 09:30 [UKNA, HW 5/498, CX/MSS/T212/122, KV 7557]; HQ 4th Infantry Division, *IPW Report No.1, from 082000 June 44 to 092000 June 44*, 9 June 44, p.1 [NARA, via Richard Anderson]
337. AOK 7 Ia, *KTB 6.6.-25.7.44*, p.24 [T312 R1569 F242]
338. Keil, G. (1948a), p.64 & Anl.11
339. HQ 4th Infantry Division, *IPW Report, from 102000 June 44 to 112000 June 44*, 12 June 44, p.1 [NARA, via Richard Anderson]
340. AOK 7, Ia Nr.3023/44 g.K., 12.6.44 [T312 R1565 F992]
341. Stadlhofer (1944), p.4; HQ 4th Infantry Division, *IPW Report, from 092000 June 44 to 102000 June 44*, 11 June 44, p.1 [NARA, via Richard Anderson] Keil states that von Schlieben mentioned the III./921 in his monograph, but this mention could not actually be found. The battalion is also missing from the order of battle of the reinforced *91. LL.Div.* on 10 June. This strongly suggests that the battalion was committed in the sector of the *709. I.D.* [**Keil, G. (1948b)**, Germ. p.15; **Keil, G. (1948a)**, Germ., p.65; **Schlieben, K.W. von (1948)**]
342. Hoffmann (1944), *Bericht über Kampfgruppe v. Schlieben*, p.9 [T312 R1566 F368]; C.S.D.I.C (UK) S.R. REPORT - S.R.M.622 [UKNA, WO 208/4138]; **Keil, G. (1948a)**, p.51; **Schlieben, K.W. v. (1948)**, p.31
343. HQ 4th I.D., AG 319.1, *Action Against Enemy, Reports After/After Action Reports*, 22 Jul. 44, Annex A - Order of Battle Team No.2 [MCoE HQ Donovan Research Library, D328/I2179]; C.S.D.I.C. (UK) S.R. Report - S.R.M.564 [UKNA, WO 208/4138]; C.S.D.I.C. (UK) S.R. Report - S.R.M.579 [UKNA, WO 208/4138]
344. Baret, J. (2014), *Une Tombe en Normandie - Vie et Mort du Sergent Adolph Greter*, Valognes: Imprimerie ICL, p.96
345. Also see the chapters on the *709. I.D.* and *Sturm-Bataillon AOK 7* (the latter in a future volume).
346. Keil, G. (1948a), p.66
347. Gruppe Hellmich, Ia Nr.896/44, 15.6.44 [UKNA, HW 5/507, CX/MSS/T221/56, KV 3956] The document mentions both 15 and 17 June, but *KG Keil* no longer belonged to *Gruppe Hellmich* on the latter date, making it more likely that the document covered 15 June.
348. Criegern, F. von (1948), MS # B-784 (Germ.), Teil I, *Die Kämpfe des LXXXIV. A.K. in der Normandie von der alliierten Landung bis 17.6.44*, p.16 & Skizze 1
349. GR 1057, Ia, *Regimental order for the defence of the Merderet Sector*, 8.6.44 [copied and translated as Enclosure No.2 to 82nd Airborne Division, G-2 Report No.61, 11 Jun 44, NARA]
350. HQ 82nd Airborne Div., G-2, *Interrogation Report No.5*, 10 Jun. 44 & HQ 82nd Airborne Div., G-2, *G-2 Report Nr.61*, 10 Jun. 44 [bothboth NARA, via Egbert van de Schootbrugge]; Anl. zu OKH/AHA/Abwicklungsstab, Anl. z. Sachgeb. 91 Nr.6.44 g., *Kriegsgliederung (91. LL.Div.), Unterstellungen Stand: 10.6.44* [T78 R672 H41/61b]
351. WFSt Op (H) *Lage West, Stand: 10.6.44*, Chef WFSt [NARA, via www.wwii-photos-maps.com]
352. Anl. zu OKH/AHA/Abwicklungsstab, Anl. z. Sachgeb. 91 Nr.6.44 g., *Kriegsgliederung (91. LL.Div.), Unterstellungen Stand: 10.6.44* [T78 R672 H41/61b]

353. Stadlhofer (1944), p.5
354. Anl. zu OKH/AHA/Abwicklungsstab, Anl. z. Sachgeb. 91 Nr.6.44 g., *Kriegsgliederung (91. LL.Div.), Unterstellungen Stand: 10.6.44* [T78 R672 H41/61b]
355. Phone call 505PIR S-2 at 17:32 on 10 Jun. 44 & HQ 82nd Airborne Div., G-2, *Interrogation Report No.5*, 10 Jun. 44 & HQ 82nd Airborne Div., G-2, *G-2 Report Nr.61*, 10 Jun. 44 [all NARA, via Egbert van de Schootbrugge]
356. The Merderet prevented direct contact between German and US forces, which could explain why they failed to notice the presence of the *I./921*.
357. Historical Division, War Dept. (1948), p.95 & 101-2 & Map 20; 4th ID, Operations D+5, p.1 [MCoE HQ Donovan Research Library, D328/I2180, *The Invasion of France*, file titled 'Miscellaneous Notes']; HQ 82nd Airborne Div., G-2, *Interrogation Report No.6*, 11 Jun. 44, p.1-2 & HQ 505th Infantry Regt., *S-2 Report*, 12 Jun. 44 [both NARA, via Egbert van de Schootbrugge]
358. See the chapter *"91.Luftlande-Infanterie-Division"*.
359. Gruppe Hellmich, Ia, 9.6.44 at 09:30 [UKNA, HW 5/498, CX/MSS/T212/122, KV 7557]
360. See the chapter *"91.Luftlande-Infanterie-Division"*.
361. A soldier of the *77. I.D.* reported them relieving the forces of Klosterkemper and Simon, which indicates they were both battlegroup commanders. [UKNA, WO 208/4138, S.R.M. 576]
362. See the chapter *"77.Infanterie-Division"*.
363. AOK 7 Ia, Anlage zum KTB Führungsabteilung, Lagekarten A.O.K.7 vom 6.6.44-30.6.44, *Stand: 15.6.44, 22 Uhr*. [T312 R1570 F23]
364. Stadlhofer (1944), p.5-8
365. OKH/AHA/Abwicklungsstab, Anl. z. Sachgeb. 91 Nr.6.44 g., *Kriegsgliederung Kampfgruppe 91.I.D., Stand: 18.6.44* [T78 R672 H41/61b]
366. 90th Inf.Div., *IPW Summary No.5*, 16 Jun. 44 [NARA, RG 407, Box 3282, File 207-2.1, Periodic Reports 90th Inf.Div. Jun. 44]
367. **Leichtfuss**, C.S.D.I.C. (UK) S. R. Report, S.R.M. 576 [UKNA, WO 208/4138] — Hereafter referred to as **Leichtfuss**, S.R.M.576
368. Volksbund
369. HQ 82nd Airborne Div., G-2, *Total number of POW captured*, 17 Jun. 44 [NARA, via Egbert van de Schootbrugge]
Historical Division, War Dept. (1948), *Utah Beach to Cherbourg (6 June-27 June 1944)*, United States Army, Washington, D.C., Map X, *Securing the Douve Line. 14-16 June 1944*. The 82nd AB captured a total of 123 members of the *243. I.D.* up to 17 June, of which the bulk belonged to the *I./921* (33) and the *II./922* (48). As it had already been in contact with the *II./922* around Le Ham, the capture of members of the battalion during the entire period up to 17 June cannot be linked to a specific sector without additional details or dates.
370. **Leichtfuss**, S.R.M.576; *77. I.D.*, orders issued by *Gen.* Stegmann regarding the move of the division towards the south, 17.6.44, copied and translated in Annex 1 to G-2 Periodic Report Nr.9, HQ First US Army, 19 June 1944 [Available at: https://firstdivisionmuseum.nmtvault.com/jsp/viewer.jsp?doc_id=iwfd0000%2F20141124%2F165&page_name=799 & 800, accessed on 4 August 2018]
371. AOK 7 Ia, *KTB 6.6.-25.7.44*, p.38 [T312 R1569 F257]
372. AOK 7, Ia Nr.80/44 g.Kdos Chefs., *Weisung an LXXXIV. Korps*, 14.6.44 [T312 R1565 F1026]
373. The confusing role of the *77. I.D.* has already been discussed at length in the division's dedicated chapter.
374. AOK 7, Ia Nr.3113/44 g.K., p.3 [T312 R1565 F1042]; Gen. Kdo.LXXXIV. A.K., *Korpsbefehl*, 15.6.44, copied and translated in Annex 1 to G-2 Report Nr.9, HQ First US Army, 19 June 44 [Available at: https://firstdivisionmuseum.nmtvault.com/jsp/viewer.jsp?doc_id=iwfd0000%2F20141124%2F165&page_name=798, accessed on 4 Aug, 2018]; AOK 7 Ia, Ia-Vormittagsmeldung, 16.6.44 [T312 R1565 F1064]; **Criegern, F. von (1948)**, MS # B-784 (Germ.), *Teil I, Die Kämpfe des* LXXXIV. A.K. *in der Normandie von der alliierten Landung bis 17.6.44*, p.30
375. IAOK 7 Ia, *KTB 6.6.-25.7.44*, p.44-45 [T312 R1569 F263-4]
376. Message from the *243. I.D.* to the *77. I.D.*, 16.6.44 at 16:11, copied and translated in Annex 1 to G-2 Periodic Report Nr.9, HQ First US Army, 19 June 1944 [Available at: https://firstdivisionmuseum.nmtvault.com/jsp/viewer.jsp?doc_id=iwfd0000%2F20141124%2F165&page_name=800, accessed on 4 Aug. 2018]
377. Historical Division, War Dept. (1948), p.136-41
378. AOK 7, Ia Nr.3169/44 g.K., 17.6.44 [T312 R1565 F1095]; See the chapter *"77.Infanterie-Division"* for more detailed information.
379. Stadlhofer (1944), p.5-8 [T78 R672 H41/61b]
380. See the chapter *"77.Infanterie-Division"*; *77. I.D.*, orders issued by *Gen.* Stegmann regarding the move of the division towards the south, 17.6.44, copied and translated in Annex 1 to G-2 Periodic Report Nr.9, HQ First US Army, 19 June 1944 [Available at: https://firstdivisionmuseum.nmtvault.com/jsp/viewer.jsp?doc_id=iwfd0000%2F20141124%2F165&page_name=799 & 800, accessed on 4 August 2018]
381. Report from the *243. I.D.* to the LXXXIV. A.K. on 17.6.44 [UKNA, HW 5/508, CX/MSS/R.222 (C), p.19; **Hayn, F. (1954)**, *Die Invasion - Von Cotentin bis Falaise*, Scharnhorst Buchkameradschaft der Soldaten, Heidelberg, p.54
382. *Kriegsgliederung Kampfgruppe 91.I.D., Stand: 18.6.44* [T78 R672 H41/61b]; AOK 7 Ia, *KTB 6.6.-25.7.44*, p.51 [T312 R1569 F269]; See the chapter *"91.Luftlande-Infanterie-Division"*.
383. Examples: AOK 7 Ia, AOK 7 *Kriegstagebuch Ia, 6 June 1944 - 16 Aug 1944*, p.112 [T312 R1569 F115] — Hereafter referred to as: AOK 7 Ia, *KTB 6.6.-16.8.44*; Okdo.d.H.Gr.B, Ia Nr.4541/44 g.K., 9.7.44, p.7 [T311 R3 F7002516]; Gen.Kdo.LXXXIV. A.K., Ia, Ia-Morgenmeldung, 18.7.44 [T314 R604 F1368]
384. German general staff officers files, index cards of *Gen.Maj.* Klosterkemper [T78 R888 H6/26]
385. AOK 7, Ia (no number), 21.6.44 [T312 R1565 F1212]
386. German general staff officers files, index cards of *Gen.Lt.* Hellmich [T78 R887 H6/26]
387. Historical Division, War Dept. (1948), *Utah Beach to Cherbourg (6 June-27 June 1944)*, United States Army, Washington, D.C., p.141-9
388. Elements of *Pi.Btl. 243* were again reported in the course of July and August. It is possible some elements of *Pi.Btl. 243* had been in action away from the battalion and were able to escape or the battalion may have been partially reconstituted using replacements or regimental engineer platoons.
389. AOK 7, Ia Nr.3282/44 g.K., 21.6.44 [T312 R1565 F1219]
390. AOK 7, Ia Nr.1645/44 g., *21.6.1944*, p.1 [T312 R1565 F1206]
391. AOK 7 Ia, *KTB 6.6.-25.7.44*, p.51 [T312 R1569 F270]; **Schlieben, K.W. v. (1948)**, p.74 & Anl.17; **Keil, G. (1948a)**, p.74
392. Keil, G. (1948a), p.75
393. C.S.D.I.C. (UK) S.R. Report - S.R.M.622, p.2 [UKNA, WO 208/4138]
394. **Hornung, A. (1944)**, report on the operations of *Pi.Btl. 709* by the battalion commander, 23.10.44, sheet 2, back [T78 R672 H41/61a]
395. C.S.D.I.C. (UK) S.R. Report - S.R.M.622, p.1 [UKNA, WO 208/4138]
396. **Hornung, A. (1944)**, sheet 2, back & sheet 3, front
397. Keil, G. (1948a), p.82-83
398. Keil, G. (1948a), p.83
399. AOK 7, Kriegsgliederungen zum KTB der Führungsabteilung AOK 7 ab 6.6.44 bis 30.6.44, *Stand 29.6. 17 Uhr* [T312 R1566 F24]
400. C.S.D.I.C. (UK) S.R. Report - S.R.M.619, p.1 [UKNA, WO 208/4138]; Headquarters Ninth Infantry Division, APO No.9, *Report of operation conducted by Ninth Infantry Division US Army - Cotentin peninsula France - 14 June-1 July*, 14.7.44, p.18
401. Tannhauser (*243. I.D.*) Ia, 18.6.44 at 07:00 [UKNA, HW 5/506, CX/MSS/T220/12, KV 8776]
402. Report (possibly *AOK 7*), 18.6.44 at 08:00 [UKNA, HW 5/506, CX/MSS/T220/54]
403. Flivo LXXXIV. A.K., 19.6.44 at about 14:00 [UKNA, HW 5/506, CX/MSS/T220/71]
404. Gefechtsbericht Kampfgruppe Klosterkemper for 19 June in AOK 7, Ia Nr. 1746/44 g.K., 26.6.44 [BAMA, RH 19-IX/2]
405. Flivo LXXXIV. A.K., 20.6.44 at 11:45 [UKNA, HW 5/508, CX/MSS/T222/63, 64]
406. Gefechtsbericht Kampfgruppe Klosterkemper for 20 June, attachment to *Heeresgruppe B*, Ia Nr.3277/44 g.K. [BAMA, RH 19-IX/2]
407. LXXXIV. A.K. on 20.6.44 at 22:00 [UKNA, HW 5/515, CX/MSS/T229/10, KV 9910]
408. OKH/AHA/Abwicklungsstab, Anl. z. Sachgeb. 91 Nr.6.44 g., *Kriegsgliederung Kampfgruppe 91.I.D., Stand: 18.6.44* [T78 R672 H41/61b]
409. Ibid.
410. Ibid.
411. CX/MSS/R.222 (C), 22.6.44, p.19 [UKNA, HW 5/508]
412. OKH/AHA/Abwicklungsstab, Anl. z. Sachgeb. 91 Nr.6.44 g., *Kriegsgliederung Kampfgruppe 91.I.D., Stand: 18.6.44* [T78 R672 H41/61b]

413. AOK 7, Ia Nr.3454/44 g.K., 27.6.44, p.2 [T312 R1565 F1376]
414. 21 AGp/Int/1070, App. Y to 21 Army Group Intelligence Summary No. 143, Part II, 8 Jul. 44 [UKNA, WO 171/131]
415. Gefechtsbericht Kampfgruppe Klosterkemper for 22 June [BAMA, RH 19-IX/3]
416. Gefechtsbericht Kampfgruppe Klosterkemper for 22 and 23 June [BAMA, RH 19-IX/3]
417. Ibid.
418. Report (unclear origin), 23.6.44 at 22:30 [UKNA, HW 5/514, CX/MSS/T228/77, KV 9868]; AOK 7, Anlage zum KTB Führungsabteilung, Lagekarten A.O.K.7 vom 6.6.44-30.6.44, Lage Normandie, Stand: 25.6.44, 22.00 Uhr [T312 R1570 F33]; AOK 7, Anlage zum KTB Führungsabteilung, Lagekarten A.O.K.7 vom 6.6.44-30.6.44, Lage Normandie, Stand: 24.6.44, 22.00 Uhr [T312 R1570 F34]
419. Gefechtsbericht Kampfgruppe Klosterkemper for 24 June, attachment to H.Gr.B., Ia Nr. 4167/44 g.K [BAMA, RH 19-IX/3]; Gefechtsbericht Gruppe König for 23 June in AOK 7, Ia Nr.1819/44 g.K., 26.6.44 [BAMA, RH 19-IX/3]
420. Report from the LXXXIV. A.K., Ia, 25.6.44 [UKNA, HW 5/514, CX/MSS/T228/81, KV 9864]
421. Gefechtsbericht Kampfgruppe Klosterkemper for 25 June, attachment to H.Gr.B.,Ia Nr. 3518/44 [BAMA, RH 19-IX/3]; Gefechtsbericht Kampfgruppe Klosterkemper for 27 June, attachment to H.Gr.B., Ia Nr.3518/44 [BAMA, RH 19-IX/3]; Gefechtsbericht Kampfgruppe Klosterkemper for 30 June, attachment to H.Gr.B., Ia Nr.3554/44 g.K. [BAMA, RH 19-IX/3]
422. OKH/AHA/Abwicklungsstab, Anl. z. Sachgeb. 91 Nr.6.44 g., *Kriegsgliederung Kampfgruppe König, Stand: 18.6.44 - 28.6.44* [T78 R672 H41/61b]
423. Ibid.
424. Ibid.
425. OKH/AHA/Abwicklungsstab, Anl. z. Sachgeb. 91 Nr.6.44 g., *Kriegsgliederung Kampfgruppe König, Stand: 18.6.44 - 28.6.44* [T78 R672 H41/61b]
426. *Gruppe König* reported 31 *7,62 cm F.K.39's*. Only two formations in the area had had such guns on D-Day: 24 in *AR 243* and eight in *KG 265*. The *3./Ost-Art.Abt. 752* had been sent to the *Nordfront* with 7.62 cm guns, but the type is unclear.
427. OKH/AHA/Abwicklungsstab, Anl. z. Sachgeb. 91 Nr.6.44 g., *Kriegsgliederung Kampfgruppe König, Stand: 18.6.44 - 28.6.44* [T78 R672 H41/61b]
428. Stadlhofer (1944), p.8 [T78 R672 H41/61b]; *Kriegsgliederung Kampfgruppe König, Stand: 18.6.44 - 28.6.44* [T78 R672 H41/61b] This is confirmed by German records. Twelve 12.2 cm howitzers were reported with *Gruppe König* on 27 June. On D-Day, the *III./AR 243* had 12 such guns and the *9./AR 265* had four. Based on their actions and late arrival, the losses of the *9./AR 265* are likely to have been minimal.
429. Stadlhofer (1944), p.8 [T78 R672 H41/61b]
430. OKH/AHA/Abwicklungsstab, Anl. z. Sachgeb. 91 Nr.6.44 g., *Kriegsgliederung Kampfgruppe König, Stand: 18.6.44 - 28.6.44* [T78 R672 H41/61b]

431. OKH/AHA/Abwicklungsstab, Anl. z. Sachgeb. 91 Nr.6.44 g., *Kriegsgliederung Kampfgruppe König, Stand: 18.6.44 - 28.6.44* [T78 R672 H41/61b]
432. AOK 7, Ia Nr.3454/44 g.K., 2.Teil, 27.6.44 [T312 R1565 F1377]
433. Ibid.
434. OKH/AHA/Abwicklungsstab, Anl. z. Sachgeb. 91 Nr.6.44 g., *Kriegsgliederung Kampfgruppe 91.I.D., Stand: 18.6.44* [T78 R672 H41/61b]; OKH/AHA/Abwicklungsstab, Anl. z. Sachgeb. 91 Nr.6.44 g., *Kriegsgliederung Kampfgruppe König, Stand: 18.6.44 - 28.6.44* [T78 R672 H41/61b]
435. Zetterling, N. (2000), *Normandy 1944, German Military Organisation, Combat Power and Organisational Effectiveness*, Winipeg: J.J.Fedorowicz Publishing, p.210. The information is based on *StuG-Lage der Sturmartillerie, Stand 1.7.44*, BaMa RH 11 II/v. 4
436. AOK 7, Anlage zum KTB Führungsabteilung, Lagekarten A.O.K.7 vom 6.6.44-30.6.44, *Lage Normandie, Stand: 28.6.44, 22.00 Uhr* [T312 R1570 F37]; The *I./1050* had arrived in the area south of the Olonde River around the time the Cotentin was cut and remained in place when the *243. I.D.* took over that sector of the *Nordfront*.
437. AOK 7, Anlage zum KTB Führungsabteilung, Lagekarten A.O.K.7 vom 6.6.44-30.6.44, *Lage Normandie, Stand: 29.6.44, 22.00 Uhr* [T312 R1570 F38]
438. AOK 7, Ia Nr.3454/44 g.K., 2.Teil, 27.6.44 [T312 R1565 F1377]; this will be addressed in more detail in the chapter *"Wolga-Tatarisches-Infanterie-Btl. 627"* in a future volume.
439. The *Regimentsgruppe* and battalion will be addressed in detail in seperate chapters in a future volume.
440. Nauroth, H.S. & B. Steinberg (2017), *Die Geschichte der 91.Luftlande-Division - Rekonstruktion eines Großverbandes der Deutschen Wehrmacht*, Hamburg: tredition GmbH, p.118-119
441. Report from Flivo LXXXIV. A.K. on 2.7.44 at 11:10 [UKNA, HW 5/519, CX/MSS/T233/53, XL 509]
442. C.S.D.I.C. (UK) S.I.R. 621, 23 Jul 44, p.1 [UKNA, WO 208/4367]; Report from Flivo LXXXIV. A.K. on 2.7.44 at 11:10 [UKNA, HW 5/519, CX/MSS/T233/53, XL 509]
443. AOK 7, Ia Nr.3505/44 g.K., 29.6.44 [T312 R1565 F1432]; **Mahlmann, P. (1946a)**, MS # A-983 (Germ.), *353. Inf.Division*, p.14-15 & Anl 7-8; AOK 7 Ia, *KTB 6.6.-16.8.44*, p.96 [T312 R1569 F99]; see also the chapters *"77.Infanterie-Division"* and the *"353.Infanterie-Division"*.
444. Flivo LXXXIV. A.K., evening 2.7.44 [UKNA, HW 5/519, CX.MSS/T234/3, XL 557 and XL 559]
445. LXXXIV. A.K. on 3.7.44 at 22:00 [UKNA, HW 5/520, CX/MSS/T235/23, XL]; this will be addressed in more detail in the chapters *"Ost-Regimentsgruppe Bunjatschenko"*, *"Ost-Bataillon 635"* and *"Ost-Bataillon Huber"* in a future volume.
446. WFSt Op (H), Situation maps (Lage West) 4.-15.7.44 (1:50.000 and 1:200.000) [NARA, via www.wwi-photos-maps.com]; also see chapters *"91.Luftlande-Infanterie-Division"* and *"265.Infanterie-Division"*.

447. Flivo LXXXIV. A.K. on 4.7.44 at 11:00 [UKNA, HW 5/520, CX/MSS/T235/39, XL 711]
448. Flivo LXXXIV. A.K. on 4.7.44 at 16:00 [UKNA, HW 5/520, CX/MSS/T235/84, XL 750 & XL 765]
449. AOK 7 Ia, *KTB 6.6.-25.7.44*, p.94 [T312 R1569 F314]
450. AOK 7 Ia, *KTB 6.6.-16.8.44*, p.115 [T312 R1569 F118]; Okdo.d.H.Gr.B, Ia Nr.4408/44 g.K., 5.7.44, p.2-3 [T311 R4 F7004837-8]
451. AOK 7 Ia, *KTB 6.6.-16.8.44*, p.112-113 [T312 R1569 F115-6]
452. Mahlmann, P. (1946a), MS # A-983 (Germ.), Anl.8
453. AOK 7 Ia, *KTB 6.6.-16.8.44*, p.118 [T312 R1569 F121]; PWIS(H)/LF/520, 15 Aug 44 [UKNA, WO 208/3645]
454. Okdo.d.H.Gr.B, Ia Nr.4421/44 g.K., 5.7.44, p.1-2 [T311 R4 F7004834-5]
455. Okdo.d.H.Gr.B, Ia Nr.4442/44 g.K II.Ang., 6.7.44 [T311 R3 F7002498]
456. Okdo.d.H.Gr.B, Ia Nr.4428/44 g.K., 5.7.44, p.2 [T312 R4 F7004833]
457. Okdo.d.H.Gr.B, Ia Nr.4442/44 g.K., 6.7.44, p.6 [T311 R3 F7002497]
458. LXXXIV. A.K., Ia on the morning of 6.7.44 [UKNA, HW 5/522, CX.MSS.T237/108, XL 1038]
459. Flivo LXXXIV. A.K. on 6.7.44 at 15:30 [UKNA, HW 5/522, CX/MSS/T237/118, XL 1043]; Okdo.d.H.Gr.B, Ia Nr.4451/44 g.K., 6.7.44 [T311 R4 F7004829]; Okdo.d.H.Gr.B, Ia Nr.4480/44 g.K., 7.7.44, p.2 [T311 R3 F7002500]
460. AOK 7 Ia, *KTB 6.6.-25.7.44*, p.102 [T312 R1569 F322]
461. Weidinger, O. (1954), *Bericht über den Einsatz bei La Haye de Puits*, p.31-32 & map 4 [pages in Anlagenband A and map in Anlagenband B to **Stückler, A. (1954)**, MS # P-159]; Okdo.d.H.Gr.B, Ia Nr.4483/44 g.K., 7.7.44, p.2-3 [T311 R4 F700425-26]; Okdo.d.H.Gr.B, Ia Nr.4489/44 g.K., 7.7 [T311 R4 F7004822-3]; Okdo.d.H.Gr.B, Ia Nr.4516/44 g.K., 8.7.44, p.3 -4 [T311 R3 F7002507-8] The document speaks of „Le Mans", but there is no such place in the area. It is assumed "Le Mont" was meant.
462. AOK 7 Ia, *KTB 6.6.-16.8.44*, p.126 [T312 R1569 F129]; Okdo.d.H.Gr.B, Ia Nr.4520/44 g.K., 8.7.44, p.2 [T311 R4 F7004819]
463. Flivo LXXXIV. A.K., 8.7.44 (late) [UKNA, HW 5/525, CX/MSS/T240/13, XL 1328]; Okdo.d.H.Gr.B, Ia Nr.4525/44 g.K., 8.7.44 [T311 R4 F7004814]
464. Weidinger, O. (1954), p.32-33 [in of Anlagenband A to **Stückler, A. (1954)** MS # P-159]; Okdo.d.H.Gr.B, Ia Nr.4529/44 g.K., 8.7.44, p.2 [T311 R4 F7004812]
465. Okdo.d.H.Gr.B, Ia Nr.4541/44 g.K., 9.7.44, p.7 [T311 R3 F7002516]; already preceded by a request from *AOK 7* on 7.7.44 in: AOK 7 Ia, *KTB 6.6.-16.8.44*, p.128 [T312 R1569 F131]
466. Flivo (likely the *LXXXIV. A.K.*) at 16:30 on 9.7.44 [UKNA, HW 5/525, CX/MSS/T240/108, XL 1431]; Okdo.d.H.Gr.B, Ia Nr.4571/44 g.Kdos, 9.7.44, p.2 [T311 R4 F7004806]; Okdo.d.H.Gr.B, Ia Nr.4585/44 g.K., 10.7.44, p.5 [T311 R3 F7002521]
467. Okdo.d.H.Gr.B, Ia Nr.4590/44 g.K., 10.7.44, p.2 [T311 R4 F7004804]

468. Flivo LXXXIV. A.K., 10.7.44 at 01:00 [UKNA, HW 5/526, CX/MSS/T241/39, XL 1498]; Okdo.d.H.Gr.B, Ia Nr.4632/44 g.K., 11.7.44, p.5-6 [T311 R3 F7002528-9]
469. Okdo.d.H.Gr.B, Ia Nr.4686/44 g.K., 12.7.44, p.2 [T311 R3 F7002530]; **Mahlmann, P. (1946a),** MS# A-983 (Germ.), p.18; AOK 7 Ia, *KTB 6.6.-16.8.44*, p.140 [T312 R1569 F144]
470. Okdo.d.H.Gr.B, Ia Nr.4696/44 g.K., 12.7.44 [T311 R4 F7004787]; Okdo.d.H.Gr.B, Ia Nr.4700/44 g.K., 12.7.44 [T311 R4 F7004785]; AOK 7 Ia, *KTB 6.6.-25.7.44*, p.114 [T312 R1569 F334]; AOK 7 Ia, *KTB 6.6.-16.8.44*, p.143-4 [T312 R1569 F147-8]; Okdo.d.H.Gr.B, Ia Nr.4704/44 g.K., 12.7.44, p.2 [T311 R4 F7004784
471. Flivo LXXXIV. A.K., 13.7.44 at 18:00 [UKNA, HW 5/529, CX/MSS/T244/121, XL 1925]; Flivo LXXXIV. A.K., 14.7.44 at 02:00 [UKNA, HW 5/530, CX/MSS/T245/78, XL 1974]
472. AOK 7 Ia, *KTB 6.6.-25.7.44*, p.113 [T312 R1569 F333]; WFSt. Op (H), *Lage West, Stand: 14.7.44*, Chef. WFSt. (1:200.000) [NARA, via www.wwii-photos-maps.com]
473. Okdo.d.H.Gr.B, Ia Nr.4753/44 g.K., 14.7.44 [T311 R3 F7002545]
474. Flivo LXXXIV. A.K., 15.7.44 AT 10:30 [UKNA, HW 5/531, CX/MSS/T246/49, XL 2173]; Okdo.d.H.Gr.B, Ia Nr.4924/44 g.K., 18.7.44, p.7 [T311 R3 F7002569]
475. Okdo.d.H.Gr.B., Ia Nr.4924/44 g.K., 18.7.44, p.7 [T311 R3 F7002569]
476. Information provided by Simon Trew based on a captured document giving the organisation of the 7th Army front on 19 July. (private collection)
477. AOK 7 Ia, KTB 6.6.-16.8.44, p.180 [T312 R1569 F184]; AOK 7 Ia, KTB 6.6.-16.8.44, p.185 [T312 R1569 F189]
478. Document (page 1 missing) [UKNA, HW 5/540, CX/MSS/T255/136]
479. Gen.Kdo.LXXXIV. A.K., Ia, 23.7.44 [T314 R1604 F1380]
480. Gen.Kdo.LXXXIV. A.K., Ia Nr.048/44 g.K., 23.7.44, p.2-3 [T314 R1604 F1374-5] The document mentions six light batteries from the *91. LL.Div.* being with the division. The entries concerning this division only mention three. Since two batteries had been lost on D-Day, a presence of three batteries is most likely, especially since a fourth light battery was attached to *"Das Reich"*. The number of six probably referred to all batteries that the *91. LL.Div.* had provided.
481. Gen.Kdo.LXXXIV. A.K., Ia Nr.035/44, 22.7.44 [T314 R1604 F1388]
482. Gen.Kdo.LXXXIV. A.K., Ia Nr.048/44 g.K., 23.7.44, p.2-3 [T314 R1604 F1374-5]
483. H.Gr.D, *K.T.B. (Tekst) 1.-31.7.44*, p.192 [T311 R16 F7016788]
484. 21 AGp/Int/1070, App. A to 21 Army Group Intelligence Summary No. 147, Part II, 20 Jul. 44 [UKNA, WO 171/131]
485. HQ V Corps, Annex No1 to G-2 Periodic Report Nr.59, Order of Battle Notes, 5 Aug. 44 [Available at https://firstdivisionmuseum.nmtvault.com/jsp/viewer.jsp?doc_id=iwfd0000%2F20141124%2F170&page_name=402 Accessed on 6 August 2018] It is assumed that the loss numbers also refer to 28 July, but without the original documents their exact meaning cannot be determined.

486. (LXXXIV. A.K.), Tagesmeldung, 26.7.44, p.2; Okdo.d.H.Gr.B, Ia Nr.5260/44 g.K., 28.7.44 [T311 R4 F7004687]; H.Gr.D (Ob.West), *Kriegstagebuch (Text) 1.-31.7.44*, p.286 [T311 R16 F7016882]
487. Okdo.d.H.Gr.B, Ia Nr.5272/44 g.K., 28.7.44 p.2 [T311 R4 F7004686]; Okdo.d.H.Gr.B, Ia Nr.5260/44 g.K., 28.7.44 [T311 R4 F7004687]
488. Okdo.d.H.Gr.B, Ia Nr.5288/44 g.K., 29.7.44, p.2 [T311 R4 F7004684]; Okdo.d.H.Gr.B, Ia Nr.5288/44 g.K., 29.7.44, p.1 [T311 R4 F7004680]; LXXXIV. A.K., 29.7.44 at 20:15 [UKNA, HW 5/548, CX/MSS/T263/121, XL 4396]; **Gemmrig (1945)**, p.2 [T78 R672 H/41/61a]; **König, E. (1946)**, p.8
489. Jagdkorps II, Ic, 30.7.44 at 06:00 [UKNA, HW 5/546, CX/MSS/T261/90 / XL 4112]
490. WFSt. Op (H), *3.Lage West, Stand: 30.7.44*, Chef WFSt. (1:50.000) [NARA, via www.wwii-photos-maps.com]; Okdo.d.H.Gr.B, Ia Nr.5322/44 g.K., 30.7.44, p. [T311 R4 F7004677]
491. Okdo.d.H.Gr.B, Ia Nr.5372/44 g.K., 31.7.44, p.2 [T311 R4 F7004668]; Okdo.d.H.Gr.B, Ia Nr.5339/44 g.K., 31.7.44, p.5 [T311 R3 F7002661]
492. Okdo.d.H.Gr.B, Ia Nr.5407/44 g.K., 1.8.44, p.1 [T311 R4 F4664]
493. Number of maps from NARA, via www.wwii-photos-maps.com: WFSt. Op.(H), *Lage West, Stand: 1.8.44*, Chef WFSt. (1:80.000); WFSt. Op (H), *3.Lage West, Stand: 1.8.44*, Chef WFSt. (1:80.000); WFSt. Op.(H), *3.Lage West*, 2.8.44, Chef West (1:80.000); WFSt Op.(H), *Lage West, Stand: 3.8.44*, Chef WFSt (1:80:000)
494. See WFSt. Op.(H), *Lage West*, Chef WFSt. for period 3-16 August (1:80.000 and 1:200.000) [NARA, via www.wwii-photos-maps.com]
495. AOK 7, 8.8.44 (morning) [UKNA, HW 5/558, CX/MSS/T273/150, XL 5778]; AOK 7 communications log for the period 3.-16.8.44, p.12-14, 27 [T312 R1568 F646-8, 660]; AOK 7, Ia Nr.3192/44 g., 25.8.44, p.2-3 [T312 R1568 F406-7]
496. On 5 October he was put in command of the *180.Div.*, which later became the *180. Inf.Div.* [German general staff officers files, index cards of *Gen.Maj.* Klosterkemper in T78 R888 H6/26]
497. OKH/GenStdH/Org.Abt. Nr.I/18698/44 g.K., 10.8.44, p.1-2 [T78 R421 F6390495-6]; **Tessin, G. (1973)**, *8.Band*, p.186; OKW/WFSt/Op. /West Nr.009810/44, 15.8.44 [UKNA, HW 5/574, CX/MSS/T289/160, XL 8279]
498. Okdo.d.H.Gr.B, Ia Nr.6712/44 g.K., 28.8.44 [T311 R4 F7004070]
499. OKH/GenStdH/Org.Abt.I Nr.I/19995/44 g.K., 16.10.44 [T78 R432 F6403685]
500. *Div. Verbände, II. Teil, 243.Inf.Div.* [T78 R412 F6380328]
501. Anlage zu Okdo.d.H.Gr.B, Ia Nr.10076.44 g.K., 21.11.44 [T78 R410 F6378806]; *Übersicht über aufgelöste Divisionen, H.Gr. Ob West* [T78 R410 F6378876]
502. Block, M., 8.1.2009, www.feldgrau.net/forum/viewtopic.php? f=24&t=30202, accessed 28.1.2012
503. Anlage zu Okdo.d.H.Gr.B, Ia Nr.10076.44 g.K., 20.11.44 [T78 R410 F6378806]; **Tessin, G. (1976)**, *13.Band*, p.319. Six replacement assault guns were sent to the the 2nd Company in October 1944. This could indicate that the original *2.(StuG)/Pz.Jg.Abt. 243* still had four assault guns left after Normandy. On the other hand, Ultra had intercepted information on the allocation of nine assault guns to the division on 24 August, which would suggest more serious losses. [UKNA, HW 5/574, CX/MSS/T289/160, XL 879, referring to T288/20]
504. Block, M., 14.7.2009, www.feldgrau.net/forum/viewtopic.php? f=24&t=31018, accessed 28.1.2012. Tessin however states that the 1st and the 3rd Companies were new units. [**Tessin, G. (1976)**, *13.Band*, p.319]

265. Infanterie-Division

1. Tessin, G. (1973), *8.Band*, p.278; Anl. zu OKH/GenStdH/Org. Abt. Nr.I/4500/43 g.K., 4.10.43, *Kriegsgliederung des Feldheeres (Sollgliederung), Band I, Stand: September 1943*, p.3 [T78 R409 F6377967] — Hereafter referred to as: OKH, *Kriegsgliederung des Feldheeres September 1943*
2. OKW, Abwicklungsstab Sachgebiet 265, *Taktischer Bericht für 265. I.D.*, 29.10.44 [T78 R672 H41/61b]; see *Schematische Kriegsgliederung* from 25.7.1943 to 12.4.1945 [T78 R649 F328-397]
3. *Ibid.*
4. Tessin, G. (1973), *8.Band*, p.278
5. German general staff officers files, index cards of *Gen.Lt.* Düvert [T78 R885 H6/26]; German general staff officers files, index cards of *Gen.Maj.* Junck [T78 R888 H6/26]
6. Anl.1 zu OKH/Chef H Rüst u.BdE AHA Ia(I) Nr.2529/43 g.K. [T78 R849 H36/156]
7. OKH, *Kriegsgliederung des Feldheeres September 1943*, p.108 [T78 R409 F6377967]
8. *Ibid.*
9. *Ibid.*
10. Feldpostübersicht
11. OKH, *Kriegsgliederung des Feldheeres September 1943*, p.108 [T78 R409 F6377967]
12. Anl.1 zu OKH/Chef H Rüst u.BdE AHA Ia(I) Nr.2529/43 g.K. [T78 R849 H36/156]
13. OKH, *Kriegsgliederung des Feldheeres September 1943*, p.108 [T78 R409 F6377967]
14. Anl.3 zu OKH/Chef H Rüst u.BdE/AHA/Ia(I) Nr.2529/43 g.K., *Liste der gültigen Stärken (bodstg.) Inf.Div.*, p.2 [T78 R849 H36/156]
15. OKH, *Kriegsgliederung des Feldheeres September 1943*, p.108 [T78 R409 F6377967]
16. Anl.1 zu OKH/Chef H Rüst u.BdE AHA Ia(I) Nr.2529/43 g.K. [T78 R849 H36/156]
17. Anl.3 zu OKH/Chef H Rüst u.BdE/AHA/Ia(I) Nr.2529/43 g.K. [T78 R849 H36/156]

18. Anl.1 zu OKH/Chef H Rüst u.BdE AHA Ia(I) Nr.2529/43 g.K. [T78 R849 H36/156]

19. 265.I.D., Zustandsbericht, Meldung vom 1.6.1944 [T314 R747 F9]

20. OKW, Abwicklungsstab Sachgebiet 265, Taktischer Bericht für 265. I.D., 29.10.44, p.1 [T78 R672 H41/61b]

21. Ob.West (Obkdo.H.Gr.D) Ia Nr.7058/43 g.K., 2.12.43, p.2 [BaMa, RH 19-IV/18]

22. Anl.2 zu Ob.West (Obkdo.H.Gr.D) Ia Nr.7183/44 g.K., 9.12.32 [BaMa, RH 19-IV/18]

23. *21 Army Group Intelligence Summary No.145*, Part II, 13 July 1944 [UKNA, WO 171/131/21, AGp/INT/1070]

24. Data obtained from the DRK *Vermisstenbildliste* and death cards in the Ancestry.com "Germany, Military Killed in Action, 1939-1948" collection.

25. The MIRS study examined 688 paybooks of the *266. I.D.*

26. See **Zetterling, N. (2000)**, *Normandy 1944, German Military Organisation, Combat Power and Organisational Effectiveness*, Winipeg: J.J.Fedorowicz Publishing, p.247-8.

27. Anl.2 zu Ob.West (Obkdo.H.Gr.D) Ia Nr.7183/44 g.K., 9.12.32 [BaMa, RH 19-IV/18]

28. 265. I.D., Zustandsbericht, *Meldung vom 1.6.1944* [T314 R747 F9]

29. 265. I.D., Zustandsbericht 265. I.D., *Meldung vom 1.6.1944* [T314 R747 F9]; Anlage zu 265. I.D., Ia Nr.283/44 g.K., (Kriegsgliederung) *265. I.D.*, 4.6.44 [T314 R747 F11]

30. 265. I.D., Zustandsbericht, *Meldung vom 1.12.1943* [T314 R745 F205]

31. 265. I.D., Zustandsbericht 265. I.D., *Meldung vom 1.6.1944* [T314 R747 F9]; Anlage zu 265. I.D., Ia Nr.283/44 g.K., (Kriegsgliederung) *265. I.D.*, 4.6.44 [T314 R747 F11]

32. Anlage zu 265. I.D., Ia Nr.283/44 g.K., (Kriegsgliederung) *265. I.D.*, 4.6.44 [T314 R747 F12]; Corps records refer to the "*Gewehr 98*", but POW reports only mention the "*K98k*".

33. Anlage zu 265. I.D., Ia Nr.283/44 g.K., (Kriegsgliederung) *265. I.D.*, 4.6.44 [T314 R747 F11]

34. Gen.Kdo.XXV. A.K., *Kriegstagebuch Nr.11 Gen.Kdo.XXV. A.K. Führungsabteilung (Ia) 1.10.43 - 31.12.43* [T314 R745 F21] — Hereafter refered to as: Gen.Kdo.XXV. A.K. Ia, *KTB Nr.11*; Anlage 2 zu OKH/Chef H Rüst u.BdE AHA / ZAst. Nr.7000/43 g.K., *Frontnachweiser (9. Neudruck)*, p.153 [T78 R401 F6371591]

35. Gen.Kdo.XXV. A.K. Nr.Ia Nr.3252/43 g., 6.11.1943 [T314 R745 F110]

36. Gen.Kdo.XXV. A.K. Nr.2939/43 g., 11.10.43 [T314 R745 F326]; Gen.Kdo.XXV. A.K. Nr.2965/43 g., 13.10.43 [T314 R745 F332]; Gen.Kdo.XXV. A.K. Ia, *KTB Nr.11* [T314 R745 F21]

37. Gen.Kdo.XXV. A.K., Nr.93/44 g. II.Ang., 12.1.44 [T314 R745 F1028]; AOK 7, *Kriegsgliederung 7. Armee, Stand 18.5.44, 265. I.D., Stand 1.5.1944* [T312 R1566 F228]

38. Anlage zu 265. I.D., Ia Nr.283/44 g.K., (Kriegsgliederung) *265. I.D.*, 4.6.44 [T314 R747 F11]

39. Anlage zu 265. I.D., Ia Nr.283/44 g.K., (Kriegsgliederung) *265. I.D.*, 4.6.44 [T314 R747 F11]

40. PWIS(H)/LF/289, 14 Jul 44, p.3 [UKNA, WO 208/3632]; C.S.I.D.C. (UK) S.I.R. 440, 28 Jun 44, p.3 [NARA, RG 165, Box 659, Folder 2]

41. PWIS(H)/LF/289, 14 Jul 44, p.3 [UKNA, WO 208/3632]; C.S.I.D.C. (UK) S.I.R. 440, 28 Jun 44, p.3 [NARA, RG 165, Box 659, Folder 2]; FID-DZ No.324, Interrogation Report, 27 July 1944 [NARA, RG 498, Box 1326]

42. C.S.I.D.C. (UK) S.I.R. 440, 28 Jun 44, p.3 [NARA, RG 165, Box 659, Folder 2]; FID-DZ No.324, Interrogation Report, 27 July 1944 [NARA, RG 498, Box 1326]; FID-DZ No.207, 11 July 1944 [NARA, RG 498, Box 1326]

43. FID-DZ No.324, 27 July 1944 [NARA, RG 498, Box 1326]

44. *K.St.N. (Heer, Nr.211F, Teileinheit, Bespannungsstaffel eines Infanterieregiments (bodenständig)*, 1.12.42 [T78 R397 F6366332]

45. PWIS(H)/LF/289, 14 Jul 44, p.3 [UKNA, WO 208/3632]; C.S.I.D.C. (UK) S.I.R. 440, 28 Jun 44, p.3 [NARA, RG 165, Box 659, Folder 2]; FID-DZ No.207, 11 July 1944 [NARA, RG 498, Box 1326]

46. C.S.D.I.C. (UK) S.I.R. 558, 12 Jul 44 [NARA, RG 155, Box 659, Folder 2]

47. PWIS(H)/LF/283, 12 Jul 44, p.1 [UKNA, WO 208/3631]

48. C.S.D.I.C. (UK) S.I.R. 558, 12 Jul 44 [NARA, RG 155, Box 659, Folder 2]

49. PWIS(H)/LF/283, 12 Jul 44, p.1 [UKNA, WO 208/3631]

50. OKH, *Kriegsgliederung des Feldheeres September 1943*, p.108 [T78 R409 F6377967]; Anlage zu 265. I.D., Ia Nr.283/44 g.K., (Kriegsgliederung) *265. I.D.*, 4.6.44 [T314 R747 F11]

51. C.S.I.D.C. (UK) S.I.R. 440, 28 Jun 44, p.1-2 [NARA, RG 165, Box 659, Folder 2]; PWIS(H)/KP/115, 7 Jul 44 [UKNA, WO 208/3624]; PWIS(H)/KP/132, 10 Jul 44 [UKNA, WO 208/3624]; PWIS(H)/KP/135, 11 Jul 44, p.1 [UKNA, WO 208/3624]; PWIS(H)/LDC/107, 12 Jul 44 [UKNA, WO 208/3646]; PWIS(H)/LF/177, 26 Jun 44, p.2 [UKNA, WO 208/3630]; PWIS(H)/LF/283, 12 Jul 44, p.1 [UKNA, WO 208/3631]

52. PWIS(H)/LF/197, 29 Jun 44 [UKNA, WO 208/3630]

53. PWIS(H)/KP/115, 7 Jul 44 [UKNA, WO 208/3624]; PWIS(H)/KP/132, 10 Jul 44 [UKNA, WO 208/3624]; PWIS(H)/KP/135, 11 Jul 44, p.1 [UKNA, WO 208/3624]; PWIS(H)/LF/197, 29 Jun 44 [UKNA, WO 208/3630]; PWIS(H)/LF/283, 12 Jul 44, p.1 [UKNA, WO 208/3631]; C.S.D.I.C. (UK) S.I.R. 440, 28 Jun 44, p.1-2 [NARA, RG 165, Box 659, Folder 2]; PWIS(H)/LF/177, 26 Jun 44, p.2 [UKNA, WO 208/3630]

54. PWIS(H)/LDC/117, 13 Jul 44, p.1 [UKNA, WO 208/3646]

55. PWIS(H)/LF/197, 29 Jun 44 [UKNA, WO 208/3630]

56. PWIS(H)/LF/177, 26 Jun 44, p.2 [UKNA, WO 208/3630]; PWIS(H)/LF/283, 12 Jul 44, p.1 [UKNA, WO 208/3631]

57. C.S.D.I.C. (UK) S.I.R. 558, 12 Jul 44 [NARA, RG 165, Box 659, Folder 2]

58. PWIS(H)/KP/132, 10 Jul 44 [UKNA, WO 208/3624]

59. 90th Infantry Div., *Ob Report No.20*, 4 July 1944 [NARA, RG 407, Box 3498, File 208-7.2]

60. C.S.D.I.C. (UK) S.I.R. 440, 28 Jun 44, p.1 [NARA, RG 165, Box 659, Folder 2]

61. PWIS(H)/KP/115, 7 Jul 44 [UKNA, WO 208/3624]

62. PWIS(H)/LDC/117, 13 Jul 44, p.1 [UKNA, WO 208/3646]

63. FID-DZ No.287, 22 July 1944 [NARA, RG 498, Box 1326]

64. FID-DZ, No.195, 9 July 1944, p.1-2 [NARA, RG 498, Box 1326]; FID-DZ No.163, 3 July 1944 [NARA, RG 498, Box 1326]

65. OKH, *Kriegsgliederung des Feldheeres September 1943*, p.108 [T78 R409 F6377967]; For the *Sollgliederung* of the divisions see *Kriegsgliederung des Feldheeres September 1943* [T78 R409 F6377954]

66. Anlage zu 265. I.D., Ia Nr.283/44 g.K., (Kriegsgliederung) *265. I.D.*, 4.6.44 [T314 R747 F11]

67. AOK 7/O.Qu., *Kriegstagebuch der Oberquartiermeisterabteilung AOK 7 für die Zeit vom 1.6.44 - 30.6.44* [T312 R1571 F496]

68. AOK 7, Ia Nr.3263/44 g.K., 21.6.44, p.1 [T312 R1565 F1215]; *XXV. A.K., Gemäß AOK 7 Abt. Ia Nr.3288/44 g.K., 21.6.44 herauszulösende Teile der 265. I.D.* [T314 R757 F31]

69. Anlage zu 265. I.D., Ia Nr.283/44 g.K., (Kriegsgliederung) *265. I.D.*, 4.6.44 [T314 R747 F11]

70. PWIS(H)/KP/135, 11 Jul 44, p.1 [UKNA, WO 208/3624]; S.D.I.C. (UK) S.I.R. 558, 12 Jul 44 [NARA, RG 165, Box 659, Folder 2]

71. FID-DZ No.195, 12 July 1944, p.2 [NARA, RG 498, Box 1326]

72. C.S.D.I.C. (UK) S.I.R. 440, 28 Jun 44, p.2 [NARA, RG 165, Box 659, Folder 2]

73. PWIS(H)/LDC/107, 12 Jul 44, p.1 [UKNA, WO 208/3646]; FID-DZ No.195, 12 July 1944, p.2 [NARA, RG 498, Box 1326]

74. Anlage zu 265. I.D., Ia Nr.283/44 g.K., (Kriegsgliederung) *265. I.D.*, 4.6.44 [T314 R747 F11]

75. FID-DZ No.264, 22 July 1944 [NARA, RG 498, Box 1326]

76. Anlage zu 265.I.D., Ia Nr.283/44 g.K., (Kriegsgliederung) *265. Inf.Div.*, 4.6.44 [T314 R747 F11]; PWIS(H)/KP/135, 11 Jul 44, p.1 [UKNA, WO 208/3624]]

77. PWIS(H)/KP/135, 11 Jul 44, p.1 [UKNA, WO 208/3624]

78. **Post, G. (1944)**, *Bericht über den Einsatz des schweren Pak-Zuges der 14.Kompanie Gren.Rgt.895 in der Invasionsfront vom 15.6. - 2.8.1944.*, p.1 [T78 R672 H41/61a]

79. Anlage zu 265. I.D., Ia Nr.283/44 g.K., (Kriegsgliederung) *265. I.D.*, 4.6.44 [T314 R747 F11]; AOK 7, Kriegsgliederung 7. Armee, Stand 18.5.44, 265. I.D., Stand 1.5.44 [T312 R1566 F228]

80. Anlage zu 265. I.D., Ia Nr.178/44 g.K., (Kriegsgliederung) *265. I.D., Stand vom 1.4.44* [T314 R746 F443]; Anlage zu 265. I.D., Ia Nr.283/44 g.K., (Kriegsgliederung) *265. I.D.*, 4.6.44 [T314 R747 F11]

81. OKH, *Kriegsgliederung des Feldheeres September 1943*, p.108 [T78 R409 F6377967]

82. Gen.Kdo.XXV. A.K. Abt.Ia Nr.1180/43 g.K., 13.11.1943, p.2 [T314 R745 F116]; Anlage zu 265. I.D., Ia Nr.6/44 g.K., (Kriegsgliederung) *265. I.D.*, 5.1.44 [T314 R745 F649]

83. Gen.Kdo.XXV. A.K., Abt. Ia Nr.18/44 g., 3.1.44 [T314 R745 F1014]

84. AOK 7, Kriegsgliederung 7. Armee, Stand 18.5.44, 265. I.D., Stand 1.5.1944 [T312 R1566 F228]; Anlage 2 zu AOK 7 Ia/Stoart Nr.318/43 g.K., 2.12.1943, Blatt 1 [T314 R745 F239]

85. Anlage zu 265. I.D., Ia Nr.283/44 g.K., (Kriegsgliederung) *265. I.D., 4.6.44* [T314 R747 F11]
86. Anl.1 zu AOK 7 O.Qu. /Ia/ Nr.2500/44 g.K., 7.5.44, [T312 R1565 F649]
87. Anlage zu 265. I.D., Ia Nr.283/44 g.K., (Kriegsgliederung) *265. I.D., 4.6.44* [T314 R747 F11]; OKH, *Kriegsgliederung des Feldheeres September 1943*, p.108 [T78 R409 F6377967]
88. Anlage zu 265. I.D., Ia Nr.235/44 g.K., (Kriegsgliederung) *265. I.D., Stand vom 1.5.44* [T314 R746 F459]
89. FID-DZ No.205, 11 July 1944 [NARA, RG 498, Box 1326]; FID-DZ No.181, 8 July 1944 [NARA, RG 498, Box 1326]
90. AOK 7, Kriegsgliederung 7. Armee, Stand 18.5.44, *265. I.D., Stand 1.5.1944* [T312 R1566 F228]
91. Anlage zu 265. I.D., Ia Nr.71/44 g.K., (Kriegsgliederung) *265. I.D., 4.2.44* [T314 R745 F666]
92. Gen.Kdo.XXV. A.K. Abt.Ia Nr.165/44 g.K.,14.2.44, p.1-2 [T314 R745 F1107-1108]
93. *Ibid.*; Anlage zu 265. I.D., Ia Nr.178/44 g.K., (Kriegsgliederung) *265. I.D., Stand vom 1.4.44* [T314 R746 F443]
94. Anlage zu 265. I.D., Ia Nr.323/44 g.K., *(Kriegsgliederung 265. I.D., 3.7.44* [T314 R747 F203]
95. Anlage zu 265. I.D., Ia Nr.283/44 g.K., (Kriegsgliederung) *265. I.D., 4.6.44* [T314 R747 F11]
96. OKH, *Kriegsgliederung des Feldheeres September 1943,* p.108 [T78 R409 F6377967]
97. *K.St.N. (Heer) Nr.859F, Kriegsetat, Infanteriedivisionsfunkkompanie (bodenständig)*, 1.1.44 [T78 R397 F6366377-9]; PWIS(H)/LF/289, 14 Jul 44, p.1-2 [UKNA, WO 208/3632]; FID-DZ No.193, 9 July 1944 [NARA, RG 498, Box 1326]. Both prisoners belonged to the same section. The section leader mentions 100W transmitters in the company, while the other man refers to 80W transmitters. This does not rule out the option that the 1st Platoon may actually have matched *KStN 859F*.
98. AOK 7, Kriegsgliederung 7. Armee, Stand 18.5.44, *265. I.D., Stand 1.5.1944* [T312 R1566 F228]; Anl. zu 265. I.D., Ia Nr.6/44 g.K., Kriegsgliederung, *Stand vom 1.1.44* [T314 R745 F645]
99. AOK 7, Kriegsgliederung 7. Armee, Stand 18.5.44, 265. I.D., *Stand 1.5.1944* [T312 R1566 F228]
100. Anlage zu 265. I.D., Ia Nr.283/44 g.K., (Kriegsgliederung) *265. I.D., 4.6.44* [T314 R747 F11]
101. Gen.Kdo.XXV. A.K., Abt. Ia Nr.3295/43 g., 10.11.43 [T314 R745 F412]
102. Gen.Kdo.XXV. A.K., Abt. Ia Nr.3476/43 g., 25.11.43 [T314 R745 F457]; Gen.Kdo.XXV. A.K. Ia Nr.3548/43 g., 2.12.43, p.1 [T314 R745 F479]; Gen.Kdo.XXV. A.K., Abt. Ia Nr.3626/43 g., 8.12.43 [T314 R745 F497]
103. AOK 7, Ia Nr.926/44 g., 24.5.44 [T312 R1565 F759]
104. AOK 7, Kriegsgliederung 7. Armee, Stand 18.5.44, 265. I.D., *Stand 1.5.1944* [T312 R1566 F228]
105. Anlage zu 265. I.D., Ia Nr.283/44 g.K., (Kriegsgliederung) *265. I.D., 4.6.44* [T314 R747 F11]
106. Anlage zu 265. I.D., Ia Nr.235/44 g.K., (Kriegsgliederung) *265. I.D.,* 1.5.44 [T314 R746 F459]
107. Anlage zu 265. I.D., Ia Nr.283/44 g.K., (Kriegsgliederung) *265. I.D., 4.6.44* [T314 R747 F11]
108. AOK 7, Kriegsgliederung 7. Armee, Stand 18.5.44, 265. I.D., *Stand 1.5.1944* [T312 R1566 F228]
109. Anlage zu 265. I.D., Ia Nr.283/44 g.K., (Kriegsgliederung) *265. I.D., 4.6.44* [T314 R747 F11]
110. *Ibid.*; AOK 7, Kriegsgliederung 7. Armee, Stand 18.5.44, 265. I.D., *Stand 1.5.1944* [T312 R1566 F228]
111. Anlage zu 265. I.D., Ia Nr.178/44 g.K., (Kriegsgliederung) *265. I.D., Stand vom 1.4.44* [T314 R746 F443]
112. AOK 7, Kriegsgliederung 7. Armee, Stand 18.5.44, 265. I.D., *Stand 1.5.1944* [T312 R1566 F228]
113. Gen.Kdo.XXV. A.K., Ia Nr.831/44 g., 18.3.44 [T314 R745 F961]; AOK 7, Kriegsgliederung 7. Armee, Stand 18.5.44, 265. I.D., *Stand 1.5.1944* [T312 R1566 F228]
114. This will be addressed in more detail in a future volume.
115. AOK 7, Kriegsgliederung 7. Armee, Stand 18.5.44, *Stand 1.5.1944* [T312 R1566 F228]; AOK 7, Kriegsgliederung 7. Armee, Stand 18.5.44, *275. I.D., Stand: 1.5.44* [T312 R1566 F230]
116. AOK 7, Kriegsgliederung 7. Armee, Stand 18.5.44, 265. I.D., *Stand 1.5.1944* [T312 R1566 F228]
117. Gen.Kdo.XXV. A.K., 14.2.44., p.1-2 [T314 R745 F1107-8]
118. AOK 7/O.Qu., *Besprechunspunkte O.Qu. bei O.Qu.West.*, 12.5.44, p.1 [T312 R1571 F389]
119. 265. I.D., Zustandsbericht, *Meldung vom 1.6.1944* [T314 R747 F9]
120. 265. I.D., Zustandsbericht, *Meldung vom 1.6.1944* [T314 R747 F10]
121. Gen.Kdo.XXV. A.K. Ia, *Kriegstagebuch Nr.14 Gen.Kdo.XXV. A.K. Ia, 6. Juni 1944 - 30. Juni 1944* [T314 R746 F542] — Hereafter referred to as: Gen.Kdo.XXV. A.K. Ia, *KTB Nr.14*
122. AOK 7, Ia Nr.3268/44 g.K., 21.6.44, p.1 [T312 R1565 F1215]
123. AOK 7/O.Qu., *Kriegstagebuch der Oberquartiermeisterabteilung AOK 7 für die Zeit vom 1.6.44 - 30.6.44* [T312 R1571 F496]
124. 265. I.D., Zustandsbericht, *Meldung vom 1.7.1944* [T314 R747 F202]
125. Gen.Kdo.XXV. A.K., Ia Nr.2284/44 g., 2.7.44 [T314 R747 F63]
126. AOK 7, *Qu.1-Besprechung am 9.11.1943*, 9.11.43 [T312 R1562 F832]; Gen.Kdo.XXV. A.K., Abt. Ia Nr.1242/43 g., 18.11.1943, p.1-2 [T314 R745 F129-30]; Gen.Kdo.XXV. A.K., Abt. Ia Nr.1286/43 g.K., 27.11.43, p.2 and Anl.5 [T314 R1745 F151 & 158];
127. AOK 7, Ia Nr.5670/43 g.K., 7.11.43, p.1-2 [T312 R1559 F35-6]; BvTO b. AOK 7, Bv.T.O. Nr.13/44 g.K., *Tätigkeitsbericht für die Zeit vom 1.Jul bis 31. Dezember 1943.*, 2.1.44, p.13 [T312 R1563 F15]
128. Gen.Kdo.XXV. A.K. Abt.Ia Nr.1242/43 g.K., 18.11.1943, p.1 [T314 R745 F129]
129. Gen.Kdo.XXV. A.K. Abt.Ia Nr.1242/43 g.K., 18.11.1943, p.1-2 [T314 R745 F129-30]
130. Anl. zu 265. I.D., Ia Nr.261/43 g.K., undated (in turn used as Anl.5 z. Gen.Kdo.XXV. A.K., Ia Nr.1286/44 g.K., 29.11.43 [T314 R745 F158]
131. Gen.Kdo.XXV. A.K., Abt. Ia Nr.1286/43 g.K., 29.11.43, p.2 [T314 R745 F151]
132. AOK 7 Ia, notes titled *Vorbereitung zum Kampf*, 2.8.43, p.1 [T312 R1559 F267]; AOK 7, *Qu.1-Besprechung am 9.11.1943*, 9.11.43 [T312 R1562 F832]
133. AOK 7 Ia Nr.6200/43 g.K., 1.12.43, p.2 [T312 R1559 F285]
134. AOK 7 Ia, notes titled *Vorbereitung zum Kampf*, 2.8.43, p.1 [T312 R1559 F267]
135. AOK 7 Ia Nr.6200/43 g.K., 1.12.43, p.2 & 5 & 9 [T312 R1559 F285 & 88 & 92]
136. Gen.Kdo.XXV. A.K., Abt. Ia Nr.1388/43, 27.12.1943, p.4 [T314 R745 F277]
137. Anlage 2 zu AOK 7, Ia Nr.6200/43 g.K., 2-3.1.1944 [T314 R745 F1055]
138. AOK 7, Ia Nr.397/44 g.K., 23.1.44, p.1-3 & Anl.2 [T312 R1564 F503-5 & 507]
139. AOK 7, Ia Nr.830/44 g.K., 14.2.44, p.2 [T312 R1565 F112]
140. AOK 7, *Besprechung bei Ia über Beweglichmachung 265. und 266. I.D.*, 11.2.44, p.1 [T312 R1565 F94]
141. Gen.Kdo.XXV. A.K. Abt.Ia Nr.165/44 g.K., 14.2.44 [T314 R745 F1107]
142. Gen.Kdo.XXV. A.K., Abt.Ia Nr.159/44 g.K., 20.2.44 [T314 R745 F1131]
143. Gen.Kdo.XXV. A.K. Abt.Ia Nr.165/44 g.K., 14.2.44 [T314 R745 F1107]
144. 265. I.D., Zustandsbericht, *Meldung vom 1.März 1944* [T314 R745 F682]
145. AOK 7, Kriegsgliederung 7. Armee, Stand 18.5.44, *Kampfgr. 265. I.D. Neubearbeitung, Stand: 1.4.44* [T312 R1566 F229]
146. Anlage zu Gen.Kdo.XXV. A.K. Abt. Ia Nr.1930/44 g., *Gliederung der Kampfgruppe der 265. ID, Stand vom 1.6.1944*, 8.6.44 [T314 R747 F38]
147. AOK 7, Kriegsgliederung 7. Armee, Stand 18.5.44, *Kampfgr. 265. I.D. Neubearbeitung, Stand: 1.4.44* [T312 R1566 F229]
148. AOK 7, Kriegsgliederung 7. Armee, Stand 18.5.44, *Kampfgr. 265. I.D. Neubearbeitung, Stand: 1.4.44* [T312 R1566 F229]; Anlage zu Gen.Kdo.XXV. A.K. Abt. Ia Nr.1930/44 g., *Gliederung der Kampfgruppe der 265. ID, Stand vom 1.6.1944*, 8.6.44 [T314 R747 F38]
149. Anlage zu Gen.Kdo.XXV. A.K. Abt. Ia Nr.1930/44 g., *Gliederung der Kampfgruppe der 265. ID, Stand vom 1.6.1944*, 8.6.44 [T314 R747 F38]
150. Gen.Kdo.XXV. A.K., Abt. Ia Nr.680/44 g.K., 2.6.44, p.1 [T314 R746 F414]
151. OKH/Chef H Rüst u.BdE AHA Ia(I) Nr.2529/43 g.K., 20.5.1943, p.1, 2 & 4 [T78 R849 H36/156]
152. Anl.1 zu OKH/Chef H Rüst u.BdE AHA Ia(I) Nr.2529/43 g.K., 20.5.43 [T78 R849 H36/156]; OKW, Abwicklungsstab Sachgebiet 265, *Taktischer Bericht für 265. I.D.*, 29.10.44, p.1 [T78 R672 H41/61b]
153. OKH/GenStdH Op. Abt. III / Prüf-Nr.31059, *Schematische*

Kriegsgliederung, Stand: 21.6.43, part III [T78 R649 F320]

154. Armee-Ober-Kommando Ia Nr.3584/43 g.K., 24.7.1943, p.2 [T312 R1563 F1033]; AOK 7/O.Qu., *Kriegstagebuch Nr.41, 1. Juli 1943 - 31. Juli 1943* [T312 R1562 F78]

155. BvTO b. AOK 7, Bv.T.O. Nr.13/44 g.K., *Tätigkeitsbericht für die Zeit vom 1.Jul bis 31. Dezember 1943.*, 2.1.44, p.7 [T312 R1563 F9]; OKH/GenStdH Op. Abt. III / Prüf-Nr.36279, *Schematische Kriegsgliederung, Stand: 25.7.44*, Part 3 [T78 R649 F329]

156. OKH/Chef H Rüst u.BdE AHA/Ia(I) Nr.3305/43 g.K., 5.7.1943, p.1 [T78 R849 H36/157]; OKH/Chef H Rüst u.BdE AHA Ia(I) Nr.3435/43 g.K., 10.7.1943 [T78 R849 H36/157]

157. Situation map, *Lage* 7. Armee, *Stand: 8.7.-20.8.43* [T312 R1558 F600-1]; Situation map, *Lage* 7. Armee, *Stand: 23.8.43* [T312 R1559 F504]

158. Gen.Kdo.XXV. A.K. Ia, *KTB Nr.11* [T314 R745 F6]

159. OKW, Abwicklungsstab Sachgebiet 265, *Taktischer Bericht für 265. I.D.*, 29.10.44, p.1 [T78 R672 H41/61b]; Situation map, *Lage 7. Armee, Stand: 23.8.43* [T312 R1559 F504]

160. Situation map, *Lage* 7. Armee, *Stand: 23.8.43* [T312 R1559 F504]

161. AOK 7, Ia Nr.4589/43 g., 12.9.44 [T312 R1558 F799]

162. Situation map, *Lage* 7. Armee, *Stand: 23.8.43* [T312 R1559 F504]

163. *Ibid.*; AOK 7, Ia Nr.3899/43 g., 8.8.43 [T312 R1558 F492]; AOK 7, Ia Nr.4450/43 g., 6.9.43 [T312 R1558 F747]

164. Situation map, *Lage* 7. Armee, *Stand: 23.8.43* [T312 R1559 F504]

165. Der Oberbefehlshaber West, Ia Nr.550/43 g.K. Ch., 28.10.1943, p.31 [T78 R11 78/311 F6263258]

166. OKH Abwicklungsstab Sachgebiet 265, *Taktischer Bericht für 265. I.D.*, 29.10.44, p.1; AOK 7, Armee-Nachrichten Führer Nr.2314/43 g.K., Feste-Ausbau im Bereich des A.O.K.7, 11.8.1943 [T312 R1563 F45]

167. Gen.Kdo.XXV. A.K. Ia, *KTB Nr.11* [T314 R745 F8]; Gen.Kdo. XXV. A.K. Nr.2939/43 g., 11.10.43 [T314 R745 F326]; Gen.Kdo. XXV. A.K. Nr.2965/43 g., 13.10.43 [T314 R745 F332]; Gen.Kdo. XXV. A.K. Nr.3061/43 g., 21.10.43 [T314 R745 F355]

168. Gen.Kdo. XXV. A.K. Ia, *KTB Nr.11* [T314 R745 F11]

169. AOK 7, Ia Nr.5307/43 g., 18.10.43 [T312 R1558 F1104]; AOK 7, Ia Nr.5356/43 g., 21.10.43, p.2 [T312 R1558 F1123]

170. AOK 7, Ia Nr.5502/43 g., 29.10.43 [T312 R1558 F1148]

171. Gen.Kdo. XXV. A.K., Abt. Ia Nr.3295/43 g., 10.11.43 [T314 R745 F412]; Gen.Kdo.XXV. A.K., Abt. Ia Nr.3311/43 g., Taktische Tagesmeldung, 11.11.43 [T314 R745 F415]

172. Gen.Kdo.XXV. A.K., Ia Nr.3476/43 g., 25.11.43 [T314 R745 F457]; Gen.Kdo.XXV. A.K., Ia Nr.3548/43 g., 2.12.43, p.1 [T314 R745 F479]; Gen.Kdo.XXV. A.K., Ia Nr.3626/43 g., 8.12.43 [T314 R745 F497]

173. Gen.Kdo.XXV. A.K. Ia, *KTB Nr.11* [T314 R745 F37]

174. BvTO b. AOK 7, *Tätigkeitsbericht für die Zeit vom 1.Januar bis 31. März 1944.* p.2 [T312 R1571 F878]

175. 265. I.D., Zustandsbericht, *Meldung vom 1.Februar 1944* [T314 R745 F665]

176. Gen.Kdo.XXV. A.K. Nr.692/44 g., 8.3.44 [T314 R745 F930]

177. *Kriegstagebuch Nr.12 Gen.Kdo.XXV. A.K. Führungsabteilung (Ia) 1.1.1944 - 31.3.1944* [T314 R745 F597]; Gen.Kdo.XXV. A.K., Abt. Ia Nr.163/44, 16.1.44, p.2 [T314 R745 F745]

178. Gen.Kdo.XXV. A.K. Nr.125/44 g., 13.1.44, p.2 [T314 R745 F735]; Gen.Kdo.XXV. A.K. Nr.138/44 g., 14.1.44 [T314 R745 F738]; Gen.Kdo.XXV. A.K. Nr.149/44 g., 15.1.44 [T314 R745 F741]

179. Gen.Kdo.XXV. A.K., Ia Nr.831/44 g., 18.3.44 [T314 R745 F961]; AOK 7, Kriegsgliederung 7. Armee, Stand 1.5.44, 265. I.D., *Stand 1.5.1944* [T312 R1566 F228]

180. Gen.Kdo.XXV. A.K., Ia Nr.842/44 g., 19.3.44 [T314 R745 F964]

181. AOK 7, Kriegsgliederung 7. Armee, Stand 1.5.44, 265. I.D., *Stand 1.5.1944* [T312 R1566 F228]; AOK 7, Kriegsgliederung 7. Armee, Stand 10.4.44, *275. I.D., Stand 1.3.1944* [T312 R1566 F179]

182. Gen.Kdo. XXV. A.K. Ia, *Kriegstagebuch Nr.13 Gen.Kdo. XXV. A.K. Führungsabteilung (Ia) 1.4.44 - 5.6.44* [T314 R746 F35] — Hereafter refered to as: Gen.Kdo.XXV. A.K. Ia, *Kriegstagebuch Nr.13*; Gen.Kdo.XXV. A.K., Ia Nr.1038/44 g., 4.4.44 [T314 R746 F86]

183. Gen.Kdo.XXV. A.K., Ia Nr.1068/44 g., 6.4.44 [T314 R746 F91]; AOK 7, Ia Nr.187/44 g., 8.4.44 [T312 R1565 F451]

184. Gen.Kdo.XXV. A.K., Ia Nr.1090/44 g., 8.4.44 [T314 R746 F99]

185. Gen.Kdo.XXV. A.K., Ia Nr.1106/44 g., 9.4.44 [T314 R746 F102]

186. AOK 7, Ia Nr.439/44 g., 24.4.44 [T312 R1565 F534]; AOK 7, Ia Nr.926/44 g., 24.5.44 [T312 R1565 F759]

187. AOK 7 Ia, Anlage zum K.T.B. Führungsabt. AOK 7 Ia, Lage-Karten A.O.K.7 vom 6.1.-5.6.44, *Stand: 5.6.44* [T312 R1570 F9-10, original in BaMa RH 20-7/138K] — Hereafter referred to as: AOK 7, Situation map 5.6.44

188. AOK 7, Ia Nr.187/44 g., 18.5.44 [T312 R1565 F723]

189. Gen.Kdo.XXV. A.K., Abt. Ia Nr.652/44 g., 4.3.44 [T314 R745 F913]

190. Gen.Kdo.XXV. A.K., Ia Nr.1117/44 g., 10.4.44 [T314 R746 F105]; Gen.Kdo.XXV. A.K., Abt. Ia Nr.630/44 g., 2.3.44 [T314 R745 F904]; Gen.Kdo.XXV. A.K., Abt. Ia Nr.872/44 g., 22.3.44 [T314 R745 F974]

191. AOK 7 Ia, Anlage zum K.T.B. Führungsabt. AOK 7 Ia, Lage-Karten A.O.K.7 vom 6.1.-5.6.44, *Stand: 22.5.44* [T312 R1570 F9-10, original in BaMa RH 20-7/138K] — Hereafter referred to as: AOK 7, Situation map 22.5.44 [T312 R1570 F7-8]; AOK 7, Kriegsgliederung 7. Armee, Stand 18.5.44, *Kampfgr. 265. I.D. (Neuaufstellung), Stand 1.4.1944* [T312 R1566 F229]

192. Gen.Kdo XXV A.K., Ia Nr.1795/44 g., 31.5.44 [T314 R746 F275]

193. AOK 7, Situation map 22.5.44 [T312 R1570 F7-8]; AOK 7, Situation map, 5.6.44; Gen.Kdo.XXV. A.K., Abt. Ia Nr.530/44 g., 24.2.44 [T314 R745 F876]; Gen.Kdo.XXV. A.K., Abt. Ia Nr.652/44 g., 4.3.44 [T314 R745 F913]

194. Gen.Kdo. XXV. A.K., Ia Nr.1503/44 g., 10.5.44 [T314 R746 F200]; Gen.Kdo.XXV. A.K., Ia Nr.1635/44 g., 21.5.44 [T314 R746 F235] The last reported location of the 3rd Company is from 14 November 1943; Gen.Kdo. XXV. A.K. Nr.3343/43 g., 14.11.43 [T314 R745 F424]

195. AOK 7, Situation map 22.5.44 [T312 R1570 F7-8]; AOK 7, Situation map, 5.6.44; Gen.Kdo.XXV. A.K., Abt. Ia Nr.3146/43 g., 29.10.1943 [T314 R745 F378]

196. AOK 7, Ia Nr.1093/44 g., 2.6.44 [T312 R1565 F827]

197. PWIS(H)/LDC/151, 21 Jul 44, p.1-3 [UKNA, WO 208/3646]

198. AOK 7, Situation map, 5.6.44

199. AOK 7, Ia Nr.872/44 g., 21.5.44 [T312 R1565 F740]

200. PWIS(H)/KP/135, 11 Jul 44, p.1 [UKNA, WO 208/3624]

201. AOK 7, Situation map 22.5.44 [T312 R1570 F7-8]; AOK 7, Situation map, 5.6.44; Gen.Kdo.XXV. A.K., Abt. Ia Nr.125/44 g., 13.1.44, p.1 [T314 R745 F734]; AOK 7, Ia Nr.267/44 g., 13.1.44 [T312 R1564 F446]

202. Gen.Kdo. XXV. A.K., Abt. Ia Nr.34763/43 g., 25.11.43 [T314 R745 F457]

203. Gen.Kdo. XXV. A.K., Abt. Ia Nr.1023/44 g., 11.1.44 [T314 R745 F729]

204. AOK 7, Ia Nr.926/44 g., 24.5.44 [T312 R1565 F759]

205. AOK 7, Situation map 22.5.44 [T312 R1570 F7-8]; AOK 7, Situation map, 5.6.44; Gen.Kdo.XXV. A.K. Nr.3438/43 g., 22.11.43 [T314 R745 F448]; Der Kommandierende General XXV. A.K., Ia Nr.781/44 g., 15.3.44. [T314 R745 F1203]; Gen.Kdo. *XXV. A.K.* Nr.3496/43 g., 28.11.43 [T314 R745 F466]

206. AOK 7, Ia Nr.3620/43 g., 25.6.43 [T312 R1558 F376]

207. AOK 7, Situation map, 5.6.44

208. FID-DZ No.260, 19 July 1944 [NARA, RG 498, Box 1326]

209. AOK 7, Situation map, 5.6.44; AOK 7, Situation map 22.5.44 [T312 R1570 F7-8]

210. AOK 7, Ia Nr.809/44 g., 18.5.44 [T312 R1565 F723]; C.S.D.I.C. (UK) S.I.R. 440, 28 Jun 44, p.3 [NARA, RG 165, Box 659, Folder 2]

211. AOK 7, Ia Nr.641/44 g., 8.5.44, p.2 [T312 R1565 F659]; FID-DZ No.264, 22 July 1944 [NARA, RG 498, Box 1326]

212. AOK 7, Ia Nr.439/44 g., 24.4.44 [T312 R1565 F534]; AOK 7, Ia Nr.926/44 g., 24.5.44 [T312 R1565 F759]

213. Gen.Kdo.XXV. A.K., Ia Nr.1289/44 g., 23.4.44, p.1 [T314 R746 F147]

214. Anlage 2 zu Gen.Kdo. *XXV. A.K.* Abt.Ia Nr.282/44 g.K., 8.3.44. [T314 R745 F1202]

215. AOK 7, Ia Nr.926/44 g., 24.5.44 [T312 R1565 F759]

216. Anlage 2 zu Gen.Kdo. *XXV. A.K.* Abt.Ia Nr.282/44 g.K., 8.3.44. [T314 R745 F1202]; *Sicherheitsbesatzung Festung „Lorient"*, 24.6.44 [T314 R746 F1015]

217. *Sicherheitsbesatzung Festung „Lorient"*, 24.6.44 [T314 R746 F1015]

218. Gen.Kdo.XXV. A.K., Ia Nr.842/44 g., 19.3.44 [T314 R745 F964]

219. AOK 7, Ia Nr.187/44 g., 8.4.44 [T312 R1565 F451]

220. Gen.Kdo.XXV. A.K., Ia Nr.831/44 g., 18.3.44 [T314 R745 F961]

221. AOK 7, Ia Nr.971/44 g., 26.5.44 [T312 R1565 F773]; Gen.Kdo. XXV. A.K., Abt. Ia Nr.454/44 g., 17.2.44 [T314 R745 F851]; AOK 7, Ia Nr.2538/44 g., 13.5.1944, p.2 [T312 R1565 F694]

222. Gen.Kdo.XXV. A.K., Abt. Ia Nr.454/44 g., 17.2.44 [T314 R745 F851]

223. AOK 7, Situation map, 5.6.44; Der Kommandierende General *XXV. A.K.*, Ia Nr.781/44 g., 15.3.44. [T314 R745 F1203]
224. Gen.Kdo.XXV. A. K. Abt.Ia Nr.1180/43 g.K., 13.11.1943, p.2 [T314 R745 F116]
225. AOK 7, Situation map, 5.6.44
226. Gen.Kdo.XXV. A. K. Nr.692/44 g., 8.3.44 [T314 R745 F930]
227. FID-DZ No.181, 8 July 1944 [NARA, RG 498, Box 1326]
228. Der Kommandierender General der Sicherungstruppen und Befehlshaber im Heeresgebiet Mitte, Ia Br.B.Nr.508/42 g.K., 31.8.42, p.1 [T501 R26 F1159]
229. Ob.West (Obkdo. H.Gr.D), Ic Nr.5238/43 g., 26.10.43 [T311 R25 F7030544-5]
230. Der Kommandierende General *XXV. A.K.*, Abt. Ia Nr.1356/44 g., 28.4.44, p.1 [T314 R746 F373]
231. Gen.Kdo. *XXV. A.K.*, Abt. Ia Nr.1168/44 g., 14.4.44 [T314 R746 F347]
232. Gen.Kdo.XXV. A. K., Abt. Ia Nr.1202/44 g., 16.4.44, p.1 [T314 R746 F350]
233. Gen.Kdo.XXV. A. K. Ia, *Kriegstagebuch Nr.13 Gen.Kdo.XXV. A.K. Führungsabteilung (Ia) 1.4.44 - 5.6.44* [T314 R746 F44]; Gen. Kdo.XXV. A. K., Abt. Ia Nr.1270/44 g., 21.4.44 [T314 R746 F140]
234. Gen.Kdo.XXV. A. K., Ia Nr.1234/44 g., 18.4.44 [T314 R746 F131]
235. Gen.Kdo.XXV. A. K., Abt. Ia Nr.1331/44 g., 26.4.44 [T314 R746 F368]
236. Gen.Kdo.XXV. A. K., Ia Nr.1541/44 g., 13.5.44, p.1 [T314 R746 F209]; Gen.Kdo.XXV. A. K., Abt. Ia Nr.1619/44 g., 20.5.44, p.2 [T314 R746 F232]
237. *Meldung vom 1.5.1944, Verband 265. I.D.* [T314 R746 F458]
238. Gen.Kdo.XXV. A. K., Ia Nr.1598/44 g., 18.5.44 [T314 R746 F225]
239. AOK 7, Ia Nr.885/44 g., 22.5.44 [T312 R1565 F744]; AOK 7, Ia Nr.906/44 g., 23.5.44 [T312 R1565 F753]
240. Gen.Kdo.XXV. A. K. Ia, *Kriegstagebuch Nr.13* [T314 R746 F56]
241. Gen.Kdo.XXV. A. K., Abt. Ia Nr.591/44 g.K., 10.5.44, p.1 [T314 R746 F392]
242. Gen.Kdo.XXV. A. K., Ia Nr.564/44 g., 9.5.44, p.1 [T314 R746 F384]; Gen.Kdo.XXV. A. K., Abt. Ia Nr.624/44 g.K., 20.5.44 [T314 R746 F403]
243. Gen.Kdo.XXV. A. K., Abt. Ia Nr.591/44 g., 10.5.44, p.1-2 [T314 R746 F392-3]
244. Gen.Kdo.XXV. A. K., Ia Nr.1683/44 g., 25.5.44 [T314 R746 F250]
245. Gen.Kdo.XXV. A. K., Abt. Ia Nr.1829/44 g., 2.6.44 [T314 R746 F283]; Gen.Kdo.XXV. A. K., Ia Nr.656/44 g., 27.5.44 [T314 R746 F410]
246. Anlage 2 zu AOK 7, Ia Nr.3000/44 g.K., 4.4.44 [T312 R1565 F426]
247. AOK 7, Ia Nr.2161/44 g., 13.4.44, p.2 [T312 R1563 F958]
248. Gen.Kdo.XXV. A. K., Abt.Ia Nr.441/44 g., 15.4.44 [T314 R746 F348]
249. Anlage zu AOK 7, Ia Nr.2710/44 g.K., p.2, 28.5.44 [T312 R1565 F795]
250. AOK 7, Ia Nr.2750/44 g.K., p.2, 31.5.44 [T312 R1565 F807]
251. AOK 7, Kriegsgliederung 7. Armee, Stand 18.5.44, *Kampfgr. 265. I.D. (Neuaufstellung), Stand 1.4.1944* [T312 R1566 F229]
252. Gen.Kdo.XXV. A. K., Ia Nr.1795/44 g., 31.5.44 [T314 R746 F275]
253. PWIS(H)/KP/135, 11 Jul 44, p.1 [UKNA, WO 208/3624]
254. BvTO b. AOK 7, *Tätigkeitsbericht für die Zeit vom 1. Januar bis 31. März 1944*, p.5 [T312 R1571 F881]; AOK 7 BvTO, Anl.15 zum Tätigkeitsbericht BvTO AOK 7, *Zusammenstellung der in der Zeit vom 1.4. - 30.6.44 im Armeebereich durchgeführten Bewegungen.*, p.1 [T312 R1571 F982]
255. Anlage zu *343. I.D.*, Ia Nr.1641/44 g.K., *343.Infanterie-Division, Stand vom 1.6.44*, 3.6.44 [T314 R747 F7]; **Kogard, R. (1947)**, MS # B-427 (Engl.), *Brest - 343rd Infantry Division (May - 18 Sep 44)*, p.14
256. C.S.D.I.C. (UK) G.R.G.G. 176, App., p.1 [UKNA, WO 208/4363]
257. Gen.Kdo.XXV. A. K. Ia, *KTB Nr.14* [T314 R746 F511-2]
258. AOK 7 Ia, *AOK 7 Kriegstagebuch Ia - 6 Jun 1944 - 25 Jul 1944*, p.7 [T312 R1569 F225] — Hereafter referred to as: AOK 7 Ia, *KTB 6.6.-25.7.44*
259. AOK 7, Ia Nr.2847/44 g.K., 6.6.44 [T312 R1565 F870]
260. PWIS(H)/KP/135, 11 Jul 44, p.1-2 [UKNA, WO 208/3624]
261. Gen.Kdo.XXV. A. K. Ia, *KTB Nr.14* [T314 R746 F513]
262. Alba (Gen.Kdo.XXV. A.K.) Ia, *Mittagsmeldung*, 7.6.44 [T314 R746 F659]
263. AOK 7 BvTO, *Tätigkeitsbericht für den Monat Juni 1944*, p.38 [T312 R1571 F908]; AOK 7 BvTO, Anl.15 zum Tätigkeitsbericht BvTO AOK 7, *Zusammenstellung der in der Zeit vom 1.4. - 30.6.44 im Armeebereich durchgeführten Bewegungen.*, p.1 [T312 R1571 F982]
264. AOK 7 BvTO, *Tatigkeitsbericht für den Monat Juni 1944*, p.38-39 [T312 R1571 F908-9]; BvTO b. AOK 7, Br.B.Nr.1304/44 g., 11.6.44 [T312 R1571 F991]; Message from *Hptm.* Treitschke at 08:05 on 8.6.44 [T314 R746 F670]
265. AOK 7, Ia Nr.1190/44 g.,7.6.44, p.1-2 [T312 R1565 F881-2]; Gen.Kdo.XXV. A. K., Ia Nr.1924/44 g., 8.6.44 [T314 R746 F678]
266. AOK 7, Ia Nr.1190/44 g.,7.6.44, p.1-2 [T312 R1565 F881-2]
267. Gen.Kdo.XXV. A. K. Ia, *KTB Nr.14* [T314 R746 F515]
268. AOK 7, Ia Nr.1190/44 g.,7.6.44, p.1 [T312 R1565 F881]
269. *Ibid.*, p.1-2 [T312 R1565 F881-2]
270. *Ibid.*, p.1 [T312 R1565 F881]; AOK 7, Kriegsgliederung 7. Armee, Stand 18.5.44, *353.Inf.-Div., Stand: 1.5.44* [T312 R1566 F232]
271. Anruf: AOK 7 Ia / Chef des Stabes Gen.Kdo.XXV. A.K., 6.6.44, 9. Uhr [T314 R746 F599]
272. AOK 7 Ia, *AOK 7 Kriegstagebuch Ia, 6 June 1944 - 16 Aug 1944*, p.3 [T312 R1569 F6] — Hereafter referred to as: AOK 7 Ia, *KTB 6.6.-16.8.44*
273. BvTO b. AOK 7, *Tätigkeitsbericht für den Monat Juni 1944*, p.39-40 [T312 R1571 F913-4]
274. AOK 7, Ia Nr.1532/44 g., 19.6.44, p.1 [T312 R1565 F1143]; AOK 7 Ia, *KTB 6.6.-25.7.44*, p.55 [T312 R1569 F274]; the presence of German armour is reported in HQ 325th Glider Infantry, *S-2 Journal - Operation Neptune, Cotentin Peninsula, France*, p.15-16 [NARA, via Egbert van de Schootbrugge]
275. AOK 7, *Übersicht über die aus der Bretagne nach der Normandie zugeführten oder noch zuzuführenden Kräfte*, 22.6.44, p.1 [T312 R1565 F1248]; AOK 7, Kriegsgliederungen zum KTB der Führungsabteilung AOK 7 ab 6.6.44 bis 30.6.44, *Stand: 23.6. 14 Uhr*, 23.6.44 [T312 R1566 F16] – Collection hereafter referred to as: Kriegsgliederungen z. KTB 6.-29.6.44
276. Anl.16 zum Tätigkeitsbericht BvTO b. AOK 7, 10.6.44 [T312 R1571 F989]; Gen.Kdo.XXV. A. K. Ia, *KTB Nr.14* [T314 R746 F523]
277. Anruf Hptm. Diepolder, 9.6.44, 01.00 Uhr [T314 R746 F701]; Gen.Kdo.XXV. A. K. Ia, *KTB Nr.14* [T314 R746 F519]; BvTO b. AOK 7, *Tätigkeitsbericht für den Monat Juni 1944*, p.38 [T312 R1571 F912]
278. Anl.16 zum Tätigkeitsbericht BvTO b. AOK 7, 10.6.44 [T312 R1571 F989]
279. CX/MSS/R.212 (C), 12.6.44, p.37-38 [UKNA, HW 5/498]
280. Gen.Kdo.XXV. A. K., Abt. Ia Nr.1961/44 g., 10.6.44, p.1 [T314 R746 F739]
281. Anruf Lt. v. Brand (to *XXV. A.K.*), 11.6.44, 07:35 [T314 R746 F755]
282. BvTO b. AOK 7, *Tätigkeitsbericht für den Monat Juni 1944*, p.39-43 [T312 R1571 F913-917]
283. Gen.Kdo.XXV. A. K., Ia Nr.1924/44 g., 8.6.44 [T314 R746 F678]
284. PWIS(H)/LF/177, 26 Jun 44, p.1 [UKNA, WO 208/3630]
285. Gen.Kdo.XXV. A. K., Ia Nr.1924/44 g., 8.6.44 [T314 R746 F678]
286. Ferngespräch Chef (*XXV. A.K.*) mit Maj. Johannes (265. I.D.), 8.6.44, 10:50 [T314 R746 F672]; Ferngespräch: Rittm. Engelken (Ib 265. I.D.) - Oblt. Brand (*XXV. A.K.*), 8.6.44, 07:25 [T314 R746 F669]
287. Fernspruch [to *XXV. A.K.*): 265. I.D. Lt.v.Brandt, 8.6.44, 23:00 [T314 R746 F677]
288. Report from the 265. I.D. to *XXV. A.K.* at 21:40 on 8.6.44 [T314 R746 F686]
289. Gen.Kdo.XXV. A. K., Abt. Ia Nr.1925/44 g., 8.6.44, p.1 [T314 R746 F692]
290. Gen.Kdo.LXXXIV. A. K., Ia Nr.1951/44 g., 9.6.44 [T314 R746 F719]
291. Gen.Kdo.LXXXIV. A. K., Ia Nr.1932/44 g., 9.6.44 [T314 R746 F716]
292. Gen.Kdo.XXV. A. K. Ia, *KTB Nr.14* [T314 R746 F521]
293. *Ibid.*
294. **Kreibig (1945)**, *Ergänzung zu taktischem Bericht für 265. I.D. des Hauptmann Kastner vom 29.10.1944*, p.1 [T78 R672 H41/61b]
295. Gen.Kdo.XXV. A. K., Ia Nr.1962/44 g., 10.6.44 [T314 R746 F726]; *XXV. A.K.* records, Meldung (unknown origin), 10.6.44 [T314 R746 F728]
296. FID-DZ No.264, 22 July 1944 [NARA, RG 498, Box 1326]
297. *XXV. A.K.* records, Meldung (unknown origin), [T314 R746 F728]
298. *Ibid.*; **Kreibig (1945)**, p.1
299. Report on the losses of *KG 265* in the records of the *XXV.*

AK., titled *Ausfälle am 10. Juni 1944* [T314 R746 F754]

300. Report on the losses of KG 265 in the records of the XXV. AK., titled *Ausfälle am 10. Juni 1944* [T314 R746 F754]; FID-DZ No.195, 9 July 1944, p.2-3 [NARA, RG 498, Box 1326] The witnesses speak of the headquarters of the III./894 losing three lorries, but official records refer to the reinforced battalion as have lost two in total.

301. XXV. A.K. records, Meldung (unknown origin), 10.6.44 [T314 R746 F728]

302. Gen.Kdo.XXV. A.K. Ia, *KTB Nr.14* [T314 R746 F526-527]

303. Gen.Kdo. Ia Nr.1962/44, 10.6.44 [T314 R746 F726]

304. According to Jäger, the attack near Juvigny took place at 10:00. The troops had been delayed for 45 minutes by a large fir-tree that had been felled across the road and needed to be blown out of the way. 20 men were killed and 40 wounded in the air attack. 12 lorries were lost as well as 10-tonnes of ammunition. [UKNA, WO 208/4363 C.S.D.I.C. (UK) G.R.G.G. 176, p. 3]

305. Gen.Kdo.XXV. A.K. Ia, *KTB Nr.14* [T314 R746 F526-527]

306. Gen.Kdo.XXV. A.K., Ia Nr.1962/44 g., 10.6.44 [T314 R746 F726]

307. Gen.Kdo.XXV. A.K. Ia, *KTB Nr.14*, entry 11.6.44 [T314 R746 F000527]

308. AOK 7, Ia Nr.2976/44 g.K., 11.6.44, p.2 [T312 R1565 F958]

309. AOK 7 Ia, *KTB 6.6.-25.7.44*, p.30 [T312 R1569 F247]

310. Nordyke, P. (2005), *All American All the Way*, St.Paul MN: Zenith Press, MN, p.369-372

311. AOK 7 Ia, *KTB 6.6.-25.7.44*, p.35 [T312 R1569 F254]; AOK 7 Ia, KTB 1.1.-30.6.1944 [T312 R1564 F311]

312. AOK 7 Ia, Nr.3052/33 g.K., 13.6.44 [T312 R1565 F1002]

313. AOK 7 Ia, *KTB 6.6.-25.7.44*, p.36-8 [T312 R1569 F255-7]

314. Kreibig (1945), p.2; See chapter "91.Luftlande-Infanterie-Division".

315. C.S.D.I.C. (UK) G.R.G.G. 176, App., p.1 [UKNA, WO 208/4363]

316. Kampfgruppe Eitner, *Kampfgruppenbefehl für die Verteidigung im Abschnitt la Rivière - les Moitiers*, 15.6.44 [T78 R672 H41/61b]

317. Captured order of **Kampfgruppe Eitner**, 18.6.44, copied and translated in HQ 82nd AB Div., G-2, *Interrogation Report No.13*, 19 June 44 [NARA, via Egbert van de Schootbrugge]

318. 82nd Airborne Div., G-2, *Interrogation Report No.13*, p.2, 19 June 44 [NARA, via Egbert van de Schootbrugge]

319. OKH/AHA/Abwicklungsstab, Anl. z. Sachgeb. 91 Nr.6.44 g., *Kriegsgliederung Kampfgruppe 91.I.D., Stand: 18.6.44* [T78 R672 H41/61b]

320. LXXXIV. A.K., 19.6.44 at 14:00 [UKNA, HW 5/506, CX/MSS/T220/72, KV 8835]

321. AOK 7, Ia Nr.3363/44 g.K., 24.6.44 [T312 R1565 F1295]; also see chapter '353.Infanterie-Division'

322. Kampfgruppe Eitner, *Kampfgruppenbefehl für die Verteidigung im Abschnitt la Rivière - les Moitiers*, 15.6.44. [T78 R672H41/61b]; **Nordyke, P. (2005)**, p.385-388

323. Nordyke, P. (2005), p.387-389; AOK 7, Ia Nr.3241/44 g.K. II Ang., 20.6.44, p.1 [T312 R1565 F1168]; AOK 7 Ia, *KTB 6.6.-25.7.44*, p.55 [T312 R1569 F274]

324. 82d Airborne Division, *Interrogation Report No.13*, 19 Jun 44, p.1 && 82d Airborne Division, *Interrogation Report No.14*, 20 Jun 44, p.1 [both NARA, via Egbert van de Schootbrugge]

325. AOK 7 Ia, *Kriegstagebuch der Führungsabteilung AOK 7 für die Zeit vom 1.Jan. - 30.Juni 1944* [T312 R1564 F334] — Hereafter referred to as: AOK 7 Ia, KTB 1.1.-30.6.1944

326. OKH/AHA/Abwicklungsstab, Anl. z. Sachgeb. 91 Nr.6.44 g., *Kriegsgliederung Kampfgruppe 91.I.D., Stand: 18.6.44* [T78 R672 H41/61b]; AOK 7, Kriegsgliederungen z. KTB 6.-29.6.44, orders of battle for the period 23.-29.6.44 [T312 R1566 F16-24]

327. OKH/AHA/Abwicklungsstab, Anl. z. Sachgeb. 91 Nr.6.44 g., (Kriegsgliederung) 91.I.D. (Div.25.Welle) mit Unterstellungen, Stand vom 20.6.44 [T78 R672 H41/61b]

328. AOK 7, Ia Nr.3268/44, 21.6.44, p.1 [T312 R1565 F1215]

329. Gen.Kdo.XXV. A.K., Abt. Ia Nr.2145/44 g., 23.6.44 [T314 R746 F1010]

330. 265. I.D., Ia Nr.1185/44 g., 22.6.44 [T314 R746 F971-2]

331. OKW, Abwicklungsstab Sachgebiet 265, *Taktischer Bericht für 265. I.D.*, 29.10.44, p.3; OKH/AHA/Abwicklungsstab, Anl. z. Sachgeb. 91 Nr.6.44 g., *Kriegsgliederung Kampfgruppe König, Stand: 18.6.44 - 28.6.44* [T78 R672 H41/61b]; the II./894 was reportedly used to relieve the II./895, but this was more likely carried out by the III./894. The latter battalion has also been linked to the relief of the II./1049 but, in turn, this was probably handled by the II./894. An explanation for these mix-ups has not been found. [**Post, G. (1944)**, p.1 in T78 R672 H41/61b; **Kreibig (1945)**, p.2 in T78 R672 H41/61b]

332. Nauroth, H.S. & B. Steinberg (2017), *Die Geschichte der 91.Luftlande-Division - Rekonstruktion eines Großverbändes der Deutschen Wehrmacht*, Hamburg: tredition GmbH, p.118-119

333. AOK 7, Kriegsgliederungen z. KTB 6.-29.6.44, Stand: 23.6.44, 14 Uhr [T312 R1566 F16]

334. see the chapter '77.Infanterie-Division'

335. OKH/AHA/Abwicklungsstab, Anl. z. Sachgeb. 91 Nr.6.44 g., *Kriegsgliederung Kampfgruppe König, Stand: 18.6.44 - 28.6.44* [T78 R672 H41/61b]

336. AOK 7, Kriegsgliederungen z. KTB 6.-29.6.44, Stand 29.6. 17 Uhr [T312 R1566 F24]

337. AOK 7 Ia, Anlage zum KTB Führungsabteilung, Lagekarten A.O.K.7 vom 6.6.44-30.6.44, *Lage Normandie, Stand: 22.6.44, 2200 Uhr* [T312 R1570 F30]

338. OKW, Abwicklungsstab Sachgebiet 265, *Taktischer Bericht für 265. I.D.*, 29.10.44, p.2 [T78 R672 H41/61b]; Flivo LXXXIV. A.K., 16.6.44 [CX/MSS/T218/103, KV 8568]; AOK 7 Ia, Anlage zum KTB Führungsabteilung, Lagekarten A.O.K.7 vom 6.6.44-30.6.44, situation maps from 20.6.44, 22:00 hours to 30.6.44 22:00 hours [T312 R1570 F28-39]

339. AOK 7, Kriegsgliederungen z. KTB 6.-29.6.44, Stand: 23.6.44, 14 Uhr [T312 R1566 F16]

340. OKH/AHA/Abwicklungsstab, Anl. z. Sachgeb. 91 Nr.6.44 g., *Kriegsgliederung Kampfgruppe König, Stand: 18.6.44 - 28.6.44* [T78 R672 H41/61b]; OKW, Abwicklungsstab Sachgebiet 265, *Taktischer Bericht für 265. I.D.*, 29.10.44, p.2 [T78 R672 H41/61b]

341. Flivo LXXXIV. A.K., 16.6.44 [CX/MSS/T218/103, KV 8568]; 17.SS-Pz.Gren.Division "Götz von Berlichingen" Ia/Op. Tgb. Nr.418/44 g.K., 22.6.44 [Published in **Wind, M. & H. Günther (2004)**, *Kriegstagebuch 17. SS-Panzer-Grenadier-Division "Götz von Berlichingen" - Auswahl von Dokumenten - 30. Oktober 1943 bis 6. Mai 1945*, St.Ingbert: Dengmerter Heimatverlag]; AOK 7, Kriegsgliederungen z. KTB 6.-29.6.44, Stand: 23.6.44, 14 Uhr [T312 R1566 F16]

342. OKH/AHA/Abwicklungsstab, Anl. z. Sachgeb. 91 Nr.6.44 g., *Kriegsgliederung Kampfgruppe König, Stand: 18.6.44 - 28.6.44* [T78 R672 H41/61b]

343. AOK 7, Kriegsgliederungen z. KTB 6.-29.6.44, Stand 29.6. 17 Uhr [T312 R1566 F24]

344. *Ibid.*

345. HQ 82nd Airborne Div., G-2, *G-2 Periodic report No.71*, 20 June 44 && HQ 82nd Airborne Div., G-2, *Interrogation Report No.14*, 20 June 44 [both NARA, via Egbert van de Schootbrugge] Instead of the III./894, it was the II./894 that was identified, but this makes no sense considering the date. On 20 June the 82AB had however identified the 5. or 6./894 through the capture of a member of the battalion. It is possible this man had been a recent transfer or actually a member of the 5./895, which had been attached to the II./894. Either way, the division mistakenly interpreted the information as the arrival of elements of the II./894 on the southern wing of the front.

346. AOK 7 Ia, Anlage zum KTB Führungsabteilung, Lagekarten A.O.K.7 vom 6.6.44-30.6.44, *Lage Normandie, Stand: 29.6.44, 22.00 Uhr* [T312 R1570 F38]

347. Nordyke, P. (2005), p.388

348. This will be addressed in more detail in the chapter "Ost-Bataillon Huber" in a future volume

349. HQ 90th Infantry Division, G-2, *IPW Report No.17*, 30 June 44 [NARA]

350. HQ 325th Glider Infantry, *S-2 Journal - Operation Neptune, Cotentin Peninsula France*, p.29 [NARA, via Egbert van de Schootbrugge]

351. HQ 508th Parachute Inf., *IPW Report - Consolidated*, 4 July 1944 [NARA, via Egbert van de Schootbrugge]

352. AOK 7 Ia, *KTB 6.6.-25.7.44*, p.81 [T312 R1569 F301]

353. *Ibid.*, p.81 & 83 [T312 R1569 F301 & 303]

354. Gen.Kdo.XXV. A.K., Ia Nr.794/44 g.K., 28.6.44 [T314 R746 F1055-6]

355. Gen.Kdo.XXV. A.K., Abt. Ia, Tagesmeldung, 11 30.6.44 [T314 R746 F1091]

356. Nauroth, H.S. & B. Steinberg (2017), p.118-119

357. Kreibig (1945), p.2. The document speaks of the 77. I.D., but the elements of KG 265 were part of Gruppe König at this time.

358. OKW, Abwicklungsstab Sachgebiet 265, *Taktischer Bericht für 265. I.D.*, 29.10.44, p.3 [T78 R672 H41/61b]; This will be addressed in more detail in the chapter "Ost-Regimentsgruppe Bunjatschenko" in a future volume

359. Annex #1 to HQ 82nd Airborne Division, G-2 Report #84, *IPW Report No.18*, 3 July 1944, p.3 [NARA, via Egbert van de Schootbrugge]
360. 21 AGp/Int/1070, App. Y to 21 Army Group Intelligence Summary No. 143, Part II, 8 Jul. 44 [UKNA, WO 171/131]
361. Blumenson, M. (1961, 1993 reprint), *Breakout and Pursuit*, Center of Military History, United States Army, Washington D.C., p.53-55 & Map 3
362. AOK 7 Ia, Anlage zum KTB Führungsabteilung, Lagekarten A.O.K.7 vom 6.6.44-30.6.44, *Lage Normandie, Stand: 29.6.44, 22.00 Uhr* [T312 R1570 F38]
363. AOK 7 Ia, *KTB 6.6.-25.7.44*, p.120-121 [T312 R1569 F340-1]. The document reported it as the area of Vindefontaine, which was a bit too far to the east.
364. HQ 82nd Airborne Div., G-2, *Interrogation Report No. 19*, 4 Jul. 44, p.2 [NARA, via Egbert van de Schootbrugge]
365. AOK 7 Ia, *KTB 6.6.-16.8.44*, p.112-113 [T312 R1569 F115-6]; see the chapter "77.Infanterie-.Division"; see chapter "91. Luftlande-Infanterie-Division".
366. OKW, Abwicklungsstab Sachgebiet 265, *Taktischer Bericht für 265. I.D.*, 29.10.44, p.3 [T78 R672 H41/61b]
367. AOK 7 Ia, *KTB 6.6.-25.7.44*, p.118 [T312 R1569 F333]
368. HQ 82nd Airborne Div., G-2, (Annex #1 to G-2 Report #84) *IPW Report No. 18*, 3 Jul. 44, p.1 [NARA, via Egbert van de Schootbrugge]
369. HQ 82nd Airborne Div., G-2, *Interrogation Report No. 19*, 4 Jul. 44, p.2 [NARA, via Egbert van de Schootbrugge]
370. HQ 82nd Airborne Div., G-2, (Annex #1 to G-2 Report #86) *Interrogation Report No. 20*, 5 Jul. 44, p.1 [NARA, via Egbert van de Schootbrugge]
371. HQ 90th Infantry Division, G-2, *IPW Summary No.20*, 5 July 1944 [NARA]
372. 82d Airborne Division, Interrogation Report No.21, 6 July 1944, p.1 [NARA, via Egbert van de Schootbrugge]
373. HQ 90th Infantry Div., *IPW Summary No.29*, 14 July 1944 [NARA, RG 407, Box 3498, File 208-7.2]
374. 21 AGp/Int/1070, App. A to 21 Army Group Intelligence Summary No. 147, Part II, 20 July 1944 [UKNA, WO 171/131]
375. OKH/AHA/Abwicklungsstab, Anl. z. Sachgeb. 91 Nr.6.44 g., *Kampfgruppe 91.I.D. Stand vom 17.7.* [T78 R672 H41/61b]
376. Ibid.; see the chapter '77.Infanterie-.Division'; see chapter '91.Luftlande-Infanterie-Division'
377. OKH/AHA/Abwicklungsstab, Anl. z. Sachgeb. 91 Nr.6.44 g., *Kampfgruppe 91.I.D. Stand vom 17.7.* [T78 R672 H41/61b]; OKW, Abwicklungsstab Sachgebiet 265, *Taktischer Bericht für 265. I.D.*, 29.10.44, p.3 [T78 R672 H41/61b]
378. OKW, Abwicklungsstab Sachgebiet 265, *Taktischer Bericht für 265. I.D.*, 29.10.44, p.3 [T78 R672 H41/61b]
379. Information provided by Simon Trew based on a captured document giving the organisation of the 7th Army front on 19 July. (private collection)
380. OKH/AHA/Abwicklungsstab, Anl. z. Sachgeb. 91 Nr.6.44 g., *Kampfgruppe 91.I.D., Stand vom 20.7.* [T78 R672 H41/61b]

— Hereafter referred to as 91.I.D., *Kriegsgliederung KG 91.I.D.*, 20.7.44 [T78 R672 H41/61b]
381. Gen.Kdo.LXXXIV. A.K., Ia Nr.048/44 g.K., 23.7.44, p.2 [T314 R1604 F1374]
382. OKH/AHA/Abwicklungsstab, Anl. z. Sachgeb. 91 Nr.6.44 g., *Kampfgruppe 91.I.D., Stand vom 26.7.* [T78 R672 H41/61b]
— Hereafter referred to as 91.I.D., *Kriegsgliederung KG 91.I.D.*, 26.7.44 [T78 R672 H41/61b]
383. Post, G. (1944), p.3-4 [T78 R672 H41/61a]; OKW, Abwicklungsstab Sachgebiet 265, *Taktischer Bericht für 265. I.D.*, 29.10.44, p.3-4 [T78 R672 H41/61b]
384. OKW, Abwicklungsstab Sachgebiet 265, *Taktischer Bericht für 265. I.D.*, 29.10.44, p.4 [T78 R672 H41/61b]
385. Post, G. (1944), p.4 [T78 R672 H41/61a]
386. OKW, Abwicklungsstab Sachgebiet 265, *Taktischer Bericht für 265. I.D.*, 29.10.44, p.4 [T78 R672 H41/61b]; OKH/Abwicklungsstab - Sachgebiet 243 (**Schoch, H.**), *Vorläufiger Bericht über den Kampf der 243. I.D. auf the Halbinsel Cotentin v. 6.6 bis 7.8 1944*. 22.12.44, p.6 [T78 R672 H41/61b]
387. See War Journals of Gen.Kdo.XXV. A.K. for June and July 1944 [T314 R746 F507-1099; T314 R747 F41-565]
388. Gen.Kdo.XXV. A.K., Abt. Ia Nr.2013/44 g., 14.6.44, p.1 [T34 R746 F828]
389. Gen.Kdo.XXV. A.K. Ia Nr.735/44 g.K., 12.6.44, Blatt I [T314 R746 F780]
390. *Ibid.*, Blatt II [T314 R746 F781]
391. 265. I.D., Ia Nr.302/44 g.K., 12.6.44 [T314 R746 F796]; Gen.Kdo.XXV. A.K. Nr.2021/44 g., 14.6.44, p.1 [T314 R746 F837]
392. *275. I.D.*, Ia Nr.306/44 g.K., 12.6.44 [T314 R746 F794]
393. 265. I.D., Ia Nr.302/44 g.K., 12.6.44 [T314 R746 F796]
394. Gen.Kdo.XXV. A.K. Ia, *KTB Nr.14* [T314 R746 F534]; Gen.Kdo. XXV. A.K. Nr.2021/44 g., 14.6.44, p.1-2 [T314 R746 F837-8]
395. Gen.Kdo.XXV. A.K., Ia Nr.735/44 g.K., 12.6.44 [T314 R746 F781]
396. Anruf F.K. Quimper, 15.6.44 12:20 Uhr [T314 R746 F842]
397. AOK 7/O.Qu., *Kriegstagebuch der Oberquartiermeisterabteilung AOK 7 für die Zeit vom 1.6.44 - 30.6.44* [T312 R1571 F496]
398. Gen.Kdo.XXV. A.K., Ia Nr.764/44 g.K., 18.6.44 [T314 R746 F884]
399. Gen.Kdo/*XXV. A.K.*, Abt. Ia Nr.2076/44 g., 19.6.44, p.1 [T314 R746 F913]
400. Alba (Gen.Kdo.XXV. A.K.) Ia Nr.2080/44 g., 19.6.44 [T314 R746 F915]
401. Gen.Kdo.XXV. A.K., Abt. Ia Nr.2098/44 g., 20.6.44 [T314 R746 F930]; Gen.Kdo.XXV. A.K., Abt. Ia Nr.21178/44 g., 21.6.44, p.1 [T314 R746 F961]
402. Gen.Kdo.XXV. A.K., Abt. Ia Nr.2098/44 g., 20.6.44 [T314 R746 F930]
403. AOK 7, Ia Nr.3268/44, 21.6.44, p.1 [T312 R1565 F1215]; Gen.Kdo.XXV. A.K., Abt. Ia Nr.2145/44 g., 23.6.44 [T314 R746 F1010]
404. Der Kommandierende General XXV. Armeekorps Ia Nr.2130/44 g., 22.6.44 (Anlage and map included) [T314 R746 F979-84]

405. AOK 7 Ia, KTB 1.1.-30.6.1944 [T312 R1564 F364-5]
406. Ob.West, Abt.Ia Nr.1332/44 g.K., 27.6.44 [T311 R24 F7029940]
407. See AOK 7 Ia, KTB 1.1.-30.6.1944 [T312 R1564 F319, 345-6 & 354]
408. Gen.Kdo.XXV. A.K., Ia Nr.2297/44 g., 2.7.44 [T314 R747 F71]
409. Gen.Kdo.XXV. A.K., Abt. Ia Nr.2145/44 g., 23.6.44 [T314 R746 F1010]
410. Gen.Kdo.XXV. A.K., Abt. Ia Nr.2330/44 g., 5.7.44 [T314 R747 F122]
411. Der Kommandierende General XXV. Armeekorps Ia Nr.864/44 g.K., 15.7.44 [T314 R747 F343]
412. AOK 7, Ia Nr.3590/44 g.K., 3.7.44 [T314 R747 F77]
413. Gen.Kdo.XXV. A.K., Ia Nr.815/44 g.K., p.1-2 [T314 R747 F92-3]
414. AOK 7, Ia Nr.3604/44 g.K., 3.7.44 [T314 R747 F703]
415. Gen.Kdo.XXV. A.K., Abt. Ia Nr.811/44 g.K., 3.7.44 [T314 R747 F79]
416. Gen.Kdo.XXV. A.K., Ia Nr.815/44 g.K., 4.7.44, p.1 [T314 R747 F92]; Gen.Kdo.XXV. A.K., Abt. Ia Nr.2343/44 g., 6.7.44 [T314 R747 F136]
417. Gen.Kdo.XXV. A.K., Ia Nr.2323/44 g., 4.7.44 [T314 R747 F106]
418. Gen.Kdo.XXV. A.K., Ia Nr.815/44 g.K., 4.7.44, p.1-2 [T314 R747 F92-3]
419. Gen.Kdo.XXV. A.K., Abt. Ia Nr.2330/44 g., 5.7.44 [T314 R747 F122]
420. Gen.Kdo.XXV. A.K., Abt. Ia Nr.820/44 g.K., 5.7.44, p.2 [T314 R747 F108]; BvTO b. AOK 7 Abt Ia Br.B.Nr.1491/44 g., 9.7.44 [T312 R1571 F1286]
421. Gen.Kdo.XXV. A.K., Abt. Ia Nr.2362/44 g., 7.7.44, p.2 [T314 R747 F149]
422. Gen.Kdo.XXV. A.K., Abt. Ia Nr.2391/44 g., 9.7.44 [T314 R747 F175]
423. Gen.Kdo.XXV. A.K., Abt. Ia Nr.820/44 g.K., 5.7.44, p.2 [T314 R747 F108]; Gen.Kdo.XXV. A.K., Abt. Ia Nr.2405/44 g., 10.7.44 [T314 R747 F190]
424. Gen.Kdo.XXV. A.K., Abt. Ia. Nr.2005/44 g., 13.6.44 [T314 R746 F818]
425. Gen.Kdo.XXV. A.K Ia, *Kriegstagebuch Nr.15 (II. Teil)* Gen.Kdo.XXV. A.K. (Ia), *11.7. - 31.7.44* [T314 R747 F258] — Hereafter referred to as: Gen.Kdo.XXV. A.K. Ia, *KTB Nr.15(II)*; Gen.Kdo.XXV. A.K., Abt. Ia Nr.2455/44 g., 14.7.44 [T314 R747 F333]; Gen.Kdo. XXV. A.K., Abt. Ia Nr.2474/44 g., 15.7.44 [T314 R747 F356]
426. Gen.Kdo.XXV. A.K., Ia Nr.856/44 g.K.1, 15.7.44, p.1-2 [T314 R747 F339-40]
427. Gen.Kdo.XXV. A.K., Abt. Ia Nr.2478/44 g., 16.7.44 [T314 R747 F371]
428. Gen.Kdo.XXV. A.K., Abt. Ia Nr.2491/44 g., 17.7.44 [T314 R747 F379]
429. Gen.Kdo.XXV. A.K., Abt. Ia Nr.2511/44 g., 19.7.44 [T314 R747 F396]
430. Gen.Kdo.XXV. A.K., Abt. Ia Nr.2522/44 g., 20.7.44 [T314 R747 F410]

431. Zusammenstellung der in der Zeit vom 1.7. - 6.8. durch den Bv.T.O. bearbeite Anträge auf Truppen - Einzeltransporte., p.2 [T312 R1571 F1030]; BvTO. b. AOK 7, Br.B Nr.1579/44 g., 20.7.44 [T312 R1571 F1298]
432. Gen.Kdo.XXV. A.K. Ia, *KTB Nr.15(II)* [T314 R747 F269]
433. Der Kommandierende General XXV. Armeekorps Ia Nr.880/44 g.K., 21.7.44 [T314 R747 F420]
434. Gen.Kdo.XXV. A.K. Ia, *KTB Nr.15(II)* [T314 R747 F267]
435. *Ibid.* [T314 R747 F271 & 273]; Gen.Kdo.XXV. A.K. Nr.2575/44 g., 25.7.44, p.1 [T314 R747 F462]
436. Gen.Kdo.XXV. A.K. Ia, *KTB Nr.15(II)* [T314 R747 F271 & 273]; Gen.Kdo.XXV. A.K. Nr.2574/44 g., 25.7.44, p.1-2 [T314 R747 F462-3]; *Ost-Art.Abt. 752* will be addressed in its own chapter in a future volume; **Wilbrand (1944)**, p.16.
437. Gen.Kdo.XXV. A.K., Ia Nr.2284/44 g., 2.7.44 [T314 R747 F63]
438. Gen.Kdo.XXV. A.K., Ia Nr.932/44 g.K., 2.8.44 [T315 R1841 F78]; Kampfgruppe Spang, Ia Nr.2475/44 g., 3.8.44 [T315 R1841 F93]; also see the chapter "77.Infanterie-.Division"; see chapter "91.Luftlande-Infanterie-Division".
439. Kampfgruppe Spang, Ia Nr.537/44 g.K., 4.8.44, p.1 [T315 R1841 F97]
440. *266. I.D.*, Ia Nr.2463/44 g., 6.8.44 [T315 R1841 F112]
441. Der Kommandierende General XXV. A.K. Ia, *Befehl für weitere Kampfführung*, p.2 [T501 R157 F14]; Kampfgruppe Spang Ia Nr.537/44 g.K., 4.8.44, p.1-2 [T315 R1841 F97-8]
442. Fernspruch der Kommandierende General XXV. A.K., Ia Nr.935/44 g.K., 3.8.44, p.3 [T315 R1841 F87]
443. OKW, Abwicklungsstab Sachgebiet 265, *Taktischer Bericht für 265. I.D.*, 29.10.44, p.5 [T78 R672 H41/61b]
444. OKH/GenStdH/Org.Abt.(I), Nr.I/19008/44 g.K. [T78 R398 H1/38]; **Tessin, G. (1973)**, *8.Band*, p.278

353. Infanterie-Division

1. Anl. zu OKH/GenStdH/Org.Abt. Nr.I/4500/43 g.K., 4.10.43, *Kriegsgliederung des Feldheeres (Sollgliederung), Band I, Stand: September 1943*, p.152 [T78 R409 F6378013] — Hereafter referred to as: OKH, *Kriegsgliederung des Feldheeres September 1943*
2. Anl.1 zu OKH/GenStdH/Org.Abt. Nr.I/16900/44 g.K., *Grundgliederung der Inf.Div.44 mit Stärkeberechnung*, 20.5.44, p.2 [T78 R410 F6378466]
3. Anl. zu Gen.Kdo.XXV. A.K., Abt. Ia Nr.148/44 g.K., 15.2.44, (Zustandsbericht) *353. I.D.*, *1.2.44* [T314 R745 fr.000672]; Anl. zu Gen.Kdo.XXV. A.K., Abt. Ia Nr.699/44 g.K., 6.6.44, (Zustandsbericht) *353. I.D.*, *1.6.44* [T314 R747 F17] — Hereafter referred to as: *353. I.D., Zustandsbericht*, 1.6.44;
4. Anl. zu Gen.Kdo.XXV. A.K., Abt. Ia N.554/44 g.K., 7.5.44, (Zustandsbericht) *353. I.D.*, *1.5.44* [T314 R746 F466]
5. *353.I.D., Kriegsgliederung, Stand: 1.6.44* [T314 R747 F20] — Hereafter referred to as: *353.I.D., Kriegsgliederung, Stand: 1.6.44*

6. Leleu, J.L. (2022), *Combattre en Dictature*, Paris: Perrin, Appendix 13 (based on MIRS (b), Various age groups studies, 12.8.1944)
7. Data obtained from the DRK *Vermisstenbildliste* and death cards in the Ancestry.com "Germany, Military Killed in Action, 1939-1948" collection.
8. *353. I.D., Zustandsbericht*, 1.6.44 [T314 R747 F17]
9. *353. I.D., Kriegsgliederung, Stand: 1.6.44* [T314 R747 F20] — Hereafter referred to as: *353. I.D., Kriegsgliederung, Stand: 1.6.44*
10. *Ibid.* [T314 R747 F19]; *K.St.N. (Heer) Nr.21 n, Kommando einer Infanteriedivision 44*, 1.4.44 [CAMO, Bestand 500, Findbuch 12451, Akte 142]; **Mahlmann, P. (1946a)**, MS # F-983 (Germ.), *353. Inf.Division*, Anl.1
11. *353. I.D., Kriegsgliederung, Stand: 1.6.44* [T314 R747 F19]; **Mahlmann, P. (1946a)**, Anl.2b
12. **Tessin, G. (1974)**, *9.Band*, p.193; **Tessin, G. (1975)**, *10.Band*, p.1; Gen.Kdo.XXV. A.K., Abt. Ia Nr.2892/43 g., 6.10.43 [T314 R745 F310]; Anl. zu Gen.Kdo.XXV. A.K., Abt. Ia Nr.1196/43 g.K., 7.11.43, (Kriegsgliederung) *Kampfgruppe Bretagne, Stand vom 1.11.43* [T314 R745 F134]; Gen.Kdo.XXV. A.K., Abt. Ia Nr.2908/43 g., 8.10.43 [T314 R745 F83]; Anl. zu Gen.Kdo.XXV. A.K., Abt. Ia Nr.1333/43 g.K., 7.12.1943, (Kriegsgliederung) *353.Inf.Div. (21.Welle), Stand: 1.12.43* [T314 R745 F214]
13. Anl. zu AOK 7 O.Qu./IIa/Nr.5850/43 g.K., 14.11.43 [T312 R1559 F143]; AOK 7, Ia Nr.5940/43 g.K., 20.11.43 [T312 R1559 F190]
14. Gen.Kdo.XXV. A.K., Abt. Ia Nr.3548/43 g., 2.12.43, p.1 [T314 R745 F479]; Gen.Kdo.XXV. A.K., Abt. Ia Nr.3562/43 g., 3.12.43, p.1 [T314 R745 F483]; Gen.Kdo.XXV. A.K., Abt. Ia Nr.3744/43 g.K., 20.12.43, p.1 [T314 R745 F531]
15. **Tessin, G. (1976)**, *13.Band*, p.147-8
16. Gen.Kdo.XXV. A.K., Abt. Ia Nr.3603/43 g., 6.12.43 [T314 R745 F492]; Gen.Kdo.XXV. A.K., Abt. Ia Nr.3744/43 g., 20.12.43, p.1 [T314 R745 F531]
17. **Tessin, G. (1975)**, *11.Band*, p.132; **Tessin, G. (1976)**, *13.Band*, p.147
18. **Tessin, G. (1975)**, *11.Band*, p.193 & 220; **Tessin, G. (1976)**, *13.Band*, p.147-8
19. Tessin states that the *I./569* became the *I./943*, which is contradicted by other records and the *Feldpost* number. He also states that *GR 581* staffs were used for the field-replacement battalion, but the *II./942* would still have required a headquarters. The *Feldpost* numbers are inconclusive since new numbers were used.
20. Anl. zu Gen.Kdo.XXV. A.K., Ia Nr.30/44 g.K., 7.1.44, (Kriegsgliederung) *353.Inf.Div. (Div. 21.Welle), Stand v. 1.1.1944* [T314 R745 F656] — Hereafter referred to as: *353. I.D., Kriegsgliederung, 1.1.44*; *353. I.D., Kriegsgliederung, Stand: 1.6.44* [T314 R747 F19]
21. *353. I.D., Kriegsgliederung, Stand: 1.6.44* [T314 R747 F19]
22. *Ibid.* All six infantry battalions had 40 light MG's each instead of the authorised 43.
23. Anl.1 zu OKH/GenStdH/Org.Abt. Nr.I/16900/44 g.K., 20.5.44, p.2 [T78 R410 F6378466]

24. PWIS(H)/LDC/120, 12 Jul 44, p.1 [UKNA, WO 208/3646]
25. PWIS(H)/KP/134, 11 Jul 44 [UKNA, WO 208/3624]; PWIS(H)/LDC/82, 5 Jul 44 [UKNA, WO 208/3646]; PWIS(H)/LDC/120, 12 Jul 44, p.1 [UKNA, WO 208/3646]; C.S.D.I.C. (UK) S.I.R. 568, p.1-2 [NARA, RG 165, Box 659, Folder 2]
26. FID-DZ No.206, 11 July 1944 [NARA, RG 498, Box 1326]. The *2./942* is said to have had only two rifle platoons instead of three. The former interrogation report (from the commander of the *2./942*, another officer and an NCO from the *I./942*) does not contradict this as it speaks of two or three platoons in most companies. Additional confirmation is not available though. [FID-DZ No.187, 9 July 1944 [NARA, RG 498, Box 1326]
27. FID-DZ No.206, 11 July 1944 [NARA, RG 498, Box 1326]; FID-DZ No.187, 9 July 1944 [NARA, RG 498, Box 1326]
28. FID-DZ No.361, 1 Aug. 1944 [NARA, RG 498, Box 1326]
29. FID-DZ No.206, 11 July 1944 [NARA, RG 498, Box 1326]; FID-DZ No.187, 9 July 1944 [NARA, RG 498, Box 1326]; C.S.D.I.C. (UK) S.I.R. 568, p.1-2 [NARA, RG 165, Box 659, Folder 2]
30. FID-DZ No.206, 11 July 1944 [NARA, RG 498, Box 1326]; FID-DZ No.187, 9 July 1944 [NARA, RG 498, Box 1326]
31. PWIS(H)/LDC/120, 12 Jul 44, p.2 [UKNA, WO 208/3646]; PWIS(H)/LF/383, 29 Jul 44 [UKNA, WO 208/3633]; PWIS(H)/LF/379, 29 Jul 44 [UKNA, WO 208/3633]; C.S.D.I.C. (UK) S.I.R. 568, p.2 [NARA, RG 165, Box 659, Folder 2]
32. FID-DZ No.206, 11 July 1944 [NARA, RG 498, Box 1326]; FID-DZ No.187, 9 July 1944 [NARA, RG 498, Box 1326]
33. PWIS(H)/LDC/120, 12 Jul 44, p.2 [UKNA, WO 208/3646]
34. C.S.D.I.C. (UK) S.I.R. 568, p.2 [NARA, RG 165, Box 659, Folder 2]
35. PWIS(H)/LDC/82, 5 Jul 44 [UKNA, WO 208/3646]; PWIS(H)/LDC/120, 12 Jul 44, p.1 [UKNA, WO 208/3646]
36. *K.St.N. (Heer) Nr.131 n, Schützenkompanie (n.A.)*, 1.5.44 [T78 R391 F6359520-22]
37. PWIS(H)/LDC/82, 5 Jul 44 [UKNA, WO 208/3646]; *353. I.D., Kriegsgliederung, Stand: 1.6.44* [T314 R747 F19]
38. PWIS(H)/LDC/120, 12 Jul 44, p.1 [UKNA, WO 208/3646]
39. *353. I.D., Zustandsbericht*, 1.6.44 [T314 R747 F18]; Anl. zu Gen.Kdo.XXV. A.K., Abt. Ia. Nr.4099/44 g.K., 8.4.44, (Zustandsbericht *353. I.D.*, 1.4.44 [T314 R746 F449] — Hereafter referred to as: *353. I.D., Zustandsbericht*, 1.4.44
40. Anl.1 zu OKH/GenStdH/Org.Abt. Nr.I/16900/44 g.K., *Grundgliederung der Inf.Div.44 mit Stärkeberechnung*, 20.5.44, p.2 [T78 R410 F6378466]
41. AOK 7/O.Qu., *Kriegstagebuch Nr.46, 1.Dez.1943 - 31.Dez.1943* [T312 R1562 F977 & 982]; AOK 7/O.Qu., *Kriegstagebuch Nr.47, 1.Jan.1944 - 31.Jan.1944* [T312 R1567 F9 & 19]
42. 353. I.D., *Zustandsbericht*, 1.6.44 [T314 R747 F18]
43. AOK 7, Kriegsgliederung 7. Armee, Stand 18.5.44, *353.Inf.-Div., Stand: 1.5.44* [T312 R1566 F232]
44. PWIS(H)/LF/379, 29 Jul 44 [UKNA, WO 208/3633]; Anl.1 zu OKH/GenStdH/Org.Abt. Nr.I/16900/44 g.K., 20.5.44, p.3 [T78 R410 F6378467]
45. PWIS(H)/LF/379, 29 Jul 44 [UKNA, WO 208/3633]

46. *Ibid.*; PWIS(H)/LDC/82, 5 Jul 44 [UKNA, WO 208/3646]
47. PWIS(H)/LF/379, 29 Jul 44 [UKNA, WO 208/3633]
48. Mahlmann, P. (1946a), Germ., p.6
49. Alph. Kartei von Allen Inf. Offiziere einschliesslich Oberst, index card of *Maj.d.R.* Görtmüller [T78 R917 H6/355]
50. Mahlmann, P. (1946a), Germ., Anl.2
51. Anl.1 zu OKH/GenStdH/Org.Abt. Nr.I/16900/44 g.K., 20.5.44, p.5 [T78 R410 F6378469]
52. OKH/GenStdH/Org.Abt. Nr.I/4367/43 g.K., 22.9.1943, p.1-3 [T78 R419 F6388565-7]; Gen.Kdo.XXV. A.K. Abt.Ia Nr.213.44 g., 22.1.44 [T314 R745 F766]
53. OKH/GenStdH/Org.Abt. Nr.I/4367/43 g.K., 22.9.43, p.3 [T78 R531 F384]
54. Anl.1 zu OKH/GenStdH/Org.Abt. Nr.I/16900/44 g.K., p.5 [T78 R410 F6378469]
55. 353. I.D., *Kriegsgliederung, Stand: 1.6.44* [T314 R747 F19]; Anl.1 zu OKH/GenStdH/Org.Abt. Nr.I/16900/44 g.K., 20.5.44, p.2 [T78 R410 F6378466]
56. PWIS(H)/KP/107, 4 Jul 44, p.1 [UKNA, WO 208/3624]; PWIS(H)/LF/259, 7 Jul 44, p.1-2 [UKNA, WO 208/3631]
57. C.S.D.I.C. (UK) S.I.R. 536, p.1 & App. [NARA, RG 165, Box 659, Folder 2]; PWIS(H)/LF/259, 7 Jul 44, p.1-2 [UKNA, WO 208/3631]
58. C.S.D.I.C. (UK) S.I.R. 536, p.1 [NARA, RG 165, Box 659, Folder 2]
59. Anl.1 zu OKH/GenStdH/Org.Abt. Nr.I/16900/44 g.K., 20.5.44, p.7 [T78 R410 F6378471]
60. Anl.3 zu OKH/Chef H Rüst u. BdE AHA Ia(I) Nr.6009/43 g.K., 5.11.43, p.2-3 [T78 R849 H36/159]; Gen.Kdo.XXV. A.K., Abt. Ia Nr.1196/43 g.K., (Kriegsgliederung) *Kampfgruppe Bretagne, Stand vom 1.11.43*, 7.11.43 [T314 R745 F184]; Gen.Kdo.XXV. A.K., *Kriegstagebuch Nr.11 Gen.Kdo.XXV. A.K. Führungsabteilung (Ia) 1.10.43 - 31.12.43* [T314 R745 F8] — Hereafter referred to as: Gen.Kdo.XXV. A.K. Ia, *KTB Nr.11*
61. Gen.Kdo.XXV. A.K., Abt. Ia Nr.3603/43 g., Taktische Tagesmeldung, 6.12.43 [T314 R745 F492]
62. Gen.Kdo.XXV. A.K., Abt. Ia Nr.3791/43 g., 27.12.43 [T314 R745 F551]; **Tessin, G. (1975)**, *10.Band*, p.3
63. Feldpostübersicht
64. 353. I.D., *Kriegsgliederung, 1.1.44* [T314 R745 F656]
65. Gen.Kdo.XXV. A.K. Abt.Ia Nr.30/44 g.K., 7.1.44, (Zustandsbericht) *353. I.D., Meldung vom 1.1.44* [T314 R745 F655]
66. Gen.Kdo.XXV. A.K., Abt. Ia Nr.102/44 g., 11.1.44 [T312 R1564 F432]
67. Feldpostübersicht
68. Gen.Kdo.XXV. A.K., Abt. Ia Nr.82/44 g., 9.1.44, p.1-2 [T314 R745 F4723-4]; Gen.Kdo.XXV. A.K., Abt. Ia Nr.84/44 g., 10.1.44, p.1 [T314 R745 F727]
69. Gen.Kdo.XXV. A.K., Nr.125/44 g., 13.1.44 [T314 R745 F734]
70. Gen.Kdo.XXV. A.K., 14.1.44 [T314 R745 F738]; Gen.Kdo.XXV. A.K., Nr.149/44 g., 15.1.44 [T312 R1564 F741]
71. Gen.Kdo.XXV. A.K., Abt. Ia Nr.245/44 g., 26.1.44 [T314 R745 F779]
72. Gen.Kdo.XXV. A.K., Ia Nr.148/44, 15.2.44, *353.Inf.Div. (Div. 21.Welle), Stand v. 30.1.1944* [T314 R745 F674]
73. AOK 7/O.Qu., *Kriegstagebuch Nr.45, 1.Nov.1943 - 30.Nov.1943* [T312 R1562 F763]; AOK 7/O.Qu., *Kriegstagebuch Nr.46, 1.Dez.1943 - 31.Dez.1943* [T312 R1562 F977]
74. AOK 7/O.Qu., *Kriegstagebuch Nr.46, 1.Dez.1943 - 31.Dez.1943* [T312 R1562 F979]; AOK 7/O.Qu., *Kriegstagebuch Nr.46, 1.Dez.1943 - 31.Dez.1943* [T312 R1562 F981]
75. AOK 7/O.Qu., *Kriegstagebuch der Oberquartiermeisterabteilung AOK 7 für die Zeit vom 1.Febr.1944 - 29.Febr.1944* [T312 R1570 F869]; AOK 7/O.Qu., *Kriegstagebuch der Oberquartiermeisterabteilung AOK 7 für die Zeit vom 1.Febr.1944 - 29.Febr.1944* [T312 R1570 F882]
76. 353. I.D., *Kriegsgliederung, 1.1.44* [T314 R745 F656]
77. Gen.Kdo.XXV. A.K., Ia Nr.270/44 g.K., 7.3.44, (Kriegsgliederung) *353.Inf.Div. (Div. 21.Welle), Stand v. 1.3.1944* [T314 R745 F690]; Zustandsbericht *353. I.D.* for 1 Febr. 1944 [T314 R745 F673]
78. Anl. zu 353. I.D., Ia Nr.971/44 g., (Kriegsgliederung) *353.Inf.Div., Stand: 1.6.44*, 3.6.1944 [T314 R747 F19]
79. AOK 7, Kriegsgliederung 7. Armee, Stand 18.5.44, *353. Inf.-Div., Stand: 1.5.44* [T312 R1566 F232]; Gen.Kdo.XXV. A.K., Ia Nr.554/44 g., 7.5.44, (Kriegsgliederung) *353.Inf.Div., Stand: 1.5.1944* [T314 R746 F467]; 353. I.D., *Kriegsgliederung, Stand: 1.6.44* [T314 R747 F19]
80. 353. I.D., *Kriegsgliederung, Stand: 1.6.44* [T314 R747 F19]
81. FID-DZ No.258, 19 July 1944 [NARA, RG 498, Box 1326]
82. PWIS(H)/LF/246, 6 Jul 44, p.1 [UKNA, WO 208/3631]
83. FID-DZ No.258, 19 July 1944 [NARA, RG 498, Box 1326]
84. 353. I.D., *Zustandsbericht 1.6.44* [T314 R747 F18]; Anl. zu Gen.Kdo.XXV. A.K., Ia Nr.554/44 g., 7.5.44, (Zustandsbericht) *353. I.D., Meldung vom 1. Mai 1944* [T314 R746 F466] — Hereafter referred to as: 353.I,D, Zustandsbericht, 1.5.44
85. Because of their origin the symbol used on the *Kriegsgliederung* for these weapons was still that of an anti-tank rifle. Nine of them had arrived at the division on 11 January. [AOK 7/O.Qu., *Kriegstagebuch Nr.47, 1.Jan.1944 - 31.Jan.1944* in T312 R1567 F13]
86. 353. I.D., *Kriegsgliederung, Stand: 1.6.44* [T314 R747 F19]
87. PWIS(H)/KP/133, 11 Jul 44 [UKNA, WO 208/3624]
88. PWIS(H)/KP/161, 17 Jul 44 [UKNA, WO 208/3624]; FID-DZ No.330, 27 July 1944 [NARA, RG 498, Box 1326]
89. FID-DZ No.254, 19 July 1944 [NARA, RG 498, Box 1326]
90. Ibid.; FID-DZ No.330, 27 July 1944 [NARA, RG 498, Box 1326]
91. *KStN 711n* and *723n* (engineer company on foot and on bicycles, both dated 1.4.44 [CAMO, Bestand 500, Findbuch 12451, Akte 142]
92. FID-DZ No.254, 19 July 1944 [NARA, RG 498, Box 1326]
93. PWIS(H)/KP/136, 11 Jul 44 [UKNA, WO 208/3624]
94. FID-DZ No.255, 19 July 1944 [NARA, RG 498, Box 1326]
95. *KStN 711n* and *723n* (engineer company on foot and on bicycles, both dated 1.4.44 [CAMO, Bestand 500, Findbuch 12451, Akte 142]
96. FID-DZ No.254, 19 July 1944 [NARA, RG 498, Box 1326] This report distinguishes *Hiwi's* and legionaries, suggesting the presence of troops in both roles in the companies.
97. 353. I.D., *Kriegsgliederung, Stand: 1.6.44* [T314 R747 F19]
98. Anl.1 zu OKH/GenStdH/Org.Abt. Nr.I/16900/44 g.K., 20.5.44, p.2 [T78 R410 F6378466]
99. 353. I.D., *Kriegsgliederung, Stand: 1.6.44* [T314 R747 F19]
100. Anl.1 zu OKH/GenStdH/Org.Abt. Nr.I/16900/44 g.K., 20.5.44, p.2 [T78 R410 F6378466]
101. PWIS(H)/LF/338, POW taken on 7 Jul 44, p.1 [UKNA, WO 208/3632]
102. FID-DZ No.236, 17 July 1944 [NARA, RG 498, Box 1326]
103. PWIS(H)/LF/338, POW taken on 7 Jul 44, p.1-2 [UKNA, WO 208/3632]; *353. I.D., Kriegsgliederung, Stand: 1.6.44* [T314 R747 F19]
104. PWIS(H)/LF/338, POW taken on 7 Jul 44, p.1 [UKNA, WO 208/3632]
105. Mahlmann, P. (1946a), Germ., p.7; *353. I.D., Kriegsgliederung, Stand: 1.6.44* [T314 R747 F19-20]
106. Mahlmann, P. (1946a), Germ., p.7
107. Gen.Kdo.XXV. A.K., Abt. Ia Nr.1612/44 g., 19.5.44 [T314 R746 F228]
108. 353. I.D., *Kriegsgliederung, Stand: 1.6.44* [T314 R747 F19]
109. Mahlmann, P. (1946a), Germ., p.11
110. 353. I.D., *Kriegsgliederung, Stand: 1.6.44* [T314 R747 F20]
111. FID-DZ No.199, 11 July 1944 [NARA, RG 498, Box 1326]
112. FID-DZ No.323, 27 July 1944 [NARA, RG 498, Box 1326]
113. OKH, *Kriegsgliederung des Feldheeres September 1943*, p.152 [T78 R409 F6378013]
114. OKH, *Kriegsgliederung des Feldheeres September 1943*, p.152 [T78 R409 F6378013]
115. AOK 7, Ia Nr.4900/43 g.K., 25.9.43, p.1 [T314 R1604 F944]; Gen.Kdo.XXV. A.K., Abt. Ia Nr.1196/43 g.K., (Kriegsgliederung) *Kampfgruppe Bretagne, Stand vom 1.11.43*, 7.11.43 [T314 R745 F184]
116. OKH, *Kriegsgliederung des Feldheeres September 1943*, p.152 [T78 R409 F6378013]
117. Anl zu Gen.Kdo.XXV. A.K., Abt. Ia Nr.1333/43 g.K., (Zustandsbericht) *353. I.D., Meldung vom 1. Dezember 1943* [T314 R745 F213]
118. AOK 7, Anl.5 zu AOK 7 O.Qu./IIa/Ia Nr.5850/43 g.K., 14.11.43, p.1 [T312 R1559 F146]
119. Gen.Kdo.XXV. A.K., Abt. Ia Nr.3603/43 g., Taktische Tagesmeldung, 6.12.43 [T314 R745 F492]; **Tessin, G. (1974)**, *9.Band*, p.169
120. AOK 7, Ia Nr.273/44 g.K., 15.1.44 [T312 R1564 F455-8]
121. *Ibid.*, p.1-2 [T312 R1564 F455-6]
122. Gen.Kdo.XXV. A.K., Abt. Ia Nr.400/44 g., Taktische Tagesmeldung, 12.2.44 [T314 R745 F833]
123. AOK 7, Ia Nr.273/44 g.K., 15.1.44, p.3 [T312 R1564 F457]
124. *Ibid.*, p.2 [T312 R1564 F456]; *K.St.N. (Heer) Nr.446a, Stu. Gesch.Battr.(mot)*, 1.11.42 [Available at: www.wwiidaybyday.com/KStN/KStN446a1nov42.htm, accessed 18 September 2018]
125. Anl. 1 zu OKH/GenStdH/Org.Abt. Nr.I/16900/44 g.K., 20.5.44, p.4 [T78 R410 F6378468]; *K.St.N. (Heer) Nr.1149,*

Sturmgeschützabteilung (in Panzer-Jager-Abteilung) (10 oder 14 Geschütze), 1.2.44 [T78 R393 F6361812-7]
126. AOK 7, Ia Nr.273/44 g.K., 15.144, p.2 [T312 R1564 F456]
127. OKH/GenStdH/Org.Abt. Nr.I/15710/44 g.K., 14.2.44 [T78 R269 F6216933]; OKH/GenStdH/Org.Abt. Nr.I/15710/44 g.K. II. Ang., 25.2.44, p.1-3 [T78 R398 H1/39]
128. AOK 7, Kriegsgliederung 7. Armee, Stand: 9.2.1944, (Kriegsgliederung) *353.Inf.-Div., Stand: 1.1.1944* [T312 R1566 F40]
129. AOK 7, Kriegsgliederung 7. Armee, Stand 14.2.44, (Kriegsgliederung) *353.Inf.-Div., Stand: 30.1.44* [T312 R1566 F108] The division's first two towed AT guns arrived with *Füs.Btl. (A.A.) 371* in the autumn of 1943 and six *7,5 cm Pak 40's* arrived on 5 December 1943. The final 14 *Pak 40's* arrived on 8 January 1944, which brought the total in the division to 22. [AOK 7, Kriegsgliederung 7. Armee, Stand 15.11.43, (Kriegsgliederung) *Kampfgr. Bretagne (353. I.D.), Stand: 10.10.44* in T312 R1559 F682; AOK 7/O.Qu., *Kriegstagebuch Nr.46, 1.Dez.1943 - 31.Dez.1943* in T312 R1562 F965; AOK 7/O.Qu., *Kriegstagebuch Nr.47, 1.Jan.1944 - 31.Jan.1944* in T312 R1567 F12; Zustandsbericht *353. I.D.* for 1.2.44 T314 R745 F672]
130. Gen.Kdo.XXV. A.K., Abt. Ia Nr.235/44 g., 24.1.44 [T314 R745 F773]
131. Gen.Kdo.XXV. A.K., Abt. Ia Nr.3143/43 g., 28.10.43 [T314 R745 F375]; Gen.Kdo.XXV. A.K., Abt. Ia Nr.554/44 g., 26.2.44 [T314 R745 F884]
132. Gen.Kdo.XXV. A.K., Abt. Ia Nr.240/44 g., Taktische Tagesmeldung, 25.1.44 [T314 R745 F776]
133. OKH/Ch H Rüst u BdE/ AHA Ia (I) Nr.609/44 g.K. v. 28.1.44 [BaMa H36/ 153]
134. Gen.Kdo.XXV. A.K., Abt. Ia Nr.285/44 g., Taktische Tagesmeldung, 31.1.44 [T314 R745 F793]
135. Gen.Kdo.XXV. A.K., Abt. Ia Nr.361/44 g., 8.2.44 [R314 R745 F819]
136. Gen.Kdo.XXV. A.K., Abt. Ia Nr.515/44 g., 23.2.44 [R314 R745 F872]
137. AOK 7, Kriegsgliederung 7. Armee, Stand 12.3.44, (Kriegsgliederung) *353.Inf.-Div., Stand: 30.1.1944* [T312 R1566 F143]
138. AOK 7, Kriegsgliederung 7. Armee, Stand 18.5.44, (Kriegsgliederung) *353.Inf.-Div., Stand: 1.5.44* [T312 R1566 F232]
139. OKH/GenStdH/Org.Abt. (I), Nr.I/3197/43 g.K.II.Ang., 2.10.43, Anl.1 [T78 R527 F117]; Anl. 1 zu OKH/GenStdH/Org.Abt. Nr.I/16900/44 g.K., 20.5.44, p.2 [T78 R410 F6378466]
140. AOK 7, Kriegsgliederung 7. Armee, Stand 18.5.44, (Kriegsgliederung) *352.Inf.Div., Stand: 1.5.44* [T312 R1566 F216]; OKH/ Ch H Rüst u BdE/ AHA Ia (I) Nr.214/44 g.K., 11.1.44, p.1 [T78 R848 H36/153]; Photos of these are in **Morgan, M.K.A. (2004)**, *Down to Earth: The 507th Parachute Infantry Regiment in Normandy*, Atglen PA: Schiffer Publishing, p.140. The 1 May *Kriegsgliederung* of the *352. I.D.* uses the symbol for towed *Flak* and a wrecked *Sd.Kfz. 7/2* from this company in Pont-l'Abbé uses that same tactical symbol. The presence of self-propelled 3,7 cm *Flak* in these companies may be explained by OKH/GenStdH/Org.Abt. Nr.I/5640/43 g.K. II. Ang. von 31.12.43, but this order has not been found.
141. Gen.Kdo.XXV. A.K., Abt. Ia Nr.498/44 g., 21.2.44 [R314 R745 F865]
142. AOK 7/O.Qu., *Kriegstagebuch der Oberquartiermeisterabteilung AOK 7 für die Zeit vom 1.3.44 - 31.3.44* [T312 R1570 F1011]
143. AOK 7/O.Qu., *Kriegstagebuch der Oberquartiermeisterabteilung AOK 7 für die Zeit vom 1.3.44 - 31.3.44* [T312 R1570 F1022]
144. *353. I.D., Zustandsbericht*, 1.4.44 [R314 R746 F449]; Gen.Kdo.XXV. A.K., Abt. Ia Nr.992/44 g., 1.4.44 [R314 R746 F77]; AOK 7/O.Qu., *Kriegstagebuch der Oberquartiermeisterabteilung AOK 7 für die Zeit vom 1.4.44 - 30.4.44* [T312 R1571 F6]; AOK 7/O.Qu., *Kriegstagebuch der Oberquartiermeisterabteilung AOK 7 für die Zeit vom 1.4.44 - 30.4.44* [T312 R1571 F12]
145. Anl. zu Gen.Kdo.XXV. A.K., Nr.409/44 g.K., 8.4.44, (Kriegsgliederung) *353.Inf.Div., Stand v.1.4.1944* [T314 R746 F450] Some records of *AOK 7* appear to have been somewhat outdated. Its *Kriegsgliederung* of 1 April puts the number of *Marders* at only nine and lists the number of towed guns as eight. The *AOK 7 Kriegsgliederung* of 1 May is actually the first to show the complete *Pz.Jg.Abt. 353*.
146. AOK 7/O.Qu., *Kriegstagebuch der Oberquartiermeisterabteilung AOK 7 für die Zeit vom 1.4.44 - 30.4.44* [T312 R1571 F17]
147. AOK 7/O.Qu., *Kriegstagebuch der Oberquartiermeisterabteilung AOK 7 für die Zeit vom 1.5.44 - 31.5.44* [T312 R1571 F298]
148. *353. I.D., Zustandsbericht*, 1.4.44 [T314 R746 F449]
149. *353. I.D, Zustandsbericht*, 1.5.44 [T314 R745 F466]
150. AOK 7/O.Qu., *Kriegstagebuch der Oberquartiermeisterabteilung AOK 7 für die Zeit vom 1.5.44 - 31.5.44* [T312 R1571 F298]
151. AOK 7/O.Qu., *Kriegstagebuch der Oberquartiermeisterabteilung AOK 7 für die Zeit vom 1.5.44 - 31.5.44* [T312 R1571 F297]
152. *353. I.D., Zustandsbericht 1.6.44* [T314 R747 F18]
153. C.S.D.I.C. (UK) S.I.R. 758, p.1 [NARA, RG 165, Box 661]
154. *353. I.D., Zustandsbericht 1.6.44* [T314 R747 F17]; Anl. zu AOK 7, Ia Nr.3000/44 g.K., 4.4.44, *Übersicht über Bewegl. Truppenteile bei eingesetzten oder in Reserve befindlichen Div.* [T312 R1565 F431]
155. 353. I.D., *Zustandsbericht 1.6.44* [T314 R747 F17]
156. AOK 7, Ia Nr.1542/44 g.K., 14.3.44, p.1 [T312 R1565 F280]
157. AOK 7, Ia Nr.1542/44 g.K. (a second version), 14.3.44, p.1-2 [T312 R1565 F283-4]
158. AOK 7, Ia Nr.3000/44 g.K., 4.4.44, p.3-4 [T312 R1565 F421-2]; Anl. zu AOK 7, Ia Nr.3000/44 g.K., 4.4.44, *Übersicht über Bewegl. Truppenteile bei eingesetzten oder in Reserve befindlichen Div.* [T312 R1565 F431]
159. Anl.1 zu AOK 7 O.Qu./Ia Nr.3508/44 g.K., 7.5.44, *Art der zusätzl. Bewegungmachung (über KStN-Soll)* [T312 R1565 F646]; [T312 R1565 F639-40]
160. Anl.2 zu AOK 7 O.Qu./Ia Nr.3508/44 g.K., 7.5.44, *Kriegsstärkenachweisung für behelfsmäßige Beweglichmachung (Bedarf an Beweglichmachungmitteln) KStN (beh.Bew.)* [T312 R1565 F651]
161. *353.I.D, Zustandsbericht*, 1.5.44 [T314 R746 F466]; *353. I.D., Zustandsbericht 1.6.44* [T314 R747 F18]
162. AOK 7/O.Qu., *Besprechungspunkte bei O.Qu.West*, 12.5.44, p.1-2 [T312 R1571 F389-90]; **Ziegelmann, F. (1946a)**, MS # B-432 (Germ.), *Die Geschichte der 352.Inf.Div.*, p.17; Anl. zu AOK 7, Ia Nr.3000/44 g.K., 4.4.44, *Übersicht über Bewegl. Truppenteile bei eingesetzten oder in Reserve befindlichen Div.* [T312 R1565 F431]
163. Mahlmann, P. (1946a), Germ., p.7-8
164. AOK 7, Ia Nr.6697/43 g.K., 28.12.43, p.1 [T312 R1563 F965]
165. Tessin, G. (1974), *9.Band*, p.265
166. Hubatsch, W. (reprint 2005b), *Kriegstagebuch des Oberkommandos der Wehrmacht (Wehrmachtführungsstab), Band III: 1. Januar 1943 - 31. Dezember 1943*, Augsburg: Verlagsgruppe Weltbild GmbH, p.1132; AOK 7, Ia Nr.4900/43 g.K., 25.9.43, p.2 [T314 R1604 F945] sent to LXXXIV. A.K. by AOK 7 in response to Ob.West (Okdo.d.H.Gr.) Nr.5395/43 g.K. v.25.9. (nur an A.O.K.); OKH/GenStdH/Org Abt. Nr.I/4367/43 g.K., 22.9.1943, p.1-3 [T78 R419 F6388565-7]; **Tessin, G. (1974)**, *9.Band*, p.279 & 286
167. OKH/GenStdH/Org.Abt. Nr.I/4367/43 g.K., 22.9.1943, p.1-2 [T78 R419 F6388565-6]
168. For examples from the *AOK 7* sector see the *371., 384., 77. I.D.*, etc.
169. AOK 7, Ia Nr.4900/43 g.K., 25.9.43, p.2 [T314 R1604 F945]
170. OKH/GenStdH Op.Abt.III/Prüf-Nr.45363, *Schematische Kriegsgliederung, Stand: 15.9.43* [T78 R649 F347]; OKH/GenStdH/Org.Abt. (I) Nr.993/43 g.K. Chefs., 28.1.43, p.1-4 & Anl. [T78 R431 F6402868-72]; OKH/Chef H Rüst und BdE, AHA Ia(I) Nr.2640/43 g.K., 26.5.43, p.1 [T78 R849 H36/156]; **Tessin, G. (1974)**, *9.Band*, p.193; **Tessin, G. (1975)**, *10.Band*, p.1
171. Tessin, G. (1975), *10.Band*, p.1
172. AOK 7 Ia, Karten u. Kriegsgliederungen zum Kriegstagebuch AOK 7 Ia vom 1.7.43 bis 31.12.43, *Lage 7. Armee, Stand: 17.9.43* [T312 R1559 F504]; AOK 7, Kriegsgliederung 7. Armee, Stand: 20.10.43, (Kriegsgliederung) *371.Inf.-Div., Stand: 1.9.43* [T312 R1559 F645]; p.158 [T78 R409 F6378021]; AOK 7/O.Qu., *Kriegstagebuch Nr.43, 1.Sept-1943 - 30.Sept.1943* [T312 R1562 F419]
173. Gen.Kdo.XXV. A.K. Ia, *KTB Nr.11* [T314 R745 F8 & 10]
174. AOK 7, Ia Nr.4900/43 g.K., 25.9.43, p.1-2 [T314 R1604 F944-5]. The *1./Pz.Jg.Abt. 371* was incorrectly listed as the 2nd Company on the document. The transfer actually involved the self-propelled company which was the 1st Company. In his monograph, Mahlmann incorrectly stated that the three infantry battalions originated from the *371. I.D.* Instead, just one infantry battal on and the fusilier battalion came from that division. [**Mahlmann, P. (1946a)**, Germ., p.2]
175. Gen.Kdo.XXV. A.K. Abt. Ia Nr.2871/43 g., 5.10.1943 [T314 R745 F63]; Gen.Kdo.XXV. A.K. Ia, *KTB Nr.11* [T314 R745 F8]; Gen.Kdo.XXV. A.K., Abt. Ia Nr.3574/43 g., 4.12.43 [T314 R745 F486]

176. Gen.Kdo.XXV. A.K. Abt.Ia Nr.2892/43, 6.10.43 [T314 R745 F310]; Gen.Kdo.XXV. A.K. Abt.Ia Nr.2904/43, 7.10.43 [T314 R745 F312]
177. Gen.Kdo. Ia Nr.2908/43 g., 8.10.43 [T314 R745 F88]
178. Gen.Kdo.XXV. A.K., Abt. Ia Nr.1196/43 g.K., (Kriegsgliederung) *Kampfgruppe Bretagne, Stand vom 1.11.43*, 7.11.43 [T314 R745 F184]
179. AOK 7, Ia Nr.5711/43 g.K., 9.11.43, p.1-3 [T314 R745 F111-3]
180. Gen.Kdo.XXV. A.K. Ia, *KTB Nr.11* [T314 R745 F26]
181. AOK 7, Ia Nr.6009/43 g.K., 27.11.43 [T314 R745 F148]; Gen. Kdo. *XXV. A.K.* Nr.3533/43 g., 1.12.43., p.1 [T314 R745 F474]; Gen.Kdo.XXV. A.K., Abt. Ia Nr.3548/43 g., 2.12.43, p.1 [T314 R745 F479]
182. Gen.Kdo.XXV. A.K., Abt. Ia Nr.3574/43 g. 4.12.43 [T314 R745 F486]
183. Gen.Kdo.XXV. A.K. Abt.Ia Nr.3562/43 g., 3.12.43 [T314 R745 F483]; Gen.Kdo.XXV. A.K. Abt.Ia Nr.3572/43 g. 4.12.43 [T314 R745 F486]
184. Gen.Kdo.XXV. A.K. Abt.Ia Nr.3603/43 g., 6.12.43 [T314 R745 F492]; **Tessin, G. (1974)**, *9.Band*, p.169
185. Gen.Kdo.XXV. A.K., Abt. Ia Nr.3744/43 g., 20.12.1943 [T314 R745 F531]; **Tessin, G. (1974)**, *9.Band*, p.94
186. Gen.Kdo.XXV. A.K. Ia Nr.213/44 g.K., 22.2.44 [T314 R745 F1138]
187. Gen.Kdo.XXV. A.K. Abt. Ia Nr.1585/44 g., 17.5.44 [T314 R746 F222]
188. Gen.Kdo.XXV. A.K. Abt.Ia Nr.1553/44 g., 14.5.44 [T314 R746 F213]
189. Gen.Kdo.XXV. A.K. Ia Nr.309/44 g.K., 14.3.44 [T314 R745 F1201]
190. Gen.Kdo.XXV. A.K., Ia Nr.1152/44 g., 12.4.44 [T314 R746 F113]
191. Gen.Kdo.XXV. A.K., Ia Nr.1503/44 g., 10.5.44 [T314 R746 F200]
192. Gen.Kdo.XXV. A.K., Ia Nr.1152/44 g., 12.4.44 [T314 R746 F113]
193. Gen.Kdo.XXV. A.K., Abt. Ia Nr.1503/44 g., 10.5.44 [T314 R746 F200]
194. Gen.Kdo.XXV. A.K., Abt. Ia Nr.1419/44 g., 3.5.44 [T314 R746 F178]
195. Gen.Kdo.XXV. A.K., Ia Nr.1152/44 g., 12.4.44 [T314 R746 F113]
196. Gen.Kdo.XXV. A.K. Abt.Ia Nr.1466/44 g., 7.5.44 [T314 R746 F191]
197. AOK 7, Ia Nr.2168/44 g.K., 13.4.44, p.2 [T312 R1565 F483]
198. Gen.Kdo.XXV. A.K., Abt. Ia Nr.599/44 g.K., 14.5.44 [T314 R746 F397]
199. Gen.Kdo.XXV. A.K., Abt. Ia Nr.1661/44 g., 23.4.44 [T314 R746 F242]
200. Der Kommandierende General XXV. A.K., Ia Nr.366/44 g.K., 27.3.44, p.1 [T314 R745 1241]
201. Gen.Kdo.XXV. A.K., Abt. Ia Nr.1007/44 g., 2.4.44 [T314 R746 F80]; Gen.Kdo.XXV. A.K., Abt. Ia Nr.1022/44 g., 3.4.44 [T314 R746 F83]; Gen.Kdo.XXV. A.K., Ia Nr.1038/44 g., 4.4.44 [T314 R746 F86]
202. AOK 7, Ia Nr.148/44 g., 6.4.44 [T312 R1565 F446]
203. PWIS(H)/LF/259, 7 Jul 44, p.1 [UKNA, WO 208/3631]
204. Gen.Kdo.XXV. A.K., Ia Nr.161/44 g.K., 9.2.44 [T314 R745 F1097]
205. Gen.Kdo.XXV. A.K., Ia Nr.539/44 g., 25.2.44, p.1 [T314 R745 F880]
206. Gen.Kdo.XXV. A.K. Ia Nr.1424/44 g., 4.5.44 [T314 R746 F181]
207. Gen.Kdo.XXV. A.K. Ia, *Kriegstagebuch Nr.13* Gen.Kdo.XXV. A.K. *Führungsabteilung (Ia) 1.4.44 - 5.6.44* [T314 R746 F46]
208. AOK 7, Ia Nr.716/44 g., 3.2.44 [T312 R1565 F23]
209. AOK 7, Ia Nr.738/44 g., 4.2.44 [T312 R1565 F30]
210. Gen.Kdo.LXXIV. A.K. Ia, Ia-Tagesmeldung, 29.5.44 [T314 R1568 F612]. For both the 2nd and 3rd Battalions the distances were measured from the churches in the respective localities.
211. AOK 7 Ia, Anlage zum K.T.B. Führungsabt. AOK 7 Ia, Lage-Karten A.O.K.7 vom 6.1.-5.6.44, *Lage 7. Armee, Stand: 12.3.44* [T312 R1570 F6]; Gen.Kdo.XXV. A.K., Abt. Ia Nr.600/44 g., 1.3.44 [T314 R745 F899]
212. AOK 7, Ia Nr.1710/44 g., 14.3.44 [T312 R1565 F270]
213. Gen.Kdo.XXV. A.K., Abt. Ia Nr.887/44 g., 19.5.44 [T314 R745 F977]. Only map coordinates are given. Since no maps area available for this sector to pinpoint the locations, these have been calculated instead, but can be off by as much as 1 km.
214. Gen.Kdo.*LXXIV. A.K.*, Führungsabt., *Kriegstagebuch Nr.2, 1.1.44-30.6.44* [T314 R1568 F454-5] AOK 7 Ia, *Kriegstagebuch der Führungsabteilung* AOK 7 für die Zeit vom 1.Jan. - 30.Juni 1944 [T312 R1564 F185]
215. Gen.Kdo.*LXXIV. A.K.* Ia, 19.2.44 [T314 R1568 F550]
216. Gen.Kdo.*LXXIV. A.K.* Ia, Ia-Tagesmeldung, 10.3.44 [T314 R1568 F562]
217. Gen.Kdo.XXV. A.K., Ia Nr.1598/44 g., 18.5.44 [T314 R746 F225]
218. Gen.Kdo.XXV. A.K., Abt. Ia Nr.1612/44 g., 19.5.44 [T314 R746 F228]
219. Gen.Kdo.XXV. A.K., Abt. Ia Nr.1499/44 g., 19.5.44 [T314 R746 F402]
220. Gen.Kdo.XXV. A.K., Abt. Ia Nr.1695/44 g., 26.5.44 [T314 R746 F254]; Gen.Kdo.XXV. A.K., Ia Nr.1714/44 g., 27.5.44 [T314 R746 F258]
221. Gen.Kdo.XXV. A.K., Ia Nr.1714/44 g., 27.5.44 [T314 R746 F258]
222. Gen.Kdo.XXV. A.K., Abt. Ia Nr.184/44 g., 19.144 [T314 R745 F756]
223. Gen.Kdo.XXV. A.K. Abt. Ia Nr.285/44 g., 31.1.44 [T314 R745 F793]; AOK 7, Ia Nr.1267/44 g., 26.2.44 [T312 R1565 F176]
224. AOK 7, Ia Nr.1267/44 g., 26.2.44 [T312 R1565 F176]
225. Gen.Kdo.XXV. A.K., Abt. Ia Nr.285/44 g., 31.1.44 [T314 R745 F793]
226. Gen.Kdo.XXV. A.K., Ia Nr.564/44 g., 27.2.44 [T314 R745 F887-9]
227. Gen.Kdo.XXV. A.K., Abt. Ia Nr.515/44 g., 23.2.44 [R314 R745 F872]
228. AOK 7, Ia Nr.1267/44 g., 26.2.44 [T312 R1565 F176]
229. Gen.Kdo.XXV. A.K., Abt. Ia Nr.564/44 g., 27.2.44, p.3 [T314 R745 F889]
230. Gen.Kdo.XXV. A.K., Abt. Ia Nr.1405/44 g., 2.5.44 [T314 R746 F175]
231. Gen.Kdo.XXV. A.K., Abt. Ia Nr.570/44 g., 28.2.44 [T314 R745 F892]
232. FID-DZ No.236, 17 July 1944 [NARA, RG 498, Box 1326]
233. Gen.Kdo.XXV. A.K., Abt. Ia Nr.1612/44 g., 19.5.44 [T314 R746 F228]
234. Gen.Kdo.XXV. A.K., Abt. Ia Nr.1695/44 g., 26.5.44 [T314 R746 F254]
235. *XXV. A.K.*, report on confirmation of Alarmstufe II, 6.6.44 [T314 R746 F595]
236. AOK 7 Ia, AOK 7 *Kriegstagebuch Ia, 6 June 1944 - 16 Aug 1944*, p.22 [T312 R1569 F25] — Hereafter referred to as: AOK 7 Ia, *KTB 6.6.-16.8.44*
237. Gen.Kdo.XXV. A.K. Ia, *Kriegstagebuch Nr.14* [T314 R746 F512] — Hereafter referred to as: Gen.Kdo.XXV. A.K. Ia, *KTB Nr.14*; *XXV. A.K.*, Anruf AOK 7 Ia / Chef.d.St. Gen.Kdo.XXV. A.K., 6.6.44 [T314 R746 F599]; *XXV. A.K.*, Rücksprache Obst. Bader (*XXV. A.K.* C.o.S.) - Obst. Helmdach (AOK 7), 6.6.44 [T314 R746 F600]
238. Gen.Kdo.XXV. A.K., Kurze Vormittagsmeldung, 6.6.44 [T314 R746 F616]
239. Gen.Kdo.XXV. A.K., 6.6.44 [T314 R746 F607]
240. Gen.Kdo.XXV. A.K., telephone call Maj. Witte (Ia *353. I.D.*), 6.6.44 [T314 R746 F608]; Gen.Kdo.XXV. A.K., Abendmeldung, 7.6.44 [T314 R746 F661]
241. Gen.Kdo.XXV. A.K., Ia Nr.1907/44 g., 7.6.44 [T314 R746 F635]; Gen.Kdo.XXV. A.K., Ia Nr.1908/44 g., 7.6.44 [T314 R746 F637]
242. *353. I.D.*, Ia Nr.1015/44 g., 8.6.44 [T314 R746 F679-80]
243. *353. I.D.*, Ia Nr.1016/44 g., 8.6.44 [T314 R746 F698-9]; Gen.Kdo.XXV. A.K., Ia Nr.1932/44 g., 9.6.44 [T314 R746 F715]
244. Gen.Kdo.XXV. A.K., telephone call Maj. Witte (Ia *353. I.D.*), 9.6.44 [T314 R746 F704]
245. Gen.Kdo.XXV. A.K. Ia, *KTB Nr.14* [T314 R746 F521]
246. Anl. zu AOK 7/BvTO Nr.357/44 g.K., *Tätigkeitsbericht des BvTO b. AOK 7, 1.1.1944 - 30.6.1944*, p.39 [T312 R1571 F913]; BvTO b. AOK 7, Br.B.Nr.1304/44 g., 11.6.44 [T312 R1571 F991]
247. Anl. zu AOK 7/BvTO Nr.357/44 g.K., *Tätigkeitsbericht des BvTO b. AOK 7*, p.40 [T312 R1571 F914]
248. AOK 7 Ia, AOK 7 *Kriegstagebuch Ia - 6 Jun 1944 - 25 Jul 1944*, p.55 [T312 R1569 F274] — Hereafter referred to as: AOK 7 Ia, *KTB 6.6.-25.7.44*
249. AOK 7, *Übersicht über die aus der Bretagne nach der Normandie zugeführten oder noch zuzuführenden Kräfte*, 22.6.44, p.1 [T312 R1565 F1248]; The battalion had been listed under *KG 265* on 19.6.44, see AOK 7, Ia Nr.1532/44 g., 19.6.44, p.1 [T312 R1565 F1143]; AOK 7, Kriegsgliederungen zum KTB der Führungsabteilung AOK 7 ab 6.6.44 bis 30.6.44, *Stand: 23.6. 14 Uhr*, 23.6.44 [T312 R1566 F16]
250. AOK 7, Ia Nr.2926/44 g.K., 9.6.44 [T312 R1565 F915]; AOK 7, Ia Nr.2926/44 g.K., 9.6.44 [T314 R746 F707]

251. Gen.Kdo.XXV. A.K., Ia Nr.719/444 g.K., 9.6.44 [T314 R746 F711]
252. *353. I.D.*, Ia Nr.1040/44 g., 10.6.44 [T314 R746 F723]
253. Gen.Kdo.XXV. A.K., Ia Nr.723/44 g.K., 10.6.44 [T314 R746 F724]; Gen.Kdo.XXV. A.K. Ia, *KTB Nr.14* [T314 R746 F523]
254. AOK 7, Ia Nr.2943/44 g.K., 10.6.44 [T312 R1565 F948]
255. Gen.Kdo.XXV. A.K., Ia Nr.725/44 g.K., 10.6.44 [T314 R746 F733-4]
256. Gen.Kdo.XXV. A.K., Abt. Ia Nr.1961/44 g., 10.6.44, p.1 [T314 R746 F739]
257. Gen.Kdo.XXV. A.K., Ia Nr.725/44 g.K., 10.6.44 [T314 R746 F733-4]; AOK 7, Ia Nr.2943/44 g.K., 10.6.44 [T312 R1565 F948]
258. **Mahlmann, P. (1946a)**, Germ., p.7
259. Gen.Kdo.XXV. A.K., Ia Nr.725/44 g.K., 10.6.44 [T314 R746 F733-4]
260. Gen.Kdo.XXV.A.K., number not known, 11.6.44, 01:00 [T314 R746 F750-2]. The numbers of the *Fahrschwadrone* are peculiar, since the division only had two.
261. Ibid. [T314 R746 F752]
262. **Mahlmann, P. (1946a)**, p.8-9
263. Gen.Kdo.XXV. A.K., Taktische Tagesmeldung, 11.6.44 [T314 R746 F768]
264. AOK 7, Ia Nr.2964/44 g.K., 11.6.44 [T312 R1565 F967]
265. Gen.Kdo.XXV. A.K. Ia, Mittagsmeldung, 11.6.44 [T314 R746 F766]; Gen.Kdo.XXV. A.K., Ia Nr.1986/44 g. 12.6.44 [T314 R746 F801]; AOK 7, Ia Nr.3045/44 g.K., Teil II, 13.5.44 [T312 R1565 F1005]
266. Gen.Kdo.XXV. A.K. Ia, Mittagsmeldung, 11.6.44 [T314 R746 F766]
267. Okdo.d.H.Gr.B., Ia Nr.3369/44 g.K., 12.6.44 [T311 R4 F7004962]
268. AOK 7, Ia Nr.3045/44 g.K., Teil II, 13.6.44 [T312 R1565 F1005]
269. Gen.Kdo.XXV. A.K. Ia, *KTB Nr.14* [T314 R746 F534]; AOK 7, Ia Nr.3075/44 g.K., 14.6.44, p.2 [T312 R1565 F1024]
270. AOK 7 Ia, *KTB 6.6.-25.7.44*, p.39-40 [T312 R1569 F258-9]; *Maj.i.G. Prinz zu Holstein, Besprechung zwischen der Oberbefehlshaber der 7. Armee und dem Komm. General des LXXXIV. A.K. am 14.6.1944 in St. Lô*, 15.6.1944, p.2 [T312 R1565 F1028]
271. AOK 7, Ia, *KTB 6.6.-25.7.44*, p.41-2 [T312 R1569 F260-1]
272. AOK 7, Ia Nr.3115/44 g.K., p.2 [T312 R1565 F1041]
273. **Ziegelmann, F. (1946g)**, MS # B-438 (Germ.), *Die Geschichte der 352.Inf.Div., Die Kämpfe vom 15.6. bis 17.6.44*, map; AOK 7, Ia Nr.3144/44 g.K., 16.6.44, p.1 [T312 R1565 F1077]; AOK 7 situation maps for the period of 6-16 June [T312 R1570 fr.000015-24]; Gliederungen of AOK 7 for the period of 11-17 June [T312 R1566 F3-7]
274. AOK 7, Ia Nr.3115/44 g.K., p.2 [T312 R1565 F1041]
275. Gen.Kdo.XXV. A.K., Abt. Ia Nr.2027/44 g., 15.6.44 [T314 R746 F849]
276. AOK 7, Ia Nr.3117/44 g.K., 15.6.44, p.1 [T312 R1565 F1049]
277. AOK 7, Ia Nr.3147/44 g.K., 16.6..44, p.3 [T312 R1565 F1068]
278. AOK 7 Ia, *KTB 6.6.-25.7.44*, p.44 [T312 R1569 F263]; **Ziegelmann, F. (1946g)**, Germ., p2-.4
279. Ibid.
280. Ibid., p.45 [T312 R1569 F264]; **Ziegelmann, F. (1946g)**, Germ., p.2-4
281. **Ziegelmann, F. (1946g)**, Germ., p.4
282. 352.I.D., Abt. Ia, *Gefechtsbericht vom 16.6.44*, 18.6.44 [BAMA, RH 19-IX/2]. The report was signed by Ziegelmann.
283. AOK 7, Ia Nr.3144/44 g.K., p.1 [T312 R1565 F1077]
284. Gen.Kdo.XXV. A.K., Abt. Ia Nr.2035/44 g., 16.6.44 [T314 R746 F861]
285. **Ziegelmann, F. (1946g)**, Germ., p.4-6
286. 352.I.D., Abt. Ia, *Gefechtsbericht vom 17.6.44*, 18.6.44 [BAMA, RH 19-IX/2]; [**Ziegelmann, F. (1946g)**, Germ., p.5-6]
287. AOK 7 Ia, KTB 6.6.-25.7.44, p.50 [T312 R1569 F268]; AOK 7, Ia Nr.1481/44 g., 17.6.44 [T312 R1565 F1089]; AOK 7, Ia Nr.3166/44 g.K., 17.6.44 [T312 R1565 F1090]
288. AOK 7 Ia, *KTB 6.6.-25.7.44*, p.50 [T312 R1569 F269]
289. Gen.Kdo.XXV. A.K., Abt. Ia Nr.2043/44 g., 17.6.44 [T314 R746 F873]; AOK 7, Ia Nr.3167/44 g.K., 17.6.44 [T312 R1565 F1097]; WFSt. Op.(H), Chef WFst, *Lage West, Stand: 17.6.44* (1:200.000) [NARA, via www.wwii-photos-maps.com]
290. AOK 7, Ia, *KTB 6.6.-25.7.44*, p.52 [T312 R1569 F271]
291. AOK 7, Ia Nr.3186/44 g.K., 18.6.44, p.2 [T312 R1565 F1116]
292. AOK 7, Ia Nr.3198/44 g.K., 18.6.44, p.2 [T312 R1565 F1124]; WFSt Op.(H), *Lage West Stand: 18.6.44*, Chef WFSt (1:200.000) [NARA, via www.wwii-photos-maps.com]
293. AOK 7, Ia Nr.3231/44 g.K., 19.6, p.1 [T312 R1565 F152]; WFSt Op.(H), *Lage West Stand: 19.6.44*, Chef WFSt (1:200.000) [NARA, via www.wwii-photos-maps.com]
294. AOK 7, Ia Nr.3264/44 g.K., 20.6.44, p.1 [T312 R1565 F1197]; WFSt Op.(H), *Lage West Stand: 20.6.44*, Chef WFSt (1:200.000) [NARA, via www.wwii-photos-maps.com]
295. AOK 7, Ia Nr.3310/44 g.K., 22.6.44 [T312 R1555 F1244]
296. AOK 7, Ia Nr.3312/44 g.K., 22.6.44, p.1 [T312 R1565 F1251]; AOK 7, Ia Nr.3347/44 g.K., 23.6.44, p.2 [T312 R1565 F1273]
297. AOK 7, Ia Nr.3371/44 g.K., 24.6.44, p.3 [T312 R1565 F1298]
298. **Mahlmann, P. (1946a)**, Germ., p.9-10.
299. See chapters "77.Infanterie-Division", "91.Luftlande-Infanterie-Division" and "243.Infanterie-Division".
300. AOK 7, Ia Nr.3238/44 g.K., 19.6.44, p.2 [T312 R1565 F1133]; AOK 7, Ia Nr.3241/44 g.K., 20.6.44, p.3 [T312 R1565 F1177]
301. AOK 7, Ia Nr.3241/44 g.K., 20.6.44, p.3 [T312 R1565 F1177]; AOK 7, Ia Nr.3363 g.K., 24.6.44 [T312 R1565 F1295]; AOK 7 Ia, KTB 1.1.-30.6.1944 [T312 R1564 F366]; AOK 7, Ia Nr.3492/44 g.K., p.2 [T312 R1565 F1429]; **Mahlmann, P. (1946a)**, Germ., p.12; **Choltitz, D. von (1947)**, MS # B-418 (Germ.), *Kämpfe des LXXXIV. A.K. in der Normandie vom 18.6.144 ab*, p.7
302. This is indeed possible, as the first elements of the division were reported to have joined the *Mahlmann-Linie* on the 20th. The headquarters of *Pi.Btl. 353* and the 3rd Company were part of the most mobile *Marschgruppe* of the division and *Pz.Jg.Abt. 353* was the first element of the division to actually leave for Normandy. [LXXXIV. A.K., 20.6.44 at 16:30 in UKNA, HW 5/508, CX/MSS/T222/64, KV 9075]
303. AOK 7 Ia, *KTB 6.6.-25.7.44*, p.55 [T312 R1569 F274]; 82nd AB, *Action in Normandy*, Narrative, p.23
304. AOK 7, Ia Nr.3238/44 g.K., 19.6.44, p.2 [T312 R1565 F1133]; AOK 7, Ia Nr.1595/44 g., 20.6.44 [T312 T1565 F1172]; **Mahlmann, P. (1946a)**, Germ., p.13; LXXXIV. A.K., 20.6.44 at 16:30 [UKNA, HW 5/508, CX/MSS/T222/64, KV 9075]
305. **Mahlmann, F. (1946a)**, Germ., Anl.7
306. AOK 7, Ia Nr.3259/44 g.K., 20.6.44 [T312 R1565 F1199]
307. **Ziegelmann (1947)**, MS # B-439, *Die Kämpfe vom 23.6. bis 10.7.44*, p.1
308. AOK 7 Ia, *KTB 6.6.-25.7.44*, p.69 [T312 R1569 F289]
309. AOK 7, Ia Nr.3373/44 g.K., 25.6.44 [T312 R1565 F1323]
310. AOK 7, Ia Nr.3373/44 g.K., 25.6.44 [T312 R1565 F1324]
311. **Harrison, G.A. (1951, reprint 1984)**, Cross-Channel Attack, Office of the Chief of Military History United States Army: Washington D.C., p.379-85 & 444
312. 352.I.D., Abt. Ia, *Gefechtsbericht vom 29.6.1944*, attachement to H.Gr.B. Ia 3554/44 g.K. [BAMA, RH 19-IX/3]; Report of 352.I.D., Abt. Ia to Gen.Kdo.II.Fs.K., 29.6.44 [BAMA, RH 19-IX/3]. KG Boehm lost at least 22 men killed on the 29th and another 14 the next day. [Kartei der Verlust- und Grabmeldungen gefallener deutscher Soldaten 1939-1945 (-1948) via Ancestry.com]
313. AOK 7 Ia, *KTB 1.1.-30.6.1944* [T312 R1564 F380-1]
314. **Harrison, G.A. (1951, reprint 1984)**, p.384, 444; For the fighting for St.Lô in July see **Blumenson, M. (1961, 1993 reprint)**, Breakout and Pursuit, Center of Military History, United States Army, Washington D.C., p.146-174 & Map III
315. **Mahlmann, P. (1946b)**, MS # A-984 (Engl.), *353.Inf.Div. (24 Jul - 10 Sep 44), Report of the Commander*, p.12
316. AOK 7, Ia Nr.3492/44 g.K., 29.6.44, p.2 [T312 R1565 F1429]; **Nauroth, H.S. & B. Steinberg (2017)**, *Die Geschichte der 91.Luftlande-Division - Rekonstruktion eines Großverbändes der Deutschen Wehrmacht*, Hamburg: tradition GmbH, p.118-119
317. AOK 7, Ia Nr.3492/44 g.K., 29.6.44, p.3 [T312 R1565 F1430]
318. AOK 7, Ia Nr.3505/44 g.K., 29.6.44 [T312 R1565 F1432]; **Mahlmann, P. (1946a)**, Germ., p.15; AOK 7 Ia, *KTB 6.6.-16.8.44*, p.96 [T312 R1569 F99]
319. **Mahlmann, P. (1946a)**, Germ., *353. Inf.Division*, p.14-15 & Anl.7; **Wilbrand (1944)**, *Gefechtsbericht des Grenadier Regimentes 1050 (77.Infanterie-Division)*, p.13 [T78 R672 H41/61b]
320. AOK 7, Ia Nr.3492/44 g.K., 29.6.44, p.3 [T312 R1565 F1430]; AOK 7, Ia Nr.3535/44 g.K., 30.6.44 [T312 R1565 F1474]
321. AOK 7, Ia Nr.3558/44 g.K., 30.6.44 [T312 R1565 F1467]
322. **Wilbrand (1944)**, p.13 [T78 R672 H41/61b] Mahlmann mixed up the I. and IV./AR 353 in his account. Period records link the 1st Battalion only to the right wing of the *Nordfront*, which means the 4th Battalion supported the 243. I.D. on the left. For example, on 17 and 21 July, the I./AR 353 was still supporting the right wing of the front, again with the *91. LL.Div*. [Anl. z. Sachb. 91 Nr.6.44 g., *KG 91.I.D., Stand: 17.7*. in T78 R672 H41/61b; Gen.Kdo.LXXXIV. A.K., Ia Nr.035/44, *Takt. Gliederung der Artillerie, Stand: 21.7.44*, 22.7.44 in T314 R1604 F1388]

323. Wilbrand (1944), p.12-13 [T78 R672 H41/61b]
324. Blumenson, M. (1961, 1993 reprint), p.54-55 and Map 3'
325. AOK 7 Ia, *KTB 6.6.-25.7.44*, p.91-92 [T312 R1569 F311-2]; LXXXIV. A.K., 3.7.44 at 22:00 [UKNA, HW 5/520, CX/MSS/T235/23, XL 697]; **Hausser, P. (1946)**, p.10; **Mahlmann, P. (1946)**, Anl.8
326. Mahlmann, P. (1946a), Germ., p.15
327. AOK 7 Ia, *KTB 6.6.-16.8.44*, p.108 [T312 R1569 F111]
328. WFSt Op.(H) zu Lage West, Stand: 4.7.44 (1:50.000) [NARA, via www.wwii-photos-maps.com]
329. LXXXIV. A.K., 3.7.44 at 22:00 [UKNA, HW 5/520, CX/MSS/T235/23, XL 697]; AOK 7 Ia, *KTB 6.6.-16.8.44*, p.108 [T312 R1569 F111]; **Mahlmann, P. (1946a)**, Germ., Anl.8
330. Mahlmann, P. (1946a), Germ., p.15 & Anl.8
331. AOK 7 Ia, *KTB 6.6.-16.8.44*, p.112 [T312 R1569 F115]
332. Okdo.d.H.Gr.B, Ia Nr.4408/44 g.K., 5.7.44, p.2 [T311 R4 F7004837]
333. Mahlmann, P. (1946a), Germ., p.15-16 & Anl.8. The fighting in this sector will be addressed in more detail in the chapters *"Ost-Rgts.Gr. Bunjatschenko"*, *"Ost-Btl. 635"* and *"Ost-Btl. Huber"* in a future volume.
334. Wilbrand (1944), p.16
335. Okdo.d.H.Gr.B, Ia Nr.4408/44 g.K., 5.7.44, p.2 [T311 R4 F7004837]; Okdo.d.H.Gr.B, Ia Nr.4421/44 g.K., 5.7.44, p.1 [T311 R4 F7004834] Okdo.d.H.Gr.B, Ia Nr.4428/44 g.K., 5.7.44, p.1-2 [T311 R4 F7004832-3]; [Okdo.d.H.Gr.B, Ia Nr.4442/44 g.K., 6.7.44 T311 R3 F7002498]
Hausser, P. (1946), MS # A-974 (Germ.), *Normandie - 7. Armee vom 29.6. - 24.7.1945*, p.13; AOK 7 Ia, *KTB 6.6.-25.7.44*, p.97 [T312 R1569 F317]
336. Mahlmann, P. (1946a), Germ., p.16-17; Okdo.d.H.Gr.B, Ia Nr.4516/44 g.K., p.3 [T311 R3 F7002507]
337. AOK 7 Ia, *KTB 6.6.-16.8.44*, p.119 [T312 R1569 F122]
338. Flivo LXXXIV. A.K., 5.7.44 at 16:30 [UKNA, HW 5/521, CX/MSS/T236/95]
339. AOK 7 Ia, *KTB 6.6.-25.7.44*, p.98 [T312 R1569 F318]
340. *Ibid.*, p.97-98 [T312 R1569 F317-8]
341. Weidinger, O. (1954), *Bericht über den Einsatz bei La Haye de Puits*, p.30-33 & map 4 [pages in Anlagenband A and map in Anlagenband B to **Stückler, A. (1954)**, MS # P-159]
342. Okdo.d.H.Gr.B, Ia Nr.4451/44 g.K., 6.7.44 [T311 R4 F7004829]
343. Okdo.d.H.Gr.B, Ia Nr.4464/44 g.K., 6.7.44, p.2 [T311 R4 F7004828]; Okdo.d.H.Gr.B, Ia Nr.4480/44 g.K., 7.7.44, p.2 & 5 [T311 R3 F7002500 & 3]; Okdo.d.H.Gr.B, Ia Nr.4483/44 g.K., 7.7.44, p.2-3 [T311 R4 F700425-26] The document refers to "Le Mans", but there is no such place in the area. It is assumed "Le Mont" was meant.
344. Okdo.d.H.Gr.B, Ia Nr.4480/44 g.K., 7.7.44, p.2 & 5 [T311 R3 F7002500 & 3]; Okdo.d.H.Gr.B, Ia Nr.4483/44 g.K., 7.7.44, p.2-3 [T311 R4 F700425-26;] Okdo.d.H.Gr.B, Ia Nr.4451/44 g.K., 6.7.44 [T311 R4 F7004829]
345. AOK 7 Ia, *KTB 6.6.-16.8.44*, p.120 [T312 R1569 F123]
346. Okdo.d.H.Gr.B, Ia Nr.4483/44 g.K., 7.7.44, p.2-3 [T311 R4 F700425-26]; Okdo.d.H.Gr.B, Ia Nr.44501/44 g.K., 7.7.44, p.2 [T311 R4 F7004821]
347. AOK 7 Ia, *KTB 6.6.-16.8.44*, p.125 [T312 R1569 F128]; Okdo.d.H.Gr.B, Ia Nr.44501/44 g.K., 7.7.44, p.2 [T311 R4 F7004821]
348. AOK 7 Ia, *KTB 6.6.-16.8.44*, p.125-6 [T312 R1569 F128-9]; Okdo.d.H.Gr.B, Ia Nr.4489/44 g.K., 7.7.44, p.2 [T311 R4 F7004823]; Okdo.d.H.Gr.B, Ia Nr.4516/44 g.K., 8.7.44, p.3 [T311 R3 F7002507]; **Mahlmann, P. (1946a)**, Germ., p.17
349. AOK 7 Ia, *KTB 6.6.-16.8.44*, p.119 & 127-129 [T312 R1569 F122, 130-2]
350. *Ibid.*, p.130-131 [T312 R1569 F133-4]
351. Okdo.d.H.Gr.B, Ia Nr.4523/44 g.K., 8.7.44, p.2 [T311 R4 F7004817]
352. Okdo.d.H.Gr.B, Ia Nr.4524/44 g.K., 8.7.44 [T311 R4 F7004817]; Okdo.d.H.Gr.B, Ia Nr.4525/44 g.K., 8.7.44 [T311 R4 F7004814]; Okdo.d.H.Gr.B, Ia Nr.4529/44 g.K., 8.7.44, p.2 [T311 R4 F7004812]; Okdo.d.H.Gr.B, Ia Nr.4516/44 g.K., 9.7.44, p.2 & 5-6 [T311 R3 F7002511 & 4-5]; Flivo LXXXIV. A.K., 8.7.44 at 23:30 [UKNA, HW 5/525, CX/MSS/T240/13, XL 1328]
353. Weidinger, O. (1954), p.32-33 [in Anlagenband A to **Stückler, A. (1954)**, MS # P-159]; Okdo.d.H.Gr.B, Ia Nr.4529/44 g.K., 8.7.44, p.2 [T311 R4 F7004812
354. Okdo.d.H.Gr.B, Ia Nr.4523/44 g.K., 8.7.44, p.2 [T311 R4 F7004817]
355. Okdo.d.H.Gr.B, Ia Nr.4529/44 g.K., 8.7.44, p.2 [T311 R4 F7004812]; Okdo.d.H.Gr.B, Ia Nr.4516/44 g.K., 9.7.44, p.5-6 [T311 R3 F7002514-5]
356. AOK 7 Ia, *KTB 6.6.-16.8.44*, p.132 [T312 R1569 F135]; Flivo LXXXIV. A.K., 8.7.44 at 23:30 [UKNA, HW 5/525, CX/MSS/T240/13, XL 1328]
357. Okdo.d.H.Gr.B, Ia Nr.4516/44 g.K., 9.7.44, p.6 [T311 R3 F7002515]
358. Flivo LXXXIV. A.K. at 09:00 on 9.7.44 [UKNA, HW 5/525, CX/MSS/T240/62, XL 1383]; Okdo.d.H.Gr.B, Ia Nr.4544/44 g.K., 9.7.44, p.2 [T311 R4 F7004810]; Okdo.d.H.Gr.B, Ia Nr.4547/44 g.K., 9.7.44, p.2 [T311 R4 F7004808]; Okdo.d.H.Gr.B, Ia Nr.4585/44 g.K., 10.7.44, p.5 [T311 R3 F7002521]
359. Okdo.d.H.Gr.B, Ia Nr.4547/44 g.K., 9.7.44, p.2 [T311 R4 F7004808]; Flivo LXXXIV. A.K., at 16:30 on 9.7.44 [UKNA, HW 5/525, CX/MSS/T240/108, XL 1431]; Okdo.d.H.Gr.B, Ia Nr.4571/44 g.K., 9.7.44, p.2 [T311 R4 F7004806]
360. Flivo LXXXIV. A.K. at 09:00 on 9.7.44 [UKNA, HW 5/525, CX/MSS/T240/62, XL 1383]; Okdo.d.H.Gr.B, Ia Nr.4544/44 g.K., 9.7.44, p.2 [T311 R4 F7004810]
361. Okdo.d.H.Gr.B, Ia Nr.4571/44 g.K., 9.7.44, p.2 [T311 R4 F7004806]
362. Okdo.d.H.Gr.B, Ia Nr.4547/44 g.K., 9.7.44, p.2 [T311 R4 F7004808]
363. AOK 7 Ia, *KTB 6.6.-16.8.44*, p.134-5 [T312 R1569 F137-8]; Okdo.d.H.Gr.B, Ia Nr.4585/44 g.K., 10.7.44, p.2 [T311 R3 F7002518]
364. AOK 7 Ia, *KTB 6.6.-16.8.44*, p.137 [T312 R1569 F140]; Flivo LXXXIV. A.K., 10.7.44, 01:00 [UKNA, HW 5/526, CX/MSS/T251/63, XL 1526]
365. Flivo LXXXIV. A.K., 10.7.44 at 01:00 [UKNA, HW 5/526, CX/MSS/T241/39, XL 1498]
366. Okdo.d.H.Gr.B, Ia Nr.4632/44 g.K., 11.7.44, p.5 [T311 R3 F7002527]
367. AOK 7 Ia, *KTB 6.6.-16.8.44*, p.139 [T312 R1569 F143]
368. *Ibid.*, p.140 [T312 R1569 F144]
369. *Ibid.*, p.142 [T312 R1569 F146]
370. Mahlmann, P. (1946a), MS# A-983 (Germ.), p.18; AOK 7 Ia, *KTB 6.6.-16.8.44*, p.140 [T312 R1569 F144]
371. Okdo.d.H.Gr.B, Ia Nr.4724/44 g.K., 13.7.44, p.4 [T311 R3 F7002539]; **Mahlmann, P. (1946a)**, Germ., p.19
372. Flivo LXXXIV. A.K., 13.7.44 at 01:30 [UKNA, HW 5/529, CX/MSS/T244/75, XL 1883]; AOK 7 Ia, *KTB 6.6.-16.8.44*, p.145 [T312 R1569 F149]
373. AOK 7 Ia, *KTB 6.6.-16.8.44*, p.148 [T312 R1569 F152]; AOK 7 Ia, *KTB 6.6.-25.7.44*, p.116 [T312 R1569 F336]; Flivo LXXXIV. A.K., 14.7.44 at 02:00 [UKNA, HW 5/530, CX/MSS/T245/78, XL 1974]
374. AOK 7 Ia, *KTB 6.6.-16.8.44*, p.148-9 [T312 R1569 F152-3]
375. AOK 7 Ia, *KTB 6.6.-16.8.44*, p.152 [T312 R1569 F156]; **Mahlmann, P. (1946a)**, Germ., p.19-20 & Anl.10; WFSt Op.(H), *4.Lage West Chef. WFSt*, 15.7.44 (1:50.000) [NARA, via www.wwii-photos-maps.com]
376. Okdo.d.H.Gr.B, Ia Nr.4753/44 g.K., 14.7.44, p.4-5 [T311 R3 F7002544-5]; Flivo LXXXIV. A.K., 10.7.44 at 01:00 [UKNA, HW 5/526, CX/MSS/T241/39, XL 1498]; Gen.Kdo.LXXXIV. A.K., Ia Nr.1758/44 g.K., 13.7.44, p.1 [published in **Wind M. & G. Günther (2004)**, *Kriegstagebuch 17.SS-Panzer-Grenadier-Division "Götz von Berlichingen"*, St.Ingbert: Dengmerter Heimatverlag]. As part of the withdrawal, the corps had ordered the following boundaries: *77. I.D./353. I.D.*: Coutances (77.) - Muneville-le-Bingard (353.) - Millières (77.) - as before; *353. I.D/243.I.D*: Montchaton (353.) - Boisroger (243.) - Nicolle (353.) - railway crossing 1 km southeast of Lessay - as before. Here "as before" presumably refers to the boundaries of 10 July.
377. Mahlmann, P. (1946a), Germ., Anl.10
378. AOK 7 Ia, *KTB 6.6.-16.8.44*, p.168 [T312 R1569 F172]; also see chapters *"77.Infanterie-Division"* and *"91.Luftlande-Infanterie-Division"*.
379. Mahlmann, P. (1946a), Germ., p.17
380. AOK 7 Ia, *KTB 6.6.-16.8.44*, p.137 [T312 R1569 F140]
381. Okdo.d.H.Gr.B, Ia Nr.4686/44 g.K., 12.7.44, p.6 [T311 R3 F7002534]; **Mahlmann, P. (1946a)**, Germ., p.19; PWIS(H)/LF/463, 8 Aug 44, p.2 [UKNA, WO 208/3634]
382. Mahlmann, P. (1946a), Germ., p.20
383. AOK 7 Ia, *KTB 6.6.-16.8.44*, p.152 [T312 R1569 F156]
384. CX/MSS/R.253 (C) [UKNA, HW 5/538]
385. AOK 7 Ia, *KTB 6.6.-16.8.44*, p.153 [T312 R1569 F157]
386. Information provided by Simon Trew based on a captured document giving the organisation of the 7th Army front on 19 July. (private collection)
387. Blumenson, M. (1961, 1993 reprint), p.90-101, 146-182;

WFSt Op.(H), Situation maps (Lage West) for period 7-23 Jul 44 (1:50.000 and 1:200.000) [NARA, via www.wwii-photos-maps.com]; The commitment and performance of the *5. Fj.Div.* in the period of 13-18 Jul 44 is covered by AOK 7 Ia, *KTB 6.6.-25.7.44*, p.117-126 [T312 R1569 F337-46]; LXXXIV. A.K., Ia Nr.048/44 g.K., 23.7.44, p.1-3 [T314 R1604 F1373-5]

388. LXXXIV. A.K., Ia Nr.048/44 g.K., 23.7.44, p.1 [T314 R1604 F1373]; **Pemsel, M. (1949a)**, MS # C-056 (Germ.), *Stellungnahme zur Arbeit über die Schlacht in der Normandie des Gen. v. Choltitz (MS # B-418)* (6.6.-15.7.), p.4-5 & 7

389. AOK 7 Ia, *KTB 6.6.-16.8.44*, p.180 [T312 R1569 F184]

390. *Ibid.*, p.183 [T312 R1569 F187]

391. Gen.Kdo.LXXXIV. A.K. Ia, Ia-Morgenmeldung, *22.7.44* [T314 R1604 F1370]; LXXXIV. A.K. Ia, *Morgenmeldungen der Divisionen*, 23.7.44 [T314 R1604 F1379]; Gen.Kdo.LXXXIV. A.K. Ia, Ia-Morgenmeldung, 23.7.44 [F1371]

392. Gen.Kdo.LXXXIV. A.K., Ia Nr.048/44 g.K., 23.744, p.2-3 [T314 R1604 F1374-5]; **Mahlmann, P. (1946a)**, Germ., Anl.8

393. HQ 4th AD, Annex No 2 to accompany G-2 Periodic Report No 16, *Order of Battle Report*, 2 Aug. 44 [Available at: http://firstdivisionmuseum.nmtvault.com/jsp/ viewer.jsp?doc_id=iwfd0000%2F20141124%2F170&page_name=282, accessed on 14 August 2018]

394. LXXXIV. A.K., 23.7.44 at 04:30 [UKNA, HW 5/539, CS/MSS/T254/25, XL 3173]

395. Gen.Kdo.LXXXIV. A.K., Ia Nr.035/44, *Takt. Gliederung der Artillerie, Stand: 21.7.44*, 22.7.44 [T314 R1604 F1388]

396. Gen.Kdo.LXXXIV. A.K., Ia Nr.048/44 g.K., 23.744, p.2 [T314 R1604 F1374]

397. Mahlmann, P. (1946b), Engl., App.2. His numbers on the weaponry of the division are ignored as they appear to be overly pessimistic and are at odds with period records.

398. On D-Day, the division had 10 towed *Pak 40's* and 14 *Marders*. The three *Pak 40's* of the *14./GR 943* were with the *II. Fs.K.*; this would have left a total of seven towed guns. Provided that no extra AT guns had been obtained, at least six out of the 13 *Pak 40's* on 23 July should thus have been *Marders*.

399. LXXXIV. A.K., Ia Nr.048/44 g.K., 23.7.44, p.1-3 [T314 R1604 F1373-5]

400. Blumenson, M. (1961, 1993 reprint), p.224-246

401. Okdo.d.H.Gr.B, Ia Nr.5172/44 g.K., 26.7.44, p.5 [T311 R3 F7002622]; AOK 7 Ia, *KTB 6.6.-25.7.44*, p.130 [T312 R1569 F350]; Artillerie-Kommandeur 474, (Tagesmeldung vom 25.7.44), 26.7.44; **Mahlmann, P. (1946b)**, Engl., p.3-4

402. LXXXIV. A.K. Ia, Ia-Morgenmeldung, 26.7.44 [T314 R1604 F1386]; **Mahlmann, P. (1946b)**, Engl., p.4

403. LXXXIV. A.K. Ia, Ia-Tagesmeldung, 26.7.44, p.1 [T314 R1604 F1381]

404. *Ibid.*; LXXXIV. A.K. Ia, Ia-Tagesmeldung, 26.7.44 [T314 R1604 F1383]

405. Blumenson, M. (1961, 1993 reprint), p.252-256 & Map V *'Breakthrough 25-27 July 1944'*

406. *Ibid.*, p.258; **Mahlmann, P. (1946b)**, Engl., p.5

407. Okdo.d.H.Gr.B, Ia Nr.5277/44 g.K., 28.7.44, p.5 [T311 R3 F7002641]; **Mahlmann, P. (1946b)**, Engl., p.5-7

408. Okdo.d.H.Gr.B, Ia Nr.5288/44 g.K., 29.7.44, p.2 [T311 R4 F7004684]

409. Mahlmann, P. (1946b), Engl., p.7-9

410. *Ibid.*, p.9-10

411. AOK 7 Ia, Ferngespräche Gen.Feldm. von Kluge - Gen.Lt. Speidel, 31.7.44 [T312 R1568 F631]

412. Mahlmann, P. (1946b), Engl., p.10

413. *Ibid.*, App.13

414. Heydte, F.A. von der (1952), MS # B-839, p.76-77; **Mahlmann, P. (1946b)**, Engl., p.11-12

415. Mahlmann, P. (1946b), Engl., p.11

416. 7th Armored Division, *7 Armd Div Intelligence Summary No 77, Part II*, p.2, 26 Aug 44 [Available at: http://firstdivisionmuseum.nmtvault.com/jsp/viewer.jsp?doc_id=iwfd0000%2F20141124%2F266&page_name=377, accessed on 14 August 2018]

417. Mahlmann, P. (1946b), Engl., p.12 & App.14

418. Okdo.d.H.Gr.B, Ia Nr.5486/44 g.K., 3.8.44, p.6 [T311 R3 F7002677]; Flivo LXXXIV. A.K., 2.8.44 at 07:15 [UKNA, HW 5/549, CX/MSST264/134 XL 4517]; WFSt Op.(H), 3. *Lage West, Chef West*, 2.8.44 (1:80.000) [NARA, via www.wwii-photos-maps.com]

419. AOK 7, 2.8.44 (evening) [UKNA, HW 5/550 CX/MSS/265/92, XL 4625]. The records speak of *"Kampfgruppe 353"*, but this seems to refer to the weakened division rather than *KG Boehm*.

420. Mahlmann, P. (1946b), Engl., App.14 - Although the map is supposed to show the situation in 1 August, period maps suggest it shows the situation on 2 August at the earliest.

421. AOK 7, Ia Nr.502/33 g. II.Ang. nach Eing. g.K., p.1 [T312 R1569 F366]

422. Mahlmann, P. (1946c), MS # A-985 (Engl.), *353.Inf.Div. (11 - 21 Aug 44), Report of the Commander*, p.12

423. Mahlmann, P. (1946c), Engl., p.12-13 & App.15; **Heydte, F.A. von der (1952)**, MS # B-839 (Germ.), p.77

424. Mahlmann, P. (1946c), Engl., App.15

425. Okdo.d.H Gr.B, Ia Nr.5517/44 g.K., 3.8.44 [T311 R4 F7003877-8]; **Criegern, F. v. (1948)**, MS # B-784 (Germ.), *Teil II, Die Kämpfe des LXXXIV. A.K. in der Normandie vom 30.7.-20.8.44*, p.45-47; **Elfeldt, O. (1946)**, MS # A-968 (Engl.), *LXXXIV Corps, 28 July to 20 August 1944*, p.12-13; The period of 2-6 Aug 44 is also covered in the daily reports (*Tagesmeldungen*) of *Heeresgruppe B*. [T311 R3 F7002607-708]; WFSt Op.(H), Situation maps (Lage West) 2-6 Aug 44 (1:80.000 and 1:200.000) [NARA, via www.wwii-photos-maps.com]

426. AOK 7, Ia Nr.526/44 g., 4.8.44 [T312 R1569 F383]; AOK 7, Ia Nr.532/44 g., 4.8.44, p.2 [T312 R1569 F385]

427. LXXXIV. A.K., 5.8.44 at 06:00 [UKNA, HW 5/552, CX/MSS/T267/21, XL 4797]; **Mahlmann, P. (1946b)**, Engl., App.16; WFSt Op.(H), *Lage West, Chef West*, 5.8.44 (1:80.000) [NARA, via www.wwii-photos-maps.com]

428. Number of maps from NARA, via www.wwii-photos-maps.com: WFSt Op.(H), 4. *Lage West, Chef West*, 4.8.44 (1:80.000); WFSt Op.(H), *Lage West, Chef West*, 4.8.44 (1:80.000); WFSt Op.(H), *Lage West, Chef West*, 5.8.44 (1:80.000)

429. LXXXIV. A.K., 5.3.44 at 05:30 [UKNA, HW 5/552, CX/MSS/T267/30 XL 4805]; AOK 7, Ia Nr.539/44 g., 5.8.44 [T312 R1569 F388]

430. Mahlmann, P. (1946b), Engl., App.17

431. AOK 7, Ia Nr.537/44 g., 6.8.44, p.2 [T312 R1569 F406]; **Mahlmann, P. (1946c)**, Engl., p.13

432. AOK 7, Ia Nr.604/44 g., 7.8.44, p.1 [T312 R1569 F413]

433. LXXXIV. A.K., 7.8.44, 20:30 [UKNA, HW 5/554, CX/MSS/T269/139, XL 5187]

434. Akten-Notiz, 8.8.44, 21:15 [T312 R1569 F434]

435. Situation report (LXXXIV. A.K.), 9.8.44 at 17:00 [UKNA, HW 5/556, CX/MSS/T271/131, XL 5463]

436. AOK 7, Ia Nr.664/44 g., 9.8.44, p.1-2 F443-4]

437. Okdo.d.H.Gr.B, Ia Nr.5890/44 g.K., 9.8.44, p.2 [T311 R4 F7004601]; Flivo LXXXIV. A.K., 10.8.44 at 03:00 [UKNA, HW 5/557]

438. LXXXIV. A.K., 10.8.44 at 00:01 [UKNA, HW 5/557, CX/MSS/T272/7, XL 5489]; **Mahlmann, P. (1946b)**, Engl., p.14

439. AOK 7, Ia Nr.636/44, Ia-Tagesmeldung, 10.8.44, p.2 [T312 R1569 F456]

440. *Ibid.*, p.3 [T312 R1569 F457]; WFSt Op.(H), Situation map (Lage West) 11.8.44 (1:80.000) [NARA, via www.wwii-photos-maps.com]

441. Flivo LXXXIV. A.K., 11.8.44 at 09:00 [UKNA, HW 5/558, CX/MSS/T273/121, XL 5739]

442. Mahlmann, P. (1946b), Engl., p.15 & App.20

443. AOK 7, Ia Nr.707/44 g., Ia-Tagesmeldung, 11.8.44, p.3 [T312 R1569 F468]; AOK 7, Ia Nr.730/44 g., 12.8.44 [T312 R1569 F477]; WFSt Op.(H), Situation maps (Lage West) 11.-12.8.44 (1:80.000) [NARA, via www.wwii-photos-maps.com]

444. There are some questions about the composition of this force. It appears to have been a reinforced regiment formed around *GR 558* and may have included the *I./557* as well. When the main body of the *331. I.D.* arrived at the front, it was rerouted and assigned to the *LXXXI. A.K*. As a result, *Rgt. Dobeneck* remained with the *353. I.D.*

445. LXXXIV. A.K., 14.8.44 at 03:30 [UKNA, HW 5/561, CX/MSS/T276/81]; **Mahlmann, P. (1946c)**, Engl., p.16-17; WFSt Op.(H), Situation maps (Lage West) 13.8.44 (1:80.000) [NARA, via www.wwii-photos-maps.com]

446. Mahlmann, P. (1946c), Engl., App.3; LXXXIV. A.K., 15.8.44 at 01:00 [UKNA, HW 5/562, CX/MSS/T277/73, XL 6381] *Gen.* Mahlmann was not sure about the sector and suggests that it ran from north of Les Hardouinières to Larchamp. Most of that sector should have been under the control of the *84. I.D.*, however.

447. LXXXIV. A.K., 16.8.44 at 13:00 [UKNA, HW 5/564, CX/MSS/T279/38, XL 6735]

448. AOK 7 Ia, AOK 7 *Kriegstagebuch la 6 Jun 1944 - 16 Aug 1944*, page for 16 August, not numbered [T312 R1569 F215]; AOK 7, 16.8.44 at 11:00 [UKNA, HW 5/564, CX/MSS/T279/112, XL 6792]; Flivo LXXXIV. A.K., 16.8.44 at 19:00 [UKNA, HW 5/564, CX/MSS/T279/32, XL 6732] Mahlmann suggests that this entire sector was held by the reinforced *353. I.D.* but admits being uncertain

about this. In reality, the northern part of the sector was assigned to the *II. Fs.K.*
449. LXXXIV. A.K., 17.8.44 at 08:00 [UKNA, HW 5/564, CX/MSS/T279/162, XL 6830]; LXXXIV. A.K., 17.8.44 at 08:45 [UKNA, HW 5/564, CX/MSS/T279/162, XL 6830]; **Mahlmann, P. (1946c)**, Engl., p.18-19 & App.5
450. AOK 7, Ia Nr.851/44 g.K., 17.8.44 [T312 R1569 F547]
451. Okdo.d.H.Gr.B, Ia Nr.6288/44 g.K., 19.8.44 [T311 R3 F7002787]
452. Mahlmann, P. (1946c), Engl., p.21-2
453. *Ibid.*, p.22
454. *Ibid.*, p.22-26
455. Mahlmann, P. (1946d), MS # A-986 (Engl.), *353.Inf.Div. (21 Aug - 7 Sep 44), Report of the Commander*, p.31-33
456. Mahlmann, P. (1946c), Engl., p.27
457. Mahlmann, P. (1946d), Engl., p.33-34
458. *Ibid.*, p.38
459. *Ibid.*, p.31-43
460. Mahlmann, P. (1946e), MS # A-987 (Engl.), *353.Inf.Div. (8 - 14 Sep Aug 44), Report of the Commander*, p.44-50
461. Tessin, G. (1974), *9.Band*, p.265

709. Infanterie-Division

1. Index carts of infantry divisions, Verband 709.Inf.Div. [T78 R412 F6380540];·OKH (Chef H Rüst u.BdE) Nr.1153/41 g.K. AHA Ia VIII, 26.3.41 [Available at www.lexikon-der-wehrmacht.de/Zusatz/Heer/15.welle.pdf. Accessed on 10 October 2018]; Documents showing the most basic background of the various 15.Welle divisions [T78 R412 F6380554]
2. OKH, GenStdH Op.Abt.III/Prüf-Nr.15433, *Schematische Kriegsgliederung. Stand: 5.6.41.* [T78 R708]
3. Gen.Kdo.LXXXIV. A.K., *KTB Ia vom 1.10-31.12.42* [T314 R1603 F400]
4. Anl. zu Sonderstab Oehmichen z.Zt. AOK 7 Ia/Stopak Nr.67./44 g.K., 13.5.44, *Übersicht der Küsten- und Eingreifsdivisionen mit panzerbrechenden Waffen, Stand vom 1.5.44* [T312 R1568 F718]
5. OKH/GenStdH/Org.Abt. Nr.I/18298/44 g.K., 24.7.44 [T78 R398 H1/44]
6. Kartei von Inf.-Kommandeuren, index card of *Gen.Maj.* v. Bessel [T78 R908 H6/354]
7. German general staff officers files, index cards of *Gen.Lt.* Nake [T78 R890 H6/26]; Gen.Kdo.LXXXIV. A.K., *Kriegstagebuch vom 1. Jan. bis 30. Juni 1943 des Gen.Kdo.LXXXIV. A.K. Ia* [T314 R1603 F882]; German general staff officers files, index cards of *Gen.d.Art.* Jahn [T78 R887 H6/26]
8. Gen.Kdo.LXXXIV. A.K., *Kriegstagebuch vom 1. Juli bis 31. Dez. 43 des Gen.Kdo.LXXXIV. A.K., Ia* [T314 R1603 F954]; German general staff officers files, index cards of *Gen.d.Art.* Jahn [T78 R887 H6/26]
9. Gen.Kdo.LXXXIV. A.K., *Kriegstagebuch vom 1. Juli bis 31. Dez. 43 des Gen.Kdo.LXXXIV. A.K., Ia* [T314 R1603 F1022]; German general staff officers files, index cards of *Gen.Lt.* von Schlieben [T78 R892 H6/26]

10. Keil's reconstruction of the fighting of his regiment immediately after the beginning of the invasion appears to be accurate. He seems to skip ahead one day around 9 June, however, reporting dates that are one day later than they actually were. This worsens when discussing the fighting on the Montebourg-Quinéville Ridge. Events are linked to different days, when they likely happened on the same day. As a result, the period of fighting in his account is longer than it actually was. On the other hand, the timeline for the fighting after the withdrawal to Cherbourg seems to be mostly correct again. The fact that it is difficult to correct Keil's timeline for even major events illustrates how few accurate German records are available.
11. Keil, G. (1948a), Engl., *Grenadier Regt. 919, Kampfgruppe Keil*, p.117
12. OKH (Chef H Rüst u.BdE) Nr.1153/41 g.K. AHA Ia VIII, 26.3.41 [Available at www.lexikon-der-wehrmacht.de/Zusatz/Heer/15.welle.pdf. Accessed on 10 October 2018]
13. Anl. zu OHH/GenStdH Org.Abt. (I) Nr.400/41 g.K., 19.2.41, *Kriegsgliederung des Feldheeres, Stand: 10. Febr. 1941*, p.15/950 [T78 R404 F6374367] — Hereafter referred to as: OKH, *Kriegsgliederung des Feldheeres, Stand: 10. Febr. 1941*
14. For examples of other divisions see OKH, *Kriegsgliederung des Feldheeres, Stand: 10. Febr. 1941* [T78 R404 H1/88]
15. Hubatsch, W. (reprint 2005a), *Kriegstagebuch des Oberkommandos der Wehrmacht (Wehrmachtsführungsstab), Band II: I. Januar 1942 - 31. Dezember 1942*, Augsburg: Verlagsgruppe Weltbild GmbH, p.704
16. OKH, Anl.2 zu OKH/GenStdH Org.Abt.(I) Nr.4730/42 g.K., 7.10.42 [T78 R405 F6375223]
17. Anl. zu OHH//GenStdH/Org.Abt.(I) (no number), *Kriegsgliederung des Feldheeres (ohne Heerestruppen), Stand: Sommer-Sept.1943*, p.168 T78 R407 F6376341] — Hereafter referred to as: OKH, *Kriegsgliederung des Feldheeres (ohne Heerestruppen), Stand: Sommer-Sept.1943*; OKH, Anl. z. OKH/GenStdH/Org.Abt. Nr.4500/43 g.K., *Kriegsgliederung des Feldheeres (Sollgliederung), Band I: Kommandobehörden u. Divisionsverbände, Stand: September 1943*, 4.10.43, p.168 [T78 R409 F6378033] — Hereafter referred to as: OKH, *Kriegsgliederung des Feldheeres September 1943*
18. OKH, *Kriegsgliederung des Feldheeres September 1943*, p.168 [T78 R409 F6378033]
19. *Ibid.*
20. OKH, *Kriegsgliederung des Feldheeres, Stand: 10. Febr. 1941*, p.15/950 [T78 R404 F6374367]; OKH, Anl.2 zu OKH/GenStdH Org.Abt.(I) Nr.4730/42 g.K., 7.10.42 [T78 R405 F6375223]
21. Anl.2 z. 709. I.D., Abt. Ia Nr.850/43 g.K., (Kriegsgliederung) *709. I.D., Stand: 1.8.43*, 3.8.43 [T314 R1604 F796]
22. OKH, *Kriegsgliederung des Feldheeres September 1943*, p.168 [T78 R409 F6378033]
23. *Ibid.*
24. Gen.Kdo.LXXXIV. A.K., *Kriegstagebuch vom 1. Juli bis 31. Dez. 43 des Gen.Kdo.LXXXIV. A.K., Ia* [T314 R1603 F988]; Gen.Kdo.LXXXIV. A.K., *Kriegstagebuch vom 1. Juli bis 31. Dez. 43 des Gen.*

Kdo.LXXXIV. A.K., Ia [T314 R1603 F991]; **Keil, G. (1948a)**, MS # C-018 (Germ.), *Bericht über die Kämpfe des hessisch-thüringischen Grenadier-Regiments 919 und der Kampfgruppe Keil*, p.4
25. AOK 7, Kriegsgliederung 7. Armee, Stand 18.5.44, (Kriegsgliederung) *709. I.D. Stand: 1.5.44* [T312 R1566 F217]; 709. I.D., (Kriegsgliederung) *709.Inf.Division, Stand: 1.5.1944* [T78 R672 H41/61b]
26. 709. I.D., (Kriegsgliederung) *709.Inf.Division, Stand: 1.5.1944* [T78 R672 H41/61b]
27. Kartei von Inf.-Kommandeuren, index cards of *Obst.* Köhn, *Gen.Maj.* Manussi and *Obst.* Rohrbach [T78 R908 H6/354]
28. C.S.D.I.C. (UK) S.R. Report, S.R.M.621 [UKNA, WO 208/418]
29. OKH GenStdH/Org.Abt. Nr.II3/2784/44 g. 19.4.44, p.2 [T78 R533 F1019]
30. Gen.Kdo.LXXXIV. A.K., *Kriegstagebuch vom 1. Juli bis 31. Dez. 43 des Gen.Kdo.LXXXIV. A.K., Ia* [T314 R1603 F1009]; OKH, Anl.2 zu OKH Chef H Rüst u. BdE, AHA / ZASt. Nr.7000/43 g.K., p.146 [T78 R401 F6371583]
31. AOK 7, Kriegsgliederung 7. Armee, Stand 18.5.44, (Kriegsgliederung) *709. I.D. Stand: 1.5.44* [T312 R1566 F217]; **Tessin, G. (1975)**, *12.Band*, p.322 & 324; OKH/GenStdH/Org.Abt. Nr.II/32784/44 g., 19.4.44, p.2 [T78 R420 F6389544]
32. 709. I.D., (Kriegsgliederung) *709.Inf.Division, Stand: 1.5.1944* [T78 R672 H41/61b]
33. AOK 7, Kriegsgliederung 7. Armee, Stand 18.5.44, (Kriegsgliederung) *709. I.D. Stand: 1.5.44* [T312 R1566 F217]; PWIS(H)/100, PW taken on 9 Jun 44 [UKNA, WO 208/3621]
34. 709. I.D., (Kriegsgliederung) *709.Inf.Division, Stand: 1.5.1944* [T78 R672 H41/61b]; PWIS(H)/LF/169, 23 Jun 44 [UKNA, WO 208/3630]
35. AOK 7, Kriegsgliederung 7. Armee, Stand 18.5.44, (Kriegsgliederung) *709. I.D. Stand: 1.5.44* [T312 R1566 F217]
36. PWIS(H)/KP/74, 29 Jun 44 [UKNA, WO 208/3623]
37. AOK 7, Kriegsgliederung 7. Armee, Stand 18.5.44, (Kriegsgliederung) *709. I.D. Stand: 1.5.44* [T312 R1566 F217]; 709. I.D., (Kriegsgliederung) *709.Inf.Division, Stand: 1.5.1944* [T78 R672 H41/61b]
38. PWIS(H)/100, POW taken on 9 Jun 44 [UKNA, WO 208/3621]
39. OKH, *Kriegsgliederung des Feldheeres September 1943*, p.168 [T78 R409 F6378033]; K.St.N. (Heer) Nr.131F, Notetat, *Schützenkompanie (bodenständig)*, 1.12.42 [T78 R397 F6366295-8]
40. PWIS(H)/LF/169, 23 Jun 44 [UKNA, WO 208/3630]; PWIS(H)/LF/181, 27 Jun 44 [UKNA, WO 208/3630]
41. 709. I.D., (Kriegsgliederung) *709.Inf.Division, Stand: 1.5.1944* [T78 R672 H41/61b]; PWIS(H)/LF/169, 23 Jun 44 [UKNA, WO 208/3630]; PWIS(H)/LF/181, 27 Jun 44 [UKNA, WO 208/3630]
42. PWIS(H)/LF/169, 23 Jun 44 [UKNA, WO 208/3630]; PWIS(H)/LF/181, 27 Jun 44 [UKNA, WO 208/3630]
43. *Ibid.*
44. 709. I.D., (Kriegsgliederung) *709.Inf.Division, Stand: 1.5.1944* [T78 R672 H41/61b]
45. AOK 7, Kriegsgliederung 7. Armee, Stand 12.3.44, *709. Infanterie-Division, Stand: 1.2.44* [T312 R1566 F156]; AOK 7,

Kriegsgliederung 7. Armee, Stand 10.4.44, *709. Infanterie-Division, Stand: 1.3.44* [T312 R1566 F194]
46. Schlieben, K.W. v. **(1948)**, MS # B-845 (Germ.), *Die deutsche 709.Infanterie - Division vor und während der anglo-amerikanischen Invasion vom 6. Juni 1944*, p.3; PWIS(H)/KP/74, 29 Jun 44 [UKNA, WO 208/3623]; Gen.Kdo.LXXXIV. A.K., Ia Nr.2127/43 g.K., 14.12.43, p.1-3 [T314 R1604 F1281-3]
47. PWIS(H)/KP/74, 29 Jun 44 [UKNA, WO 208/3623]
48. See the Kriegsgliederungen from 1.2. to 1.11.43 in T312 R1553 & T312 R1559; AOK 7, Anl.1 zu AOK 7, O.Qu./Qu.1 Nr.1271/43 g.K.v.8.11.43, *Übersicht über vorhandene s.Pak* [T312 R1562 F830]
49. 709. I.D., Anl.2 zu *709. I.D.*, Abt. Ia Nr.1240/43 g.K., *Kriegsgliederung, Stand: 1.11.43*, 3.11.43 [T314 R1604 F1133]
50. 709. I.D., Anl.2 zu *709. I.D.*, Abt. Ia Nr.1240/43 g.K., *Kriegsgliederung, Stand: 1.11.43*, 3.11.43 [T314 R1604 F1133]
51. Gen.Kdo.LXXXV. A.K., Ia Nr.2127/43 g.K., 14.12.43, p.3 [T314 R1604 F1283]
52. AOK 7, Kriegsgliederung 7. Armee, Stand 10.4.44, *709. Infanterie-Division, Stand: 1.3.44* [T312 R1566 F194]; PWIS(H)/KP/74, 29 Jun 44 [UKNA, WO 208/3623] The *Gliederung* suggests there were six 5 cm and three 7.5 cm AT guns, but this is probably a mix up because it does not match the weapons total of the division in the same document.
53. AOK 7, Kriegsgliederung 7. Armee, Stand 18.5.44, (Kriegsgliederung) *709. I.D. Stand: 1.5.44* [T312 R1566 F217]
54. Anl. zu Sonderstab Oehmichen z.Zt. AOK 7 Ia/Stopak Nr.67./44 g.K., 13.5.44, *Übersicht der Küsten- und Eingreifsdivisionen mit panzerbrechenden Waffen, Stand vom 1.5.44* [T312 R1568 F718]
55. Keil, G. **(1948a)**, Germ., p.29
56. AOK 7, Kriegsgliederung 7. Armee, Stand 18.5.44, (Kriegsgliederung) *709. I.D. Stand: 1.5.44* [T312 R1566 F217]; PWIS(H)/KP/74, 29 Jun 44 [UKNA, WO 208/3623]
57. AOK 7, Kriegsgliederung 7. Armee, Stand 18.5.44, (Kriegsgliederung) *709. I.D. Stand: 1.5.44* [T312 R1566 F217]; PWIS(H)/LDC/68, 3 Jul 44 [UKNA, WO 208/3646]
58. PWIS(H)/LDC/68, 3 Jul 44 [UKNA, WO 208/3646]
59. This will be discussed in detail later
60. AOK 7/O.Qu./Qu.1, *Kriegstagebuch der Oberquartiermeisterabteilung für die Zeit vom 1.Febr. 1944 bis 29. Febr. 1944* [T312 R1570 F887]; See the later information on Art.Rgt.1709
61. BvTO b. AOK 7, Bv.T.O. Nr.13/44 g.K., *Tätigkeitsbericht für die Zeit vom 1. Jul bis 31. Dezember 1943.*, 2.1.44, p.8 [T312 R1563 F10]
62. 709. I.D., (Kriegsgliederung) *709.Inf.Division, Stand: 1.5.1944* [T78 R672 H41/61b]
63. AOK 7, Kriegsgliederung 7. Armee, Stand 18.5.44, (Kriegsgliederung) *709. I.D. Stand: 1.5.44* [T312 R1566 F217]
64. PWIS(H)/102, POW taken on 9 Jun 44, p.1 [UKNA, WO 208/3622]; PWIS(H)/LF/153, 18 Jun 44 [UKNA, WO 208/3622]; PWIS(H)/LF/242, 5 Jul 44 [UKNA, WO 208/3631]; **Keil, G. (1948a)**, Engl., p.1
65. AOK 7, Kriegsgliederung 7. Armee, Stand 18.5.44, (Kriegsgliederung) *709. I.D. Stand: 1.5.44* [T312 R1566 F217]
66. Chazette, A. **(2012)**, *Atlantikwall Utah Beach - de la baie des Veys à Quinéville*, p.28, Editions Histoire & Fortifications, Vertou
67. Anl.1 zu OKH Chef H Rüst u. BdE AHA Ia (I) Nr.3414/43 g.K., 9.7.43, *242. Bodenständige Inf.Div.* [T78 R849 H36/157]
68. 709. I.D., Anl.2 zu *709. I.D.*, Abt. Ia Nr.1240/43 g.K., *Kriegsgliederung, Stand: 1.11.43*, 3.11.43 [T314 R1604 F1133]
69. AOK 7, Kriegsgliederung 7. Armee, Stand 12.1.44, *709. Infanterie-Division, Stand: 1.1.1944* [T312 R1566 F53]
70. 709. I.D., (Kriegsgliederung) *709.Inf.Division, Stand: 1.5.1944* [T78 R672 H41/61b]
71. Keil, G. **(1948a)**, Germ., p.29; AOK 7, Kriegsgliederung 7. Armee, Stand 10.4.44, *709. Infanterie-Division, Stand: 1.3.44* [T312 R1566 F194]
72. AOK 7, Kriegsgliederung 7. Armee, Stand 12.1.44, *709. Infanterie-Division, Stand: 1.1.1944* [T312 R1566 F53]; **Keil, G. (1948a)**, Germ. p.29
73. AOK 7, Kriegsgliederung 7. Armee, Stand: 20.10.43, *709. Infanterie-Division, Stand: 1.9.43* [T312 R1559 F655]
74. AOK 7, Kriegsgliederung 7. Armee, Stand: 20.10.43, *709. Infanterie-Division, Stand: 1.9.43* [T312 R1559 F655]; AOK 7, Kriegsgliederung 7. Armee, Stand: 15.11.43, *709.Infanterie-Division, Stand: 9.10.43* [T312 R1559 F690]
75. PWIS(H)/LF/221, 4 Jul 44 [UKNA, WO 208/3631]
76. AOK 7, Kriegsgliederung 7. Armee, Stand: 20.10.43, (Kriegsgliederung) *709.Infanterie-Division, Stand: 1.9.43* [T312 R1559 F655]; AOK 7, Kriegsgliederung 7. Armee, Stand: 15.11.43, (Kriegsgliederung) *709.Infanterie-Division, Stand: 9.10.43* [T312 R1559 F690]; **Keil, G. (1948a)**, Engl., p.30
77. PWIS(H)/LF/221, 4 Jul 44 [UKNA, WO 208/3631]
78. **Keil, G. (1948a)**, Engl., p.1 & 6; 709. I.D., (Kriegsgliederung) *709.Inf.Division, Stand: 1.5.1944* [T78 R672 H41/61b]
79. AOK 7, Kriegsgliederung 7. Armee, Stand 10.4.44, *709. Infanterie-Division, Stand: 1.3.44* [T312 R1566 F194]; AOK 7, Kriegsgliederung 7. Armee, Stand 18.5.44, (Kriegsgliederung) *709. I.D. Stand: 1.5.44* [T312 R1566 F217]; Anl.3 zu AOK 7 Ia 3000/44 g.K., *Übersicht über Bewegl. Truppenteile bei Eingesetzten oder im Reserve befindlichen Div.*, p.1, 4.4.44 [T312 R1565 F427]; C.S.D.I.C. (UK), S.I.R.360, p.1 [NARA, RG 165, Box 560, Folder 4]; PWIS(H)/102, POW taken on 9 Jun 44, p.1 [UKNA, WO 208/3622]
80. **Keil, G. (1948a)**, Engl., p.4-6; Armee-Oberkommando Ia Nr.900/44 g.K., 5.2.44, p.2 [T312 R1565 F46]
81. Anl.3 zu AOK 7 Ia 3000/44 g.K., p.1, 4.4.44 [T312 R1565 F427]
82. **Keil, G. (1948a)**, Engl., p.22 & (Germ.) Anl.3
83. Ibid.
84. PWIS(H)/LF/169, 23 Jun 44 [UKNA, WO 208/3630]
85. PWIS(H)/LF/153, 18 Jun 44 [UKNA, WO 208/3622]
86. PWIS(H)/LDC/124, 14 Jul 44 [UKNA, WO 208/3646]
87. OKH, *Kriegsgliederung des Feldheeres, Stand: 10. Febr. 1941*, p.15/950 [T78 R404 F6374367]; OKH, Anl.2 zu OKH/GenStdH Org.Abt.(I) Nr.4730/42 g.K., 7.10.42 [T78 R405 F6375223]
88. OKH, *Kriegsgliederung des Feldheeres (ohne Heerestruppen), Stand: Sommer-Sept.1943*, p.168 [T78 R407 F6376341]; Gen.Kdo. LXXXIV. A.K., Ia-Tagesmeldung, 31.8.43 [T314 R1604 F837]
89. AOK 7, Kriegsgliederung 7. Armee, Stand 18.5.44, (Kriegsgliederung) *709. I.D. Stand: 1.5.44* [T312 R1566 F217]
90. PWIS(H)/LDC/76, 4 Jul 44, p.2 [UKNA, WO 208/3646]
91. AOK 7, Kriegsgliederung 7. Armee, Stand 18.5.44, (Kriegsgliederung) *709. I.D. Stand: 1.5.44* [T312 R1566 F217]
92. OKH, *Kriegsgliederung des Feldheeres, Stand: 10. Febr. 1941*, p.15/950 [T78 R404 F6374367]
93. For the latest report before the changes see: AOK 7, Kriegsgliederung 7. Armee, Stand: 21.5.43, (Kriegsgliederung) *709.Infanterie-Division, Stand: 1.5.43* [T312 R1553 F631]
94. Gen.Kdo.LXXXIV. A.K., *Kriegstagebuch vom 1. Jan. bis 30. Juni 1943 des* Gen.Kdo.LXXXIV. A.K. *Ia* [T314 R1603 F910]
95. AOK 7 Ia/Stoart Nr.638/43 g., 15.6.43 [T314 R1604 F575]
96. Gen.Kdo.LXXXIV. A.K., Ia Nr.5777/43 (2973) g., 11.7.43 [T314 R1604 F683]
97. 709. I.D., Anl.2 zu *709. I.D.*, Abt. Ia Nr.850/43 g.K., (Kriegsgliederung) *709. I.D., Stand: 1.8.43*, 3.8.43 [T314 R1604 F796]
98. 709. I.D., Anl.2 zu *709. I.D.*, Abt. Ia Nr.1112/43, (Kriegsgliederung) *709.Inf.Div., Stand: 1.10.1943*, 3.10.43 [T314 R1604 F1007]
99. AOK 7, GenStdH Op.Abt.III/Prüf-Nr.36278, *Schematische Kriegsgliederung, Stand: 25.7.43* [T78 R708 H22/339a]
100. 709. I.D., Anl.2 zu *709. I.D.*, Abt. Ia Nr.1112/43, (Kriegsgliederung) *709.Inf.Div., Stand: 1.10.1943*, 3.10.43 [T314 R1604 F1007]
101. OKH, Anl. 4 zu OKH/GenStdH/Org.Abt.Nr.I/5700/43 g.K., *Artillerie im Bereich A.O.K.7*, 19.12.43, p.1 [T78 R528 F888]; 709. I.D., Anl.2 zu *709. I.D.*, Abt. Ia Nr.10/44 g.K., *Kriegsgliederung, Stand: 1.1.44*, 3.1.44 [T314 R1604 F1353]
102. Ob.West Obkdo.H.Gr.D, II. Ausfertigung Ia, K.T.B. vom 1.10 - 31.10.43, p.21 [T311 R20 F7023238]; Gen.Kdo.LXXXIV. A.K., Ia Nr.8301/43 (4231) g.II.Ang., 3.10.43 [T314 R1604 F1012]
103. Tessin, G. **(1975)**, *12.Band*. p.77
104. OKH, Anl. 1 zu OKH/GenStdH/Org.Abt.Nr.I/5700/43 g.K., *Gültige K.St.N.* [T78 R528 F879]; The *KStN's* can be found in T78 R397.
105. PWIS(H)/LF/258, 7 Jul 44, p.1 [UKNA, WO 208/3631]
106. Ibid.; PWIS(H)/LDC/93, 9 Jul 44, p.1 [UKNA, WO 208/3646]
107. PWIS(H)/LF/258, 7 Jul 44, p.1 [UKNA, WO 208/3631]
108. Ibid.
109. OKH, *Kriegsgliederung des Feldheeres, Stand: 10. Febr. 1941*, p.15/950 [T78 R404 F6374367]; 709. I.D., Anl.4 zu *709. I.D.* Abt.Ia Nr.5/42 g.K., 19.1.1942 [T314 R742 F79]
110. OKH, Chef H Rüst u BdE Nr.690/42 g. AHA Ib (II), 8.1.42 [T314 R742 F109]
111. OKH, Anl.2 zu OKH/GenStdH Org.Abt.(I) Nr.4730/42 g.K., 7.10.42 [T78 R405 F6375223]
112. AOK 7, Kriegsgliederung 7. Armee, Stand: 12.3.43, *709. Infanterie-Division, Stand: 1.2.43* [T312 R1553 F528]
113. 709. I.D., Anl. zu *709. I.D.*, Ia Nr.1221/42 g.K., *Kriegsgliederung, Stand: 5.12.42*, 7.12.42 [T314 R1603 F734]; AOK

7, Kriegsgliederung 7. Armee, Stand: 4.2.43, (Kriegsgliederung) *709.Infanterie-Div., Stand: 10.12.42* [T312 R1553 F474]; AOK 7, Kriegsgliederung 7. Armee, Stand: 10.2.43, (Kriegsgliederung) *709.Infanterie-Div., Stand: 10.12.42* [T312 R1553 F500] A *Gliederung* of 10 December 1942 listed the 1st Battery with French 10.5 cm light field howitzers, the 2nd battery with Czech light howitzers and the 3rd battery with *7,5 cm F.K. nA 16's*. During this period (up to about April 1943), there was a discrepancy between the *Kriegsgliederungen* in the corps and field-army records. The corps records consistently list the 2nd and 4th batteries with *7,5 cm F.K. nA 16's*.

114. AOK 7, Kriegsgliederung 7. Armee, Stand: 12.3.43, *709. Infanterie-Division, Stand: 1.2.43* [T312 R1553 F528]

115. AOK 7, Kriegsgliederung 7. Armee, Stand: 15.4.43, (Kriegsgliederung) *709. I.D., Stand: 1.4.43* [T312 R1553 F598]; AOK 7, Kriegsgliederung 7. Armee, Stand: 21.5.43, (Kriegsgliederung) *709.Infanterie-Division, Stand: 1.5.43* [T312 R1553 F631]

116. (*709. I.D.*), (Kriegsgliederung) *709. I.D., Stand: 1.6.43* [T314 R1604 F649]; AOK 7, Kriegsgliederung 7. Armee, Stand 7.12.43, (Kriegsgliederung) *709.Infanterie-Division, Stand: 1.11.43* [T312 R1559 F725]

117. AOK 7/O.Qu., *Kriegstagebuch Nr.42, 1. August 1943 - 31. August 1943* [T313 R1562 F265]; AOK 7, Kriegsgliederung 7. Armee, Stand: 20.10.43, (Kriegsgliederung) *709. I.D., Stand: 1.9.43* [T312 R1559 F654]

118. 709. I.D., Anl.2 zu *709. I.D., Abt. Ia Nr.1240/43 g.K., Kriegsgliederung, Stand: 1.11.43*, 3.11.43 [T314 R1604 F1133]

119. OKH, Anl. 4 zu OKH/GenStdH/Org.Abt.Nr.I/5700/43 g.K., *Artillerie im Bereich A.O.K.7*, 19.12.43, p.1-2 [T78 R528 F888-9]; 709. I.D., Anl.2 zu *709. I.D., Abt. Ia Nr.1335/43 g.K., Kriegsgliederung, Stand: 1.12.1943*, 3.12.43 [T314 R1604 F1255]; 709. I.D., Anl.2 zu *709. I.D., Abt. Ia Nr.10/44 g.K., Kriegsgliederung, Stand: 1.1.44*, 3.1.44 [T314 R1604 F1353]

120. OKH, Anl. 1 zu OKH/GenStdH/Org.Abt.Nr.I/5700/43 g.K., *Gültige K.St.N.* [T78 R528 F879]

121. 709. I.D., Anl.2 zu *709. I.D., Abt. Ia Nr.10/44 g.K., Kriegsgliederung, Stand: 1.1.44*, 3.1.44 [T314 R1604 F1353] The descriptions of the guns in 1st, 2nd and 4th Batteries were vague or even a bit off, but the types are clear from other documents.

122. AOK 7, Kriegsgliederung 7. Armee, Stand 10.4.44, *709. Infanterie-Division, Stand: 1.3.44* [T312 R1566 F194] The microfilms of these documents are very dark, presumably because certain areas were in colour. The originals are likely to be better, but these have not been examined.

123. 709.I.D., (Kriegsgliederung) *709.Inf.Division, Stand: 1.5.1944* [T78 R672 H41/61b]; AOK 7, Kriegsgliederung 7.Armee, Stand 18.5.44, (Kriegsgliederung) *709.I.D. Stand: 1.5.44* [T312 R1566 F217]; AOK 7/O.Qu., *Kriegstagebuch der Oberquartiermeister-abteilung AOK 7 für die Zeit vom 1.3.44 - 31.3.44* [T312 R1570 F1017]; FID-DZ No.196, 11 July 1944, p.1-2 [NARA, RG 498, Box 1326]

124. PWIS(H)/LDC/93, 9 Jul 44, p.1 [UKNA, WO 208/3645]

125. FID-DZ No.196, 11 July 1944, p.1-2 [NARA, RG 498, Box 1326]

126. C.S.D.I.C. (UK) S.I.R.511, p.1 [NARA, RG 165, Box 659, Folder 2]; KStN 403F, 433F and 582F [T78 R397 F6366341-8 & 62-5]

127. FID-DZ No.196, 11 July 1944, p.2 [NARA, RG 498, Box 1326]

128. *K.St.N. (Heer) Nr.433F, Kriegsetat, Batterie leichte Feldhaubitzen (zu 3 oder 4 Geschützen) (bodenständig), 1.11.43* [T78 R397 F6366342-8]

129. *K.St.N. (Heer) Nr.582F, Kriegsetat, Stabsbatterie einer Artillerie-Abteilung (bodenständig), 1.11.43* [T78 R397 F6366362-5]

130. Gen.Kdo.LXXXIV. A.K., Ia Art. Nr.1958/43 g.K., 11.11.43, p.2 [T314 R1604 F1168]; OKH, Anl. 4 zu OKH/GenStdH/Org.Abt. Nr.I/5700/43 g.K., *Artillerie im Bereich A.O.K.7*, 19.12.43, p.1 [T78 R528 F888]; 709. I.D., Anl.2 zu *709. I.D., Abt. Ia Nr.10/44 g.K., Kriegsgliederung, Stand: 1.1.44*, 3.1.44 [T314 R1604 F1353]

131. Gen.Kdo.LXXXIV. A.K., Ia Art. Nr.1958/43 g.K., 11.11.43, p.2 [T314 R1604 F1168]; OKH, Anl. 4 zu OKH/GenStdH/Org.Abt. Nr.I/5700/43 g.K., *Artillerie im Bereich A.O.K.7*, 19.12.43, p.1 [T78 R528 F888]

132. OKH, Anl. 1 zu OKH/GenStdH/Org.Abt.Nr.I/5700/43 g.K., *Gültige K.St.N.* [T78 R528 F879]

133. OKH, Anl. 4 zu OKH/GenStdH/Org.Abt.Nr.I/5700/43 g.K., *Artillerie im Bereich A.O.K.7*, 19.12.43, p.1 [T78 R528 F888]; 709. I.D., Anl.2 zu *709. I.D., Abt. Ia Nr.10/44 g.K., Kriegsgliederung, Stand: 1.1.44*, 3.1.44 [T314 R1604 F1353]

134. PWIS(H)/LDC/115, 13 Jul 44, p.2 [UKNA, WO 208/3646]; AOK 7, Kriegsgliederung 7. Armee, Stand 10.4.44, *709. Infanterie-Division, Stand: 1.3.44* [T312 R1566 F194]

135. PWIS(H)/LDC/93, 9 Jul 44, p.1 [UKNA, WO 208/3646]

136. KStN 403F, 433F, 459F and 582F [T78 R397 F6366341-8, 53-55 & 62-5]

137. 709. I.D., (Kriegsgliederung) *709.Inf.Division, Stand: 1.5.1944* [T78 R672 H41/61b]

138. FID-DZ No.174, 5 July 1944, p.2 [NARA, RG 498, Box 1326]

139. PWIS(H)/LDC/115, 13 Jul 44, p.2 [UKNA, WO 208/3646]

140. C.S.D.I.C. (UK) S.I.R. 491, p.1 [NARA, RG 165, Box 659, Folder 2]; FID-DZ No.158, 2 July 1944 [NARA, RG 498, Box 1326]

141. 709. I.D., Anl.2 zu *709. I.D., Abt. Ia Nr.1240/43 g.K., Kriegsgliederung, Stand: 1.11.43*, 3.11.43 [T314 R1604 F1133]; Some records state the guns actually were the similar *7,62 cm F.K.297(r)*, which fired the same ammunition. [Gen.Kdo.LXXXIV. A.K., Ia Art. Nr.1958/43 g.K., 11.11.43, p.3 in T314 R1604 F1169]

142. Gen.Kdo.LXXXIV. A.K., Ia Art. Nr.1958/43 g.K., 11.11.43, p.3 [T314 R1604 F1169]

143. AOK 7/O.Qu., *Kriegstagebuch Nr.46, 1.Dez.1943 - 31.Dez.1943* [T312 R1562 F984]

144. 709. I.D., (Kriegsgliederung) *709.Inf.Division, Stand: 1.5.1944* [T78 R672 H41/61b]

145. PWIS(H)/LF/258, 7 Jul 44, p.1 [UKNA, WO 208/3631]

146. PWIS(H)/LDC/31, 28 Jun 44, p.1 [UKNA, WO 208/3645]

147. *Ibid.*, p.1-2. Identifying the exact equipment is complicated by the use of names rather than official German terminology and use of Allied classifications which used its own numbering system. In the case of the "Type 6", the equipment has not been identified.

148. *Ibid.*, p.1-3

149. AOK 7/O.Qu., *Kriegstagebuch Nr.46, 1.Dez.1943 - 31.Dez.1943* [T312 R1562 F979]; 709. I.D., Anl.2 zu *709. I.D., Abt. Ia Nr.10/44 g.K., Kriegsgliederung, Stand: 1.1.44*, 3.1.44 [T314 R1604 F1353]

150. 709. I.D., Anl.2 zu *709. I.D., Abt. Ia Nr.10/44 g.K., Kriegsgliederung, Stand: 1.1.44*, 3.1.44 [T314 R1604 F1353]; AOK 7, Kriegsgliederung 7. Armee, Stand 10.4.44, *709. Infanterie-Division, Stand: 1.3.44* [T312 R1566 F194] AOK 7, Kriegsgliederung 7. Armee, Stand 12.1.44, *709. Infanterie-Division, Stand: 1.1.1944* [T312 R1566 F53]

151. AOK 7, Kriegsgliederung 7. Armee, Stand 14.2.44, *709. Infanterie-Division, Stand: 1.2.44* [T312 R1566 F120]

152. Ob.West, Anl.4 zu Gen.d.Art.b.Ob.West, Ib Nr.484/44 g.K., *Heeres-Küsten-Artillerie (situation 1.2.44)*, 20.2.44 [CAMO, Bestand 500, Findbuch 12451, Akte 418]; Ob.West, Anl.4 zu Gen.d.Art.b.Ob.West, Ib Nr.788/44 g.K., *Heeres-Küsten-Artillerie, Stand vom 1.3.44*, 20.3.44 [CAMO, Bestand 500, Findbuch 12451, Akte 418]; AOK 7 Ia, Anlage zum KTB Führungsabteilung, Lagekarten A.O.K.7 vom 6.6.44

153. AOK 7/O.Qu./Qu.1, *Kriegstagebuch der Oberquartiermeisterabteilung für die Zeit vom 1.Febr. 1944 bis 29. Febr. 1944* [T312 R1570 F887]

154. Gen.d.Art.b.Ob.West Ib Nr.1077/44 g.K., *Nicht eingesetzte Geschütze, Stand v.1.4.44*, 18.4.44 [CAMO, Bestand 500, Findbuch 12451, Akte 418]; General d.Art.b.Ob.West Ib Nr.1077/44 g.K., *Landesabwehrgeschütze, Stand v. 1.4.44*, 18.4.44 [CAMO, Bestand 500, Findbuch 12451, Akte 418]

155. Schlieben, K.W. v. (1948), Germ., p.16-17

156. General d.Art.b.Ob.West Ib Nr.1077/44 g.K., *Divisions-Artillerie: Stand v.1.4.44*, 18.4.44 [CAMO, Bestand 500, Findbuch 12451, Akte 418]

157. AOK 7, Kriegsgliederung 7. Armee, Stand 10.4.44, *709. Infanterie-Division, Stand: 1.3.44* [T312 R1566 F194] AOK 7, Kriegsgliederung 7. Armee, Stand 12.1.44, *709. Infanterie-Division, Stand: 1.1.1944* [T312 R1566 F53]

158. General d.Art.b.Ob.West Ib Nr.1077/44 g.K., *Nicht eingesetzte Geschütze, Stand v.1.4.44*, 18.4.44 [CAMO, Bestand 500, Findbuch 12451, Akte 418]

159. Historical Section (G.S.), Army Headquarters (1951), *Report No. 41, The German Defences in the Courseulles St.Auvin Area of the Normandy Coast - Information from German sources*, App. C, D & G; PWIS(H)/LDC/16, p.2 [UKNA, WO 208/3645]

160. AOK 7, Kriegsgliederung 7. Armee, Stand 18.5.44, (Kriegsgliederung) *709. I.D. Stand: 1.5.44* [T312 R1566 F217]; **Hoffmann (1944)**, *Bericht über Kampfgruppe v. Schlieben*, p.4 [T312 R1566 F363]

161. OKH/GenStdH/Org.Abt. Nr.I/16998/44 g.K., 15.5.44 [T78 R526 F92-3]

162. Gen.Kdo.LXXXIV. A.K., Ia Nr.9855/43 (5007) g., 25.11.43 [T314 R1604 F1197]; Inv.-Gespräch (AOK 7) Ia mit Chef LXXXIV. A.K., 20.11.43 [T312 R1559 F191]

163. Sonderstab Oehmichen, z.Zt. AOK 7 Ia Stopak Nr.67/44

g.K., *Bericht über das Kommando des Sonderstabes zum AOK 7*, 13.5.44, p.18 [T312 R1568 F701]
164. Feldpostübersicht
165. AOK 7, Kriegsgliederung 7. Armee, Stand 18.5.44, (Kriegsgliederung) *709. I.D. Stand: 1.5.44* [T312 R1566 F217];
166. Zetterling, N. (2000), *Normandy 1944, German Military Organisation, Combat Power and Organisational Effectiveness*, Winipeg: J.J.Fedorowicz Publishing, p.292
167. *Kriegsgliederung des Feldheeres, Stand: 10. Febr. 1941*, p.15/950 [T78 R404 F6374367] Tessin states that *Pz.Jg.Kp. 709* had been raised on 2 May 1941, along with the rest of the division, but this does not match the earliest known *Sollgliederung* of the division. [**Tessin, G. (1975)**, *12.Band*, p.164]
168. OKH, Anl.2 zu OKH/GenStdH Org.Abt.(I) Nr.4730/42 g.K., 7.10.42 [T78 R405 F6375223]
169. AOK 7/O.Qu., *Kriegstagebuch Nr.45, 1.Nov.1943 - 30.Nov.1943* [T312 R1562 F769]; **Rösgen, P.W. (1944)**, *Bericht über den Heldenkampf der Panzerjäger Abteilung 709 im Raume Cherbourg / Frankreich*, p.1 [T78 R672 H41/61a]
170. 709. I.D., Anl.3 zu *709. I.D.*, Abt. Ia Nr.115/43 g.K., *Kriegsgliederung, Stand: 1.2.43*, 3.2.43 [T314 R1604 F247]
171. AOK 7, Kriegsgliederung 7. Armee, Stand: 15.4.43, (Kriegsgliederung) *709.Infanterie-Division, Stand: 1.4.43* [T312 R1553 F598]; AOK 7, Kriegsgliederung 7. Armee, Stand: 21.5.43, (Kriegsgliederung) *709.Infanterie-Division, Stand: 1.5.43* [T312 R1553 F631]
172. (*709. I.D.*,) (Kriegsgliederung) *709. I.D., Stand: 1.6.43* [T314 R1604 F649]
173. Gen.Kdo.LXXXIV. A.K., Ia Nr.5345/43 (2743) g., 30.6.43 [T314 R1604 F600]; 709. I.D., Anl.2 zu *709. I.D.*, Abt. Ia Nr.741/43 g.K., *Kriegsgliederung, Stand: 1.7.43*, 3.4.43 [T314 R1604 F670]
174. Gen.Kdo.LXXXIV. A.K., Ia Nr.5053/43 (2575) g., 16.6.43 [T314 R1604 F577]
175. 709. I.D., Anl.2 zu *709. I.D.*, Abt. Ia Nr.741/43 g.K., *Kriegsgliederung, Stand: 1.7.43*, 3.4.43 [T314 R1604 F670]
176. Gen.Kdo.LXXXIV. A.K., Ia Nr.5664/43 (2907) g., 8.7.43 [T314 R1604 F680-1]
177. Gen.Kdo.LXXXIV. A.K., Ia Nr.5920/43 (3041) g., 16.7.43 [T314 R1604 F698]
178. Gen.Kdo.LXXXIV. A.K., Ia Nr.6230/43 (3208) g., 26.7.43 [T314 R1604 F729]
179. Gen.Kdo.LXXXIV. A.K., Ia Nr.6673/43 (3423) g., 8.8.43, p.1 [T314 R1604 F804]
180. *Ibid.*, p.1-2 [T314 R1604 F804-5]
181. AOK 7/O.Qu., *Kriegstagebuch Nr.42, 1. August 1943-31. August 1943* [T312 R1562 F264-5]
182. *Ibid.* [T312 R1562 F274]
183. *Ibid.* [T312 R1562 F264]
184. AOK 7, Kriegsgliederung 7. Armee, Stand: 20.10.43, (Kriegsgliederung) *709. I.D., Stand: 1.9.43* [T312 R1559 F655]
185. Pz.Jg.Kp. 709, Az. 12, Nr.291/43 g., 5.9.43 [BaMa RH 10/248]
186. Gen.Kdo.LXXXIV. A.K., Anl. zu Gen.Kdo.LXXXIV. A.K., Ia Nr.1808/43 g.K., *Fragebogen über die Verteidigungsfähigkeit des LXXXIV. A.K. nach dem Stande vom 1.10.1943*, 410.43, p.3 [T314 R1604 F1023]; Gen.Kdo.LXXXIV. A.K., Ia Nr.6673/43 (3423) g., 8.8.43, p.1 [T314 R1604 F804]
187. Pz.Jg.Kp. 709, Az. 12, Nr.291/43 g., 5.9.43 [BaMa RH 10/248]
188. 709. I.D., Anl.2 zu *709. I.D.*, Abt. Ia Nr.1112/43, (Kriegsgliederung) *709.Inf.Div., Stand: 1.10.1943*, 3.10.43 [T314 R1604 F1007]; AOK 7, Kriegsgliederung 7. Armee, Stand: 15.11.43, *709.Infanterie-Division, Stand: 9.10.43* [T312 R1559 F690]
189. AOK 7, Kriegsgliederung 7. Armee, Stand 7.12.43, (Kriegsgliederung) *709.Infanterie-Division, Stand: 1.11.43* [T312 R1559 F725]; 709. I.D., Anl.2 zu *709. I.D.*, Abt. Ia Nr.1240/43 g.K., *Kriegsgliederung, Stand: 1.11.43*, 3.11.43 [T314 R1604 F1133]
190. Conversation between *Ia AOK 7* and *Chef LXXXIV. A.K.*, 19.11.43 [T312 R1559 F188]
191. Conversation between *Ia AOK 7* and *Chef LXXXIV. A.K.*, 23.11.43 [T312 R1559 F208]; AOK 7, Ia Nr.5927/43 g., 23.11.43, p.1-2 [T312 R1559 F209-10]
192. Gen.Kdo.LXXXIV. A.K., Ia Nr.9855/43 (5007) g., 25.11.43 [T314 R1604 F1197]
193. AOK 7/O.Qu., *Kriegstagebuch Nr.45, 1.Nov.1943 - 30.Nov.1943* [T312 R1562 F769]
194. Anl.3 zu OKH/Chef H Rüst u. BdE AHA Ia(I) Nr.6009/43 g.K., 5.11.43, p.3 [T78 R849 H36/159]; Gen.Kdo.XXV. A.K., Abt. Ia Nr.1195/43 g.K., (Kriegsgliederung) *Kampfgruppe Bretagne, Stand vom 1.11.43*, 7.11.43 [T314 R745 F184]; AOK 7 /O.Q.U., Qu.1 Nr.1128/43 g.K., *Besondere Anordnungen für die Versorgung der 371. I.D. für den Fall des Abtransportes nach dem Osten*, 26.9.43, p.2 [T312 R1562 F553]; AOK 7, Anl.1 zu AOK 7, O.Qu.1 Nr.1271/43 g.K.v.8.11.43, *Übersicht über vorhandene s.Pak* [T312 R1562 F830]
195. AOK 7, Anl.5 zu AOK 7 O.Qu./IIa/Ia Nr.5850/43 g.K., 14.11.43, p.1 [T312 R1559 F146]; AOK 7/O.Qu., *Kriegstagebuch Nr.45, 1.Nov.1943 - 30.Nov.1943* [T312 R1562 F755]
196. 709. I.D., Anl.2 zu *709. I.D.*, Abt. Ia Nr.1335/43 g.K., *Kriegsgliederung, Stand: 1.12.1943*, 3.12.43 [T314 R1604 F1255]
197. AOK 7/O.Qu., *Kriegstagebuch der Oberquartiermeisterabteilung AOK 7 für die Zeit vom 1.Febr.1944 - 29.Febr.1944* [T312 R1570 F876]
198. Gen.Kdo.LXXXIV. A.K., 13.12.43, p.1-2 [T314 R1604 F1277-8]
199. Gen.Kdo.LXXXIV. A.K., Ia Nr.2127/43 g.K., 14.12.43, p.1-3 [T314 R1604 F1281-3]
200. Gen.Kdo.LXXXIV. A.K., Ia Nr.2127/43 g.K., 14.12.43, p.1-3 [T314 R1604 F1281-3]; Gen.Kdo.LXXXIV. A.K., Ia Nr.9855/43 (5007) g., 25.11.43 [T314 R1604 F1197]
201. Gen.Kdo.LXXXIV. A.K., Ia Nr.2127/43 g.K., 14.12.43, p.2 [T314 R1604 F1282]
202. 709. I.D., Anl.2 zu *709. I.D.*, Abt. Ia Nr.10/44 g.K., *Kriegsgliederung, Stand: 1.1.44*, 3.1.44 [T314 R1604 F1353]
203. AOK 7, Kriegsgliederung 7. Armee, Stand 10.4.44, *LXXXIV. Armee-Korps, Stand: 1.2.44* [T312 R1566 F191]
204. Rösgen, P.W. (1944), p.1; AOK 7, Ia Nr.122/44 g., 4.4.44 [T312 R1565 F417]; **Ryan, C. (1958)**, Wilhelm Hümmerich Interview, 25 June 1958, p.2 [Cornelius Ryan Collection of World War II Papers, Mahn Center for Archives and Special Collections, Ohio University Libraries]
205. AOK 7, Kriegsgliederung 7. Armee, Stand 18.5.44, (Kriegsgliederung) *709. I.D. Stand: 1.5.44* [T312 R1566 F217]
206. Sonderstab Oehmichen, z.Zt. AOK 7 Ia Stopak Nr.67/44 g.K., *Bericht über das Kommando des Sonderstabes zum AOK 7*, 13.5.44, p.18 [T312 R1568 F701]; **Schlieben, K.W. v. (1948)**, Germ., p.3; PWIS(H)/LF/237, 5 Jul 44, p.1 [UKNA, WO 208/3631]
207. Rösgen, P.W. (1944), Anl.3 zum Tätigkeitsbericht des Gen.Kdos. LXXXIV. A.K. für Juni 1942, *Personalveränderungen Stab/Gen.Kdo.LXXXIV. A.K.* [T314 R1603 F295]
208. PWIS(H)/LF/237, 5 Jul 44, p.1-2 [UKNA, WO 208/3631]
209. Ryan, C. (1958), Wilhelm Hümmerich Interview, p.5-6
210. Some American accounts from the Ste. Mère-Église area also speak of armoured cars, although such claims are often unreliable. Perhaps more important is the recovery of a number of triangular armoured hubcaps, typical for early war German four-wheel armoured cars, in the area of Neuville-au-Plain.
211. AOK 7, Kriegsgliederung 7. Armee, Stand 18.5.44, (Kriegsgliederung) *709. I.D. Stand: 1.5.44* [T312 R1566 F217]
212. PWIS(H)/LF/237, 5 Jul 44, p.1 [UKNA, WO 208/3631]
213. AOK 7, Kriegsgliederung 7. Armee, Stand 18.5.44, (Kriegsgliederung) *709. I.D. Stand: 1.5.44* [T312 R1566 F217]; **Ryan, C. (1958)**, Wilhelm Hümmerich Interview, p.4
214. AOK 7, Kriegsgliederung 7. Armee, Stand 18.5.44, (Kriegsgliederung) *709. I.D. Stand: 1.5.44* [T312 R1566 F217]; PWIS(H)/LF/237, 5 Jul 44, p.2 [UKNA, WO 208/3631]
215. PWIS(H)/KP/81, 1 Jul 44 [UKNA, WO 208/3624]; Feldpostübersicht
216. Feldpostübersicht
217. AOK 7 Ia, *Kriegstagebuch der Führungsabteilung AOK 7 für die Zeit vom 1.Jan. - 30.Juni 1944* [T312 R1564 F226]; AOK 7, Ia Nr.122/44 g., 4.4.44 [T312 R1565 F417]
218. PWIS(H)/LF/237, 5 Jul 44, p.1 [UKNA, WO 208/3631]
219. PWIS(H)/KP/81, 1 Jul 44 [UKNA, WO 208/3624]
220. PWIS(H)/LDC/66, 3 Jul 44 [UKNA, WO 208/3646]
221. PWIS(H)/LF/237, 5 Jul 44, p.1 [UKNA, WO 208/3631]
222. PWIS(H)/LDC, 3 Jul 44 [UKNA, WO 208/3646]
223. PWIS(H)/LF/237, 5 Jul 44, p.1 [UKNA, WO 208/3631]
224. *Ibid.*; PWIS(H)/LDC/66, 3 Jul 44 [UKNA, WO 208/3646]
225. PWIS(H)/LF/237, 5 Jul 44, p.2 [UKNA, WO 208/3631]; PWIS(H)/LDC/66, 3 Jul 44 [UKNA, WO 208/3646]
226. 709. I.D., (Kriegsgliederung) *709.Inf.Division, Stand: 1.5.1944* [T78 R672 H41/61b]
227. Der O.Qu. Heeresgruppe B, Qu 1, Br.B.Nr.396/44 g., 27.4.44, p.1 [T311 R1 F7000517]
228. Der O.Qu. Heeresgruppe B, Qu 1/Mun., Br.B.Nr.396/44 g., 30.3.44, p.1 [T311 R1 F7000252]
229. 709. I.D., (Kriegsgliederung) *709.Inf.Division, Stand: 1.5.1944* [T78 R672 H41/61b]

230. AOK 7, Kriegsgliederung 7. Armee, Stand 10.4.44, *716. Infanterie-Division, Stand: 1.3.44* [T312 R1566 F194]
231. AOK 7/O.Qu., *Kriegstagebuch der Oberquartiermeisterabteilung AOK 7 für die Zeit vom 1.4.44 - 30.4.44* [T312 R1571 F25]
232. AOK 7, Kriegsgliederung 7. Armee, Stand 10.4.44, *716. Infanterie-Division, Stand: 1.3.44* [T312 R1566 F194]
233. Anl. zu Gen.Kdo.LXXXIV. A.K., Ia Nr.1402/43 g.K., *709. I.D. (bodenständige Division 15. Welle)*, 24.7.43 [T314 R1604 F719]
234. Gen.Kdo.LXXXIV. A.K., Ia Nr.117/43 g.K., 16.1.43 [T314 R1604 F32]
235. Gen.Kdo.LXXXIV. A.K., Ia Nr.116/43 g.K., 15.1.43, p.1-2 & Anl. [T314 R1604 F33-5]
236. Gen.Kdo.LXXXIV. A.K., Ia Nr.234/43 g.K., 31.1.43, Anl. [T314 R1604 F60]
237. Gen.Kdo.LXXXIV. A.K., Ia Nr.235/43 g.K., 31.1.43, p.1-2 [T314 R1604 F57-58]; also see: Anl. zu Gen.Kdo.LXXXIV. A.K., Ia Nr.116/43 g.K., 15.1.43 [T314 R1604 F35]
238. Gen.Kdo.LXXXIV. A.K., Ia Nr.303/43 g.K., 13.2.3 [T314 R1604 F152]; for changes in March 1943 see: Gen.Kdo.LXXXIV. A.K., Ia Nr.705/43 g.K., 29.3.43 [T314 R1604 F319]
239. Gen.Kdo.LXXXIV. A.K., Ia Nr.1269/43 g.K., 28.6.43, p.4 [T314 R1604 F593]; Gen.Kdo.LXXXIV. A.K., Anl. zu Gen.Kdo.LXXXIV. A.K., Ia Nr.1303/43 g.K., 4.7.44 [T314 R1604 F665]
240. Gen.Kdo.LXXXIV. A.K., Ia Nr.8412/43 (4276) g., 5.10.43 [T314 R1604 F1019]; Gen.Kdo.LXXXIV. A.K., Ia Nr.1836/43 g.K., 9.10.43, p.1-2 & 4-5 [T34 R1604 F1042-3 & 45-46]
241. AOK 7, Ia Nr.5670/43 g.K., 7.11.43, p.1-2 [T312 R1559 F35-6]
242. Gen.Kdo.LXXXIV. A.K., Ia Nr.1985/43 g.K., 12.11.43, p.1 [T314 R1604 F1175]
243. AOK 7, Ia Nr.5670/43 g.K., 7.11.43, p.4-5 & Anl. [T312 R1559 F38-9 & 42] There are indications that some of these forces are incorrect. For example, the *III./739* seems more likely than the *I./739*.
244. AOK 7, Der Oberquartiermeister, Qu.1 Nr.4935/43 g., 30.11.43, p.1 [T312 R1562 F852]
245. AOK 7, Ia Nr.900/44 g.K., 6.2.44, p.1-2 [T312 R1565 F45-6]
246. AOK 7/O.Qu., *Kriegstagebuch der Oberquartiermeisterabteilung AOK 7 für die Zeit vom 1.3.44 - 31.3.44* [T312 R1570 F1012]
247. Anl.3 zu AOK 7 Ia Nr.3000/44 g.K., *Übersicht über Bewegl. Truppenteile bei Eingesetzten oder im Reserve befindlichen Div.*, p.1, 4.4.44 [T312 R1565 F427]
248. OKH, *Kriegsgliederung des Feldheeres September 1943*, p.168 [T78 R409 F6378033]
249. AOK 7 Qu./A.O.Kraft/Ia Nr.2500/44 g.K., 7.5.44, p.2-3 [T312 R1565 F639-40]
250. AOK 7 O.Qu./A.O.Kraft/Ia Nr.2500/44 g.K., 7.5.44, p.3 [T312 R1565 F640]
251. AOK 7, *Besprechungspunkte O.Qu. bei O.Qu.West.*, 12.5.44, p.2 [T312 R1571 F390]
252. 709. I.D., (Kriegsgliederung) *709.Inf.Division, Stand: 1.5.1944* [T78 R672 H41/61b]

253. WFST/Op. (H) West, Nr.004662/44 g.K., 3.5.44, *Fehlstellen der Divisionen im Bereich* Ob.West, *Stand 1.4.44*, p.2 [T77 R1421 F238] Referred to in **Zetterling, N. (2000)**, p.292 & 294
254. Hoffmann (1944), p.1 [T312 R1566 F360]
255. Harrison, G.A. (1951, reprint 1984), *Cross-Channel Attack*, Office of the Chief of Military History United States Army: Washington D.C., p.147. Harrison refers to Hoffmann's account. Some examples of other authors, in chronological order: **Carell, P. (1960)**, p.27; **Crookenden, N. (1976)**, *Dropzone Normandy - The Story of the American and British Airborne Assault on D Day 1944*, New York: Charles Scribner's Sons, p.71; **Paine, L. (1981)**, *D-Day*, London: Robert Hale Ltd., p.54; **Ambrose, S.E. (1994)**, *D-Day - June 6, 1944: The Climactic Battle of World War II*, New York (NY): Simon & Schuster, p.34 & 116; **Balkoski, J. (2006)**, *Utah Beach: The Amphibious Landing and Airborne Operations on D-Day*, Mechanicsburg, PA: Stackpole Books, p.50; **Zaloga, S.J. (2015)**, *Cherbourg 1944 - The First Allied Victory in Normandy*, Oxford: Osprey Publishing, p.13; **Caddick-Adams, P. (2019)**, p.24, 485 & 487
256. Der Bef.H.d.Heeresgruppe B, Ia Nr.4257/44 g.K. Chefs., *Betrachtungen*, 3.7.44, p.1 [T311 R3 F7003764]
257. Anl. zu Gen.Kdo.LXXXIV. A.K., Ia Nr.1402/43 g.K., *709. I.D. (bodenständige Division 15. Welle)*, 24.7.43 [T314 R1604 F719]
258. Gen.Kdo.LXXXIV. A.K., Beil.1 zu Anl. Zu Gen.Kdo.LXXXIV. A.K., Ia Nr.1808/43 g.K., 4.10.1943 [T314 R1604 F1032]
259. Ob.West (Obkdo.H.Gr.D) Ia Nr.7058/43 g.K., 2.12.43, p.2 [BaMa, RH 19-IV/18]; Anl.2 zu Ob.West (Obkdo.H.Gr.D) Ia Nr.7183/44 g.K., 9.12.32 [BaMa, RH 19-IV/18]
260. Keil, G. (1948a), Germ., p.3, 5
261. C.S.D.I.C. (UK) S.I.R.477, p.1 [NARA, RG 165, Box, Folder 2]
262. Data obtained from the DRK *Vermisstenbildliste* and death cards in the Ancestry "Germany, Military Killed in Action, 1939-1948" collection.
263. Zaloga, S.J. (2015), *Cherbourg 1944 - The First Allied Victory in Normandy*, Osprey Publishing, Oxford, p.14
264. OKH/GenStdH/Org.Abt. Nr.I./4263/43 g.K., 22.9.43 AOK 7, *Kriegstagebuch der Führungsabteilung* AOK 7 für die Zeit vom 1.7.43 - 31.12.43 [T312 R1558 F61]; AOK 7 IIa/IIb, *Tätigkeitsbericht der Abt. IIa/IIb für die Zeit vom 1.7. - 30.9.43*, p.2 [T312 R1562 F5]
265. See chapter 'The Heer Infantry Division'
266. OKH, GenStdH Op.Abt. III/Prüf Nr.14549, *Schematische Kriegsgliederung, Stand: 1.5.41* [T78 R708 H22/337a]
267. OKH, GenStdH Op.Abt. III/Prüf Nr.15180, *Schematische Kriegsgliederung, Stand: 27.5.41* [T78 R708 H22/337a]
268. OKH, GenStdH Op.Abt. III/Prüf Nr.15433, *Schematische Kriegsgliederung, Stand: 5.6.41* [T78 R708 H22/337a]
269. OKH/GenStdH/Op.Abt. Prüf Nr.15325, *Lage West am 3.6.41 abends* [CAMO, Bestand 500, Findbuch 12465, Akte 44]
270. OKH/GenStdH/Op.Abt.IIIb Prüf Nr.73314, *Lage West, Stand: 29.8.42* (1:1.000.000) [NARA, via www.wwii-photos-maps.com]
271. OKH/GenStdH/Op.Abt.IIIb Prüf Nr.43167, *Lage West, Stand: 4.11.1942* (1:1.000.000) [NARA, via www.wwii-photos-maps.com]

272. AOK 7, Ia Nr.5180/42 g.K., 20.11.42 [T314 R743 F191]; Gen. Kdo.XXV. A.K., *Korps-Befehl Nr.44*, 25.11.42 [T314 R743 F201]
273. AOK 7, Ia Nr.5221/42 g.K., 22.11.43 [T314 R1603 F654]
274. Gen.Kdo.LXXXIV. A.K., *Lagekarte* Gen.Kdo.LXXXIV. A.K., *Stand 1.11.1942* [T314 R1603 F608]
275. Gen.Kdo.LXXXIV. A.K., *KTB Ia vom 1.10-31.12.42* [T314 R1603 F362]
276. Gen.Kdo.LXXXIV. A.K., *KTB Ia vom 1.10-31.12.42* [T314 R1603 F398]; AOK 7, Ia Nr.5368/42 g., 2.12.42, p.1 [T312 R1553 F70]; AOK 7, Ia Nr.5352/42 g., 1.12.42 [T312 R1553 F74]
277. Gen.Kdo.LXXXIV. A.K., Ia Nr.2739/42 g.K., 27.11.42, p.1 [T314 R1603 F663]; *320. I.D., Kriegstagebuch Nr.2, 1.1.42 - 31.12.42* [T315 R2032 F197]; Gen.Kdo.LXXXIV. A.K., Ia Nr.2802/42 g., 30.11.42, p.1-2 [T314 R1603 F675-6]
278. 165. Div., Kriegstagebuch Nr.1, 1. Dezember 1942 - 25. Februar 1943, *Darstellung der Ereignisse usw. der 165. Division* [T315 R1475 F164-6]; OKH, GenStdH Op.Abt.(II) Nr.327/43 g.K., 9.1.43, p.3 [T78 R314 F6267394]
279. Gen.Kdo.LXXXIV. A.K., *Lagekarte des LXXXIV. A.K., Stand: 8.1.43* [T314 R1604 F12]
280. AOK 7, Ia Nr.5233/42 g.K., 23.11.42 [T314 R1603 F653]; AOK 7, Ia Nr.5352/42 g., 1.12.42 [T312 R1553 F74]; AOK 7, Ia Nr.5397/42 g., 3.12.42 [T312 R1553 F69]
281. Gen.Kdo.LXXXIV. A.K., Ia-Tagesmeldung, 19.10.42 [T314 R1603 F578]
282. Gen.Kdo.LXXXIV. A.K., Ia-Tagesmeldung, 29.11.42 [T314 R1603 F706]; *165. Div., Kriegstagebuch der 165. Division*, p.1 [T315 R1475 F161]
283. *165. Div., Kriegstagebuch der 165. Division*, p.1-2 [T315 R1475 F161-2]; Art.Abt. Römer, Abt. Ia, Tätigkeitsbericht, 22.10.42 [T315 R1475 F140-1]; Gen.Kdo.LXXXIV. A.K., Ia Nr.2739/42 g.K., 27.11.42, p.2 [T314 R1603 F664]
284. 320.Inf.Div., Abt. Ia Nr.1551/42 g.K., 28.11.42, p.1 [T315 R2032 F740]
285. Gen.Kdo.LXXXIV. A.K., Ia Nr.2739/42 g.K., 27.11.42, p.1-3 [T314 R1603 F663-5]; *320. I.D.* Abt. Ia Nr.1551/42 g.K., 28.11.42, p.1 [T315 R2032 F740]
286. Gen.Kdo.LXXXIV. A.K., Ia Nr.2739/42 g.K., 27.11.42, p.2 [T314 R1603 F664]; Gen.Kdo.LXXXIV. A.K., Ia Nr.2794/42 g., 30.11.42 [T314 R1603 F674]; Gen.Kdo.LXXXIV. A.K., Ia-Tagesmeldung, 8.12.42 [T314 R1603 F798]; Gen.Kdo.LXXXIV. A.K., *Arko 118* Nr.2803/42 g.K., 30.11.42 [T314 R1603 F670]; Gen.Kdo.LXXXIV. A.K., Ia-Tagesmeldung, 10.12.42 [T314 R1603 F800]
287. Gen.Kdo.LXXXIV. A.K., Ia-Tagesmeldung, 21.11.42 [T314 R1603 F698]; Gen.Kdo.LXXXIV. A.K., *Lagekarte Gen.Kdo.LXXXIV. A.K., Stand: 8.10.43* [T314 R1604 F1034]
288. AOK 7, Ia Nr.5579/43 g., 2.11.43 [T312 R1559 F6]
289. Gen.Kdo.LXXXIV. A.K., Ia Nr.2739/42 g.K., 27.11.42, p.1 [T314 R1603 F663]; Gen.Kdo.LXXXIV. A.K., Ia Nr.9555/42, 4.12.42 [T314 R1603 F729]
290. Gen.Kdo.LXXXIV. A.K., Ia-Tagesmeldung, 29.11.42 [T314 R1603 F706]
291. AOK 7, Ia Nr.5368/42 g., 2.12.42 [T312 R1553 F72]; Gen.Kdo.

LXXXIV. A.K., *KTB Ia vom 1.10-31.12.42* [T314 R1603 F404]
292. AOK 7, Ia Nr.5397/42 g., 3.12.42 [T312 R1553 F69]
293. Gen.Kdo.LXXXIV. A.K., Ia-Tagesmeldung, 4.12.42 [T314 R1603 F794]; Gen.Kdo.LXXXIV. A.K., Ia-Tagesmeldung, 5.12.42 [T314 R1603 F795]
294. Gen.Kdo. LXXXIV. A.K., *KTB Ia vom 1.10-31.12.42* [T314 R1603 F408]
295. AOK 7, Ia Nr.5457/42 g., 6.12.42 [T312 R1553 F63]; Gen.Kdo.LXXXIV. A.K., Ia-Tagesmeldung, 6.12.42 [T314 R1603 F796]
296. Example of the rotation system: Gen.Kdo.LXXXIV. A.K., Ia Nr.2915/42 g.K., 13.12.42 [T314 R1603 F754]
297. Gen.Kdo.LXXXIV. A.K. Abt.Ia Nr.854/43 g.K., 17.4.43, p.1 [T314 R1604 F393]
298. Gen.Kdo.LXXXIV. A.K., Ia Nr.2830/42 g.K., 5.12.42 [T314 R1603 F730]; Gen.Kdo.LXXXIV. A.K., Ia-Tagesmeldung, 3.1.43 [T314 R1604 F91]; Gen.Kdo.LXXXIV. A.K., Ia-Tagesmeldung, 4.1.43 [T314 R1604 F90]; AOK 7 Ia, Lagekarten 7. Armee, Ia, Januar-Juni 1943, *Lage 7. Armee, Stand: 3.1.1943* [T312 R1553 F671]
299. Gen.Kdo.LXXXIV. A.K., Ia-Tagesmeldung, 3.1.43 [T314 R1604 F91]; Gen.Kdo.LXXXIV. A.K., Ia-Tagesmeldung, 7.1.43 [T314 R1604 F87]
300. Gen.Kdo.LXXXIV. A.K., Ia-Tagesmeldung, 4.1.43 [T314 R1604 F90]
301. Gen.Kdo.LXXXIV. A.K., Ia-Tagesmeldung, 17.1.43 [T314 R1604 F77]
302. Gen.Kdo.LXXXIV. A.K., Ia-Tagesmeldung, 5.1.43 [T314 R1604 F89]
303. Gen.Kdo.LXXXIV. A.K., Ia-Tagesmeldung, 27.1.43 [T314 R1604 F67]; Gen.Kdo.LXXXIV. A.K., *KTB Ia 1.1.-30.6.43* [T314 R1603 F850]
304. AOK.7, Ia Nr.380/43 g.K., 31.1.43, p.1 [T314 R1604 F54]
305. Gen.Kdo.LXXXIV. A.K., Ia-Tagesmeldung, 2.2.43 [T314 R1604 F231]; Gen.Kdo.LXXXIV. A.K., *KTB Ia 1.1.-30.6.43* [T314 R1603 F854]
306. Gen.Kdo.LXXXIV. A.K., Ia-Tagesmeldung, 19.2.43 [T314 R1604 F214]; Gen.Kdo.LXXXIV. A.K., Ia-Tagesmeldung, 23.2.43 [T314 R1604 F210]; Gen.Kdo.LXXXIV. A.K., *KTB Ia 1.1.-30.6.43* [T314 R1603 F862]
307. Gen.Kdo.LXXXIV. A.K., Ia-Tagesmeldung, 23.2.43 [T314 R1604 F210]
308. AOK 7, Ia Nr.592/43 g.K., 11.2.43 [T314 R1604 F145]
309. Gen.Kdo.LXXXIV. A.K., Abt.Ia Nr.317/43 g.K., 12.2.43 [T314 R1604 F146]
310. Gen.Kdo.LXXXIV. A.K., Ia Nr.344/43 g.K., 15.2.43 [T314 R1604 F160]
311. Gen.Kdo.LXXXIV. A.K., Ia-Tagesmeldung, 16.2.43 [T314 R1604 F217]
312. Gen.Kdo.LXXXIV. A.K., *KTB Ia 1.1.-30.6.43* [T314 R1603 F864]
313. Gen.Kdo.LXXXIV. A.K., Ia-Tagesmeldung, 17.2.43 [T314 R1604 F216]
314. Gen.Kdo.LXXXIV. A.K., Ia Nr.432/43 g.K., 25.2.43 [T314 R1604 F181]

315. AOK 7, Ia Nr.513/43 g., 7.2.43 [T314 R1604 F121]; Gen.Kdo. LXXXIV. A.K., Ia-Tagesmeldung, 17.2.43 [T314 R1604 F216]
316. AOK 7, Ia Nr.513/43 g., 7.2.43 [T314 R1604 F121]; Gen.Kdo. LXXXIV. A.K., Ia Nr.294/32 g.K., 9.2.43, p.1 & 3 [T314 R1604 F133 & 135]; Gen.Kdo.LXXXIV. A.K., Ia Nr.317/43 g.K., 12.2.43 [T314 R1604 F146]
317. Gen.Kdo.LXXXIV. A.K., Ia-Tagesmeldung, 23.2.42 [T314 R1604 F210]
318. Gen.Kdo.LXXXIV. A.K., Ia-Tagesmeldung, 20.2.43 [T314 R1604 F213]
319. Gen.Kdo.LXXXIV. A.K., Ia-Tagesmeldung, 22.2.43 [T314 R1604 F211]
320. Gen.Kdo.LXXXIV. A.K., Ia Nr.681/43, 16.2.43 [T314 R1604 F162]
321. Gen.Kdo.LXXXIV. A.K., *KTB Ia 1.1.-30.6.43* [T314 R1603 F862]; AOK 7/Stoart/Ia Nr.652/43 g., 15.2.43 [T314 R1604 F162]
322. Gen.Kdo.LXXXIV. A.K., *Kriegstagebuch vom 1. Juli bis 31. Dez. 43 des Gen.Kdo.LXXXIV. A.K., Ia* [T314 R1603 F964]; Gen.Kdo. LXXXIV. A.K., *KTB Ia vom 1.1.-30.6.43* [T314 R1603 F922]
323. Gen.Kdo.LXXXIV. A.K., Ia Nr.1349/43 (664) g. [T314 R1604 F155]
324. Gen.Kdo.LXXXIV. A.K., *KTB Ia 1.1.-30.6.43*[T314 R1604 F908 & 922]
325. Gen.Kdo.LXXXIV. A.K. Ia 358/43 g.K., 17.2.43 [T314 R1604 F164]
326. Gen.Kdo.LXXXIV. A.K., *KTB Ia 1.1.-30.6.43* [T314 R1603 F876]
327. Gen.Kdo.LXXXIV. A.K., Ia-Tagesmeldung, 17.3.43 [T314 R1604 F336]; Gen.Kdo.LXXXIV. A.K., Ia Nr.353/43 g.K., 19.2.43, p.2 [T314 R1604 F167]
328. Gen.Kdo.LXXXIV. A.K., Ia-Tagesmeldung, 24.2.43 [T314 R1604 F209]; Gen.Kdo.LXXXIV. A.K., Ia-Tagesmeldung, 25.2.43 [T314 R1604 F208]; Gen.Kdo.LXXXIV. A.K., *KTB Ic 1.1.-30.6.43* [T314 R1603 F866]
329. AOK 7, Ia Nr.726/43 g., 19.2.43 [T314 R1604 F171]
330. Gen.Kdo.LXXXIV. A.K., *KTB Ia 1.1.-30.6.43* [T314 R1603 F878]
331. Gen.Kdo.LXXXIV. A.K., Ia-Tagesmeldung, 3.3.43 [T314 R1604 F350]; Gen.Kdo.LXXXIV. A.K., *KTB Ia 1.1.-30.6.43* [T314 R1603 F894]
332. Gen.Kdo.LXXXIV. A.K., Ia-Tagesmeldung, 27.9.43 [T314 R1604 F966]
333. AOK 7, Ia Nr.169/44 g., 9.1.44 [T312 R1564 F426]
334. Gen.Kdo.LXXXIV. A.K., Ia-Tagesmeldung, 22.3.43 [T314 R1604 F331]
335. Gen.Kdo.LXXXIV. A.K., Ia-Tagesmeldung, 10.4.43 [T314 R1604 F448]
336. Gen.Kdo.LXXXIV. A.K., Ia-Tagesmeldung, 9.4.43 [T314 R1604 F449]; Gen.Kdo.LXXXIV. A.K., *Lagekarte Gen.Kdo.LXXXIV. A.K., Stand: 5.5.43* [T314 R1604 F481]
337. Gen.Kdo.LXXXIV. A.K., *KTB Ia 1.1.-30.6.43* [T314 R1603 F900]
338. Gen.Kdo.LXXXIV. A.K., *KTB Ia 1.1.-30.6.43* [T314 R1603 F904]

339. Gen.Kdo.LXXXIV. A.K., *KTB Ia 1.1.-30.6.43* [T314 R1603 F916]; Gen.Kdo.LXXXIV. A.K., Ia-Tagesmeldung, 29.5.43 [T314 R1604 F523]
340. Gen.Kdo.LXXXIV. A.K., *Lagekarte Gen.Kdo.LXXXIV. A.K., Stand: 5.6.43* [T314 R1604 F565]
341. Gen.Kdo.LXXXIV. A.K., *Lagekarte Gen.Kdo.LXXXIV. A.K., Stand: 5.7.43* [T314 R1604 F671]; Gen.Kdo.LXXXIV. A.K., *Lagekarte Gen.Kdo.LXXXIV. A.K., Stand: 5.8.43* [T314 R1604 F801]; Gen.Kdo. LXXXIV. A.K., *Lagekarte, Stand: 6.9.43* [T314 R1604 F909]
342. Gen.Kdo.LXXXIV. A.K., Ia Nr.1726/43 g.K. II.Ang., 17.9.43 [T314 R1604 F923]; Gen.Kdo.LXXXIV. A.K., Ia Nr.1734/43 g.K., 18.9.43 [T314 R1604 F924]; Gen.Kdo.LXXXIV. A.K., Ia Nr.1735/43 g.K., 18.9.43, p.1-3 [T314 R1604 F925-7]; AOK 7, Ia Nr.4738/43 g.K., 19.9.43 [T314 R1604 F931]; Gen.Kdo.LXXXIV. A.K., Ia-Tagesmeldung, 26.9.43 [T314 R1604 F967]
343. Gen.Kdo.LXXXIV. A.K., Ia Nr.1171/43 g.K., 5.6.43 [T314 R1604 F564]
344. Gen.Kdo.LXXXIV. A.K., Ia-Tagesmeldung, 17.7.43 [T314 R1604 F755]
345. Gen.Kdo.LXXXIV A.K., *Kriegstagebuch vom 1. Juli bis 31. Dez. 43 des Gen.Kdo.LXXXIV. A.K., Ia* [T314 R1603 F962] — Hereafter referred to as: Gen.Kdo.LXXXIV. A.K., *KTB Ia 1.7.-31.12.43*
346. Gen.Kdo.LXXXIV. A.K., Ia-Tagesmeldung, 21.8.43 [T314 R1604 F846]
347. Gen.Kdo.LXXXIV. A.K., Ia Nr.1523/43 g.K. II.Ang., 18.8.43, p.2 [T314 R1604 F821]
348. Gen.Kdo.LXXXIV. A.K., Ia-Tagesmeldung, 16.9.43 [T314 R1604 F977]
349. Gen.Kdo.LXXXIV. A.K., Ia-Tagesmeldung, 12.11.43 [T314 R1604 F1227]; Gen.Kdo.LXXXIV. A.K., Ia-Tagesmeldung, 18.12.43 [T314 R1604 F1320]
350. AOK 7, Ia Nr.2152/44 g.K., 11.4.44, p.1 [T312 R1565 F467]
351. AOK 7 Ia, Anlage zum K.T.B. Führungsabtl. AOK 7 Ia, Lage-Karten A.O.K.7 vom 6.1.-5.6.44, *Stand: 5.6.44* [T312 R1570 F9-10, original in BaMa FH 20-7/138K] — Hereafter referred to as AOK 7, *Situation map, 5.6.44*
352. Gen.Kdo.LXXXIV. A.K., Ia Nr.1537/43 g.K., 19.8.43, p.1 [T314 R1604 F822]
353. Gen.Kdo.LXXXIV. A.K., *KTB Ia 1.7.-31.12.43* [T314 R1603 F970-1 & 3 Gen.Kdo.LXXXIV. A.K., Ia Nr.1537/43 g.K., 19.8.43, p.1 [T314 R1604 F822]; Gen.Kdo.LXXXIV. A.K. Ab. Ia Nr.1559/43 g.K., 21.8.43, p.1 [T314 R1604 F828]
354. Gen.Kdo.LXXXIV. A.K., Ia-Tagesmeldung, 26.8.43 [T314 R1604 F841]
355. Gen.Kdo.LXXXIV. A.K., Ia-Tagesmeldung, 8.10.43 [T314 R1604 F1107]
356. Gen.Kdo.LXXXIV. A.K., Ia Nr.1559/43 g.K., 21.8.43, p.2 [T314 R1604 F829]; Gen.Kdo.LXXXIV. A.K., Ia-Tagesmeldung, 23.8.43 [T314 R1604 F844]
357. Gen.Kdo.LXXXIV. A.K., Ia-Tagesmeldung, 25.9.43 [T314 R1604 F968]
358. Gen.Kdo.LXXXIV. A.K., Ia Nr.8301/43 (4231) g. II.Ang., 3.10.43 [T314 R1604 F1012]
359. Gen.Kdo.LXXXIV. A.K., Ia/Nr.1811/43 g.K., 3.10.43, p.1 [T314

R1604 F1017]; Gen.Kdo.LXXXIV. A.K., Ia-Tagesmeldung, 6.10.43 [T314 R1604 F1109]
360. Gen.Kdo.LXXXIV. A.K., Ia-Tagesmeldung, 7.10.43 [T314 R1604 F1108]
361. Gen.Kdo.LXXXIV. A.K., Ia-Tagesmeldung, 6.10.43 [T314 R1604 F1109]; Gen.Kdo.LXXXIV. A.K., Ia Nr.8301/43 (4231) g. II.Ang., 3.10.43 [T314 R1604 F1012]
362. Gen.Kdo.LXXXIV. A.K., Ia-Tagesmeldung, 9.10.43 [T314 R1604 F1106]
363. Gen.Kdo.LXXXIV. A.K., Ia Nr.8412/43 (4276) g., 5.10.43 [T314 R1604 F1019]; Gen.Kdo.LXXXIV. A.K., Ia Nr.1873/43 g.K., 17.10.43 [T314 R1604 F1058]
364. Gen.Kdo.LXXXIV. A.K., Ia-Tagesmeldung, 17.10.43 [T314 R1604 F1098]; Gen.Kdo.LXXXIV. A.K., Ia-Tagesmeldung, 24.10.43 [T314 R1604 F1090]
365. Gen.Kdo.LXXXIV. A.K., Ia Nr.1845/43 g.K., 11.10.43 [T314 R1604 F1051]; Gen.Kdo.LXXXIV. A.K., Ia-Tagesmeldung, 19.10.43 [T314 R1604 F1096]
366. Gen.Kdo.LXXXIV. A.K., Ia-Tagesmeldung, 17.10.43 [T314 R1604 F1098]
367. Gen.Kdo.LXXXIV. A.K., Ia-Tagesmeldung, 19.10.43 [T314 R1604 F1096]; Gen.Kdo.LXXXIV. A.K., Ia-Tagesmeldung, 25.10.43 [T314 R1604 F1089]
368. Gen.Kdo.LXXXIV. A.K., *Lagekarte Gen.Kdo.LXXXIV. A.K., Stand: 8.10.43* [T314 R1604 F1034]
369. Gen.Kdo.LXXXIV. A.K., Ia-Tagesmeldung, 22.10.43 [T314 R1604 F1092]
370. Gen.Kdo.LXXXIV. A.K., Ia-Tagesmeldung, 13.10.43 [T314 R1604 F1102]
371. Gen.Kdo.LXXXIV. A.K.**,** Ia Nr.1845/43 g.K., 11.10.43 **[**T314 R1604 F1051]
372. Gen.Kdo.LXXXIV. A.K., Ia-Tagesmeldung, 14.10.43 [T314 R1604 F1101]
373. OKH/GenStdH/Org.Abt. Nr.II/32784/44 g., 19.4.44, p.2 [T78 R420 F6389544]
374. Gen.Kdo.LXXXIV. A.K., Ia Nr.1873/43 g.K., 17.10.43 [T314 R1604 F1058]
375. Gen.Kdo.LXXXIV. A.K., Ia-Tagesmeldung, 24.10.43 [T314 R1604 F1090]; Gen.Kdo.LXXXIV. A.K., Ia-Tagesmeldung, 26.10.43 [T314 R1604 F1088]
376. Gen.Kdo.LXXXIV. A.K., Ia-Tagesmeldung, 12.11.43 [T314 R1604 F1227]
377. Gen.Kdo.LXXXIV. A.K., Ia-Tagesmeldung, 2.10.43 [T314 R1604 F1113]; Anlage zu *243. I.D.*, Ia Nr.242/43 g.K., (Kriegsgliederung) *243.Inf.Div., Stand vom 1.11.43*, 4.11.1943 [T314 R745 F180]
378. Gen.Kdo.LXXXIV. A.K., Ia-Tagesmeldung, 2.10.43 [T314 R1604 F1113]
379. AOK 7, Ia Nr.6132/43 g., 30.11.43 [T312 R1559 F259]; Gen. Kdo.LXXXIV. A.K., Ia-Tagesmeldung, 4.12.43 [T314 R1604 F1334]
380. Gen.Kdo.LXXXIV. A.K., Ia-Tagesmeldung, 2.12.43 [T314 R1604 F1336]
381. OKH/GenStdH/Org.Abt. Nr.II/32784/44 g., 19.4.44, p.2 [T78 R420 F6389544]
382. Gen.Kdo.LXXXIV. A.K., Ia-Tagesmeldung, 5.12.43 [T314 R1604 F1333]; Gen.Kdo.LXXXIV. A.K., Ia-Tagesmeldung, 6.12.43 [T314 R1604 F1332]
383. AOK 7, Ia Nr.106/44 g., 6.1.44 [T312 R1564 F410]; AOK 7, Ia Nr.133/44 g., 7.1.44 [T312 R1564 F414]
384. For some reason, the return of the I./729 has not been properly recorded. The *AOK 7* daily report for 25 January 1943 is missing, however.
385. AOK 7, Ia Nr.382/44 g., 19.1.44 [T312 R1564 F474]
386. AOK 7, Ia Nr.839/44 g., 9.2.44 [T312 R1564 F67]
387. AOK 7, Ia Nr.153/44 g., 8.1.44 [T312 R1564 F418]; AOK 7, Situation map, 5.6.44; OKW, Abwicklungsstab Rudolstadt, Ob.West, *Oblt.* Becker, *Vorläufiger Gefechtsbericht der 709. I.D. über die Kämpfe vom 6. bis 30.6.1944*, p.2 [T78 R672 H41/61a] — Hereafter referred to as: **Becker**, *Vorläufiger Gefechtsbericht der 709. I.D.*
388. AOK 7, Ia Nr.194/44 g.K., 10.1.44 [T312 R1564 F429]
389. AOK 7, Ia Nr.365/44 g.K., 18.1.44 [T312 R1564 F472]; AOK 7, Ia Nr.433/44 g., 21.1.44, p.2 [T312 R1564 F484]; AOK 7, Ia Nr.473/44 g., 23.1.44 [T312 R1564 F502]
390. AOK 7, Ia Nr.985/44 g.K., 15.2.44, p.2 [T312 R1565 F115]
391. AOK 7, Ia Nr.66/44 g., 4.1.44 [T312 R1564 F403]; AOK 7, Ia Nr.225/44 g., 11.1.44 [T312 R1564 F432]; AOK 7, Ia Nr.925/44 g., 13.2.44 [T312 R1565 F106]
392. Der Oberbefehlshaber der 7. Armee, Ia Nr.765/44 g.K., 6.2.44, p.1 [T312 R1565 F41]
393. AOK 7, Ia Nr.832/44 g., 8.2.44 [T312 R1565 F63]
394. AOK 7, Ia Nr.795/44 g., 7.2.44 [T312 R1565 F57]
395. AOK 7, Ia Nr.1288/44 g., 27.2.44, p.1 [T312 R1565 F180]
396. AOK 7, Ia Nr.1930/44 g.K., 24.3.44 [T312 R1565 F347]; AOK 7, Ia Nr.332/44 g., 17.4.44 [T312 R1565 F499]
397. AOK 7, Ia Nr.1565/44 g., 8.3.44 [T312 R1565 F235]; AOK 7, Ia Nr.1592/44 g., 9.3.44 [T312 R1565 F237]; AOK 7, Ia Nr.1649/44 g., 11.3.44 [T312 R1565 F253]
398. AOK 7, Ia Nr.1891/44 g., 22.3.44, p.1 [T312 R1565 F320]; AOK 7, Ia Nr.1910/44 g., 23.3.44 [T312 R1565 F328]; AOK 7, Ia Nr.138/44 g., 5.4.44 [T312 R1565 F442]
399. AOK 7, Ia Nr.1926/44 g., 24.3.44 [T312 R1565 F335]
400. AOK 7, Ia Nr.187/44 g., 8.4.44 [T312 R1565 F451]; AOK 7, Ia Nr.798/44 g., 17.5.44 [T312 R1565 F714]
401. AOK 7, Ia Nr.122/44 g., 4.4.44 [T312 R1565 F417]
402. AOK 7, Ia Nr.2152/44 g.K., 11.4.44, p.1 [T312 R1565 F467]
403. AOK 7, Ia Nr.25386/44 g.K., 13.5.44, p.2 [T312 R1565 F694]; AOK 7, Ia Nr.798/44 g., 17.5.44 [T312 R1565 F714]; **Keil, G. (1948a)**, Engl., p.32
404. AOK 7, Ia Nr.610/44 g., 6.5.44 [T312 R1565 F628]
405. AOK 7, Kriegsgliederung 7. Armee, Stand 18.5.44, *Kriegsgliederung AOK 7, Stand: 18.5.1944* [T312 R1566 F208]
406. Order from Ob.West (H.Gr.D) Ia, 13.5.44 [UKNA, HW 5/489, CX/MSS/T197/31, KV 5416]
407. AOK 7, Ia Nr.885/44 g., 22.5.44 [T312 R1565 F744]
408. AOK 7, Ia Nr.1146/44 g., 5.6.44 [T312 R1565 F851]
409. AOK 7, Ia Nr.971/44 g., 26.5.44 [T312 R1565 F773]; AOK 7, Ia Nr.1005/44 g., 29.5.44, p.1 [T312 R1565 F782]
410. Rolf, R. (2014), *Atlantikwall, Batteries and Bunkers*, p.305; AOK 7, Ia Nr.809/44 g., 18.5.44 [T312 R1565 F723]
411. AOK 7, Ia Nr.575/44 g., 3.5.44 [T312 R1565 F596]; AOK 7, Ia Nr.798/44 g., 17.5.44 [T312 R1565 F714]; AOK 7, Ia Nr.1061/44 g., 18.2.44 [T312 R1565 F137]
412. AOK 7, Ia Nr.798/44 g., 17.5.44 [T312 R1565 F714]; AOK 7, Ia Nr.809/44 g., 18.5.44 [T312 R1565 F723]; AOK 7, Ia Nr.834/44 g., 19.5.44 [T312 R1565 F731]
413. AOK 7, Situation map, 5.6.44; order from Ob.West (H.Gr.D) Ia on 13.5.44 [UKNA, HW 5/489, CX/MSS/T197/31, KV 5416]
414. AOK 7, Ia Nr.2567/44 g.K., 16.5.44, p.1 [T312 R1565 F710]; AOK 7, Ia Nr.834/44 g., 19.5.44 [T312 R1565 F731]
415. AOK 7, Ia Nr.1093/44 g., 2.6.44 [T312 R1565 F827]
416. AOK 7, Situation map, 5.6.44
417. *Ibid.*
418. Becker, *Vorläufiger Gefechtsbericht der 709. I.D.*, p.2 [T78 R672 H41/61a]; **Schlieben, K.W. v. (1948)**, Germ., Anl.5; *Festungs-Stamm-Abteilung LXXXIV* will be addressed in its own chapter in a future volume.
419. AOK 7, Ia Nr.187/44 g., 8.4.44 [T312 R1565 F451]
420. AOK 7, Situation map, 5.6.44
421. AOK 7, Ia Nr.1093/44 g., 2.6.44 [T312 R1565 F827]
422. AOK 7, Situation map, 5.6.44; C.S.D.I.C. (UK) S.I.R.483, p.1 [NARA, RG 165, Box 659, Folder 2]; **Triepel, G. (1946)**, MS # B-260 (Germ.), *I.Abschnitt, Cotentin (6.Juni - 18.Juni 1944)*, p.12
423. AOK 7, Situation map, 5.6.44
424. Rolf, R. (2014), *Atlantikwall, Batteries and Bunkers*, p.442; **Schlieben, K.W. v. (1948)**, Germ., Anl.6
425. AOK 7, Ia Nr.1146/44 g., 5.6.44 [T312 R1565 F851]
426. Rolf, R. (2014), *Atlantikwall, Batteries and Bunkers*, p.442; **Schlieben, K.W. v. (1948)**, Germ., Anl.6; a discussion on the locations of German artillery can be found at https://forum.axishistory.com/viewtopic.php?f=54&t=171480&start=60#p1529033.
427. No evidence has been found that *KVU St. Vaast* was split up to create a new *KVU* for the *II./919*. The sector was apparently held by both the *I./729* and the *II./919*.
428. AOK 7, Situation map, 5.6.44
429. AOK 7, Ia Nr.575/44 g., 3.5.44 [T312 R1565 F596]
430. AOK 7, Situation map, 5.6.44
431. AOK 7, Ia Nr.575/44 g., 3.5.44 [T312 R1565 F596]
432. *Ibid.*; AOK 7, Kriegsgliederung 7. Armee, Stand 18.5.44, (Kriegsgliederung) *709. I.D. Stand: 1.5.44* [T312 R1566 F217]
433. AOK 7, Ia Nr.575/44 g., 3.5.44 [T312 R1565 F596]
434. PWIS(H)/100, PW taken on 9 Jun 44 [UKNA, WO 208/3621]; AOK 7, Ia Nr.839/44 g., 9.2.44 [T312 R1565 F67]; AOK 7, Ia Nr.985/44 g.K., 15.2.44, p.2 [T312 R1565 F115]; HQ 4th Infantry Division, *IPW Report, from 132000 June 44 to 142000 June 44*, 15 June 44, p.2 [NARA, via Richard Anderson]
435. Schwellenbach (1944), *Erlebnisbericht über Kampfhandlungen des II./GR 729 im Kampfraum Cherbourg*

(Cotentin-Halbinsel), p.1 [T78 R672 H41/61a]
436. Rolf, R. (2014), *Atlantikwall, Batteries and Bunkers*, p.442; **Schlieben, K.W. v. (1948)**, Germ., Anl.6; AOK 7, Situation map, 5.6.44
437. AOK 7, Ia Nr.1146/44 g., 5.6.44 [T312 R1565 F851]
438. AOK 7, Situation map, 5.6.44
439. Keil, G. (1948a), Engl., p.12-13
440. *Ibid.*, p.32
441. *Ibid.*, p.13-14, 25, 31-32, 50 & (Germ.) Anl.5; **Rohweder, H. (1944)**, *Erlebnisbericht zürückkehrender Offiziere der 709. I.D. (Cherbourg)*, 19.10.44, p.1 [T78 R672 H41/61a]
442. Either the St. Martin west of Les Mézières or St. Martin-de-Varreville to the east.
443. Keil, G. (1948a), Engl., p.32-33
444. *Ibid.*, p.14 & (Germ.) Anl.5; AOK 7, Ia Nr.453/44 g., 22.1.44 [T312 R1564 F496]
445. Keil, G. (1948a), (Engl.) 33 & (Germ.) Anl.5: AOK 7, Ia Nr.798/44 g., 17.5.44 [T312 R1565 F714]; AOK 7, Kriegsgliederung 7. Armee, Stand 18.5.44, (Kriegsgliederung) 709. I.D. Stand: 1.5.44 [T312 R1566 F217], **Keil, G. (1948a)**, MS # C-018
446. Keil, G. (1948a), Engl., p.29
447. *Ibid.*, p.29-30
448. Keil, G. (1948a), Germ., p.28-29
449. See chapter "*91. LL.Div.*"; **Keil, G. (1948b)**, MS # B-844 (Germ.), p.2
450. Keil, G. (1948a), Engl., p.46, (Germ.), p. 29; **Keil, G. (1948b)**, MS # B-844 (Germ.), p.4; **Schlieben, K.W. v. (1948)**, Germ., p.75; Unidentified Ia very late on 13.6.44 [UKNA, HW 5/501, CX.MSS/T215/54]
451. Hornung, A. (1944), sheet 1, front [T78 R672 H41/61a]
452. AOK 7, Situation map, 5.6.44
453. Ryan, C. (1958), Wilhelm Hümmerich Interview, p.1
454. AOK 7, Ia Nr.122/44 g., 4.4.44 [T312 R1565 F417]; PWIS(H)/LDC/66, 3 Jul 44 [UKNA, WO 208/3646]
455. Ryan, C. (1958), Wilhelm Hümmerich Interview, p.1
456. Gen.Kdo.LXXXIV. A.K., Ia-Tagesmeldung, 16.2.43 [T314 R1604 F217]; Gen.Kdo.LXXXIV. A.K., Ia-Tagesmeldung, 3.9.43 [T314 R1604 F989]; AOK 7, Ia Nr.656/44 g., 1.2.44 [T312 R1565 F3]
457. Ryan, C. (1958), Wilhelm Hümmerich Interview, p.1
458. AOK 7, Ia Nr.575/44 g., 3.5.44 [T312 R1565 F596]
459. Ryan, C. (1958), Wilhelm Hümmerich Interview, p.1
460. Keil, G. (1948a), Germ., p.28; **Keil, G. (1948b)**, MS # B-844 (Germ.), *Bericht zu der Anfrage der Historischen Division über den Einsatz des Inf. Regiments 1058 und der Kampfgruppe Keil.*, p.5
461. Rösgen, P.W. (1944), p.1
462. HQ 4th Infantry Division, *IPW Report, from 132000 June 44 to 142000 June 44*, 15 June 44, p.3 [NARA, via Richard Anderson] The prisoner was identified as belonging to the "*2./Pz.Jg.Abt. 319*", but his information clearly shows that he was assigned to the 2./Pz.Jg.Abt. 709.
463. Rolf, R. (2014), p.422
464. Schlieben, K.W. v. (1948), Germ., Anl.6

465. *Ibid.*, p.22-24
466. AOK 7 Ia, Ia-Morgenmeldung, 6.6.44 [T312 R1565 F860]; AOK 7 Ia, AOK 7 *Kriegstagebuch Ia - 6 Jun 1944 - 25 Jul 1944*, p.2 [T312 R1569 F219]
467. Schwellenbach (1944), p.1 [T78 R672 H41/61a]; Seekdt. Normandie, 6.6.44 at 09:15 [UKNA, HW 5/494, CX/MSS/T207/47, KV 6622]; **Hoffmann (1944)**, p.6 [T312 R1566 F365]; **Schlieben, K.W. v. (1948)**, Germ., p.23; AOK 7, Ia Nr.1162/44 g., 6.6.44, p.1 [T312 R1565 F861]; AOK 7 Ia, *KTB 6.6.-25.7.44*, p.3 & 5 [T312 R1569 F221 & 223]
468. Keil, G. (1948a), Engl., p.54-55
469. Keil states that the company commander also evacuated *Wn. 10a* and *Wn. 11* and assembled the garrisons at *St.P. 12*. Yet, the 4th ID only captured *Wn. 10a* on 9 June and *Wn. 11* and *St.P. 12* on 11 June. [**Keil, G. (1948a)**, Engl. p.45; **Historical Division, War Dept. (1948)**, p.108; MCoE HQ Donovan Research Library, D328/I2180, *The Invasion of France*, file titled 'Miscellaneous Notes', (D+3, p.5 and D+5, p.1]
470. Keil, G. (1948a), Engl., p.53-54
471. *Ibid.*, p.49-50
472. There is a St. Martin to the west of Les Mézières. It seems less likely that the force attempted to move east to St. Martin-de-Varreville.
473. Keil, G. (1948a), Engl., p.51-52
474. AOK 7 Ia, AOK 7 *Kriegstagebuch Ia - 6 Jun 1944 - 25 Jul 1944*, p.2 [T312 R1569 F220] — Hereafter referred to as: AOK 7 Ia, *KTB 6.6.-25.7.44*; AOK 7 Ia, Ia-Morgenmeldung, 6.6.44 [T312 R1565 F860]
475. Keil, G. (1948a), Engl., p.43-44
476. Ryan, C. (1958), Wilhelm Hümmerich Interview, p.5-7
477. Nordyke, P. (2006), *Four Stars of Valor - The Combat History of the 505th Parachute Infantry Regiment in World War II*, p.163-167
478. Keil, G. (1948a), Engl., p.45-46; **Keil, G. (1948b)**, MS # B-844 (Germ.), p.4-5
479. After the war, Hümmerich stated that he had dispatched the six AT guns soon after receiving an urgent phone call around 06:00. The force moved from Huberville around Montebourg and was then ambushed as it approached St. Floxel. In minutes, all equipment was destroyed and the 40 men involved killed, the sole survivor dying of wounds soon after. [**Ryan, C. (1958)**, Wilhelm Hümmerich Interview, p.4-5]
480. Keil, G. (1948a), Engl., p.45-46
481. Schlieben, K.W. v. (1948), Germ., p.24-25 & 27-28
482. *Ibid.*, p.28
483. Nordyke, P. (2006), p.166-167
484. Schlieben, K.W. v. (1948), Germ., p.28-29
485. Hornung, A. (1944), sheet 1, front [T78 R672 H41/61a]
486. Schlieben, K.W. v. (1948), Germ., p.31-2
487. AOK 7 Ia, Ia-Tagesmeldung , 6.6.44, p.2 [T312 R1565 F868]; AOK 7 Ia, AOK 7 *Kriegstagebuch Ia, 6 June 1944 - 16 Aug 1944*, p.2 [T312 R1569 F5] — Hereafter referred to as AOK 7 Ia, *KTB 6.6.-16.8.44*; **Schlieben, K.W. v. (1948)**, Germ., p.31-32; **Keil, G. (1948a)**, Germ., p.51-52

488. Keil, G. (1948b), MS # B-844 (Germ.), p.10; **Schlieben, K.W. v. (1948)**, Germ., p.32; **Becker**, *Vorläufiger Gefechtsbericht der 709. I.D.*, p.4 [T78 R672 H41/61a]
489. 4th ID, Operations D plus 1, p.2-3 [MCoE HQ Donovan Research Library, D328/I2180, *The Invasion of France*, file titled "Miscellaneous Notes"]; **Historical Division, War Dept. (1948)**, p.65-71 & Map 12
490. Becker, *Vorläufiger Gefechtsbericht der 709. I.D.*, p.4 [T78 R672 H41/61a]; **Keil, G. (1948a)**, Engl, p.59-60 & (Germ.) Anl.10
491. Keil, G. (1948a), Engl., p.60 & 72; (unknown) Ia, 9.6.44 at 09:30 [UKNA, HW 5/498, CX/MSS/T212/122, KV 7557
492. Historical Division, War Dept. (1948), p.71 & Map 12
493. 4th ID, Operations D plus 1, p.2 [MCoE HQ Donovan Research Library, D328/I2180, *The Invasion of France*, file titled "Miscellaneous Notes".]
494. Schlieben, K.W. v. (1948), Germ., p.32; for the presence of *Pz.Jg.Abt. 243*, see chapter "*243.Infanterie-Division*".
495. Schlieben, K.W. v. (1948), Germ., p.32
496. *Ibid.*; C.S.D.I.C. (UK) S.R. Report, S.R.M.612, p.3 [UKNA, WO 208/4138]; **Nordyke, P. (2006)**, *Four Stars of Valor - The combat history of the 505th Parachute Infantry Regiment in World War II*, Zenith Press, St. Paul, MN, p.178-95; also see chapter "*91. Luftlande-Infanterie-Division*".
497. Schlieben, K.W. v. (1948), Germ., p.32-33 & Anl. 10
498. Stadlhofer (1944), p.2 [T78 R672 H41/61b]
499. Keil, G. (1948a), Engl., p.58
500. Hoffmann (1944), p.1 & 9 [T312 R1566 F360 & 368]; also see chapter "*91.Luftlande-Infanterie-Division*".
501. (possibly a *Luftwaffe Flak* element), 7.6.44 [UKNA, HW 5/495, CS/MS/T209/25, KV 6919 & KV 6932] A report actually includes Ste. Mère-Église in the lines, stating that it was in both German and American hands. This matches the common, albeit incorrect, German claim that the town was recaptured and again lost on 7 June.
502. Schlieben, K.W. v. (1948), Germ., p.33
503. Keil, G. (1948a), Engl., p.58-59; **Schlieben, K.W. v. (1948)**, Germ., p.33-34
504. C.S.D.I.C. (UK) S.R. Report, S.R.M.612, p.3 [UKNA, WO 208/4138]
505. *Ibid.*, **Hoffmann (1944)**, p.7-8
506. Keil, G. (1948a), Engl., p.60; **Keil, G. (1948b)**, Germ., p.13-14
507. Hoffmann (1944), p.8; **Schwellenbach (1944)**, p.3-4 [T78 R672 H41/61a]; **Stadlhofer (1944)**, *Bericht über den Einsatz der III./AR 243 vom 6.6.1944 bis 25.6.1944*, p.4-5 [T78 R672];
508. Keil, G. (1948a), Engl., p.58-59; **Becker**, *Vorläufiger Gefechtsbericht der 709. I.D.*, p.4 [T78 R672 H41/61a]
509. Schwellenbach (1944), p.1-2 [T78 R672 H41/61a]. In his account, Schwellenbach mentions Hill 177, but there are no hills of that height in the area. Instead, Hill 117 would appear to refer to the area of the Bois de Montebourg.
510. Keil, G. (1948a), Engl., p.69 & 72; **Schlieben, K.W. v. (1948)**, Germ., p 34
511. Hornung, A. (1944), sheet 1, back [T78 R672 H41/61a];

Becker, *Vorläufiger Gefechtsbericht der 709. I.D.*, p.4 [T78 R672 H41/61a]
512. Keil, G. (1948a), Engl., p.58-59
513. *Ibid.*, p.13 & 42, Anl.5
514. *Ibid.*, p.69-70
515. Becker, *Vorläufiger Gefechtsbericht der 709. I.D.*, p.4-5 [T78 R672 H41/61a] Keil mentions two companies, but records only support one.
516. Hornung, A. (1944), sheet 1, back [T78 R672 H41/61a]
517. Schlieben, K.W. v. (1948), Germ., p.34-35; **Becker**, *Vorläufiger Gefechtsbericht der 709. I.D.*, p.5 [T78 R672 H41/61a]; **Keil, G. (1948a)**, Engl., p.57
518. Schlieben, K.W. v. (1948), Germ., p.34-35
519. Seekdt. Normandie, 8.6.44 at 03:00 [UKNA, HW 5/495, CX/MSS/T209/13, KV 6918]. It is not clear, if the batteries or villages are meant but, considering these are map references, the latter seems more likely.
520. Becker, *Vorläufiger Gefechtsbericht der 709. I.D.*, p.4 [T78 R672]; Schwellenbach (1944), p.2 [T78 R672 H41/61a]
521. Historical Division, War Dept. (1948), p.95-96, Map 20 & Map X
522. Schwellenbach (1944), p.3 [T78 R672 H41/61a]
523. Historical Division, War Dept. (1948), p.103 & Map X
524. Keil, G. (1948a), Engl., p.72
525. Historical Division, War Dept. (1948), p.103 & Map X; **Becker**, *Vorläufiger Gefechtsbericht der 709. I.D.*, p.5 [T78 R672 H41/61a]; **Rösgen**, *Bericht über den Heldenkampf der Panzerjäger Abteilung 709 im Raume Cherbourg / Frankreich*, 21.8.44, p.2 [T78 R672 H41/61a]; HQ 4th I.D., AG 319.1, *Action Against Enemy, Reports After/After Action Reports*, 22 Jul. 44, p.4 [MCoE HQ Donovan Research Library, D328/I2179]; 4th ID, Operations D+2, p.4-7 [MCoE HQ Donovan Research Library, D328/I2180, The Invasion of France, file "Narrative Account of Operation"]. Rösgen actually refers to Joganville, but there was no fighting at Joganville until 9 June. Instead, it more likely took place at Émondeville, where the 4th ID reported being counter-attacked by a tank-infantry force on the afternoon of 8 June. The same document (Rösgen's) already mentions fighting at Joganville on 7 June, which seems much too early and this supports a mix-up.
526. Historical Division, War Dept. (1948), p.104 & Map X
527. Keil, G. (1948a), Engl., p.62-63
528. *Ibid.*, p.69-70
529. *Ibid.*, p.60-62
530. Gen.Kdo.LXXXIV. A.K., Ia Nr.1273/44 g.K., 8.6.44, p.3 [T312 R1565 F939]; Criegern, F. von (1948), *Teil I*, p.21
531. Hornung, A. (1944), p.2 [T78 R672 H41/61a]
532. (unknown) Ia, 9.6.44 at 09:30 [UKNA, HW 5/498, CX/MSS/T212/122, KV 7557]. Some locations in the report are impossible to confirm without a copy of the map used: "through the 'ss' of Écausseville" and "from the 'e' of Joganville". Considering the troops deployed east of the highway, the latter location was probably east of the village.

533. Becker, *Vorläufiger Gefechtsbericht der 709. I.D.*, p.5 [T78 R672 H41/61a]
534. (unknown) Ia, 9.6.44 at 09:30 [UKNA, HW 5/498, CX/MSS/T212/122, KV 7557]
535. Flak-Rgt 30, 9.6.44 [UKNA, HW 5/497, CX/MSS/T211/72 KV 7333]
536. Historical Division, War Dept. (1948), p.103-4 & 107 & Map VIII; 4th ID, Operations D+3, p.5 [MCoE HQ Donovan Research Library, D328/I2180, *The Invasion of France*, file titled "Narrative Account of Operation"]
537. Keil, G. (1948a), Engl., p.63-64; **Becker**, *Vorläufiger Gefechtsbericht der 709. I.D.*, p.5 [T78 R672 H41/61a] Keil states it happened on 10 June, but information from *Oblt.* Grabbe suggests it took place on 9 June.
538. Historical Division, War Dept. (1948), p.103 & Map VIII; 4th ID, Operations D+3, p.4-5 [MCoE HQ Donovan Research Library, D328/I2180, *The Invasion of France*, file titled "Miscellaneous Notes"]
539. Keil, G. (1948a), Engl., p.64, 72-73
540. Historical Division, War Dept. (1948), p.103 and Map VIII; 4th ID, overlay 9 June 44, 22:00 [MCoE HQ Donovan Research Library, D328/I2180, *The Invasion of France*, file titled "Position Overlays"]
541. AOK 7 Ia, AOK 7 *Kriegstagebuch Ia - 6 Jun 1944 - 25 Jul 1944*, p.24 [T312 R1569 F242]
542. 13.*Flak*-Division. 8.6.44, 20:00 [UKNA, HW 5/495, CX/MSS/T209/172, KV 7065]
543. Becker, *Vorläufiger Gefechtsbericht der 709. I.D.*, p.5 [T78 R672 H41/61a]; Schwellenbach (1944), p.3-4 [T78 R672 H41/61a]; 4th ID, Operations D+3, p.1-4 [MCoE HQ Donovan Research Library, D328/I2180, *The Invasion of France*, file titled "Miscellaneous Notes"]
544. AOK 7 Ia, Ia-Tagesmeldung, 9.6.44 [T312 R1565 F907]
545. AOK 7 Ia, AOK 7 *Kriegstagebuch Ia - 6 Jun 1944 - 25 Jul 1944*, p.25 [T312 R1569 F243]
546. Keil, G. (1948a), Engl., p.64 & 72-73
547. Hornung, A. (1944), sheet 1, back [T78 R672 H41/61a]
548. AOK 7 Ia Nr.1273/44 g., 10.6.44 [T312 R1565 F923]
549. 4th ID, Operations D+4, p.2 [MCoE HQ Donovan Research Library, D328/I2180, *The Invasion of France*, file titled "Miscellaneous Notes"]; **Historical Division, War Dept. (1948)**, p.103-104 & Map VIII; 4th ID, overlay 10 June 44, 22:00 [MCoE HQ Donovan Research Library, D328/I2180, *The Invasion of France*, file titled 'Position Overlays']
550. 4th ID, Operations D+4, p.2-3 [MCoE HQ Donovan Research Library, D328/I2180, *The Invasion of France*, file titled "Miscellaneous Notes"]; **Historical Division, War Dept. (1948)**, p.108
551. Hoffmann (1944), p.9 [T312 R1566 F368]; Stadlhofer (1944), *Bericht über den Einsatz der III./AR 243 vom 6.6.1944 bis 25.6.1944*, p.4-5 [T78 R672]; Schwellenbach (1944), p.4 [T78 R672 H41/61a]
552. Becker, *Vorläufiger Gefechtsbericht der 709. I.D.*, p.5 [T78 R672 H41/61a]

553. Stadlhofer (1944), p.4-5 [T78 R672]
554. See the chapter "243.Infanterie-Division"
555. Historical Division, War Dept. (1948), p.100-102
556. 709. I.D., 10.6.44 at 21:30 [UKNA, HW 5/498, CX/MSS/T212/66, KV 7474]
557. Keil, G. (1948a), Engl., p.66-67
558. AOK 7 Ia, Ia-Morgenmeldung,*Teil 1*, 11.6.44 [T312 R1565 F954]
559. Keil, G. (1948a), Engl., p.74-75
560. *Ibid.*, Engl., p.75
561. Historical Division, War Dept. (1948), p.104
562. Keil, G. (1948a), Engl., p.65-66 & (Germ.) Anl.11
563. Becker, *Vorläufiger Gefechtsbericht der 709. I.D.*, p.6 [T78 R672 H41/61a]
564. Historical Division, War Dept. (1948), p.95 & 101-2 & Map 20; 4th ID, Operations D+5, p.1 [MCoE HQ Donovan Research Library, D328/I2180, *The Invasion of France*, file titled "Miscellaneous Notes"]; HQ 82nd Airborne Div., Interrogation Report No.6, 11 Jun. 44, p.1-2 and HQ 505th Infantry Regt., *S-2 Report*, 12 Jun. 44 [both NARA, via Egbert van de Schootbrugge]
565. Hoffmann (1944), p.9 [T312 R1566 F368] On the evening of 10 June, the first elements of the division reached the area south of Valognes. [T312 R1569 R1565 F24] It is, however, unclear how strong these were and/or if these needed to assemble before being able to start their preparations to take over part of the front. Hoffmann's claim is supported by AOK 7 records, which first report the deployment of the lead battalion on the Merderet at 19:00 on 11 June. AOK 7 Ia, *KTB 6.6.-25.7.44*, p.30 [T312 R1569 F248]
566. Hoffmann (1944), p.9 [T312 R1566 F368]
567. Becker, *Vorläufiger Gefechtsbericht der 709. I.D.*, p.6 [T78 R672 H41/61a]; Schwellenbach (1944), p.5 [T78 R672 H41/61a]
568. Keil, G. (1948a), Engl., p.75-76. Evidence shows that Keil took over the *Kampfgruppe* on either 11 or 12 June, but the exact date is difficult to confirm due to conflicting information. According to Keil himself, he took command on the day of the failed counterattack, but after *Gen.* Marcks' death on 12 June. A comparison of his account against other records and accounts shows that this order of events is unlikely. It is possible that taking over the *Kampfgruppe* was actually a process and, including reorganisations, took place over both days.
569. *Ibid.*, p.69-70 & 75-76; Gruppe Hellmich, Ia Nr.896/44, 15.6.44 [UKNA, HW 5/507, CX/MSS/T221/56, KV 8956]; **Hoffmann (1944)**, p.1 [T312 R1566 F360] According to Keil, *ObstLt.* Hoffmann's forces were still formed by *Sturm-Btl. AOK 7*, remnants of *GR 1058* and, possibly, the *II./921*, which held the front west of Montebourg. Hoffmann, however, states these were being relieved, and the sector taken over by the *77. I.D.* on 12 June. After this, he was in command of the troops defending Montebourg itself.
570. Keil, G. (1948a), Engl., p.76-78
571. *Ibid.*, p.77-8
572. *Ibid.*, p.84-85
573. 4th ID, Operations D+6, p.1 [MCoE HQ Donovan Research

Library, D328/I2180, *The Invasion of France*, file titled "*Miscellaneous Notes*"]; **Historical Division, War Dept. (1948)**, p.109 & Map VIII-IX
574. Keil, G. (1948a), Engl., p.78; App. No. 1 - Narrative report of engagements of 70th Tank Battalion during the period 1 to 30 June 1944, p.2 [NARA]
575. Keil, G. (1948a), Engl., p.78-79
576. 4th ID, Operations D+6, p.1-2 [MCoE HQ Donovan Research Library, D328/I2180, *The Invasion of France*, file titled "*Miscellaneous Notes*"]; **Historical Division, War Dept. (1948)**, p.108-109 & Map IX
577. Schwellenbach (1944), p.5-6 [T78 R672 H41/61a]; **Keil, G. (1948a)**, Engl., p.82. According to Keil, two counterattacks were launched. It is possible the first had been halted, when the battalion commander was wounded at the start.
578. Keil, G. (1948a), Engl., p.82
579. *Ibid.*, p.86 & (Germ.) p.73
580. *Ibid.*, Engl., p.79
581. Triepel, G. (1946), MS # B-260, *I.Abschnitt, Cotentin (6.Juni - 18.Juni 1944)*, p.11; **Becker**, *Vorläufiger Gefechtsbericht der 709. I.D.*, p.6 [T78 R672 H41/61a]; **Carell, P. (revised edition 1994, reprint 1997)**, *Sie Kommen! Die Invasion 1944*, Berlin: Ullstein Buchverlage GmbH, p.234-235; C.S.D.I.C. (UK) S.I.R.511, p.1-2 [NARA, RG 165, Box 659, Folder 2] Triepel states that the batteries included the *1.* and *2./AR 1709.* but these were 1st and 3rd battery, according to the commander of the 1st Battalion. This information is considered more reliable.
582. Historical Division, War Dept. (1948), p.110-114; **Keil, G. (1948a)**, Engl., p.68 & 79-80. The division had ordered *St.P. 16* and *Wn. 17* to be abandoned, and the personnel to withdraw to *St.P. 18*. This may explain why there was no fighting for *Wn. 17*.
583. Keil, G. (1948a), Engl., p.80
584. *Ibid.*, 84-85 & (Germ.) Anl. 13. Keil actually mentions *Wn.20* instead of *Wn. 21*, but this resistance nest was neither on the coast nor north of the Sinope River. He also linked the Le Bourg de Lestre railway station to the *7./919* and the highway to *Kompanie Schimpf*, but those are essentially the same area. It is assumed that the *7./919* was on the left (east) and Schimpf on the right.
585. Historical Division, War Dept. (1948), p.110-115 & 118
586. Gruppe Hellmich, Ia Nr.896/44, 15.6.44 [UKNA, HW 5/507, CX/MSS/T221/56, KV 8956]
587. AOK 7 Ia Nr.3116/44 g.K., 15.6.44 [T312 R1565 F1048]
588. AOK 7 Ia, *KTB 6.6.-25.7.44*, p.42 [T312 R1569 F261]
589. Ob.West, Anlage zum KTB, Einzelnotizen 6.6.-30.6.44, document on losses as reported by *Heeresgruppe B* on 16.6.44 [T311 R25 F7030072]
590. AOK 7, Ia Nr.3113/44 g.K., p.3 [T312 R1565 F1042]; **Criegern, F. von (1948)**, *Teil I*, p.30
591. AOK 7, Ia Nr.3113/44 g.K., p.3 [T312 R1565 F1042]; AOK 7, Ia Nr.3114/44 g.K., 15.6.44 [T312 R1565 F1046]
592. AOK 7, Ia.Fü., Nr.3113/44 g.K., p.3 [T312 R1565 F1042]; AOK 7, Ia Nr.3114/44 g.K., 15.6.44 [T312 R1565 F1046]

593. AOK 7 Ia, Ia-Vormittagsmeldung, 16.6.44 [T312 R1565 F1064]
594. Schlieben, K.W. v. (1948), Germ., p.60-61
595. AOK 7 Ia, *KTB 6.6.-25.7.44*, p.44 [T312 R1569 F263]
596. AOK 7, Ia Nr.3147/44 g.K., 16.6.44, p.1-2 [T312 R1565 F1066-7]; AOK 7, Ia Nr.3136/44 g.K., 16.6.44, p.1-2 [T312 R1565 F1074-5]; AOK 7, *KTB 6.6.-25.7.44*, p.46 [T312 R1569 F265]
597. AOK 7, *KTB 6.6.-25.7.44*, p.48 [T312 R1569 F267]
598. AOK 7, *KTB 6.6.-25.7.44*, p.49 [T312 R1569 F268]; AOK 7, Ia Nr.3169/44 g.K., 17.6.44, p.1-2 [T312 R1565 F1095-6]
599. AOK 7 Ia, 16.6.44 [T312 R1565 F1073]
600. AOK 7 Ia, *KTB 6.6.-25.7.44*, p.49 [T312 R1569 F268]
601. AOK 7 Ia, *KTB 6.6.-25.7.44*, p.51 [T312 R1569 F270]
602. Keil, G. (1948a), Engl., p.82-83; **Schlieben, K.W. v. (1948)**, Germ., p.60-61; **Hornung, A. (1944)**, sheet 2, front [T78 R672 H41/61a]
603. Triepel, G. (1946), MS # B-260, *I.Abschnitt, Cotentin (6.Juni - 18.Juni 1944)*, p.11
604. AOK 7, Ia Nr.1481/44 g., 17.6.44 [T312 R1565 F1089]
605. Hoffmann (1944), *Bericht über Kampfgruppe v. Schlieben*, p.10 [T312 R1566 F369]
606. Hornung, A. (1944), sheet 2, front [T78 R672 H41/61a]
607. *Ibid.*; **Hoffmann**, *Bericht über Kampfgruppe von Schlieben*, 27.6.44, p.15 [T312 R1568 F374]
608. Hornung, A. (1944), sheet 2, front [T78 R672 H41/61a]
609. Historical Division, War Dept. (1948), p.141-9
610. AOK 7, Ia Nr.1496/44 g., 18.6.44, p.1 [T312 R1565 F1104]
611. AOK 7 Ia *KTB 6.6.-25.7.44*, p.52 [T312 R1569 F271]
612. AOK 7, Ia Nr.3187/44 g.K., 18.6.44 [T312 R1565 F1114]; AOK 7, Ia Nr.3186/44 g.K., 18.6.44, p.1 [T312 R1565 F1115]
613. Keil, G. (1948a), Engl., p.84; **Keil, G. (1948b)**, MS # B-844 (Germ.), p.20
614. Schlieben, K.W. v. (1948), Germ., p.70
615. Gen.Lt. von Schlieben, 18.6.44, 20:00 [UKNA, HW 5/506, CX/MSS/T220/55, KV 8815]
616. Historical Division, War Dept. (1948), p.150-3; **Historical Division, War Dept. (1948)**, p.103 & Map VIII; 4th ID, report on period 19-27 June, p.1-3 [MCoE HQ Donovan Research Library, D328/I2180, *The Invasion of France*, file titled "*Miscellaneous Notes*".]
617. Keil, G. (1948b), MS # B-844 (Germ.), p.20; **Carell, P. (1962)**, *Invasion - They're coming!*, London: Georg G. Harrap & Co. Ltd, p.172; C.S.D.I.C.(UK) G.R.G.G.155, p.2 [UKNA, WO 208/4363] The code word has not been found in German records, but it was mentioned by Carell and, more importantly, also by *Obst* Rohrbach in captivity.
618. Keil, G. (1948a), Engl., p.85-86
619. *709. I.D.* Ia, 20.6.44 at 08:00 [UKNA, HW 5/507, CX/MSS/T221/22, KV 8913]
620. AOK 7, Ia Nr.1549/44 g., 19.6.44 [T312 R1565 F1131]
621. AOK 7, Ia Nr.1573/44 g., *Lageorientierung 19.6.*, p.2 [T312 R1565 F1137]
622. Hornung, A. (1944), sheet 2, back [T78 R672 H41/61a]

623. Schlieben, K.W., von (1948), Germ., p.73
624. Keil, G. (1948a), Engl., p.86
625. Hoffmann (1944), p.12 [T312 R1566 F371]
626. *Ibid.*; **Keil, G. (1948a)**, Engl., p.85-6; **Schlieben, K.W. v. (1948)**, Germ., p.74
627. *709. I.D.* Ia, 20.6.44 at 08:00 [UKNA, HW 5/507, CX/MSS/T221/22, KV 8913]
628. AOK 7, Ia Nr.1607/44 g., 20.6.44, p.2 [T312 R1565 F1179]; C.S.D.I.C. (UK) S.I.R. 526, 9 Jul 44, p.3 [NARA, RG 165, Box 659, Folder 2]; **Schlieben, K.W. v. (1948)**, Germ., p.73 & 76
629. Hornung, A. (1944), sheet 2, front [T78 R672 H41/61a]
630. C.S.D.I.C. (UK). S.I.R. 526, 9 Jul 44, p.3 [NARA, RG 165, Box 659, Folder 2]
631. *709. I.D.* Ia, 20.5.44 at 08:00 [UKNA, HW 5/507, CX/MSS/T221/22, KV 8913]
632. AOK 7, Ia Nr.1586/44 g., 20.6.44, p.1-2 [T312 R1565 F1170-1]
633. AOK 7, Ia Nr.1510/44 g., 21.6.44 [T312 R1565 F1201-2]
634. AOK 7, Ia Nr.1528/44 g., 21.6.44 [T312 R1565 F1204]
635. AOK 7, Ia Nr.1513/44 g., 21.6.44 [T312 R1565 F1203]
636. AOK 7, Ia Nr.1545/44 g., 1.6.44, p.1-3 [T312 R1565 F1206-8]
637. Keil, G. (1948b), MS # B-844 (Germ.), p.21; Von Schlieben, 21.6.44 (very early) [UKNA, HW 5/507, CX/MSS/T221/108, KV 9001]
638. Schlieben, K.W. v. (1948), Germ., Anl.14
639. *Ibid.*, p.74 & Anl.14; AOK 7, Anl. 2 zu AOK 7 /A.Pi.Fü., map of the resistance nests in *V.B. Cherbourg, KVU Barfleur* and *KVU Jobourg* [T312 R1569 F711]
640. Hoffmann (1944), p.12-13 [T312 R1566 F371-2]; **Hornung, A. (1944)**, sheet 2, back [T78 R672 H41/61a]
641. Keil, G. (1948a), Engl., p.89 & 100-101
642. C.S.D.I.C. (UK) S.R. Report - S.R.M.622, p.2 [UKNA, WO 208/4138]
643. Keil, G. (1948a), Engl., p.88
644. Schlieben, K.W. v. (1948), Germ., p.74; **Keil, G. (1948a)**, Engl., p.88. Keil, Hoffmann and von Schlieben give different boundaries. Priority is given to Keil, followed by Hoffmann. The latter two men place the boundary between Keil and Hoffmann further to the east at *Wn. 463* (Keil). It is possible Keil's sector originally was wider, but it seems unlikely that Keil would have forgotten the sector he was directly responsible for during the fighting.
645. Keil, G. (1948a), Engl., p.90-91 & (Germ.) p.76
646. Polo (AOK 7) Ia Nr.1341/44 g., 22.6.44 [T312 R1565 F994]; **Keil, G. (1948a)**, Engl., p.90-91; Order of Gren.Rgt.919, 22.6.44, copied and translated in Annex 1 to G-2 Periodic Report Nr.15, HQ First US Army, 25 June 1944 [available at http://firstdivisionmuseum.nmtvault.com/jsp/viewer.jsp?doc_id=iwfd0000%2F20141124%2F166&page_name=237; Accessed on 12 October 2018]
647. Keil, G. (1948a), Engl., p.92-93
648. Hoffmann, *Bericht über Kampfgruppe von Schlieben*, 27.6.44, p.13 [T312 R1566 F372]; **Schlieben, K.W. v. (1948)**, Germ., p.74; **Keil, G. (1948a)**, Engl., p.88; AOK 7, Anl. 2 zu AOK 7 /A.Pi.Fü., map of the resistance nests in V.B. Cherbourg, KVU Barfleur and KVU Jobourg [T312 R1569 F711]

649. Hoffmann (1944), p.1 [T312 R1566 F360]; AOK 7 Ia, KTB 1.1.-30.6.1944 [T312 R1564 F357]
650. Schlieben, K.W. v. (1948), Germ., Anl. 14
651. Hoffmann (1944), p.12-13 [T312 R1566 F371-2]; C.S.D.I.C (UK) S.R. REPORT - S.R.M.622, p.2 [UKNA, WO 208/4138]
652. C.S.D.I.C (UK) S.R. REPORT - S.R.M.622, p.2 [UKNA, WO 208/4138]
653. IPW Reports of the 4th ID for the period of 20:00 on 21 June to 20:00 on 29 June 1944 [NARA, via Richard Anderson]
654. AOK 7, Anl. 2 zu AOK 7 /A.Pi.Fü., map of the resistance nests in V.B. Cherbourg, KVU Barfleur and KVU Jobourg [T312 R1569 F711]
655. Schlieben, K.W. v. (1948), Germ., p.74 & Anl.14; AOK 7, Anl. 2 zu AOK 7 /A.Pi.Fü., map of the resistance nests in V.B. Cherbourg, KVU Barfleur and KVU Jobourg [T312 R1569 F711]
656. IPW Reports of the 4th ID for the period of 20:00 on 21 June to 20:00 on 29 June 1944 [NARA, via Richard Anderson]
657. Carell, P. (revised edition 1994, reprint 1997), p.245
658. Von Schlieben to Heeresgruppe B, 24.6.44 at 10:00 [UKNA, HW 5/511, CX/MSS/T225/24 KV 4396]
659. C.S.D.I.C. (UK) S.I.R.511, p.1-2 [NARA, RG 165, Box 659, Folder 2]
660. For the composition of his forces see C.S.D.I.C. (UK). S.I.R. 511 [NARA, RG 165, Box 659, Folder 2]
661. PWIS(H)/LDC/93, 9 Jul 44, p.1 [UKNA, WO 208/3646]
662. Schlieben, K.W. v. (1948), Engl., page with corrections
663. HQ 4th Infantry Division, *IPW Report, from 222000 June 44 to 232000 June 44*, 24 June 44, p.2 [Nara, via Richard Anderson]; **Carell, P. (revised edition 1994, reprint 1997)**, p.243-245
664. The background of this officer is not clear. It seems clear he was not a battalion commander in *AR 1709*. Instead, he may have been in the headquarters of *AR 1709* or assigned to *H.K.A.R. 1261* or *1262*.
665. C.S.D.I.C. (UK), S.I.R. 542, p.1 [NARA, RG 165, Box 659]
666. AOK 7/O.Qu., Kriegstagebuch der Oberquartiermeisterabteilung AOK 7 für die Zeit vom 1.6.44 - 30.6.44 [T312 R1571 F575]; FID-DZ No.196, 11 July 1944, p.1 [NARA, RG 498, Box 1326]
667. (possibly *709. I.D.*), 21.6.44 at 17:00[UKNA, HW 5/508, CX/MSS/T222/122, KV 9136]; AOK 7, Ia Nr.1645/44 g., 21.6.44, p.1-2 [T312 R1565 F1206-7]
668. 4th ID, report on period 19-27 June, p.3 [MCoE HQ Donovan Research Library, D328/I2180, *The Invasion of France*, file titled *"Miscellaneous Notes"*.]
669. AOK 7, Ia Nr.1654/44 g., 22.6.44 [T312 R1565 F1224]
670. Historical Division, War Dept. (1948), p.171-2
671. *Ibid.*, p.172-3
672. *Ibid.*, p.179-80; AOK 7 Ia, *KTB 6.6.-16.8.44*, p.66 [T312 R1569 F69]
673. Keil, G. (1948a), Engl., p.93-94 & (Germ.) p.78
674. AOK 7 Ia, *KTB 6.6.-16.8.44*, p.66 [T312 R1569 F69]; **Harrison, G.A. (1951, reprint 1984)**, *Cross-Channel Attack*, Office of the Chief of Military History United States Army: Washington D.C., p.429 & Map XXIV; **Historical Division, War Dept. (1948)**, p.177-8

675. AOK 7, Ia Nr.1687/44, 22.6.44, p.1 [T312 R1565 F1228]
676. AOK 7, Ia Nr.1698/44 g., 23.6.44, p.2-3 [T312 R1565 F1256-7]
677. C.S.D.I.C. (UK), S.R. Report, S.R.M.622, p.1 [UKNA, WO 208/4138]
678. Keil, G. (1948a), Engl., p.90. Tanks were reported near the railway between Cherbourg and Tourlaville in the final stages of the fighting, just like the *III./922*. [C.S.D.I.C. (UK), S.R. Report, S.R.M.613, 29 Jun 44, p.3 in UKNA, WO 208/4138]
679. AOK 7, Ia Nr.1698/44 g., 23.6.44, p.2-3 [T312 R1565 F1256-7]; **Historical Division, War Dept. (1948)**, p.173-4
680. AOK 7, Ia Nr.1687/44, 22.6.44, p.1 [T312 R1565 F1228]; AOK 7, Ia Nr.1687/44 g. II.Ang., 23.6.44, p.1-2 [T312 R1565 F1230 & F1232]
681. AOK 7, Ia Nr.1655/44 g., 22.6.44 [T312 R1565 F1225]; AOK 7, Ia Nr.1672/44 g., 22.6.44 [T312 R1565 F1227]; AOK 7 Ia, *KTB 6.6.-16.8.44*, p.66 [T312 R1569 F69]; AOK 7, Ia Nr.1698/44 g., 23.6.44, p.2-3 [T312 R1565 F1256-7]; **Historical Division, War Dept. (1948)**, p.175
682. Hornung, A. (1944), sheet 2, back [T78 R672 H41/61a] The name of the sector commander was omitted, but it was an *Oberstleutnant*. This means it was either Keil or Müller, but the battalion seems to have operated in the sector of the former during this period, not on the Jobourg Peninsula.
683. *Ibid.*
684. Polo (AOK 7) Ia Nr.1694/44 g., 23.6.44, p.2 [T312 R1565 F1254]
685. AOK 7, Ia Nr.3324/44 g.K., 23.6.44 [T312 R1565 F1258]; **Keil, G. (1948a)**, Engl., p.94-95
686. Keil, G. (1948a), Engl., p.95-96; **Historical Division, War Dept. (1948)**, p.182 & Map XIV; **Rawson, A. (2004)**, *Cherbourg - 4th, 9th and 79th Infantry Divisions*, Pen & Sword Military: Barnsley, p.91-92
687. AOK 7, Ia Nr.3324/44 g.K., 23.6.44 [T312 R1565 F1258]; **Historical Division, War Dept. (1948)**, p.182 & Map XIV
688. Keil, G. (1948a), Engl., p.95-96
689. AOK 7, Ia Nr.3324/44 g.K., 23.6.44 [T312 R1565 F1258]
690. *709. I.D.* Ia, Lageorientierung Festung Cherbourg, 23.6.44 [T312 R1565 F1267]; AOK 7 Ia 3334/44 g.K., 23.6.44 [T312 R1565 F1268]; AOK 7, Ia Nr.3334/44 g.K., II.Ang. 23.6.44 [T312 R1565 F1269]
691. Hornung, A. (1944), sheet 2, back [T78 R672 H41/61a]
692. *709. I.D.* Ia, Lageorientierung Festung Cherbourg, 23.6.44 [T312 R1565 F1267]; AOK 7, Ia Nr.3334/44 g.K., II.Ang., 23.6.44 [T312 R1565 F1269]
693. AOK 7 Nr.1735/44 g., 23.6.44, p.1-2 [T312 R1565 F1261-2]
694. AOK 7, Ia Nr.3334/44 g.K., II.Ang., 23.6.44 [T312 R1565 F1269]
695. AOK 7, Ia Nr.1718/44 g., 23.6.44 [T312 R1565 F1266]
696. AOK 7, Ia Nr.3349/44 g.K., 23.6.44 [T312 R1565 F1265]
697. (pres. Gruppe von Schlieben), 23.6.44 at 11:00 [UKNA, HW 5/511, CX/MSS/T225/6, KV 9384]
698. AOK 7, Ia Nr.1748/44 g., 24.6.44, p.1 [T312 R1565 F1282]

699. Keil, G. (1948a), Engl., p.96
700. *Ibid.*, Engl., p.96-97
701. Hornung, A. (1944), sheet 2, back [T78 R672 H41/61a]
702. AOK 7, Ia Nr.1748/44 g., 24.6.44 [T312 R1565 F1282]
703. AOK 7, Ia Nr.1743/44 g., 24.6.44 [T312 R1565 F1290]
704. Historical Division, War Dept. (1948), p.185-6; AOK 7, Ia Nr.1764/44 g., 24.6.44 [T312 R1565 F1285]
705. AOK 7, Ia Nr.1748/44 g., 24.6.44 [T312 R1565 F1282]
706. AOK 7, Ia Nr.1743/44 g., 24.6.44 [T312 R1565 F1290]
707. 4th ID, report on period 19-27 June, p.6 [MCoE HQ Donovan Research Library, D328/I2180, *The Invasion of France*, file titled *'Miscellaneous Notes'*]; **Schlieben, K.W. v. (1948)**, Engl., page with corrections; **Historical Division, War Dept. (1948)**, p.184-5; C.S.D.I.C (UK) S.R. REPORT - S.R.M.603, p.1 [UKNA, WO 208/4138]
708. Schlieben, K.W. v. (1948), Engl., page with corrections
709. C.S.D.I.C. (UK), S.R. Report, S.R.M. 613, p.1-4 [WO 208/4138];
710. Historical Division, War Dept. (1948), p.184-5; 4th ID, report on period 19-27 June, p.6-7 [MCoE HQ Donovan Research Library, D328/I2180, *The Invasion of France*, file titled *"Miscellaneous Notes"*.]
711. The railway has been replaced by a bicycle route. The crossing was located at the intersection of today's *Rue du Gen. Leclerc* and *Rue du Grand Pré*.
712. C.S.D.I.C. (UK), S.R. Report, S.R.M. 613, p.1-4 [WO 208/4138]
713. AOK 7 Ia, *KTB 6.6.-25.7.44*, p.68 [T312 R1569 F288]
714. AOK 7, Ia Nr.1764/44 g., 24.6.44 [T312 R1565 F1285]; AOK 7, Ia Nr.1772/44 g., 24.6.44, p.1 [T312 R1565 F1286]
715. AOK 7, Ia Nr.3349/44 g.K., 24.6.44 [T312 R1565 F1288]
716. Keil, G. (1948a), Engl., p.98-99
717. *Ibid.*, p.99
718. *Ibid.*, p.99-100
719. According to Keil, another battalion was in position behind the right wing of *GR 922* as a reserve. This claim is odd, since there should only have been two battalions left after the transfer of the *III./922* to the east of Cherbourg. Since the *III./919* was later deployed on the right wing of *U.KG Müller*, it is possible Keil misidentified the battalion.
720. Keil, G. (1948a), Engl., p.100-101
721. *Ibid.*, p.101
722. *Ibid.*, p.102
723. Hornung, A. (1944), sheet 2, back [T78 R672 H41/61a]
724. *Ibid.*, sheet 3, front [T78 R672 H41/61a]; **Harrison, G.A. (1951, reprint 1984)**, p.443-444
725. Hornung, A. (1944), Sheet 3, front and back [T78 R672 H41/61a] Maj. Hornung lost an arm. After being transferred to the United Stated, he returned to Germany as part of a prisoner exchange. A Swedish ship was used to transfer them, leaving New York harbour on 23 August 1944. His return to Germany gave him the chance to write a report about his battalion while his memory was still fresh.
726. Historical Division, War Dept. (1948), p.192- & Map XIV; 9th I.D., *Report of operation, 14 June-1 July 1944*, p.14-15

727. 4th I.D., report on period 19-27 June, p.7 [MCoE HQ Donovan Research Library, D328/I2180, *The Invasion of France*, file titled *"Miscellaneous Notes"*]; **Historical Division, War Dept. (1948)**, p.185 & 192
728. AOK 7, Ia Nr.1796/44 g., 25.6.44, p.1-2 [T312 R1565 F1311-2]; AOK 7, Ia Nr.1790/44 g., 25.6.44 [T312 R1565 F1326]
729. AOK 7, Ia Nr.1817/44 g., 25.6.44, p.2 [T312 R1565 F1314]; AOK 7, Ia Nr.1755/44 g., 24.6.44, p.2 [T312 R1565 F1284]
730. AOK 7 Ia, *KTB 6.6.-25.7.44*, p.73 [T312 R1569 F293]; **Keil, G. (1948a)**, Engl., p.103
731. AOK 7 Ia, *KTB 6.6.-25.7.44*, p.73 [T312 R1569 F293]
732. AOK 7 Ia, *KTB 6.6.-25.7.44*, p.73 [T312 R1569 F293]; Achilles (AOK 7) Ia Nr.1827/44, 26.6.44 [T312 R1565 F1333-4]
733. Historical Division, War Dept. (1948), p.193-4; 4th ID, report on period 19-27 June, p.9 [MCoE HQ Donovan Research Library, D328/I2180, *The Invasion of France*, file titled *"Miscellaneous Notes"*]
734. Rawson, A. (2004), p.143-148; HQ Ninth Infantry Division, *Report of Operations*, 14 July 1944, p.15; AOK 7, Ia Nr.1845/44 g., 26.6.44 [T312 R1565 F1347]
735. Schlieben, K.W. v. (1948), Germ., p.108; **Harrison, G.A. (1951, reprint 1984)**, p.438; **Carell, P. (1960, revised edition 1994, reprint 1997)**, p.250
736. Harrison, G.A. (1951, reprint 1984), p.437; HQ Ninth Infantry Division, *Report of Operations*, 14 July 1944, p.15; AOK 7, Ia Nr.1859/44 g., I. Teil, 26.6.44 [T312 R1565 F1348]
737. Harrison, G.A. (1951, reprint 1984), p.438 & 440; AOK 7, Ia Nr.1838/44 g., 26.6.44, p.1 [T312 R1565 F1345]; AOK 7, Ia Nr.1845/44 g., 26.6.44 [T312 R1565 F1347]
738. AOK 7, Ia Nr.1859/44 g., I. Teil, 26.6.44 [T312 R1565 F1348]; **Keil, G. (1948a)**, Engl., p.106; AOK 7 Ia, *KTB 6.6.-25.7.44*, p.75 [T312 R1569 F295]
739. AOK 7, Ia Nr.1885/44 g., 27.6.44 [T312 R1565 F1369]; **Historical Division, War Dept. (1948)**, p.195 & 197
740. Rawson, A. (2004), p.160-2
741. C.S.D.I.C. (UK) S.R. Report, S.R.X.1693 [UKNA, WN 208/4164]; C.S.D.I.C. (UK) S.R. Report, S.R.N.3935 [UKNA, WO 208/4154]; **Carell, P. (1960, revised edition 1994, reprint 1997)**, p.254
742. Harrison, G.A. (1951, reprint 1984), p.441
743. Havers, R.P.W. (2004), p.147-9
744. AOK 7, Ia Nr.3440/44 g.K., 27.6.44, p.1 [T312 R1565 F1387]; AOK 7 Ia, AOK 7 Ia, *KTB 6.6.-16.8.44*, p.89 [T312 R1569 F92]; AOK 7 to *KG Keil*, 27.6.44 [T312 R1565 F1391]
745. AOK 7 Ia, *KTB 6.6.-25.7.44*, p.78 [T312 R1569 F298]
746. Keil, G. (1948a), Engl., p.107-108
747. AOK 7 Ia, *KTB 6.6.-25.7.44*, p.68 [T312 R1569 F288]
748. Keil, G. (1948a), Engl., p.102
749. AOK 7, Kriegsgliederungen zum KTB der Führungsabteilung AOK 7 ab 6.6.44 bis 30.6.44, *Stand: 28.6.44* [T312 R1566 F21]
750. AOK 7, Ia Nr.1919/44 g., 28.6.44 [T312 R1565 F1403]; AOK 7, Ia Nr.1930/44 g., 28.6.44, p.2 [T312 R1565 F1410]; AOK 7, Ia Nr.1930/44 g. II.Ang., *Nachtrag*, 28.6.44: [T312 R1565 F1411]
751. Rolf, R. (2014), inside front cover
752. Keil, G. (1948a), Engl., p.107; AOK 7 Ia Nr.1937/44 g., 29.6.44 [T312 R1565 F1418]
753. AOK 7, Ia Nr.1952/44 g., 29.6.44, p.2 [T312 R1565 F1420]
754. AOK 7, Ia Nr.1956/44 g., 29.6.44 [T312 R1565 F1423]; Telephone conversation between ObstLt. Keil and AOK 7, 30.6.44 at 01:00 [T312 R1565 F1443-4]; AOK 7, Ia Nr.1965/44, 29.6.44, p.1-2 [T312 R1555 F1425-6]; **Keil, G. (1948a)**, Engl., p.108-109
755. AOK 7, Ia Nr.1965/44 geh, II.Ang., 29.6.44 [T312 R1565 F1427]; **Keil, G. (1948a)**, Engl., p.109
756. Telephone conversation between ObstLt. Keil and AOK 7, 30.6.44 at 01:00 [T312 R1565 F1443-4]
757. *Ibid.*
758. AOK 7, Ia Nr.1977/44 g., 30.6.44 [T312 R1565 F1448]
759. *Ibid.*; Telephone conversation between ObstLt. Keil and AOK 7, 30.6.44 [T312 R1565 F1449]
760. AOK 7, Ia Nr.1977/44 g., 30.6.44 [T312 R1565 F1448]; **Keil, G. (1948a)**, Engl., p.111; Telephone conversation between ObstLt. Keil and AOK 7, 30.6.44 [T312 R1565 F1449]; AOK 7, Ia Nr.1977 g., Nachtrag, 30.6.44 [T312 R1565 F1458]
761. HQ First US Army, *G-2 Periodic report Nr.21*, 1 July 1944, p.1 [Available at: http://firstdivisionmuseum.nmtvault.com/jsp/viewer.jsp?doc_id=iwfd0000%2F20141124%2F167&page_name=103, accessed on 12 October 2018]
762. AOK 7, Ia Nr.1977/44 g., 30.6.44 [T312 R1565 F1448]; **Keil, G. (1948a)**, Engl., p.111
763. *Ibid.*; **Keil, G. (1948a)**, Engl., p.111
764. AOK 7, Ia Nr.1977 g., Nachtrag, 30.6.44 [T312 R1565 F1458]; **Keil, G. (1948a)**, Engl., p.113
765. AOK 7, Ia Nr.1977/44 g., 30.6.44 [T312 R1565 F1448]; AOK 7, Ia Nr.1977 g., Nachtrag, 30.6.44 [T312 R1565 F1458]
766. Telephone conversation between ObstLt. Keil and AOK 7, 30.6.44, 17:00 [T312 R1565 F1449]
767. Keil, G. (1948a), Engl., p.112-113
768. AOK 7, Ia Nr.1997/44 g., 30.6.44 [T312 R1565 F1459]; AOK 7, Ia Nr.2000/44 g., 30.6.44, p.1-2 [T312 R1565 F1463-4]
769. AOK 7 Ia, *KTB 6.6.-25.7.44*, p.88 [T312 R1569 F308]
770. 9th I.D., *Report of operation, 14 June-1 July 1944*, p.17-18
771. AOK 7, Ia Nr.2000/44 g. II.Ang., 1.7.44, p.2 [T312 R1565 F1466]
772. Keil, G. (1948a), Engl., p.11
773. AOK 7 Ia, *KTB 6.6.-25.7.44*, p.88 [T312 R1569 F308]
774. Keil, G. (1948a), Engl., p.114-115
775. *Ibid.*, p.112 & 115; AOK 7 Ia, *KTB 6.6.-16.8.44*, p.103 [T312 R1569 F106]
776. Keil, G. (1948a), Engl., p.115-116
777. 21 AGp/Int/1070, App. Y to 21 Army Group Intelligence Summary No. 143, Part II, 8 Jul. 44 [UKNA, WO 171/131] These numbers do not include those hospitalised, meaning that the number of captured troops was even higher and, of course, not everyone was necessarily identified.
778. 21 AGp/Int/1070, App. A to 21 Army Group Intelligence Summary No. 147, Part II, 20 Jul. 44 [UKNA, WO 171/131]

1. Rolf, R. (2014), *Atlantikwall - Batteries and Bunkers*, Middelburg: PRAK publishing, p.151
2. Gen.Kdo.LXXXIV. A.K. Ia, *Tätigkeitsbericht des H.Kdos. LX für den Monat Mai 1942*, p.1 [T314 R1603 F205]
3. Gen.Kdo.LXXXIV A.K, Abt. Ia Nr.2920/42 g.K., 15.12.42, p.2-3 [T314 R1603 F765-6]
4. The *LXXXIV. A.K.* records started to commonly mention the names of the (sub)sectors in May and June 1943. The situation maps, however, already showed identical sectors as of March 1943. [T314 R1604 F000265, 590-1, 828-9]
5. Gen.Kdo.LXXXIV. A.K., Ia Nr.1260/43 g.K., 28.6.43 [T314 R1604 F590-1]
6. Gen.Kdo.LXXXIV. A.K., *Lagekarte Gen.Kdo.LXXXIV. A.K., Stand: 8.10.43* [T314 R1604 F1034]
7. Gen.Kdo.LXXXIV. A.K., *Kriegstagebuch vom 1. Juli bis 31. Dez. 43 des Gen.Kdo.LXXXIV. A.K., Ia* [T314 R1603 F996]
8. Gen.Kdo.LXXXIV. A.K., *Lagekarte Gen.Kdo.LXXXIV. A.K., Stand: 6.11.1943* [T314 R1604 F1162]; Gen.Kdo.LXXXIV. A.K., Ia-Tagesmeldung, 9.10.43 [T314 R1604 F1096]; Gen.Kdo.LXXXIV. A.K., Ia Nr.1845/43 g.K., 11.10.43 [T314 R1604 F1051]
9. Gen.Kdo.LXXXIV. A.K., Ia Nr.1944/43 g.K., 30.10.43, p.1 [T314 R1604 F1079]
10. Gen.Kdo.LXXXIV. A.K., Ia Nr.2280/43 g.K., 28.12.43, p.1-3 [T314 R1604 F1292-4]; AOK 7 Coastal defence maps of January 1944 [T312 R1569 F708-13 & F716-8]
11. AOK 7, Ia Nr.832/44 g., 8.2.44 [T312 R1565 F63]; AOK 7, Ia Nr.881/44 g., 11.2.44, p.1 [T312 R1565 F89]
12. AOK 7, Ia Nr.832/44 g., 8.2.44 [T312 R1565 F63]
13. AOK 7, Ia Nr.1930/44 g.K., 24.3.44 [T312 R1565 F347 AOK 7, Ia Nr.1644/44 g.K II.Ang., 14.3.44, p.1 [T312 R1565 F274]
14. Gen.Kdo. LXXXIV. A.K., Abt. Ia Nr.730/44 g.K., 25.3.44, p.1-2 [T314 R1568 F765-6]
15. *Ibid.*
16. AOK 7, Ia Nr.91/44 g., 2.4.44 [T312 R1565 F393]
17. AOK 7, Ia Nr.399/44 g., 21.4.44, p.1 [T312 R1565 F521]
18. AOK 7, Ia Nr.1714/44 g.K., 16.3.44 [T312 R1565 F295]
19. AOK 7, Ia Nr.399/44 g., 21.4.44, p.1 [T312 R1565 F521]
20. See the information for May 1944 in the chapter *"LXXXIV. Armee-Korps: Normandy from 1941 to D-Day"*.

Acknowledgements

This book is a culmination of everything I have learned since I first participated in online history forums as a teenager. Complete strangers became friends, setting an example with their incredible knowledge, kindness, patience and all-round support, sometimes even financially. This book is a tribute to all of them, most of whom I have only met online. I could never have accomplished my research without the help of those friends and colleagues, who provided me with key information, ranging from a single (but significant!) page to thousands of pages of documents.

Many people have generously shared materials that they had gathered during their own specialised research efforts. They include Greg Way, who supplied me with documents from his Fallschirmjäger research, as well as Egbert van de Schootbrugge and Richard Anderson, both of whom shared vitally important Allied records. All three of them helped to fill frustrating lacunae in my research after I had exhausted my own options. Helge Nauroth has also made a key contribution to this project. By sharing many of the documents that are at the very heart of this book, he gave my research much needed impetus, when my spirit had begun to flag.

I would be remiss if I failed to acknowledge the indispensable support given me by Sam Wren, who graciously shared thousands of pages of documents he had painstakingly photographed at different archives and which were often not relevant to his own research. His palpable delight in sharing materials with other researchers has been an inspiration to me.

Specialist support was provided by Emmanuel Ferey. His unique expertise on German artillery has saved me from embarrassing mistakes on many an occasion and has been essential to interpretating related documents. Although he only took part in the final year or two of the writing phase of this project, Dr. Simon Trew's contribution is also worthy of note. Not only did he set aside his own ambitions for a similar project, he also made his research materials available to me, enabling me to add more depth where it was still needed. Moreover, he painstakingly proofread my manuscript. Most of all, however, I am grateful for the enthusiasm he brought to my project. For it did wonders to eliminate the doubts I had as to whether my research was truly worth the years of effort I had dedicated to it.

Dr. Philip Blood has been of great assistance in reevaluating my manuscript and correcting many unfortunate choices I had made. With his critical observations, he made many vital suggestions to improve the endproduct.

The editing work on this book was done by Nick Soulsby and Robert Edwards. They identified some issues and many instances where a less than-expert reader would need clarifications. In addition, they did mammoth work to tighten up the language, which has made this work much more pleasurable to read. Through their work and historical and military expertise they have also provided me with a format to work with, which should benefit future volumes tremendously. The final editing and layout were done by Toni Canfora, who used all his experience to make the books look as good as they do. Of course, my gratitude very much includes Lee Archer, who was prepared to step out of his comfort zone and took on this project of text heavy books with thousands of endnotes. Not only has he allowed me to keep updating my writings, he has also made the Panzerwrecks photo collection available to help find the right balance between text and illustrations.

Indeed, assembling photographs for this book was a challenge. I did not want to use generic photographs, but only those that had been taken in the actual areas. Mark A. Bando was kind enough to share some very special photographs from his unrivalled 101st Airborne Division collection, which made it possible to illustrate key weapons and equipment. Martin K.A. Morgan was also instrumental in tracking down requisite photographs, while also giving advice on how to procure them.

Despite the support of so many people, researching and writing this book would have been a lonely (and hopeless) endeavour without Sean Claxton. Not only did he serve as my permanent eyes on the ground in Normandy, but his role as a sounding board was of inestimable value to me, and for that I am deeply grateful. His keen interest in my work motivated me and made sure I did not waver. And, of course, I will always fondly remember his (and Jackie's and Boris') hospitality in Normandy.

Last, but certainly not least, I thank my family and friends, who have supported me in more ways than I could ever put into words. This is particularly true of my parents, who may have had their doubts but knew just how much this project meant to me.

Niels Henkemans, October 2024

More books at
panzerwrecks.com